ENCYCLOPEDIA OF

WOMEN
IN THE
ANCIENT
WORLD

ENCYCLOPEDIA OF

WOMEN
IN THE
ANCIENT
WORLD

Joyce E. Salisbury

FOREWORD BY
Mary Lefkowitz

A B C 🔖 C L I O

Santa Barbara, California   Denver, Colorado   Oxford, England

© 2001 by Joyce E. Salisbury

Library of Congress Cataloging-in-Publication Data

Salisbury, Joyce E.
Encyclopedia of women in the ancient world / Joyce E. Salisbury;
    foreword by Mary Lefkowitz.
        p. cm.
Includes bibliographical references and index.
ISBN 1-57607-092-1 (hard: acid-free paper) — ISBN 1-57607-585-0 (e-book)
1. Women—History—To 500—Encyclopedias. 2. Women—Biography—To
500—Encyclopedias. 3. Civilization, Ancient—Encyclopedias. I. Title.

HQ1127 .S25 2001
305.4'09'0103—dc21   00-013117

06 05 04 03 02 01   10 9 8 7 6 5 4 3 2 1

This book is also available on the World Wide Web as an e-book. Visit abc-clio.com for details.

ABC-CLIO, Inc.
130 Cremona Drive, P.O. Box 1911
Santa Barbara, California 93116-1911

This book is printed on acid-free paper ⊗.
Manufactured in the United States of America

To
Lydia Anne Hillesheim

CONTENTS

ENCYCLOPEDIA OF WOMEN
IN THE ANCIENT WORLD

ENTRIES BY CATEGORY

FOREWORD

"Women are more like men than anything else on earth." Although that observation seems perfectly reasonable in today's world, with its women astronauts and Supreme Court justices, when the English writer Dorothy Sayers made it in 1938 she meant to surprise, shock, and make her readers question whether women were as different from men as they had supposed. The idea that women are a different species from men has a long history. We encounter it in the story of Adam and Eve in the Old Testament, and in the Greek versions of the creation story that date from the eighth century B.C. In these the poet Hesiod tells how the god Zeus sent the first woman to men as punishment: "from her is descended a great pain to mortal men, the race of female women, who live with men and cannot put up with harsh poverty, but only with plenty." In the sixth century B.C. the Greek poet Semonides complained that Zeus made the female mind separately. Not only did women not think like men, but most of them did nothing to help men, and often undid the work that men had struggled to accomplish.

Perhaps if Hesiod and Semonides had been able to read through this encyclopedia they might have judged women less harshly. Here we can find women from almost 4,000 years of human history who played a variety of important roles. There are queens of vast empires, like Cleopatra VII. There are military commanders like Queen Artemisia of Halicarnassus in Asia Minor, who led her ships against the Athenians in the battle of Salamis, and who served as an advisor to Xerxes, the great king of the Persian Empire. There are the women who served as priestesses to the important goddesses, like Enhaduenna, priestess of Ishtar, and the vestal virgins in Rome, and women martyrs like Perpetua of Carthage who died rather than give up her faith in Christianity. There are women who were poets and writers, like Sappho and Anyte, women philosophers like Hipparchia and Hypatia, and prophets like Sosipatra. And there are the women who served as close advisors and confidants of men in important positions, like Cornelia and Caerellia. Similar roles, less visible and prominent, were played by many ordinary women in the ancient world, although their names were not known to many people outside their own families and they do not appear in this encyclopedia. Despite Semonides' claim that women's minds are different from men's, women could and did do men's work and worked along with men. No one who reads the material collected in this encyclopedia will be able to imagine that all ancient women spent their lives in silence, sitting near the fire, guarding the house and working in wool.

Mary Lefkowitz
Andrew W. Mellon Professor in the
Humanities, Wellesley College

PREFACE

When did women first begin to work? When did they first become rulers, athletes, soldiers, heroines, and villains? When did they become responsible for their children, their families, and themselves? Such questions come up often in my history classes, and the easy answer to all of them is "they always did." There never was a time when some women did not participate in all aspects of society. Was it easy for them? Never, because just as in today's society, women struggled with cultural expectations and with competing family obligations. This encyclopedia tells the stories of many women from the ancient world and shows the choices they made in their lives as they looked for happiness or wealth or power or well-being for their families. In their stories, we can perhaps see that women in the distant past were not so very different from ourselves.

Coverage

The women in this book are drawn from the region historians roughly call ancient Western civilization. This term does not define one specific location; instead it refers to a series of cultures that have slowly changed and spread until Western civilization has made an impact all over the world today. The cradle of Western culture lay in the fertile crescent in the Middle East, from the river valleys of the Tigris and Euphrates Rivers over to the eastern shore of the Mediterranean Sea down to the rich Nile valley of Egypt. Here Stone Age peoples developed agriculture from the rich native plants and domesticated the first animals. Here also great cities grew up that brought with them social stratification, hierarchy, and a changed way of life for women (and men). This encyclopedia looks at many of the women in this dawn of history, from Mesopotamian priestesses and poets to Jewish matriarchs and heroines to Egyptian queens and consorts.

This core area of the Middle East never existed in isolation. In fact, part of its success came from the fact that it lay at the center of the great east-west trade routes that led all the way to China. Kingdoms and individuals moved throughout the region bringing conquests, trading, and rich new ideas. For most of the ancient world, the key to this large trading nexus was the great Persian Empire that extended all the way from India to the shores of the Mediterranean, and this encyclopedia includes entries about women from this empire at the eastern edge of Western civilization. At the height of the Persian Empire, it confronted a growing culture to the west: small Greek city-states actually challenged and defeated the great Persian military (which was ably led by a woman naval officer!).

The core of Western civilization then moved westward to the Aegean Sea and Greece, where men and women made dramatic innovations in the arts, sciences, and politics. Many look to Greece as the home of our democratic institutions and our intellectual styles. In about 338 B.C., the individualistic Greek city-states were conquered by the Macedonians, their neighbors to the north. The young Macedonian king, Alexander the Great, took Greek culture (which he loved) and spread it eastward with his conquests of Egypt and the Persian Empire. Western civilization was irrevocably and, for women, beneficially transformed into a new cosmopolitan society found in great cities all over the region. This introduced a period that historians have come to call the Hellenistic, which means "Greeklike," to indicate that classical Greek culture spread and was changed.

After Alexander the Great's death in 323 B.C., his huge (though short-lived) empire broke up into Hellenistic kingdoms. Here in these new cosmopolitan kingdoms, women found new freedom and new opportunities. Wealthy queens made an impact on their societies even as they struggled for power as ruthlessly as their brothers. This book tells their stories but also relates the tales of women philosophers, poets, and artists who found room to express themselves in the new large kingdoms.

These wealthy and mighty kingdoms in their turn fell to an even stronger power that arose to the west: Rome. The city-state began modestly among seven hills in the center of Italy, then proceeded not only to conquer the Hellenistic kingdoms to the east, but also western Europe from Britain to Spain. Just as during the Hellenistic period, many Roman women found that empire brought them wealth and opportunity (and, for some, tragedy).

The Roman Empire carefully guarded its borders on the north from Germanic tribes who had first come from Scandinavia and moved south to threaten the empire (and in the fifth century A.D. to topple the western portion). Also threatening on the north were Celtic tribes that advancing Roman armies had pushed to the fringes of Europe—Britain, Ireland, and Wales. This encyclopedia includes some entries on the Germanic and Celtic women who played a critical role in the decline and transformation of the Roman Empire.

Even before its fall, the Roman Empire was changed by the growth of Christianity. Throughout the centuries of the empire, Christians slowly converted their neighbors, and the Christian communities grew. Sometimes Christians came into conflict with the power of Rome, and some women and men were killed. This encyclopedia tells the stories of many of the martyrs who died for their faith. Their deaths actually helped forward the spread of the religion, and in the fourth century A.D. even the emperors had converted and the Roman Empire had become a Christian one. In the course of this change, some women (such as the queens of the Theodosian dynasty) were able to use the new power of the church to enhance their own

sovereignty. The time period covered by this encyclopedia ends with the Christian empire that was conquered by the Germanic tribes. The heartland of Western civilization would move north in the Middle Ages.

Thus the geographic area covered by this book is roughly the old cradle of Western civilization from the Middle East and the Persian Empire around the Mediterranean Sea and northern Europe. The time period is equally broad. Some entries, which cover the prehistoric period, look at Stone Age art, clothing, jewelry, work, and so on. Most of the encyclopedia, however, explores the historical period beginning in about 3,000 B.C. (B.C. means "before the birth of Christ") in which written texts offer more information about women (and men). I have ended the entries at about A.D. 500 (A.D. means "Anno Domini," "the year of our Lord," or "after the birth of Christ"), which is approximately when scholars begin to speak of the medieval period instead of the ancient world.

I must offer a caution about the dates that are included here. When I indicate by the use of "ca." that the dates are approximate, that really means that we do not know exactly what the date is. I have tried to include a general date for women whose precise dates are unknown to try to help students locate the women generally in time. In most cases, I have omitted dates for women who are clearly fictional, since it is too difficult to determine whether I should use the date of the composition of the work or the date when the fictional woman was supposed to have lived. Within such entries, readers can find dates to help place the characters. In my desire to approximately place many of the women, I will surely run into disagreement from some scholars who might choose other dates, but I believe the attempt at dating will be most helpful to general readers.

The Women

The heart of this encyclopedia is the biographies of some 150 women of the ancient world. They range from the very famous—such as Cleopatra VII, immortalized even by Hollywood—to the barely remembered—such as the Roman wife Turia or the poet Nossis. As I wrote these biographies, I was profoundly impressed by the range of the women and their activities. There is no single formula for creating a satisfying (or disastrous) life, and the study of these women of the ancient world (like that of the women of today) reveals a broad range of choices.

There is much to learn from biographies, but there are also more general themes that illuminate the lives of ancient women. Therefore, I have included over thirty general entries that explain various aspects of the ancient world. Some look at women in different cultures—*see* Roman Women, Etruscan Women, Germanic Tribal Women, and other similar entries—while other subject entries analyze topics about women from a cross-cultural perspective. The general entries include themes such as clothing, cosmetics, work, sexuality, prostitution, gynecology, and others. These general entries allow readers to look at the biographical entries in a rich context that I hope will help bring the ancient world to life.

Finally, I have included a third category of entries—mythological or legendary women and goddesses. Perhaps strangely, these "women" and deities were probably more influential to ancient (and modern) people's ideas about women than were the actual women of the times. For example, the legendary story of the faithful wife Penelope certainly shaped people's perceptions of wives more than that of the real faithful wife, Turia. Therefore, to facilitate an understanding of women of the ancient world, I have included the stories about the most famous of the mythological women and goddesses.

Features

Throughout this book I have tried to address readers who have no background in ancient history. In this way I depart from many works on women's history that assume people know the general history and want to add women back into the narrative. In this encyclopedia, each entry begins with a paragraph or so that places the relevant women in their historical context. For example, students who read about Calpurnia and Servilia will learn about the fall of the Roman Republic and the assassination of Julius Caesar. All the women in this book were central to (or at least involved in) the historical events of

their lives. Therefore, we can readily learn about ancient history through the lens of their lives. Students who are curious about historical events or men can find them by referring to the extensive general index in the back of the book. Thus, students interested in Jerome or Alexander the Great or Zoroastrianism or many other topics will find this book a rich source of information.

As part of writing these entries for an audience of general readers, I tried to make the information interesting and accessible. These are good stories, and I have tried to write them as such. Therefore, there are no very short entries (as one might expect in an encyclopedia). All are long enough to set the stage and tell the tale. I have also tried to keep them from being too long; they can be easily read in one sitting. Readers can go to related entries by following the cross references listed at the end of each entry; these will lead interested students to a fuller exploration of the time period. For example, the Christian church father Jerome wrote to a number of women, and the encyclopedia entries for each of these women explore different aspects of Jerome's thought—virginity, asceticism, heresy, and so on. Each entry in the encyclopedia also includes a Suggested Readings section to lead interested readers to further research. The list of "Entries by Category" at the beginning of the book will also help guide readers to entries from specific geographic regions or belief systems, thus again making this reference work easy to use.

Since this book is for a general reader, for the most part it does not engage in the many scholarly controversies that surround much of the material in the ancient world. I believed it was essential first for people to become aware of the general outlines of the stories of the ancient women rather than to hear about the controversies that have engaged scholars for years. For example, scholars disagree about the historicity of figures such as Esther or Dinah or Deborah and question the accuracy of ancient accounts of women philosophers or martyrs. Thus, readers are urged to remember that many of the accounts that are presented here are subject to various interpretations, and I have tried to present the accounts that people in the ancient world told and believed, regardless of whether modern scholars believe them. Readers interested in pursuing scholarly controversies can do so by beginning with the lists of suggested readings at the end of each entry.

While written texts offer the most information about women in the ancient world, there is another fascinating source: visual images. People have always portrayed women in art, and this is the best way literally to see women as their contemporaries saw them. This encyclopedia is lavishly illustrated and offers readers a wonderful window into the past as they see the women discussed in the text. I have also included some genealogical charts, which follow this introduction, to help readers keep track of some of the dynasties that produced a number of famous women.

Last, but certainly not least, this encyclopedia recognizes that one of the most difficult challenges to students of the ancient world is keeping track of the geography. The ancient names are unfamiliar, and the ancient kingdoms repeatedly shifted or disappeared. I have included ten maps at the front of the text to help people keep track of the ancient spaces. Most of the entries cross-reference the appropriate map, and I hope readers will take a minute to find the appropriate locations on the maps as they read about the women. In this way, students will learn about ancient spaces as well as ancient times.

We have created a website to support and enhance the material presented here. Please visit www.uwgb.edu/sophia to see animated timelines, more illustrations, and other changing features.

I hope readers find this encyclopedia accessible, informative, and enjoyable and see that women have always been rulers, athletes, soldiers, heroines, and villains. Perhaps more importantly, just as did men of the ancient world, women bravely worked to shape a satisfying life, whatever that meant to each of them. I have enjoyed retelling their stories, and I am pleased to present them here.

Joyce E. Salisbury
University of Wisconsin–Green Bay

ACKNOWLEDGMENTS

As for intellectual training, the prince must read history . . . so that he can do what eminent men have done before him, taken as their model some historical figure who has been praised and honored, and always kept his deeds and actions before them.
Niccolo Machiavelli, *The Prince*

During the Italian Renaissance, Machiavelli (like many others) believed one key to great accomplishments was to learn from the deeds of great men in the ancient world. He was right, but what he missed was that women, too, needed to know that the classical world offered significant models for their lives. I have written this encyclopedia to bring to life some of the many women of the ancient world; we have much to learn from them.

Central to the success of this project was the Editorial Board: Professors Mary Gardner, Judith Hallett, Ross S. Kramer, Mary Lefkowitz, and Joyce Tyldesley are scholars who have worked for years building our knowledge of women in the ancient world—indeed, they have been instrumental in developing the field. They were generous with their time, knowledge, and comments, and any remaining errors are my own.

I extend my thanks to Jim Graves for creating the website at www.uwgb.edu/sophia that so lavishly supports the book.

I would also like to thank Gary Kuris of ABC-CLIO for luring me into what has turned out to be a fascinating project and for being so easy to work with.

Finally, this book is dedicated to my young granddaughter, Lydia, who will grow up with plenty of role models to help her be whatever she wants and accomplish whatever she chooses.

GENEALOGICAL CHARTS

Chart 1. House of Theodosius

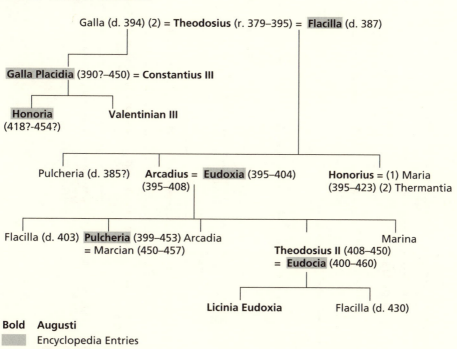

Galla (d. 394) (2) = **Theodosius** (r. 379–395) = Flacilla (d. 387)

Galla Placidia (390?–450) = **Constantius III**

Honoria (418?-454?)   **Valentinian III**

Pulcheria (d. 385?)   **Arcadius** = Eudoxia (395–404)   **Honorius** = (1) Maria
(395–408)   (395–423) (2) Thermantia

Flacilla (d. 403) Pulcheria (399–453) Arcadia   Marina
= **Marcian** (450–457)   **Theodosius II** (408–450)
= Eudocia (400–460)

Licinia Eudoxia   Flacilla (d. 430)

Bold   Augusti

      Encyclopedia Entries

=   Indicates marriage

Chart 2. The Herodian Family

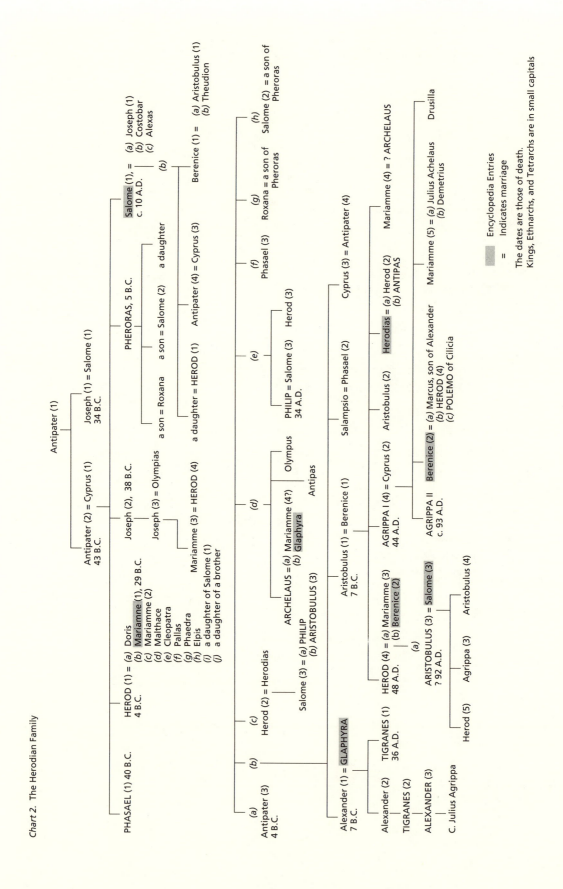

Chart 3. The Family of Augustus

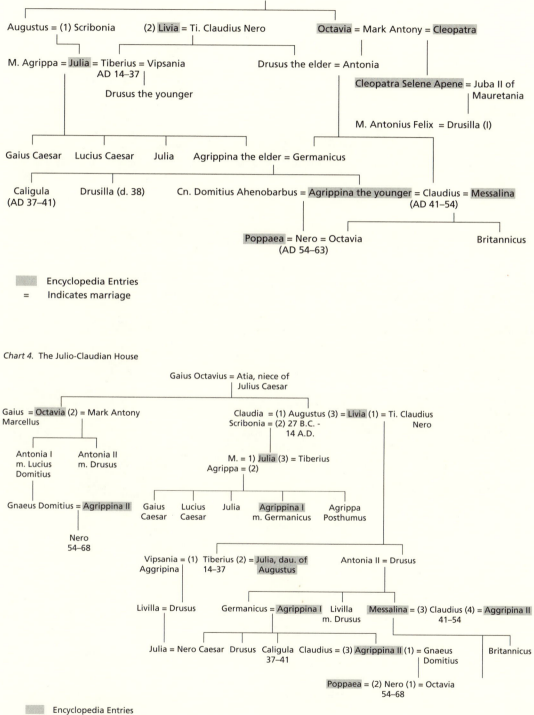

Augustus = (1) Scribonia   (2) Livia = Ti. Claudius Nero   Octavia = Mark Antony = Cleopatra

M. Agrippa = Julia = Tiberius = Vipsania   Drusus the elder = Antonia
AD 14–37
          Drusus the younger   Cleopatra Selene Apene = Juba II of
                                                                            Mauretania

          M. Antonius Felix = Drusilla (I)

Gaius Caesar   Lucius Caesar   Julia   Agrippina the elder = Germanicus

Caligula   Drusilla (d. 38)   Cn. Domitius Ahenobarbus = Agrippina the younger = Claudius = Messalina
(AD 37–41)   (AD 41–54)

                    Poppaea = Nero = Octavia   Britannicus
                            (AD 54–63)

    Encyclopedia Entries
=   Indicates marriage

Chart 4. The Julio-Claudian House

Gaius Octavius = Atia, niece of
            Julius Caesar

Gaius = Octavia (2) = Mark Antony   Claudia = (1) Augustus (3) = Livia (1) = Ti. Claudius
Marcellus   Scribonia = (2) 27 B.C. -   Nero
                                                        14 A.D.

Antonia I   Antonia II   M. = 1) Julia (3) = Tiberius
m. Lucius   m. Drusus   Agrippa = (2)
Domitius

Gnaeus Domitius = Agrippina II   Gaius   Lucius   Julia   Agrippina I   Agrippa
                                  Caesar   Caesar   m. Germanicus   Posthumus
            Nero
            54–68

                    Vipsania = (1) Tiberius (2) = Julia, dau. of   Antonia II = Drusus
                    Aggripina   14–37   Augustus

            Livilla = Drusus   Germanicus = Agrippina I   Livilla   Messalina = (3) Claudius (4) = Aggripina II
                                               m. Drusus   41–54

                    Julia = Nero Caesar Drusus Caligula Claudius = (3) Agrippina II (1) = Gnaeus   Britannicus
                                                  37–41   Domitius

                            Poppaea = (2) Nero (1) = Octavia
                                          54–68

    Encyclopedia Entries
=   Indicates marriage

MAPS

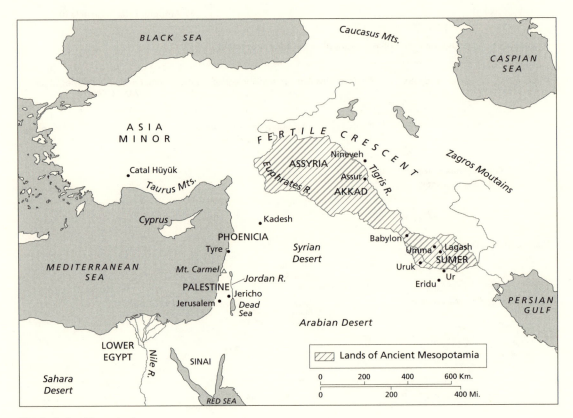

Map 1. Ancient Mesopotamia

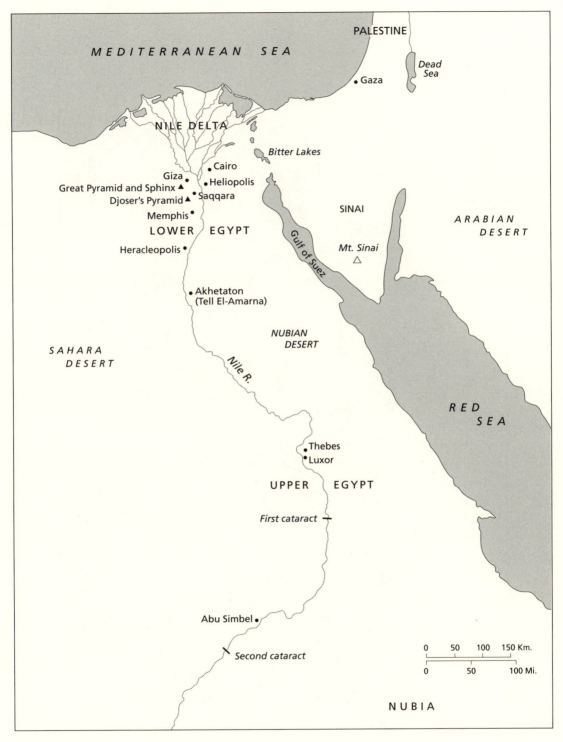

Map 2. Ancient Egypt

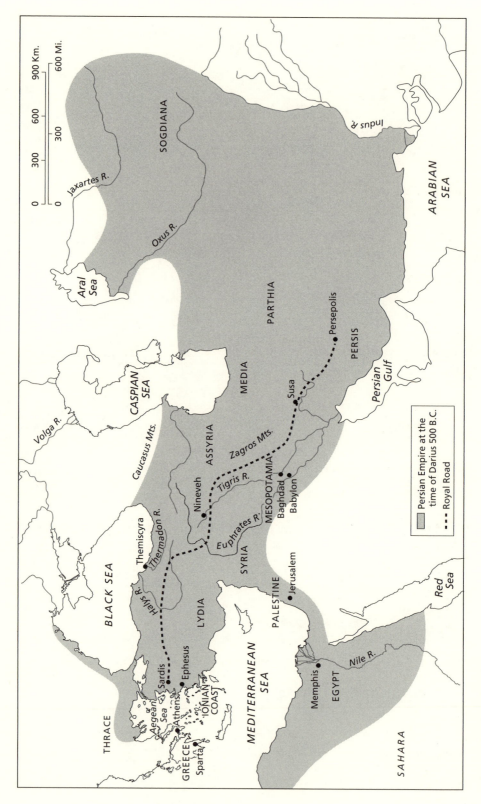

Map 3. Persian Empire

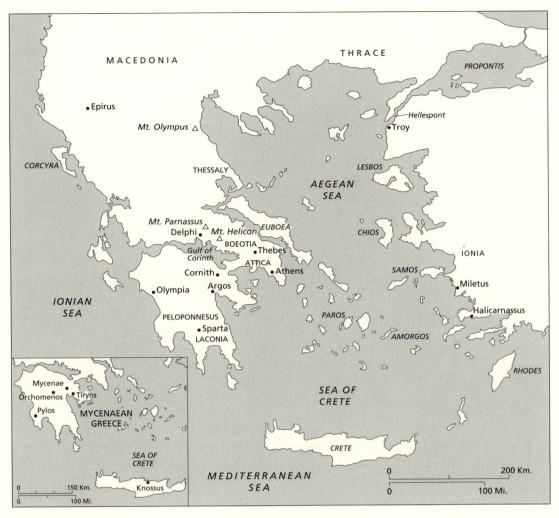

MACEDONIA

THRACE

PROPONTIS

Epirus

Mt. Olympus △

Hellespont

Troy

CORCYRA

THESSALY

LESBOS

AEGEAN
SEA

CHIOS

IONIA

Mt. Parnassus △
Delphi △ Mt. Helicon
BOEOTIA
Gulf of
Corinth
ATTICA
Cornith
Athens
Thebes

EUBOEA

SAMOS

Miletus

IONIAN
SEA

Olympia
Argos

Halicarnassus

PELOPONNESUS

PAROS

Sparta
LACONIA

AMORGOS

RHODES

Mycenae
Orchomenos Tiryns
Pylos
MYCENAEAN
GREECE

SEA OF
CRETE

SEA OF
CRETE

CRETE

MEDITERRANEAN
SEA

Knossus

150 Km.

100 Mi.

0   200 Km.

0   100 Mi.

Map 4. Ancient Greece

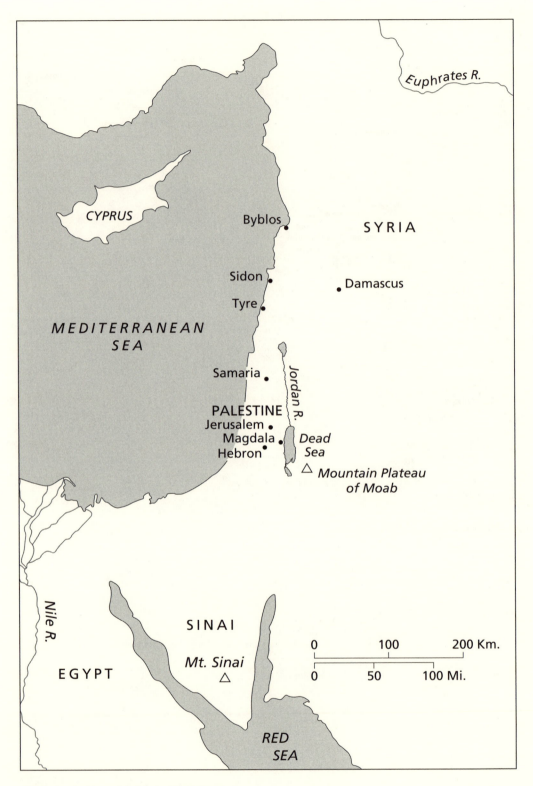

Map 5. Ancient Hebrew Kingdoms

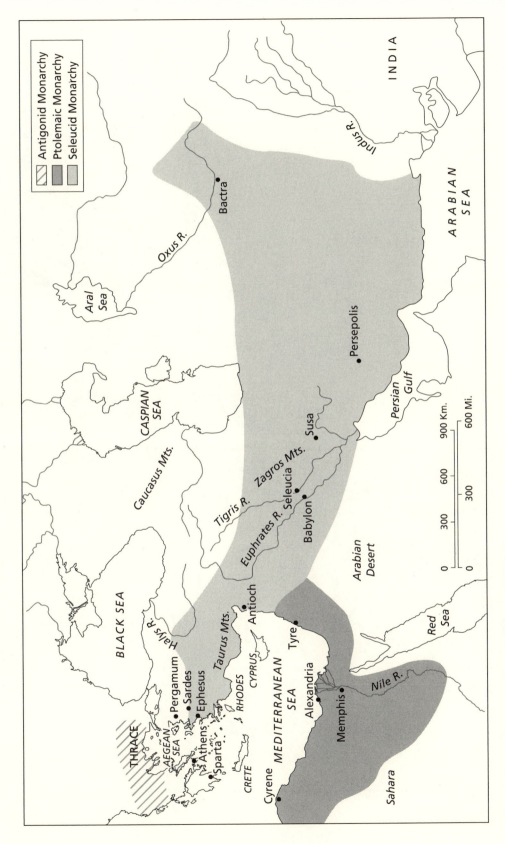

Map 6. The Hellenistic Monarchies, ca. 250 B.C.

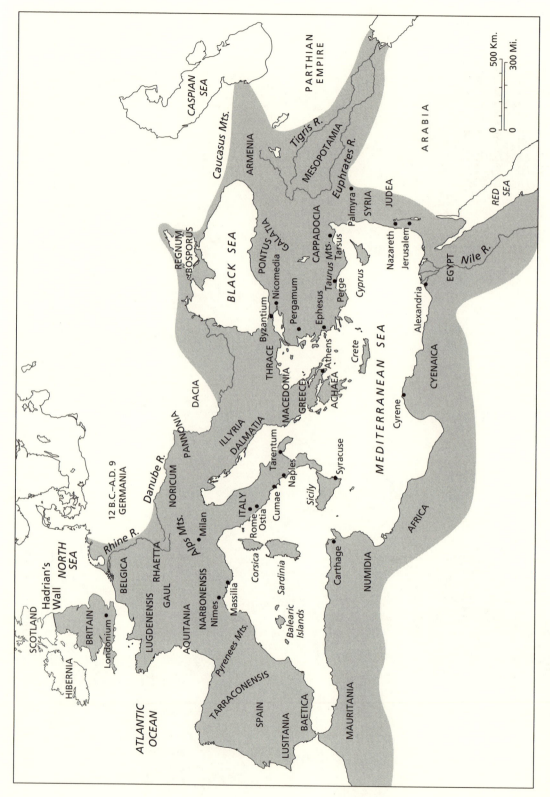

Map 7. The Roman Empire

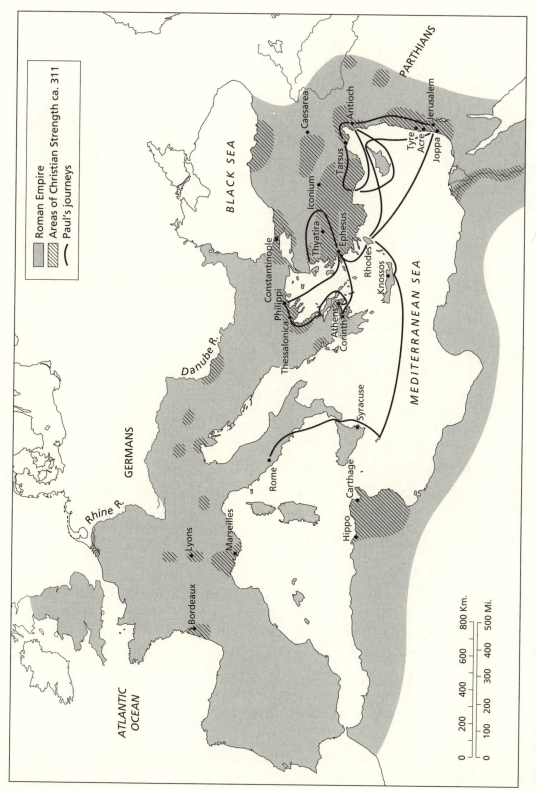

Map 8. The Spread of Christianity

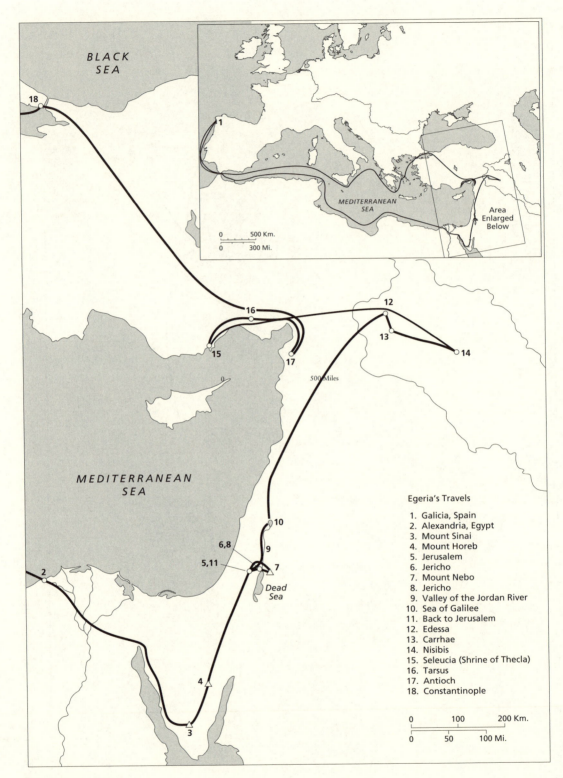

BLACK
SEA

MEDITERRANEAN
SEA

MEDITERRANEAN
SEA

Area
Enlarged
Below

0   500 Km.
0   300 Mi.

500 Miles

Dead
Sea

Egeria's Travels

1. Galicia, Spain
2. Alexandria, Egypt
3. Mount Sinai
4. Mount Horeb
5. Jerusalem
6. Jericho
7. Mount Nebo
8. Jericho
9. Valley of the Jordan River
10. Sea of Galilee
11. Back to Jerusalem
12. Edessa
13. Carrhae
14. Nisibis
15. Seleucia (Shrine of Thecla)
16. Tarsus
17. Antioch
18. Constantinople

0   100   200 Km.
0   50   100 Mi.

Map 9. Egeria's Travels

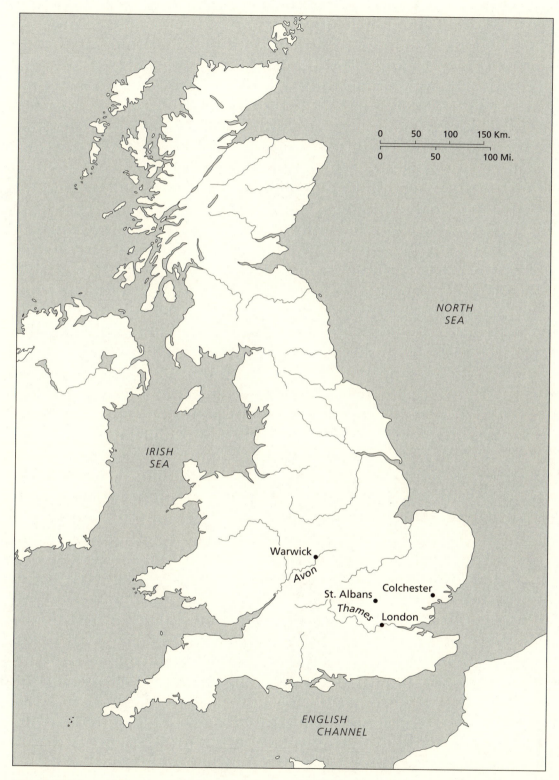

Labels on map:
NORTH SEA
IRISH SEA
Warwick
Avon
St. Albans
Colchester
Thames
London
ENGLISH CHANNEL

Scale:
0 50 100 150 Km.
0 50 100 Mi.

Map 10. Britain

ENCYCLOPEDIA OF
WOMEN
IN THE
ANCIENT
WORLD

Abortion

Our oldest records indicate that the practice of inducing abortions was used throughout the ancient world. There were many methods for inducing abortions, from surgery to irritating the cervix to taking abortifacient herbs. For example, an ancient Egyptian papyrus dating from 1550 B.C. recommended inserting strips of papyrus into the cervix to irritate it and stimulate an abortion. Most of these methods involved risk for the mothers; for example, some ancient cultures recommended eating ergot, a fungus that grows on rye. While effective as an abortifacient, this fungus can cause severe poisoning, even death, if consumed in too great a concentration.

The ancient Greeks wrote extensively on medicine and gynecology, and they included frequent references to abortions. Midwives passed on information about herbs that would stimulate uterine contractions and induce abortion or prescribed irritating the uterus by inserting laurel and peppers. Abortions must have been fairly frequent, since the practice is mentioned in various sources. For example, Greek temple inscriptions show that the Greeks considered that abortion made a woman impure for forty days.

Since Greeks exposed unwanted infants to the elements, they had no particular objection to abortion, but nevertheless they did forbid it in some instances. For example, if a pregnant woman's husband died, she was not to have an abortion because the child should inherit the father's estate. Physicians who took the Hippocratic Oath promising to do their patients no harm were not supposed to administer abortifacients, but this prohibition was probably aimed at not harming the mother rather than at protecting the fetus.

Roman physicians built on Greek medicine and continued many of the same approaches to abortions. Soranus, a physician who favored abortion, gave the most complete description of how to induce abortions. The least intrusive (and least effective) of his recommendations involved the pregnant woman's leaping and carrying heavy objects. Then the woman could try injecting hot olive oil into her uterus. If those techniques did not work, Soranus recommended a list of herbs that could be used as poultices or injections or taken internally, usually as a vaginal suppository. Soranus warned women to be careful not to use anything too strong for fear of injury: "[B]eware of things that are too powerful and of separating the embryo by means of something sharp-edged, for danger arises that some of the adjacent parts be wounded" (Lefkowitz and Fant 161).

The Roman Empire produced people with opinions on both sides of the abortion issue. Soranus strongly recommended abortion when the woman was so young that her uterus was still small. Indeed, he claimed that there were only two reasons for a doctor to refuse to help a woman abort: when the child was the product of adultery and when the woman's only reason for wanting an abortion was to preserve her beauty. The Stoic philosophers, too, supported abortion, claiming that the fetus resembled a plant and only became an animal at birth; therefore they found abortion perfectly acceptable.

However, the Romans always had a problem maintaining their population, so there were many who argued against abortions. The earliest Roman laws—the Laws of Romulus—gave the husband the right to divorce his wife if she used "drugs or magic" to prevent childbirth, and other Roman critics from Ovid to Juvenal argued that women used abortion to hide the results of adultery. In all these critiques, the men of the ancient world were not concerned about the rights of the unborn child. Instead, their legislation was aimed at controlling their wives and maintaining power over the decision about whether they should raise a child or not.

In A.D. 211, Emperor Caracalla for the first time banned abortion as a crime against the rights of parents and punished it with temporary exile. By that time, Christianity was spreading through the empire, and Christian writers, including Tertullian in the third century A.D., condemned abortion. Later Christian writers would continue this prohibition, although some continued to allow abortion during the first trimester, after which they believed the soul entered the fetus. At this point, for the first time in the ancient world, abortion became an issue about the unborn child rather than about the woman or about parental rights.

See also Contraception; Gynecology; Motherhood, Roman

Suggested Readings

Lefkowitz, Mary R., and Maureen B. Fant. *Women in Greece and Rome.* Toronto: Samuel-Stevens, 1977.

Pomeroy, Sarah B. *Goddesses, Whores, Wives, and Slaves: Women in Classical Antiquity.* New York: Schocken Books, 1975.

Rousselle, Aline. *Porneia: On Desire and the Body in Antiquity.* New York: Basil Blackwell, 1988.

Agnes

Virgin Martyr (d. ca. A.D. 304)

The Emperor Diocletian in about A.D. 304 instituted a persecution of Christians that was intended once and for all to resolve the question of whether Christians could be loyal Romans. Diocletian required everyone to come forward and perform a ritual sacrifice to the emperor, proving his or her loyalty to the state. All citizens were to obtain a certificate testifying to their sacrifice, which could be checked later. This persecution caused many Christians to flock to the marketplaces of the empire and perform the required sacrifice, but it also led to examples of resistance that created large groups of martyrs. Among the faithful probably martyred during this persecution was a young Roman girl, Agnes, who became one of the most esteemed martyrs of the fourth century.

The earliest sources praise the martyrdom of Agnes: Ambrose, Jerome, and Augustine all wrote of her bravery, and the fourth-century bishop of Rome, Damasus (A.D. 366–384), had an inscription engraved on marble commemorating her martyrdom. However, the most beautiful account of her death comes from the pen of the Iberian poet Prudentius, who published a hymn to Agnes in about A.D. 400. This account gives the details of the martyrdom (whether accurate or not we cannot know) and outlines the story that captured the imagination of Christians and was retold for centuries.

According to the account of the poet Prudentius, when Emperor Diocletian called for sacrifices, Agnes, a young twelve- or thirteen-year-old virgin, came forward to defy the decree. The judge threatened her with torture, but her resolve remained firm. The judge then commanded that she be shamed and placed naked in the public square for all to see. Most turned their eyes away from the modest maiden, but one young man looked at her with lust. As the poet wrote:

> It chanced that one man was forward
>   enough to fix
> His gaze upon the maiden and did not fear
> To look with lustful eye on her sacred form.
> But lo, a flame as swift as a lightning flash
> Quick struck his wanton eyes with its
>   trembling dart. (Prudentius 276)

The youth was blinded, and Agnes sang praises to God for protecting her chastity. (The poet recounts that some people said the generous girl prayed to restore the reckless youth's eyesight.) The furious judge put an end to the spectacle and had the girl beheaded by his swordsman. Prudentius ends his hymn with the virgin's ascent into heaven.

Agnes's body was placed in a sepulcher in Rome, where many came to venerate her. During the reign of Constantine (A.D. 306–337), the emperor caused a church to be erected in Agnes's honor over her grave. This church was remodeled in the seventh century and has remained substantially unaltered since then. Since the fourth century, the veneration of St. Agnes has been included in church calendars, and the young, courageous virgin has become a symbol of purity and faith.

See also Constantina; Helena; Martyrs
Suggested Readings
Prudentius. *The Poems of Prudentius.* Trans. M. C. Eagan. Washington, DC: Catholic University of America Press, 1962.

Agrippina the Elder
Granddaughter of Caesar Augustus
(ca. 14 B.C.–A.D. 33)

In the Julio-Claudian dynasty founded by Caesar Augustus, one of the main qualifications for emperor was to belong to Augustus's family. Thus, daughters were as significant as sons, for they could offer legitimacy to a claimant of the throne of the Roman Empire. However, their political significance also caused some of these daughters to suffer in the political struggles of the day. It would seem that a granddaughter of the great Caesar Augustus would have her fortunes guaranteed, but Agrippina the Elder would not be so fortunate.

Agrippina was one of the five children of Augustus's daughter Julia, and since Augustus had no more children of his own, the succession to the imperial throne lay clearly through Julia's children. Augustus was proud of Agrippina—the ancient historian Suetonius claims her grandfather wrote a letter praising her intelligence and directing her education. Augustus arranged a good match for Agrippina: she married Germanicus, the grandson of Augustus's sister, Octavia. Germanicus was a popular military commander who was greatly loved by the people of Rome. He had a charismatic personality, and he seemed the perfect successor to Augustus.

As Augustus aged, he decided to adopt Tiberius, his stepson, as his heir. Tiberius was not popular; he was reclusive and morose, but Augustus believed he would secure the succession. Augustus did insist that Tiberius adopt Germanicus as his own son, promising the succession to him. However, this was not to be.

In A.D. 19, Germanicus died in Antioch during a campaign. Contemporaries (and historians ever since) have wondered whether his death was an accident or whether Tiberius had managed to rid himself of his popular rival by murdering him. Agrippina was certain her husband had been assassinated, and she voiced her opinion widely. Tiberius's popularity dropped even lower. The relations between Agrippina and Tiberius finally ended at a dinner party, when the emperor offered Agrippina an apple. She refused to accept it from his hand, thus implying it was poisoned. He never invited her to dine again and began to look for a way to remove her and her family from the imperial succession.

Finally, in A.D. 29, Agrippina and her two teenaged sons were accused of plotting to overthrow Tiberius. They were tried and condemned to exile. Agrippina's son Nero committed suicide soon after the trial, and her other son, Drusus, died of starvation while imprisoned in Rome a few years later. Agrippina was exiled to the island of Pandateria (where her mother had been exiled years before). Suetonius writes of her ill treatment, which had been ordered by Tiberius: "In punishment for her violent protests he [Tiberius] ordered a centurion to give her a good flogging; in the course of which she lost an eye. Then she decided to starve herself to death and, though he had her jaws pried open for forcible feeding, succeeded" (Suetonius 140). Whether she succeeded in starving herself or whether Tiberius had her killed in this way we do not know.

Tiberius was not content solely with Agrippina's death. He slandered her memory, persuading the senate to decree her birthday a day of ill omen. Historians, however, have been much kinder to the memory of Agrippina the Elder, whose fierce defense of her husband led her to such a tragic end.

See also Julia; Octavia
Suggested Readings
Suetonius. *The Twelve Caesars.* Trans. Robert Graves. New York: Penguin, 1979.

Agrippina the Younger
Roman Empress (A.D. 15–59)

The Julio-Claudian dynasty of emperors defined their legitimacy to rule based on their relationship to the great Caesar Augustus, who had been the first emperor of the Romans. This significant tie of blood made the female relatives highly important, because through marriage with them and creation of heirs one could legitimately claim the imperial throne. At least one woman, however, was not content to be the passive conduit of imperial power; she wanted to rule in her own right—at least as regent. Agrippina the Younger, niece and fourth wife of the Emperor Claudius, was an active and perhaps violent emperor maker, and the ancient historians were not kind to her.

Agrippina was one of eight children of Germanicus and Agrippina the Elder, and she was only four years old when her father died tragically in Syria. The Emperor Tiberius was no friend of the family, since most Romans had wished for the popular Germanicus to become emperor. It did not take long for imperial politics to strike the family: her mother and her eldest brother were banished in A.D. 29. By then, Agrippina the Younger was already out of the household. She had been married in A.D. 28—when she was thirteen—to C. Domitius Ahenobarbus, a man whom contemporaries described as "in every aspect of his life utterly detestable." It seemed as if her life were destined to be miserable and short. In a few years, however, her fortunes dramatically changed.

By A.D. 37, Agrippina's parents were dead, but so was Tiberius. Two days after Tiberius's death, Agrippina's brother Gaius Caligula was emperor. Caligula was extremely attached to his sisters, and they received unusual public honors. One distinction was particularly bizarre: all three were awarded the status of "honorary vestal virgins" even though they were all married. Agrippina was even pregnant at that time, and on 15 December 37 she gave birth to Nero. Her husband was reputed to have said on that occasion that "any child of Agrippina and himself must be a loathsome object and a public disaster" (Suetonius 216). Her husband died within two years, but for Agrippina the overriding fact was that she had a son, and for the next fourteen years she held the ambition to be the mother of an emperor. Her impatience, it turned out, almost led to her downfall.

Agrippina became the lover of her deceased sister's husband Lepidus, which in itself would not have caused much scandal. However, Lepidus was involved in a plot to overthrow Caligula and take power himself. Was the ambitious Agrippina involved? We cannot know, but when Caligula discovered the plot he had Lepidus executed in A.D. 39. Caligula handed Agrippina the urn containing Lepidus's ashes, with the instruction that she should bury it. She and her sister were banished, and Caligula himself auctioned off their possessions. A year later, Caligula banished one of his guard on the allegation that Agrippina had been his mistress. It seemed that having an imperial princess alive was hazardous to Caligula. Surely she would have been next to die, but Caligula himself was assassinated in January 41.

The new Emperor Claudius recalled his niece Agrippina and restored her property. In A.D. 44 she married an extremely wealthy Roman (Passienus Crispus), and she no doubt hoped his money and position might help forward the prospects of her son, Nero. He was moved further from the throne, however, by the birth of the son Britannicus to Claudius and his wife Messalina. Agrippina's moment came when the young Messalina betrayed her husband.

When the Emperor Claudius had discovered the adultery of his third wife Messalina and arranged for her execution, a power gap was left in the court, raising the question of who would become the emperor's next wife. Almost at once he considered marrying the previous emperor's widow or remarrying an ex-wife of his; however, his niece Agrippina won his heart. According to the ancient historian Suetonius, she seduced Claudius: "She had a niece's privilege of kissing and caressing Claudius, and exercised it with a noticeable effect on his passions" (Suetonius 203). He persuaded a group of senators to propose that a union between them be arranged "in the public interest" and that the laws against incest be changed to allow other uncles to marry their nieces. The wedding took place a day later in A.D. 49. (Suetonius claims that only two other men took advantage of the change in the incest law to marry their nieces—most men were not interested.)

Now Claudius fell under the spell of a woman

with more experience and ambition than his previous wife, and the ancient historian Tacitus was not generous to her influence: "From this moment the country was transformed. Complete obedience was accorded to a woman. . . . This was a rigorous, almost masculine despotism. In public, Agrippina was austere and often arrogant. Her private life was chaste—unless power was to be gained. Her passion to acquire money was unbounded. She wanted it as a stepping-stone to supremacy" (Tacitus 253).

Within a year of the marriage, Agrippina persuaded Claudius to adopt her son, Nero. As Claudius's eldest son, Nero was Claudius's heir. He was married to Claudius's daughter Octavia to further ensure that the dynasty of the Julio-Claudians would continue through her son.

Agrippina was not content to ensure that her son would inherit; she wanted to exert some authority in her own right. She took the title Augusta—empress—and became the third woman in Roman history (after Livia and Octavia) to carry this honorable title in her lifetime. Unlike the other two women, she was the first to carry it during the lifetime of her husband; she seems to have considered herself as coruler with Claudius. Tacitus even describes an incident in which she sat on a throne before the Roman army to receive prisoners, an occasion described by the historian as a "novelty, quite alien to ancient manners." However, Tacitus continues, "In fact, Agrippina boasted that she was herself a partner in the empire which her ancestors had won" (Tacitus 267).

Claudius seems to have regretted marrying Agrippina and displacing his son Brittanicus. His advisers began to urge him to intervene to weaken the hold his wife had on the household and the state, but it was too late. Claudius grew sick after eating and died the next day. Some of the ancient historians claimed he was poisoned, and some even suggested that Agrippina poisoned a dish of mushrooms, which were his favorite food. Agrippina's hope had come to pass: her seventeen-year-old son Nero was proclaimed emperor. She planned to continue her authority as imperial mother. In time, however, her son would chafe at her authority.

When Nero protested at his mother's presence everywhere, Agrippina threatened the young emperor with the existence of his half-brother, Britannicus. She said she would reveal the sinister facts of Nero's accession to the throne and support Britannicus's claims. Nero had learned from his mother and had Britannicus poisoned at an imperial dinner party. In the same year—A.D. 55—he evicted his mother from the palace to live in a private house in Rome.

Now her old enemies found her vulnerable and went to the emperor with charges of her conspiring against him. She demanded an audience with the emperor and persuaded him of her unstinting devotion to him. Her enemies were exiled, and Nero's aunt died from poison. Agrippina, however, would find an enemy who was even closer to her son than she—Nero's mistress Poppaea. The ancient historians claimed that Agrippina appeared in broad daylight elaborately made up and kissed her son "with indecent passion" (Suetonius 228), with the unmistakable suggestion of incest. Such scandals affected the emperor and his mistress, and they decided that it was time for Agrippina to die.

The assassination plans were elaborate. They wanted her death to appear an accident to prevent political opponents from using her death against Nero. They also did not trust poison, for it was said that Agrippina dosed herself regularly on antidotes. In the end, they tried a ruse by which she would be lured onto a ship that had been set up to fall apart at sea, where she could drown "by accident." However, it did not work. The ship fell apart, and one of her handmaidens unwisely called out: "I am Agrippina. Help for the Emperor's Mother." She was bashed to death with oars, and the real Agrippina escaped by swimming until she was picked up by a small boat. She knew that the assassination order had been placed and attempted to save herself.

The situation seemed desperate for Nero, for the senate and the army still loved the dead Germanicus, and his daughter still generated sympathy. A freedman of Nero's household said he would do the deed. When he and his escort entered her chamber, she knew that she would die. When the officer drew his sword, she pointed to her womb and said, "This is the place to strike." She received many blows and died. Reputedly, when she had been younger, she had consulted astrologers about Nero and had received the answer, "He will be Emperor and will kill his mother." She responded, "He is welcome to kill me, as long as he becomes Emperor" (Tacitus 326). The ambitious woman seems to have gotten her wishes—both for her own authority and her son's power. The historian Suetonius claimed that for the remaining nine years of his rule Nero suffered from bad dreams over the murder of his mother, who had committed many crimes to be sure he would rule Rome (Suetonius 232).

See also Agrippina the Elder; Messalina; Poppaea Sabina

Suggested Readings

Barrett, A. A. *Agrippina*. New York: Routledge, 1999.
Hawley, R., and B. Levick, eds. *Women in Antiquity: New Assessments*. New York: Routledge, 1995.
Suetonius. *The Twelve Caesars*. Trans. Robert Graves. New York: Penguin, 1979.
Tacitus. "The Annals." In *Complete Works of Tacitus*. New York: The Modern Library, 1942.

Alexandra Salome

Queen of Judea (140–67 B.C.)

In about 168 B.C., the Jews of Judea led by Judas Maccabeus led a revolt against the Hellenistic monarchy and succeeded in establishing a theocratic state ruled by the Hasmonean kings, who were strong enough to extend the dynasty's powers over some neighboring states. The dynasty was soon drawn into the politics of the Roman Empire, which became involved in the dynastic struggles and would ultimately replace the Hasmonean dynasty with the Herodian one in 37 B.C. Queen Alexandra Salome, one of the late Hasmonean rulers, successfully preserved the dynasty through an excellent reign; she was praised by the ancient historian Josephus as a far more successful sovereign than the men of her family.

Alexandra was first married to Aristobulus I, who may have been the first formal king of Judea, although the sources are contradictory. Aristobulus ruled briefly—only from 104 to 103 B.C.—but he accomplished quite a lot. He extended the lands of Judea by taking the neigh-boring area of Galilee, and he forced all the men of that land to be circumcised and live according to Jewish customs. Aristobulus was particularly brutal to his family members—he imprisoned and starved his mother, had one of his brothers killed, and imprisoned the other three. At his death in 103 B.C., Alexandra Salome had his brothers released from prison and married one of them, Alexander Jannaeus, thus making him the official king of Judea.

Alexander Jannaeus ruled for twenty-seven years, and the reign was filled with bloodshed, civil wars, and foreign conquests. He died of drunkenness and other excesses in 76 B.C., and the historian Josephus related his deathbed conversation with his wife. The dying king told Alexandra Salome to take over the kingdom and to reconcile with his enemies, the Pharisees, and give them a share in the government. She took his advice and remained the sole ruler from 76 to 67 B.C.

The Pharisees were a sect of Judaism that, unlike the religiously conservative Sadducees, adopted a more flexible approach to the Laws of Moses and emphasized tradition as well as written scriptures. Some historians suggest that the Pharisees' opposition to established order drew the patronage of aristocratic women; it is certainly likely that the support of the queen helped strengthen the position of the Pharisees during this period. Josephus was less enthusiastic about her support of the Pharisees; he praised her rule, but he said that though she ruled the nation, the Pharisees ruled her.

Josephus's overall laudatory assessment of the queen's administration seems to overwhelm any criticism he might offer of her support of the Pharisees. Josephus writes: "She was sagacious in the highest degree in the exercise of authority and demonstrated by her acts her practical understanding of politics, which far exceeded that of the men, who constantly came to grief in affairs of government. She always counted the bird in the hand preferable to the bird in the bush and held that an iron will in government was a *sine qua non*, from which policy she was not deterred by considerations of honor or justice. . . . She did keep her people in peace throughout her reign" (Macurdy 66).

Like many fine rulers of the ancient world, Alexandra Salome was less able to control her sons, Hyrcanus and Aristobulus, who soon after her death began fighting each other for power. The rivalry between them gave Pompey—the Roman general—an excuse to annex Judea in 63 B.C. Imprudent alliances on the part of the Judean rulers caused the Romans to end the Hasmonean dynasty in 37 B.C. and appoint Herod the Great to be king of Judea, thus introducing the Herodian dynasty to the area. Through these tumultuous times, the Jews had cause to look back fondly to the rule of Alexandra Salome, who had brought peace and justice to the troubled land.

See also Glaphyra; Mariamne; Salome I
Suggested Readings

Josephus, Flavius. *Jewish Antiquities.* Trans R. Marcus. Cambridge: Harvard University Press, 1963.
———. *Josephus, The Jewish War.* Trans. H. St. James Thackeray. Cambridge: Harvard University Press, 1927.
Kokkinos, Nikos. *The Herodian Dynasty: Origins, Role in Society and Eclipse.* Sheffield, UK: Sheffield Academic Press, 1998.
Kraemer, Ross Shepard, and Mary Rose D'Angelo. *Women and Christian Origins.* New York: Oxford University Press, 1999.
Macurdy, Grace Harriet. *Vassal-Queens and Some Contemporary Women in the Roman Empire.* Baltimore: Johns Hopkins University Press, 1937.
Richardson, Peter. *Herod: King of the Jews and Friend of the Romans.* Philadelphia: Fortress Press, 1999.
Sandmel, Samuel. *Herod: Profile of a Tyrant.* Philadelphia: J. B. Lippincott, 1967.

Amazons
Ancient Warrior Women

Many ancient Greek writers told of a race of women warriors who were descended from Ares, the god of war, and the nymph Harmonia. They were said to live without men, wear masculine clothing, and spend their days hunting, farming, and above all fighting; their favorite goddess was Artemis, the virgin huntress. There has been no archaeological evidence that proves the existence of such a tribe of women warriors (although archaeologists have found evidence of a

Figure 1. Amazon in Oriental dress on horseback, Athenian red-figure amphora, ca. 420 B.C. (Staatliche Antikensammlungen, Munich, inv. 2342)

people—the Sauromatians—whose women hunted and fought alongside their men). Nevertheless, the myth of the Amazons was popular; classical writers repeated the tales, and artists portrayed the Amazon women prominently in their art. Even in the modern period, the myth has held an allure—Spanish explorers of Brazil named the great river "Amazon" because they saw native women fighting alongside their men to repel the invaders. How did ancient writers describe this imaginary tribe of powerful, independent women?

The Amazons were placed in a variety of geographical locations, and the one mentioned most frequently is the area bordering on the southeastern shore of the Black Sea (in modern northern Turkey) around the city of Themiscyra and the Thermadon River—see Map 3 for the location. When Greek travelers in the sixth century B.C. went to that region and discovered no Amazons, they did not abandon the myth; they simply moved the location to distant Scythia or north Africa. What was most important about the presumed location of the Amazons was that they were outside the "civilized" world inhabited by the Greeks.

For most of the writers, the Amazons lived not only far away but also in a distant time—usually before or during the Trojan War, and thus at least 500 years before the first mention of them in the Greek literature (in Homer's work). One set of narratives did set the Amazons in a historical period—late in the fourth century B.C. when Alexander the Great was reputed to have met a troop of Amazons led by their queen Thalestris when he traveled in the far north of the Persian Empire. The historian Arrian mentions a contact between Alexander and the Amazons but does not give it much credence, since he said he thought that Amazons no longer lived during the time of Alexander. Even the ancient historian who was recording the supposed contact placed the Amazons in a time before memory—a time of myth.

Amazonian customs generated a great deal of attention from ancient authors who were drawn to speculations about exotic women who were so different from the ideal Greek women. The Greek geographer Strabo said that in order to reproduce themselves, the Amazons set aside two months every year for visits to the mountainous area on the border between their own country and that of a people called Gargarians. The men from the other side of the border met them and all participated in promiscuous sexual relationships. If the babies born as a result were female, they were kept by the Amazons; if they were male, they were returned to their fathers to be raised as Gargarians.

Some writers said that the right breasts of the young girls were either cut off or seared with a hot iron so that all the strength and bulk that might otherwise have gone to the breast went instead to the right shoulders and arms, strengthening them for fighting. One reason why this story was popular was that it explained to the Greeks a possible origin of the name: the

Greek word *a-mazon* could be translated as "without a breast." However, this explanation probably did not accompany the early stories, for all the visual representations of the Amazons produced in the fifth century B.C. show them with two breasts.

While some ancient authors (such as Strabo) claimed that the Amazons lived entirely without men, other authors (such as Diodorus) claimed that the Amazons lived with men but simply inverted the normal sex roles of Greek society. Diodorus said that women were the fighters, rulers, and administrators; the men, "like married women in our own society," looked after the home, reared the children, and obeyed the orders given to them by their wives. To ensure this inverted order, Diodorus claimed that mothers dislocated the legs of infant boys to make them crippled when they grew up. This ensured that they were unfit for war and thus would not challenge the women's predominance in this arena.

While all the authors claimed that the women in some way wanted to stay separate from men, they also claimed that the Amazons were susceptible to sexual desire. The fifth-century Greek historian Herodotus told of a group of Amazons who were seduced by men of the Scythian tribe who lived on the northern shore of the Black Sea. Although in love with the Scythians, the Amazons were nevertheless unwilling to enter into conventional Scythian society because they would have to give up the customs they had become used to. According to Herodotus, the couples decided to establish a new community separate from both, and this was the origin of the Sauromatians, whose women in his day still engaged in hunting and fighting (and who modern archaeologists have discovered were buried with their precious weapons).

If Herodotus claimed that Amazons could be "tamed" by sexual intercourse, other authors insisted that their way of life came to an end by force of arms. At least as far back as the fifth century B.C., the story circulated that the Greek hero Heracles (known to the Romans as Hercules) was given the task of bringing back to Greece the girdle of the Amazon queen Hippolyta. To achieve this, he and his followers fought a battle against the women warriors during which Heracles killed Hippolyta and took the girdle from her dead body.

Some of the versions of the Heracles episode claim that the hero was accompanied on this adventure by his Athenian comrade Theseus. Theseus became the consort of Hippolyta's sister Antiope, and he took her to Athens. This incident became one of the major events in Athens's mythical past, for according to the story, the Amazons invaded Greece from the north and marched on Athens. They launched a siege of the Acropolis, which lasted three months until Theseus's forces finally defeated the Amazon army.

In one other incident, the Amazons were represented as enemies of the Greeks: The Amazon queen Penthesilea brought her army to Troy to defend the city against the Greeks after the death of the Trojan hero Hector. According to the myth, the hero Achilles met Penthesilea on the battlefield, and it was only after his spear had pierced her breast that he noticed her beauty and fell in love with her; but it was too late—he had killed her.

Since there was no real basis for these myths, their origins remain obscure. There can be no doubt, however, about the popularity of the Amazon stories to the ancient Greeks. Several places in mainland Greece boasted tombs that were reputed to be of defeated Amazons. For example, there was a marker by one of the Athenian gates that was said to mark the grave of the Amazon Antiope, and there were several other tombs farther from Athens that were explained as the burial places of Amazons who had died while fleeing the battle against Theseus. Art, too, revealed the popularity of the legend, for there were many portrayals of Amazon women in sculptures and vase paintings. Why was this legend so popular, and what did it mean for the ancient Greeks who happily repeated the stories?

The Amazons represented the enemies of Greece, and in some vase paintings the Amazons were shown in Persian dress to emphasize both that they were "foreign" and enemies. The Amazon shown in Figure 1 is shown in Oriental dress as she rides the horse into battle. But the message of the Amazons had implications for Athenian society as well, for the myth reminded men and

women alike that anyone who did not follow ordinary family life with its carefully circumscribed roles was dangerous to society. While we sometimes admire the independent women of the Amazon myths, most of the ancient Greeks would have recognized that the message of the myth of the Amazons was that an ordered society depended upon women's behaving in ways completely opposite from the Amazons—leaving the fighting to the men and staying indoors to keep the home and society in order. Yet, one can imagine that some young girls dreamed of fighting and hunting and ruling as the mythological Amazon women did.

See also Greek (Athenian) Women; Nymphs

Suggested Readings

Blundell, Sue. *Women in Ancient Greece.* Cambridge: Harvard University Press, 1995.

Grimal, Pierre. *The Dictionary of Classical Mythology.* Oxford: Blackwell, 1996.

Larson, Jennifer. *Greek Heroine Cults.* Madison: University of Wisconsin Press, 1995.

Lefkowitz, Mary R. *Women in Greek Myth.* Baltimore: Johns Hopkins University Press, 1986.

Tyrrell, William Blake. *Amazons: A Study in Athenian Mythmaking.* Baltimore: Johns Hopkins University Press, 1984.

Anna

Jewish Prophet (ca. A.D. 10)

Throughout the ancient world, prophecy was seen as one of the significant marks of the presence of the divine. This was true among pagans, Jews, and early Christians—people who possessed the gift of prophecy were accorded great respect. Prophecy could include speaking with the voice of a spirit or foretelling the future. Jesus' divinity was "seen" by two prophets during his childhood—Simon (a blind man) and Anna.

In the Gospel of Luke, he describes how after Jesus was born, Mary and Joseph fulfilled two ritual requirements: circumcising the infant and taking him to the Temple for purification. When they arrive at the Temple, Simon the blind prophet praises the child in song. At the same time, another prophet—Anna—sees the child.

Luke (Luke 2:36–39) says that Anna had been married and had lived with her husband seven years before he died, leaving her as a widow. Instead of remarrying, Anna lived in the forecourt of the Temple, "worshiping with fasting and prayer night and day." Since Anna was eighty-four years old at this point, that would mean she had lived in the Temple for over fifty years. This is a curious statement; for while it was possible for a woman to live within the women's court of the Temple, no other known examples attest to anyone living there for so long. However, it may be that this is a reference to an early practice of widows dedicating themselves to the service of the church in good works.

When Anna saw Jesus, she "gave thanks to God, and spoke of him to all who were looking for the salvation of Jerusalem" (Luke 2:38). That is all that we know about Anna the prophet, but she forecasts more than Jesus' mission; she also introduces a tradition of Christian women prophets who will be instrumental in spreading the Christian message.

See also Christian Women; Mary; Perpetua the Martyr
Suggested Readings
Meyers, Carol, Toni Craven, and Ross S. Kraemer. *Women in Scripture.* New York: Houghton Mifflin, 2000.

Anyte of Tegea
Hellenistic Poet (ca. third century B.C.*)*
Anyte of Tegea in southern Greece was a poet who received much contemporary acclaim. A first-century literary critic—Antipater of Thessalonica—described her as the "female Homer" because her poetry was so admired. Unlike her contemporary Nossis of Locri, Anyte wrote on varying themes. Like male poets, she wrote celebrating war, and she was one of the first Hellenistic poets to write bucolic poetry praising country life. Anyte's verses appealed to both men and women.

Anyte also wrote epigrams, which were probably intended for inscriptions on graves, and several of these epigrams reveal her deep sensitivity to women. A number of the most poignant verses mourn girls who died before they were married. In the ancient world, marriage was considered the most important event in a woman's life, so when a girl died unwed, the lamentations were greater

for a "life unfulfilled." Two of Anyte's verses capture these feelings:

No bed-chamber and sacred rites of
    marriage for you.
Instead, your mother put upon this marble
    tomb
A likeness which has your girlish shape and
    beauty,
Therisis; you can be addressed even though
    you are dead.
I mourn for the maiden Antibia, to whose
father's house many suitors came, drawn by
Report of her beauty and wisdom. But
    deadly Fate
Whirled away the hopes of all of them.

This last verse includes a praise of Antibia's intelligence as well as her beauty, and it shows the value Hellenistic families placed on the education of their daughters.

Finally, one verse reveals poignantly the love that existed within ancient families:

Throwing her arms around her dear father,
Erato, melting away in moist tears, spoke
these last words.
"Father, I am no more; dark black Death
covers my eyes as already I perish."
    (Fantham et al. 166)

While we may lament that more of Anyte's verses have not survived, we can be grateful that these beautiful lines remain to give us a glimpse of the emotions of ancient men and women.

See also Corinna of Tanagra; Nossis of Locri
Suggested Readings
Fantham, E., et al. *Women in the Classical World.* New York: Oxford University Press, 1994.
Lefkowitz, Mary R., and Maureen B. Fant. *Women in Greece and Rome.* Toronto: Samuel-Stevens, 1977.

Aphrodite
Greek Goddess
Aphrodite was the goddess of desire, an important deity highly respected throughout the ancient world under various names. The myths

about her recognized the central place that love, beauty, and desire took in the lives of the ancient peoples. The myths said Aphrodite was born by rising naked from the foam of the sea, riding on a scallop shell. She first stepped ashore on the island of Cythera, which she found too small. She continued on until she landed at Paphos in Cyprus, where the Seasons welcomed her and adorned her and led her to the home of the Immortals. Grass and flowers sprang from the soil wherever she walked, and Paphos became the main center of her worship.

All the myths agree she came from sea foam, but they differ in their accounts of her parentage. Some say she sprang from the genitals of Uranus when he was castrated by his son Cronos, who threw his father's genitals into the sea. Other myths say that her father was Zeus, who sired her with a sea nymph. She was called "she who was born of the sea" or "she who was born of the god's seed," and her associations with the sea caused her to be venerated as a patron of seafaring. In all her functions, she was a powerful goddess not to be trifled with.

Various legends arose about Aphrodite, and instead of a coherent story, these consisted of different episodes in which the goddess played a part. In one, Zeus had given Aphrodite in marriage to Hephaestus, the lame smith-god. However, Aphrodite loved Ares, the god of war. Aphrodite bore several children by Ares—Eros and Anterus, Phobus and Deimus (Terror and Fear), and Harmonia. Some legends add Priapus, the protecting deity of gardens—a god with enormous genitals—to this list.

Homer tells how the love affair between Aphrodite and Ares was discovered when the lovers stayed too long together in bed at Ares's palace, and the Sun saw them when he arose. He told Hephaestus about the affair. The smith angrily went to his forge and made a bronze hunting net as fine as gauze, but unbreakable, to entrap the lovers. He attached it to Aphrodite's bed, and one night when Aphrodite summoned Ares, Hephaestus closed the net over them and summoned all the Olympian gods to witness his dishonor. Poseidon persuaded Hephaestus to release them, and Aphrodite fled to Paphos, where she renewed her virginity in the sea.

Some myths say that Zeus grew angry with Aphrodite and wanted to humiliate her by having her fall in love with a mortal—the handsome Anchises, king of the Dardanians. She appeared to him disguised as a human and slept with him. When they parted at dawn, she revealed her identity and made him promise not to tell anyone. Once when he had been drinking, however, the mortal bragged about his accomplishment; Zeus was so angry that he hurled a thunderbolt at Anchises. Aphrodite saved her lover, making the bolt land on the ground in front of him, but the force was so strong he was left crippled. Aphrodite bore him a son—Aeneas, who would become famous as the mythological founder of Rome. The powerful Aphrodite protected her son Aeneas during the Trojan War and helped him found Rome. Thus, Aphrodite, under the name Venus, became one of the special patrons of Rome.

Aphrodite's power was also manifested in her anger at humans who offended her. For example, she reputedly punished the women of Lemnos for not honoring her by making them smell so horrible that their husbands abandoned them. She also punished the daughters of Cinyras in Paphos by compelling them to become prostitutes for strangers. One of the most famous examples of the effects of her rage concerned one of the daughters of Cinyras named Smyrna (or Myrrha). Aphrodite made Smyrna fall in love with her own father and Smyrna deceived him into sleeping with her. When Cinyras realized he had been deceived, he chased his daughter with a knife. The gods took pity on Smyrna and turned her into a myrrh tree. Nine months later the bark of the tree burst open and a child emerged; he was called Adonis.

Aphrodite showed that her capacity for compassion was as great as her wrath by taking in the beautiful child Adonis. She entrusted him secretly to Persephone, Queen of the Dead. When Aphrodite returned to claim the child, Persephone, who loved him, would not give him up. The two powerful goddesses submitted the matter to Zeus, who decided that the youth should spend one-third of the year with Aphrodite, one-third with Persephone, and one-third wherever he wanted. Adonis so favored the goddess of love that he ended up spending two-thirds of the year with her. Soon afterwards, Adonis was wounded by a wild boar and died, possibly a victim of the jealousy of Ares. A popular cult arose about Adonis, the beloved of Aphrodite, which spread throughout the Mediterranean world.

Through all these stories, the Greeks recognized the power of Aphrodite, the goddess of love. She was a divinity who was strong in her passions, her rage, and her compassion, and she was venerated throughout the ancient world.

See also Athena; Helen of Troy in Greek
    Mythology; Ishtar; Mythology; Venus
Suggested Readings
Grimal, Pierre. *The Dictionary of Classical
    Mythology.* Oxford: Blackwell Publishers, 1996.

Apocryphal Acts of the Apostles
(ca. A.D. 200)

Sometime between A.D. 160 and A.D. 250 in Asia Minor or Greece, a number of fascinating texts were produced by early Christians. These texts told of heroic Christian women and often purported to recount the activities of such early followers of Jesus as John, Peter, and Paul, thus giving the texts greater authority. Because of the inclusion of these apostles, the texts collectively are called Acts of the Apostles. These stories derive from a period in Christian history when the Christian communities were changing. The early church of charismatic leadership in which some women who could prophesy could take a leadership role (*see* Perpetua the Martyr) was becoming more institutional, and leadership was moving to officials who did not necessarily derive their authority from charismatic powers. As women moved from leadership in the communities as a whole, they continued to play central roles in ascetic communities of women. These Acts were composed in these times of tension between charisma and hierarchy—between women's power and men's authority. As such, they offer fascinating insights into a critical time in the development of Christian thought.

Among the many texts with names of the apostles, the ones that most likely date from this period are the following: The Acts of John, The Acts of Peter, The Acts of Paul, The Acts of Andrew, The Acts of Thomas, and The Acts of Xanthippe. These are anonymous, but a number of scholars have made a compelling case arguing that they were most likely written by women for communities of women. There were plenty of Christian women with opportunity and interest in creating such texts, for most of the Christian communities by this time had a group of women associated with the church. This "order of widows" included Christian women whose husbands had died and who had taken vows of chastity, but the sources indicate that it also included young virgins, who also wanted to dedicate themselves to God. These women served a number of functions for the communities, but most importantly they were to pray for the congregation and, in return, the church had an obligation to offer these women financial support and care. The number of these women by the late second century was significant—for example, the records of the church in Rome show that 1,500 widows and "other needy" were supported by the congregation. It is probable that women in these orders of widows produced the Acts of the Apostles for themselves and each other. If this is so, these texts offer an excellent window into the outlook of a too-silent group of women, and by looking at the themes within the texts we analyze this point of view.

The overriding lesson of all these Acts is that chastity is the most important quality for a Christian. In The Acts of Paul, the authors transform the beatitudes of Jesus into a praise of chastity, saying: "Blessed are they who have kept the flesh pure, for they shall become a temple of God. Blessed are the continent, for to them will God speak. Blessed are the bodies of the virgins, for they shall be well pleasing to God, and shall not lose the reward of their purity" ("Apocrypha" 487). This extreme position even included a rejection of producing children, which most church leaders advocated. The Acts of Thomas argues that children are not blessings, for "the majority of children become unprofitable . . . either lunatic or half-withered or crippled or deaf or dumb or paralytic or stupid. Even if they are healthy, again will they be unserviceable, performing useless and abominable deeds . . ." (537). This suggests that these Acts were taking a strong antisocial position, and indeed this was the case.

In their advocacy of chastity, the authors of the Acts make villains of suitors, husbands, fathers, and even occasionally mothers who stand for the social life of marriage. Thecla (*see* Thecla) rejects her mother's entreaties and her suitor's pressure to follow Paul in chastity. In The Acts of Peter, the apostle has converted many women, including the beautiful Xanthippe. Her husband was "filled with fury and passionate love for Xanthippe, and amazed that she would not even sleep in the same bed with him, was raging like a wild beast and wished to do away with Peter; for he knew that he was responsible for her leaving his bed. And many other women besides fell in love with the doctrine of purity and separated from their husbands . . ." (Burrus 123). The story blames the martyrdom of Peter on the crowds of women who converted to chastity at his words, which highlights the fact that Christian virtue comes with the rejection of family ties—and sexuality.

The apostles who are the charismatic role models in the stories sometimes are not even strong enough to support the women against the pressures of society and family, thus making the women even more heroic than the male apostles. In The Acts of Thomas, Mygdonia's husband threatens Thomas with death if he will not encourage Mygdonia to return to him. Thomas tells the wife to "obey what your husband says." Mygdonia reprimands the apostle, saying: "If thou couldst not name the deed in word, how dost thou compel me to endure the act?" ("Apocrypha" 547). By this exchange, the woman is shown to be even stronger in faith than the apostle, and she withstands her husband's pressure. Repeatedly, then, in these stories chaste women are praised as models of heroic Christians, and in all of them men are shown to be weaker than the women. This reversal of the standard view must have been highly satisfying to the women who were reading these widely circulated texts!

Another striking feature of the Acts is the absence of mention of the church hierarchy, which by the second century was certainly visible in the Christian congregations. There is virtually no mention of priests or even deacons, in spite of the fact that they were the ones organizing the payments to the orders of widows, and the very absence of mention suggests some criticism of hierarchy. Instead, the heroes of the works—aside from the chaste women themselves—were the apostles, who wandered from city to city preaching and performing healings and other miracles. During the second century, there were still prophets who went from city to city visiting the Christian congregations. In some regions, these wandering prophets were called "apostles," so the Acts of the Apostles serve as praise for these charismatic holy men. It is perhaps not surprising that texts written for communities of women would praise these wandering prophets, because when they dominated the church, there was a good deal of space for women to exert their own charismatic authority. The Acts urge rebellion against husbands, and they nowhere encourage subservience to the authority of bishops or priests. These are texts about freedom from restriction. Under the increasing guidance of priests and bishops, women's roles were receding from the Christian communities, and these texts seem to offer one source of information about how some women felt about the change.

The works also point directly to a time when women had authority in the Christian communities. Thecla baptizes herself in the arena, and she preaches to a queen and a governor to convert them. Another Christian heroine, Polyxena, also preached to the prefect of the city and converted him to Christianity. The Acts of Xanthippe (probably written the latest) show a strange ambiguity about women's preaching, which may show how women were being affected by the changing status that was restricting their voices. Xanthippe says, "I desire to keep silence, and am compelled to speak, for some one inflames and sweetens me within. If I say, I will shut my mouth, there is some one that murmurs in me" (Burrus 125). By this speech, Xanthippe begins a tradition that will continue for centuries: Christian women who are forbidden to speak the words of God claim that they are divinely inspired to such speech; thus it is God who is speaking through them. They claim the gift of prophecy that had inspired women in the earliest congregations to speak out and take charismatic leadership of the communities. Even though that leadership role had been transformed by the beginning of the third century, and women were to be silent, these texts preserved the idea of a different role for women.

Beyond these larger issues of spirituality and power, the Acts of the Apostles record incidents that point to the everyday problems of widows living in orders and depending upon the charity of the congregations. Repeatedly the Acts urge generosity to widows. In one incident, the Apostle Peter reputedly raised a boy from the dead. The grateful mother claimed that she would give some of her property to newly freed slaves in gratitude, but the apostle immediately told her to distribute the money "to the widows." In another incident in The Acts of Thomas, a woman tells of a vision she had of hell and of the devil, and the people were so impressed that they "brought much money for the service of the widows," and they sent them "both clothing and provision for their nourishment" ("Apocrypha" 546).

The widows did not only need food and clothing; they were also preoccupied with ill health and the problems of aging. In The Acts of John, the apostle heard about the condition of one of the orders of widows: "Out of the old women over sixty that are here I have found only four in good bodily health; of the others some are paralytic and others sick." After reprimanding the men of Ephesus for neglecting the elderly women, John healed them all. Peter, too, restored the sight to blind widows in a miraculous act. Since most of the Acts show specific concern for the health and financial security of widows over and above a general concern for the poor and weak, it seems that there were communities of widows known to the composers of the Acts and that the Acts show intense respect for these communities. The women writing these works must have believed that the widows did not always receive the care they needed, since the references often include some sort of rebuke. Through these writings, we can perhaps glimpse some of the struggles of elderly women living in communities devoted to prayer.

How did men of the official church respond to these texts that clearly empowered women?

Not well at all. The influential third-century church father, Tertullian, railed against The Acts of Paul because within them women were assumed to have the right to preach and to baptize, both activities he forbade. Many churchmen condemned these Acts as heretical because they seemed to be too much against marriage and contained other elements that seemed suspect. In the late fourth century A.D., Pope Gelasius even issued a decree specifically condemning the Acts of Peter, Philip, and Andrew. The church had changed from the early centuries—now the authority of bishops and priests was paramount, and wandering charismatic preachers and women who claimed divine inspiration were suspect. These ancient Acts were called "apocryphal," meaning they were not genuinely biblical.

We can be grateful, however, that in spite of the condemnations, these texts have survived. They offer us a rare and precious glimpse into the lives of some anonymous ancient women who would otherwise have been lost. Widows and virgins living together in semiofficial orders were instrumental in building the Christian communities that so transformed the Western world during the late antique period. Through these texts that were probably written by and for women, we can see that they thought of their roles as heroic and that they struggled to maintain their status in spite of difficulties of every sort from hostile families to financial hardship to neglected old age. The texts also show that these Christian women never lost their taste for fast-paced, lively stories. The Apocryphal Acts of the Apostles remain entertaining reading today.

See also Anna; Christian Women; Eve; Perpetua the Martyr; Thecla

Suggested Readings

"Apocrypha." In *Ante-Nicene Fathers.* Vol. 8, *Fathers of the Third and Fourth Centuries,* ed. by A. Roberts. Peabody, MA: Hendrickson Publishers, 1995.

Burrus, Virginia. *Chastity as Autonomy: Women in the Stories of Apocryphal Acts.* Lewiston, NY: Edwin Mellen Press, 1987.

Davies, Stevan L. *The Revolt of the Widows: The Social World of the Apocryphal Acts.* Carbondale: Southern Illinois University Press, 1980.

James, M. R., trans. *The Apocryphal New Testament.* Oxford: Clarendon Press, 1969.

Aristodama of Smyrna

Hellenistic Poet (ca. 218 B.C.)

During the Hellenistic age there were more opportunities than ever before for women to get an education and, perhaps more important for us, to become public figures and use their education in the arts. These circumstances contributed to the emergence of women poets throughout the Greek world, and some of these poets were honored in their lifetimes by their contemporaries. One such poet was Aristodama of Smyrna.

Unfortunately, none of Aristodama's lyrics have survived; we only know of her fame because of an inscription erected in her honor by the citizens of Lamia. The inscription describes the honors she won for her poetry:

> Since Aristodama, daughter of Amyntas, a citizen of Smyrna in Ionia, epic poet, while she was in our city, gave several public recitations of her poems in which the nation of the Aitolians and the People's ancestors were worthily commemorated and since the performance was done with great enthusiasm, she shall be a "friend of the state" and benefactor, and she shall be given citizenship and the right to purchase land and a house and the right of pasture and inviolability and security on land and sea in war and peace for herself and her descendants and their property for all time. (Fantham et al. 163)

The grateful citizens awarded the rights of citizenship to her brother as well.

This was an extraordinary reward for a poet in the ancient world, and that it was given to a woman is particularly noteworthy. It not only testifies to Aristodama's skill but also points out that during the Hellenistic centuries some ancient women were able to succeed in public creative enterprises.

See also: Erinna of Telos; Nossis of Locri; Sappho of Lesbos

Suggested Readings

Fantham, E., et al. *Women in the Classical World.* New York: Oxford University Press, 1994.

Arsinoë II

Ptolemaic Queen of Egypt (315–ca. 270 B.C.)

The generation of Macedonians who took power after the death of Alexander the Great in 323 B.C. boasted a number of remarkable women who became queens and engaged in the violent political intrigues of the times. Out of these intrigues grew great kingdoms that lasted for centuries (until conquered by the greater power of Rome). The richest of these kingdoms was that of the Ptolemies, ruled by the Macedonian family who conquered and established a dynasty in the land of the Nile—the old kingdom of the pharaohs. The early queens were instrumental in establishing this spectacular dynasty, which had its capital at Alexandria. Historians agree that one of the most talented of these women was Arsinoë II, wife of kings.

Arsinoë was the daughter of the first Ptolemy of Egypt (the successor of Alexander) and his wife Berenice I. The sources praise Arsinoë's beauty, and surviving busts show that she was regularly portrayed in the traditional Greek way with perhaps an idealized beauty. When she was only about fifteen years old, her parents arranged an exceptional marriage for her to Lysimachus, the king of Thrace (east of Macedonia, by the Black Sea). As was customary in the ancient world, this older king already had taken two wives. One was a Persian woman to whom he had been married for two years and who had borne him a son named Alexander. Upon Arsinoë's arrival, the Persian wife returned to her lands in the east. Lysimachus had another son, named Agathocles, whose mother was Nicaea (a daughter of Antipater, Alexander's regent). Agathocles was twenty years old when Arsinoë arrived at the court, and some sources suggest the new teenaged bride found the son much more attractive than her husband. (And after all, her acquaintance, Stratonice, had married her husband's son, and Arsinoë must have been aware of this.) However, Agathocles rejected her advances. Arsinoë bore three sons to Lysimachus before trouble arose between her and Agathocles. Her stepson, a successful general, was married to Arsinoë's half-sister, Lysandra, when Arsinoë accused him of disloyalty to Lysimachus. According to one source, Arsinoë prepared the poison for the old king (who was now almost

Figure 2. Queen Arsinoë (Metropolitan Museum of New York)

eighty years old) to give to his son, and the young man died, paving the way for Arsinoë's son to inherit his father's throne.

At the end of his life, the old king had to fight a war against the Seleucid dynasty of Syria. In the course of the battles, Lysimachus died and his armies defected to Seleucus; Arsinoë was no longer safe in her city and developed a strategy to escape: She dressed as a beggar, rubbing dirt on her face, and dressed her maid in her royal robe. The unfortunate maid was killed by men who thought she was the queen, while Arsinoë escaped to shore where ships sped her and her three children to Macedonia. She had great wealth and could have lived in retirement, but the Hellenistic queens were seldom willing to be far from the centers of power. Arsinoë hoped her son Ptolemy would be able to take the throne of Macedonia with the help of her brother, the king of Egypt.

However, a new general rose up to claim the Macedonian throne—Arsinoë's half-brother Ceraunus. Ceraunus sent Arsinoë a message offering to marry her, make her queen of Macedonia, and adopt her children so young Ptolemy would be his heir. She and her son were suspicious of his offer—Ptolemy fled the city before the pretender's arrival, and Arsinoë insisted that she be proclaimed queen by the army before opening the city gates. Ceraunus consented and Arsinoë heard herself hailed queen of Macedonia as she threw open the gates. She should have been more prudent—Ceraunus marched into the town and killed her two younger children as they clung to their mother for protection. Strangely, Arsinoë lived and escaped to Egypt to the protection of her brother the king. There her ambitions were finally fulfilled.

Within her brother's household, Arsinoë II first accused her stepdaughter Arsinoë I, her brother's wife, of plotting against him. Her brother Ptolemy believed her, exiled his wife, and in about 265 B.C. married his full sister Arsinoë II; she was now queen of Egypt. The marriage of brother and sister was traditional among Egyptian pharaohs but forbidden among the Greeks and Macedonians. This act began to move the Macedonian dynasty of the Ptolemies closer to the traditional Egyptian rulers, and to note this,

Ptolemy II and his sister were called Philadelphus, which means "sibling-lover." A new blending was occurring that would help shape this new strong dynasty of Egypt. The bust of Arsinoë II shown in Figure 2 shows the new queen wearing the headdress of the traditional Egyptian rulers. She is also portrayed in the Egyptian manner with eye makeup and presumably a shaved head. This treatment of the figure shows that the Greek queen has become an Egyptian one.

Arsinoë II served as queen of Egypt for only five years, and historians have disagreed on how many of the accomplishments of Ptolemaic Egypt at that time were due to her influence or her brother's rule. The reign of Ptolemy Philadelphus and his sister-wife is remembered for several accomplishments. One is the linking of the Macedonian dynasty with the Egyptian tradition (shown in Figure 2). Another is a series of military victories that allowed Egypt to win the Syrian War (between 276 and 274 B.C.). Arsinoë traveled to the borders in Egypt in 273 B.C. to survey the defenses, so some historians suggest that she was instrumental in the planning that led to Egypt's military victory. During this period, Egypt built a large navy, which made the nation into a sea power, and again historians are divided about how much influence Arsinoë had in this decision. Finally, Ptolemy II Philadelphus founded the great museum in Alexandria, which would serve as the center of learning in the Mediterranean world for almost the next thousand years.

Whatever modern historians think of the queen's influence, her contemporaries—including her brother-husband—had no doubt about her power. She was the first Macedonian queen to be worshipped as a goddess during her lifetime, and she was venerated in many temples. Poems that survive praise the newly declared goddess and testify that prayers to her would help sailors and others in distress. After her death in 270 B.C., her husband did not remarry but continued to bestow honors upon Arsinoë II. He awarded her the title King of Upper and Lower Egypt, which strongly suggests that he credited her with an active role in his reign; that she served as a coruler. Furthermore, to stimulate her worship, he diverted taxes from other temples to the cult of Arsinoë Philadelphus. Finally, it is certain that the model of this strong, capable queen would serve as precedent for other rulers in the Ptolemy dynasty, which had more than its share of competent female rulers.

See also (Julia) Berenice; Cleopatra VII; Egyptian Women; Phila; Stratonice I

Suggested Readings

Burstein, Stanley Mayer. "Arsinoë II Philadelphos: A Revisionist View." In *Philip II, Alexander the Great, and the Macedonian Heritage,* ed. by W. Lindsay Adams and Eugene N. Borza, 197–212. Washington, DC: University Press of America, 1982.

Macurdy, Grace Harriet. *Hellenistic Queens.* Baltimore: Johns Hopkins University Press, 1932.

Pomeroy, Sarah B. *Women in Hellenistic Egypt: From Alexander to Cleopatra.* New York: Schocken Books, 1984.

Arsinoë III

Ptolemaic Egyptian Queen (ca. 224–ca. 203 B.C.)

In the dynasty of the Ptolemies in Egypt, one of the worst kings was Ptolemy IV, the son of Berenice II. This young man had killed his brother and mother when he took the throne, and in the Egyptian manner, her married his very young sister, Arsinoë III. Ptolemy's reign was dominated by Sosibius, an unscrupulous prime minister, who indulged the weak king's drunkenness and debauchery. The histories preserve only a bit of information about the life of Arsinoë, who must have had a difficult time in the decadent court of her brother. We know of her travels through inscriptions and artwork. One incident, however, suggests that even as a young girl she had the strong spirit of her mother and grandmother.

Early in his reign, Ptolemy IV was engaged in the Fourth Syrian War (221–217 B.C.) against the Hellenistic kingdom of the Seleucids. At first, he had lost much of the Syrian coast to Antiochus III, but the final battle of Raphia in 217 B.C. turned the tide. The apocryphal book of the Bible *III Maccabees* and the historian Polybius relate the role of the girl Arsinoë in this decisive battle. Ptolemy brought the young girl to the front, and she repeatedly appeared before the disheartened Egyptian troops to urge them to

bravery. She stood before them weeping, with hair flying loose in the wind, as she told them to fight bravely for their wives and children and for their own safety. Thus stirred, the Egyptian troops won the decisive victory, and Antiochus was driven back, leaving Syria and Phoenicia in Egyptian hands.

For the next three months, Ptolemy and Arsinoë traveled in the region, and according to *III Maccabees* Ptolemy demanded to be allowed to enter the inner sanctum of the Jewish Temple in Jerusalem. He was told he could not, and when he was about to use force, the text says that God struck him with a fit that left him shaking on the ground. He gave up his attempt to enter the forbidden parts of the temple. After touring, the couple returned to Alexandria.

Arsinoë did not have a child until 209 B.C., and historians suggest that the delay was due to her very young age at marriage. She had a son, Ptolemy. When the boy was six years old, he succeeded to the throne after his father's mysterious death. Arsinoë was probably murdered at the same time, for Polybius tells how the young Ptolemy was crowned before the soldiers with urns containing the ashes of Ptolemy VII and his young sister-wife Arsinoë III.

See also Berenice II; Egyptian Women

Suggested Readings

Macurdy, Grace Harriet. *Hellenistic Queens.* Baltimore: Johns Hopkins University Press, 1932.

Polybius. *Histories.* Trans. Evelyn S. Shuckburgh. New York: Macmillan, 1889.

Pomeroy, Sarah B. *Women in Hellenistic Egypt: From Alexander to Cleopatra.* New York: Schocken Books, 1984.

Artemis

Greek Goddess

Artemis was the virgin goddess of the hunt and the protector of small children and suckling animals. She was very popular and was worshiped in many shrines in ancient Greece. According to some Greek myths, Artemis was the sister of Apollo (the god of archery, music, medicine, prophecy, and so on). Their mother was Leto, daughter of Titans, and their father was Zeus. Zeus transformed himself and Leto into quails so he could seduce her without his sister-wife

Figure 3. Artemis of Ephesus (Ann Ronan Picture Library)

from her anger. Artemis took part in the battle against the Giants, where she killed the giant Gration with the help of Heracles. She also destroyed other monsters and Orion, the giant huntsman. In all the myths, Artemis is portrayed as a ferocious goddess of the woods and mountains, who shunned cities and hunted in the hills. She was held in honor in all the wild and mountainous areas of Greece and was the protecting deity of the Amazons, who were warriors and huntresses like her.

The most famous shrine of this goddess was at Ephesus, where the temple was one of the seven wonders of the ancient world. At this shrine the worship of Artemis was integrated with veneration of an ancient fertility goddess, Cybele. The statue of Artemis there (shown in Figure 3) shows her covered with breasts to mark her connection with childbirth and with suckling animals. Artemis is mentioned in the New Testament of the Bible, which in the Book of Acts describes the Apostle Paul when he preached at Ephesus. Paul gained so many converts that the followers of Artemis were concerned. A silversmith who made small silver shrines of the goddess gathered people to remind them that their economy rested on the worship of Artemis. He said: "And there is danger not only that this trade of ours may come into disrepute but also that the temple of the great goddess Artemis may count for nothing and that she may even be deposed from her magnificence" (Acts 19:27). Hearing this, the crowd rioted, saying "Great is Artemis of the Ephesians," and they attacked some of Paul's companions. The riot was finally quieted and Paul moved on.

This incident shows how popular the worship of the virgin huntress was throughout the ancient Mediterranean world. She was a goddess who commanded respect even as the message of Christianity was slowly spreading through the Roman Empire. There would continue to be many men and women who found comfort in the worship of this powerful deity.

See also Cybele; Diana; Hera; Niobe
Suggested Readings
Grimal, Pierre. *The Dictionary of Classical Mythology.* Oxford: Blackwell Publishers, 1996.

Hera's finding out. However, Zeus's jealous wife sent the serpent Python to pursue Leto and decreed that she would not deliver her children anywhere that the sun shone. Carried on the wings of the south wind, Leto came near Delos, where she bore Artemis, who then helped her mother give birth to her brother. Women in labor prayed to Artemis as the patron of childbirth because her mother Leto bore her without pain. Artemis was eternally young—a wild young goddess who loved to hunt more than anything else.

Artemis used a silver bow to kill stags but also to inflict sudden death, often upon women who died in childbirth. She was vindictive, and many, such as the children of Niobe, suffered

Artemisia

Admiral in the Persian Navy (480 B.C.)

By 500 B.C., the Greek city-states were well established and had placed colonies on the mainland of Asia Minor. These colonies became more prosperous, and it was perhaps inevitable that the Greeks would clash with the neighboring and powerful Persian Empire. The first dramatic confrontation came in 490 B.C., when the Persian great king Darius I sent an army against Greece. It was resoundingly defeated at the Battle of Marathon, when an outnumbered Athenian army beat the invading Persians. Although the Greeks celebrated their victory, everyone knew the Persians would be back to take revenge. Ten years later, Darius's son, Xerxes, gathered the full strength of the Persian forces and coordinated a land and sea attack against the Greek city-states. The famous Greek historian Herodotus (ca. 484–424 B.C.) was from Asia Minor near Persia, so he knew of many of the details of the Persian advance. Within his history, Herodutus recounts the details of these great Persian wars, including the story of a brilliant admiral who commanded ships in the Persian navy—Artemesia, queen of Caria (in the Persian Empire) and Xerxes's trusted admiral.

Xerxes's armies swept down the Greek peninsula, and while the Spartans made a brave stand at the mountain pass of Thermopylae, they were eventually defeated by the Persian forces. Now the way to Athens was open to the invading armies, and it looked as if the Persians would avenge their humiliating loss at the Battle of Marathon. The outmatched Athenians consulted the Delphic oracle, who told them to trust to wooden walls. The Athenian leader, Themistocles, persuaded the people that the oracle meant the wooden "walls" of their ships, not the walls of Athens, so the Athenians scattered, taking refuge in their fleet and abandoning the city for nearby islands. Many horrified Greeks were close enough to watch as the Persians plundered Athens and burned the temples on the Acropolis, the hill that was the center of Athens. Yet as in Marathon, the tide once again turned against the mighty Persians—this time in the bay of Salamis.

Themistocles had devised a plan to trap the Persian navy in the narrow straits near Salamis. He sent a spy to the Persians to try to persuade them that the Greek fleet was fleeing and that swift action would allow the Persians to catch it unawares and defeat it. Xerxes consulted his admirals, including the skilled Artemisia, who commanded five ships in his navy. Artemisia advised Xerxes against confronting the Greek fleet at Salamis, but the king ignored her advice and sent his ships into the straits. At dawn, the 380 Greek ships faced a much larger Persian fleet, but the narrow straits worked to the Greek advantage. When the Greeks sprang their trap and the battle began to go badly for the Persians, Artemisia demonstrated her skill and resourcefulness. Herodotus described the battle. When the Persian forces had been reduced to utter confusion, a Greek ship was pursuing Artemisia's ship. She could not escape because the way was blocked by other ships of the Persian allies. Artemisia conceived of a bold plan: she turned her ship and rammed a friendly ship—that of the Persian ally, the king of the Calyndians. Herodotus did not know whether the queen took the advantage of battle to settle an old score with the king, or whether the Calyndian ship just happened to be in her way, but she sank it. When the Greek ship that was pursuing her saw her action, the captain assumed that she was helping the Greeks, so he stopped chasing her and turned his attention to other ships. She was free to escape the destruction (Herodotus 85).

Artemisia's good luck continued; as the Persians on shore watched her action they misunderstood what had happened, for as they saw the ramming, one of the king's advisers said, "Master, do you see Artemisia, how well she fights? And, lo, she has sunk a vessel of the enemy." Xerxes asked if the action was really that of Artemisia, and the adviser said absolutely, for they could read her identifying mark on the ship. None of the men in the Calyndian ship survived to accuse the queen of betrayal, so Xerxes gave her remarkable credit for skill in battle. He was reputed to have said as he watched the Persians lose the struggle: "My men have become women, and my women men" (Herodotus 85–86). Perhaps he also remembered her sound advice that he avoid this devastating battle in the straits of Salamis.

The Persian fleet was destroyed, and the Greeks once again had beaten back the Persian menace. Artemisia seems to have kept her favored status with Xerxes, for when she and her ships returned to the great king, he asked her what he should do now that he had lost much of his fleet. She prudently suggested that he retreat, and this time he listened. He then entrusted to her his children who had accompanied him, and she returned them safely to Asia Minor. Historical records do not tell the rest of Artemisia's career—she disappears from the sources, but luckily Herodotus preserved this account of a highly skilled woman of the ancient world.

See also Persian Women
Suggested Readings
Herodotus. *The History.* Vol. 4. Trans. A. D. Godley. Cambridge: Harvard University Press, 1925.

Artists, Hellenistic

During the Hellenistic period (beginning with the death of Alexander the Great in 323 B.C.), there were many more opportunities for women to be involved in work and in the arts than there had been in ancient Greece. In these new cosmopolitan cities, women were not restricted to the household and frequently were employed in trades or shops. Most such women learned their vocations from their families, and girls sometimes worked in the workshops of their fathers; this was true of painters and sculptors. Most of the artists (male and female) of the ancient world worked anonymously; their names have been forgotten even though we still admire their works.

Thanks to the work of the Roman, Pliny the Elder (A.D. 23–79), we do know a few names of ancient women painters. Pliny, in his large work *Natural History,* compiled much information about the ancient world. He assiduously collected information about many subjects, and this book remained hugely popular for centuries. Within his catalog, Pliny named some women painters: "Timarete the daughter of Micon, who painted the very ancient picture of Artemis at Ephesus; Irene, daughter and pupil

of the painter Cratinus, who did the girl at Eleusis, a Calypso, an old woman, and Theodore the juggler and Alcisthenes the dancer; and Aristarete, daughter and pupil of Nearchus, who painted an Asclepius" (Fantham et al. 168). In his catalog, Pliny inadvertently shows the typical pattern of ancient women painters: they studied and worked with their fathers. However, Pliny also recorded an exceptional artist, a woman who was not associated with either father or husband:

> When Marus Varro was a young man [mid-first century B.C.], Laia [or Lala] of Cyzicus, who never married, painted pictures with the brush in Rome, chiefly portraits of women, as well as a large picture on wood of an old woman, at Naples, and a self-portrait done in a looking glass. No one else had a quicker hand in painting, while her artistic skill was such that the prices she obtained far outstripped the most celebrated portraitists of the day. (Fantham et al. 168)

It is unfortunate that we know no more about these reputedly talented women. However, Pliny's record serves to show us that during the ancient world some women painted and earned a reputation (and a living) from their skill.

Suggested Readings:
Fantham, E., et al. *Women in the Classical World.* New York: Oxford University Press, 1994.
Pliny. *Natural History.* Trans. H. Rackham. Cambridge: Harvard University Press, 1960.

Asella

Roman Christian Virgin (b. ca. A.D. 334)
In the fourth century A.D., a number of wealthy Roman families were becoming Christian, and in the process, many women practiced their faith by living lives strikingly different from those of other contemporary women. Some believed that the way to follow Christ was to renounce society, families, and the luxuries that had marked their lives, and as they did so, they brought a form of monasticism to the great city of Rome itself. Many women who chose these special ascetic paths to God were influenced by

family members, so we can see asceticism running in families in some of the great households of the late Romans. One such household was that of the virgin Asella—sister of Marcella—in which the daughters grew to be influential founders of the monastic life.

Asella's parents were wealthy, influential Romans, but they were also Christians, and their religious beliefs were passed on to their daughters. While Asella's mother was pregnant with Asella, her father had a dream that she was delivered to him as a virgin in a bowl of shining glass "brighter than a mirror." Believing this a call from God, the father consecrated her to a life of virginity and serving God, while placing the family's hopes for heirs in her sister Marcella. At the age of ten, Asella was consecrated to the religious life in a formal ceremony. Since there were as yet no established convents for women, the dedicated young girl continued to live at home, creating a religious life within the busy household.

It would be easy to imagine that a young girl dedicated to a religious life before she was born might rebel against this role, but Asella was fully committed to it. The church father, Jerome (ca. A.D. 340–420), wrote how by the age of twelve, Asella demonstrated that she felt a deep call to a religious life of renunciation. At that age, she took her gold necklace and sold it without her parents' knowledge (an unusual sign of rebellion for a well-brought-up Roman girl). She then put on a dark dress "such as her mother had never been willing that she should wear," and by these acts she demonstrated that she was renouncing the world of Roman society. As Jerome wrote, "She sought all her delight in solitude, and found for herself a monkish hermitage in the center of busy Rome" (Jerome 43).

She lived very privately within her home, shutting herself up in a small room and rarely speaking to anyone, especially men. She even avoided the company of her elder sister, Marcella, who was being raised to marry. Asella fasted all year, eating only bread and salt and cold water, and sometimes going for three days eating nothing. Jerome (who was always an advocate of fasting) praised her ways, saying "Fasting was her recreation and hunger her refresh-

ment" (43). He further noted that even at the age of fifty, this life had not weakened her digestion or caused her any stomach pains. Fasting was not her only austerity, for she slept on the hard ground and wore rough cloth that scratched her skin. She prayed constantly, making "her holy knees hardened like those of a camel from the frequency of her prayers" (43), and her only visits outside the home were to martyrs' shrines.

In one way she kept the traditional life of a Roman woman—in her work. In her solitude she worked with her hands—probably spinning, weaving, and sewing to keep herself busy. When her sister, Marcella, made their house a center of religious gatherings for women, Asella joined them. Later she became the leader of the group of religious women who gathered in the palace on the Aventine hill in the rich southern side of the great city of Rome. When Jerome had to leave Rome amid a frenzy of criticism and accusations that he was traveling inappropriately with women (Paula and Eustochium), he turned to the quiet, gentle Asella. While he was on the ship preparing to depart, he sent her a letter (which has survived) reassuring her of the purity of his life and intentions and urging her not to listen to the gossip. Perhaps he felt that the gentle, quiet, elderly woman who had lived a holy life for so long would be one who could understand his motives for leaving Rome in the company of two other holy women. Or perhaps he had written his letter to quiet the fears of one critic whose opinion he valued—Asella herself. We shall never know, for the silent Asella lives on in our memory only through the words of Jerome, not through any writings of her own. But, certainly, her example spurred other women to choose a religious life within their own homes.

See also Eustochium; Marcella; Melania the Elder; Paula

Suggested Readings

Jerome. *Jerome: Letters and Select Works. Nicene and Post-Nicene Fathers,* vol. 6. Ed. Philip Schaff and Henry Wace. Peabody, MA: Hendrickson Publishers, 1995.

Kelly, J. N. D. *Jerome: His Life, Writings, and Controversies.* New York: Harper and Row, 1975.

Aspasia

*Greek Philosopher, Politician, and Courtesan
(ca. 470–ca. 401 B.C.)*

At the time that Aspasia was born in Miletus, a Greek city in Asia Minor (see Map 4), it was clear that Athens had become the dominant power among the Greek city-states. Athens had led the Greek coalition to victory against Persia by 480 B.C., and in 478 B.C. had established the Delian League, a coalition of city-states that would prepare for any future aggression by Persia. Organized as a coalition of equals, the league soon became an Athenian Empire, for Athens would not allow any member to withdraw. The strength of Athens became clear when Pericles—a great orator—became leader in Athens. From about 461 to 430 B.C. he would guide Athens in what would become its golden age. In 454 B.C., Pericles moved the treasury of the Delian League to Athens (ostensibly to protect the funds from the Persians), then used the money to build Athens into the artistic center that has made it so memorable. At Pericles's side was the most famous woman in Athenian history—Aspasia the courtesan, who many claimed shaped some of his policies and even his speeches.

We know nothing of Aspasia's youth in Miletus; in fact, Aspasia probably was not even her given name, since it means "the desired one," so she likely took this name as a courtesan. She was either orphaned, sold into slavery, or born of a prostitute, but she seems to have been raised to be a courtesan—a highly trained professional prostitute. In ancient Greek society, there was a large distinction between prostitutes, who plied their trade as streetwalkers, and courtesans, who stayed at home and entertained wealthy clients. Aspasia was one of the latter—a respected, cultured courtesan. Probably when she was in her late teens, she moved to Athens, along with many merchants and others who wanted to take advantage of Athens's growing prosperity. There she established a house of prostitution; there were many public and private ones in the city, and they were legal as long as they were registered and paid the required tax. According to the ancient biographer Plutarch (ca. A.D. 46–120), "she managed a business that was neither seemly nor respectable; she raised young girls as courte-

sans" (Kebric 132). While Plutarch objected, the Athenians permitted this occupation for noncitizen women, and it was customary to raise young girls to learn the trade, which was a profitable profession in Athens, where there were very few professions open to women.

Aspasia's house quickly became the fashionable place for gentlemen of quality to gather. Politicians, playwrights, philosophers, artists, and literary celebrities passed through her doors, and she came to know the most famous architects of the Athenian golden age. One of her renowned visitors was the philosopher Socrates, and through this relationship Aspasia acquired a reputation for skill in philosophy. The philosopher Plato, in his work *Menexenus*, created a dialogue between Aspasia and Socrates, and this work, which has generated much scholarly controversy, offers information about the brilliant woman. Some scholars argue that Plato recognized Aspasia's reputation as a philosopher/rhetorician but disapproved of the influence philosophers like her had on Greece. What was Aspasia's influence? It seems that Plato regarded her as representing the abuses of philosophy: of using wisdom and the truth in the form of her mastery of rhetoric to control and deceive the people. In a sense, he accused her of being a consummate politician. However Plato's work is to be interpreted, it is clear that he—and many others—believed in Aspasia's talent and influence.

Perhaps it is not surprising that this remarkable woman became the mistress of the most powerful man in Athens—Pericles. The influential statesman was in his fifties when he met Aspasia (who was perhaps thirty or younger). Pericles had been married and had children, but he divorced his wife (either before or after he met Aspasia) and came to live with the courtesan. This arrangement was highly unusual in Athens—influential men visited their courtesans; they did not live with them. Athenians were also surprised at the depth of Pericles's love for Aspasia because they reported in shock that the statesman kissed her every morning when he left and again when he returned home. Aspasia bore Pericles an illegitimate son, also named Pericles. Later in his life, after plague claimed his legitimate sons, the elder Pericles pleaded before the assembly to confer citizenship on Aspasia's son. The Athenians were not compelled to take this unusual act, but they did so, perhaps in return for all that Pericles had done for Athens. Young Pericles would later serve the state at the highest levels.

For all that the Athenians loved Pericles, they were not pleased with the influence of the brilliant courtesan. Comic poets wrote satires that ridiculed Aspasia—calling her a "dog-eyed whore." At one point, citizens brought charges of impiety against Aspasia in court, and it was said that Pericles himself handled her defense. She was found innocent of those charges, but in the marketplace of Athens, people repeatedly claimed she exerted too much influence on the smitten Pericles. For example, some were convinced she had prodded him into a nasty war with Samos in 441 B.C. to support her native city of Miletus. Others even made her responsible for the outbreak of the Peloponnesian War between Athens and Sparta that decimated the Greek states. (She may have supported the enterprise, but the war surely would have begun without her support.) Plato later even offered the hint that Aspasia composed Pericles's famous "Funeral Oration" in which he extolled the virtues of Athenian democracy. Her rhetorical skills were well known, and it is certainly plausible that she influenced Pericles's style.

Pericles died of the plague in 429 B.C., while the war still raged. It is perhaps testimony to Aspasia's skills that her influence did not recede even after the death of her powerful patron. Shortly after his death, she became consort to Lysicles, a rich wool merchant. She used her influence to help this commoner obtain high office, and he became a general in the war. He died in battle a year later, however, and after that Aspasia fades from the direct sources—although we know her son grew to take high office in Athens. If the philosophers' references are accurate, she probably lived on in Athens—training young girls to be courtesans and continuing to entertain the brightest minds of a golden age.

See also Greek (Athenian) Women; Philosophers, Greek; Prostitution

Suggested Readings
Henry, Madeline. *Prisoner of History: Aspasia of*

Miletus and Her Biographical Tradition. New York: Oxford University Press, 1995.

Kebric, Robert B. *Greek People.* Mountain View, CA: Mayfield Publishing, 1989.

Lefkowitz, M. R., and M. B. Fant. *Women's Life in Greece and Rome.* Baltimore: Johns Hopkins University Press, 1982.

Robinson, C. A. *Athens in the Age of Pericles.* Norman: University of Oklahoma Press, 1959.

Waithe, Mary Ellen. *A History of Women Philosophers.* Vol. 1: *600 B.C.–A.D. 500.* Boston: Martinus Nijhoff Publishers, 1987.

Athena
Greek Goddess

Athena was one of the most important deities of ancient Greece, and although she was worshiped in temples all over the peninsula, she was particularly venerated in Athens, where she was the special protector of that city. She was the goddess of war and wisdom and was also known as the goddess of crafts. She was essentially a civilized and urban goddess (the opposite in many respects of the outdoor goddess, Artemis).

The myth of Athena's birth reinforces her traditionally male attributes of wisdom and war by making her not born of a woman. According to Hesiod's version, Zeus, the father of the gods, lusted after a Titaness named Metis, who tried to escape from Zeus. *Metis* means "prudence" or "intelligence," and she passed these qualities on to her divine offspring. Zeus finally caught Metis and impregnated her. An oracle of mother earth, however, then proclaimed that this would be a girl-child, but if Metis conceived again, she would bear a son who would depose Zeus just as Zeus had deposed his father. To stop the cycle, Zeus wanted to ensure that Metis would never bear another child, so he swallowed the pregnant Metis.

When the time came for the child to be born, Zeus told Hephaestus, the smith-god, to split Zeus's skull with an axe. The goddess Athena sprang fully armed from Zeus's head, thus preserving all her parents' wisdom as well as the military prowess usually given to men. As she leaped, she uttered a war cry that resounded in heaven and earth. A new powerful goddess had been born. She was armed with a spear and aegis (a goatskin breastplate). Later she added to her shield the head of the Gorgon (which Perseus

Figure 4. The Varaklon, a Roman marble copy (ca. A.D. 130) of Phidias's gold and ivory statue of Athena (438 B.C.) (Alinari/Art Resource, NY)

had given her), which turned anything that looked at it to stone. She was described as being tall, majestic, with calm features—the "goddess with the gray eyes."

She played an important part in the struggle against the Giants, ruthlessly killing opponents. In the narrative of the *Iliad,* she participated in the fighting on the side of the Greeks, and she also helped Odysseus to return home in the narrative of the *Odyssey.* The help Athena gave heroes such as Odysseus and Heracles is a symbol of the help that intellect can bring to brute strength, and especially in Athens, she was viewed as the goddess of Reason. While strong and ruthless, the goddess brought intellect to the mighty warfare of the Greeks.

Some myths say that Athena and Poseidon competed to see who would receive the worship of Attica. Poseidon bribed the people with the horse or, some myths say, with a saltwater spring, but Athena gave them olive trees. Olives were perceived to be the most valuable (indeed, Athenian economy depended upon olive cultivation), and Athena won their allegiance.

In her role of the goddess of intelligent activity, Athena was credited with many inventions: the flute, the trumpet, earthenware pots, plows, rakes, the horse bridle, the ox-yoke, chariots, and ships. She gave people the science of mathematics and all of women's arts—cooking, weaving, and spinning. She also represented the intellectual and civilized side of war instead of just bloodlust. She brought victories because of her skill in tactics and strategy, and she was the goddess of good counsel. Wise warriors always consulted her.

While the myths said that many of the gods wanted to marry Athena, she rebuffed them all. She remained a virgin goddess, which the ancient Greeks believed was a key to her preservation of her powers. One myth claims that she had a child even though she remained a virgin. In this legend, Hephaestus, who had been deserted by Aphrodite, fell in love with Athena and began to chase her. She fled, but Hephaestus caught up with her and embraced her. She did not yield to him, but in his passion, Hephaestus ejaculated on the goddess's leg. In her revulsion, she wiped her leg with some wool and threw it on the ground. From the earth that was fertilized in this way, Ericthonius was born, and Athena regarded him as her son. She brought him up without the knowledge of the other gods and entrusted him to the daughters of the kings of Athens.

After the Athenian victory in the Persian Wars in the mid-fifth century B.C., the grateful Athenians built a magnificent temple on the Acropolis (the high ground) of their city. They called the temple the Parthenon, which means "virgin," after their virgin goddess. The greatest sculptor of the day, Phidias, built a huge statue of Athena out of gold and ivory to reside in the Parthenon. The statue is lost, but we know it from Roman copies made in marble, such as the one shown in Figure 4. Athena is commonly shown in ancient art with her helmet, spear, and shield as she is shown here.

According to the playwright Aeschylus, Athena was credited with founding the Areopagus, Athens's citizen council. She further shaped this body's decision making by breaking a deadlock of the judges in favor of the defendant. This set the precedent, followed throughout Athens's history, that a tie vote signified acquittal.

All these myths suggest that although she could be fierce, Athena was compassionate, intelligent, and profoundly civilized. There is one myth, however, that reminded people that none of the ancient gods would put up with challenges from humans. In one legend, a girl named Arachne challenged Athena to a tapestry-weaving contest. Athena searched Arachne's work for a flaw but could not find one. Furious, Athena destroyed the tapestry. When the terrified Arachne tried to hang herself to escape the goddess's wrath, Athena turned her into a spider, so she could spend her life (and all other spiders' lives) weaving endless webs.

Athena made a perfect patroness for a city that valued its skill in war, peace, the arts, and the creation of a perfectly governed society. Her favorite animal was the owl and her favorite plant the olive tree. Athenians had been blessed by the favor of a magnificently powerful goddess who brought that city greatness.

See also Artemis; Danaë; Minerva
Suggested Readings
Aeschylus. *Agamemnon, Choephoroe, Eumenides.* Trans. G. M. Cookson. London: Chapman Hall, 1924.
Grimal, Pierre. *The Dictionary of Classical Mythology.* Oxford: Blackwell Publishers, 1996.
Lefkowitz, Mary R. *Women in Greek Myth.* Baltimore: Johns Hopkins University Press, 1986.

B

Baodicea

See Boudicca

Bathsheba

Hebrew Queen and Mother of a King
(ca. 1000 B.C.)

In the late second millennium B.C., the Hebrew tribes who had been seminomadic began to settle in the eastern Mediterranean and to become farmers and craftsmen. These permanent settlements changed the social patterns of the ancient Hebrews, and one significant transformation was in leadership. During the period of settlement, a new kind of leader arose—the "judge"—who confronted external military threats and mediated internal stresses (*see* Deborah). In time, however, as the tribes moved toward a national unity, the elders began to see the need for a king. They persuaded Samuel, the last of the judges, to anoint their first king—Saul (ca. 1020–1000 B.C., although there is much scholarly controversy about his dates). After Saul died in battle against the Philistines, David was accepted as king, and he united the southern tribes of Judah and the northern tribes of Israel. Shortly after his reign began, David captured the city of Jerusalem and made it his capital.

The account of the reign of David is told in the Bible in the Second Book of Samuel, known as 2 Samuel. Historians credit this book with a good deal of accuracy and assume it was written in the generation after David's death. Within this account the author tells of Bathsheba, the beautiful and influential woman who became King David's favorite wife. This story also reveals once again the informal influence of individual women as the history of the ancient Hebrews unfolded.

One warm moonlit night early in David's reign, the king was unable to sleep and paced restlessly along the rooftop of his palace in Jerusalem. Glancing down, he was startled to see a beautiful young woman bathing herself on a nearby roof. In the hot Middle East, it was not unusual for people to seek a private place outdoors to bathe (*see* Susanna), and the flat roofs of the houses were frequently used for sleeping or bathing on hot nights. Ordinarily, people could assume a good deal of privacy on their roofs, but the king's palace was higher than the other buildings, so Bathsheba's bath was exposed to David's sight.

The king sent to find out who the lovely woman was and discovered she was the granddaughter of his chief councillor and the wife of Uriah, an army officer serving in David's command. Unable to forget the lovely woman, David sent servants to bring Bathsheba to him. He made love to her, and she returned secretly to her own home. Some time later, she sent word to David that she was pregnant. To avoid scandal, David summoned Uriah home, ostensibly to report on the campaign, but mostly to sleep with Bathsheba so that the unborn child might be thought to be her husband's. However, Uriah was not interested in his wife, and he spent his leave in Jerusalem with his army companions. David had to find another way to save Bathsheba from the scandal created by his lust.

The king sent his commander a letter: "Set Uriah in the forefront of the hardest fighting, and then draw back from him, that he may be struck down and die" (2 Sam. 11:15). It happened as the king commanded, and Uriah was killed in battle. Bathsheba fulfilled the necessary period of mourning required by a widow, but then David brought her to the palace and married her. In due course, the new queen bore David a son. However, the infant fell sick and died. Soon, she was pregnant again, and this time she bore a son who would grow to be a great king—Solomon.

Bathsheba continued to exert influence at the court in Jerusalem. When David had grown old and frail, Bathsheba made him promise that Solomon would succeed him on the throne, even though David had older sons. But even before the king died, one of his elder sons—Adonijah—began to gather support and make the necessary religious sacrifices to become king. David's chief adviser, Nathan, warned Bathsheba once again to use her influence on the aging king. She went to him, bowed low on the floor, and reminded him of his promise to her. He acknowledged his pledge and showed he still had the political wisdom that had marked his long reign: He had his son Solomon crowned king immediately and gave him the throne while David still lived. Solomon forced his half-brother Adonijah to swear allegiance, then let him leave.

When King David died, Bathsheba continued to be influential in the court of her son, the new king. We can see evidence for this influence in the actions of Adonijah, who wanted a favor from King Solomon, but approached his mother. Bathsheba went to Solomon, who received her with all honor: "And the king rose to meet her, and bowed down to her; then he sat on his throne, and had a seat brought for the king's mother; and she sat on his right." (1 Kings 2:19). However, Solomon was not to grant Bathsheba's request, for Adonijah had asked to marry a beautiful young woman who had been a concubine of the old king David. Traditionally, the members of the king's household were considered royal property to be passed on to the next king, so Adonijah was treading on royal prerogative by asking for her hand. Was he so in love with the woman that he was willing to risk the new king's wrath? Was this a political move to claim the throne after he claimed the king's concubine? We cannot know, for Solomon used the inappropriate request as an excuse to execute his half-brother. His respect for his mother did not extend to politics.

The story of Bathsheba captured the imagination of readers for millennia. Many women learned to hope that if their beauty caught the eye of a king, they could achieve a measure of power. In modern times, painters have loved to depict the moment in a moonlit night when a modest bather captivated a king and changed the course of ancient Hebrew history.

See also Deborah; Jewish Women; Susanna
Suggested Readings
Meyers, Carol, Toni Craven, and Ross S. Kraemer. *Women in Scripture.* New York: Houghton Mifflin, 2000.
Wiseman, D. J., ed. *Peoples of Old Testament Times.* Oxford: Society for Old Testament Study, 1973.

(Julia) Berenice
Jewish Queen (ca. A.D. 28–after 80)

At the time Jesus was born in Judea, it was a subject kingdom of the Roman Empire. King Herod the Great (37–4 B.C.) had been appointed king of Judea by the Roman senate, and he expanded the Temple there, making it a magnificent building. Herod was disliked by many of the Jewish factions, however, and was never able to bring peace to the stormy province. Jesus was probably born shortly after Herod's death, and the followers of Jesus added to the controversial religious disputes that often led to violence in the territory. In A.D. 70, Rome finally lost patience with the revolts of the Jews, destroyed Jerusalem, and placed Palestine under direct Roman rule. The last queen of this Herodian dynasty—Julia Berenice—was intimately involved with both the Christian controversy and the Roman destruction.

Berenice (also known as Julia Berenice) was born about A.D. 28; she was one of the five children of Agrippa I as well as a great-granddaughter of Herod the Great. At a relatively young age (probably in her early teens), she was married to a man from a wealthy Alexandrian Jewish family—Marcus Julius Alexander. When Marcus died, her father then married her to Herod of Chalcis, with whom she had two sons. By A.D. 50, she was a widow for the second time. The historian Josephus claims that Berenice next arranged her own marriage to Polemo, the king of Cilicia. He was not Jewish but agreed to be circumcised for the marriage. The marriage soon failed, however, when Berenice divorced Polemo. The Roman historian Josephus claimed that she was motivated by "inappropriate sexual desire," leading to the divorce, but again it is impossible to tell what motivated her action. Was it personal or political?

Instead of marrying again, she ruled as queen with her brother Agrippa II, and an inscription on a statue set up to honor her in Athens refers to her as a "great" queen. Josephus (who was no fan of Berenice) claimed that she was living incestuously with her brother during their joint rule, but there is no other evidence for this claim.

During her joint rule with her brother, Berenice became involved with the early Christian movement and secured a place in the Christian Bible in the Book of Acts. The Apostle Paul had come to Jerusalem as he traveled about preaching. There, many Jews rose up against him, accusing him of overturning the Laws of Moses that had identified Jews as a people. Paul addressed the Jews and explained how he had been miraculously called to Christianity and told to preach to the gentiles (non-Jews). But many were unpersuaded and plotted to kill the apostle. The Romans were warned of the plot and took Paul away to protect him, since he was a Roman citizen. They brought him to Caesarea (shown on Map 8) so the governor there could decide what to do. The governor, Felix, was accompanied by his Jewish wife, Drusilla, and he sent for Paul and heard him speak about the Christian faith. Felix did not make a judgment in the case; instead, "desiring to do the Jews a favor, Felix left Paul in prison" (Acts 25:24). Two years later, Felix was succeeded by Festus as governor.

The chief priests of Jerusalem wanted to persuade Festus to allow Paul to go to Jerusalem because they planned an ambush to kill him. But Festus said he would keep Paul in Caesarea in order to hear the case. When Festus questioned Paul, the Apostle said he wanted to appeal to Caesar, which was his right as a Roman citizen. Some days later, Agrippa and Berenice, king and queen of Judea, arrived at Caesarea to welcome Festus, and the governor presented Paul's case to them. Agrippa said he wanted to hear the case himself.

The next day, Agrippa and Berenice entered the hall with great ceremony. Paul was brought in, and Festus asked the king to question him and prepare charges for him to send to the emperor. Paul was pleased to present his case to Agrippa, saying "because you are especially familiar with all customs and controversies of the Jews" (Acts 26:3). After hearing Paul's testimony, Agrippa, Berenice, and Festus said to one another, "This man is doing nothing to deserve death or imprisonment" (Acts 26:31). But since Paul had appealed to the emperor, they let him set sail to Italy.

By A.D. 66, the Romans sent an army to put down a general rebellion in Judea. Vespasian commanded three legions, and his son Titus accompanied him. In A.D. 69, the armies were besieging Jerusalem itself after subduing the countryside, and at that time Vespasian heard he had been named emperor. He returned to Rome, leaving his son Titus to finish the subjection of Judea. When Vespasian left, King Agrippa and Queen Berenice were in Titus's camp as guests, for they had put their allegiance with Rome. (This was the source of the historian Josephus's animosity toward Berenice.) Although the queen was forty-one years old and Titus was twenty-eight, the two fell in love. In the next year, Titus sacked Jerusalem and burned down Herod's great Temple, which has never been rebuilt. Titus continued the suppression of the revolt, and in A.D. 73, he destroyed Masada—near the Dead Sea—which was the last pocket of rebellion. As he was about to take this mountain fortress, all the inhabitants committed suicide rather than surrender to Rome. With peace in the province, Titus returned to Rome, and Berenice joined him.

In A.D. 75, Berenice was in Rome as Titus's lover. She was a queen and immensely wealthy, and it seems likely that she expected to become empress of Rome at Titus's accession. It may be that he even proposed marriage to her, but Rome was not prepared to have a Jewish queen in the imperial palace. Philosophers spoke against her, the Roman people reacted strongly, and Titus was persuaded to send her away. When he was proclaimed emperor in A.D. 79, Berenice returned to Rome once more, perhaps hoping that as emperor he would be able to marry her. Titus succumbed to popular pressure again and sent her away for good. That is the last record we have of this extraordinarily independent woman who influenced some of the pivotal events in the history of Judaism, Christianity, and the Roman Empire.

See also Alexandra Salome; Glaphyra; Mariamne

Suggested Readings
Balsdon, J. P. V. D. *Roman Women: Their History and Habits.* New York: John Day, 1963.
Crook, J. A. "Titus and Berenice." *American Journal of Philology* 72 (1951): 162–175.
Kokkinos, Nikos. *The Herodian Dynasty: Origins, Role in Society and Eclipse.* Sheffield, UK: Sheffield Academic Press, 1998.
Kraemer, Ross Shepard, and Mary Rose D'Angelo, eds. *Women and Christian Origins.* New York: Oxford University Press, 1999.
Macurdy, Grace H. "Julia Berenice." *American Journal of Philology* 56 (1935): 246–253.
Richardson, Peter. *Herod: King of the Jews and Friend of the Romans.* Philadelphia: Fortress Press, 1999.

Figure 5. Gem with portrait of Berenice I as Isis (Boston Museum of Fine Arts)

Berenice I

Egyptian Queen, Dynasty of the Ptolemies
(b. ca. 340 B.C.)

After the death of Alexander the Great in 323 B.C., his closest supporters founded dynasties of their own from the lands they carved from his empire. Ptolemy went to Egypt and established a dynasty there that would last for centuries. In this Macedonian dynasty, most of the rulers were named Ptolemy—after the founder—and many of the queens were given the famous Macedonian name of Cleopatra. The Ptolemies—like the other Hellenistic kings—conducted much of their diplomatic negotiations through marriages of their high-born princesses. The women of this dynasty in Egypt began to wield considerably more power than had previously been the case in the land of the Nile. The early female head of the dynasty of the Ptolemies—Berenice I—was by all accounts an extraordinary woman.

As soon as Ptolemy took control of Egypt, in 322 B.C., Alexander's friend and regent, Antipater, arranged to have his daughter Eurydice marry Ptolemy to be certain his family would share in the new emerging power structure. (Antipater had married another of his daughters, Phila, to the successor kings in Syria.) Eurydice

dutifully bore Ptolemy four children, and it seemed as if Antipater's family would be the founders of the new Egyptian dynasty. Competition, however, would come from a surprising source.

Several years after the marriage, Ptolemy fell in love with a young widow—Berenice—who had come from Macedonia as a lady-in-waiting to Eurydice, to whom she was related as a cousin. Berenice had two children with her when she came to Egypt, but by 316 B.C. she was at least Ptolemy's mistress, if not his second wife. The king so favored her company that he took her with him on campaign to Greece in 309 B.C. Certainly by 287 B.C., Ptolemy had repudiated Eurydice and married Berenice.

It is remarkable that Berenice, with no family position to speak of, should have replaced the politically connected Eurydice in an age when the successors married for political reasons. It seems that he was won over to her by her personal charm and her good sense (such sources as Plutarch praise her intellectual power). The carving on the gem in Figure 5 shows a Ptolemaic queen in the form of the goddess Isis, and scholars believe it is probably Berenice I. If so, the queen was certainly beautiful, and the contemporary poet Theocritus praised the affection between Ptolemy and Berenice, writing: "They say that no woman ever won such love from a husband as that with which Ptolemy loved his wife, and still greater love did he receive from her" (Macurdy 106).

Ptolemy renounced his children by Eurydice in favor of Berenice's, and her son Ptolemy II was proclaimed king in 284 B.C. It is not clear whether Berenice was alive to see her son become king, but it is certain that the new king remembered his parents fondly, for he was the first of the Hellenistic kings to build temples to his parents. Berenice was given the sacred title "savior," and she and Ptolemy were put in the official list of deified kings along with Alexander. Two towns were named in her honor, but her greatest accomplishment was the long-standing dynasty she founded.

See also Berenice II; Egyptian Women; Isis; Phila
Suggested Readings
Appian. *Appian's Roman History.* Trans. H. White. Cambridge: Harvard University Press, 1964.
Macurdy, Grace Harriet. *Hellenistic Queens.* Baltimore: Johns Hopkins University Press, 1932.

Berenice II
Ptolemaic Queen of Egypt
(ca. 273–ca. 223 B.C.)

When Alexander the Great's empire dissolved in the early fourth century B.C., several kingdoms arose in its place. Many queens of these Hellenistic kingdoms came to prominence. Their contemporaries and modern historians record their political machinations during these violent times, and many proved as ruthless as their fathers and husbands as they struggled to maintain the power they believed was their birthright. Occasionally, however, one of these rulers stands out precisely because she was able to be remembered for virtue and peaceful pursuits in an age of turmoil. One such queen was the founder of the Egyptian dynasties of the Ptolemies, Berenice I; another was her granddaughter, Berenice II.

Berenice II was the daughter of Magas, Berenice I's son by her first husband, and Apame, daughter of Stratonice, one of the indomitable Macedonian queens. This high-born woman could expect a good marriage, and her parents selected the son of Demetrius the Besieger and Phila. The young man, called Demetrius the Fair because he was so handsome, was to be king of Cyrene, in North Africa. Berenice was very young at the time of this marriage, which would come to a violent end. Demetrius was so good-looking that Berenice's mother, Apame, fell in love with him and took him as her lover. This behavior so outraged Berenice and the others at the court that they arranged for his death. Soldiers entered Apame's bedchamber while Demetrius was there. Berenice stood at the door and watched, warning the murderers not to kill her mother, who tried unsuccessfully to shield Demetrius's body from the swords.

The young widow found a happier second marriage with her cousin, Ptolemy III of Egypt. By all accounts, this marriage was exceptionally happy in contrast to the scandals that plagued so many of the marriages of the Ptolemies. They had four children—Ptolemy, Arsinoë, Magas, and Berenice. The young Berenice died while she was still a child, and the couple mourned her by establishing a temple in her honor. Beyond this tragedy, Berenice's married life seems to have been filled with pleasures—at least that is what the sources report.

The queen—rich as all the Hellenistic royal women were—indulged her passion for horseback riding. She even entered some chariot teams in the Olympic Games and won a prize—a high honor indeed. (After her death, when her son inaugurated a cult in her honor, he called the presiding priest *athlophore,* meaning "prize-bearer," and he may have been referring to Berenice II's victorious teams in the Olympics.) She also loved perfume made of roses and encouraged the rose growers to develop particularly fragrant blooms. She is possibly most remembered as a literary patron, for she supported the poet Callimachus (ca. 305–240 B.C.), whose surviving works remain masterpieces of hymns and epigrams. Callimachus's poem "The Lock of Berenice" preserves a charming incident of the queen's dedicating a lock of her hair to guarantee her husband's safe return from a war.

All these incidents suggest that this queen remained fairly distant from the political events that so tormented many of her contemporaries. The Greek writer Aelian does preserve one incident in which Berenice was shown to have some sensitivity to the plight of her people. Her husband was playing dice while a page read him a list of people condemned to death. Berenice reprimanded her husband, saying it was right to give one's full attention when deciding matters of life and death. Ptolemy was pleased with her insights and promised never again to judge while engaged in frivolous pastimes.

Berenice's life may have been peaceful, but she would die by violence, as did so many other Hellenistic rulers. Her son Ptolemy IV inherited the throne at his father's death, and the sources say he was a violent man. He ordered his brother, Magas, scalded to death in the bath, and when he believed that his mother favored Magas over him, he had her murdered as well. She died bravely, and the people remembered the gentle queen fondly.

See also Berenice I; Egyptian Women; Olympic Games; Phila; Stratonice I

Suggested Readings

Macurdy, Grace Harriet. *Hellenistic Queens.* Baltimore: Johns Hopkins University Press, 1932.

Pomeroy, Sarah B. *Women in Hellenistic Egypt: From Alexander to Cleopatra.* New York: Schocken Books, 1984.

Blaesilla

Roman Christian Widow (A.D. 364–384)

Rome in the fourth century A.D. included a vigorous Christian community, and wealthy Roman women were in the forefront of this Christian life. Some widows—such as Paula and Marcella—surrounded themselves with women who prayed, studied scripture, and formed almost monastic communities within their great mansions. The women in these households did not follow monastic rules, but instead selected lifestyles that suited their individual temperaments. All rejected the luxurious lives of wealthy pagan women, but some, such as Marcella, chose moderate lives in which they ate plain food and drank a bit of wine while wearing modest attire. Others, such as

Asella, secluded themselves in the households, withdrawing from the company of other people. Some, however, believed that Christian worship included a requirement for more rigorous asceticism. Asella ate only bread and water in her fasts, and Paula always slept on the hard floor. The church father Jerome, who served as spiritual adviser to many of the women, was a strong advocate of asceticism, and he believed that severe fasts would control the flesh and help people focus on God. One woman—Blaesilla—took his advice to heart, with mortal consequences.

The widow Paula had four daughters, of whom the eldest was Blaesilla. She was a beautiful, talented young girl who loved the merry life of aristocratic Rome. She enjoyed dinner parties, theater, and the company of other young people. At the age of about eighteen, she made a good marriage, but her husband died only seven months after the wedding, leaving her a prosperous widow. Although Blaesilla mourned his death, she was still too young to be willing to forgo the exciting life she had loved. She lavished time and money on her dress and her appearance as she continued to enjoy the pleasant company she loved.

Jerome, who spent a great deal of time in Blaesilla's household talking to her pious mother, Paula, and her equally religious sister, Eustochium, was deeply worried about the state of Blaesilla's soul. He reprimanded her in the strongest terms against her frivolous life. Her relatives were very annoyed at his interference with the bright young woman, but it seems that she took his words to heart.

Blaesilla became very ill with a fever. She recovered, but she was a changed woman. Instead of returning to her previous habits, she took on the ways of an extreme ascetic. She dressed in the plainest clothes, described as "no better than her maids," and she indulged in extreme fasts that weakened her dramatically. Jerome wrote that "her steps tottered with weakness, her face was pale and quivering, her slender neck scarcely upheld her head" (48). This behavior delighted Jerome, for he saw it as a sign of intense spirituality, but it outraged her previous friends and some relatives, who feared for the health of the young woman.

In addition to ascetic practices, Blaesilla began to study scriptures, and she demonstrated a remarkable intellectual talent. Jerome wrote, "Who can recall without a sigh the earnestness of her prayers, the brilliancy of her conversation, the tenacity of her memory, and the quickness of her intellect?" (49). She learned Greek with a perfect accent and mastered Hebrew within a few months. She carried books with her everywhere and demanded that Jerome write Bible commentaries for her to study. However, her young body was not up to the rigorous demands. Before four months had passed, she was dead from her ascetic extremes. Many Romans were outraged at the premature death of the bright young woman and blamed Jerome for influencing her to practice extreme fasts.

Blaesilla's mother, Paula, collapsed in grief at her daughter's funeral, but she did not reject her mentor. Jerome wrote her a letter to console her for Blaesilla's death, and many modern readers find it a little unsympathetic. Jerome reminds Paula that he, too, loved Blaesilla and that the mother's grief was excessive. He told her that Blaesilla should not be mourned, but instead they should be pleased that she had gone to Christ and that the daughter would be distressed to see her mother's grief. Jerome concluded his letter by promising to keep Blaesilla's name alive by including her in all his writings. "Everlasting remembrance will make up for the shortness of her life. . . . In my writings she will never die. She will hear me conversing of her always, either with her sister or with her mother" (54).

Blaesilla's death polarized Roman opinion against Jerome and his seemingly endless calls to rigid asceticism. The following year, the church father decided to leave Rome to go to the Holy Land, and he was accompanied by Paula and Eustochium, the mother and sister of the dead widow. They seemingly did not blame him for the asceticism of Blaesilla and seemed certain that she had died in a state of grace. Jerome's writings did keep alive the name of this ancient woman who starved herself to death in the name of Christ.

See also Asella; Eustochium; Marcella; Paula
Suggested Readings

Jerome. *Jerome: Letters and Select Works. Nicene and Post-Nicene Fathers,* vol. 6. Ed. Philip Schaff and Henry Wace. Peabody, MA: Hendrickson Publishers, 1995.

Kelly, J. N. D. *Jerome: His Life, Writings, and Controversies.* New York: Harper and Row, 1975.

Blandina
Martyr (d. A.D. 177)

A brisk trade along the River Rhone in Gaul (in modern France) brought goods and people from the east to the cities of Gaul. As early as the first century A.D., Christians had come from the Greek-speaking cities of the east—from as far away as Syria—and taken up residence in these Latin towns along the Rhone. Many of these Christians were wealthy and well educated—physicians and lawyers as well as merchants—and many had slaves. Some of the slaves were Christians, but some were pagans, who would testify against their masters when trouble began. In the summer of A.D. 177, trouble did come to the Christians of Lyons and Vienne, and pagans turned on their Christian neighbors as persecution escalated. Among those who would be killed was the slave woman Blandina, whose courage raised her far above her social status. A Christian eyewitness wrote of the events of the persecution in a letter circulated to Christians in the churches of Asia, whence the Gallic Christians had come. The fourth-century historian Eusebius reproduced the letter in his *History of the Church,* and it offers a remarkable glimpse into the early Christian communities of ancient western Europe.

The Christians in Gaul began to experience persecution of various sorts from pagan neighbors who were suspicious of them. The text does not say what triggered the animosity, so we cannot know for certain. In some parts of the empire, Christians were falsely reputed to engage in practices from cannibalism to sexual promiscuity, but we cannot know whether pagans in Lyons and Vienne had heard these rumors. For whatever reason, Christians were first banned from the public places of the town—the baths and the forum—and finally were told they could not be seen anywhere at all. If they did appear, crowds attacked them, beating them and dragging them on the ground. Finally, officials became involved, and many Christians were imprisoned and brought to trial. Some renounced their faith in the face of such pressure, but others continued on to face martyrdom.

The writer of the letter spoke of the trial and of the tortures that many of the Christians experienced, and the author introduced with wonder a brave slave woman. The narrator described Blandina as "worthless and ugly and despicable," but he noted with wonder that God's grace could make even such a one "worthy of great glory." Blandina withstood "every kind of torture from morning to evening," but "like a noble athlete, she gained her strength by her confession, finding refreshment and freedom from pain in saying 'I am a Christian'" (Eusebius 196). After the trial and torture, the intransigent Christians—including Blandina—were sentenced to death in the amphitheater of Lyons.

Blandina was hung on a stake, exposed as food for wild beasts who were driven into the arena. However, she gladly accepted that trial, imagining that the stake was a cross like that of Jesus' torture, and her courage inspired other Christians to hold firm to their faith while they were attacked in the arena. Blandina's ordeal was not over, however. The beasts refused to touch her, so she was taken down from the stake and sent back to prison to wait for another day. The narrator again commented on the contrast between her lowly stature and her inspiring courage: "for she, small and weak and despised as she was . . . won through conflicts" (200).

Finally, on the last day of the games, Blandina was again brought forward with a boy of about fifteen. They both had been brought each day to witness the deaths of the others and had been pressed to worship the pagan gods. Because Blandina and the boy had remained constant in their faith, the people had grown very angry with their stubbornness, and "they respected neither the youth of the boy nor the sex of the woman; but they made them pass through every form of terrible suffering, and through the whole round of punishments, urging them to swear after each one" (202). The writer said that Blandina was like the Maccabean mother who urged her seven sons to die before her, because she encouraged the youth to die bravely as he was tortured. Finally, they placed Blandina in a basket and threw her to a bull. Time after time the animal tossed her, but she was at last insensitive to any pain, and she died. As the text concluded, "even the heathen themselves confessed that never yet amongst them had a woman suffered such manifold and great tortures" (202).

Blandina was an early martyr, but she was only one of many women who would die bravely for their faith. Her example, which was circulated widely, spurred other women and slaves to confess their faith bravely and demonstrated that even those who were "despised" could find a privileged place in the new religion.

See also Agnes; Felicity; Maccabean Martyrs; Martyrs; Perpetua the Martyr

Suggested Readings

Eusebius. *The History of the Church from Christ to Constantine.* Trans. G. A. Williamson. Harmondsworth, UK: Penguin, 1965.

Frend, W. H. C. "Blandina and Perpetua: Two Early Christian Heroines." In *Women in Early Christianity,* ed. by D. M. Scholer, 87–97. New York: Garland, 1993.

———.*Martyrdom and Persecution in the Early Church.* Grand Rapids, MI: Baker Book House, 1965.

LaPorte, Jean. *The Role of Women in Early Christianity.* Lewiston, NY: Edwin Mellen Press, 1982.

Boudicca
British Queen (ca. A.D. 26–60)

The island of Britain in the first century A.D. was inhabited by Celtic tribes, each led by its own ruler, and each fiercely independent. The Celts fought almost endless wars, and their war leaders used light wicker chariots to lead into battle as their fierce but undisciplined armies swarmed behind them shouting loud battle cries. The victorious bands of armies expected to plunder the defeated and bring home booty. All the while, the women and children of the warriors followed the bands to watch the carnage and the victory, and at times women fought as well. This way of life had continued for centuries, but contact with the Roman Empire changed the way of life and the traditional warfare of the Celts.

In A.D. 43, the Emperor Claudius sent Rome's legions to Britain, and they conquered eleven tribes of Britain, all located in the south. Among the conquered were the Iceni, probably located on the eastern edge of the island, shown on Map 10. (This is the modern location of Norfolk and Suffolk.) The tribes must not easily have given up their freedom to the Roman rulers, so in A.D. 47 the governor of Britain (Ostorius Scapula) disarmed all the British "allies," but that did not bring peace. In about A.D. 49, the Iceni led a rebellion against the Romans, which was put down. This would not be the last revolt of the Iceni; indeed, their queen Boudicca would lead a violent revolt that almost eliminated the Roman presence in Britain.

After the rebellion of A.D. 49 was put down, the Iceni became a client kingdom of Rome, led by their king Prasutagus. He was married to Boudicca, and they had two daughters. Prasutages was very wealthy, but he knew that his wealth was tempting to the Roman overlords. Therefore, he tried to protect his daughters' legacy by preparing a will in which half his wealth was bequeathed to the emperor Claudius and half to his two daughters (to be held in trust by Boudicca). The king had probably hoped that his attention to the emperor would demonstrate his loyalty enough to allow Rome to protect his family. He was mistaken.

The local Roman administrators reacted immediately to King Prasutagus's will—they seized all the king's estate and the total of his treasury. In general, the Romans had been taking profits (often illegally) from the conquered Britons, and resentment was growing as the old nobility often began to feel they had nothing to lose by rebellion. This was not the end of the insult, however. Perhaps to prove their dominance, the Romans flogged Boudicca and raped her two daughters. The queen then called her people together for revenge.

The Roman historian Dio Cassius (who could not have witnessed the events) described Boudicca: She had a wild mass of red hair hanging to her waist, and she was very tall, "in appearance almost terrifying" (Fraser 59). This description is plausible for the Celtic tribes of the time and has been fixed in the imaginations of modern Britons who see in Boudicca's actions the struggle of freedom over tyranny. Dio said that the queen gave an elaborate speech stirring her people, calling upon them to prefer freedom over slavery, and reminding them how the Britons had suffered under the Romans. Then she pulled a hare from the folds of her dress, using it as a means of divination. When she released the hare, it ran "in an auspicious direction," so the people believed the signs were right to revolt. Boudicca then prayed to a goddess named Andraste, calling upon her "as woman speaking to woman" and evoking this goddess of war and victory (71).

The queen mounted her chariot and led an initial army of about 120,000, according to Dio (although those figures are probably exaggerated). Their first target was Camulodunum (the modern city of Colchester shown on Map 10). This was a newly established town that the Romans used to give land to their veterans. Within this town they were building a huge, opulent temple dedicated to the Emperor Claudius, and the building costs further oppressed the local Britons. Camulodunum was not walled and had a token presence of only about 200 troops. Boudicca overran the town easily and sacked and burned it. The temple itself (made of durable stone) held out for two more days before the veterans were overrun by the British forces. All were killed and the temple battered down and burned. Modern excavations at Colchester testify to the destruction and burning of the city.

A Roman force—the IXth Legion Hispana—set off for Camulodunum to rescue the Romans in the area and to end the rebellion. The British were waiting for them, however; they laid an ambush that was strikingly effective. The Roman infantry was cut to pieces, and the commander and the cavalry took refuge back at the legionary camp. The Romans had lost another 2,500 men and were no nearer to stemming the British advance.

Boudicca then went south to London—known as Londinium. The Roman governor Suetonius had rushed back from quelling rebellions in the west of Britain and reached Londinium before Boudicca. However, he decided that the city—which probably had about

30,000 inhabitants—was not defensible. As the Roman historian Tacitus (who was contemporary with the events) said, "He decided to save the whole situation by the sacrifice of a single city" (Tacitus 339). This caused panic among the inhabitants, who had heard of the ruthlessness with which Boudicca had sacked the first city, and as Tacitus was later to write, "Never before or since has Britain ever been in a more disturbed and perilous state" (339).

The queen led the armies into Londinium, and the earlier massacre was repeated. The Roman sources described many brutalities that the angry British inflicted on the residents of Londinium. They did not take prisoners, and as Tacitus wrote, "They could not wait to cut throats, hang, burn, and crucify" (Tacitus 339). Captives—both men and women—were tortured and sacrificed, and the city was burned. Excavations have found a red layer of scorched earth under the modern city of London that preserves the memory of Boudicca's wrath. After the armies had taken everything of value, they turned north to take yet one more city.

The British army swept north to Verulamium (modern St. Albans, shown on Map 10). This city was different from the previous two because it was populated not by Romans but by Britons who were friendly to Rome. Once again the city was burned, as the Romans had not yet brought their legions to confront the queen's forces. However, in the glory of their victories, the British armies showed their weakness: their love of plunder. As Tacitus described Boudicca's strategy: "The natives enjoyed plundering and thought of nothing else. Bypassing forts and garrisons, they made for where the loot was richest and protection weakest" (Tacitus 340). This desire prevented Boudicca from striking at the Roman commander Suetonius before he was prepared and while she was at her strongest. This would prove a fatal mistake.

Even though the British forces greatly outnumbered the available Roman legions, Suetonius finally decided it was time to confront Boudicca—while he could select the terrain and the time. He chose a position at the end of a deep ravine with a thick, impenetrable woods at his back. Modern historians have searched for

this site, and most believe it is in the Midlands area, possibly near Warwick. Regardless of the uncertainty of the location, the final results were well described.

The battle was preceded by a series of speeches that Tacitus described. He said Queen Boudicca drove round and round the assembled troops in her chariot, spurring them on. She told them to win the battle or perish: "That is what I, a woman, plan to do! Let the men live in slavery if they will" (Tacitus 340). The Roman commander commented on the presence of women in the army, scornfully dismissing their force and urging his own troops to rely on their experience and discipline. Suetonius was right that the Romans were better armed and had armor, while the Britons fought seminaked with swords. But perhaps the greatest advantage of the Romans was their strategy.

As was their custom, the Britons brought their women and children in wagons to watch the battle, and the lay of the land dictated that the wagons would be at the end of the ravine (sadly blocking any retreat). As the Britons charged up the ravine, their greater numbers were not useful in the narrow terrain, and the Romans methodically killed the recklessly charging Britons. Tacitus says that according to one source, 80,000 Britons died compared to 400 Romans. The women and children watching the fray were also slaughtered as the Romans made sure to take revenge for the previous losses.

Queen Boudicca did not die in the battle. Instead, Tacitus said that she took poison and died rather than let herself be taken captive. Tacitus did not tell what happened to her daughters, but later historians claimed that they, too, took poison.

The Romans' victory and the subsequent repression of the local population ensured the Roman presence on the island that would last another 350 years. But Boudicca was not forgotten. Dio Cassius says that her people gave her a splendid burial, and even today, the British remember the valiant uprising of the native queen, who came to be called Baodicia. Indeed, there is a romantic (and rather fanciful) statue of her in London, in which she is shown riding in her chariot with her two daughters and led by rearing horses. The spirit of this brave woman of the ancient world has been adopted by modern men and women alike.

See also Cartimandua; Dynamis; Germanic Tribal Women

Suggested Readings

Dio Cassius. *Dio's Roman History.* Trans. E. Cary. Cambridge: Harvard University Press, 1961.

Dudley, Donald R. *The Rebellion of Boudicca.* London: Routledge, 1962.

Fraser, Antonia. *The Warrior Queens.* New York: Alfred A. Knopf, 1989.

Tacitus. "Annals." In *Complete Works of Tacitus.* New York: The Modern Library, 1942.

C

Caerellia
Wealthy Roman Matron (ca. 116–ca. 36 B.C.)
In the Roman world, if a woman had wealth and family connections, she was able to exert a good deal of independence and influence. Many such women pursued their interests, whether in the arts (such as Clodia) or making money (such as Terentia), and maintained love affairs or friendships with whomever they chose. Most of these women's lives are forgotten now, but one wealthy independent woman is remembered because she was the good friend of Cicero, the famous orator who wrote speeches and letters that continue to be much studied today. Within his letters, he tells of his friend Caerellia, a wealthy woman ten years older than he.

Cicero and Caerellia seem to have become friends based on a mutual love of philosophy and literature. Cicero rejoiced to find in her an admirer whose ability gave him as much pleasure as her enthusiasm, and he even sent her advance copies of some of his works. Caerellia repeatedly exchanged letters with Cicero that reveal this ongoing intellectual interest.

Perhaps not surprisingly, the scandalmongers in Rome accused Cicero of having a more carnal interest in Caerellia. People who wanted to attack the orator claimed that she had been his mistress and that he continued to court her when he was in his sixties and she in her seventies. However, his letters belie the rumors; he repeatedly calls her his friend, and there is no indication of any other form of the relationship.

Cicero, who frequently had money problems, turned to his wealthy friends for help, and he was not shy about approaching Caerellia. In 45 B.C., when his finances were at a low point, Caerellia advanced him a large loan. Cicero's secretary bluntly told Cicero that if he valued his dignity, he must repay this loan immediately, but Cicero postponed repayment and used her money liberally.

The extent to which Caerellia's friendship was important to Cicero may be seen toward the end of his life, when his daughter Tullia had died and when his second marriage to the very young Publilia seemed to be failing (which it did within a few months of the wedding). Publilia and her family approached Caerellia to serve as an intermediary to try to smooth things out between Cicero and his bride. Her efforts to dissuade Cicero from seeking a divorce were unsuccessful, but her role is indicative of how influential Cicero's acquaintants perceived her to be.

Unfortunately, most of our information about Caerellia comes from Cicero, so we do not know her feelings about all these events. However, we may draw a few conclusions: Her wealth gave her the independence to pursue her love of philosophy, to befriend Cicero, and to ignore the rumors that circulated through the city. She could follow her own inclinations and did so, and it is likely that other anonymous Roman women similarly placed were able to do the same thing.

See also Clodia; Terentia; Tullia
Suggested Readings
Bailey, D. R. Schackleton. *Cicero.* New York: Charles Scribner's Sons, 1971.
Carcopino, Jerome. *Cicero: The Secrets of His Correspondence.* New York: Greenwood Press, 1969.

Calpurnia
Roman Wife of Julius Caesar (ca. 85–45 B.C.)
In the last decades of the Roman Republic, Rome was swept with civil war as powerful men

used their popularity with the Roman people and their leadership of the armies to take control. The government was still nominally a republic, where men were elected to administer the increasingly complex government, but the constitution allowed for the office of "dictator"—in which a man could take full powers during emergencies. This office became the coveted one as men sought to circumvent the constitution, and the old system of checks and balances no longer worked. One group of popular leaders bypassed most of the formal structures and made a private alliance to share power. Modern historians have called this agreement the First Triumvirate, or the rule by three men. Contemporaries called it a three-headed monster.

The First Triumvirate (ca. 60–49 B.C.) was made up of three men who appealed to various sectors of Roman society. Pompey was a brilliant general who had won striking battles in the east. Julius Caesar was probably an even more talented general and brilliant orator, who had the support of the people. The third man was Crassus, a fabulously rich leader of the business community. Instead of bringing peace, however, the triumvirate simply became an arena in which the three powerful figures jockeyed for control. Throughout this struggle for power, marriage alliances were used to cement political alliances.

Julius Caesar was known for being attracted to many women, and his sexual escapades were the talk of Rome, even during a time when sexual mores had become somewhat loose. In his youth, he had a long affair with a married woman named Servilla, and at the end of his life he scandalized Rome with his liaison with the Egyptian queen Cleopatra VII. He also married women to form political alliances (as was common in the senatorial class at that time). His first wife was Cornelia, whom he married in 84 B.C. when he was only sixteen years old; she was the daughter of a leading follower of the popular leader Marius. After her death, he married Pompeia, whom he later renounced after a scandal. His last wife was Calpurnia, who earned Rome's admiration by her support of her talented but errant husband.

Calpurnia was the daughter of an influential man named Piso; Caesar married her in 59 B.C.

Her father was made consul the next year, a reward for this influential marriage. This political match caused Cato—a Roman critic—to remark that it was intolerable that the government "should be prostituted by marriages, and that they should advance one another to commands of armies, provinces, and other great posts, by means of women" (Plutarch 862). Although Cato's accusation was true and the marriage was made for political reasons, Calpurnia remained by Caesar's side through the civil wars that brought Caesar to the highest power that a Roman had yet achieved.

The triumvirate fell apart by 49 B.C., and Caesar's armies crossed the Rubicon River into Italy from Gaul, beginning the civil war against Pompey. As Caesar led his armies across the Mediterranean (and into Egypt where he fell in love with Cleopatra), Calpurnia remained faithful in Rome. By 48 B.C., Caesar had accepted the office of dictator, and four years later he took the title dictator for life in a shocking breach of Roman custom. He may have turned down the title of king, but there were many who believed he was acting like one. He struck coins with his own image on them (as a king did), and he wielded total power over the state. Finally, in 44 B.C. a coalition of senators conspired to kill him to end this threat to the republican constitution.

According to Roman historians, soothsayers had warned Caesar to beware of the Ides of March (15 March), and Calpurnia, too, worried about her husband. The night before his assassination, when he was in bed with his wife, all the doors and windows flew open from a wind. Caesar was awakened by the noise, and by the moonshine saw Calpurnia asleep. She was dreaming, and Caesar heard her speaking and groaning in her sleep. Later she said that she dreamed she was weeping over Caesar and holding his bleeding body in her arms.

When it was morning, she begged Caesar not to go out, but to adjourn the senate to another day. She further said if he did not believe her dream, he should consult his fate by other forms of divination. He, too, was concerned, as Plutarch writes, "for he never before discovered any womanish superstition in Calpurnia, whom he now saw in such great alarm" (Plutarch 891).

He tried to delay the senate meeting, but some of the conspirators mocked his fears, asking whether they should hold up government until Calpurnia had better dreams. Caesar went ahead to the senate meeting, where he was stabbed to death on the Ides of March in 44 B.C. Calpurnia's dream had come true.

See also Cleopatra VII; Pompeia; Porcia; Servilia
Suggested Readings
Grant, Michael. *Caesar.* Chicago: Follett Publishing, 1975.
Plutarch. *The Lives of the Noble Grecians and Romans.* Trans. J. Dryden. New York: The Modern Library, n.d.

Cartimandua

British Queen (ca. A.D. 47–69)
When the Romans began their northward conquest of Britain, they encountered a loose confederation of tribes, collectively called the Brigantes. In A.D. 47, the Romans noted that one of the tribes was led by an effective queen, Cartimandua (whose name means "sleek pony"). The Roman historian Tacitus (ca. A.D. 56–ca. 120) wrote that she was of "noble lineage" and "flourishing in all the splendor of wealth and power" (Ellis 83). Cartimandua decided to become an ally of the Romans and retained power as a client ruler of the empire. Internal dissent, however, would threaten the peace treaty she had made.

In A.D. 48, a tribe in the southwest portion of her kingdom threatened the peace with Rome by attacking Roman armies that were heading into what is now Wales. The Roman army defeated the rebellious forces of Caractacus, who fled to Cartimandua's court looking for sanctuary. The queen honored her treaty with Rome, however, and handed over Caractacus and his family to the Romans. They were taken to Rome in chains, where they lived out the rest of their lives. Cartimandua had proven her loyalty to Rome, and it would stand her in good stead.

The queen had married a British chieftain, Venutius, who was known as a valiant warrior. Within a few years, however, there was strife within the royal household. According to Tacitus, many of the subjects were unwilling to support their queen: "They scorned to submit to a female government . . ." (Ellis 84). It is more likely, however, that the civil war grew out of a power struggle between Venutius and Cartimandua. The queen called on the Roman governor to send his troops to protect her rule, and he did so. With the presence of the Roman legion, the queen and her husband reconciled, and peace seemed once again ensured under the strong rule of Cartimandua. The close association between the queen and the Romans probably explains why the Brigantes did not join in the rebellion of Boudicca in A.D. 61.

Cartimandua's marital problems were to bring the Roman legions again into her territory. In A.D. 69, she divorced Venutius in favor of his charioteer. The spurned husband raised an army from tribes outside the Brigantian confederation and threatened Cartimandua's rule. The queen again called on her Roman allies to help her, but this time they were less successful. Tacitus says that the Romans suffered several losses at the hands of Venutius and were unable to restore Cartimandua to her throne. They settled for removing the queen and her new husband safely from the disputed territory, leaving Venutius as king of the Brigantes. Cartimandua disappears from the historical sources at this point. The Romans would eventually defeat Venutius and take over the independent kingdom of the Brigantes. This resolution suggests the wisdom of Queen Cartimandua in preserving her rule by allying with the powerful Romans.

See also Boudicca
Suggested Readings
Ellis, P. B. *Women in Celtic Society and Literature.* Grand Rapids, MI: W. B. Eerdmans Publishing, 1995.
Fraser, Antonia. *The Warrior Queens.* New York: Alfred A. Knopf, 1989.

Cassandra

Mythological Greek Prophet
The Trojan War was fought between Greeks and Trojans over the abduction of the beautiful Helen, and according to the ancient legends, many tragedies arose from this long and brutal war. One of the popular ones described the fate of Cassandra, the most beautiful daughter of Priam and Hecuba (Hecabe)—king and queen of Troy. Hecabe had borne Priam many children

(some legends place the number at over nineteen), and among her youngest children were the twins Cassandra and Helenus. At their birthday feast, the twins fell asleep in a corner, while their forgetful parents went home without them. When Hecabe returned to the temple, she found sacred serpents licking the children's sensory organs in order to purify them. The queen screamed in terror, and the serpents disappeared at once. From that hour, both Cassandra and Helenus possessed the gift of prophecy that had been given them by the purification of the serpents.

Another legend gives a different version of how Cassandra came to have the gift of prophecy. One day she fell asleep in the temple, and Apollo appeared and promised to teach her the art of prophecy if she would yield to his advances. Cassandra accepted his gift, but then went back on the bargain, refusing him. Apollo begged her to give him one kiss. As she did, he spat into her mouth, thus ensuring that no one would believe what she prophesied.

Cassandra vainly tried to warn the Trojans against pursuing the disastrous war, and when the Greeks left the great horse outside the walls, Cassandra uselessly warned the Trojans not to bring the wooden horse within the walls. As her warnings fell on deaf ears, Troy fell in flames. As the citizens were being massacred, Cassandra fled to the temple of Athena for safety. She was pursued there by Ajax, one of the Greek heroes, who tore her from the statue of the goddess. In doing so, he loosened the statue. Confronted by this act of sacrilege, the Greeks were ready to stone Ajax, but he saved himself by demanding sanctuary at the altar of the goddess he had insulted.

When the booty of the war was divided up, Agamemnon claimed Cassandra as his prize and forced the virgin to his bed. Cassandra continued to prophesy disaster even as Agamemnon took her back to his home in Greece. Some sources say she bore Agamemnon twin sons. All were murdered by Agamemnon's wife, Clytemnestra, when they returned to Greece.

The popularity of this legend has led to a continued use of the word *Cassandra* to mean anyone who repeatedly predicts disaster, but who is never believed. This is a sad heritage of this ancient myth of Cassandra.

See also Clytemnestra; Helen of Troy in Greek Mythology
Suggested Readings
Grimal, Pierre. *The Dictionary of Classical Mythology.* Oxford: Blackwell, 1996.

Çatal Hüyük
Neolithic Settlement (ca. 6500 B.C.)

People first began living in relatively large settled communities in the Neolithic (New Stone Age), when tribes began to change from hunting and gathering societies to a culture that practiced agriculture and kept domestic animals. Since this development took place sometime around 8000 B.C., it is extremely difficult to find information about women's roles in these early settlements. One remarkable excavation, however, has offered some tantalizing information about women in these early cities. Çatal Hüyük, in modern Turkey, is the largest Neolithic site excavated to date, and it sheds light on the hidden period when people began to shift from hunting to agriculture. It covers about thirty-two acres, and perhaps as many as 8,000 people lived there. It was founded about 6500 B.C. and was inexplicably abandoned about 5650 B.C.

Families in this extensive village lived in mud-brick houses packed closely together, and it seems that the town layout was planned, not random. These houses had neither doors nor windows; people entered by descending a ladder through a hole in the roof. The hole also served as a vent for smoke from the family's hearth. This construction provided excellent insulation from the elements and offered another important advantage: safety from threatening neighbors. This seems to have been quite effective, for there is no evidence of warfare at Çatal Hüyük at any point in its 850 years of existence.

The interior of the buildings had plastered walls that were sometimes painted with geometric patterns. Many of the houses had walls that had been replastered repeatedly, so we can assume that people gave a great deal of care to the interior of their homes. Within the houses, men and women slept on separate sleeping platforms. Archaeologists designate the occupants of these areas because adults were buried under them by

Figure 6. Anatolian cultural relic (Ann Ronan Picture Library)

skeletons have been found only under the women's beds, which suggests that women had most of the responsibility for the children. It may also suggest that in this society inheritance passed through the women's line, but the information is too scarce to be certain.

The many skeletons have also provided information about the lives of the people themselves. The average height for women was between 5 feet and 5 feet 4 inches, while men were between 5 feet 4 inches and 5 feet 10 inches. None of the skeletons showed signs of violent death, which again argues for a peaceful existence. As one would expect, a few had had broken limbs, which had been set. None seem to have lived beyond the age of about forty years, and it seems that childbirth, infection, and pneumonia were the main causes of death. Among the skeletons, women and children far outnumber men, but scholars have no speculation about why this is so.

Excavations at this rich site also reveal the religious interests of the inhabitants. Within the town there were many buildings that were larger and more elaborately decorated than the others, and archaeologists assume these were religious shrines. They had decorative wall paintings, including representations of animals, and they also had plaster images of great bulls' horns and stags' heads set into the walls. In other shrines there were many plaster representations of breasts set in the walls. In all levels, there are both male and female deities worshiped (although the males are only represented by the animals' horns), and in the earliest levels there are wall paintings that depict lively hunting scenes. After 5800 B.C., art increasingly focused on a mother goddess—pregnant with large breasts. Presumably, this shift in religious emphasis accompanied a shift from hunting-gathering to agricultural activities, and the villagers were concerned with fertility to ensure their survival.

The Çatal Hüyük villagers first settled in the area probably because of its proximity to great grasslands that had huge herds of wild cattle and deer. Figure 6 shows a stylized deer with a great rack of antlers that was excavated from the site. Hunters also had abundant wild sheep to bring to the table, but paintings also show

gender. The bones of the dead were buried in the houses only after the flesh had decomposed or had been removed by vultures or other animals. Then the bones were carefully wrapped in cloth and placed in the earth graves below the sleeping platforms. This burial pattern has allowed archaeologists to speculate on some of the gender relationships in this ancient town, since the burials allow scholars to identify the owners of the sleeping platforms.

The women's platforms were larger and fixed, while the men's were smaller and more portable, suggesting that the men moved around more often. Some archaeologists suggest that this arrangement indicates matrilocal marriage; that is, arrangements in which the bridegroom moves to live with the bride's family. Children's that they confronted leopards and lions in their hunts. Soon after the settlement began, there is evidence for a growth of agriculture—barley and lentils were planted, and people (probably women) brewed ale. They also had domesticated sheep and goats, which were kept largely for milk, and women may have used the acid in the local acorn caps to make yogurt.

The Çatal Hüyük residents proved so successful at farming that they began developing specialized skills. For example, some workers made traditional tools of stone, wood, and bone. Others specialized in the new skills of textile weaving and pottery making. Trade was also a prominent feature of the economy of Çatal Hüyük. Residents imported decorative shells from the Mediterranean Sea and exported obsidian, a volcanic rock from a nearby mountain. This site also shows the beginnings of metalworking, an innovation that ultimately freed people from reliance on stone. That would take time, though, for the Çatal Hüyük townspeople began to experiment with metals first for ornament, not tools, by pounding copper and lead into jewelry. Life in Çatal Hüyük shows a growing complexity that marks the beginnings of civilization. In addition, the provocative site offers tantalizing evidence of a time when women's roles were central in religion and in the community.

See also Jewelry; Stone Age Art
Suggested Readings
Ehrenberg, M. *Women in Prehistory.* Norman: University of Oklahoma Press, 1989.
Gimbutas, M. *The Civilization of the Goddess: The World of Old Europe.* San Francisco: HarperCollins, 1991.
Mellaart, J. *Çatal Hüyük: A Neolithic Town in Anatolia.* New York: McGraw-Hill, 1967.

Ceres
Roman Goddess
Ceres was an ancient goddess representing the regenerative power of nature. She was worshiped in a temple on the Aventine hill in Rome, with games in her honor and a popular spring festival that took place in April. During a famine in Rome in 496 B.C., the Sybilline books recommended that the Greek deities Demeter, Persephone, and Bacchus be identified with the Roman gods Ceres, Liber, and Libera. Therefore, the myths associated with Demeter and Persephone became identified with the Italian corn-goddess Ceres.

See also Demeter
Suggested Readings
Adkins, Lesley, and Roy A. Adkins. *Handbook to Life in Ancient Rome.* New York: Oxford University Press, 1994.
Grant, M. *Roman Myths.* London: Weidenfeld and Nicolson, 1971.
Grimal, Pierre. *The Dictionary of Classical Mythology.* Oxford: Blackwell, 1996.
Ogilvie, R. M. *The Romans and Their Gods.* London: Chatto and Windus, 1969.

Christian Women
(ca. A.D. 30–400)
As soon as Jesus began his brief ministry in Palestine, his followers included women. We glimpse some of these women in the Gospels (which were written from 75 to 100 years after Christ's crucifixion) and others in the Acts and letters of the apostles written slightly earlier. These sources, however, seem to have been shaped by contemporary ideas and also at times contain contradictory information, so historians (and theologians) sometimes disagree on the exact roles women played in the formative centuries of Christianity. This issue is particularly significant—and controversial—because many people believe that the precedents set in the early church should inform modern issues, such as whether women should serve as priests and pastors. In spite of the controversies that surround elements of interpretation of these early sources, it is possible to draw some general conclusions about women in the early Christian centuries and to say definitively that women were centrally important during Christ's ministry and beyond.

Women in the New Testament
All the Gospels indicate that women followed Jesus as he traveled, spoke, and worked miracles. Some of the anonymous women mentioned in the Bible had been healed of demon possession or illness and followed Jesus in gratitude. The Gospel of Luke includes such examples as Jesus'

curing a woman who had been bleeding (probably from her uterus) for twelve years and curing another woman who had been crippled and bent over for eighteen years. Jesus even cured the mother-in-law of his apostle Simon Peter; she then showed her gratitude by serving the men.

These women "ministered to" or "served" Jesus and the Twelve Apostles, supporting them with finances as well as with their labor. Women such as Martha invited Jesus to stay in their homes and supported them there, and she was not unique. In fact, the early movement depended upon the wealth of patrons, many of whom seem to have been women. After Jesus' death, the religion spread through "house churches" where the faithful met, and many of these churches were owned by wealthy women who offered their homes within which the new congregations could gather.

Women also served as the catalyst for Jesus to offer significant points of his teachings, and the fact that the Gospels include women at these moments indicates that women were important in the early movement. For example, one woman sinner described in the Gospel of Luke washed Jesus' feet with her tears and dried them with her hair. In another example, Jesus used this story to show that sins can be forgiven by great love, and he used the example of a woman to teach this important message. Jesus spoke to Martha about the resurrection of the dead before he raised her brother Lazarus from his tomb, and this formed the core of his teaching about the afterlife. The Gospels also report that Jesus cured a Canaanite woman—a non-Jewish (or Gentile) woman—after first refusing, saying that his mission was only for Jews, then relenting because of her faith. This incident is often thought to forecast Christianity's spread to Gentiles. All these incidents point to women at the central moments of the teachings that would become the core of the growing Jesus movement.

Women were present at Jesus' last hours, for the Gospels say that many women who had followed Jesus from Galilee to Jerusalem watched the crucifixion. Mark (15:40) says that three women—Mary Magdalene, Mary the mother of James the younger, and Salome—stood closely and witnessed Jesus' death. (Luke agrees that

Mary Magdalene was a witness but names two other women—Joanna and Susanna—as her companions.) These women were included as significant witnesses to Jesus' death and burial when the male disciples had all fled.

Three days later, it was women who discovered that Jesus had risen from the dead, and he spoke to Mary Magdalene. It was she who brought the news to the apostles. Finally, the Gospel of Luke describes how Jesus ascended into heaven after telling his followers wait for a sign to begin their ministry. The book of Acts picks up the account of the apostles gathering to pray in an upstairs room in Jerusalem. With them are Mary the mother of Jesus a number of unnamed women. These included those who had witnessed the crucifixion

Acts then talks primarily about deeds of the male apostles. It is surprising Mary Magdalene and Mary the mother Jesus did not continue the missionary activ se two Marys are important in the Apl Acts and in other noncanonical work early church, so it may have been that hor of Acts was interested in only a por the history of the early church. Within s, the role of women is played down, brtainly does not disappear.

The Acts of the Apostles talk a e missionary work of Paul and the apostles. They traveled throughout the R empire preaching about Jesus and estab small congregations in house churches th often run by women. We have more nation about women in these house church m the letters of Paul as he wrote to vario urches within his ministry. Within these let—that became scripture—we can see the for tion of the attitudes toward the role of wo n that came to characterize the early Christian hurch, and we can also see the many controversies that began to arise on the subject of women.

In his first letter to the Corinthians, Paul addressed the issue of marriage and established principles that have continued to affect women (and men) today. While Paul preferred people to remain unmarried and devote their lives to serving God, he nevertheless acknowledged that marriage was a central part of the Roman world.

Thus, he told married women to continue to have sexual relations with their husbands to keep their husbands from being lured into sins of lust. Furthermore, in a world in which divorce was common (see Roman Women), Paul told women not to divorce their husbands if they were Christian. Even if their husbands were pagans, women were not to initiate divorce; instead they were to stay with their spouses and try to convert them. This latter requirement proved influential in converting many Romans, for women often seemed to have converted first and their husbands and families followed the women's lead. (Monica is an excellent example of this pattern.)

The letter to the Corinthians also contains other requirements that have proven much more ambiguous and troubling to many feminist scholars. It is clear that in the Corinthian church a number of women prophets took the lead in speaking in tongues and prophesying in this. This tradition of Corinth went back to origins of this church, when women such as and Phoebe (mentioned in Rom. 16:1) served as leaders. Tension seems to have grown up in the church, however, and to bring harmony once more to the congregations, Paul wrote to emphasize love rather than spiritual gifts as prophecy). In the process, he wrote regarding women's participation.

Paul also took up a conflict in the Corinthian church about appropriate costume during worship. In the course of this discussion, he urged women to cover (or veil) their heads or else shave their heads. "Any woman who prays or prophesies with her head unveiled dishonors her head—it is the same as if her head were shaved. For if a woman will not veil herself, then she should cut off her hair; but if it is disgraceful for a woman to be shorn or shaven, let her wear a veil" (1 Cor. 11:5–6). Readers of these rather ambiguous passages have found evidence for both the subordination of women (to men's leadership) and the freedom of veiled women—later interpreted as nuns—to conduct their own affairs.

Paul's further comments have been even more criticized by feminists. In the famous passage of 1 Cor. 14, Paul writes of the spiritual gifts that came to the early congregations, when people spoke in tongues and prophesied in the church. He wrote, "When you come together, each one has a hymn, a lesson, a revelation, a tongue, or an interpretation" (1 Cor. 14:26). This passage describes what the early services in the house churches would have looked like—all the faithful contributing something as the Spirit moved them. Then Paul rapidly inserts a statement that is surprising, since he had already acknowledged that women within the church were prophesying: "As in all the churches of the saints, the women should keep silence in the churches. For they are not permitted to speak, but should be subordinate, as even the law says. If there is anything they desire to know, let them ask their husbands at home. For it is shameful for a woman to speak in church" (1 Cor. 14:33–35). Paul then concludes this verse by saying that no one should forbid speaking in tongues but that "all things should be done decently and in order" (1 Cor. 14:40).

This passage has been used for most of Christian history to deny women participation and leadership in the Christian community. Not surprisingly, these verses have received an enormous amount of scholarly scrutiny to try to resolve the apparent contradiction within Paul's words. Should women speak out in the church when they feel moved by the Spirit? Some scholars suggest that the passage was a later insertion into scripture, written by someone who wanted to exclude women from an active part of the services. Other scholars say that Paul wrote it, but he simply wanted to reprimand women who were gossiping during the service. These questions are not resolved, and it is certain that these passages will continue to generate much scholarly (and nonscholarly) discussion.

Women in the Postapostolic Churches

Even if Paul had intended for women to be silent within the churches, it is clear that they were not. As Christianity spread to more and more house churches throughout the Roman Empire in the next two centuries, women continued to speak and take leadership roles within the church. In the third century and the beginning of the fourth century, women took leadership roles in four principal ways: (1) as owners of the house churches and wealthy patrons of the congregations, (2) as members of an order of "widows" who served the church in charitable and other ways, (3) as prophets who spoke in tongues and manifested other forms of spiritual gifts, and (4) as deaconesses, ordained to perform some liturgical functions specifically for women in the congregations.

Throughout the third and fourth centuries, there were periodic tensions within the churches about the roles and powers of women within the congregations. Sometimes women who spoke of prophecies seemed to claim more respect and authority than priests or bishops, and it was increasingly difficult to identify a clear and organized hierarchy. For example, the North African church father Tertullian (at the beginning of the third century A.D.) described the Christian community as being led by elders of high moral character and presided over by a hierarchy of deacons, presbyters, and bishops. At the same time, Tertullian wanted to preserve the expression and value of charismatic gifts that were at the heart of the earliest communities. As long as prophecy yielded leadership, women would remain in positions of authority in the congregations. However, that situation would not remain in effect, and even Tertullian was condemned for trying to preserve an earlier form of worship.

By the fourth century, as the church became more and more linked to the established order of the Roman Empire and as it began to appeal to wealthy and influential people, the congregations increasingly became organized in a hierarchical fashion. Now women would be excluded from leadership roles. This did not happen immediately (and the tendency began earlier than the fourth century), but slowly it was so. Some Christian leaders wrote to reduce the power of widows, placing them under vows of obedience to their bishops. It appears that this group of women was the first to be regulated within the church. When the church was no longer persecuted, the house churches were replaced by public buildings, and the female owners of the houses no longer held the privileged positions that came with being the acknowledged heads of the households.

As early as the third century, prophecy within the church came to be restricted. Owing to the popularity of heretical groups like the Montanists and Gnostics, both of which offered significant roles for women prophets, the official church began to restrict the right of women to prophesy in church. Churchmen also slowly began to exclude texts that gave women a significant leadership role—texts such as The Gospel of Mary that depicted Mary Magdalene as a church leader or The Acts of Paul and Thecla that showed Thecla preaching and baptizing were called apocryphal, that is, false. As prophecy faded from the churches, so did the women who had spoken loudly as the Spirit moved them.

The deaconesses (such as Olympias) were the group most easily integrated into a church hierarchy, and thus they remained central through the fourth century. Deaconesses were to help priests in their ministry and tend specifically to the women of the congregations. For example, deaconesses were needed to assist the priest in the baptism of women, for in these early ceremonies, women emerged naked from the baptismal pool and were then anointed all over with oil. It would have been unseemly for men to perform the anointment. This procedure did not give women permission to perform the baptism—indeed by the late third century, texts specifically forbade women's performing this sacred act. Deaconesses also were permitted to teach women as they were preparing for baptism. Thus, deaconesses—under careful supervision—performed many of the day-to-day acts central to the Christian congregations. Later, beginning sometime in the late fourth century, women were excluded from these church offices as well.

Does all this mean that women had leadership roles in the early centuries of Christianity? Certainly it does. Can we then assume that in today's church women should be ordained as priests and ministers? This remains controversial because the modern roles of priest do not exactly parallel the early leadership roles, and the churches of modern times are not the simple house churches of the earliest centuries of Christianity. Others say that women should be church leaders today, for it was in large part under the initiative of brave and enterprising women of the ancient world that Christianity spread. This argument will not be resolved easily.

See also Apocryphal Acts of the Apostles; Martha [Christian Woman]; Mary; Mary Magdalene; Monica; Olympias [Christian Deaconess]; Perpetua the Martyr; Thecla

Suggested Readings

Corley, Kathleen E. *Private Women, Public Meals: Social Conflict in the Synoptic Tradition.* Peabody, MA: Hendrickson Publishers, 1993.

Kraemer, Ross Shepard. *Her Share of the Blessings: Women's Religions among Pagans, Jews, and Christians in the Greco-Roman World.* New York: Oxford University Press, 1992.

Kraemer, Ross Shepard, and Mary Rose D'Angelo. *Women and Christian Origins.* New York: Oxford University Press, 1999.

Meyers, Carol, Toni Craven, and Ross S. Kraemer. *Women in Scripture.* New York: Houghton Mifflin, 2000.

Salisbury, Joyce E. *The Death and Memory of a Young Roman Woman.* New York: Routledge, 1997.

Wire, Antoinette Clark. *The Corinthian Women Prophets: A Reconstruction through Paul's Rhetoric.* Minneapolis: Fortress Press, 1990.

Cleopatra I ("The Syrian")

Ptolemaic Egyptian Queen (d. ca. 173 B.C.)

King Ptolemy V (203–180 B.C.) was a young boy when he succeeded his father to the throne. He was faced with many problems, both domestic and foreign. In 197 B.C., when Ptolemy was twelve years old, he officially came of age, and he had to negotiate careful compromises to bring peace to his land. In 201 and 200 B.C., there had been uprisings against Macedonian rule among Egyptian natives in the Nile Delta, and Ptolemy needed the support of the old Egyptian priesthood to maintain his power. He had himself crowned as a pharaoh—laden with traditional sacred titles and gold snake-crowns—in the old capital of Memphis, instead of Alexandria, which had been preferred by the Macedonians. Now the Macedonian kingship was seen as truly Egyptian by the priests and the people, and the riots were quelled. The great decree proclaiming Ptolemy's acceptance of the old gods was inscribed on the famous Rosetta Stone in three languages—Greek, sacred hieroglyphics, and common Egyptian script. It was this stone that helped nineteenth-century scholars break the code of the ancient hieroglyphics.

Ptolemy's foreign problems were resolved in a way more traditional for the Hellenistic kings—marriage. The powerful Seleucid king Antiochus III, "the Great" (223–187 B.C.), had once more gone to war against a weakened Egypt and had taken back Syria and other lands won by Egypt in part through the courage of the young queen Arsinoë III. To seal the peace treaty, Antiochus insisted that Ptolemy V take Antiochus's daughter Cleopatra as wife. The terms were generous—Cleopatra would receive the lands of Syria as dowry, returning to Egypt that territory that Antiochus had won. It may be that Antiochus hoped eventually to unite the Seleucid territory with that of Egypt by this marriage, but that was not to be. Whatever his motives, the marriage took place in 193 B.C. at Raphia—the old battleground where Ptolemy V's mother Arsinoë III had stirred the troops to victory against the previous Seleucid forces. Instead of weakening the Egyptian Ptolemies, however, this marriage brought a strong woman to power who invigorated the dynasty.

The historian Livy calls Ptolemy V and Cleopatra I "kings of Egypt" (Macurdy 144), which suggests that Cleopatra's prestige as daughter of Antiochus and her enormous dowry gave her a position equal to that of her husband. Her personal talents further secured her place as a competent ruler. The couple had three children; the eldest of the three may have been Cleopatra II (although we are not sure of her birth date), and the other two were sons, both named Ptolemy. The elder was born in 186 B.C. and the younger shortly thereafter.

In 180 B.C., Ptolemy V died, and Cleopatra's elder son Ptolemy VI—who was called Philomater, which means "mother loving"—became pharaoh. Ptolemy VI was only five years old at his accession, so Cleopatra I became regent during his minority. She seems to have governed well during her regency, maintaining peace with the Seleucid kingdom, the increasingly powerful Rome, and her own people. She was the first Ptolemaic queen to issue coins in her name alone, which increased the precedent for strong queens in Egypt.

It is perhaps testimony to her strength that the name Cleopatra—originally a Macedonian royal name—became entrenched in Egypt. It replaced Berenice and Arsinoë as dynastic names and became almost equal to Ptolemy in signaling royalty. She was the first of a long line of Cleopatras who would rule in Egypt.

See also Arsinoë III; Cleopatra II; Cleopatra Thea
Suggested Readings
Livy. *Livy.* Vol. 37. Trans B. O. Foster. Cambridge: Harvard University Press, 1963.
Macurdy, Grace Harriet. *Hellenistic Queens.* Baltimore: Johns Hopkins University Press, 1932.
Pomeroy, Sarah B. *Women in Hellenistic Egypt from Alexander to Cleopatra.* New York: Schocken Books, 1984.

Cleopatra II
Ptolemaic Egyptian Queen
(ca. 190–ca. 116 B.C.)

Cleopatra II was the eldest child of Cleopatra I and Ptolemy V, and with the precedent of her strong mother's regency, the new queen might have expected to enjoy a good deal of power and peace during her reign. The events of her life, however, would turn out to be as dramatic as any of the Hellenistic queens.

Cleopatra and her brother Ptolemy VI Philomater were married in about 173 B.C. after their mother's death; Ptolemy was about fourteen at that time. Philomater was persuaded to enter into a war against his uncle, the Seleucid Antiochus IV, over the endlessly contested lands in Syria that bordered the two kingdoms. Antiochus defeated the Egyptian troops soundly, and Philomater was captured by the Seleucid king. Antiochus invaded Egypt itself, perhaps to have himself crowned king. When he arrived, however, he discovered that the younger brother—Ptolemy VII Euergetes (meaning "benefactor")—had been chosen king in Alexandria in place of the fleeing Philomater and was reigning there along with his sister Cleopatra II, Philomater's wife. Antiochus threw his support to Philomater, leaving him in Memphis with a strong garrison. It is likely that Antiochus hoped that dissension among the siblings would weaken Egypt.

However, the three Ptolemies came to terms, and all three reigned jointly in Alexandria. Rome got involved in this dispute and ordered Antiochus to cease the warfare against his two nephews. The Seleucid king was forced to agree. The Roman documents were addressed to the "rulers of Egypt, Ptolemy and Cleopatra," which shows the regard that Rome gave to the queen. Cleopatra's difficulties in the future would not come from afar but from her position of having to be peacemaker between her two brothers.

Cleopatra II and Philomater seem to have enjoyed a reasonable family life. They had four children. The two sons were named Eupator and Ptolemy Neos Philopater; the two daughters were both named Cleopatra. Philomater made political marriages for his daughters: One, known as Cleopatra Thea, would marry into the Seleucid dynasty; the other would marry her uncle Ptolemy Euergetes, who had been persuaded to rule in a North African country, leaving Egypt to Philomater and Cleopatra. All seemed in order in the land and in the Ptolemy household until Philomater was thrown from his horse; he landed on rocky ground and received a wound from which he died. He was forty-one years old, and his wife a few years older. Now, she faced the most serious challenge of her life.

Cleopatra II became regent with her son Ptolemy Neos Philopater, but her younger brother Euergetes wanted to rule. The sources describe Ptolemy VII Euergetes as a thoroughly cruel man. He was abnormally fat—his people gave him the nickname of "fat-belly"—and he wore transparent robes to reveal his bulk. The Greek sources hate him because he exiled or killed many Greek scholars and other professional men. This despicable man killed his nephew Ptolemy Neos Philopater. One source says he killed the boy while he was in his mother's arms, but that may have been sensationalism.

One might imagine that Euergetes would have killed his sister as well, but remarkably he married her instead. It may be that he was more secure on the throne with his popular sister as queen; her motives for the marriage may have been simple survival or a desire for power. In any case, they had a son called Memphites. Cleopatra II now was once again mother to the heir to the throne. After several years of marriage, however, Euergetes fulfilled the engagement promised by his brother and married his niece Cleopatra III (Cleopatra II's daughter). There were thereafter two queens named Cleopatra married to the king. The formula in documents and inscriptions reads "King Ptolemy and queen Cleopatra the Sister and queen Cleopatra the Wife." This situation became untenable.

In 130 B.C. Euergetes was driven out of Alexandria, and Cleopatra II ruled the city. The king fled to Cyprus with his wife, Cleopatra III, and their children. He also took with him his son by his sister, Memphites, who was about fourteen years old. The Greek historian Diodorus claims that the king killed their son and sent his dismembered body in a birthday box to his sister. There followed a period of warfare in Egypt between supporters of Cleopatra II and those of the king. Finally, and again remarkably after all that had transpired, the king and sister made peace in 118 B.C. Ptolemy VII Euergetes died in 116 B.C., and Cleopatra II lived for a few months longer, sharing rule with her daughter.

Perhaps the most extraordinary thing about Cleopatra II was her longevity. She was queen for almost fifty-seven years and was probably over seventy when she died. To have stayed alive in such a violent age, particularly with a murderous brother, testified to an extraordinary resilience. She was not able, however, to keep her sons alive to inherit the throne of Egypt. Instead, her indomitable daughter Cleopatra III would rule next.

See also Cleopatra I; Cleopatra III; Cleopatra Thea
Suggested Readings
Macurdy, Grace Harriet. *Hellenistic Queens.* Baltimore: Johns Hopkins University Press, 1932.
Pomeroy, Sarah B. *Women in Hellenistic Egypt from Alexander to Cleopatra.* New York: Schocken Books, 1984.

Cleopatra III

Ptolemaic Egyptian Queen
(ca. 160–ca. 101 B.C.)

Cleopatra III was faced with the difficult situation of being the second wife of her uncle, Ptolemy VII Euergetes, who was also married to her mother, Cleopatra II. Cleopatra III bore five children to her husband—Ptolemy VIII Soter II, Ptolemy Alexander, Tryphaena, Cleopatra IV, and Cleopatra V Selene. Cleopatra III's married life began in family turmoil as her husband and her mother went to war. In time, the family reconciled, and by 124 B.C. all three ruled together again—although uneasily. Ptolemy VII Euergetes died in 116 B.C., and Cleopatra II and Cleopatra III ruled jointly with Ptolemy Soter. When Cleopatra II died (or was murdered by her daughter), Cleopatra III was left to try to manipulate her high-strung children—while keeping power herself.

The people of Alexandria preferred her elder son, Ptolemy Soter, as joint ruler with her, and he married his sister Cleopatra IV in traditional fashion. However, Cleopatra III found both her elder son and her eldest daughter too strong, and the mother conspired to weaken the pair. She forced her son to divorce Cleopatra IV, whom he loved, and made him marry his more tractable younger sister, Cleopatra V Selene. Cleopatra IV had money and spirit enough to challenge this move, so she went to Cyprus, where her brother Ptolemy Alexander ruled, and raised an army.

Cleopatra IV went with her army to Syria and offered her services to her cousin Antiochus Cyzicenus, who was at war with his half-brother Antiochus Grypus. Both of these men were sons of Cleopatra Thea, sister of Cleopatra III of Egypt. The eldest daughter of Cleopatra III—Tryphaena—was married to Grypus. Thus, this war was fully a family affair between the several branches of this dynasty as they struggled for power. Cleopatra IV married Cyzicenus to strengthen his ability to rule.

Unfortunately, Cleopatra IV was in Antioch when that city was besieged by Grypus. The city fell, and Cleopatra fell into the hands of her sister Tryphaena. Grypus wished to spare Cleopatra IV—and a speech is preserved in which he asks his wife to consider their common blood and the sanctuary of the temple in which Cleopatra had taken refuge. However, Tryphaena thought her husband loved her sister and in a rage had Cleopatra IV killed at the altar where she clasped the image of Artemis. When Cleopatra IV's husband Cyzicenus was again victorious, he killed Tryphaena—offering her to appease the spirit of his murdered wife.

Cleopatra III had thus lost two daughters and sown discord among her nephews. She also continued her struggle against her elder son, trying to replace him with her younger, Alexander. The succeeding wars were fought in Palestine and the eastern Mediterranean, and they involved the people of Alexandria, who became involved in favoring one son and then another. Finally, sometime about 102 B.C., Cleopatra III's favored son, Alexander, seems to have tired of his mother's involvement and raised an army against her. She sued for peace, and her name soon vanishes from the records, so she must have agreed to retire from political life. She died sometime in the summer of 101 B.C., and some contemporary historians claim she was killed by Alexander. It might well have been the case. She had fostered discord among her family but had outlived many of them in the turmoil. Her sister, Cleopatra Thea, had long been dead, and Cleopatra III survived the longest of the children of Cleopatra II and Philomater. Cleopatra III was survived by both of her sons and by her daughter Cleopatra V Selene, who would be the next Hellenistic queen to fight for power in the Mediterranean world.

See also Cleopatra II; Cleopatra V Selene; Cleopatra Thea

Suggested Readings

Macurdy, Grace Harriet. *Hellenistic Queens.* Baltimore: Johns Hopkins University Press, 1932.

Pomeroy, Sarah B. *Women in Hellenistic Egypt from Alexander to Cleopatra.* New York: Schocken Books, 1984.

Cleopatra V Selene

Ptolemaic Egyptian Queen (ca. 131–69 B.C.)

Cleopatra V Selene was the youngest daughter of Cleopatra III and Ptolemy VII Euergetes. Early in her life she became a pawn in the struggles between her mother and her brothers for power, and her life perhaps best illustrates the way marriage was used among the families of the Hellenistic monarchies. Some queens had been able to exert some independent authority on their own; others like Selene used their own noble birth and great wealth as an instrument to influence the politics of power that brought almost incessant warfare to the Hellenistic dynasties.

Selene's first husband was her brother Ptolemy VIII Soter II, when her mother made her replace her sister Cleopatra IV as his wife so Cleopatra III might more easily control her son. When that marriage proved politically inexpedient, Cleopatra III found another husband for Selene. In 102 B.C., Selene was sent to Syria with an army and a great deal of money as a dowry to marry Antiochus Grypus, widower of Selene's sister Tryphaena. When Grypus's power failed, Selene married his enemy Antiochus Cyzicenus, who had killed Tryphaena.

The wealthy queen was still not through marrying. In her forties, she married once again to Antiochus Eusebes, son of Cyzicenus and nephew of Grypus. The contemporary commentator Appian claimed—surely sarcastically—that the Syrians gave Eusebes the title "the pious" because he had honored his father's and uncle's wishes so much that he was willing to marry his stepmother. She did have two sons by Eusebes, and Selene wanted them to claim as much of the Hellenistic world as they could. She turned to the great power emerging in the west—Rome.

According to Cicero, she sent these two sons to claim the throne of Egypt, which was occupied by Ptolemy XII Auletes, a bastard son of Ptolemy VIII Soter II, Selene's first husband. Cicero stated with some surprise that they did not come to claim the Syrian throne, for they undisputedly held that through their father. Instead, they claimed that their ties through their mother gave them the throne of Egypt as well. Rome was not impressed and refused to intervene.

For all of Selene's marriages, the Syrian branch of the family was soon to lose power. Cleopatra Selene herself was murdered in 69 B.C. by political enemies in Seleuceia on the Euphrates River. Her son Antiochus XIII (by her husband Grypus) was the last of the Seleucid kings; he was killed by an Arab chief. Rome annexed the province of Syria in 64 B.C., ending the Hellenistic kingdom of the Seleucids that had produced a dynasty of strong queens as well as ruthless kings.

See also Cleopatra III; Cleopatra Thea
Suggested Readings
Macurdy, Grace Harriet. *Hellenistic Queens.* Baltimore: Johns Hopkins University Press, 1932.
Pomeroy, Sarah B. *Women in Hellenistic Egypt from Alexander to Cleopatra.* New York: Schocken Books, 1984.
Cicero. *The Verric Orations.* Cambridge: Harvard University Press, 1928–1935.

Cleopatra VII

Ptolemaic Egyptian Queen (69–30 B.C.)

The last of the Ptolemaic rulers of Egypt is by far the most famous of the Hellenistic queens—celebrated in theater and literature into modern times. This Cleopatra—like many of her ancestors—boldly played the power politics of the day and used all her talents to try to preserve the Ptolemaic line of rulers in Egypt. Ultimately she failed, but she did so with such courage that her story is still told today as an example of a bold woman of the ancient world.

Cleopatra VII was the daughter of Ptolemy XII Auletes, the illegitimate son of Ptolemy VIII Soter II whom Cleopatra Selene had tried to have deposed in favor of her sons. Cleopatra Selene had appealed to Rome—the new strong power in the west—and although the Romans decided that Ptolemy XII Auletes should retain the right to rule, the family of the Ptolemies clearly saw that no ruler in Egypt would be secure without Rome's blessing. Cleopatra would remember this lesson. When Ptolemy XII Auletes died in 51 B.C., he willed Egypt to his seventeen-year-old daughter and his ten-year-old son, who ruled jointly as Cleopatra VII and Ptolemy XIII Philopater.

The young Ptolemy soon fell under the influence of advisers who persuaded the boy that he should rule without his energetic and intelligent sister. As a result, Cleopatra VII was driven from Alexandria. At this point, the history of Egypt becomes intimately intertwined with the history of Rome, for Julius Caesar, who was engaged in a civil war against his rival Pompey, entered Egypt pursuing his opponent. When Caesar arrived, Cleopatra was on the eastern border of Egypt using her great wealth to raise an army against her brother. Caesar—as Rome's official representative—believed he had the right to mediate between the two siblings, but young Ptolemy refused. In the resulting war, Caesar won. Ptolemy and his advisers were all killed, and Cleopatra was restored to the throne, this time with Ptolemy XIV, her younger brother, as consort. By 48 B.C., Cleopatra was in control of Egypt.

Cleopatra was a shrewd enough politician to realize that linking Egypt's fortunes with those of Rome would be the best way to secure her kingdom, and in the traditional way of Hellenistic queens, she used dynastic ties to try to protect her rights. While Cleopatra was not traditionally beautiful (she is shown in Figure 7), all the sources indicate she was intelligent, charming, and highly educated; she spoke at least five languages. Julius Caesar, then in his fifties, fell in love with the twenty-one-year-old queen—much to the horror of many Romans. Cleopatra bore him a child named Caesarion, and it seemed as if a new dynasty would rule in Egypt, but first Caesar would have to marry the queen and declare the child legitimate.

When Julius Caesar returned to Rome in 46 B.C., he celebrated a triumph in which he demonstrated the subjugation of Egypt by having Cleopatra's younger sister—Arsinoë—march in chains. Yet, Cleopatra was still the acknowledged queen of Egypt, and Caesar placed a statue of her made of gold in the temple of Venus. Cleopatra, her son, Caesarion, and her consort Ptolemy XIV joined Caesar in 46 B.C., and they stayed in Caesar's villa outside Rome. Caesar may have planned to gain special permission from the Roman people to marry Cleopatra, but his plans were cut short by his assassination in 44 B.C. Cleopatra would need all her wits and charm to hold her throne without her champion.

As was customary in the Hellenistic dynasties, Cleopatra first placed her hopes in her son, Caesarion, expecting that he could rule and that as a son of Caesar he would receive Rome's support. Her younger brother stood in the way of a clear succession, and he was poisoned about the time of Caesar's death. Historians differ about Cleopatra's role in her brother's death. Cleopatra

Figure 7. Cleopatra VII (Reuters NewMedia Inc./Corbis)

quickly returned to Egypt with Caesarion to await the power struggle that was sure to come.

Power in Rome was soon split among three men—Mark Antony, Lepidus, and Caesar's heir and nephew Octavian—who were called the Second Triumvirate. In his eastern campaigns, Mark Antony saw that the wealth of Egypt and the strength of its queen would be extremely useful to him. Or perhaps, like Caesar before him, he simply fell in love with the extraordinary woman. In 41 B.C., Antony stayed in Egypt, being entertained by Cleopatra and ignoring the reality of his life in Rome—where his first wife, Fulvia, was conducting a war. A year later, Antony could no longer ignore Roman politics, so he returned to Italy. After he left, Cleopatra had twin children that he had fathered—Alexander Helios and Cleopatra Selene Apene. Cleopatra bore Antony a total of three children—the third was a son, Ptolemy Philadelphus.

While he was in Italy, Antony's first wife, Fulvia, died. Some sources suggest that his anger at her drove her to suicide. Her death paved the way for a reconciliation between Octavian and Antony, which was sealed by Antony's marriage to Octavian's half-sister, Octavia. Octavia was beautiful and wise, and she won the heart of her new husband for a time—he did not return to Cleopatra for some years. Octavia bore him a daughter their first year together. The ancient biographer Plutarch says that Cleopatra was afraid of losing Antony and that she "conquered him by her weakness and her tears" (Plutarch 1134). Perhaps more likely she offered him the vision of a kingship in the Hellenistic model that was still impossible in Rome.

Antony came to Alexandria in about 37 B.C. and the couple celebrated a great triumph there (much to the horror of Romans, who felt this was a serious breach of custom). Shortly after this triumph another magnificent ceremony was celebrated, which announced to the world that Antony and Cleopatra were emperor and empress of the east and that their children were their heirs. They sat on golden thrones, with their children arrayed before them, and Antony proclaimed Cleopatra as queen of Egypt with Caesarion as coregent. He also distributed Roman provinces in the east to his three children by Cleopatra.

For the next few years, Romans listened with horror to reports of drunken revels coming from Egypt. Romans believed that Antony had come completely under the control of Cleopatra—her charms, her wealth, and her great navy. Romans also questioned whether Caesarion was indeed Caesar's son, for Octavian—Caesar's heir—would have much preferred if the child did not exist. All this came to a head in 32 B.C. when Antony formally divorced Octavia. War broke out between Octavian and Antony. In September of 31 B.C., the fleets met in the great battle of Actium. Cleopatra fled the battle and Antony followed her, leaving Octavian with a decisive victory.

In Alexandria, Antony was surrounded by Octavian's forces and believed that Cleopatra—who was hiding in her tomb—was dead. Recognizing that he had no political future without her, he took a sword and stabbed himself. The blow was not immediately mortal, and she brought him into her hiding place, where he died in her arms.

Even in this desperate situation, Cleopatra did not give up her desire to have her children rule. She tried to charm Octavian, who would not be moved. Octavian planned to bring her to Rome in shame to march in his triumph, but according to the contemporary sources (who have been doubted on this point), Cleopatra arranged for poisonous snakes (asps) to be delivered to her in a basket of fresh figs. She died by the asp bites, and Octavian was robbed of his captive. Her son Caesarion would not live to rule—Octavian had him killed to make sure there would be no other heir of Caesar to challenge his own position.

Cleopatra VII was the last Ptolemaic queen of Egypt. After her death, Egypt was made into a Roman province, and the great Hellenistic kingdom that had lasted for almost 300 years passed into the hands of a greater kingdom. Of Cleopatra's children, only one survived to rule—her daughter, Cleopatra Selene Apene.

See also Cleopatra V Selene; Cleopatra Selene Apene; Fulvia; Octavia

Suggested Readings
Lindsey, Jack. *Cleopatra*. New York: Coward-McCann, 1971.
Macurdy, Grace Harriet. *Hellenistic Queens*. Baltimore: Johns Hopkins University Press, 1932.
Plutarch. "Antony." In *The Lives of the Noble Grecians and Romans*. Trans. J. Dryden. New York: The Modern Library, n.d.
Pomeroy, Sarah B. *Women in Hellenistic Egypt from Alexander to Cleopatra*. New York: Schocken Books, 1984.
Volkmann, H. *Cleopatra: A Study in Politics and Propaganda*. New York: Sagamore Press, 1958.

Cleopatra Selene Apene
Queen of Numidia (ca. 40 B.C.–ca. A.D. 11)

When the last Ptolemaic queen of Egypt, Cleopatra VII, committed suicide, she left three children that she had borne Mark Antony: Alexander Helios, Cleopatra Selene, and Ptolemy Philadelphus. Remarkably for the violent times, the victor Octavian—soon to be called Caesar Augustus—spared the children's lives. When Octavian celebrated his triumph in 29 B.C., they marched in the procession, and a statue of their mother with an asp on her arm was also carried in the celebration. The children were then given over to the care of Octavia—Mark Antony's second wife and Octavian's sister. She raised them together with her two daughters by Antony and Antony's son by his first wife, Fulvia. Octavia continued her reputation for dignity and virtue by raising the children of her rival with impeccable care.

When Cleopatra Selene was of marriageable age, Octavian arranged for her marriage to Juba, a prince of the province of Numidia in North Africa. Caesar Augustus was fond of the young man, who had a passion for historical research and travel, and he gave him the kingdom in North Africa to rule. Cleopatra, with her high birth, ruled jointly with him. We have an epigram by Crinagoras of Mitylene, probably written to celebrate the wedding of Juba and Cleopatra, which expresses the hope of a new dynasty that seemed to be created by this wedding: "Great lands of the earth, whose borders touch, which the Nile with waters swelling separates from the black Aethiopians, you have got sovereigns in common by marriage and you make one race of Egypt and Libya. From generation to generation may the scepter pass from father to son, firmly established forever over both lands" (Macurdy 225).

The sovereigns clearly reigned together, for Cleopatra issued coins in her own name, and her head and legend were associated with those of Juba on his coins. She must have considered her lineage superior to his, and the coins showed this.

She had a son, whom she named Ptolemy, suggesting that she was expecting to continue the Ptolemaic dynasty of which she was so rightfully proud. We hear little more of this royal couple. Plutarch claims that Juba, with his love of history, traveled to Asia and took as a second wife Glaphyra, the daughter of king Archelaus of Cappadocia. We know from the testimony of the coins that Cleopatra lived until after the year A.D. 11, and it is possible that she served as regent for her husband during his travels in the east.

Her son, Ptolemy, succeeded his father and reigned until A.D. 40, when he was killed by Caligula, the Roman emperor, and the North African kingdom was divided into Roman provinces. Young Ptolemy seems to have had no children, so the ancient line of the Ptolemies that stretched back to the successors of Alexander the Great had died out. It was a dynasty that produced some of the most impressive women of the ancient world.

See also Cleopatra VII; Glaphyra; Mariamne
Suggested Readings
Macurdy, Grace Harriet. *Hellenistic Queens.*
 Baltimore: Johns Hopkins University Press, 1932.
Pomeroy, Sarah B. *Women in Hellenistic Egypt from Alexander to Cleopatra.* New York: Schocken Books, 1984.
Volkmann, H. *Cleopatra: A Study in Politics and Propaganda.* New York: Sagamore Press, 1958.

Cleopatra Thea
Seleucid Queen (d. ca. 121 B.C.)
The history of the queens in the Seleucid dynasty is a catalog of dynastic marriages, wars, and violence that reflects the ferocity of the Hellenistic kingdoms. Even in an age noted for its upheavals, one queen—Cleopatra Thea—was caught up in a series of particularly violent struggles and emerged late in her life to rule on her own.

Cleopatra Thea was the wife of three Seleucid kings—a testimony to the power of her family ties that made her a prize to be won. She was the daughter of Cleopatra II of Egypt and her brother Ptolemy VI Philomater—perhaps their eldest, but her date of birth is not known. In 150 B.C., her father gave her in marriage to Alexander Balas, an ambitious man who claimed to be the son of Antiochus IV and thus a pretender to the throne of the Seleucid kingdom in Syria and the east. Alexander killed the reigning king—Demetrius I—and was received in Antioch with much rejoicing. Alexander received the blessing of the Roman senate to hold power, and he returned to Antioch to reign. In the tradition of the Hellenistic kings, Alexander killed many of the family of the old king in hopes of preserving his reign. Cleopatra Thea bore Alexander a son, called Antiochus (one of the popular family names of the Seleucids).

Alexander proved to be a poor king. According to Diodorus—the Greek historian—Alexander "proved useless in the rank of king because of the weakness of his soul" (Macurdy 95). The king abandoned himself to drunken debauchery and lost the support of many of the people. Then, a serious threat appeared: a young son of the late king Demetrius arrived with mercenaries from Crete and the support of Cleopatra Thea's father, Philomater. Philomater renounced his son-in-law, Alexander, and gave his daughter in marriage to the young Demetrius (the son of the late king of the same name) in 146 B.C. This was to be her second husband-king. Alexander Balas was assassinated by one of his officers, and his head was brought to his ex-father-in-law.

However, the death of Alexander did not bring peace to the Seleucid kingdom. There was a time of anarchy, when soldiers could pillage at will. Demetrius was too young to govern effectively, and Cleopatra had not yet found the ability to rule on her own. It was a time of civil war, and a new pretender to the throne appeared—a mercenary leader named Diodotus, who took

Figure 8. Cleopatra Thea, 125 B.C. (British Museum)

the name King Tryphon. Diodotus came to power by finding the young son of Cleopatra Thea and Alexander Balas, who had been hidden, and establishing him as the nominal king Antiochus VI. Antiochus ruled in Antioch (see Map 6) from 145 to 142 B.C., when he died. Some said Diodotus had killed him and then taken the title King Tryphon.

Now, Cleopatra Thea sought out her third king—someone who could displace King Tryphon, who had perhaps killed her first son. She sent a message to the younger brother of Demetrius—Antiochus VII—and invited him to marry her and claim the kingdom. This new Antiochus was tremendously popular—people called him the "pious" and "savior"—and he drove King Tryphon from the city and chased him to Phoenicia, where he committed suicide.

Cleopatra Thea had lost her first son, but in her next two marriages she had borne other children. By her second husband, Demetrius, she had two sons—Seleucus V and Antiochus Grypus—and by her third husband she had another son—Antiochus Cyzicenus. Antiochus VII had proved a strong and energetic king, and he could well have brought the order that the Seleucid kingdom desperately needed after all the years of civil war. But the perils of battle interfered—Antiochus died fighting in the east. In the power vacuum that suddenly emerged, Cleopatra's sec-

ond husband, Demetrius, returned to resume his throne. Demetrius was unpopular with the people and with Cleopatra. This time, the queen was prepared to take action.

She sought the support of her relatives in Egypt, the ruling Ptolemies, who defeated Demetrius in battle. When Demetrius was captured, Cleopatra Thea reputedly ordered him killed. Immediately, Cleopatra's son by Demetrius, Seleucus V, assumed the crown without Cleopatra's permission, and the Roman historians say she killed her son by her own hand.

Cleopatra Thea now assumed the crown, ruling as queen beginning in 125 B.C. Her son Antiochus VIII Grypus seems to have shared the rule, but Cleopatra Thea was able to be the senior ruler for a time. She was the first Hellenistic queen to strike coins in her name only, and the silver tetradrachm shown in Figure 8 shows the face of the queen (with her characteristic hairstyle and the large nose of her family) on the front and on the obverse the horn of plenty. The inscription reads "of queen Cleopatra, goddess of Plenty."

Two years later, her son Antiochus Grypus became more powerful and in a position to threaten his mother's rule. In 123 B.C., he married a daughter of the Egyptian Ptolemies, a political match that would allow him to displace Cleopatra Thea. The contemporary account by Justin tells how the aging queen tried to hold on to power by killing her son. Antiochus Grypus came in overheated from hunting, and Cleopatra greeted him with a cool drink of poisoned wine. Feigning courtesy, the young man insisted that his mother drink first. At first she refused, and he insisted. Finally, he produced evidence of her malicious intent toward him, and she drank the poisoned wine and died. Ironically, in one of the inscriptions purchased by Grypus, he has among his titles that of Philomater—"mother-loving."

Historians have remembered Cleopatra Thea as one of the cruelest of the Seleucid queens—killing her own sons for power. Of course, it is always possible that the contemporary accounts were shaped by Antiochus Grypus, who gave his mother a poisoned cup and who had good reason to spoil her reputation and enhance his own. We shall never know; all we have produced by her are the images of this strong queen—on her coin and in a bust—who was able to rule in her own right in these turbulent times.

See also Cleopatra II; Laodice I; Stratonice I
Suggested Readings
Appian. *Appian's Roman History.* Trans. H. White. Cambridge: Harvard University Press, 1964.
Macurdy, Grace Harriet. *Hellenistic Queens.* Baltimore: Johns Hopkins University Press, 1932.

Clodia

Influential Roman Matron
(ca. 97–after 45 B.C.)
During the Roman period, probably the single most important thing to Romans was family ties. The old and great families had alliances, property, wealth, and influence. Their daughters married well, and their sons could look forward to powerful political careers. Sons and daughters of the most influential families could also look forward to a degree of independence not available to their less well placed contemporaries, and this independence sometimes took the form of ignoring social conventions. One of the most illustrious families of the republic was the Claudii, whose members from the third century B.C. served as consuls and senators in Rome. In the first century B.C., a daughter of this illustrious family was so wealthy, beautiful, and talented that she became one of the most notorious figures of the time.

Clodia was born in about 97 B.C., and in the tradition of Roman patrician families, her father arranged a good marriage for her when she was fifteen years old. She married Q. Metellus Celer, a twenty-year-old military man who could look forward to a good career rising to politics through the military ranks. It seems that as part of her dowry, Clodia brought a great house on the Palatine Hill in Rome—the most expensive area of the city—and the couple settled there. She bore him one child, a girl named Metella.

During her years of marriage, like so many of the wealthy Romans, Clodia surrounded herself with writers and entertainers. She seems to have written mimes herself and perhaps even learned to dance and perform. She was accused by her most vocal detractor (the orator Cicero) of dancing lasciviously at her own dinner parties. She may well have done so, for the highborn Claudii did not feel themselves bound by the same rigorous standards that constrained other republican Romans. In about 62 B.C., Clodia became acquainted with a poet, who would ensure her fame.

Catullus (ca. 84–54 B.C.) was a young poet who was born in the province of Gaul. He went to Rome in about 62 B.C. when he was in his early twenties, and the lyrics he wrote during his short life would transform Roman poetry. This "new poetry" was personal, direct, often insulting, and blunt and continues to be admired today. Perhaps it is not surprising that this talented young man came to the attention of Clodia, the wealthy patron of the arts, and Catullus fell insanely in love with her. He wrote poetry chronicling their love affair, but since she was married, he gave her the pseudonym of Lesbia (after the Greek women of Lesbos who were reputed to be beautiful, and perhaps indicating his debt to the poet Sappho of Lesbos).

In Catullus's poetry, we learn that a friend brought him to Clodia's house, where he fell in love—"My radiant goddess appeared to me"—and they quickly began an affair. Perhaps his most famous poem (#5) celebrates their passion:

Lesbia, let us live and love,
And think what crabbed old men resent

With all their talk, not worth a cent.
The sun which sets returns above
But once our short-lived light shall die
In endless darkness we must lie.
So kiss me, give me a thousand kisses,
Another thousand, hundreds more.
(Catullus 7–9)

The love affair did not last, for Clodia moved on to other lovers. Catullus wrote of his pain: "Wretched Catullus, leave off playing the fool:/Give up as lost what is forever past" (#8) (Catullus 11), but he continued to write painful poems that immortalized his love for Clodia, whose free ways would bring her more notoriety.

In 59 B.C., her husband died, but the widow continued her social life in her house on the Palatine Hill. In the same year as her husband's death, another influential young man moved to the Palatine. The twenty-nine-year-old Caelius moved into an apartment owned by Clodia's brother, Clodius, and Caelius soon became Clodia's latest lover. Caelius was handsome, with a taste for an extravagant lifestyle, and in the best Roman manner, he combined his passions with politics.

The relationship between Caelius and Clodia was made more complicated by the struggle among the strong men of the First Triumvirate. As Julius Caesar, Crassus, and Pompey jockeyed for power, no one of the Roman upper classes was left out. Clodia and her brother were supporting Crassus, but Caelius secretly allied himself with Pompey. Perhaps this caused the lovers to separate, or perhaps the affair between these two strong-willed people simply could not last. They fought, and Clodia even claimed that Caelius tried to have a slave poison her. This private scandal would soon become very public.

In 54 B.C., Caelius was brought to trial on charges of political violence. He was accused of beating up envoys and other disruptive acts. The charges were pressed by the influential Claudii—including Clodia. Caelius (who was probably guilty) found a powerful advocate to press his case—the brilliant orator, Cicero. Cicero (supporter of Julius Caesar) had no love for the Claudii, and his defense of Caelius rested upon an attack on Clodia and her lifestyle. Through Cicero's accusations, Clodia's infamy was sealed.

While the Claudii began by accusing Caelius of a decadent life, Cicero turned the accusations back on Clodia. He accused Clodia of being "a widow living loosely, a wanton living promiscuously, a rich woman living extravagantly and a randy woman living like a harlot" (Fantham et al. 284). Through his rhetorical skill, Cicero succeeded in proving that Clodia was morally disreputable and that Caelius was not. Cicero persuaded the jury that Clodia was a scorned woman who wanted to get revenge on her old lover. Caelius was found innocent, and Clodia's reputation was damaged (for all time, due to the endurance of Cicero's and Catullus's writings).

What happened to Clodia after this public humiliation? Probably not much—her wealth and connections continued to protect her and allowed her to live as she pleased. She dropped out of public life for the next eleven years, but she probably continued to enjoy her properties and her friends. She reappears briefly in the texts in 45 B.C., when she was fifty-two years old. Ironically, perhaps, her old adversary Cicero wanted to buy her riverside gardens, for he was looking for an agreeable property in which to retire. She refused his offer, and Cicero probably quite accurately explained her motivation for refusing: "She likes the place and she's not short of money" (Wiseman 98). This short summary might serve to indicate that the public loss did not appreciably affect this rich, powerful, and eccentric woman of the ancient world who chose to conduct her life on her own terms.

See also Calpurnia; Sappho of Lesbos
Suggested Readings
Catullus. *Catullus: The Complete Poems*. Trans. R. Myers. New York: E. P. Dutton, 1970.
Fantham, E., et al. *Women in the Classical World*. New York: Oxford University Press, 1994.
Wiseman, T. P. *Catullus and His World: A Reappraisal*. London: Cambridge University Press, 1985.

Cloelia

Legendary Roman Heroine (ca. 508 B.C.)
In 509 B.C., the Romans had thrown off the rule of the Etruscan monarchy and established their republic. A year later, the young republic was

threatened by an invasion of the Etruscans, who under their leader, Porsena, sought to reimpose their sovereignty. Romans remembered the deeds of three heroic Romans who saved their city in this dark hour: Horatius Cocles, Mucius Scaevola, and a brave young woman, Cloelia.

The Etruscan general first thought to sweep across the Tiber River and invade the small city. All that lay between him and his goal was a bridge across the river that offered access to the city. A brave man, Horatius Cocles, said he would stand alone on the far side of the bridge to keep the invaders from crossing while other Romans destroyed the bridge behind him, preventing the Etruscans from crossing. At first Horatius was joined by two companions, and they bravely held off the armies. As the bridge was collapsing behind them, Horatius's companions crossed the remainder of the structure, while the hero was left holding the bridge alone. When he heard the final collapse of the bridge, he turned and dived in with full armor. He remarkably swam the rushing river and emerged safely on the other side. He was hailed as a hero and rewarded. The threat of the Etruscans, however, was only temporarily put aside.

Seeing that he could no longer storm the city, Porsena decided to besiege it. His ships controlled the river, and he blockaded the city, making sure no supplies were brought in. Famine began to affect the inhabitants hiding behind their walls. Slaves deserted what seemed to be a lost city, but a number of young Romans did not lose heart. The next hero who rose to the occasion was Q. Mucius.

The young man got permission from the senate to execute a brave plan. He left Rome, hiding his sword under his cloak, and secretly entered the enemy camp. He arrived as the Etruscan king and his paymaster were distributing the money for the troops. This was the opportunity for him to fulfill his mission—to kill King Porsena. The only problem was that the king and the paymaster were dressed alike. Throwing his fate in the hands of the gods, Mucius drew his sword and struck—and killed the wrong man. The paymaster died, and the king arrested the Roman.

Porsena threatened to torture Mucius until he told of the nature of the conspiracy that sent the assassin to the camp. Mucius defied the king and scoffed at the threatened torture by fire. Instead, he held his own right hand in an open flame and watched as the flames burnt away his flesh. As the historian Livy wrote, "The king was beside himself with wonder" (Livy 259), and he told Mucius he would be permitted to go free. Porsena said he had never seen such bravery and rewarded it. Mucius was henceforth known as Scaevola, or "left-handed," for he had burned away his right hand.

Mucius then said he would give Porsena the information that the king was not able to extract by torture. Mucius said there were 300 young Romans who had vowed to come to the camp and murder Porsena. Although Mucius had failed, he warned the king that there were many more brave youths like himself who would dare anything to kill the Etruscan leader. Porsena was frightened by the threat, imagining he would have to constantly watch his back against the fanatic, patriotic Romans. He freed Mucius and sued for peace with the Romans.

Porsena's conditions for peace included the taking of many Roman hostages to guarantee that the Romans would remain peaceful as the Etruscan garrisons left the region. Included in the hostages was the young maiden Cloelia, and in the tales of the ancient Romans, her bravery matched that of Horatius and Mucius.

As the Etruscans camped near the banks of the Tiber on their return to their lands, Cloelia saw her chance and led a band of girls who leaped into the Tiber in the midst of the arrows their captors sent at the escapees. The girls successfully swam the river, and Cloelia led the girls safely back to their families. Porsena was as impressed with the girl's heroism as he had been with that of Mucius and agreed that if the Romans would give her back as a hostage, he would release her. Both parties kept their word.

The Etruscan king not only honored Cloelia by releasing her and praising her brave deed, but he allowed her to take with her half the hostages. She could choose the ones she wished. She selected the young boys to return with her, because as Livy wrote, the hostages themselves agreed she should save the ones "who were of an age which particularly exposed them to injury" (Livy 263). The girls presumably were safer as hostages than boys.

The Romans rewarded her valor with an honor that had never before been accorded a woman: they erected a statue of Cloelia riding a horse. This statue was erected on the summit of the Sacred Way. The later encyclopedist Pliny the Elder (d. A.D. 79) was horrified at the statue, for she was portrayed not only on a horse but also clad in a toga (which was reserved as a ceremonial costume for men). He believed that she did not deserve such an honor, when others— like Lucretia—did not receive them.

Did this strong-swimming brave maiden really exist? We have no way of knowing for sure. These early years of Roman history mixed legend and reality in a bewildering combination. It is certain, however, that ancient Romans *believed* she existed; they observed her statue and were proud of the strength and courage of this ancient woman who helped save the Republic in its early years.

See also Lucretia
Suggested Readings
Fantham, E., et al. *Women in the Classical World.* New York: Oxford University Press, 1994.
Gardner, Jane F. *Roman Myths.* Austin: University of Texas Press, 1995.
Livy. *History.* Bk. II. Trans. B. O. Foster. Cambridge: Harvard University Press, 1917.

Clothing

Throughout the ancient world, clothing was made from a relatively limited number of things. Animal skins and leather were the oldest materials; they then gave way to woven fabric made from wool of domesticated sheep and goats. In time, ancient peoples learned to pound the fibers of the flax plant into threads to make linen, which was woven into cloth. In Asia, silk was produced from the cocoons of silk worms, but silk remained scarce and expensive. With these materials, people in the ancient world created a range of clothing that kept them warm and satisfied desires for decoration and style. Some societies used clothing for modesty, but many found nudity (particularly among men) perfectly acceptable, and clothing

in that case was simply for decoration or for warmth.

During the Stone Age, people used animal skins as clothing, and archaeologists have found bone needles that allowed people to sew skins together to make practical costumes. The earliest coverings for both men and women were probably simple loincloths, which were supplemented by large skins used as blankets or cloaks in inclement weather. Later, in colder climates, skins were sewn together in simple tunics to provide more warmth.

By the Neolithic period, some societies had developed agriculture along with animal husbandry. Domesticated sheep and goats provided a ready source of skins for clothing, and the earliest clothing in Sumeria seems to have used the old techniques of sewing skins together. However, when they sewed the sheepskins together, they left the wool fleece on, so the wool seemed to hang down in loops. This gave the effect of layered flounces in a skirt worn by both men and women. Figure 9 shows a drawing of this kind of garment.

Sometime relatively early in Sumerian history, people learned to spin and weave the wool to make garments (without killing the sheep). While everyday people used woven cloth draped about them in varying ways, they believed goddesses (and priestesses) had to wear clothing that resembled the traditional flounced garments, so designers made dresses of woven wool that looked as if they were made of sewn-together sheepskin. Figure 10 shows one such outfit.

Clothing designers took two directions after the Sumerians: They tanned skins to make more finished leather clothing or wove the wool into finer and finer cloth. The former had the advantage of durability and the latter of being cooler and more washable. Garments made of leather tended to be more form-fitting, while woolen cloth was loosely draped.

The Minoans on the island of Crete seem to have favored leather garments—at least for the goddesses and priestesses portrayed in the artwork. The most famous outfit is shown in Figure 11—a picture of the snake-goddess. She wears a tight-fitting (and thus probably leather) bodice over a skirt made of panels, which again were probably skins. She also wears an apron

Figure 9. Early Sumerian clothing made of fleece
(Mary G. Houston. *Ancient Greek, Roman and
Byzantine Costume & Decoration.* London: Adam and
Charles Black, 1965, p. 3)

Figure 10. Later Sumerian clothing woven to look like
flounced fleece (Mary G. Houston. *Ancient Greek,
Roman and Byzantine Costume & Decoration.* London:
Adam and Charles Black, 1965, p. 3)

and a belt, which may have been of decorative
metal. Minoan women participated with men in
a dangerous athletic contest of leaping over
bulls, and they wore the same small leather loincloth that would leave their motions unencum-
bered. Persians and Germanic peoples also used
leather garments—including trousers and capes
for durable clothing and horseback riding.

The history of woven woolen and linen clothing is much more extensive. Such clothing is
cheaper than leather and is more versatile because wool can be woven thickly to make a
warm, heavy garment or thinly to make fabric
that is transparent and almost like gauze. Not
surprisingly, the Germanic tribes of northern Europe favored thick wool, woven into a tweedlike
cloth. Germanic women wore skirts and loose
blouses of this cloth. The skirts were wrapped
around them and often secured by a belt.

The predominant clothing style in the ancient Middle East and the Mediterranean world
was woven woolen or linen cloth. This fabric
lent itself to draping in various ways, and these
folds dictated the characteristic garments of the
various cultures.

In ancient Greece, women wore a *chiton*—a
dress. The earliest form of chiton is called the
Doric style. In its most simple form, the Doric
chiton was an oblong of woollen cloth measur-
ing about twice the width of the wearer from
elbow to elbow when the arms were out-
stretched and about eighteen inches more than

Figure 12. Greek Doric chiton (Mary G. Houston. *Ancient Greek, Roman and Byzantine Costume & Decoration.* London: Adam and Charles Black, 1965, p. 40)

Figure 11. Minoan clothing (James Laver. *Costume in Antiquity.* New York: Clarkson N. Potter, Inc., 1964, p. 13)

her height from shoulder to ground. As you can see by the drawing in Figure 12, the fabric was folded in half lengthwise, then folded again at the height of the shoulders, allowing the extra eighteen inches to fall down outside in a flap. Then the whole thing was fastened at the shoulders with two huge pins, and sometimes the woman could decide to belt the dress at the waist. As Figure 13 shows, this simple design draped beautifully with finely spun wool. The garment was also practical because a woman could pull the extra fabric over her head when she was outside if the weather were inclement.

At the beginning of the sixth century B.C., Athenian women began to wear a different kind of dress—the Ionic chiton. The Greek historian Herodotus offers a political explanation for the change in fashion. He said that after a disastrous military expedition, all the Athenian soldiers were put to death by the victorious army except

Figure 13. Greek Doric chiton as worn (Mary G. Houston. *Ancient Greek, Roman and Byzantine Costume & Decoration.* London: Adam and Charles Black, 1965, p. 41)

Figure 14. Greek Ionic chiton (Mary G. Houston. *Ancient Greek, Roman and Byzantine Costume & Decoration.* London: Adam and Charles Black, 1965, pp. 48–49)

Figure 15. Greek Ionic chiton as worn (Mary G. Houston. *Ancient Greek, Roman and Byzantine Costume & Decoration.* London: Adam and Charles Black, 1965, p. 49)

one man, who escaped to tell the disconsolate women of Athens the fate of their men. The women were so angry that they took off the great pins that held their chitons and stabbed the survivor to death. The Athenians were so angry at the women that Herodotus said that from then on they were required to wear the Ionic dress that does not require pins. It is hard to know how accurate Herodotus's story was, but the fashion in Athens did change by the sixth century.

The Ionic chiton was usually made of thin linen (and sometimes thinly spun wool) that was so fine it was often transparent. It had no overfold as did the Doric chiton. Figure 14 shows a drawing of an Ionic chiton that is held together at the upper arms by hoops. (Sometimes the tops were stitched together with a seam, thus eliminating the hoops.) Notice how much more fabric there is here than in the Doric chiton, so the garment looked pleated as the women gathered it together and tied or belted it in various ways. One example is shown in Figure 15. Since the Ionic dress was made of such thin material, Greek women added a long rectangle of wool as an outer garment when they went outdoors. This cloak (called a *himation*) could also be draped in a number of ways, and Figure 16 shows one example. This basic Greek

Figure 16. Greek Ionic chiton covered with himation for outdoor wear (Mary G. Houston. *Ancient Greek, Roman and Byzantine Costume & Decoration.* London: Adam and Charles Black, 1965, p. 64)

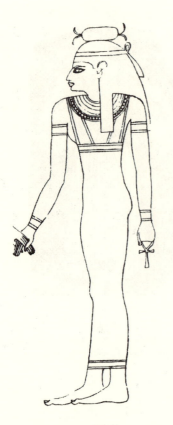

Figure 17. Egyptian sheath dress (James Laver. *Costume in Antiquity.* New York: Clarkson N. Potter, Inc., 1964, p. 30)

Figure 18. Egyptian transparent clothing (James Laver. *Costume in Antiquity.* New York: Clarkson N. Potter, Inc., 1964, p. 31)

outfit remained constant throughout the classical period, and women could vary it at will by draping, belting, or embroidering decoration on the fabric.

Ancient Egyptians had fewer considerations of modesty than even the Greeks, and men and women often worked naked. Upper-class women, however, took some pride in ornamentation, including clothing in finely woven fabrics. The wealthy favored garments of white linen, and through most of Egypt's history, women usually wore a tight-fitting sheath as shown in Figure 17. This garment with its tight seams left little room for mobility, so it was clearly ceremonial more than practical. During the reign of Queen Nefertiti, women's court costume underwent a striking change. Women in art were depicted either naked or wearing transparent cloth dresses or robes that exposed their breasts and bellies. Figure 18 shows one of these transparent garments. As elsewhere in the Mediterranean world, during cool weather, women wore shawls of wool over their dresses. The drawings of the Egyptian women indicate how important jewelry—great necklaces and earrings—was to the ensemble. The simple cloth was set off with large, elaborate pieces.

Early in their history, Roman women's costumes were almost identical with men's. Both wore long lengths of woolen cloth draped modestly about their bodies—togas. Throughout Rome's history, togas remained the ceremonial costume for men. Young girls continued to wear children's togas as did boys until puberty. Once a woman married, she changed her costume, which by the second century B.C. became almost identical with the Greek. The Ionic chiton and himation were worn, but renamed by the Romans. The dress was the *stola* and the himation the *palla.* Underneath the stola, Roman women added a tunic that could be either sleeveless or with short sleeves. This tunic offered a degree of

Figure 19. Roman matron with stola and palla (Mary G. Houston. *Ancient Greek, Roman and Byzantine Costume & Decoration.* London: Adam and Charles Black, 1965, p. 110)

modesty that the pure Greek chiton lacked. Figure 19 shows a Roman woman with her stola, draped modestly and graciously in her palla. The palla also served to veil a woman's head while she was in public.

When a Roman woman became a widow, she replaced the palla with another covering for her head. This was a square covering made of dark wool, called the *ricinium.* This ancient garment was even referred to as early as the sixth century B.C. in the Twelve Tables (the earliest recorded law code of the Romans).

From the third century A.D. until the sixth century, we can see the gradual development from Roman to Byzantine costumes. Men stopped wearing the traditional toga and began to wear long robes and long-sleeved tunics. Women, too, began to abandon the traditional stola in favor of a wide robe that was worn over a long-sleeved inner tunic. Figure 20 shows the

Figure 20. Byzantine dress (Mary G. Houston. *Ancient Greek, Roman and Byzantine Costume & Decoration.* London: Adam and Charles Black, 1965, p. 135)

simple pattern of this new style. The seams are sewn into a simple T-shaped garment that hangs loosely and modestly as was suitable to a world that was increasingly Christian and demanded modest attire.

Throughout the ancient world, all these garments could have complex patterns either dyed or embroidered on the borders of the cloth or all over the fabric. In spite of the relatively few basic shapes of the dresses, women could find variety through decoration, jewelry, and draping and belting the dresses. Like those today, ancient women enjoyed expressing their individual tastes and creativity through their wardrobe.

See also Egyptian Women; Minoan Women; Nefertiti

Suggested Readings

Houston, Mary G. *Ancient Greek, Roman and Byzantine Costume & Decoration.* London: Adam and Charles Black, 1965.

Laver, James. *Costume in Antiquity.* New York: Clarkson N. Potter, 1964.

Rubens, Alfred. *A History of Jewish Costume.* New York: Funk and Wagnalls, 1967.

Schutz, Herbert. *The Prehistory of Germanic Europe.* New Haven: Yale University Press, 1983.

Sebesta, Judith Lynn, and L. Bonfante. *The World of Roman Costume.* Madison: University of Wisconsin Press, 1994.

Clytemnestra

Mythological Greek Queen

The Trojan War, which according to myth was fought over the abduction of Greek Helen by Paris, Prince of Troy, spawned other myths that told of tragedies and strengths of Greek women. Whether these legends preserved the memory of real women or whether they were fabrications that articulated deep truths about society, the stories circulated throughout the Mediterranean world for millennia. One of the most infamous of these women was Clytemnestra, alternately portrayed as a weak woman led astray by a lover or a strong, vengeful woman.

The legends say that Clytemnestra was the sister of Helen and wife of Agamemnon, Greek king of Mycenae. Clytemnestra had small cause to love Agamemnon, for he had killed her first husband and her newborn child at her breast, then married her by force. Nevertheless, they had one son, Orestes, and three daughters: Electra, Iphigenia, and Chrysothemis. (Some myths say that Iphigenia was Clytemnestra's niece.) When the Trojan War began, Agamemnon prepared to leave with the army to avenge the insult and bring back Helen.

When the army was assembled at Aulis to leave, the winds were blowing in the wrong direction and the army could not depart. A prophet said that they would be unable to sail unless Agamemnon sacrificed the most beautiful of his daughters to Artemis. The legends were not clear about why Artemis was angry with Agamemnon: Some said he had bragged that he could hunt better than Artemis, and others claimed he had killed her sacred goat. In any case, Agamemnon said he could not sacrifice Iphigenia, for Clytemnestra would never allow it. The Greeks were adamant and devised a ruse by which Clytemnestra would allow Iphigenia to come to the shore: They said that Achilles would marry the girl, and Clytemnestra brought her.

When Achilles found out that his name had been used in the ruse, he tried to protect the girl. However, she volunteered to die for the glory of Greece and offered her neck to the sacrificial axe without a word of complaint. Some myths say that Artemis or Achilles saved her at the last minute and spirited her away. Whether she was sacrificed or not, the northeasterly gale stopped and the ships sailed to Troy. Agamemnon's willingness to sacrifice her daughter gave Clytemnestra one more grievance against her husband.

The war dragged on for ten years, and it must have seemed that the Greeks were never going to return home. In Agamemnon's absence, Clytemnestra took his cousin Aegisthus for her lover. Finally, word came that the war was over and Agamemnon was returning, and Clytemnestra was further infuriated to hear that he was bringing back his mistress Cassandra, the Trojan prophet who had borne the king twin sons. Clytemnestra and Aegisthus conspired to kill Agamemnon upon his return. Fearing that the king might arrive unexpectedly, Clytemnestra sent a message to Agamemnon telling him to light a beacon fire when he was ready to leave, and she then arranged for a chain of fires to relay the message of his return. At last, one dark night, her watchman saw the beacon blaze and ran to wake Clytemnestra. She celebrated the news with sacrifices of thanksgiving and prepared the trap.

Clytemnestra greeted her travel-worn husband with every appearance of delight. She unrolled a purple carpet for him and led him to the bathhouse, where slave-girls bathed him. Cassandra remained outside the palace, caught in a prophetic trance, crying that she smelt blood. Because it was her curse that no one should listen to her prophecies, the plot continued to unfold. As Agamemnon stepped out of the bath, Clytemnestra came forward as if to wrap a towel around him. Instead, she threw over his head a net garment that entangled and immobilized him. Aegisthus then rushed forward and struck Agamemnon with a sword. He fell back into the bath, where Clytemnestra avenged herself by beheading him with an axe. She then ran out to kill Cassandra with the same weapon. In some versions of the legend, Aegisthus killed Cassandra's twin boys.

After this battle, which took place on the thirteenth day of the month of January and in which many of Agamemnon's followers who had survived the Trojan War were killed, Clytemnestra decreed that the thirteenth day would be a monthly festival. However, the family tragedy was not over, for Agamemnon's ten-year-old son Orestes had escaped the carnage. He grew up in a household far away. Aegisthus reigned for seven years, but he always feared that Orestes would come to take vengeance for Agamemnon's murder.

Orestes was spurred on to vengeance by his sister Electra, who hated her mother for her role in the murder of her beloved father. Orestes also consulted the Delphic Oracle, who said that if Orestes neglected to avenge his father he would become an outcast from society and would be afflicted with leprosy. Thus supported by divine advice, Orestes secretly returned to Mycenae, determined to destroy both Aegisthus and his own mother.

Helped by his sister Electra, Orestes appeared at the gates of the palace. His mother did not recognize him, and he claimed to be a stranger bringing news of Orestes's death. Aegisthus was relieved, believing that the threat of vengeance was now over, and he entered the palace unarmed. Orestes easily drew his sword and killed Aegisthus. Clytemnestra then recognized her son and tried to soften his heart by baring her breast and appealing to his filial duty. Orestes, however, beheaded her with a single stroke of his sword, and she fell beside the body of her lover.

In the oldest versions of the legend, Aegisthus alone planned the murder of Agamemnon; Clytemnestra was innocent. However, the later tragic poets gave her the greater role, implying that her perfidy brought eternal disgrace upon all women. Orestes, too, came under some criticism for killing his mother, and some legends said that he just turned her over to judges, who executed her. In spite of the variations, the story of Clytemnestra—with its lessons of anger, murder, and vengeance—captured the imagination of generations of Greeks and others who followed classical mythology.

See also Cassandra; Delphic Oracle; Electra; Helen of Troy in Greek Mythology

Suggested Readings

Grimal, Pierre. *The Dictionary of Classical Mythology.* Oxford: Blackwell, 1996.

Constantina
Daughter of an Emperor (d. A.D. 354)

One of the most influential Roman emperors was Constantine the Great (ca. A.D. 280–337), who moved the capital of the empire from Rome east to the new city of Constantinople. Constantine was also significant for his support of Christians, who had experienced periodic persecutions before Constantine's time. Under this emperor Christians received special privileges, tax advantages, and a freedom to follow their consciences. The establishment of an imperial Christian church dates from his reign, and perhaps not surprisingly, Christian legends grew up about members of his family—particularly his daughter, Constantina.

Fathers and daughters during the Roman Empire enjoyed a particularly strong bond. The sources speak to strong affection between fathers and dutiful daughters and to a deep expectation that daughters would serve an important social and political function for their fathers: through their marriages family alliances would be solidified and family fortunes would be continued. These social expectations were even stronger for daughters of emperors, and Constantine's daughter seems to have served as a dutiful child.

The emperor arranged for Constantina to marry a powerful general—Hannibalianus—no doubt in part to keep the general from contesting Constantine's power. After the marriage, Hannibalianus was given the title King of Kings and sent to rule in an eastern province near the Black Sea, with Constantina as his queen. However, the young woman was to continue to be a pawn in the political game of rulers. After Constantine's death, Constantina's brother, Constantius II, had further plans for his sister that would help him in new power struggles. Constantius arranged the assassination of Hannibalianus and arranged another political marriage for Constantina. She married her cousin Gallus, who was Constantius's ally in the dynastic struggles with his brother. For a while, Gallus and Constantina enjoyed a good deal of power, but the political turmoils took their toll. Gallus was murdered in A.D. 353, and Constantina died a year later. The Roman historian Ammianus believed that Constantina had been an active participant in the political machinations that brought down her two husbands. He wrote that she was as "insatiable as Gallus in her thirst for human blood" (Salisbury 66) and that she worked closely with her husband in the conspiracies that led to his murder. All these activities would have been perfectly consistent with the role of a high-born daughter of an emperor.

Although the Roman sources portray a shrewd, ruthless woman, Christian sources have preserved a different image of Constantina. Instead of the politically expedient daughter of a powerful emperor, in legend she was described as a perfect, virginal daughter of a Christian hero. In the legend of Constantina, preserved in various manuscripts, the young woman was portrayed as a pious Christian who was plagued with leprosy as a young girl. She prayed at the tomb of St. Agnes in Rome, and the saint miraculously appeared to her and cured her illness. From then on, Constantina dedicated her life to God. In the legend, she refused to marry her father's choice of a suitor, a general, and instead proceeded to convert the general and his whole household to Christianity, all the while remaining a virgin. The legend makes a striking contrast to the politically involved daughter of an emperor.

Like many legends, the story of the fictional Constantina was made more memorable by its association with a landmark—the Tomb of Santa Constanza in Rome. The Emperor Constantine had built this church near a church he had also built and dedicated to Saint Agnes. The tomb of Santa Constanza was probably built for the emperor's half-sister, Constantia, who had been an extremely pious Christian. Constantia, too, had been a victim of the violence of the times, for the emperor had murdered her husband, Licinius, during a civil war. The widow refused to remarry and spent her days in pious prayer. While it is most likely that Constantine built this tomb to appease his pious half-sister, in time the tomb became associated with Constantina, the legendary daughter of the emperor, reputedly cured of leprosy by the saint in the adjoining church.

In this way, the legendary daughter became more influential than the real daughter. After the political marriages and assassinations were over, the world remembered a fictional religious woman immortalized in a tomb that likely belonged to someone else.

See also Agnes; Helena
Suggested Readings
Salisbury, J. E. *Church Fathers, Independent Virgins.* London: Verso, 1991.

Contraception

From evidence in the earliest records, we know that people in ancient societies sometimes used various methods to prevent contraception during sexual intercourse. The many recipes to prevent pregnancy suggest that there is a long history of the practice.

The simplest means of contraception is coitus interruptus, whereby the man withdraws from the woman just before ejaculation. There are a few mentions of this in the sources, from the biblical "sin of Onan" to a Greek poem (by the poet Archilochus) that writes of "landing in the grassy meadows" (Fantham et al. 25). The Greek philosopher Plato condemned the practice of coitus interruptus, saying he would ban it from his just society. The motives behind the condemnation of coitus interruptus were largely a concern with "wasting" sperm rather than preventing conception.

The Roman physician, Soranus, recommended that the woman take responsibility for withdrawing at the moment of orgasm. He said that when she guessed that the man was about to ejaculate, she must hold her breath and "draw herself away a little, so that the seed may not be hurled too deep into the cavity of the uterus" (Rousselle 45). After that she should squat down, sneeze, and wash out her vagina. This method was not as reliable as blocking the sperm's entrance.

Some texts recommended blocking the entrance to the cervix with a number of preparations. Ancient Egyptian scrolls called for inserting crocodile dung or honey and gumlike substances into the vagina to block the path of the sperm. The ancient Greeks recommended olive oil, and Jews used a sponge soaked in vinegar to act as a spermicide. Greek physicians also recommended intrauterine devices, but that always posed the danger of excessive bleeding.

The most comprehensive catalog of things with which to block the passage of sperm comes from Soranus. He recommended smearing the cervix with "honey or cedar resin or juice of the balsam tree—alone or with white lead—or with a paste of myrtle oil with white lead" (Lefkowitz and Fant 159). For an intrauterine device, Soranus recommended a lock of fine wool to be inserted. He also recommended things that would cause the cervix to constrict, thus blocking the sperm's entrance. His list of these items to be placed in the vagina is extensive. The following are only a few of the items he recommends: Mix pine bark and sumac with some wine and apply before coitus with some wool. After leaving it there for two or three hours, the woman can remove it and have intercourse. Similarly, women could use ground pomegranate rinds, oak galls, or ginger or dried figs. After this list, Soranus wisely ended by warning women not to use things that were too caustic because they might lead to ulcerations of the uterus.

Finally, women took herbs to stop pregnancies. The ancient sources did not really distinguish between contraception and abortifacients, so that herbs that could bring on uterine contractions and start a woman's period were the same ones that caused an abortion.

Women of the ancient world were clearly concerned about unwanted pregnancies. The extensive catalogs recorded by physicians were drawn from information from women about what they used, and the many recipes testify to women's long experimentation with avoiding unwanted pregnancies.

See also Abortion; Gynecology
Suggested Readings
Fantham, E., et al. *Women in the Classical World.* New York: Oxford University Press, 1994.
Lefkowitz, Mary R., and Maureen B. Fant. *Women in Greece and Rome.* Toronto: Samuel-Stevens, 1977.
Rousselle, Aline. *Porneia: On Desire and the Body in Antiquity.* New York: Basil Blackwell, 1988.

Corinna of Tanagra
Hellenistic Poet (ca. third century B.C.)
Like her contemporary Anyte of Tegea, Corinna of Tanagra wrote poetry that had wide appeal.

The ancient critic Antipater of Thessalonica in the first century B.C. praised Corinna for her poetry of war, calling her an earthly muse who possessed much poetic talent. Unlike some of the women poets who emphasized love, Corinna wrote of heroic deeds. Indeed, in a brief fragment she proclaims:

> But I myself sing the excellent deeds
> of male and female heroes. (Fantham et al. 166)

Yet, even within the poems chronicling victories and defeats, Corinna was acutely sensitive to feelings. For example, in a fragment of a much longer poem, she writes of the contest between Cithaeron and Helicon in which the Muses got the gods to bring "their voting pebbles to the golden bowls, and then all were counted." Cithaeron won, but Corinna dwells on Helicon's feelings: "He was overcome by harsh grief. . . . and he tore out a bare rock and from the height dashed it into countless stones" (Lefkowitz and Fant 6).

In another fragment, Corinna addressed a group of girls who were probably members of a chorus who would learn to perform Corinna's songs:

> Terpsichore summoned me to sing
> beautiful tales of old
> to the Tanagraean girls in their white robes
> And the city rejoiced greatly
> in my clear, plaintive voice. (Fantham et al. 167)

In this fragment, we can see the kind of public acclaim that some Hellenistic poets such as Corinna and Aristodama could expect to receive because of their talents.

Corinna's reputation continued throughout the ancient world. For Roman poets in the time of Caesar Augustus, the name Corinna was synonymous with talent and wisdom. Other male poets, such as Ovid, evoked the name of Corinna when they wanted people to think of poetic skill. Through the medium of her poetry, this ancient woman's reputation lasted for centuries.

See also Anyte of Tegea; Aristodama of Smyrna; Muses; Nossis of Locri

Suggested Readings

Fantham, E., et al. *Women in the Classical World.* New York: Oxford University Press, 1994.

Lefkowitz, Mary R., and Maureen B. Fant. *Women in Greece and Rome.* Toronto: Samuel-Stevens, 1977.

Cornelia

Roman Matron (191–108 B.C.)

One of the most famous women of the Roman Republic was Cornelia, who embodied all the virtues that Romans held dear. Cornelia was the daughter of the great Scipio Africanus, the conqueror of Hannibal; having so famous a father immediately endeared her to the Roman people. She married one of the more influential men of her day, Teberius Sempronius Gracchus, and she bore him twelve children—a remarkable feat in any age but particularly so during the Roman period when people praised families with three children. Cornelia's husband died, leaving her to raise all these children.

She was so well known and respected and, according to Plutarch, "such a good mother" (Plutarch 1010), that King Ptolemy of Egypt sought her hand in marriage and offered to share his throne with her. However, she refused him, preferring to remain a widow. (This, too, gained her praise, for Romans had the highest respect for women who had known only one husband.) She devoted her widowhood to raising her children. Unfortunately, only three survived. Her daughter, Sempronia, would marry the national hero Scipio the Younger, and her two sons, Tiberius and Gaius, were raised to serve the state. They did so to a remarkable degree, and many credited some of their success to their mother's teaching. In an often-told story, when a visitor asked Cornelia to display her jewels, she introduced her sons. However, they came to power in a tumultuous age and would give their lives in the service of the Roman people.

In the mid-second century, the Roman Republic suffered a sudden economic downturn. The wars of expansion had brought vast riches into Rome; this wealth drove prices up, and as part of the many economic and social problems, an unfortunate grain shortage made food prices skyrocket. The Gracchi brothers came forward to see if they could help resolve the crisis. Tiberius became tribune of the plebeians in 133 B.C.

Tiberius proposed an agrarian law that would redistribute public land to landless Romans. The idea was sound and might have made a difference, but it alarmed greedy landlords. The law passed, but the senate reluctantly voted only a tiny sum to help Tiberius administer it. Many senators were particularly worried when Tiberius announced he was running for reelection. Although in the distant past, tribunes had run for a second term, that had not been done for a long time, and Tiberius's opponents argued that it was illegal. In the ensuing turmoil, a riot occurred at an assembly meeting, and some senators with their followers beat Tiberius and 300 of his followers to death. With one stroke, a new element emerged in Roman political life: political murder.

Tiberius's land law continued to operate for a time, but not very effectively. In 123 B.C., Tiberius's brother, Gaius, became tribune in an effort to continue his brother's work. A controversial letter that has survived was purportedly written by Cornelia to Gaius denouncing his revolutionary activities. "Will our family ever desist from this madness? Will we ever feel shame at throwing the state into turmoil and confusion? But if that really cannot be, seek the tribunate after I am dead" (Fantham et al. 264). It is hard to imagine that this indomitable woman urged her son to refrain from the political life for which she had prepared him, and it is too convenient a text to support the conservative forces that destroyed the Gracchan reforms not to doubt its authenticity. In any case, Gaius continued in public office to a disastrous end.

The senate moved to undo his reforms as soon as Gaius was out of office, and he and some 250 supporters were murdered in 122 B.C.—their deaths arranged by one of the consuls supporting the senate. The Gracchi brothers were martyred for the plebeian cause in Rome; they were gone, but the admiration Rome felt for their mother only increased.

Instead of retreating in mourning after the loss of the sons, Cornelia continued in her public life. She lived as she always had and continued to entertain lavishly and correspond with the intelligent and powerful men of the age. According to Plutarch, all the reigning kings sent her gifts, and she surrounded herself with literary figures. She spoke of her sons without grief or tears, proud that they had died serving Rome.

Her contemporaries erected a great statue of her in a public place to honor this Roman mother who embodied all the virtues Romans praised. The marble base of the statue survives but the statue itself has been lost. She was portrayed seated serenely, and this pose became a model for statues of later Roman women. (The statue of Helena shown in Figure 40, page 154, was presumably modeled after Cornelia.) More than her statue became a model, however. Subsequent Romans praised this brave woman who trained her sons for public service and then accepted their loss stoically.

See also Helena; Motherhood, Roman

Suggested Readings
Dixon, Suzanne. *The Roman Mother.* Norman: Oklahoma University Press, 1988.
Fantham, E., et al. *Women in the Classical World.* New York: Oxford University Press, 1994.
Plutarch. "Tiberius Gracchus," "Gaius Gracchus." In *Plutarch.* Trans. F. C. Babbitt. Cambridge, MA: Loeb Classical Library, 1968.

Cornelia

Wife of Roman Dictator (ca. 53 B.C.)
At the end of the Roman Republic, the constitutional form of government fell apart. Strong men rose to power and used armies and popular support to hold power. During the decade of the eighties, the rise of Pompey (106–48 B.C.) was phenomenal. In 83 B.C. he brought his army to serve with Sulla as that strongman rose to power to be a dictator. In 81 B.C., Sulla gave Pompey the title "the Great," which signified how high his fortunes had already risen. Pompey was so handsome and talented that his contemporaries compared him to Alexander the Great, and Pompey even wore a robe that Alexander himself reputedly wore in order to increase the comparison. Like members of the Macedonian dynasties, Pompey knew that his fortunes depended in part upon prudent marriages.

In the course of his life, Pompey married and divorced several women; Roman marriages were more about political alliances than anything else. For example, in 82 B.C., when Sulla was made dictator, Pompey divorced his first wife, Antistia, and married Sulla's stepdaughter, Aemilia, to cement his alliance with Sulla. After Sulla's death, more civil wars erupted in Rome, and Pompey was in the thick of the power struggle. He became one of the three men who made an informal alliance—later called the First Triumvirate—to rule Rome. These three—Pompey, Crassus, and Julius Caesar—knew their alliance was tenuous, and Pompey married Caesar's daughter Julia to seal the bond. Pompey's most famous wife, however, was the one who watched him die—Cornelia, daughter of the consul in 52 B.C., Metellus Scipio.

Cornelia was one of the many talented, highborn women of the late republic. The ancient biographer Plutarch described her as follows:

> She had other attractions besides those of youth and beauty; for she was highly educated, played well upon the lute, and understood geometry, and had been accustomed to listen with profit to lectures on philosophy; all this, too, without in any degree becoming unamiable or pretentious. . . . Nor could any fault be found either with her father's family or reputation. (Plutarch 779)

Her first marriage was a fine one, with P. Crassus, a charming and gifted man and the son of Crassus who shared power with Caesar and Pompey. Cornelia's fortunes changed when the men of the Triumvirate began to fight among themselves.

The first sign of the breakdown of good relations came when Pompey's wife, Julia, died in childbirth in 54 B.C. Now there were no longer family ties holding Pompey and Caesar together. Then Crassus died in battle in the east when his armies were ambushed near Carrhae in 53 B.C. He who had served as a buffer between Caesar and Pompey was now gone. In this battle, Cornelia's young husband also died fighting with his father. The next year, Pompey negotiated a marriage with Cornelia, who was much younger than he. In fact, Plutarch notes "the disparity of their ages was not liked by everybody; Cornelia being in this respect a fitter match for Pompey's son" (Plutarch 779). Cornelia seemed fond of her elderly husband, but the marriage would be brief and end in tragedy.

In 49 B.C., Caesar entered Italy from Gaul with his armies, and Pompey decided to abandon Rome to fight Caesar in the east. Pompey took Cornelia and his son and was joined by a number of senators who supported him. In August of 48 B.C., Caesar and Pompey joined battle at Pharsalus, where Caesar won a decisive victory. Pompey had to flee.

When a messenger appeared to Cornelia telling her that things had not gone well with Pompey, she "fell into a swoon and continued a long time senseless and speechless" (Plutarch 793). When she woke, she ran to Pompey and threw herself at his feet, blaming herself for his misfortune. She said when he married her he led a fleet of fifty ships, but now he appeared for her as a fugitive with only one. She thought her own bad luck had contributed to Pompey's reduction, but Pompey comforted her and said that fortunes rose and fell.

The couple resolved to flee to Egypt, but they were caught by an Egyptian ship. Pompey was captured and brought on board the other ship, joined by his freedman and slave. He bade good-bye to Cornelia and his son. As the ships drew near shore, Cornelia took courage because she saw several well-dressed people coming to join her husband, and she believed they were going to give him an honorable reception. She was shocked, however, to see that instead they drew their swords and killed him. He died when he was fifty-eight years old. According to Plutarch, Cornelia—seeing him murdered—gave such a cry that it was heard on shore, then her galley turned, hoisted the sail, and fled. Though the Egyptians tried to pursue the ship, they were unable to catch it, so Cornelia escaped back to Italy.

The assassins decapitated Pompey's body and saved the head for Caesar. Pompey's freedman gave their general's body a solemn cremation, then carried his ashes back to Cornelia, who deposited them at his country house near Alba in Italy. Cornelia's personal accomplishments were few, but she represents many Roman women who were swept up in the civil wars that marked the end of the Roman Republic and whose personal lives were profoundly affected by politics.

See also Calpurnia; Fulvia; Turia
Suggested Readings
Greenhalgh, Peter. *Pompey: The Roman Alexander.* Columbia: University of Missouri Press, 1980.
Plutarch. "Pompey." In *The Lives of the Noble Grecians and Romans.* Trans. J. Dryden. New York: The Modern Library, n.d.

Cosmetics

As far as we can tell with scarce information, people have always used cosmetics of some kind. Just as with jewelry, cosmetics were used for magical purposes as well as to enhance attractiveness. It is difficult to know how people adorned their bodies in prehistoric times since most of the remains are only bones, which do not yield enough information. Neanderthal burial sites from the Stone Age show that the dead were covered with red ochre to color their skin, and it may be that the living, too, painted themselves for ritual purposes. One wonderful find from the Bronze Age—a hunter frozen in a glacier and known as the "ice man"—has enough soft tissue preserved to show that he had tattoos as a body adornment. Were these for beauty or symbols of other rites? Some archaeologists suggest that they were for medicinal purposes, but we do not know. Other ancient tribes—such as the Germans and Celts—also painted themselves and used tattoos as part of a war ritual. Therefore, we assume that prehistoric peoples used paints and dyes of various kinds—either applied temporarily or tattooed into the skin permanently—to enhance their appearance. By the time we reach the historical period, the evidence for such practices is more abundant.

Egypt

In the dry desert air of Egypt, men and women alike used elaborate moisturizing creams and oils for their skin. Moisturizing was made even more necessary because the main ingredient of soap was natron, which was the main drying agent used to remove the flesh's liquid and preserve dead bodies during mummification. Therefore Egyptians used oils and creams lavishly. They also believed these creams improved the health of the skin, so once again there was little difference between health and beauty aids. One recipe from a medical text sounds like a modern advertising campaign: "To remove facial wrinkles: frankincense gum, wax, fresh balanites oil and rush-nut should be finely ground and applied to the face every day. Make it and you will see!" (Tyldesley 152). Lower classes had to be content with simple castor or linseed oil, but the wealthy purchased oils and waxes scented with expensive imported perfumes.

Perfumed conditioning oils were also rubbed into the scalp after shampooing to protect the scalp and hair from the drying effects of the harsh climate. During the New Kingdom (ca. 1400 B.C.) this practice led to a custom that seems rather strange to us. At dinner parties or other social gatherings, the host provided the guests with lumps or cones of perfume that were balanced on the heads during the social event. These were made of tallow (animal fat that is now used in candles) with sweet-smelling myrrh, and they were designed to melt slowly during the evening, allowing a thin trickle of wax to run down the hair and face while releasing the perfume. As the fat melted away, servants would come and replace the cones. These are illustrated on tomb scenes and are shown as white lumps with brown streaks running down the sides, and white clothing is shown with brown stains on the shoulders, which may represent the greasy drips. No actual examples of these perfume cones have survived, so it is difficult to imagine exactly how this practice would have worked. Nevertheless, it shows how important Egyptians believed perfume and moisturizers were to the skin.

Men and women alike also used a good deal of makeup, and mirrors, like that shown in Figure 21, were used by men and women to apply their cosmetics. Indeed, from predynastic times onward (from before 3000 B.C.), men and women chose to be buried with their cosmetic cases and blocks of pigment that they used for adorning their eyes. The most important cosmetics were used on the eyes because people believed that eye makeup would protect the eyes from the fierce desert sun. Paint was applied to

Figure 21. Egyptian hand mirror, New Kingdom, 1400 B.C. (Ann Ronan Picture Library)

the upper and lower lids, outlining the eyes and lengthening the eyebrows. People would often paint a bold line from the outer corner of the eye to the hairline. Black kohl was used as an eyeliner, but two other colors were available: green and dark gray. Green (made with malachite) was the most popular during the early dynastic period, and dark gray gained popularity during the New Kingdom. The most fashionable women used both in combination. Other cosmetics were less common, although some women used a powdered rouge made from red ochre. There is little evidence of lip color, although one text shows a picture of a prostitute painting her lips using a lip brush and a mirror.

Women who earned their living depending on the attractiveness of their bodies used tattoos on their bodies, arms, and/or legs. They used small needles and lamp black mixed with oil to make intricate patterns. Tattoos seem to have been confined to entertainers and prostitutes, and only from the Middle Kingdom (ca. 1800 B.C.) do we have mummies that have been tentatively identified as royal concubines with remnants of tattoos.

Greece

We have less information about the cosmetics used by Greek women. Respectable Athenian women did not leave their houses very often, so we do not have as much evidence for cosmetic use. Women did remove their pubic hair by singeing and plucking, and some cosmetics were used by both prostitutes and respectable women. A white complexion was considered attractive, since it proved that a woman did not have to go out in the sun and work, so powder of white lead was used to whiten the complexion, and some rouge was used on the cheeks. We assume prostitutes used even more cosmetics.

Rome

Even during the republican period when men and women prided themselves on simplicity, women used cosmetics. The Roman historian Livy relates a speech in which one man explained that women could not enjoy the triumphs that came with warfare; they had to settle for other pleasures: "Cosmetics and adornment are women's decorations. They delight and boast of them and this is what our ancestors called women's estate" (Fantham et al. 261). Like the Greek women, Roman women whitened their faces with chalk and lead and used other pigments as rouge and lipstick. Some women also spread a sparkling cream made of antimony on their eyelids as an eye shadow.

Roman women favored fine perfumes and spent a good deal of money importing elaborate scents from the east. Archaeologists have found many cosmetic cases, perfume containers, and small hand mirrors, showing how prevalent these things were. Most of the cosmetics, skin creams, and perfumes were made with olive oil as a base, so the olive oil business also increased.

Romans did not favor tattoos. This practice belonged to the "barbarians" outside their borders or to slaves, soldiers, or gladiators. There is little evidence that women—even performers—used tattoos during the Roman period.

Christian fathers such as Jerome condemned the practice of wearing makeup, claiming that Christian women should renounce all such things. In a letter to a widow (Furia), Jerome wrote, "What place have rouge and white lead on the face of a Christian woman? . . . How can a woman weep for her sins whose tears lay bare her true complexion and mark furrows on her cheeks?" (Jerome 104). This passage not only shows the Christian view of cosmetic use but also points to how thick the powders were placed if tears would streak it so badly. In spite of the prohibitions of men such as Jerome, however, Christian women, too, continued to enjoy the cosmetics that had been used by women of the ancient world from time beyond memory.

See also Clothing; Jewelry

Suggested Readings

Adkins, Lesley, and Roy A. Adkins. *Handbook to Life in Ancient Rome.* New York: Oxford University Press, 1994.

Fantham, E., et al. *Women in the Classical World.* New York: Oxford University Press, 1994.

Jerome. *Jerome: Letters and Select Works. Nicene and Post-Nicene Fathers,* vol. 6. Ed. Philip Schaff and Henry Wace. Peabody, MA: Hendrickson Publishers, 1995.

Pomeroy, Sarah B. *Goddesses, Whores, Wives, and Slaves: Women in Classical Antiquity.* New York: Schocken Books, 1975.

Tyldesley, Joyce. *Daughters of Isis: Women of Ancient Egypt.* New York: Penguin, 1994.

Cybele

Roman Goddess

Cybele was the Great Mother goddess whose worship originated in Phrygia (in central Asia Minor). She was considered to be the mother of all living things—both a goddess of fertility and of wild nature—and was said to cause and cure disease. Her ancient myth claims that she was born with both male and female genitalia. The gods then castrated the infant and cast its male organ into the ground, where an almond tree sprouted. The child then grew up into the goddess Cybele. Nana, a daughter of a river god, gathered the blossom of the almond tree and then conceived Attis. Cybele loved Attis, but when he wished to marry someone else, she drove him mad, so that he castrated himself and died beneath a pine tree. This myth of love and castration formed the basis of the fertility cult that grew up around the Great Mother, which was celebrated every spring with pine trees and festivals. In this cult, followers sacrificed their own fecundity in exchange for prosperity for the land and also perhaps for a personal immortality.

By the fifth century B.C., the cult of Cybele was known in Greece. In the third century B.C., her cult was officially brought to Rome from Asia Minor after a prophecy said that this would improve Rome's fortunes in the Punic Wars against Carthage. The Roman historian Livy described how the goddess—in the form of a stone—was brought by ship into Rome. Publius Cornelius, a Roman leader, went with the matrons of the city to carry the goddess. The matrons passed the goddess from hand to hand while the whole city poured out to meet her. They carried the goddess to the Temple of Victory in the center of Rome, where she resided from then on. The rites of Cybele were popular and dramatic.

The rites began on 15 March with a procession and a sacrifice for the crops. After a week of fastings and purifications, the festival proper opened on 22 March with the bringing of the pine tree, a symbol of Attis, to the temple. The 24th was a Day of Blood, commemorating the castration and probably the death of Attis, and the 25th was a day of joy and banqueting. The procession was accompanied by ecstatic dancing and music of shrill Syrian pipes, and the priests cut their arms with swords and flogged themselves, showing their imperviousness to pain. Finally, the procession culminated in many of the initiates' self-castration. The contemporary observer Lucian described the ecstatic ceremony:

The youth for whom these things lie in store throws off his clothes, rushes to the center with a great shout, and takes up a sword. . . . He grabs it and immediately castrates himself. Then he rushes through the city holding in his hands the parts he has cut off. He takes female clothing and women's adornment from whatever house he throws these parts into. This is what they do at the Castration. (Martin 84)

The priests of the goddess were eunuchs who had sacrificed themselves this way in imitation of Attis, beloved of the goddess.

By the first century A.D., a new ceremony in honor of this popular goddess spread from Asia Minor throughout the Roman Empire. This was the *taurobolium,* in which an individual who wanted to be initiated into the mysteries of this cult stepped down into a pit and was bathed in the blood of a bull that was sacrificed on top of the pit. This seems to have represented a rebirth that would ensure the initiate's immortality by being reborn within Mother Earth. Sometimes the ceremony was conducted with a ram, and then it was called the *criobolium.*

The cult of Cybele remained enormously popular throughout the Roman Empire until the spread of Christianity. Along with the cult of Isis, this was a cult that gave a great deal of satisfaction to ancient men and women alike.

See also Isis

Suggested Readings

Adkins, Lesley, and Roy A. Adkins. *Handbook to Life in Ancient Rome.* New York: Oxford University Press, 1994.

Grimal, Pierre. *The Dictionary of Classical Mythology.* Oxford: Blackwell, 1996.

Kraemer, Ross Shepard. *Her Share of the Blessings.* New York: Oxford University Press, 1992.

Martin, Luther H. *Hellenistic Religions.* New York: Oxford University Press, 1987.

D

Danaë

Mythological Greek Woman

The ancient Greeks told a popular story about a woman named Danaë, who was beautiful above all other women of the land. But this was no comfort to her father, King Acrisius of Argos, because the Delphic Oracle had told him that his daughter's son would kill him. The only sure way to escape his fate was for the king to put Danaë to death, but he was unwilling to incur the wrath of the gods for killing his own daughter. Therefore, the king built a house all of bronze and sank it underground so it was completely sealed in. Only a part of the roof was open to the sky so that light and air could come through. He shut his daughter up and had her guarded to make sure she would never have a son.

However, Zeus fell in love with the beautiful maiden and came to her in a shower of gold that fell from the sky and filled her chamber. In this shape, Zeus impregnated Danaë, and she bore a son, named Perseus. King Acrisius was furious, but he was still afraid to kill his offspring. He decided, however, that he could place them in enough danger to secure their death and foil the prophecy that called for Perseus to kill his father. He placed the two in a great chest, closed it, and cast it into the sea. The chest washed safely on land, however, and the two were taken in by a kind fisherman named Dictys and his wife.

The two were not to have a peaceful life, however. When Perseus was grown, the evil ruler of the island Polydectes saw Danaë and fell in love with her radiant beauty. He wanted to marry her, but he also wanted to be rid of her son. So he devised a plan. He tricked Perseus into boldly promising to bring him the severed head of the monster Medusa. With the help of the gods, Perseus accomplished his task.

On the way back with his prize, Perseus saw a beautiful woman, named Andromeda, chained to a rock to be devoured by a sea serpent. The girl's mother had insulted the gods by claiming that her daughter was more beautiful than the daughters of the sea-god. In revenge, the sea-god sent a serpent who was devouring the citizens, and an oracle said they would be freed from its tyranny only if they offered it Andromeda. This was the situation that Perseus encountered, and he instantly fell in love with her. He waited until the serpent came for its prey, and he cut its head off. Perseus took Andromeda to her parents and asked for her hand in marriage. They agreed.

With Andromeda, Perseus continued his journey back to his mother with Medusa's head safely in a pouch. When he arrived home, he discovered that Danaë had had to flee from the evil king who still wanted to marry her. Perseus went straight to the king's palace, where there was a banquet going on. He walked in, pulled out the Medusa head, and turned to stone everyone who looked at the monster. He then found Danaë and decided to try to return to their original home. However, on their way, Perseus entered an athletic contest and participated in the discus-throwing contest. His throw swerved and entered the crowd, striking his father, Acrisius, who was there in the audience. In this way Apollo's oracle proved true. With the death of the old king, Danaë's problems were over, and she, Perseus, and Andromeda lived happily ever after.

From ancient times to today, many have been captivated by the image of the beautiful Danaë being visited by Zeus in the form of a golden shower. This has been portrayed by painters and other artists, and even early Christians sometimes saw the story of a metaphor of God's love coming from the heavens.

See also Delphic Oracle; Hera; Medusa
Suggested Readings
Hamilton, Edith. *Mythology.* New York: Mentor, 1955
Grimal, Pierre. *The Dictionary of Classical Mythology.* Oxford: Blackwell, 1996.

Daphne

Mythological Nymph

According to both Greek and Roman myths, Daphne was a wood-nymph, daughter of the river-god Peneus. (Some versions of the myth say she was the daughter of the River Ladon.) Daphne wanted to remain a virgin, never marrying and always hunting and frolicking in the woods. Her father despaired of having grandchildren, but Daphne wanted to be like Artemis/Diana, and her indulgent father could not refuse her. She was so lovely that she had many suitors, and even the god Apollo himself had fallen in love with her.

Apollo first saved her from one of her suitors—Leucippus—who had disguised himself as a woman to join Daphne in her mountain revels. Apollo, knowing about this deception, advised the mountain nymphs to bathe naked and thus make sure that everyone in their company was a woman. Leucippus was immediately discovered, and the nymphs tore him to pieces. However, Apollo was not content to save the nymph from other suitors; he wanted her himself.

Once Apollo saw her hunting in the woods. She had her arms bare and her hair in wild disarray. Apollo started to chase her to rape her and Daphne fled. Although Daphne was a fleet runner, Apollo soon caught up to her. He called to her not to fear, for she would be loved by a god. But Daphne ran on, even more frightened than before. As she felt Apollo's breath on her neck, she saw her father's river ahead of her. "Help me, father, help me," she called. At the words, a numbness came upon her, and her feet seemed rooted to the ground. Bark was enclosing her and leaves were sprouting forth; she had been changed into a laurel tree. The carving in Figure 22 shows Daphne slowly transforming into a tree, and this is just one of many such depictions, for the legend was a popular one among artists.

Apollo watched the transformation with dis-

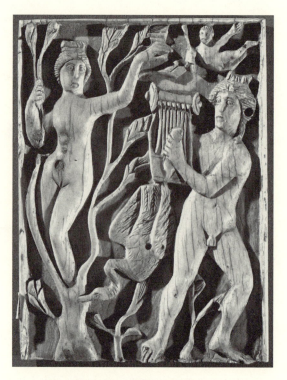

Figure 22. Daphne and Apollo, fifth century A.D. (Scala/Art Resource, NY)

may. To console himself, Apollo fashioned a crown of laurels and made it a prize for the victors in the games in his honor. The laurel crown became a symbol of victory and was worn even by the Roman emperors. In their victories, athletes and kings alike remembered the determination of the independent nymph, Daphne.

See also Artemis; Nymphs
Suggested Readings
Hamilton, Edith. *Mythology.* New York: Mentor, 1955.
Grimal, Pierre. *The Dictionary of Classical Mythology.* Oxford: Blackwell, 1996.

Deborah

Hebrew Leader (ca. 1200 B.C.)

The Book of Judges in the Bible tells of the Israelites' continuing battles with their neighbors as they tried to consolidate their rule over the region in the eastern Mediterranean known as ancient Palestine—the biblical Promised Land for the Jews. The stories in Judges preserve the exploits of the heroes of various Hebrew tribes; these leaders were called "judges" not because they held a strictly legal position but because their people accorded them much respect as charismatic leaders. The editor who recorded the tales gave them a unity by making all the judges national instead of tribal leaders and by providing a moral and religious interpretation to the political events. Readers of the Book of Judges therefore were to learn that loyalty to God was the first requirement for national success.

One of the judges included in the accounts was a woman and prophet whose name was Deborah. The story of Deborah's triumph is told in two parallel accounts in the Bible. The one in prose form is followed by a beautiful poem (or song) attributed to Deborah herself. We cannot be certain, however, who actually wrote the poem.

Deborah was identified as a "woman from [the town of] Lappidoth" or perhaps the "wife of [the man] Lappidoth"—the translation is unclear—and little else is told about her. She did serve in the legal capacity of a judge as well as a prophet, and therefore she was regularly consulted in the settlement of disputes. She habitually sat under a tree in a region north of Jerusalem where "the people of Israel came up to her for judgment" (Judg. 4:1). By Deborah's adulthood, the Israelites had been engaged in warfare for twenty years in the north against the Canaanites, who held a fertile valley that stretched from west to east across the country down to the Sea of Galilee. Deborah's song tells of the disruption caused by the Canaanites and of her call to alleviate the suffering: "Caravans ceased and travelers kept to the byways. The peasantry ceased in Israel, they ceased until you arose, Deborah, arose as a mother in Israel" (Judg. 4:6–7).

Like a good mother, Deborah set out to improve her people's plight. Commanded by God, she sent for Barak, a leader of a tribe in the Galilee highlands, and told him to muster men on the wooded slopes of Mount Tabor. The prose version of the account says that only two tribes were involved in the battle, but Deborah's song says that she sent out a general call for help and urged the tribes to rally together against the

Canaanite threat. When the forces had gathered, Deborah told Barak to take command, but he answered firmly: "If you will go with me, I will go; but if you will not go with me, I will not go" (Judg. 4:8). Deborah agreed to go with the army but gave Barak a prophetic forecast that he would not receive the glory for the victory; instead "the Lord will sell Sisera [the opposing general] into the hand of a woman" (Judg. 4:9).

Barak gathered his forces of 10,000 men on a plateau at the end of the valley, while Sisera assembled a larger army that included 900 chariots. Sisera may have assumed that in the presence of his superior force the Israelites would flee, but the weather was on the side of the Hebrews. A violent rainstorm came suddenly, turning the floor of the valley into mud, which caused Sisera's horses and chariots to bog down. The Israelites were able to charge down from the highlands and rout the Canaanites.

Sisera fled the battle and went to the encampment of an ally from a neighboring tribe. The general entered the tent of his ally's wife, Jael, who invited him in. She gave him milk to drink and covered him to allow him to rest. He told her to guard the door of the tent to keep anyone from finding him while he rested from the battle. However, Jael "took a tent peg, and took a hammer in her hand, and went softly to him and drove the peg into his temple, till it went down into the ground. So he died" (Judg. 4:21). When Barak arrived seeking his foe, Jael showed him the dead body of Sisera. Thus, Deborah's prophecy came true, for Sisera was killed by the hand of a woman. This great victory gave the Israelites momentum to crush the Canaanites so "the land had rest for forty years" (Judg. 5:31).

The account of Deborah's leadership offers an unusual example of an ancient Hebrew woman who transcended the usual expectations to take an active public role. The song of Deborah included in Judges perhaps also offers a glimpse into at least one ancient woman's perspective on warfare, for the poet includes unusual details in praise of the great victory. For example, after Deborah summoned the people to fight, the poet recognized the sacrifice this would bring: "My heart goes out to the commanders of Israel who offered themselves willingly among the people" (Judg. 5:9). Furthermore, the poetic account greatly praised the bravery of the woman Jael, calling her twice "the most blessed of women" (Judg. 5:24).

Perhaps the most poignant description of ancient warfare, however, lay in the final stanza of Deborah's song. Here Sisera's mother anxiously awaits her son's return, as mothers have always worried about their absent sons. When she wonders aloud about her son's tardiness, the ladies of her household try to comfort her, reminding her of war victors' customary taking of spoils, and the mother echoes their reflections: "Are they not finding and dividing the spoil? A maiden or two for every man; spoil of dyed stuffs for Sisera, spoil of dyed stuffs embroidered, two pieces of dyed work embroidered for my neck as spoil?" (Judg. 5:30). Here an ancient mother hopes her son will return safely bringing precious cloth for her. She also notes that women will be enslaved in war—"a maiden or two for every man." Indeed, here is a woman's perspective on warfare, but the irony is not lost on the reader: This mother will not see her son again, just as many mothers waited in vain. In the story of the praise of an exceptional woman lies the truth of the plight of many anonymous women of the ancient world.

See also Jewish Women; Judith
Suggested Readings
Ackerman, Susan. *Warrior, Dancer, Seductress, Queen: Women in Judges and Biblical Israel.* New York: Doubleday, 1998.
Meyers, Carol, Toni Craven, and Ross S. Kraemer. *Women in Scripture.* New York: Houghton Mifflin, 2000.

Delilah

Philistine Heroine (ca. 1100 B.C.)

In the Book of Judges in the Bible, the narrator recounts the feats of Israelite heroes who fought against neighboring tribes as the Hebrews were consolidating their rule over the Promised Land of ancient Palestine. One of the popular figures from the Book of Judges was Samson, a folk hero of supernatural birth and superhuman strength. Samson was from one of the Hebrew tribes—the tribe of Dan—who lived near the coastal hills of Judea. It was an area that encroached into the land of the Philistines, a sea people who had recently settled on the mainland from either the Aegean Islands or from the coast of Asia Minor. Samson was born during incessant border wars between the Israelites and the Philistines, and it was in this struggle that he both earned his reputation and met his death. Equally as famous as Samson was his lover, Delilah, heroine of the Philistines and betrayer of the Hebrews.

Samson's mother had been childless for years until an angel appeared before her and told her she would conceive a son who would "begin to deliver Israel from the hand of the Philistines" (Judg. 13:5). The angel further warned that the child would be dedicated to God's service, so he was forbidden to cut his hair or touch strong drink. While Samson grew up with superhuman strength, he also grew into a weakness for women, particularly Philistine women, and these would bring about his downfall.

As a young man, Samson fell in love with a Philistine woman and told his parents he wanted to have her for his wife. They tried to urge him to marry a woman from his own tribe, but he was adamant. When they traveled together to the girl's village, Samson was attacked by a young lion, but he tore the lion apart with his bare hands and left the carcass where it fell. Then the family continued on to negotiate with the girl's father. Samson was well pleased with the woman and continued to press his suit. As he returned from the village, he turned aside to see the carcass of the lion he had killed, and he found within it a wondrous thing: a swarm of bees had inhabited the body. Samson scraped out the sweet honey from the carcass and gave some to his parents. However, he did not tell anyone where he had gotten the sweet treat.

As was customary, Samson gave a wedding feast in his bride's village that went on for seven days. Thirty young Philistines were invited to attend, and Samson placed a bet with them. For a wager of thirty pieces of linen and thirty fine garments, Samson bet he could pose a riddle that they could not solve. He chose the incident of the lion to frame his riddle: "Out of the eater came something to eat. Out of the strong came something sweet" (Judg. 14:14). The Philistines could not think of the answer, so they threatened Samson's wife if she did not provide the answer, saying they would burn her and her father's house. The bride pestered Samson with tears until he told her the answer, which she promptly told the young men.

On the last day of the wedding feast, the Philistines gleefully produced the answer, and Samson was furious, knowing they had gotten the answer from his bride. He gained his revenge (and paid his debt) by killing thirty Philistines and taking the linen and garments from them. He then returned to his father's home, but he could not stop thinking about his Philistine wife. He sent a small goat to the girl's father as a peace offering, but the embarrassed father refused to let Samson see the woman. The father explained that he had assumed that Samson's rage meant he renounced the woman, so her father had then given her as a bride to the Philistine who had acted as best man at the wedding. Her father offered Samson her younger sister as a substitute, but Samson scorned this proposal and claimed that now he had good reason to revenge himself on his wife's people.

Samson caught three hundred foxes and tied them together by their tails. He then lighted torches between their tails and turned them loose into the Philistine wheat fields. The fires destroyed the harvest as well as vineyards and olive groves. Philistines asked in shock who had done this damage and were told that Samson had been getting even for what his wife's family had done to him. The incensed farmers took vengeance of their own by burning Samson's wife's house, killing the father and daughter within.

Again Samson reacted violently, killing many as reprisal. By now, what had started as a family incident at a wedding had escalated into a full-scale war. The Philistines sent an armed force into the territory of the tribe of Judah, demanding that Samson be handed over to them. But Samson could not be bound with ropes and he killed "thousands" of Philistines. The Philistines tried to find some way to trap Samson, and they looked for their opportunity in the strongman's weakness for women. Once, when Samson spent the night with a prostitute in town, the

men set up a trap near the city gates. Instead of waiting for the gates to open in the morning, Samson tore down the gates in the night and escaped. Samson could not escape his longing for Philistine women, however.

Samson next fell in love with Delilah, who lived in the valley near his hometown. A group of Philistine chiefs came to her and offered to pay her 1,100 silver pieces if she would persuade Samson to tell her the secret of his great strength so he might be captured. Delilah begged Samson to tell her his secret, and three times he told her lies, saying he could be captured by "seven fresh bowstrings" or "new ropes that have not been used" or "weaving the seven locks of my head with a web and making it tight with a pin" (Judg. 16:7–14). Each time, Delilah tried the secret and called in Philistines, and each time Samson broke free and proved he was as strong as ever.

Delilah continued to press Samson for his secret, saying "How can you say, 'I love you,' when your heart is not with me? You have mocked me these three times, and you have not told me wherein your great strength lies" (Judg. 16:15). Finally, Samson told her the truth: his strength lay in his long hair. This time when he slept Delilah had his head shaved, and when she summoned the Philistines, Samson was captured easily. They blinded him and bound him and set him to work as a slave pushing a millstone. But as he labored, his hair began to grow back.

Finally, the Philistines gathered in the temple of their god to celebrate the capture of their enemy, and as they feasted, they called for Samson to be brought in so they could make fun of him. The blind Israelite was led to the center of the temple, and he felt the two pillars that supported the roof. Samson prayed to God for strength and broke the pillars, killing the thousands of Philistines who were present and himself. His kinsfolk came to claim his body, and he was buried in the foothills of his childhood.

If the Philistines had written this account, Delilah would have emerged as the heroine who destroyed the enemy of her people. Instead, of course, the story was preserved by Hebrew authors. Thus, Delilah became remembered as a traitor who betrayed her lover and his people. Samson's first wife, too, became a symbol of a weak woman who could not keep a secret. Thus, in the literature of the West, Delilah represented a feminine danger that would destroy men who, like Samson, indulged their weakness for women.

See also Deborah; Jewish Women; Judith
Suggested Readings
Ball, Mieke. *Lethal Love: Feminist Literary Readings of Biblical Love Stories.* Bloomington: Indiana University Press, 1987.
Meyers, Carol, Toni Craven, and Ross S. Kraemer. *Women in Scripture.* New York: Houghton Mifflin, 2000.

Delphic Oracle

In all the religions of the ancient world, proper worship involved sacrificing a portion of human production to the gods. These sacrifices might be as small as a drop of wine or a small bit of food, or as large as a sacrificial animal—a goat, bird, or even an ox. A few societies (such as the Phoenicians) even offered human sacrifice as a way to persuade the gods to look kindly on their requests.

The ancient Greeks, too, shared this idea of sacrifice as the proper ritual behavior, but in contrast to the Mesopotamians and other ancient peoples, Greeks sacrificed things of relatively little value—thigh bones wrapped in fat or internal organs of sacrificial animals—while keeping the best parts for themselves. Furthermore, family, magistrates, and citizen assemblies were primarily responsible for observing proper respect for the gods. As a result, unlike the situation in Egypt and Mesopotamia, powerful religious institutions never developed in ancient Greek society. Each temple had a priest or priestess, but these were usually part-time activities requiring little training.

The real religious professionals were oracles—people who interpreted divine will. There were various means by which people believed they had received communication from a god—for example, drawing lots or reading signs drawn from the flames on Zeus's altar. At some shrines—particular the healing temples dedicated to Asclepius—an oracle would ask the god to send a prophetic dream about how to cure a specific illnesses. The most prestigious oracles, however, were those spoken by a priestess while she was in a trance. People believed that while an oracle was in this state, the god's voice spoke directly through her. (Occasionally male priests would prophesy in this way, but it was seldom.) Among these women, the Delphic Oracle was the most famous.

It seems that there was an oracle of Apollo at Delphi (see Map 4) as early as the ninth century B.C., and there are remains of a temple from the second half of the seventh century B.C. The oracle entered into a trance in the innermost sanctuary of the temple, which the ancient Greeks believed stood at the center of the world (the "navel" of the earth). According to Greek legend, Zeus had released two eagles to fly around the world—one from the east and one from the west—and they met at Delphi. Zeus set a stone there to mark this center spot, which was located in the temple's inner sanctum. Also within the temple's interior stood a laurel tree—sacred to the god. (Later Hellenistic tradition would claim that the oracle sat over a chasm from which vapors emerged from the earth to induce her trance, but that was absent in the early cult tradition.)

People who wanted to consult the oracle would come to the temple and pay a consultation fee and offer a sacrifice at the altar outside the temple. If this sacrifice seemed auspicious—that is, if the animal reacted properly before the sacrifice—then the petitioner could enter the temple. There he would offer a second sacrifice, depositing either a whole sacrificial victim or parts of one on the offering table in front of the inner sanctum. Then he was led to a waiting place by the interpreters (called the *prophetai*) where he could not see the oracle (called the *Pythia*).

To prepare herself for seeking a prophecy, the *Pythia* purified herself at a nearby spring, then burnt laurel leaves and barley meal on the altar inside the temple. Then, crowned with a laurel wreath, she sat on a tripod and became possessed by the god. Shaking a laurel, she prophesied under divine inspiration, in a state that modern psychologists might call a self-induced trance.

Scholars are uncertain about the exact form of the oracle's pronouncements. They may have been fragmentary phrases and words, or confused sentences. The *prophetai* then had to interpret these words into coherent, if ambiguous, responses. One would think people would be annoyed at such ambiguous responses, but the Greeks believed that imprecise messages were the nature of prophecy—that the gods do not want humans to have certain knowledge about the future. Thus, gods left some room for humans to misinterpret the messages. The *prophetai* often even offered the response in the form of a riddle, which increased the possibility for misunderstanding. However, if the *prophetai* were skilled enough to relay a correct message from the *Pythia,* and if the petitioner correctly guessed the meaning of the message, then everyone believed they had sound information directly from the gods. This seemed worth the cost and ambiguity.

Most of the petitions involved everyday questions. People asked whether they should marry a particular person, whether a woman would conceive and bear a son, or whether to travel on a certain day. Many sought advice about health issues or asked questions about their crops or financial fortunes. One of the most famous instances of a question posed to the Delphic Oracle was by an Athenian who asked who was the wisest man, and the oracle answered that it was Socrates. This prophecy reputedly set the famous philosopher on his quest to find someone wiser than he, and in the process he earned the reputation for wisdom that made him one of the most famous of the Greek philosophers.

Sometimes states asked the oracle what they should do in time of trouble. When confronted with the invasion of Persia, Athens sent to the oracle to find out what to do. The oracle said to take refuge behind "wooden walls." While many Athenians believed this meant to trust in the great wooden walls that surrounded the city, a leader was able to persuade the people that the oracle meant the "wooden walls" of ships. The city of Athens was evacuated, leaving Persians to burn it. This is given as one of the best examples of a correct interpretation of an ambiguous prophecy. Everyone was not so lucky in their assessment of the will of the gods.

Perhaps the most famous misinterpretation of an oracle's response was made by King Croesus of Lydia in about 546 B.C. Croesus was worried about Cyrus the Persian, who was threatening his kingdom, and asked the oracle whether he should wage war against Persia. The *prophetai* returned with the answer: If Croesus were to make war on the Persians, he would destroy a mighty empire. Croesus was elated, but he had misinterpreted the oracle—the mighty empire that fell was the Lydian one, as Cyrus defeated Croesus. Messages from oracles needed to be interpreted very carefully, indeed.

The Delphic Oracle served in her role for life. She was usually elderly, often a widow, who then remained chaste so that her powers would not be diluted by sexual intercourse. This series of anonymous women was among the most respected in ancient Greece, and people came great distances to consult with the women. Their pronouncements (as interpreted by male priests) often shaped the course of history.

See also Anna; Christian Women

Suggested Readings

Dempsey, T. *Delphic Oracle: Its Early History, Influence and Fall.* New York: B. Blom, 1972.

Fontenrose, Joseph. *Delphic Oracle: Its Responses and Operations.* Berkeley: University of California Press, 1978.

———. *Python: A Study of the Delphic Myth and Its Origin.* New York: Biblio and Tanner, 1974.

Demeter
Greek Goddess

Demeter was the Greek goddess of grain and other crops. In myth, she was considered the granddaughter of Gaia and sister of Zeus. Zeus fathered a child by Demeter, her beloved daughter Persephone, who was also known simply as Kore ("the maiden"). Mother and daughter were inseparable until Hades, Persephone's uncle and lord of the underworld, stole her away from her mother and took her to the underworld to be his wife.

Demeter was so distraught at the loss of her daughter that she searched the world for her. She took the disguise of an old woman and came to Eleusis, where she was welcomed by the family of King Celeus. She became the nurse of his baby son, Demophon, and tried to make the boy immortal by burning away his mortality. She was

Figure 23. Demeter, Greek goddess of corn and harvest, presenting corn to Triptolemus. (Ann Ronan Picture Library)

Persephone were the ceremonies of initiation known as the "mystery," which were celebrated all over the Greek world. The festivals were designed to bring fertility, and many of these festivals were secret and restricted to women. By far the most famous of these celebrations took place at Eleusis. The mysteries at Eleusis brought celebrants from all over the Greek-speaking world, but they were particularly favored by the Athenians. During the annual celebration, a procession went from Athens to Eleusis and culminated in a nocturnal celebration in the Hall of Initiations, which could hold thousands of the faithful. There the priest revealed "the holy things"—secret artifacts that the goddess herself was said to have brought.

Demeter was also said to have brought two gifts to humans. The first was grain, which formed the basis of a civilized, urban life. Beyond that, however, the goddess promised the hope of a happy afterlife for the initiates who had "seen" the mysteries. Priests promised initiates that death was nothing to be feared. Since Demeter rescued her daughter from the underworld, people hoped that they, too, could be rescued from death.

The gifts of Demeter—food, fertility, and hope—caused her to be a powerful goddess and much beloved of the people. She also represented the depth of the love of a mother for her daughter.

See also Ceres
Suggested Readings
Burkert, Walter. *Ancient Mystery Cults.* Cambridge: Harvard University Press, 1987.
Grimal, Pierre. *The Dictionary of Classical Mythology.* Oxford: Blackwell, 1996.

interrupted by Celeus's wife, so she could not complete the magic. Instead, she revealed her true identity and promised to endow Demophon with heroic honors. She told the Eleusinians to build her a temple and altar, and she withdrew to them to mourn for her lost Persephone. During her mourning, she brought a great famine, which threatened to destroy all humans.

Zeus was forced to intervene, and he told Hades to release Persephone, so she could return to the world. Her return was contingent upon her never having eaten of the food in the Underworld, but Hades had given her a pomegranate seed to eat. Therefore, Persephone had to return to Hades for four months every year, and during those months, Demeter caused all the crops to stop growing. With Persephone's return in the spring, however, Demeter was so happy that she restored the fertility of the fields, and she taught the princes of Eleusis the secret of agriculture.

The most important festivals of Demeter and

Diana

Roman Goddess

Diana was an ancient moon goddess and deity of the hunt and wilderness places in Italy. She was also associated with women and childbirth, although she was a virgin herself. Her most ancient cult center was at Aricia, on the shore of the volcanic Lake Nemi, which was known as Diana's Mirror. Her temple stood in a grove, and some myths said that her priest there had to be a runaway slave who must murder his predecessor. According to legend, one of the early kings of Rome—Servius Tullius—wanted to bring her cult to Rome, and he built an early temple there for her on the Aventine hill. Early in Rome's history, this popular goddess was associated with the Greek goddess Artemis, and the myths concerning Artemis were attributed to Diana.

Roman women particularly favored the worship of Diana, turning to the virgin goddess for help in childbirth and to protect their children. However, the goddess—with her silver bow—was said to bring death from natural causes to women just as her brother Apollo did to men. In spite of this aspect of the goddess, she remained one of the most popular among Roman women.

See also Artemis
Suggested Readings
Adkins, Lesley, and Roy A. Adkins. *Handbook to Life in Ancient Rome.* New York: Oxford University Press, 1994.
Grant, M. *Roman Myths.* London: Weidenfeld and Nicolson, 1971.
Grimal, Pierre. *The Dictionary of Classical Mythology.* Oxford: Blackwell, 1996.
Ogilvie, R. M. *The Romans and Their Gods.* London: Chatto and Windus, 1969.

Dido

Queen of Carthage (ca. 800 B.C.)

By the ninth century B.C., ships from the city-states of Tyre and Sidon in Phoenicia (on the eastern shore of the Mediterranean, shown on Map 5) sailed all over the Mediterranean Sea, bringing the whole region into a trading network with the ancient Middle East. The Phoenicians were driven as far away as Spain to trade; they were looking for such metals as gold, silver, copper, and tin, since their land had none. Ancient ships only sailed during the day and hugged the shore, so Phoenicians established colonies along the shore to provide safe landing spots for their merchant vessels. The most successful—and famous—of these colonies was founded by a Phoenician princess, Elissa, who is popularly remembered as Queen Dido. Her colony of Carthage would grow so powerful, it even challenged the power of Rome.

The story of the founding of Carthage is preserved in various legends, none of which can be confirmed with historical accuracy. Nevertheless, people of the ancient world credited the founding of Carthage to an indomitable woman. According to legend, there was a dynastic quarrel at Tyre, in the Phoenician homeland. Elissa, sister of King Pygmalion, married her uncle Acherbas, a priest of the god Melkart and a wealthy member of the royal house. Pygmalion had Acherbas killed, however, because the king wanted Acherbas's fortune. Accompanied by a number of people who were opposed to the king, Elissa escaped and sailed to Cyprus on her way to found a new colony where she could rule.

On Cyprus, she met the high priest of the goddess Astarte, who agreed to join her expedition on the condition that his family could continue to hold the high priesthood in the new land. Eighty virgins who had been identified to serve as sacred prostitutes in Cyprus also accompanied the party to marry and ensure that the new colony would grow in population. After Elissa left Cyprus, she wandered through the eastern Mediterranean for some time, and during this period she became known as Dido. Modern scholars have not been able to give a satisfactory derivation for this name, but the ancient writers called her a "wanderer" or a "virile woman." For subsequent history, however, the original Phoenician name, Elissa, has all but disappeared, to be replaced by Queen Dido.

The group finally landed on a peninsula offering a fine harbor on the coast of North Africa (see Map 7). Supposedly, local tribesmen objected to Dido's establishing a colony on their land, but the enterprising queen persuaded them to give her as much land as could be covered by one ox hide. However, when she began to shave the ox hide into extraordinarily thin strips, the tribesmen saw that they had been tricked. They agreed to give her the settlement by the shore that she wanted for fear that her skill with an ox hide would allow her to claim all of North Africa.

The dominant feature of Carthage (ancient and modern) is the Byrsa Hill—a high point that overlooks the ports. The word *Byrsa* seems to have been derived from the term *ox hide,* in memory of the founding legend of the skill of Dido. The whole city covered about seven square miles, with three sides protected by the sea. At the height of Carthage's power, the remaining sides had more than twenty-one miles of walls with parapets and towers. The center of the city lay near the busy and bustling ports that brought people and goods from all over the Mediterranean. Behind the center rose the Byrsa Hill, capped with a strong fortification that guarded the city. Dido's colony grew and prospered, but the queen herself came to an unhappy end.

According to legend, the king of the Libyans (a neighboring North African tribe) wanted to marry Dido. The queen, however, had vowed to stay true to the memory of her murdered husband, so she refused to marry again. To avoid her suitor, Dido pretended to preside over a religious ceremony that required a great fire for a sacrifice. Instead of marrying, she flung herself on the flames, committing suicide.

Carthaginians considered their queen's sacrifice to have served to bring prosperity to the colony, and throughout much of its history, Carthage preserved human sacrifice long after it had been abandoned elsewhere in the ancient world. Archaeologists have excavated a cemetery in Carthage where children were buried who had been offered as sacrificial victims to ensure prosperity. Between 400 and 200 B.C., as many as 20,000 sacrifices had been offered to the Carthaginian gods. The colony Dido founded demanded much from its citizens in exchange for the prosperity it offered.

The story of Dido gained popularity when the greatest of the Roman poets, Virgil, used it as a significant incident in his epic story of the founding of Rome—*The Aeneid.* In Virgil's fictional account, the hero, Aeneas, was a Trojan who had fled from the destruction of his city by the Greeks. He was Venus's favorite, so the goddess of love wanted to ensure that her champion would receive a warm welcome in Carthage—she made Dido fall in love with Aeneas. In Virgil's hands, Dido is a most sympathetic figure—he shows her as an honorable widow who had devoted herself to the memory of her murdered husband. She is lured to fall in love with Aeneas, however, and to break her oath of celibacy. She takes him as her husband and consort and shares her rule.

Aeneas's destiny lay elsewhere, however, according to the poet. Aeneas left Dido and continued his quest that would ultimately lead him to found the city of Rome. Virgil described Dido's response to her lover's departure in poignant terms, and here his epic returns to the legendary end of the queen: As Aeneas sails from Carthage, Dido builds and lights a huge funeral pyre, climbs on it, and stabs herself to death before the flames rise. Aeneas looks back and sees the pyre blazing, and he and his companions guess what has happened. Virgil offered a poetic reason for the great animosity between Carthage and Rome that would lead to three wars and the ultimate total destruction of Dido's city: a Carthaginian queen was scorned by a Roman adventurer. But Virgil also made sure that the memory of the enterprising woman from Tyre, who founded one of the greatest cities of the ancient world, would not die.

See also Prostitution, Sacred; Sophoniba
Suggested Readings
Grimal, Pierre. *The Dictionary of Classical Mythology.* Oxford: Blackwell, 1996.
Lancel, Serge. *Carthage: A History.* Oxford: Basil Blackwell, 1995.
Warmington, B. H. *Carthage: A History.* New York: Barnes and Noble, 1960.

Dinah

Hebrew Woman (ca. 1500 B.C.)

The Book of Genesis in the Bible treats the earliest history of the ancient Hebrews, spanning the time of approximately the beginning of the second millennium B.C. (from about 2000 to 1500). This book tells the history of the patriarch, Abraham, and his descendants, including his grandson Jacob. Jacob married two sisters, Rachel and Leah, and kept many concubines; consequently he fathered many children—twelve sons and one daughter. The many tribes of Israel traced their origins to this extensive family of Jacob, but the Bible also tells how the fortunes of his daughter, Dinah, led to violence in the ancient land.

Jacob's large family lived near tribes that were not Hebrews, and while the men worked hard at raising the flocks, Jacob and Leah's daughter

Dinah associated with the women of the neighboring peoples. Thus, she came to the notice of Shechem, the prince of the neighboring land, and he came to lust after her. He grabbed her and raped her, but in the process, he came to love her: His "soul was drawn to Dinah the daughter of Jacob; he loved the girl and spoke tenderly to her" (Gen. 34:3). Shechem then asked his father to talk to Jacob and obtain Dinah for his wife.

When Jacob heard that Dinah had been defiled, he was furious, but he could not take vengeance immediately for his sons were all out in the fields. When the sons returned, they too were outraged "because he had wrought folly in Israel by lying with Jacob's daughter, for such a thing ought not to be done" (Gen. 34:7). However, Shechem's father tried to appease them by offering marriage. Indeed, he suggested that the two tribes become one through many marriages: "Give your daughters to us, and take our daughters for yourselves. You shall dwell with us; and the land shall be open to you; dwell and trade in it, and get property in it" (Gen. 34:9–10). This exchange shows how important marriage ties were in the ancient world, for they could serve to unite whole peoples—their economies as well as their families.

Dinah's brothers were not willing to transcend the insult of the rape so readily, so they came up with a plan to deceive Shechem's tribe. They told the men they could not allow Dinah—or indeed any of their daughters—to marry a man who was uncircumcised. So, they said if all the men of Shechem's tribe would agree to be circumcised like the Hebrews, they would join as one people. Shechem and his father praised the idea: "Will not their cattle, their property and all their beasts be ours? Only let us agree with them, and they will dwell with us" (Gen. 34:23). So every male was circumcised in preparation for the marriages that would link the two peoples. Dinah's brothers were not willing, however, to let the original insult to their sister and their own pride go so easily.

When the men were still sore and weakened from the circumcisions, the sons of Jacob took their swords and attacked the city and killed Shechem, his father, and many men. They took the wealth of the inhabitants and their animals and all their possessions. Jacob reprimanded his sons for their deed, for he said this would cause other neighbors to come together and threaten Jacob's clan. The sons, however, gave this justification: "Should he treat our sister as a harlot?" (Gen. 34:31). In the violence, they believed their family honor was restored.

In this tale, readers are reminded that the men of the ancient world cared deeply about the virtue of their female relatives. We are never told what Dinah thought of the whole incident, for her sexuality is portrayed as a matter of her brothers' pride and property. It was also an economic matter for her prospective bridegroom, for marriage would link his people with the wealthy tribe of Jacob. Ancient women's sexuality was a public, not a private, matter.

See also Jewish Women; Rachel

Suggested Readings

Archer, L. J. *Her Price Is Beyond Rubies. The Jewish Woman in Graeco-Roman Palestine.* Sheffield, UK: Sheffield Academic Press, 1990.

Bird, P. "Images of Women in the Old Testament." In *Religion and Sexism: Images of Woman in the Jewish and Christian Traditions,* ed. by R. R. Ruether. New York: Simon and Schuster, 1974.

Meyers, Carol, Toni Craven, and Ross S. Kraemer. *Women in Scripture.* New York: Houghton Mifflin, 2000.

Sheres, Ita. *Dinah's Rebellion: A Biblical Parable for Our Times.* New York: Crossroad, 1990.

Diotima of Mantinea

Greek Philosopher and Priestess (ca. 415 B.C.)

One of the most famous of the Greek philosophers was Socrates (469–399 B.C.), who lived in Athens, where he spent his days in the streets and marketplaces talking to his neighbors. Socrates believed he had a divine mission to seek the truth by questioning all statements and urging people to aspire to the highest standards of good, beauty, and justice. Not everyone appreciated his probing questions, and eventually he was accused of corrupting the youth of Athens and of impiety (or denying the existence of the gods). He was brought to trial, and in one of the most famous cases in history, he was found guilty and sentenced to death. He bravely drank a bowl of poison hemlock, preferring to die rather than lead a life without questioning.

Socrates wrote nothing himself; but after his death, his favorite and most brilliant pupil, Plato (427–347 B.C.), established a school of philosophy in a place called the Academy—in an olive grove outside Athens. Plato then wrote his memories of what he had heard of the dialogues—the conversations—of his beloved teacher, Socrates, and it is primarily through the words of Plato that we know of Socrates's teachings. Throughout the dialogues, Plato identified the people—students of philosophy—who participated in discussions with Socrates and who served to stimulate the development of the thought of the great philosopher. Among the people Plato mentioned as talking to Socrates was Diotima, a woman who he claimed was responsible for shaping Socrates's (and his own) views on love.

Diotima appears in the dialogue called "The Symposium" (or "The Banquet"), which was purported to be a banquet that took place in the house of the poet Agathon in 416 B.C. This banquet was on the occasion of celebrating the poet's victory in a dramatic festival, and the story of the banquet—and its lively conversations—was recounted some fifteen years later. Plato recorded the discussion of the banquet, and within this dialogue he mentions the woman Diotima. According to the dialogue, the conversation had turned to the question of love and its nature. Socrates quoted Diotima's opinion on the subject: "There is a speech about Love which I heard once from Diotima of Mantineia, who was wise in this matter and in many others. . . . And she it was who taught me about love affairs" ("Symposium" 97). He further identified Diotima as a priestess and claimed that she managed to hold off the plague that struck Athens for about ten years. Socrates's long explanation of Diotima's philosophical position on love offers a complex view of the subject that is somewhat different from Plato's and Socrates's and gives insights into the development of Plato's ideas.

According to Socrates, Diotima said that love was neither fully beautiful nor good; instead it was located in a middle point between good and evil. Diotima further said that love was the child of lack (poros) and plenty (penia), which thus explained its position between good and evil, beautiful and foul. Love then served as one of the spirits that relayed messages and prayers between the gods and people: "For God mingles not with man; but through Love all the intercourse and converse of god with man, whether awake or asleep, is carried on" ("Symposium" 98). The priestess/philosopher said that Socrates had mistaken the idea of love with the idea of the beloved—"For the beloved is the truly beautiful, and delicate, and perfect, and blessed; but the principle of love is of another nature" (99). Therefore, love can cause anguish and pain. In this analysis, Diotima seems to depart from Plato's analysis of the Good as a perfect form—a Platonic idea.

Diotima also departs from Plato in her view of immortality. While Plato argued for the immortality of the soul, Diotima did not. She believed that people strive to be immortal by having their qualities survive in their offspring. She said, "Mortal nature seeks always as far as it can be to be immortal; and this is the only way it can, by birth, because it leaves something young in place of the old" ("Symposium" 102). Diotima expands her notion of pregnancy to include those who "are pregnant in soul" (101)—that is, those who conceive wisdom and virtue in general, and poets and craftsmen who produce beautiful things.

By using this imagery of procreation and growth, Diotima was led to develop a sense of how people progress to appreciate more abstract values. She said that at first—when people are young—they love and appreciate the beauty in one body. Then they grow to become lovers of all beautiful bodies, relaxing the intense passion felt for one. Then people learn that the beauty of souls is more precious than beauty in bodies and seek out people with beautiful souls. Finally, a person could turn his attention to beauty in its most abstract form—"beauty in different kinds of knowledge, and directing his gaze from now on towards beauty as a whole, . . . he should turn to the great ocean of beauty, and in contemplation of it give birth to many beautiful and magnificent speeches and thoughts in the abundance of philosophy" ("Symposium" 104). Thus, Diotima develops a philosophy that describes how love can lead people both to immortality through reproduction and to virtuous action through involvement in community.

While Diotima's ideas as they were expressed in Plato's "Symposium" represent fruitful areas of inquiry, much of modern scholarship has focused on the question of whether Diotima ever existed—some scholars argue that she was a fictional character invented by Plato to express ideas that belonged to himself or Socrates. The main arguments against her existence are as follows: (1) It was out of character for Plato to cast a woman in so central a role as Diotima holds, (2) Socrates could not have learned such important ideas from a woman, and (3) there is no reference to Diotima in sources other than "The Symposium." The arguments in favor of her existence include the following: (1) Diotima's ideas as presented in "The Symposium" are different from Plato's and Socrates's, so she represents a different philosophical position, suggesting that she existed; (2) Plato portrays Socrates learning from Diotima, which places a woman in the role of teacher, unusual for Plato; (3) Mary Ellen Waithe describes archaeological evidence—a carving—that shows Diotima speaking to Socrates, and if this carving predates "The Symposium," it might argue for the philosopher's existence (Waithe 103). The jury is still out, but certainly centuries of readers of Plato saw the priestess as a real, and important, philosopher.

It would appear that the great philosopher Socrates—who began his career of inquiry based on a prophecy by the Delphic Oracle (albeit interpreted by male priests)—turned to another priestess—Diotima—to learn about the nature of love. And he concluded his account of her speech by placing in her voice the greatest ideal of philosophy: "When he [a contemplator of beauty] has given birth to real virtue and brought it up, will it not be granted him to be the friend of God, and immortal if any man ever is?" ("Symposium" 106). Thanks to the dialogue of Plato, who preserved her words and ideas, the priestess and philosopher Diotima earned the kind of immortality that she promised Socrates.

See also: Delphic Oracle; Philosophers, Greek; Theano

Suggested Readings

Kersey, Ethel M. *Women Philosophers: A Bio-Critical Source Book.* New York: Greenwood Press, 1989.

"Symposium." In *Great Dialogues of Plato.* Trans. W. H. D. Rouse. New York: Mentor Books, 1965.

Waithe, Mary Ellen. *A History of Women Philosophers.* Vol 1: *Ancient Women Philosophers.* Boston: Martinus Nijhoff Publishers, 1987.

Dynamis

Queen of Bosporus (ca. 62 B.C.–A.D. 7)

In Bosporus, a kingdom on the Black Sea (see Map 7), lived an independent people who vigorously fought against the spreading power of the Roman Empire. During the late republic, the dictator Sulla earned much of his reputation by fighting repeated wars against Mithradates, the king of Bosporus. While Rome finally made Bosporus a client-kingdom, the independent spirit of the kings continued to be noted. One descendant of Mithradates—his daughter Dynamis—was a particularly effective and long-lived ruler of Bosporus while it was under the control of the Roman Empire.

In about 17 B.C., Bosporus was in a state of upheaval. A king had died, and a pretender to the throne named Scribonius declared that he had been given the right to rule by Caesar Augustus, the first Roman emperor. To secure his throne, Scribonius married the king's widow, Dynamis, who was an actual descendant of Mithradates. While Scribonius thus became ruler of Bosporus, his reign was not uncontested. Augustus must not have sanctioned Scribonius's rule, for his lieutenant Agreppa sent Polemo, the king of Pontus on the southern shore of the Black Sea (see Map 7), to attack Scribonius. Before Polemo could arrive, however, Scribonius was murdered by the Bosporans, leaving Dynamis as sole ruler of the country.

The queen, however, still faced the threat of the king of Pontus, and the greater threat was from the armies of Rome who were supporting Polemo. Finally, Dynamis realized that she could not hold out against the power of Rome, so she accepted marriage with Polemo, which united

Figure 24. Bronze bust of Queen Dynamis of Bosporus (Ann Ronan Picture Library)

purgus, the chief of a neighboring tribe. She married him, and the two challenged the armies of Polemo for the possession of Bosporus.

In the struggle that followed, Polemo was killed in 8 B.C. At this time, Dynamis seems to have become the sole ruler of Bosporus. That kingdom possessed the right to mint gold coins, and Dynamis did so, showing herself as the sole ruler of the kingdom. The bust in Figure 24 shows the queen wearing her royal headdress. In the statues she erected for herself, she called herself Empress and Friend of Rome, and this inscription shows the political sagacity that helped her stay on the throne. She knew that it would be foolish to fight Rome; it was better to rule with Roman support than not to rule at all.

Some historians suggest that Dynamis had the support of Augustus's influential wife, Livia, who frequently became involved in the political affairs of the empire. Dynamis had dedicated a statue of Livia in a temple of Aphrodite, and in the inscription calls the empress her own benefactress. Perhaps the highest form of compliment to the Roman empress lay in Dynamis's imitation of Livia's hairstyle, shown on her bust in Figure 24. Unfortunately, we do not have any correspondence that tells us the exact nature of the relationship between Livia and Dynamis; all we know is the Bosporus queen's success. She ruled until she died in about A.D. 7 at the age of seventy—a politically astute ancient ruler who knew how to preserve her sovereignty under the large shadow of the Roman Empire.

See also Livia
Suggested Readings
Macurdy, Grace Harriet. *Vassal-Queens and Some Contemporary Women in the Roman Empire.* Baltimore: Johns Hopkins University Press, 1937.

the two kingdoms. The Roman historian Dio Cassius claimed that Augustus did sanction this marriage, but he must not have exerted a very strong influence, for the union did not last long. Neither Dynamis nor her people liked Polemo, and the queen escaped and took refuge with As-

E

Egeria
Pilgrim (ca. A.D. 381)

In the fourth century A.D., there was a vibrant Christian life in the northwest province of the Iberian Peninsula (in modern Spain and northern Portugal). Travelers had come from the eastern Mediterranean to settle there, and groups of women lived together in early monastic communities. Most of the pious women from this time are anonymous; we know of them only from official references to their communities and from the remaining manuscripts that they copied. However, one fascinating exception to this anonymity is Egeria, an adventurous woman who left her home in northwest Iberia to travel as a pilgrim to the Holy Land in the eastern Mediterranean. The journey lasted about three years—from A.D. 381 to 384—and during her travels she wrote letters back to Iberia. These letters have survived to tell us much about life in the Holy Land during the fourth century and to offer a tantalizing glimpse into the life of this enterprising pilgrim.

We know little about Egeria herself, but we can make some assumptions from her letters. She addressed the correspondence affectionately to her "sisters," no doubt women with whom she lived in a loose-knit community. Furthermore, historians assume she came from an influential and wealthy family, for wherever she journeyed she was well received by such dignitaries as the Bishop of Edessa and the Bishop of Charrae, who both accompanied her personally to pilgrimage sites. Furthermore, when Egeria and her company moved through remote areas, they had an escort of Roman soldiers to guard them, and Egeria was able to ride comfortably throughout her travels.

As Map 9 shows, Egeria traveled first to Egypt and then crossed the Red Sea to the Sinai Peninsula. She said she wanted to retrace the steps of as many biblical figures as she could, and she began with what was reputed to be Mount Sinai where Moses stood and, as she wrote, "where the law was given, and the place where the Glory of the Lord came down on the day when the mountain was smoking." She was shown "everything which the Books of Moses tell us took place in that valley beneath holy Sinai, the Mount of God" (Salisbury 85). Egeria spent years visiting sites that ranged from the spectacular—the heights of Mount Sinai and Horeb—to the more modest, such as Jacob's reputed well where Rachel had drawn water. She continued to Jerusalem, where she visited churches, and her account represents one of the earliest surviving testimonies to the nature of early church services in the Holy Land.

From Jerusalem, Egeria took a side trip across the Dead Sea to visit Mount Nebo and nearby sites; then she traveled all the way up the valley of the Jordan River, seeing where Jesus was reputed to have been baptized. Finally, when it was time to go home, Egeria said she wanted to go by way of Constantinople to see the great cities of Edessa and Antioch. She recounts her travels through what is now Turkey, as she stopped at many famous shrines, including that of St. Thecla. She ended in Constantinople, where we assume she took a ship back home to the Iberian Peninsula.

By her travels, Egeria was claiming the biblical past and making it tangibly part of her own experience. In doing so, she was following in the tradition of Helena, the mother of Emperor Constantine, who was the first to locate the pilgrimage sites, and Egeria's account shows that by the fourth century there was a booming business in pilgrimage travel. Her guides throughout were careful to take her to all the famous biblical sites. Furthermore, Egeria's letters helped establish a precedent for other pilgrims to follow.

The young traveler did not limit her visits to archaeological sites; she was also fascinated by holy men and women who had retreated from society to live on its fringes. She was awed by their holy way of life, and she visited them in their small cells on the edge of the desert to talk to them and receive small souvenir gifts—apparently fruits or small loaves of bread.

Like many other travelers, Egeria enjoyed her journeys. She wrote vividly of the wonderful things she had seen and done, and these exuberant descriptions often had nothing to do with the spiritual good that she was presumably acquiring by her visits. She enthusiastically described the mountainous terrain and the fertile valleys and spoke cheerfully of the pleasant company that joined her in her travels. When it was time for her to return home, she stayed in order to make a detour to northwest Syria and Mesopotamia to prolong her travels.

It may be that Egeria's pleasure in travels generated some criticism. The church father, Jerome, who traveled the same pilgrimage route as Egeria some time after the Iberian's return, wrote a letter to a virgin in Italy warning her to avoid scandal. Jerome wrote: "I have lately seen a most miserable scandal traverse the entire East. The lady's age and style, her dress and mien, the indiscriminate company she kept, her dainty table and her regal appointments" (Salisbury 87) were more appropriate to an emperor's wife than a chaste virgin. While Jerome did not name the traveler, some historians have suggested that his description suited Egeria, an indomitable, independent woman, whose travel accounts have delighted readers for more than a thousand years.

See also Helena; Rachel; Thecla
Suggested Readings
Gingras, George E., trans. *Egeria: Diary of a Pilgrimage.* New York: Newman Press, 1970.
Salisbury, Joyce E. *Church Fathers, Independent Virgins.* London: Verso, 1991.

Egyptian Women

The river valley of the Nile spawned one of the earliest settled civilizations in the ancient Middle East. The river flooded annually, leaving a rich layer of fertile mud that allowed abundant crops to grow. Around 3000 B.C., a king united the small political units that had grown up along the Nile, and he created a unified kingdom that would persist for millennia. The regular flooding of the Nile and the usual abundance of the harvest convinced the Egyptians that for the most part nature had blessed them and would continue to do so, so they tended to be confident and optimistic. Egyptian art usually emphasized the good things of this world, the pleasures of the moment, and the expectation that for the rulers at least, the good life would continue into the next world after death.

Once established, Egyptian civilization remained remarkably constant over the centuries. While change did occur, it was by no means as rapid as in other places. In fact, the Egyptians consciously tried to maintain the world as they knew it, for they believed it was excellent. Their primary concern was to preserve the order that blessed their world. They had a concept called *maat,* which can be translated variously as "truth" and "justice" and "righteousness," and they wanted to preserve *maat* to prevent any chaos or disruption from interfering with their lives. They depended on their king—their pharaoh—who was seen as a divine being, a god incarnate, to ensure that justice remained in the land. All Egyptians were subject to the pharaoh's orders, and the royal family grew rich from the taxes paid by their grateful subjects.

In this stable society, women had a good deal of independence by the standards of the ancient world. The fifth-century B.C. Greek historian Herodotus wrote with surprise at the freedom of Egyptian women: "The Egyptians in most of their manners and customs, exactly reverse the common practice of mankind. The women attend the markets and trade, while the men sit at home at the loom" (Tyldesley 1). Herodotus overstated the case in his surprise at seeing women in the marketplace, for in most ancient portrayals of Egyptian women they were shown as dutiful wives, daughters, and mothers. While women could function in some public roles (unlike their Greek counterparts), the heart of their role was at home within the family. That was an important role, however, for the ancient Egyptians, from the humblest peasant to the pharaoh himself, treasured family life. Thus, wives and mothers were accorded a good deal of status.

Family Life

Through their paintings, carvings, and love songs, the ancient Egyptians showed that they valued, indeed treasured, married life. A writer in the third millennium B.C. left a list of recommendations for a good life, and he included a comment on marriage: "If you are prosperous you should establish a household and love your wife as is fitting. Fill her belly and clothe her back. Oil is the tonic for her body. Make her heart glad as long as you live" (Tyldesley 45). Evidence suggests that many shared this assessment of the joys of family life. A typical family unit probably included a husband and wife, their children, a husband's widowed mother, and any of his unmarried sisters, and many scenes show these extended families enjoying each other's company. Figure 25 shows Pharaoh Akhenaten and his wife Nefertiti playing with their daughters. The father is showing the daughter affection, and the poses are all relaxed. This portrayal of the royal family seems typical of the attitudes of other ancient Egyptian families.

Remarkably from our point of view, there seems to have been no formal marriage ceremony to bind families. It appears that simply the cohabitation of the couple marked the establishment of a new household. A young woman left her father's home with all her possessions—the "goods of a woman," as the texts say—which might have included a bed, clothing, jewelry, mirrors, a musical instrument, and other items. She then marched in great ceremony to her new home. Even though wives enjoyed the protection of their new husbands, they were allowed to continue to administer their own property, accumulate their own wealth, and retain legal rights. This legal independence was unusual in the ancient world and probably contributed to Herodotus's assessment of Egyptian women's independence.

Figure 25. Akhenaten, Nefertiti, and three of their daughters (Erich Lessing/Art Resource, NY)

Death rates in ancient Egypt were high, and marriages were frequently ended by the death of one partner. Young girls who married much older men were often widowed in their teens. However, it was equally common for widows and widowers to enter second marriages, and in fact some tombstones indicate that some people married three or even four times. Even after the death of a beloved partner, people sought to renew the pleasures of family life.

Divorce was permitted in Egyptian society, although it was without a doubt a serious matter. But just as marriages were conducted without ceremony, divorces, too, were equally simple. A wife could simply take her possessions back to her family home, and the marriage was severed. At times, however, there were disputes about property, and these were settled by the legal system. Some wealthy couples had the foresight to draw up a marriage contract, so they remained bound by the terms, but if not, the parties had to submit their disputes to judges. There were many reasons for divorce, from mutual incompatibility to one party's having fallen in love with someone else. At times men repudiated their wives because of infertility, but the Egyptian sources reveal that men were repeatedly told that they should not do so.

For all that marriage was valued, it was not uncommon for men to keep concubines. Pharaohs certainly married several women as well as keeping concubines, and by late in Egypt's history, the royal household included a harem populated by the king's wives and concubines. Egyptian men could also take advantage of the services of prostitutes, and some contemporary ancient societies believed that there were more prostitutes in Egypt than elsewhere, although that was probably reputation more than fact.

Women's Work

As we might expect, the most important job for women was to care for the needs of the household. In fact, the married woman's most coveted title was "mistress of the house," which showed the importance of her domestic role. One second-millennium B.C. scribe reminded men to trust their wives to run the household efficiently and not check on them or argue with them: "Do not control your wife in her house when you know she is efficient. Do not say to her 'Where is it? Get it' when she has put something in its correct place" (Tyldesley 82). This recognizes the complexities of household management and the important role of the wife within it.

Meals were, of course, essential to the well-being of the family, and the mistress of the house was charged with both purchasing the food and preparing it. Bread was the most important food prepared by the Egyptian housewife, and this was a daunting task. The wife and her servants had to grind the grain by hand to produce flour, which was then mixed with salt and water (or at times leavened with yeast) and cooked on a flat stone over a fire made by burning animal dung. Along with bread, the family ate various vegetables, fish, and occasionally meat. Women and men were also responsible for brewing large vats of homemade beer, which was also a staple of households. The wealthy could buy wine to go with their meals.

Although women were responsible for the households, many also worked in some capacity outside the home. Many did so to augment the family income, and the positions available to them had to do with their connections. Poor women would work as servants helping in oth-

ers' homes, while some talented women earned a good living as musicians and singers. Artistic evidence shows that women participated in agriculture, harvesting in the fields and winnowing grain.

During most of Egypt's history, the basic material for clothing, sheets, and blankets was linen. Linen was also an important component in the process of mummification, since huge amounts were used to wrap and pad the body. The manufacture of linen was therefore a major industry in Egypt. From the earliest years, women seem to have been responsible for weaving and supervising the manufacture on a large scale. Over the years, a number of women held the important title "overseer of the house of weavers," which suggests that women held managerial responsibilities in this industry. Large workshops produced great amounts of finely woven linen throughout ancient Egypt, and although the sources of information are scanty, we can assume that women continued to take a leading role in this industry.

A final profession that was dominated by women was that of mourner. These specialists were hired to enhance the status of the deceased by openly grieving at the funeral. They would wail loudly and make ostentatious displays of grief: beating exposed breasts, smearing their bodies with dirt, and tearing their hair. The women shown in Figure 26 were official mourners. The lines on their cheeks were to symbolize the tears they shed, and their dresses are colored gray-blue, perhaps to show the dust that the women have thrown over their heads to express their grief. Some women may have acted as mortuary priests and would have received payment for ensuring that the tomb of the deceased was well maintained. In a society that gave great value to the passage to the next world, mourners were highly valued and relatively well paid.

Royal Women

Just as family ties were centrally important to average Egyptians, they were equally important to the ruling household. The word *pharaoh*, which we usually use to mean "king," actually meant the "great house"—the king, his family, and administrators—that governed the land and

Figure 26. Tomb painting of mourning women (Museum of Fine Arts, Boston. William Francis Warden Fund, 68.555)

individual women involved. Some women—such as Queen Tiy—exerted immense influence while remaining within the traditional family structure. Others, such as Queen Hatshepsut, ruled completely alone, taking on the image and activities of a king. Occasionally, queens ruled as regents in the name of very young sons who inherited the throne.

A century ago, Egyptologists looked at these royal marriage patterns and the influence of some powerful royal women and concluded that pharaohs gained their throne through the maternal line, inheriting their divinity through their mothers. This has been shown to be incorrect, for sometimes kings married nonroyal women, yet kept their divine kingship. However, the misunderstanding does show that scholars recognized the importance of family in the ancient Egyptian royal families; in fact, the history of Egypt is divided into "dynasties" that show the lineage. Within these families, royal women sometimes exerted far more power than was customary in the ancient world.

brought order to it. (The word *pharaoh* always refers to the king himself as the embodiment of the full administration.) In this system, although kings had immense power, the women of the household also were able to exert a good deal of influence and independence. While kings could have many wives and concubines, they nevertheless had one woman as their main consort, and not infrequently they selected a family member—sister or half-sister—to fill this role. In this way, they imitated the brother-sister marriage of the deities Isis and Osiris and at the same time kept their own divinity in the family.

The most influential royal women could thus claim to have many titles: "king's daughter," "king's wife," and with luck and longevity, "king's mother." The royal consort was depicted with her husband fulfilling official ritual duties, and the sources indicate that sometimes these women engaged in correspondence with foreign dignitaries. Beyond these general roles, however, the actual working out of power relationships within the royal households depended upon the

Appearance

Egyptian men and women alike cared much for their appearance and spent time and resources on clothing, jewelry, and makeup. Perhaps for practical reasons of cleanliness and heat, men and women shaved their heads and bodies. Some women's tombs have many items for hair removal, such as tweezers, knives, razors, and whetstones, suggesting that the process of remaining free of hair was time-consuming. Figure 27 shows a princess with a neatly shaved head, and we assume that in the privacy of their homes they went without wigs or hats. Bodily cleanliness was also important, and although they did not have soap, they bathed with ashes and soda to get clean. Egyptian medical texts also gave recipes to "expel stinking of the body of a man or woman: ostrich-egg, shell of tortoise are roasted and the body is rubbed with the mixture" (Tyldesley 148). The wealthy would add expensive oils and perfumes to the daily routine.

Upper-class men and women who shaved their heads wore wigs and headdresses of varying kinds for ceremonial occasions. The mourners shown in Figure 26 are wearing wigs with the ends fringed into small ringlets, and the royal family shown in Figure 25 wear headdresses. Small children had their heads shaved but kept one sidelock of hair growing on the side of their heads. (The royal children shown in Figure 25 show this style.) The most elaborate wigs were made of human hairs, and the worst were made of coarse red date-palm fiber. Styles of wigs changed more rapidly than other elements of Egyptian society, favoring everything from straight locks to curly Nubian-style wigs (see Figure 77, page 352, showing Queen Tiy wearing a Nubian wig).

Men and women alike wore a good deal of makeup, imagining it offered health as well as beauty benefits. Eye paint was used, and Figure 27 shows the preferred style of eye makeup with a line extending to the temple. People believed that black color applied to the rims, lashes, and brows and lining the eye would reduce glare from the sun and thus lessen the chances of eye infections. Women also used powdered rouge for their cheeks and occasionally lip color. Prostitutes, professional dancers, and acrobats who performed with few clothes used tattoos to catch people's attention.

Nudity was not considered shocking. For example, fishermen worked naked as did others who labored outdoors. Upper classes, however, took some pride in wearing elegant garments of white linen. During most of Egypt's history, women wore a tight-fitting sheath, but during the time of Queen Nefertiti (called the Amarna period) when many conventions were overturned, women—including the queen—were depicted either naked or wearing casually unfastened robes that left the breasts and belly nude. Late in Egypt's history, women's clothing became elaborately pleated. The mourners in Figure 26 (page 95) wear simple linen dresses tied under their breasts, and these indicate the ways simple linen could be folded and worn. Finally, during cool Egyptian nights, women wore simple shawls over their dresses.

Plain white garments provided the perfect background for colorful and varied jewelry popular with men, women, and children of all classes. Mass-produced beads were inexpensive and brightened the costumes of almost anyone,

Figure 27. Head of a princess (Foto Marburg/Art Resource, NY)

while the wealthy wore jewelry of exquisite craftsmanship made of precious metals and stones. Egyptians fully expected to wear their jewelry in the afterlife, so much was buried with the dead. This led to a brisk traffic in grave robberies that was condemned throughout the dynastic periods. Yet they continued, and the very workmen who carefully buried the gold-encrusted coffins broke into the tombs later to strip the gold. Just as makeup was perceived to have medicinal value, jewelry, too, seemed to have value other than simply decorative. Fish ornaments, for example, were supposed to protect young girls from drowning, and green turquoise was to protect the wearer from all ills.

The trade in jewelry, makeup, cloth, and other elements for personal use reflected the importance Egyptians placed on enjoying a pleasurable life on earth and continuing it in the afterlife. This was a rich kingdom that lasted for two thousand years, and part of its success lay in its ability to provide a good life for many of its citizens. Events to the north, however, were to interrupt and eventually bring down the gracious society of dynastic Egypt. First the Assyrians, then the Persians, conquered Egypt and set up dynasties of their own. It was the conquest of the Macedonian Alexander the Great in the fourth century B.C. that introduced a strikingly new element to Egyptian culture. A new dynasty was established—the Ptolemaic—that consciously tried to bring Greek culture to combine with Egyptian. These Hellenistic rulers introduced the last stage of ancient Egyptian culture before its conquest by Rome.

Hellenistic Egypt of the Ptolemies

When Alexander died in 323 B.C., his generals immediately began to fight among themselves to take over his empire. None was able to prevail, and Alexander's lands were divided among his generals. The most able of them was Ptolemy, who returned to Egypt to claim that wealthy, ancient land as his own. He introduced a new Macedonian dynasty that was to rule Egypt for almost 300 years. The Ptolemies kept many of the trappings and traditions of the old pharaohs—they worshiped Egypt's deities, paid Egypt's priests, and wore the double crowns of upper and lower Egypt during ceremonial occasions. They also introduced some changes into the ancient culture—they brought the Greek language to the court, and they encouraged the settlement of Greeks and others into the Egyptian cities. Perhaps most significant, they fostered the growth of Alexandria, the city in the Nile Delta that had been founded by Alexander. These changes shifted the traditional patterns of the Egyptian ruling classes, and in the process made way for women to have more independence than they ever had before in the ancient world.

The most visible of the newly powerful women were the queens themselves. Like the ancient Egyptian queens, they controlled their own wealth, but their riches were even more substantial. Ptolemaic queens made an impact as they spent money for public works and private enterprises. As had their dynastic Egyptian counterparts, many of the Ptolemies married their siblings. The first to do so was Arsinoë II, who married and shared power with her brother Ptolemy II (266–262 B.C.). She was no figure-head consort; she exerted a strong influence that served as a model for many subsequent Ptolemaic queens. Some queens ruled solely in their own names, and they faced less controversy over the issue than their ancient Egyptian counterparts, such as Hatshepsut, had confronted. The height of the Hellenistic queens of Egypt came with the last one, Cleopatra VII, who challenged the power of Rome itself through its leaders Julius Caesar and Mark Antony.

Many women outside the royal family also benefited from the Macedonian rule. Surviving records on papyrus show that an unusual number of women owned land and other property in their own names. While most gained the land through inheritance, they nevertheless managed the estates and built and used the wealth they generated. Control of riches inevitably brought the possibility for independence.

Some women even were able to take advantage of an emphasis on education that came with the Macedonian rulers, who wanted to make sure there was a literate, Greek-speaking bureaucracy in place to manage its affairs. The royal princesses were literate and schooled in the palace, and it is likely that other noble girls joined the princesses in the classrooms. We also have small statues showing young girls working with writing slates, so that suggests that there were opportunities for other young women to learn to read and write. The fruits of these educational opportunities show in the exceptional women who became philosophers and artists in Alexandria and beyond.

In Alexandria and other Hellenistic great cities, less wealthy women were visible working in the shops and squares as they earned a living for themselves. The sources refer to a number of jobs that were specifically women's work. The most obvious was employment as wet nurses—nursing mothers who would be employed to breast-feed wealthy infants along with their own. One surviving contract for a wet nurse from the beginning of the Ptolemaic period shows that this employment was looked on as a highly formal arrangement. The woman was to serve as a wet nurse for a boy for three years (an unusually long time for nursing in the ancient world, in which women usually nursed children for two years). The wet nurse contracted to provide milk from both breasts, and in exchange she received her room and board, a decent salary, and a measure of oil each day.

Other professional women worked in food preparation and selling in shops, but the greatest numbers were employed in clothing manufacture. Just as in ancient Egypt, many women worked in large shops making linen out of flax, but the Macedonians introduced a large demand for wool clothing—the traditional Greek textile. One enterprising Greek wrote that in 250 B.C. he employed a total of 784 women making wool for him in three different villages. The pay was extremely low and must have served as a supplement to the rural family's farm income.

In general, during the Ptolemaic period in Egypt, there was much less distinction between the genders than there had been in classical Greek society from an earlier period (with the exception of Spartan women). Hellenistic women controlled property, participated in the booming Egyptian economy, became involved in the cultural life of the great cities, and mingled in the marketplaces. It was perhaps fitting that the final influential symbol of this society was a woman—Queen Cleopatra VII—under whose rule the kingdom finally came under control of the Roman Empire, ending the history of an independent ancient Egypt.

See also Arsinoë II; Cleopatra VII; Clothing; Cosmetics; Hatshepsut; Jewelry; Nefertiti; Philosophers, Greek; Prostitution; Tiy

Suggested Readings

Capel, Anne K., and G. E. Markoe, eds. *Mistress of the House, Mistress of Heaven: Women in Ancient Egypt.* New York: Hudson Hills Press, 1996.

Macurdy, Grace. *Hellenistic Queens.* Baltimore: Johns Hopkins University Press, 1932.

Pomeroy, Sarah B. *Women in Hellenistic Egypt from Alexander to Cleopatra.* New York: Schocken Books, 1984.

Tyldesley, Joyce. *Daughters of Isis: Women of Ancient Egypt.* New York: Penguin Books, 1994.

Watterson, B. *Women in Ancient Egypt.* New York: St. Martin's Press, 1991.

Electra

Legendary Greek Woman

Electra was the daughter of Agamemnon and Clytemnestra in the legendary tale about Clytemnestra's murder of Agamemnon upon his return from the Trojan Wars. Although Homer did not mention Electra, among the writers of Greek tragedy she assumed a central role in the drama of murder and revenge. Aeschylus, Sophocles, and Euripides all present her as fanatically hostile to her mother and deeply attached to her dead father. Freud in the late nineteenth century was so taken with her characterization that he used the name "Electra complex" to refer to a woman's fixation on her father. Here is the story of this single-minded legendary woman.

Clytemnestra and Agamemnon had three children: a son, Orestes, and two daughters, Electra and Iphigenia. The latter had been sacrificed to ensure a good sailing wind for the fleet going to Troy, and the other two were raised in the palace while Clytemnestra took her lover Aegisthus. On the evening of Agamemnon's return, during the carnage of the murder of the king and his followers, Electra feared that Aegisthus would kill her brother, Orestes, to prevent his growing up and taking revenge. She wrapped him in a robe embroidered with wild beasts, which she herself had woven, and smuggled him out of the city. Orestes hid for a while but then escaped and was raised far from home.

Aegisthus was afraid to let Electra marry for fear that she might bear a son who would avenge Agamemnon, and therefore he would not accept any of the many suitors from among the leading princes of Greece. He would gladly have destroyed Electra—who hated her stepfather and showed it at every opportunity—but Clytemnestra would not allow Electra's death. She did allow Aegisthus to marry her daughter to a peasant, who never consummated the marriage.

Electra lived in poverty and comparative obscurity, but she never forgot her anger at her mother. She called Aegisthus and Clytemnestra "murderous adulterers" and sent frequent messages to Orestes reminding him that he had to exact vengeance. Finally, seven years later (and some writers say twenty years later), Orestes secretly went to Mycenae to seek his revenge. His first stop was at the tomb of Agamemnon, where he cut off a lock of his hair and vowed revenge.

Meanwhile, Clytemnestra had had a terrible

dream of destruction, and she sent slave-women to the tomb to bring offerings and appease the dead. Among this party was Electra. She counteracted the prayers of conciliation offered by the slave-women and instead offered prayers for vengeance. She noticed the lock of blond hair on the tomb and decided it must have belonged to Orestes, since it so resembled her own. She followed his footsteps, and when he emerged from his hiding place, he showed her that it was his hair, and he produced the robe in which he had escaped from Mycenae so many years before.

Electra was delighted, and together they planned their revenge. With Electra's help, Orestes entered the palace in disguise, and when Aegisthus was off guard, Orestes killed him and Clytemnestra. Although the Greeks expected Orestes to avenge his father, matricide was a different story. Orestes and Electra were brought to trial.

Meanwhile, Menelaus and Helen arrived. Helen was ashamed to mourn in public for her sister Clytemnestra, since she herself had caused so much bloodshed by her own infidelities. She asked Electra to take a lock of her hair to Clytemnestra's tomb and pour libations to her ghost. Electra, believing that Helen had been too vain to cut more than a small end of hair, refused to take the offering and told Helen to send her own daughter, Hermione, instead. Menelaus entered the palace and called for both Orestes and Electra to be stoned to death as matricides. The judges decreed suicide for Orestes, Electra, and Pylades, Orestes's friend and now Electra's fiancé.

Electra waited outside the walls to capture Hermione on her return from Clytemnestra's tomb in order to hold her as a hostage to save them. Orestes and Pylades entered the palace to kill Helen, who they believed had caused all the trouble in the first place. Apollo intervened to stop the bloodshed and saved Helen. (Some stories say Apollo swept her to Olympus, where she became immortal.) Apollo also saved Hermione and decreed that she should marry Orestes and that Orestes and Electra were forgiven the crime of matricide.

In the final trial, Apollo argued that the motherhood was not important, asserting that a woman was inconsequential in reproduction for it was the man's seed that grew into a child. Therefore, he said that Orestes and Electra were justified in killing their mother to avenge their father, because the father was the more important parent. Athena voted in favor of Orestes as well, breaking a tie vote of the Athenian jurors. Although Electra's rage was vindicated, this story confirmed the rule of patriarchy in ancient Greek society.

See also Clytemnestra; Helen of Troy in Greek Mythology

Suggested Readings

Grimal, Pierre. *The Dictionary of Classical Mythology.* Oxford: Blackwell, 1996.

Lefkowitz, Mary R. *Women in Greek Myth.* Baltimore: Johns Hopkins University Press, 1986.

Elen Luyddog

British Empress (ca. A.D. 380)

In the fourth century A.D., Britain consisted of a number of Celtic tribes ruled by their local chiefs. The overarching authority, however, was the Roman Empire, which had conquered Britain centuries before. The Romans represented both an occupying army and a population that began increasingly to marry the local Celts and settle down. In this environment, sometimes local Celtic women shared the power of the Romans. This was true of the fourth-century Celtic princess, Elen Luyddog.

Elen was the daughter of a British chieftain who ruled in southwest Britain. Her father arranged an excellent match for his daughter— she was wedded to a Roman soldier named Magnus Maximus, who originally came from the Iberian Peninsula. Magnus had been stationed in Britain and became a commander who led his armies to many military victories in Britain. Praising his victories, his loyal soldiers acclaimed him emperor, and he gave Elen the comparable high status of empress. The soldier-emperor crossed the channel into Gaul and through more successful battles forced the eastern emperor, Theodosius, to acknowledge him as coemperor.

Magnus and Elen established a court in Gaul, where the empress set up an elaborate household. Elen surrounded herself with the leading scholars of the day and came to know the renowned Christian Martin of Tours (ca. A.D. 315–399), with whom she enjoyed long talks about religious philosophy. The sources say that she took a leading role in cultivating the court's intellectual life while at the same time raising many children. The pleasant life in Gaul was not to last, however. Magnus was ambitious, and in A.D. 387 he crossed the Alps to invade Italy. He was captured and executed in A.D. 388.

Wisely avoiding the subsequent turmoil, Elen left Gaul and returned to Britain, where she and her children influenced the religious and political development of the island. Elen began the missionary work of bringing Christianity to the pagan Britons, although this work would not fully bear fruit until after her death. She is credited with a more immediate contribution: she seems to have recognized both the possibility and importance of drawing the southern island together. Therefore, she was reputed to have initiated the building of roads across Britain, a significant improvement in transportation and communication.

Her sons became Celtic kings over many tribes, and her daughter, Sevira, married Vortigern, the king of Britain who first invited the Anglo-Saxons into the island. All subsequent kings of Celtic Britain and the Isle of Man traced their lineage and legitimacy to this remarkable woman.

See also Boudicca; Cartimandua; Eudocia
Suggested Readings
Ellis, Peter Berresford. *Women in Celtic Society and Literature.* Grand Rapids, MI: W. B. Eerdman's Publishing, 1995.

Elissa
See Dido

Elizabeth
Jewish Woman (ca. A.D. 1)
The Gospel of Luke in the Bible begins with a description of an elderly couple, Zechariah and Elizabeth. Both were of priestly descent, and Zechariah served as a Jewish priest. Both were "righteous before God, living blamelessly ac-

cording to all the commandments and regulations of the Lord" (Luke 1:6). They were unhappy, however, because they had no children. In the ancient Jewish culture, for a woman to be childless was a sign of God's disfavor, so the elderly couple were saddened by their state.

One day, when Zechariah was in the temple, the angel Gabriel terrified him by appearing and announcing that Elizabeth would conceive a son. Zechariah responded with doubt, and Gabriel punished the old priest by making him speechless until the child's birth. The angel did not appear to Elizabeth, but once she conceived, she was delighted, believing the Lord now looked favorably upon her and took away the disgrace she had endured. She then secluded herself within her house for five months.

In the next section of the story, Gabriel announced to Mary that she would conceive by divine visitation. Gabriel proclaimed to Mary the miracle of Elizabeth's pregnancy as proof of God's great works, and the angel promised that Mary's own conception would be an even greater miracle than Elizabeth's. Mary paid a visit to Elizabeth, Mary's relative, offering us an example of the mutual support women in the ancient world gave one another.

When Elizabeth heard Mary's voice, her infant son, John, leaped in her womb, and Elizabeth was filled with the Holy Spirit. She pronounced to Mary, "Blessed are you among women, and blessed is the fruit of thy womb!" (Luke 1:42). She further proclaimed that Mary carried her Lord, and this was the first confession in the Gospel that Jesus was the coming Lord. Mary stayed with Elizabeth for three months before returning to her home.

Elizabeth delivered a son, and on the eighth day, when he was to be circumcised, the neighbors wanted to name the child Zechariah after his father. But Elizabeth said no, he was to be named John. The neighbors asked the father, and since he had still not found his voice, he asked for a writing tablet and wrote, "His name is John." Then his voice returned to him and he foretold how his son would be the prophet for the coming Lord. The young John grew up to be John the Baptist and prepare the way for Jesus' ministry.

See also Mary
Suggested Readings
Meyers, Carol, Toni Craven, and Ross S. Kraemer. *Women in Scripture.* New York: Houghton Mifflin, 2000.

Enheduanna

Akkadian Priestess and Poet (ca. 2354 B.C.)

The earliest western civilizations developed in Mesopotamia—the region between the Tigris and Euphrates Rivers, where agriculture first developed in about 3000 B.C. (See Map 1.) Cities grew in that region, and they competed with each other for power and resources. Each city worshiped its own god or goddess, who seemed particularly to protect the residents of its city. In about 2350 B.C., a great king of the Akkadians—Sargon I—conquered a large portion of the region and established an empire throughout the Tigris-Euphrates valley and up into modern Turkey. Sargon faced the problem of how to unite the peoples of his expanded kingdom, and not surprisingly for the ancient world, he chose religion as the unifying principle. He assigned that task to his daughter Enheduanna, who performed the job with astonishing creativity and success.

Enheduanna served as high priestess of the Sumerian goddess Inanna—the queen of heaven, and she also fused this worship with the praise of the Sumerian goddess Ishtar. The advocacy of the supremacy of Inanna over the other gods served as a religious counterpart to Sargon's political empire. Enheduanna as priestess is shown in Figure 28; she is the second figure from the left, and she wears the elaborate feathered gown of a priestess. She stands behind a nude male priest who pours an offering on an altar in front of a stepped structure (probably representing a Ziggurat, the stepped pyramids of Mesopotamian worship). Enhaduanna is followed by two priestesses—one holding a wand and another a jug for worship. She proved so successful in joining the worship of the favorite goddesses, thus linking people's political loyalties to some degree, that Sargon's successors continued the practice of making their daughters high priestesses and thus forging a link between the cultures of the region. This political and religious

accomplishment is remarkable enough, but Enheduanna distinguished herself in another way. She wrote magnificent poetry in praise of Inanna, and this poetry has survived today, making Enheduanna one of the earliest authors of literature whose name has survived.

Her most famous poems are her cycle of three hymns to Inanna. In these hymns, we can glimpse the religious feelings of the ancient Sumerians and also see the transformation of religious interests on the part of her poetic priestess Enheduanna.

In the first hymn, "The Myth of Inanna," Enheduanna almost exclusively celebrates the goddess's power—she is portrayed as a fierce warrior goddess who crushed the people of Mt. Ebih:

> Since it [Ebih] didn't kiss the ground in front of me,
> Nor did it sweep the dust before me with its beard,
> I will lay my hand on this instigating country:
> I will teach it to fear me!
> . . .
> I'll bring war [to Ebih], I'll instigate combat,
> I'll draw arrows from my quiver,
> I'll unleash the rocks from my sling in a long salute,
> I'll impale it [Ebih] with my sword.
> (Hallo 21)

This hymn may refer to a historical event commemorating one of Sargon's triumphs, and if so, it serves as a perfect fusion of political and religious propaganda promoting the rule of Sargon and Inanna. His priestess-daughter served her function beautifully.

The poetess departs from this traditional warlike function of the goddess in her second hymn—"Stout-Hearted Lady"—for in this her principal theme is Inanna's omnipresent role in human affairs. Once the political conquest is over, the goddess and the ruler are involved in governing. In this poem, we can also see Enheduanna's relationship with the goddess, for she introduces herself in the poem: "I am Enheduanna, the en-Priestess of Nanna," and she tells

Figure 28. Limestone disk of Enheduanna at worship, ca. 2300 B.C. (The University Museum, University of Pennsylvania)

her own role: "My lady, I will proclaim your greatness in all the lands and your glory! Your way and great deeds I will always praise!" (Hallo 23). In her praise, Enheduanna shows her movement beyond conquest to governing, describing Inanna's function:

To build a house, to build a woman's
    chamber, to have implements,
to kiss the lips of a small child are yours,
    Inanna,
To give the crown, the chair and the scepter
    of kingship is yours, Inanna. (Hallo 23)

By the third poem—"The Exaltation of Inanna"—we can see that Enheduanna's fortunes have changed, and in the process she changes her relationship to Inanna. The poet refers to a historical event, when she lost power because of someone named Lugalanne. Since the priestess's position was primarily political, Enheduanna was banished from her temple. She appeals to Inanna to help her in her personal struggle, calling down the goddess's wrath to displace the usurper and restore Enheduanna as her priestess: "Oh my divine impetuous wild cow, Your rage is increased, your heart unassuaged"

(Hallo 27). Here in this final poem we are given an unusual glimpse into the life and feelings of an ancient woman: She feels a personal relationship with the goddess she served for so long and hopes for the goddess's direct help.

We have no other information about Enheduanna's political trouble. Sargon ruled for fifty years and was succeeded by his sons and grandson before the Akkadian dynasty fell, to be replaced by others. It may be that the priestess's displacement was part of internal politics. Because of her poetry, however, Enheduanna is remembered long after the kings and courtiers have been forgotten.

See also Artemis; Clothing; Ishtar; Mythology
Suggested Readings
Hallo, William W. "The Women of Sumer."
   Bibliotheca Mesopotamica 4 (1975).
Hallo, William W., and J. J. Van Dijh. *The Exaltation of Inanna.* New Haven: Yale University Press, 1968.
Hirshfield, Jane. *Women in Praise of the Sacred.* New York: HarperCollins, 1995.

Erinna of Telos

Hellenistic Poet (ca. fourth century B.C.)
The Hellenistic period produced a number of women poets who throve in the large cosmopolitan regions that arose after the death of Alexander the Great. One such poet who was highly praised by ancient critics was Erinna of Telos. Antipater of Thessalonica, writing at the end of the first century B.C., called Erinna one of the nine muses because her poetry seemed so inspired.

We know nothing about Erinna except that she was from the Greek island of Telos and that by the age of nineteen she had composed her most famous poem, "The Distaff." The title refers to wool working, the primary task of Greek women of all classes. This was originally a very long poem, but only a small fragment—about thirty lines—survives. The poem is a lament for Erinna's friend Baucis, who had recently died. Erinna recalls their joyous childhood:

You leaped from the white horses
   And raced madly into the deep wave—
But "I've got you, dear!" I shouted loudly.
And when you were the Tortoise

You ran skipping through the yard of the
   great court.
These are the things I lament and
Sorrow over, my sad Baucis. (Lefkowitz and
   Fant 7)

Erinna continues to remember their childhood when they played in their rooms with their dolls and times when they pretended they were young brides. She recalls how they were called to their chores and were frightened by Mormo—an imagined monster-woman. These poignant recollections not only offer beautiful poetry of grief, they also provide a small window into the childhood life of ancient young girls.

Baucis died shortly after her marriage, and in an epigraph for Baucis's tomb, Erinna writes of the irony of the sudden death of the happy bride: "Her bridegroom's father lighted her pyre with the same torches that had burned while the bridal hymn was sung. And you, Hymenaeus, changed the harmonious wedding song to the gloomy sounds of lamentation" (Fantham et al. 165).

Erinna, like her friend Baucis, died young, probably shortly after writing the few poems that survive and give such evidence of her talent. She probably died unwed, for a later poet described her as "the maiden bride of Hades." While poets ever since were saddened that her talent was cut off so prematurely, we can be grateful that the voice of this young poet has survived.

See also Anyte of Tegea; Aristodama of Smyrna; Muses; Nossis of Locri; Sappho of Lesbos
Suggested Readings
Fantham, E., et al. *Women in the Classical World.* New York: Oxford University Press, 1994.
Lefkowitz, Mary R., and Maureen B. Fant. *Women in Greece and Rome.* Toronto: Samuel-Stevens, 1977.
Pomeroy, Sarah B. *Goddesses, Whores, Wives, and Slaves: Women in Classical Athens.* New York: Schocken Books, 1975.

Esther

Hebrew Woman/Persian Queen
In about 587 to 586 B.C., the Babylonians had destroyed the city of Jerusalem, burned the Temple to the ground, and forced most of the Jewish

people into exile. This Babylonian Captivity of the Hebrews came to an end when the more tolerant Persians conquered the Babylonians. In 539 B.C., the Persian king Cyrus allowed the Jews to return to Jerusalem and rebuild their Temple, but all did not return home. Many Jews continued to live in the lands of the Persian Empire and preserved their traditional culture and their religious observances within the larger society, but sometimes tensions and persecutions arose between the two peoples. Within this setting, people told the story of how one brave woman named Esther appeared, who would help save her people from destruction. The account is written in the Book of Esther in the Hebrew scriptures (the Christian Old Testament).

The Book of Esther shows a good deal of familiarity with the Persian court, and there is external historical evidence of a man named Marduka (or Mordecai) who held an official post under the Persian king Xerxes I (485–464 B.C.). While the story may preserve a historical account of deliverance of Jews in Persia, most scholars believe the tale is mostly legendary and that it was written to enhance Purim, a festival celebrated in early spring that celebrates the deliverance of Jews from a planned persecution. This is a joyous folk festival that is celebrated with parades for children and with special foods. A central feature of Purim is the reading of the Book of Esther, which gives the following account of the people's salvation.

In the third year of his reign, King Ahasuerus (called Xerxes in English textbooks) called together all the army chiefs, the princes, and the governors of his empire to the capital at Susa for a period of banqueting and celebration. His wife, Queen Vashti, conducted banquets for the women at the same time—modestly separated from the men's feast. After seven festive days, "when the heart of the king was merry with wine" (Esther 1:10), he sent his eunuchs to fetch Queen Vashti, so that his guests could see her beauty. But the queen refused to come at the king's command. "At this the king was enraged, and his anger burned within him" (Esther 1:12). The king called together his wise men to ask how he should respond to the queen's behavior, and they all agreed that a strong response was

necessary to prevent rebellious women from asserting themselves: "For this deed of the queen will be made known to all women, causing them to look with contempt upon their husbands" (Esther: 1:17). They recommended that a law be made that Vashti would never again come into the king's presence and that her position be given to another. They further said that once this law was sent throughout the land, "all women will give honor to their husbands, high and low" (Esther 1:20). It is significant that the Bible's account sees in this tale not just the disobedience of one woman but the assumption that one woman's defiance would lead many women to also rebel. According to the text, the king took his counselors' advice and issued the decree.

Then the king's servants ordered that young virgins be brought from all over the kingdom to the capital at Susa and placed in charge of the chief eunuch of the women of the household. He provided them with cosmetics to enhance their beauty and then brought them before the king, who would choose a favorite to replace the disgraced Vashti. One of the maidens brought to the palace was Esther, a young orphaned cousin of the devout Jew named Mordecai, who had been one of the captive exiles brought to Babylon from Jerusalem. The chief eunuch was pleased with the young maiden and gave her a privileged position in the harem with the best ointments, good food, and seven maids from the king's palace. Mordecai had warned Esther not to reveal her religion, and she took his advice.

Each woman spent one year in the harem beautifying herself with oils and spices before coming before the king. Each woman spent one night with the king and then was returned to the harem in the charge of the chief eunuch. She would not be summoned again to the king unless he "delighted in her and she was summoned by name" (Esther 2:14), but he called none to return. Finally it was Esther's turn to go in to the king. He "loved Esther more than all the women, and she found grace and favor in his sight more than all other virgins, so that he set the royal crown on her head and made her queen instead of Vashti" (Esther 2:17).

Mordecai himself had a position at the court, and one day he overheard two of the king's eunuchs, who guarded the door, plotting to assassinate King Ahasuerus. Mordecai told Esther to warn the king. When the charge was investigated and found to be true, the men were both hanged. Mordecai's service to the king was recorded in the official court records.

Shortly afterward, the king appointed a man named Haman as his chief minister. Ahasuerus gave orders that everyone was to bow down before Haman, but Mordecai alone refused to do so. In his anger at the insult, Haman turned his rage against all Jews, not only Mordecai. Haman then went to the king and denounced the Jewish minority in the kingdom, saying: "There is a certain people scattered abroad and dispersed among the peoples in all the provinces of your kingdom; their laws are different from those of other people, and they do not keep the king's laws" (Esther 3:8). Haman offered to pay the king a huge sum if he got permission to persecute the Jews. The king gave Haman his signet ring to use in making the necessary orders, which gave the persecution the force of law. Haman had the orders drawn up, translated into all the languages of the great empire, and sent by special runners to authorities in each province. On the appointed day they were to have all the local Jews slaughtered and their possessions seized.

The Jews were frightened at the threatened destruction. They fasted, prayed, and tore their clothes in mourning, and Mordecai stood in front of the palace to summon Esther. When the queen saw him, she sent to ask him what had happened. Mordecai produced a copy of Haman's edict and asked her to approach the king and beg for the lives of her people. Esther was frightened because it was against the law to enter into the king's presence without being summoned, and she had not been called to him for a month. Mordecai told her she had no choice: "Think not that in the king's palace you will escape any more than all the other Jews" (Esther 4:13). He said that it might be that her whole purpose for being chosen was to help her people in their time of trouble. Esther agreed to try, first asking all the Jews of Susa to gather together and fast for three days on her behalf.

After the three-day fast, Esther put on her royal robes and stood in the inner court of the king's palace. The king noticed Queen Esther and was pleased to see her. He offered to grant her any request, and all she asked was that the king and Haman come to dine with her. At the wonderful dinner, the king again offered to grant Esther any request. She only asked for the king and Haman to come once again to dine with her the next night. Haman was highly honored at the request that he share the king and queen's table, but his anger was raised again when he saw Mordecai in the palace square. Encouraged by his wife and friends, he ordered a gallows to be constructed, intending the next morning to ask the king for permission to have Mordecai hanged. That night the king was unable to sleep, and to pass the night he ordered that the court records be read to him. He came across the entry that gave Mordecai credit for having revealed the assassination plot, and he discovered that Mordecai's good deed had gone unrewarded.

When Haman arrived in the morning to see the king, Ahasuerus asked him how the king should reward someone who pleases him. Foolishly thinking that the king was referring to him, Haman said that such a man should be dressed in royal robes, placed on the king's horse, and led in honor through the streets of Susa. To Haman's dismay, Ahasuerus ordered that Mordecai be so honored.

When the king and Haman appeared at Queen Esther's second dinner, she appeared downcast. When the king asked what she wanted, Esther pleaded that the lives of herself and her people be spared. She then accused Haman of having organized the mass murder. The king was overcome with anger and rushed out of the room. While he was away, Haman flung himself down on the queen's couch to beg for his life. At that moment, the king strode in again and seeing Haman on the couch he cried out: "Will he even assault the queen in my presence, in my own house?" (Esther 7:8). The king's attendants grabbed Haman and took him to be hanged on the gallows he had prepared for Mordecai. Haman's house and possessions were confiscated and given to Esther, while Mordecai was appointed chief minister in his place.

Esther again appeared weeping before the king, asking him to cancel Haman's order of persecution. However, that was impossible because under Persian law nothing could repeal an order given with the king's signet ring. Instead, Mordecai was authorized to send out another decree, which was taken to all the provinces. In this order, Jews were given the right to carry arms in self-defense against the coming persecution, and on the day Haman had set for their destruction, the Jews turned on their enemies and slaughtered them. Many thousands were killed along with the ten sons of Haman. After the violence subsided and the Jews were safe, Mordecai and Esther sent letters to all the Jews commanding that their deliverance from persecution be commemorated each year with the feast of Purim. And thus was the great celebration implemented.

Esther served as a positive role model for Jewish women living in diaspora (outside of the Jewish state amid other peoples). This quality has made the Book of Esther popular in its own time and into today, and Esther remains enduringly popular.

See also Cosmetics; Jewish Women; Persian
Women; Susanna
Suggested Readings
Comay, Joan. *Who's Who in the Old Testament.*
London: Routledge, 1995.
Meyers, Carol, Toni Craven, and Ross S. Kraemer.
Women in Scripture. New York: Houghton
Mifflin, 2000.

Etruscan Women

(ca. 800–500 B.C.)
The Etruscans were a people who emerged in central Italy sometime before 800 B.C. and who developed an advanced civilization that reached its height in the seventh and sixth centuries B.C. Scholars still argue over the origins of these people—some claim they came from the east, and others suggest that they developed from the indigenous peoples of Italy. Regardless of their origin, scholars agree that they produced a society that was highly influential, for by the sixth century B.C. they ruled over an extended area that included the early settlers of Rome. They were a great trading people and competed with the Greeks and Carthaginians for the wealthy trade of the western Mediterranean. The Etruscans

also were master builders, and they were skilled at reading omens; subsequent Roman society was to take many of these Etruscan developments and make them their own. In one area, however, the Etruscans contributed little to the rest of the Mediterranean world—their treatment of women. The Etruscan women took a strikingly public role, which shocked the Greeks and Romans who observed it.

It is difficult for historians to get a full picture of Etruscan society because we cannot read their language. Therefore, we must use only others' accounts of their customs, which are highly biased, and archaeological evidence, which fortunately is very rich. The most shocking thing that the Greek authors observed was that men and women dined together. Aristotle said that Etruscan husbands and wives reclined together at dinner (instead of sitting in chairs, ancient Mediterranean people reclined on couches around a table). In Greek society, the only women who joined men at banquets were prostitutes, so it seemed to the Greeks that all Etruscan women were therefore sexually free.

The longest description of the Etruscans comes from the fourth-century Greek historian Theopompus. He said the Etruscan women were "extraordinarily pleasure-loving," for they dined not only with their husbands, but with other men. Furthermore, they had free sexual lives: "It is not shame for the Etruscans to be seen having sexual experiences . . . for this too is normal: it is the local custom there" (Fantham et al. 248). He goes on to say that people shamelessly call sexual intercourse by its name if telling someone the master is busy making love.

Archaeologists are able to confirm some of these accusations on the basis of rich tomb paintings and sculptures in the Etruscan burial vaults. In the wall painting of a banqueting scene shown in Figure 29, we can see Etruscan women enjoying a dinner party in the company of men. So it appears that women did join men in public in a way that respectable Greek and early Roman women did not. Furthermore, there are paintings of women joining men to watch games and contests in public. The clothing of the women in paintings and sculptures also suggests a public life for women, for there

Figure 29. Tomb of the Triclinium at Tarquinia, ca. 470 B.C. (Alinari/Art Resource, NY)

were many more shown in shoes and mantles—public attire—than were present in comparable Greek portrayals.

The many sculptures on top of sarcophagi (stone coffins) also suggest much about the affectionate family relationships. Most show men and women reclining together on a couch, with their arms affectionately around each other. Figure 30 even shows the married couple naked together on their marriage bed. The Greeks would have found such a portrayal shocking, for although men were frequently nude, respectable women—even in a marriage bed—were not. It may be that such figures offer evidence to confirm the Greek historian's assessment that the Etruscans—men and women—were comfortable with their sexuality.

Theopompus also commented on the Etruscans' affection for their children. In contrast to Greece and Rome, where the father could determine whether the child would be raised or exposed to die, the Greek historian noted that the Etruscans raised all the children who were born, even if they did not know who the father was. The only independent confirmation we have of

differing attitudes toward children is the presence of small statues of women nursing their babies. These statues are unique in the ancient world—this was not an artistic theme for the Greeks. Some scholars suggest that these figures indicate that Etruscan women personally raised their babies.

The Roman sources imply that Etruscan women of the royal family had a strong role in governing the society. According to one legend, an ambitious Etruscan couple arrived in Rome in about 630 B.C. As the man and his wife looked down from their wagon on the city that was to be their new home, an eagle came down and plucked the man's hat off. It then swooped back down and replaced the hat. The woman—who like most Etruscans was skilled at reading omens—joyfully embraced her husband, for she explained that this was a sign that he would be king. The prophecy came true, and Lucius Tarquin became king of Rome. His wife was the powerful Etruscan queen Tanaquil. This story repeated the reputation Etruscan women had for prophecy and reading omens, which was continued throughout their history.

Figure 30. Lid of a limestone sarcophagus, mid-fourth century B.C. (Museum of Fine Arts, Boston. 86.145)

If Etruscan women reputedly had more freedom than women in the rest of the Mediterranean world, they also had the same opportunities as men for political intrigue and cruelty. The Roman historian Livy tells of an Etruscan queen named Tullia who violated the laws of family to forward her ambitions. According to Livy, the Etruscan princess persuaded her husband to kill her own father so they could rule, and she brazenly rode in an open carriage to the forum to see the results. Her husband, Tarquin, told her to go home, as the crowd might be dangerous. As she was leaving, her driver stopped the cart, for her father's mutilated body lay in their path. The "crazed woman" drove the carriage over her father's body so that blood from the corpse spattered her clothing. This story told by a Roman recounted the fall of the Etruscan monarchy, which restored a society in which women did not have the freedom they had under the Etruscans. Did he exaggerate the woman's cruelty to prove that the Etruscan way was corrupt? Perhaps. It would be centuries before respectable women again would experience the public life enjoyed by the Etruscan women of the ancient world.

See also Greek (Athenian) Women; Roman Women

Suggested Readings

Bonfante, L. *Etruscan Life and Afterlife.* Detroit: Wayne State University Press, 1986.

Fantham, E., et al. *Women in the Classical World.* New York: Oxford University Press, 1994.

Macnamara, E. *Etruscans.* London: British Museum, 1990.

———. *Everyday Life of the Etruscans.* London: Batsford, 1973.

Sprenger, M., and G. Baroloni. *The Etruscans.* New York: H. N. Abrams, 1983.

Eudocia

Empress (ca. A.D. 400–460)

During the late Roman Empire, the eastern capital in Constantinople was much influenced by women in the imperial family that had been started by Theodosius I. When Theodosius's son Arcadius died in A.D. 408, his heir Theodosius II was only seven years old. He and his sisters were raised in the secluded palace at Constantinople while the dynasty was protected by the regency of an able administrator, Anthemius, who no doubt hoped to gain entry to the royal family by arranging a marriage with one of the daughters. However, Arcadius's elder sister, Pulcheria, managed to exert a good deal of political power in her own right. She guided her brother's policies in many things, but in the process, she created critics at court. To many, the best way to weaken Pulcheria's power while securing the dynastic succession was to find a suitable wife for Theodosius II. They found in her an intelligent and beautiful newcomer to the capital.

Sometime around the beginning of the fifth century a pagan philosopher named Leontios fathered a daughter he named Athenais, after Athens, the place of her birth. All commentators remarked that she was beautiful and intelligent, and her proud father educated her carefully in classical studies and philosophy. About A.D. 419, Athenais moved to Constantinople, the bustling capital of the Roman Empire, and there she converted to Christianity. When the patriarch baptized her she took the name Eudocia, by which she has been subsequently remembered.

The sources disagree about how Eudocia came to the attention of the emperor. Some say his sister, Pulcheria, introduced him to the young woman, but others more plausibly say that Pulcheria's rivals at court brought Eudocia forward. Either way, the marriage was arranged, and Eudocia and Theodosius were married on 7 June 421. The marriage was soon blessed with a child—a daughter, Licinia Eudoxia—born the following year. Eudocia later bore another daughter, but Eudocia and Theodosius II never had a son to provide a clear transition for the dynasty to continue into the next generation.

Eudocia also seems to have continued her intellectual interests and to have immediately entered into the ongoing struggle for power with her sister-in-law Pulcheria. In A.D. 422, when Pulcheria received partial credit for the empire's military victory against Persia, Eudocia wrote a poetic praise crediting her husband with the victory. In the next year, Theodosius continued the practice of his family and awarded Eudocia the formal title of augusta—"empress." This made the domestic politics in his court more complicated, however, since his sister Pulcheria already held the title of empress. Now there were two augustae presiding in Constantinople, and both became involved in the uneasy politics that surrounded this situation.

In A.D. 431, Eudocia and Theodosius's second daughter died, which seemed to threaten the all-important imperial family connections. However, Eudocia was pleased to see her other daughter, Eudoxia, married in A.D. 437 to the western Roman emperor Valentinian III. In the course of that year, Eudocia met the holy woman Melania the Younger, who had come to Constantinople. According to Melania's biographer, the holy woman taught Theodosius and his wife, who had been a convert to Christianity. The two seem to have struck up an affectionate friendship, and the

empress conceived of a longing to see the holy places of Jerusalem. Melania persuaded Theodosius to allow Eudocia to make the pilgrimage. The following year Eudocia left for Jerusalem.

Along the way she made quite an impact, in part by distributing generous amounts of money to the needy, but the high point of her travels took place in Antioch, where she delivered such a stirring speech to the senate and people of the city that they raised a statue of her in her honor. After spending some months touring Jerusalem, she returned to Constantinople in about A.D. 439. She was at the height of her popularity, as people associated her with the saintly Helena, mother of Constantine, the last empress to visit the Holy Land.

Beginning in A.D. 440, there was a major change in the court of Theodosius, and both empresses lost some of the support they had enjoyed with the emperor. Pulcheria moved away from the capital, and the sources say that Eudocia was accused of adultery and chose to return to the Holy Land. She would never again return to Constantinople. In spite of the gossip that had driven her away from court, however, she continued to keep the title of empress (although the royal mint stopped striking coins bearing her image), and during her exile she continued to exert a good deal of authority in the Holy Land.

Part of her power certainly derived from the great wealth she continued to control. She supported monasteries and founded churches in the Holy Land. She also became involved in the theological controversies of the day. By about A.D. 449, the eastern empire was split over the belief of monophysitism—a belief that emphasized the divine nature of Christ at the expense of His human nature. This belief was popular in Jerusalem, Egypt, and Syria, and Eudocia, too, followed this doctrine. This stance put her on opposing sides from her old nemesis Pulcheria, who worked actively to condemn monophysite beliefs. Eudocia was finally persuaded to abandon monophysitism by talking to two noted holy men of the region, and in A.D. 455 she returned to the orthodox faith. She died in A.D. 460 in Jerusalem and was buried in the church of St. Stephen, which she had founded just outside the holy city.

The educated and enterprising empress exerted most of her influence through her patronage of the church and through her political influence over her husband. She was also known, however, for some of her writings. According to Roman and medieval writers, Eudocia was supposed to have written six works: some poetic paraphrases of some biblical works, her poetic praise of her husband's victory over the Persians, her successful address to the people of Antioch, a Homeric poem on the life of Christ, and an account of the martyrdom of St. Cyprian. Through these works, people remembered a wise empress who impressed with her learning as well as her piety. Although she exerted a good deal of authority during her lifetime, she did not bear a son, who would have been essential to dynastic continuity.

See also Eudoxia; Flaccilla; Helena; Melania the
    Younger; Pulcheria
Suggested Readings
Holum, Kenneth G. *Theodosian Empresses: Women
    and Imperial Dominion in Late Antiquity.*
    Berkeley: University of California Press, 1982.
Wilson-Kastner, Patricia, et al. *A Lost Tradition:
    Woman Writers of the Early Church.* New York:
    University Press of America, 1981.

Eudoxia

Roman Empress (r. A.D. 395–404)

When the emperor Theodosius I died in A.D. 395, his son Arcadius inherited the imperial throne in the eastern part of the empire. (Arcadius's brother, Honorius, ruled in the west.) Theodosius had ruled successfully in part because he had ensured the succession early by producing heirs and increasing their legitimacy by giving their mother, Flaccilla, the title of empress. As soon as he took the throne, Arcadius embarked on a similar policy. In the year in which he assumed power, the new emperor married Eudoxia, the daughter of a Roman woman and a Frankish general, who was under the care of an important general in the imperial army. Like her mother-in-law before her, Eudoxia would receive the imperial title, but Arcadius's empress would manage to convert the honorary title into real power.

Arcadius was not the strong ruler his father

had been: Sources criticized his lethargic temperament, saying "his halting speech betrayed a sluggish spirit" and claiming ministers led him "like an ox" (Holum 50). His father had so carefully established that the dynasty ruled by virtue of birth and Christian blessing, however, that even an emperor who was personally weak had the right to rule. This weakness also permitted his strong wife to exert her will in many matters.

Eudoxia's power depended upon her providing heirs for the dynasty, and her first child was born in A.D. 397. This daughter was named Flaccilla, no doubt to remind people of Theodosius's popular empress and of the continuity of the dynasty. Eudoxia proved remarkably fertile for the ancient world, and in nine years she bore five live children in the course of six pregnancies. As soon as she had children—even though they were daughters—Eudoxia used them to enhance her political position. For example, in A.D. 399, Eudoxia came into conflict with a eunuch who was her husband's most powerful minister. She appeared before Arcadius with her two infant daughters in her arms, crying and complaining about the eunuch. Arcadius dismissed his counselor on the spot, for as the sources wrote, "compassion entered him for his children" (Holum 2–3).

In A.D. 400, Eudoxia received the title of augusta—"empress"—just as Arcadius's mother, Flaccilla, had. Once again, the emperor ordered coins minted honoring the new empress. As Figure 31 shows, the gold coin cast for Eudoxia resembled that of Flaccilla (in Figure 34, page 127). The empress is shown wearing the same imperial robe as Arcadius, and she wears the imperial jeweled crown. There is an innovation on this coin, however. On the top of the coin, a disembodied hand—the right hand of God—reaches down to crown the empress, and this symbol implies that Eudoxia was crowned by God, not simply by her husband. Her title was supposed to be transcendent and even more important than that of her predecessor, Theodosius's empress. As these symbols were disseminated throughout the empire, her brother-in-law in the west, Honorius, objected to these new honors shown Eudoxia, but his voice went unheeded in the halls of power in Constantinople.

Figure 31. Coin of Empress Eudoxia, solidus minted at Constantinople (Ann Ronan Picture Library)

People soon recognized that they might appeal to the empress when usual channels did not fill their needs. For example, in A.D. 400, one monk wanted the emperor to destroy a pagan shrine, but fearing political repercussions, Arcadius refused. The monk approached the pregnant empress, promising that her child would be a much-anticipated boy if she would help him. Early in the next year, she bore a son—Theodosius II—and granted the holy man's request. The sources say that Arcadius agreed because "the lady empress nagged him incessantly" (Holum 55).

The strong-minded woman could not help but generate criticism from those who objected to an empress wielding such power. Her strongest critic was the bishop of Constantinople, the famous church father John Chrysostom. The bishop preached sermons against females in general, which the congregations interpreted (probably correctly) as an attack on the empress, and Eudoxia finally seemed to win her struggle against the popular and articulate bishop when he was sent away in A.D. 403. Disaster seemed to threaten the royal family, however, striking fear in Eudoxia's heart. Her eldest daughter, Flaccilla, died, and the superstitious empress believed that her quarrels with the bishop had brought the wrath of God upon them. She wrote a desperate letter to Chrysostom begging him to return: "Let your Holiness not think that this was my doing! I am guiltless of your blood" (Holum 75).

The crisis was not so readily solved, however. Hostile bishops fought against Chrysostom's return, while his supporters rioted in the streets. The pregnant empress was horribly frightened by the crisis, concerned that God was angry at the turmoil. Even the weather brought evil omens, for a violent hailstorm seemed to Eudoxia a reprimand from the Almighty. The terrified empress suffered a miscarriage during this turmoil, and the bleeding took her life. Eudoxia died in A.D. 404, but she had secured the dynasty with her son Theodosius II, who would be much guided by his strong sister, Pulcheria.

See also Eudocia; Flaccilla; Gynecology; Pulcheria
Suggested Readings
Holum, Kenneth G. *Theodosian Empresses: Women and Imperial Dominion in Late Antiquity.* Berkeley: University of California Press, 1982.

Eulalia of Merida
Virgin and Martyr (d. ca. A.D. 304)
During his reign, the Roman emperor Diocletian issued an edict that required everyone in the empire to prove his or her loyalty to Rome and its gods. All had to come and give sacrifice to a statue of the emperor and receive a certificate indicating their compliance. Such an act was seen as idolatry by Christians who otherwise were good citizens of the empire, so many confronted the authorities with their refusal and thousands

died as martyrs to their faith. One of the many martyrs created by Diocletian's persecution was Eulalia, a young girl in Spain.

The Spanish poet Prudentius (ca. A.D. 348–ca. 424) wrote the earliest surviving account of her martyrdom (or her "passion," as accounts of martyrdoms are called). His long, beautiful hymn was sung on Eulalia's saint's day—10 December—and this young virgin had become so popular by the fifth century that the famous church father St. Augustine wrote a sermon about her also to be delivered on her day of celebration. There is no way to know how accurate Prudentius's account is of the events surrounding her torture and death, but her contemporaries certainly believed it.

According to Prudentius, Eulalia was twelve years old when Diocletian's decree was issued. She was already a devout Christian with a wisdom well beyond her age:

When but a child she despised and ignored
Toys and sports with which girls are
    amused.
. . .
Childlike in ways, even then she possessed
Wisdom that comes with gray hair of old
    age. (Prudentius 124)

The young girl was eager to become a martyr, and her mother so feared for her life that she kept the child secluded in a rural villa, far away from the city where Christians were being persecuted. The enterprising girl escaped—"freeing herself from imprisoning walls," as Prudentius put it (130)—and walked through the night over rough roads and brambles. Eulalia walked many miles and when dawn broke, she appeared at the magistrate's court in town. She challenged the officials in a bold way:

Miserable men, for the Christians you
    search!
Lo, I am one of that odious race,
Foe to your fiendish idolatrous rites.
Witness to Christ with my heart and my
    lips,
Under my feet I will trample your gods.
    (Prudentius 131)

The Romans were angered at her impudence and began to torture her horribly—tearing her flesh and burning her. She responded with defiance, even spitting at her captors. Finally, she was burned to death. The poet claimed that at the moment of her death a dove flew from her mouth, showing the departure of her spirit to heaven. The guards were frightened by this vision and fled, leaving her body behind. Snow fell and modestly covered her burnt body until local Christians came and buried her. Her shrine, purportedly with its relics of bones, is still in Merida, Spain, today.

See also Agnes; Felicity; Maccabean Martyrs;
    Martyrs; Perpetua the Martyr
Suggested Readings
Prudentius. *The Poems of Prudentius.* Trans.
    M. Clement Eagan. Washington, DC:
    Catholic University Press, 1962.
James, E., ed. *Visigothic Spain: New Approaches.*
    Oxford: Clarendon Press, 1980.

Euphrosyne (Castissima)

Holy Woman (ca. fourth century A.D.)

In the fourth century in Alexandria, a story circulated about an independent young woman who took strong measures in order to lead an independent life as a Christian holy person. She even transcended her gender and gained fame as a holy man. Through such accounts, women during the early centuries of Christianity and later came to believe that Christian worship would bring them the possibility for freedom from social expectations that bound many women. When Euphrosyne's story was translated from Greek to Latin and spread through the west, her name was changed to Castissima. The popular story of Euphrosyne/Castissima began in Alexandria—the Egyptian city that had a large and important Christian population.

A god-fearing couple lived in Alexandria. They were wealthy and pious, and they were content in all respects except one: the wife was barren, and they very much wanted a child. They prayed, gave great wealth to the poor and sick, and did all they could to pray for a child. At last they visited a monastery, whose abbot joined his prayers to theirs. The anonymous biographer who preserved her story wrote that

God took pity on the couple and granted them one daughter, whom they named Euphrosyne. Her parents took much joy in her.

When she was twelve years old, Euphrosyne's mother died, and when her father took over her education, he focused on teaching her scriptures and "the wisdom of God." She was quick to learn, and her father was proud of her. Her name was spread throughout the city because of her wisdom, her love of learning, and her great beauty. Of course, many important men sought to acquire her as a bride for their sons. One of these men, who stood above all others in power, succeeded in persuading Euphrosyne's father to betroth her to his son. The betrothal presents were exchanged, binding the agreement.

A short time after the betrothal agreement, when Euphrosyne was eighteen, her father took her to visit the monastery where years before he had prayed for his daughter's conception. While father and daughter stayed at the monastery, the girl heard the abbot speak of purity and virginity and the fear of God. During this visit, her biographer says Euphrosyne progressed greatly in wisdom. She observed the spiritual life of the monks and said to herself: "Blessed are all who live in this place. They are like angels who praise God without ceasing. And after death they will be worthy of eternal life" (Salisbury 105). She began to repent in her heart the life that had been chosen for her. After the three-day visit, father and daughter left to return to Alexandria, but the father did not know how Euphrosyne had been transformed.

Some time later, the abbot sent one of the brothers to bring Paphnutius—Euphrosyne's father—to the monastery for a celebration. The young monk found only Euphrosyne at home, and she eagerly questioned him about life in the monastery. His answers made her long for the monastic life, but she was afraid her father would never permit her to renounce the world. The monk encouraged her desire for an ascetic life, however, saying: "No, my daughter, do not give your body up into corruption, nor surrender your beauty to shameful passion, but be whole in your purity as a bride of Christ. . . . Run and hide; join a monastery and there you will be saved." Euphrosyne's one reservation was "Who will tonsure me? For I do not wish to be shaved by a layman, but by a servant of God" (Salisbury 105).

The girl's question shows the significance of cutting her hair—her transformation from woman to eunuch of God would lie in this act. A woman's hair was a symbol and an expression of her sexuality and her gender, which was why church fathers always said that women should veil their heads to modestly hide their hair. However, church law was also adamant that women should not cut their hair short like men's either—in A.D. 390 a law was passed that forbade such tonsuring. The emperor had decreed: "Women who shall have shorn their hair contrary to divine and human laws . . . should be barred from the doors of a church" (Salisbury 105). Euphrosyne was taking a rebellious step when she asked a holy man to give her the haircut of a monk. The young monk said he would send someone to tonsure her.

An old recluse came, shaved the girl's head, dressed her in a woman's robe suitable for a penitent, and departed. Euphrosyne then considered her situation. According to her biographer, she said to herself: "If I go to a monastery of women, my father will never cease to look for me until I am found, and he will take me away by force to be given to my betrothed. Instead, I will put myself in a monastery of men in the disguise of a eunuch and no one will suspect me" (Salisbury 106). When it was evening, she took off her women's clothes, dressed herself in the clothing of a man, and left her house.

Euphrosyne went to the monastery that had played such a continuing role in her life. She presented herself to the porter, asking that he tell the abbot that a certain eunuch from the palace wanted to enter the monastery. The abbot asked the youth's name, and she gave the false name of Emerald (a precious stone that symbolized faith, purity, and the ability to overcome trials and sin). When the eunuch joined the monastic community, a problem arose. The youth was so fair of face that the monks were tempted into sin, so the abbot sent Emerald to live alone away from the monastery proper. There the youth could sing hymns, eat, and be tutored by the educated monks. Emerald peacefully withdrew to the cell and began a life of such zealous piety that all were astounded.

Meanwhile, Paphnutius discovered that his daughter had gone. He searched for her and lamented her loss, and the whole city mourned the absence of the young girl. Paphnutius went to the monastery to seek the prayers of the holy men to aid him in his search, and while most of the monks prayed that the whereabouts of the lost girl might be revealed to the father, Emerald prayed to remain hidden. The narrator praised the holiness of Euphrosyne, saying that Emerald's prayers outweighed all the rest. The abbot tried to reassure Paphnutius that God was watching out for his lost daughter.

The next time the father visited the monastery, the abbot suggested that the old man might profit from a visit with their pious recluse, Emerald. Paphnutius did not recognize his daughter, as she was so changed by much fasting and other austerities. However, the two had such a wonderful talk that Paphnutius praised the eunuch to the abbot, saying: "How much have I profited from this man. God knows how my soul has been captured by his love, as if he had been my own daughter" (Salisbury 107).

After Emerald had been in the monastery for thirty-eight years, she fell ill. During this illness, Paphnutius arrived for one of his periodic visits. He saw the sick monk for the last time and begged his prayers, asking that he be released from the grief about his missing daughter. Emerald assured him that soon he would have information about the lost Euphrosyne. The father waited three days with the sick monk. On the third day, Emerald knew she was dying and revealed herself to Paphnutius: "My father . . . end your grief for Euphrosyne your daughter. I am she" (Salisbury 107). After she had spoken, she died. When all the monks heard how the woman had lived among them all those years as a eunuch, they were amazed and sang praises to God who had wrought such miracles.

Scholars have studied the rich tradition of "transvestite saints" who transformed their gender and lived as men, only to be discovered at their death. Some have explained the popularity of these tales as showing a way that women could transcend their gender and rise above the social expectations that bound women in the ancient world. Others say the stories offered male monks

a model of a nonthreatening woman. Yet others claim that images of transgendered women who lived as eunuchs gave both men and women a model of a person who transcended not only her sexuality, but her gender as well. This was the goal of both men and women who left society to live in the desert, and the stories were thus models of the ultimately successful ascetic life. All these interpretations at the very least indicate the richness of the implications of the tales of transvestite saints that were retold for millennia.

See also Pelagia; Thecla

Suggested Readings

Delcourt, Marie. *Hermaphrodite: Myths and Rites of the Bisexual Figure in Classical Antiquity.* Trans. J. Nicholson. London: Studio, 1961.

Lewis, Agnes Smith. "The Life of Euphrosyne of Alexandria." *Vox Benedictina* (July 1984): 140–156.

Salisbury, J. E. *Church Fathers, Independent Virgins.* London: Verso, 1991.

Europa

Mythological Greek Maiden

One popular Greek myth tells of Europa, a beautiful princess, daughter of a legendary king of Tyre (on the eastern coast of the Mediterranean, shown on Map 5). One early spring morning, Europa summoned two of her young companions to go walking in the meadows near the sea. They brought baskets to collect the beautiful spring flowers that were at their height. As the young women wandered happily in the meadow, Zeus looked down from the sky and saw the beautiful sight. Although all the women were lovely, Europa stood out among them. As Zeus watched, Cupid shot one of his shafts into Zeus's heart, and he fell madly in love with the maiden. Even though his wife, Hera, was away, Zeus thought it best to approach the girl cautiously.

Zeus changed into a bull and appeared in the meadow. This was not an ordinary bull, but one more beautiful than had ever been seen before: He was a bright chestnut color with a silver circle on his brow and horns like the crescent of the young moon. He seemed so gentle that the women were not frightened of him but instead gathered around to pet him. As he approached Europa, he lowed so musically that the sound

Figure 32. Europa abducted by Zeus, from an Attic vase, fifth century B.C. (Christel Gerstenberg/Corbis)

was more beautiful than any flute. He lay down before her feet and seemed to encourage her to ride him.

Smiling, Europa sat on his back and called her companions to join her. Before they could, however, the bull leaped up and charged at full speed to the seashore. He leaped up and galloped above the water accompanied by sea nymphs riding on dolphins. Poseidon, too, appeared to escort the bull. Europa was frightened and clung to the bull's horn, but she knew this must be a god. She pleaded with the bull, begging him not to leave her in some strange place all alone. He finally spoke to her and told her he was Zeus, the greatest of the gods, and that he loved her. He said he was taking her to the island of Crete, where she would bear him sons. It happened as Zeus had said. They landed in Crete, where Zeus took his new bride. She bore him three sons, Minos, Rhadamanthus, and Sarpedon.

Zeus gave her three gifts: Talos, which was either a human or a bronze robot that guarded the coasts of Crete; a hunting dog that never let any prey escape; and a hunting spear that never missed its mark. Zeus then married her to the king of Crete, Asterion, who adopted her sons.

Europa was worshiped in Crete as a goddess, and the bull whose form Zeus had taken became a constellation and was included among the signs of the Zodiac. Her story may have been a Greek invention to explain the bull-leaping ritual found in Crete. The story has always been a popular one with artists, and many through modern times have illustrated the capture or "rape" of Europa.

See also Hera; Minoan Women
Suggested Readings
Grimal, Pierre. *The Dictionary of Classical Mythology.* Oxford: Blackwell, 1996.
Hamilton, Edith. *Mythology.* New York: Mentor, 1955.

Eurydice
Mythological Greek Nymph
According to Greek legend, Orpheus, who was the son of the muse Calliope, was the most famous musician who ever lived. Apollo gave him a lyre, which the muses taught him to use, and his music was so beautiful that he enchanted everyone, even animals, who heard it. Even rocks on the hillside followed his music. Orpheus married Eurydice, a maiden he loved deeply. Tragically, the marriage was to be brief.

Shortly after the wedding, Eurydice was walking in a field. A man tried to grab and rape her, but she ran away. In her haste, however, she stepped on a snake, and she died of its poisonous bite. Orpheus's grief was overwhelming. He was determined to go down to the underworld of death to bring her back. As he entered the dark realm, his music soothed his way. The great dog of the underworld, Cerberus, relaxed his guard, and the ferryman Charon was charmed by Orpheus's song. Even the tortures of the dead were temporarily suspended under the spell of his beautiful music. Hades, the king of the underworld, was so enchanted by the

music that he said Orpheus could take Eurydice back to the world of the living, but he imposed one condition: Orpheus was not to look at Eurydice until she was out in the world of the living.

They started the long journey back up to the world of light. and Eurydice followed the sound of Orpheus' lyre. He longed to look back at his bride but resisted the temptation. Finally, he stepped out into the daylight, and he joyfully turned to her. However, it was too soon; she was still in the cavern. He saw her in the dim lights, and he held out his arms to her. But in that instant, she was gone. She had slipped back into the darkness, and all he had was the last lingering sound of her voice as she said farewell.

While this was the most common version of the myth, some held that Orpheus was able to keep Eurydice for one day, but then Hermes (in his capacity as guide to the dead) led her back to Hades. Orpheus ended up being torn apart by Maenads (followers of Dionysus). This myth spread to Rome and was popular throughout classical times. It is likely that people were drawn to the idea of being rescued from the dead, as Eurydice almost was.

See also Maenads; Nymphs
Suggested Readings
Grimal, Pierre. *The Dictionary of Classical Mythology.* Oxford: Blackwell, 1996.

Eurydice I
Queen of Macedonia (ca. 370 B.C.)
The people of the city-states of ancient Greece had great scorn for Macedonia (see Map 4), which they considered a crude, "barbaric" backwater province to the north of the Greek mainland. Here, tribal kings fought with each other to hold power and led small armies of mounted warriors against neighbors. In the fourth century B.C. a non-Macedonian woman named Eurydice was given in marriage to the Macedonian king, Amyntas. Eurydice's husband died after she bore him three sons—Alexander, Perdiccas, and Philip—and one daughter—Eurynoe. Thanks to the resourcefulness of this strong woman, her youngest grew up to rule and change the future of Greek and western civilization.

There is virtually no information that tells us about the domestic life in ancient Macedonia—the sources are preoccupied with violence and dynastic struggles. However, Plutarch (ca. A.D. 100) describes an inscription that offers a glimpse into Eurydice's life as a mother. The inscription he quotes was a dedication to the muses: "Eurydice, daughter of Irrhas, offers this shrine to the Muses, Glad for the wish of her heart granted by them to her prayer, Since by their aid she has learned, when mother of sons grown to manhood, Letters, recorders of words; learned how to read and to write" (Macurdy 20). Plutarch used this lovely dedication as an example of perfect maternal love on the part of a woman who, though a "barbarian," learned to read and write for the sake of her children. Violence would sweep over the family, however, and Eurydice's reputation suffered as she struggled to survive and protect her sons.

When Eurydice was widowed in about 370 B.C., her eldest son, Alexander, inherited the throne. In Macedonian politics, however, inheriting was not the same thing as holding power.

Alexander was soon murdered at a Macedonian war dance, and his sister's husband Ptolemaeus took power and served as regent while waiting for Alexander's younger brothers, Perdiccas and Philip, to grow old enough to take their rightful place on the Macedonian throne. This situation was volatile, for Eurydice had lost one son, and a powerful regent could easily threaten the others. The sources offer conflicting stories about the widow queen's response.

One source written by an Athenian orator, Aeschines, shortly after the events describes the most plausible scenario. He said that after the death of Amyntas and the murder of Alexander, Eurydice looked to Athens for support. She summoned Iphicrates, the Athenian general, to help her, and she placed her two young sons in his lap, saying, "Amyntas, the father of these children, when he was alive, made you his son and counted Athens his friend, so you personally are a brother of these boys and politically a friend to us" (Macurdy 19–20). Aeschines continues to say that Eurydice expressed no trust in her son-in-law (and regent) Ptolemaeus. Iphicrates gave Eurydice the help she needed and drove another claimant to the throne out of Macedonia.

Other sources painted Eurydice in a very different light. One claims that she had fallen in love with her son-in-law and that she, herself, conspired to kill her son Alexander. This story may have arisen in the fact that Ptolemaeus took Eurydice as his second wife after the murder of Alexander. Eurydice may have voluntarily (or forcibly) taken this step to try to protect her remaining sons, or Ptolemaeus may have wanted to try to ensure his power through marriage to the queen mother. We cannot know for sure the motivations, but we do know that by whatever means, Perdiccas and Philip were kept safe to grow old enough to claim the throne. It is hard to imagine that the dedicated mother who learned to read and write so she could educate her sons could be the brutal murderer that one source describes. But we cannot know for sure.

As soon as Perdiccas took power, he had Ptolemaeus killed, which suggests at the very least that all was not well in the royal household. It also shows how difficult it was to hold the Macedonian throne—rivals were killed, not trusted. Perdiccas reigned for five years before he was killed in battle. Some of the subsequent chroniclers (those who wanted to paint Eurydice as an evil queen) accused her of arranging for Perdiccas to die to avenge the death of her second husband. However, this would presuppose a great deal more political power than she could have wielded at the time. More likely, she was pleased to have her son on the throne and to have a remaining third son who could then inherit.

Philip became the next king—Philip II of Macedon. This brilliant strategist conquered Greece and established the Macedonian Empire. He also seems to have dreamed of attacking the Persian Empire, but that feat would wait for his famous son, Alexander the Great. Eurydice fades from the sources, so we do not know when or how she died. We can hope that she lived long enough to meet her young grandson—named after her own murdered first son—for this woman who cared so much for her sons' welfare would have been delighted with the precocious boy who would conquer most of the western world and change the course of civilization.

See also Muses; Olympias [Macedonian Queen]
Suggested Readings
Macurdy, Grace Harriet. *Hellenistic Queens.*
Baltimore: Johns Hopkins University Press,
1932.

Eustochium

Roman Christian Virgin (ca. A.D. 368–ca. 419)
Controversies that swept through Rome in the late fourth century shaped many elements of later Christian thought, and one of the most influential ideas that emerged was the great valuing of virginity that was to remain a core of Christian belief. By the end of the century, church fathers would agree that Mary had been perpetually virgin (that she was a virgin both before and after the birth of Jesus) and that virginity was the highest calling, followed by chastity after marriage, and finally accepting a sexual married life as a third place—a compromise in a fallen world. For the church father Jerome, the only good thing about marriage was that it produced more virgins—marriage "is the thorn from which roses may be gathered" (Jerome 30). These ideas were not uncontested. Letters and tracts circulated arguing against this ascetic position, claiming that marriage was a properly ordered religious life, but the strongly antisexual position prevailed, largely owing to the influential writings of Jerome. His work in turn was shaped by his relationship with high-born ascetic women—especially the virgin Eustochium, who became his lifelong companion.

When Jerome came to Rome in about A.D. 382 to work in the service of Pope Damasus, he immediately came to know several wealthy women who had chosen to live quietly in their homes and devote themselves to the study and practice of Christianity. Among them was the widow Paula, who had five children. Jerome spent a great deal of time in their household, talking to them about ascetic Christianity, reading and discussing scripture with them, and simply becoming their friend and adviser. Remarkably, this irascible man in his fifties who made enemies wherever he went found a friendly haven in the company of Paula and her family. Jerome developed a special relationship with Paula's third child, her daughter Eu-

stochium. As early as A.D. 384, Eustochium sent Jerome gifts to celebrate the festival of St. Peter; she sent doves, cherries, bracelets, and a letter. We have preserved a letter from Jerome thanking her for her gifts and using the occasion to offer her moral instruction. Eustochium's presents may let us glimpse the affection the young girl had for the elder (often stern) teacher.

When Jerome came to Rome, Eustochium was probably in her early teens, a gentle, quiet child who was inseparable from her mother and (according to Jerome) invariably obedient to her. Eustochium joined Paula in Jerome's Bible classes and joined in singing the psalms and learning Hebrew. Unlike her elder sister, Blaesilla, Eustochium immediately rejected the beautiful clothes, smart hairstyles, and makeup that marked the Roman upper classes. Indeed, from an early age Eustochium dedicated herself to a life of virginity, rejecting the family life that marked the aspirations of good Roman daughters. Jerome was delighted—he called her the first aristocratic young woman in Rome to embrace this vocation—and the prolific church father would use Eustochium as his model to urge others to dedicate their sexuality to God.

Jerome (and his contemporaries) wrote letters that were not simply read by their recipients but were also copied and widely circulated. Among the more than one hundred letters of Jerome's that survive, the most famous is number 22, addressed to Eustochium. This long letter is really a long treatise on virginity, and it became the influential prototype of instruction to those who would dedicate themselves to God in this way.

The letter talks about how a woman should live a virginal life while in the cosmopolitan world of Rome, which was full of temptations. Virgins should avoid the company of married women and worldly women in general and stay only with dedicated women "pale and thin with fasting" (Jerome 28). A virgin should stay in her room most of the time, praying, reading, and studying. She should avoid wine, eat sparingly, and every night cry in her bed over the evils of the world. In this tract, Jerome reminded Eustochium (and all of Rome) of his previous work "Against Helvidius," in which he argued for the perpetual virginity of Mary and the superiority of the virgin state over the married one, and in this way the letter to the young virgin became pivotal in establishing virginity as a central ideal for Christians.

In his letter, Jerome also offered insights into prevailing beliefs of sexuality, for he not only warned Eustochium against things such as food, wine, and hot baths that might lead her to sexual feelings, but he also portrayed the virgin life in strongly erotic terms. Drawing from the imagery in the Song of Songs in the Bible, Jerome portrayed Eustochium as Christ's bride—and even depicted Paula as Christ's mother-in-law. For Jerome, Eustochium was not renouncing the sensual pleasures of marriage but was accepting as her groom Christ Himself. Jerome promised that Christ would visit the virgin at night as a bridegroom to love her. These sensual images offered to Eustochium also became the language of spiritual love that would shape the writings of nuns and mystics in the future.

Eustochium remained true to her vows of virginity throughout her life, and she remained loyal to Jerome as well. When the nettlesome man was forced to leave Rome because he had made so many enemies, Paula and Eustochium went with him. The three founded monasteries near Bethlehem, where they lived out their lives continuing the prayer, study, and ascetic renunciations that had marked them in Rome. Eustochium cared for her mother during her final illness in about A.D. 402 and continued to be Jerome's closest confidante until her own death in about A.D. 419. Jerome was almost unconsolable when Eustochium passed away, and he died about a year later.

The way of life they lived and espoused, however, continued long after them. Eustochium's place as head of the monastery they founded was taken over by Paula, Eustochium's niece, who had been raised as a dedicated virgin and who continued Eustochium's way of life. Generations of nuns would read the famous letter of Jerome to Eustochium and find in it an expression of their spirituality and a validation of their way of life. The gentle Roman virgin became the prototype of many other spiritual women—both ancient and modern.

See also Asella; Blaesilla; Marcella; Mary; Paula
Suggested Readings
Clark, Elizabeth. *Jerome, Chrysostom & Friends.* New York: Edwin Mellen Press, 1979.
Jerome. *Jerome: Letters and Select Works. Nicene and Post-Nicene Fathers,* vol. 6. Ed. Philip Schaff and Henry Wace. Peabody, MA: Hendrickson Publishers, 1995.
Kelly, J. N. D. *Jerome: His Life, Writings, and Controversies.* New York: Harper and Row, 1975.
Salisbury, Joyce E. *Church Fathers, Independent Virgins.* London: Verso, 1991.

Eve
Biblical First Woman

Probably the best-known woman of the ancient world is Eve, who appears in the Bible as the first woman created by God. Creation stories all over the world are invested with a great deal of significance because they are presumed to express an essential truth about the human condition, and as part of a creation story, Eve too takes on a striking importance. For people in the West, Eve became "everywoman" and symbolized all women. Consequently, scholars and others have studied carefully the characteristics and roles of Eve, and not surprisingly opinions about her have changed over time. Eve may be all women, but like other women her position has changed over time and remains elusive.

Eve as Partner: The Hebrew Bible

The first account of Eve is in the Book of Genesis in the Bible, where there are two accounts of the creation of man and woman. The first account is the shorter one: "So God created man in his own image, in the image of God he created him; male and female he created them. And God blessed them, and God said to them, 'Be fruitful and multiply . . .'" (Gen. 1:27–28). However, most analyses of Eve come from a second account later in Genesis. After God made the heavens and the earth, "the Lord God formed man of dust from the ground, and breathed into his nostrils the breath of life; and man became a living being" (Gen. 2:7). It is important to realize that these translations of the Bible into English are varying renditions of the Hebrew originals, which lose some of the subtleties of the originals. The Hebrew word for "dust" or "earth" is *'adamah,* and you can see the pun building on the name of Adam and earth. Carol Meyers provides another translation for this passage that provides a compelling new look at this important text. While her translation remains somewhat controversial, her reading removes the strong gendered connotations of using the word *man* for Adam while emphasizing the associations implicit in the original Hebrew: "Then God Yahweh formed an earthling of clods from the earth and breathed into its nostril the breath of life; and the earthling became a living being" (Meyers 81).

According to Genesis, after the creation of Adam, God created the Garden of Eden, but then recognized Adam's loneliness and created the beasts of the land, sea, and air. As the Bible says, among all that life, however, "for the man there was not found a helper fit for him" (Gen. 2:20). Then we have the second account of the creation of the woman: "So the Lord God caused a deep sleep to fall upon the man, and while he slept took one of his ribs and closed up its place with flesh; and the rib which the Lord God had taken from the man he made into a woman and brought her to the man. Then the man said, 'This at last is bone of my bones and flesh of my flesh; and shall be called woman, because she was taken out of man'" (Gen. 2:21–23). At this point in the narrative, the woman is not yet named Eve.

The man and woman were permitted to eat all the fruits in the Garden of Eden—which grew with no labor on their part—except the fruit of one tree, which gave the knowledge of good and evil. God forbade them to eat of this tree. According to the Bible, the serpent came and tempted the woman to eat the forbidden fruit: The serpent told her she would not die from eating the fruit, but instead "your eyes will be opened and you will be like God, knowing good and evil" (Gen. 3:5). So the woman saw that the fruit was good for food, and she ate some and gave some to her husband, and he also ate. "Then the eyes of both were opened, and they knew that they were naked; and they sewed fig leaves together and made themselves aprons" (Gen. 3:7). Then God appeared in the garden,

and the man hid himself because he knew he was naked; thus God knew that they had eaten the forbidden fruit. God asked Adam, and he blamed the woman: "She gave me fruit of the tree, and I ate." God then asked the woman and she blamed the snake: "The serpent beguiled me, and I ate" (Gen. 3:12–13).

In response, God cursed the three. The snake was made the most hated animal and would be forever the woman's enemy. Adam was cursed to toil on the ground, which would no more bring forth fruit without much labor; instead it would grow thorns and thistles unless he worked hard to grow grain. The woman, too, received a curse, and this is another biblical verse that has generated much comment. In a standard English translation, it reads: "I will greatly multiply your pain in childbearing; in pain you shall bring forth children, yet your desire shall be for your husband, and he shall rule over you" (Gen. 3:16). Carol Meyers—an eminent scholar of the Hebrew texts—has demonstrated that in the world of the ancient Hebrews, this text would more accurately be rendered something like this: "I will greatly increase your toil and your pregnancies, [along] with travail shall you beget children. Yet your desire shall be for your husband, and he will predominate over you" (Meyers 101–117).

This translation suggests that the creation story was formed in a context of the ancient highlands where the Hebrews lived—where the land was hard to work, where large families were essential to survival, and where husbands and wives labored long in partnership, yet took pleasure in each other. This story told of a reality in which both partners were needed for the people to survive, and in fact there was a shared responsibility between men and women. But this pattern would not remain, and subsequent writers would reinterpret this creation story. Indeed modern translations reflect the changed interpretation of the relationship between the first couple.

According to the Bible, after God had cursed the couple, Adam named his wife Eve (which in Hebrew resembles the word for *living*) because "she was the mother of all living" (Gen. 3:20). They left the Garden of Eden and had sexual intercourse; Eve then bore Cain and his brother, Abel. Apart from the early chapters in Genesis, there is in the Hebrew Bible (the Christian Old Testament) no further mention of Eve. It is only in later compositions that Eve is fully developed as a source of sin and evil. It is this later Eve that has become so influential in our Western consciousness.

Eve as Wise Woman: The Gnostics

When the circumstances of societies change, some people reinterpret the creation stories to make them apply to new conditions. When Christians adopted Hebrew scriptures as their own, they also adopted the stories of Eve, the first woman. Some Christians held very different views from those that were later defined as orthodox, and these who came to be called "Gnostic Christians" developed an elaborately different view of Eve. Apparently, many Gnostics were dualists who believed that people were created in a precosmic struggle between the principles of good and evil and that Christ had come to earth to free the spiritual parts of humans that were trapped within the evil flesh.

Like other early Christians, Gnostics interpreted scriptures as myths with hidden meanings that the spiritually aware could understand, and this sort of reading turned the story of Genesis into an elaborate allegory. Adam and Eve were not historical figures to the Gnostics, but instead they represented two principles that existed within everyone. Adam was the soul and Eve was the spirit—the higher self of wisdom. In Gnostic scriptures, Eve is the messenger of the divine principle of wisdom (Sophia), who awakens Adam from his sleeping state (the deep sleep he was in when God removed his rib to create Eve).

Eve's temptation by the serpent was also rendered as a positive act by the Gnostics. The serpent was an emissary of wisdom, who instructed Eve, informing her that she and Adam were of a holy origin and not mere slaves of a creator deity. When Eve and Adam ate the fruit of wisdom, they were reclaiming their divinity that had been hidden from them by a jealous evil deity. Thus, in Gnostic scriptures, Eve became a heroine who freed humanity from ignorance.

From the second to the fourth centuries A.D., orthodox churchmen fought against Gnostic beliefs. As they did so the Gnostic gospels and other such works were suppressed, and Gnostic ideas were slowly removed from the communities of the faithful. In addition, church fathers offered their own interpretations of scriptures, and in the process, Eve was transformed again.

Eve: The Gateway of the Devil

In the first and second centuries A.D., Christians wrote texts that would in time become the New Testament—the Christian portion of the Bible. In these texts, writers include Eve. In the letter to Timothy attributed to Paul, the correspondent for the first time in scriptures equates Eve with the introduction of sin: "For Adam was formed first, then Eve; and Adam was not deceived, but the woman was deceived and became a transgressor. Yet woman will be saved through bearing children. . . ." (1 Tim. 2:13–15). Here childbirth is portrayed as the one way that all women can be forgiven what has now become the "sin" of Eve—the crime of everywoman. Church fathers begin to pick up this theme as they explain the meaning of scriptures.

The early third-century church father Tertullian warned that all women tempted men as Eve had first tempted Adam to eat the forbidden fruit. Then Tertullian concluded in his famous phrase that women were the "devil's gateway" through which humanity fell into sin. As the biblical passage of Genesis is reinterpreted and given new emphasis on sin, the role of Eve becomes one of more villainy, and women receive the blame for the fall of humankind.

As church fathers also began to argue against the Gnostic position, they began to give a more literal interpretation of the Genesis creation story. In the mid-fourth century A.D., church fathers like Ambrose would still offer an allegorical interpretation of Genesis. For example, he argued that Eve's creation from Adam's rib was a command against adultery because the two were really one. In addition, Ambrose interpreted the passage that Adam and Eve were created in God's image as an instruction for women not to erase God's artwork by wearing cosmetics. But under the pressure to fight Gnostics, these allegorical messages would give way.

By the beginning of the fifth century, the most influential church father in the West—Augustine—moved to a more literal interpretation. In reacting against charges of dualist beliefs and in struggling against a growing movement against marriage, Augustine claimed that Adam and Eve were literal historical figures who had disobeyed God. In his analysis, he took seriously the biblical order to "be fruitful and multiply" as a vindication of marriage and procreation. In this he returns a bit to the Hebrew sense that childbirth was a gift, not a punishment, for Eve. But even Augustine did not attempt to vindicate the woman. He, too, shared the notion of the other early Christian fathers that Eve had introduced sin and lust into a fallen world. This was a burden that western women have carried ever since.

The final church father who was most influential in sealing the fate of the new sinful Eve was Jerome—the irascible scholar who was adamantly against sexual intercourse. He believed that marriage was a consequence of the fall that should be avoided if at all possible, and what made his opinions so overwhelmingly important was that they shaped his translation of the Hebrew scriptures—including the passage of Genesis. Jerome also believed that women should be strictly under control of men, and this idea, too, colored his translation of the troublesome passage that has so influenced how people perceive Eve.

Jerome's Latin translation of the Hebrew Bible is called the Vulgate, and it was commissioned by Pope Damasus in A.D. 382. This became the authoritative Bible of the Western church for centuries, and Jerome's version has influenced the subsequent translations. Jerome translated the Genesis passage as follows: "I will multiply your toils and your conceptions; in grief you will bear children, and you will be under the power of your husband, and he will rule over you" (Gen. 3:16). Jerome's first line follows quite closely the Hebrew original, but later modern versions emphasize the pain of childbirth. For example, the Revised Standard Version published in 1952 reads, "I will greatly multiply your pain in childbearing; in pain you shall bring forth children" (Gen. 3:16).

Eve has been transformed by these passages. Instead of a partner who shares Adam's toil on the land, she bears only one curse—to redeem her sin by painfully bearing children. Too often, subsequent women in the west have shared Eve's curse of being seen as subordinate, sinful, and shamed. Fortunately, some modern scholars have reconsidered this powerful creation story to try to find another Eve who might more readily represent everywoman's experience: a hardworking partner in the enterprise of building family and community.

See also Jewish Women; Monica; Paula

Suggested Readings

Clark, Elizabeth A. "Heresy, Asceticism, Adam, and Eve: Interpretations of Genesis 1–3 in the Later Latin Fathers." In *Ascetic Piety and Women's Faith,* ed. by Elizabeth A. Clark. Lewiston, NY: Edwin Mellen Press, 1986.

Meyers, Carol. *Discovering Eve: Ancient Israelite Women in Context.* New York: Oxford University Press, 1988.

Meyers, Carol, Toni Craven, and Ross S. Kraemer. *Women in Scripture.* New York: Houghton Mifflin, 2000.

Pagels, Elaine. *Adam, Eve, and the Serpent.* New York: Random House, 1988.

———. *The Gnostic Gospels.* New York: Vintage Books, 1981.

Salisbury, Joyce E. *Church Fathers, Independent Virgins.* London: Verso, 1991.

F

Fausta
Wife of Roman Emperor (d. A.D. 326)

During the late Roman Empire, emperors held power largely through good marriages and ruthless politics. Constantine the Great (r. A.D. 306–337) successfully took power during the tumultuous times after the abdication of the emperor Diocletian. Constantine was able to reunite the empire, and he is best known for his support of Christianity. With the help of his mother, Helena, Constantine supported Christians and started the process by which the pagan empire would become a Christian one. His religious beliefs did not exempt him from the brutal politics that dominated the age, however, and one of the casualties of his rule was his wife, Fausta.

In his youth, Constantine had fathered a son by a concubine, and this boy, Crispus, grew up to be a popular soldier. When it came to marriage, however, Constantine (like most ancient rulers) made a political alliance. He married Fausta, daughter of Maximian—Diocletian's coemperor—a marriage intended to tie the two families together. This marriage, however, did not prevent Constantine from fighting a civil war with Fausta's brother Maxentius for control of the empire. The decisive battle came in A.D. 312, when Constantine reputedly saw a vision that promised him victory over the superior forces of Maxentius if he fought under the sign of Christianity. Constantine won, and Christians attributed the victory to the intervention of God. By A.D. 324, Constantine was sole rule of the empire.

Ironically, Fausta's difficulties did not arise from any support she may have given her brother. She and Constantine had three sons—Constantius II, Constantine II, and Constans—and it would seem that these heirs to Constantine's throne should have secured her privileged position at court. According to the sources, however, Fausta brought tragedy to the house of Constantine by following her own passions.

Reputedly, Fausta fell in love with Constantine's first son, Crispus, who was about the same age as she was. When Crispus refused her advances, she became indignant at his rejection of her and told Constantine that Crispus was the one who was making improper advances. Constantine became enraged and had his son murdered in secret. However, Constantine's mother, Helena, believed Fausta was lying and had falsely accused Crispus. There were also rumors that Fausta was having an affair with a slave. Helena brought all this to her son's attention, and Constantine regretted his impulsive killing of Crispus. Then Constantine (or Helena) arranged Fausta's murder. They had the servants lock her in her bath and heat the water so much that she was scalded to death.

Some historians have suggested that Fausta had invented the story to get Crispus out of the way to make sure her sons would inherit Constantine's throne. If so, she chose a dangerous way to do so, and it certainly backfired. Her sons would all become emperors of different parts of the empire after Constantine's death, but she did not live to see it.

See also Helena

Suggested Readings

Jones, A. H. M. *Constantine and the Conversion of Europe.* London: Hodder and Stoughton, 1948.
Macmullen, Ramsay. *Constantine.* New York: Dial Press, 1969.

Faustina the Younger
Roman Empress (d. A.D. 176)

From about A.D. 90 to 180, the Roman Empire was ruled by the men who have been designated

Figure 33. Faustina the Elder and Antoninus carried up to become gods, watched by the goddess "Roma" on the right, from the base of the column of Antoninus Pius, ca. A.D. 161 (Alinari/Art Resource, NY)

as the "five good emperors." One of the things that characterized these emperors was the fact that they adopted their successors, choosing able men instead of hoping their own sons would be competent. To confirm this adoption, the emperors frequently had their adopted heirs marry their daughters, thus ensuring that there was some family continuity to the succession. Many of the daughters-turned-empresses were as able and virtuous as the "good emperors" who ruled with them.

When the emperor Hadrian died in A.D. 138, he named the next two successors (in a departure from tradition and perhaps in an attempt to ensure that the empire would have competent leadership for a long time). Hadrian's first successor was a fifty-two-year-old man from Nîmes (in modern France), who had a distinguished record of public service. Antoninus (later known as Antoninus Pius) came to power already married to a beautiful, virtuous woman—Faustina the Elder—and with a daughter—Faustina the Younger.

Faustina the Elder was awarded the title of augusta—"empress"—as soon as her husband became emperor, and she was also given the right to mint coins, which was the public statement of authority recognized by Romans. She died three years later in about A.D. 140 and was declared a divinity. The figure of Faustina the Elder is shown in Figure 33, which shows the empress and emperor rising to heaven as gods, while the female figure of Rome looks on approvingly. Antoninus Pius further commemorated her memory by establishing an endowment for poor girls in her name. Faustina the Elder left a daughter—Faustina the Younger—who cemented the succession of Antoninus Pius's adopted heir—Marcus Aurelius.

In A.D. 146, Antoninus Pius had arranged a

marriage between Marcus Aurelius and his daughter Faustina the Younger. (The two were cousins.) A year later, they had a daughter, and like her mother before her, Faustina received the title of empress and the right to issue coins. Rome was astonished at the fertility of the royal couple—Faustina gave birth to twelve children (and perhaps even more). As Romans constantly struggled with infertility, this accomplishment led to a great deal of praise—a coin was struck that showed Faustina surrounded by four children and that had an inscription reading "Fertile Empress." Not all of the children survived, but a son did—Commodus, who would succeed his father and break the streak of "good emperors."

Marcus Aurelius is best remembered not as a good emperor and a solid military commander, but as a philosopher. He had studied Stoic philosophy and wrote a series of *Meditations,* which are often looked at as the highest literary expression of Stoicism. Marcus Aurelius was a high-minded man whose ethics were above reproach and who placed duty above all else. Within his *Meditations,* he at times revealed some details about his private life that show that he was content. For example, he referred to Faustina as "obedient, loving, and devoid of affectation" (Balsdon 145).

In the tradition of many of the empresses, Faustina traveled with Marcus Aurelius as he engaged in the many wars that marked his reign. She was with him in Germany in A.D. 170–174 and was hailed as "mother of the army" after one of his victories. She accompanied Aurelius to the East, but in A.D. 176 she died there suddenly. Marcus Aurelius was deeply saddened at her loss, and he arranged a number of honors in her memory. He had her consecrated as a goddess as her mother had been. Temples were erected in her honor both in Rome and at Halala, where she had died. The place of her death was even renamed Faustinopolis ("City of Faustina"). Finally, like his father-in-law before him, he increased the endowment for poor girls. It may be a tribute to Faustina that Marcus never remarried—the emperor said that he did not want his children to have a stepmother to bully them.

Even though all the contemporary evidence from Marcus Aurelius and Faustina's reign shows a contented and prudent couple, historians who wrote almost a century later added some stories that cast blame on Faustina. Some claimed that she had taken a number of lovers, including gladiators and pantomime actors, and some even claimed that Commodus was sired by a gladiator instead of by Marcus Aurelius. Is there any truth to these accusations? It seems improbable, for the only contemporary criticism of Faustina the Younger was a mild one from Dio Cassius, who wrote of Marcus Aurelius: "Other people's misdoings, in particular his wife's, he tolerated, making no fuss and exacting no punishment."

To counter this is the record of Marcus Aurelius's affection for all his children and his clear praise of his wife after her death. Finally, if Marcus Aurelius had not believed Commodus to be his son, he would not have made him his successor—breaking the pattern of good emperors who adopted the best man as his successor. Commodus became emperor in A.D. 180 (when he was nineteen years old), and he was murdered in A.D. 192 after a disastrous reign. It may be that later Roman historians could not believe the simple-minded yet strong young emperor who was interested only in playing gladiator had descended from the serious and hardworking Marcus Aurelius. To save the reputation of the good emperor, they had to slander his good wife, Faustina the Younger.

See also Sabina

Suggested Readings

Balsdon, J. P. V. D. *Roman Women: Their History and Habits.* New York: John Day, 1963.
Dixon, Suzanne. *The Roman Mother.* Norman: Oklahoma University Press, 1988.
Hawley, R., and B. Levick, eds. *Women in Antiquity: New Assessments.* New York: Routledge, 1995.

Felicity

Martyr (d. A.D. 203)

In A.D. 203, in the prosperous vibrant North African city of Carthage, a small group of five Christians was arrested and brought to trial. There were many Christians in Carthage—probably about two thousand—but these people seem to have been selected because they were about to be baptized as Christians, thus violating Emperor Septimius Severus's edict issued the year before against new conversions to Christianity. The arrests came at the house of a wealthy Roman landowner, and these included his daughter Perpetua and two household slaves: Revocatus and Felicity. The small group was quickly tried, found guilty, and sentenced to death in the arena on the occasion of the birthday of the emperor's son Geta. The account of their ordeal is preserved in a contemporary diary written in part by Perpetua and in part by a second observer of the events. It was the second narrator who wrote of the experience of the slave girl, Felicity.

Felicity was in her eighth month of pregnancy when she was arrested, and her greatest worry was that her condition would keep her from sharing the struggle in the arena with her companions. As the narrator wrote, "She became greatly distressed that her martyrdom would be postponed because of her pregnancy, for it is against the law for women with child to be put to death. Thus she might have to shed her holy, innocent blood afterwards along with others who were common criminals" (Salisbury 115). Felicity was right about the Roman law; a pregnant woman would not be executed, even if she were a confessed Christian. Furthermore, since Felicity was a slave, Rome had an interest in her child even if it no longer valued the mother. The child represented property belonging to Felicity's owner and as such was important. In accordance with Roman law and values, a pregnant Felicity would not be executed with her companions.

The narrator said that "her comrades in martyrdom were also saddened; for they were afraid that they would have to leave behind so fine a companion to travel alone on the same road to hope" (Salisbury 116). The group prayed together, and the Lord answered their prayers by bringing on premature labor pains two days before the contest in the arena. Felicity bore her child, experiencing the pain of a difficult birth and the additional ordeal of a taunting guard:

She suffered a good deal in her labor because of the natural difficulty of an eight

months' delivery. Hence one of the assistants of the prison guards said to her: "You suffer so much now—what will you do when you are tossed to the beasts? Little did you think of them when you refused to sacrifice." "What I am suffering now," she replied, "I suffer by myself. But then another will be inside me who will suffer for me, just as I shall be suffering for him." And she gave birth to a girl; and one of her sisters brought her up as her own daughter. (Salisbury 116)

Felicity had delivered the child just in time, for the next morning was the scheduled execution in the arena. The young slave girl went straight from the birthing stool to the arena, and even members of the hostile crowd were "horrified when they saw that one . . . was a woman fresh from childbirth with the milk still dripping from her breasts" (Salisbury 142). However, the execution continued. The young slave woman joined her mistress, Perpetua, in being brutally tossed by a wild heifer before they were both executed by the sword of a gladiator. The account of the martyrdom of Perpetua and Felicity became a popular and much-read account of Christian bravery during the Roman Empire.

See also Julia Domna; Perpetua the Martyr
Suggested Readings

Musurillo, H., comp. and trans. *The Acts of the Christian Martyrs.* Oxford: Oxford University Press, 1972.
Salisbury, Joyce E. *Perpetua's Passion: Death and Memory of a Young Roman Woman.* New York: Routledge, 1997.

Flaccilla

Empress of the Roman Empire (ca. A.D. 380)
Emperor Theodosius I (A.D. 346–395) was the last emperor of the undivided Roman Empire. He was from the western portion—of Spanish origin—and he successfully made many of the Germanic tribes allies and thus withstood their threat. Theodosius was a staunch supporter of the Christian church and did much to make Christianity the official religion of the empire. In A.D. 380 he moved to Constantinople and revitalized that capital as the Christian center of

Figure 34. Gold solidus showing Empress Flaccilla, minted at Constantinople, A.D. 383 (Staatliche Museen, Munzkabinett, Berlin)

imperial power. Theodosius also believed he needed to found a dynasty that would ensure the succession within his family and thus avoid the disruptions, indeed even civil wars, that came when the heir to the throne was not certain. A wife who could produce heirs was central to Theodosius's dynastic plans, and Aelia Flavia Flaccilla filled this purpose. In gratitude, Theodosius crowned her augusta—"empress"—and she was the first woman so crowned since Constantine had awarded his mother, Helena, the title in A.D. 324.

Like Theodosius, Flaccilla was from the Spanish aristocracy, and they married probably in about A.D. 376. At the time the couple took up residence in the capital of Constantinople, Flaccilla had already given birth to two children: a son, Arcadius, and a daughter, Pulchria. In A.D. 384, she bore a second son, Honorius, in the palace of Constantinople. With the presence of heirs, Theodosius proceeded to ensure the dynastic succession. In A.D. 383, he raised Arcadius to the rank of augustus—"emperor"—at about the same time that he granted Flaccilla the rank of augusta.

Flaccilla's new rank was confirmed and spread widely through the typical Roman propaganda means—coinage. From her elevation to empress in A.D. 383 until her death in A.D. 387, Constantinople and other mints struck coins with her image in gold, silver, and bronze. Figure 34 shows a beautiful gold solidus minted at Constantinople. On the front of the coin (the obverse side) the empress is shown dressed in stately attire. Indeed, the mantle she wears along with its jeweled fastening is exactly that worn by the emperor. Furthermore, her elaborate hairstyle frames a jewel of her crown. The reverse of the coin shows a standard image on Roman coinage—the statue of the goddess victory enthroned writing a Christian symbol on a shield with the words *Salus Rei Publicae* ("well-being of the state") engraved. While the reverse was traditional, the obverse broke new ground by showing the empress in all the regalia usually attributed to the emperor. Even Constantine had not shown his empress mother in such state. The new needs of dynasty had led Theodosius to recognize the importance of his wife in securing the future of the state.

The empress was not able to enjoy her new status for very long. She died in A.D. 387, and the eloquent church father, Gregory of Nyssa, delivered an oratory at her funeral. He praised many of the elements that had characterized the empress: "This ornament of the Empire has gone from us, this rudder of justice, the image of philanthropy or, rather, its archetype. This model of wifely love has been taken away . . . dignified but approachable, clement but not to be despised, humble but exalted, modest but ready to speak boldly—a harmonious mixture of all the virtues" (Holum 23). In this praise, he recognized her support of the church, both with faith and with the amount of money that only the resources of the crown could bring. He also remembered her works of charity, for people watched in shock as the empress herself helped the sick in hospitals. The ideal of "wifely love" was expressed in the heirs that she produced to save the state. All these virtues became models for future women in this dynasty that was begun by Theodosius. Future women, too, would claim the title of empress that Flaccilla brought again to the empire of Rome in the east.

See also Eudocia; Eudoxia; Helena; Pulcheria
Suggested Reading
Holum, Kenneth G. *Theodosian Empresses: Women and Imperial Dominion in Late Antiquity.* Berkeley: University of California Press, 1982.
King, N. Q. *The Emperor Theodosius and the Establishment of Christianity.* Philadelphia: Westminster Press, 1960.

Fulvia

Roman Wife (d. 40 B.C.)

The turmoil of the later Roman Republic brought civil wars as strong men struggled to increase their power. During the First Triumvirate (an informal structure in which three men agreed to share power), Julius Caesar, Pompey, and Crassus battled to take sole control of the state. After Julius Caesar's assassination in 44 B.C., three more men struggled to rule the huge empire. Caesar's heir Octavian (later to be known as Caesar Augustus), Lepidus, and Mark Antony jockeyed for position, forged alliances, and ultimately fought great battles before Octavian made himself master of the Roman world. During these troubled times, many people died as Romans tried to ally themselves with the right patrons, and men and women alike used everything in their power—from marriage alliances to character assassination to murder—to survive. One strong woman took an active role during this time and in the process had her name slandered for a long time to come. Fulvia actively fought for Mark Antony during the civil wars, but the reputation of those who supported the losers perhaps inevitably suffers at the hands of the winners.

Fulvia was the daughter of Marcus Fulvius Bambalio, who was an extremely wealthy Ital-

ian. She was married to the famed orator and politician Publius Clodius, who was involved in the political struggle of the First Triumvirate. They had one daughter, named Clodia. Clodius supported Julius Caesar not only through his rhetorical skills but more often through violence or threat of violence. When Clodius led the people as tribune, he exiled the great orator Cicero for having put citizens to death without a trial (this was the famous Catiline conspiracy). Clodius's gang of ruffians seemed to pose such a threat to the orderly functioning of the state that many senators supported a man named Milo, who organized another, opposing gang. During the inevitable clash between these two rival factions, Clodius was murdered in 52 B.C. Clodius's death produced a great riot, in which his followers burned down the senate house. At this point, Fulvia appeared for the first time in the political arena at Rome.

As a dutifully mourning wife, Fulvia exhibited her husband's mutilated body to the mob gathered outside their residence. Her display of his wounds inflamed the people against Milo and his party, resulting in his being brought to trial. Fulvia also appeared with her mother at his trial, presumably to silently insist on justice. Even though Cicero defended Milo, he was exiled. This would be the beginning of Cicero's implacable hatred of Fulvia, as they continued to represent opposing sides in the seemingly endless struggles that brought down the Roman Republic. Fulvia next married Caius Scribonius Curio, but he died in 49 B.C. in Africa fighting in the wars. It was Fulvia's next marriage, however, that really brought her into close involvement with the political activities of her husband.

In the same year as Julius Caesar's murder, Fulvia married Mark Antony, who immediately began to vie with Octavian for control of Rome. Once again she was opposed to the great orator Cicero, whose support of Octavian made him one of Antony's deadly enemies. In his writings, Cicero used his rhetorical skills to accuse Antony of being dominated by Fulvia. Cicero further charged Fulvia with squandering wealth and of cruelly enjoying watching the execution of some riotous troops. Some modern historians have cast doubts on Cicero's characterization of Fulvia—he had too much animosity and personal interest in defaming both Fulvia and Antony for his account to be particularly accurate. Ancient Roman writers after Cicero, however, picked up the drumbeat and continued their vilification.

In 43 B.C., Cicero was killed, and the orator's head was brought to Antony and Fulvia. According to one Roman historian (not a contemporary), Antony "uttered many reproaches against it" and ordered it publicly displayed. Fulvia, however, took more vengeance. She set the head on her lap, forced open the mouth, and "pulled out the tongue, which she pierced with the pins that she used for her hair" (Dio 2–4). It is not impossible to imagine that during these violent times Fulvia took such steps against a man who had spoken so vehemently against her for some time. Her political activities increased as the violence of the wars escalated.

Antony and Octavian had first sealed their alliance by a marriage between Fulvia's daughter, Clodia, and Octavian. Fulvia apparently did not help the alliance. She intervened actively in her husband's interest (with or without his support). In 42 B.C., Antony went to the eastern part of the empire to administer the provinces and to raise funds. Fulvia remained in Italy—the territory administered by Octavian. While in the east, Antony met Cleopatra VII in 41 B.C. and began the affair that would continue until Antony's death. While Antony was still married to Fulvia, Cleopatra bore him twins. While Antony was away, it appeared that Fulvia and Antony's brother Lucius Antonius intervened in Italy, where they believed Octavian was becoming too powerful. Octavian was confiscating territories to distribute among his veterans. Antony's brother either feared that soldiers would become loyal to Octavian instead of Antony or hoped that this was an opportunity for him to increase his own power. Either way, Fulvia and Lucius instituted a rebellion.

Fulvia joined Lucius and even brought Antony's children before the legions to urge them not to forget Antony, to whom they owed their previous victories. Octavian saw this threat and used the opportunity to renounce

his wife—Clodia—and send her back (purportedly with her virginity intact) to Fulvia. There was no more marriage alliance binding the remaining triumvirs, so it seemed a final breach was imminent. Lucius marched on Rome, only to withdraw at Octavian's advance. From Rome he marched northward to Perusia, which Octavian besieged. Although Fulvia had marshaled reinforcements, her husband's generals from Gaul were reluctant to attack Octavian and lift the siege. Octavian starved the city into submission and allowed his troops to plunder it. Remarkably, Lucius was allowed to leave for Spain (he died shortly thereafter), and Fulvia was allowed to escape unharmed and go east to Greece to meet Antony, who was returning from Athens.

Fulvia's participation in this Perusine War has been controversial. Initially, she opposed Lucius as stirring up war at an inopportune time—while Antony was abroad. However, once Lucius was besieged, Fulvia became actively involved, urging Antony's generals to act. When Octavian wrote his memoirs of this event, he laid the blame for the Perusine War directly on the headstrong Fulvia instead of on Lucius or Antony, a characterization that was picked up by subsequent commentators. In 41 B.C., however, Octavian and Antony were temporarily reconciled, so making Fulvia the victim was convenient.

Equally convenient was Fulvia's fate. When she met with Antony in Greece, he was reputedly very angry at her for the unsuccessful war. Fulvia died soon afterward, and some sources suggest that it was from profound grief at Antony's displeasure. Even though her death seemed fortunate to the men who still struggled for power, the ancient historian Appian wrote that "Antony was much saddened by this event because he considered himself in some sense the cause of it" (Kebric 82). Yet, he did not grieve long. Politics intervened, and Antony sought to bind himself more closely to Octavian by marrying his sister Octavia. The truce would be short-lived.

What of the reputation of Fulvia, who had fought so actively for her husband, Antony? Few women have been so slandered as Fulvia—by Octavian the victor and by historians who followed him. Plutarch knew how to insult a Roman woman:

> She was a woman who took no interest in spinning or managing a household, nor could she be content to rule a husband who had no ambition for public life; her desire was to govern those who governed or to command a commander-in-chief. And in fact Cleopatra was indebted to Fulvia for teaching Antony to obey a wife's authority, for by the time he met her, he had already been quite broken in and schooled to accept the sway of women. (Plutarch 1111)

Was she truly as greedy, power-hungry, and vicious as these sources would have us believe? Or was her villainy a perfect foil for the perfect Roman matron, Octavia, the victor Octavian's sister? We will never know, but the story of Fulvia shows that the winners write history, and the reputations of those who back the losers will certainly suffer.

See also Cleopatra VII; Octavia; Turia
Suggested Readings
Balsdon, J. P. V. D. *Roman Women: Their History and Habits.* New York: John Day, 1963.
Delia, D. "Fulvia Reconsidered." In *Women's History and Ancient History,* ed. by S. B. Pomeroy. Chapel Hill: University of North Carolina Press, 1991.
Dio Cassius. *Dio's Roman History.* Trans. E. Cary. Cambridge: Harvard University Press, 1961.
Kebric, Robert B. *Roman People.* Mountain View, CA: Mayfield Publishing, 1993.
Plutarch. "Antony." In *The Lives of the Noble Grecians and Romans.* Trans. J. Dryden. New York: The Modern Library, n.d.

G

Gaea

The Greek Goddess Earth

All cultures have some explanation for the creation of the world, and within these creation myths lie symbolic and influential depictions of how people viewed themselves and their gods. The ancient Greek myths of creation are full of complicated and violent family relationships and a struggle by men for dominance. The definitive mythological account of the world's creation was written by Hesiod in his poem, *Theogony,* in about 700 B.C. The story begins with the goddess Earth—Gaea (also spelled Gaia and Ge)—who first generated gods and monsters.

According to Hesiod, originally there was only Chaos, a gaping void out of which appeared the Earth, Gaea. Along with Gaea, other creatures were generated out of chaos: Tartarus (the underworld), Nyx (night), Erebus (darkness), and Eros (the spirit of generative love). Gaea, without making love, gave birth to Uranus (sky), the hills, and the sea. The trouble in the world began when sexual relations generated beings.

Gaea lay with her son Uranus, and as a result produced a great brood of monstrous children, including the primitive gods known as the Titans and Titanesses, the oceans that surrounded the world, Cyclopes, and giants. Uranus hated the Cyclopes and giants and refused to let them see the light, pushing them back down again into their mother's womb so that Gaea's body was wracked with pain.

Gaea was furious at this treatment and plotted the overthrow of Uranus with her son Cronus, one of the Titans. She created a sickle from gray steel and told Cronus to castrate his father when he next came to lie with his mother Earth. Cronos did so and threw his father's genitals into the sea; from them spread a foam, which generated the Furies, other giants, and nymphs. Cronus's member floated on the sea to the island of Cyprus, where the foam that had gathered around it turned into the goddess Aphrodite.

Cronus proved to be as tyrannical as his father Uranus had been. He cast his brothers the Cyclopes down into Tartarus, and feared his own children. Cronus married his sister Rhea, but Gaea had warned him that one of his children would overthrow him, so he tried to prevent that. Rhea gave birth to four children—Hestia, Demeter, Hera, and Poseidon. As soon as each of these children emerged from the womb, Cronus promptly seized it and swallowed it. Rhea was grief-stricken, but her mother Gaea helped her. When Rhea's last child, Zeus, was born, Gaea hid him in Crete and gave Cronus a stone to swallow instead of the child. Like Cronus before him, Zeus would grow up to destroy his own father.

When Zeus grew to maturity, he prepared to attack his father and some of the Titans who supported Cronus. For the upcoming battle, Zeus freed the Cyclopes and giants that had been trapped in the underworld and armed them with thunderbolts. Rhea—Cronus's sister-wife—gave her husband a potion that made him vomit up the other deities he had swallowed, and they too helped Zeus. The battle lasted ten years, and when Zeus won, he imprisoned the hostile Titans, including his father, in the depths of Tartarus, the underworld.

Gaea found Zeus's imprisonment of her children the Titans high-handed, and she led another revolt against Zeus, but Zeus managed to remain victorious. Gaea also helped Zeus at other times. When the new leader of the gods married his first wife Metis (whose name means "intelligence"),

Gaea warned him that a son of the union would replace him as lord of the gods, reproducing the cycle that had brought Zeus to power. Zeus was determined to break this cycle, so instead of waiting for Metis to give birth, he swallowed his pregnant wife. Metis continued to live inside Zeus, advising him with her intelligence, thus giving him an intellectual advantage over the other gods. Later, he gave birth to Athena, who sprang fully armed from her father's head.

By this strategy, Zeus had escaped the cycle of hostility between fathers and sons that had marked the two preceding generations. Zeus also gave rights and privileges to the other gods that they had never had before, thus establishing a divine constitutional monarchy, which further precluded the cosmic battles that had gone before. By evading the future overthrow prophesied by his grandmother, he ensured that no son would ever succeed to his position. Instead of allowing his wife to bear a threatening son, he swallowed her and bore a powerful and favorite daughter—Athena—whose perpetual virginity and lack of a mother ensured that there would be no further source of challenge to his authority. He is thus established as the leader of the Olympian deities who would dominate classical Greek mythology.

In this myth of creation, the ancient Greeks (or at least the poet Hesiod) linked the evolution of an orderly universe with the growth of patriarchal divine power in the person of Zeus, who finally ended the family chaos. At the beginning of the story, the powerful goddess Gaea can give birth to her sons alone—she needs no consort. By the end of the story, Zeus can produce a daughter, Athena, from his own head. In the person of Zeus, the gods claim Gaea's role of reproduction as well as controlling the world. Zeus does go on to father children in the normal way; the first three (born of his marriage to Themis, his second wife) are called Order, Peace, and Justice, and they represent the high moral tone of Zeus's government. These goddesses indicate that the violence that had characterized the previous generations of the gods was over and had been replaced by peaceful rule by Zeus.

Gaea did not disappear from the Greek supernatural world with the victory of her grandson Zeus. She remained closely associated with oracles and prophecy, and according to tradition it was she who founded the oracular shrine of Delphi, which later became the shrine of Apollo. The earth-snake Python belonged to Gaea, and when Apollo killed it, he had to compensate for the murder by establishing Pythian Games and by employing the Pythian priestess to oversee his oracle. Finally, Gaea supervised oaths, many of which were made in her name, and she punished those who broke their oaths by sending the Furies to avenge her. Throughout the ancient Greek period there was a widespread cult of Gaea; people did not forget their debt to their mother Earth who spawned them all.

The myth of creation that brought Zeus to power, however, seems to validate the male domination on the human level by erecting a divine pattern in which rule by men is linked to the creation of order. The society created by the ancient Greeks would mirror this order, to the restriction of ancient Greek women.

See also Aphrodite; Athena; Delphic Oracle; Eve; Nymphs

Suggested Readings

Athanassakis, Apostolos N. *Hesiod: Theogony, Works and Days, Shield.* Baltimore: Johns Hopkins University Press, 1983.

Blundell, Sue. *Women in Ancient Greece.* Cambridge: Harvard University Press, 1995.

Grant, Michael, and J. Hazel. *Who's Who in Classical Mythology.* New York: Oxford University Press, 1993.

Grimal, Pierre. *The Dictionary of Classical Mythology.* Oxford: Blackwell, 1996.

West, M. L. *The Hesiod Catalogue of Women: Its Nature, Structure, and Origins.* New York: Oxford University Press, 1985.

Gaia

See Gaea

Galla Placidia

Roman Empress (r. ca. A.D. 390–450)

Emperor Theodosius I had established a strong dynasty with the children from his first wife, Flaccilla. When the empress died in A.D. 387, however, Theodosius remarried, joining with the imperial dynasty of the western portion of the empire by marrying the reputedly beautiful girl Galla. The new bride also sought to contribute to Theodosius's dynasty, but of the three pregnancies she had, only one child survived—a daughter named Galla Placidia. The elder Galla died in A.D. 394, but her daughter would wield influence throughout the empire well worthy of her illustrious relatives.

When Theodosius died in A.D. 395, he left his son Arcadius ruling in the eastern portion of the empire while his son Honorius and his half-sister Galla Placidia went to the western portion—the region most plagued by invading Germanic tribes, most of whom were called Goths. When the Goths invaded Italy, the royal household was unable to withstand them. Even Galla Placidia was captured in A.D. 409 or 410, and she witnessed the sack of the Eternal City of Rome itself. (During this raid, the expensive house of the holy woman Melania the Younger was burned down.) The young hostage seems to have been well treated and held in respectful captivity, and during this time Galla Placidia seems to have begun to exert influence on the Goths.

When the Goths left Italy and moved into Gaul (modern-day southern France), the royal princess went with them. In A.D. 414, the Gothic leader Athaulf made a peace treaty with Rome and established a home in the empire for him and his people. In the same year, he married Galla Placidia, thus making any children they would have heirs to the Roman Empire itself. At their wedding, he reputedly claimed to have changed his ambitions—instead of planning to establish a Gothic empire, he wanted to renew the Roman one. Sources suggest that Galla Placidia was instrumental in transforming the Gothic raider to an aspiring emperor. In A.D. 415, she bore Athaulf a son, and they gave him the royal name Theodosius. The infant soon died, however, and Athaulf was murdered in the same year; Galla Placidia would have to ensure her royal power through other means.

In the next year, the Roman general Constantius forced the Goths to come to terms with him. In exchange for food, the Goths promised a peace treaty, which included the exchange of hostages—including the royal widow, Galla Placidia. She once more moved to the center of Roman power in the west and sealed her position by marrying the victorious general, Constantius. She bore him two children: a daughter, Justa Grata Honoria, and a son, Valentinian. In A.D. 421, Constantius received the title of co-emperor with Galla Placidia's brother, and it looked as if the couple's success was ensured. The violence of the age, however, once again caused havoc in the royal household.

Shortly after he was named emperor, Constantius died, leaving Galla Placidia a widow once again. Her brother Honorius seemed to fear the political influence she wielded—especially over the always-turbulent Gothic tribes, so he sent her to Constantinople with her children to keep her out of the way. Honorius himself died two years later in A.D. 423, leaving the succession uncertain. After two years of a usurper, the eastern emperor Theodosius II restored Galla Placidia's family. In A.D. 425, her young son Valentinian III (only about six years old) was crowned emperor. She ruled for about a decade during his minority, and during that time she showed her political astuteness as she maneuvered through the difficult times when Goths and Romans were fighting for wealth and power throughout the west.

Sometime during her regency, Galla Placidia commissioned the building of a small chapel in the new Italian capital of Ravenna. This elegant building in the shape of a cross has a simple exterior, but inside it is dominated by splendid mosaics—the oldest in Ravenna. This building has come to be called the mausoleum of Galla Placidia, although it was probably intended as a chapel, not a tomb. This lovely building remains as a memorial of the life of an extraordinary fifth-century woman.

See also Eudoxia; Flaccilla; Honoria; Justina; Melania the Younger

Suggested Readings

Bury, J. B. "Justa Grata Honoria." *The Journal of Roman Studies* 9 (1919): 1–13.

Frend, W. H. C. *The Rise of Christianity.* Philadelphia: Fortress Press, 1984.

Jones, A. H. M. *The Later Roman Empire: 284–602.* Baltimore: Johns Hopkins University Press, 1986.

Ge

See Gaea

Germanic Tribal Women
(ca. 500 B.C.–ca. A.D. 300)

In about 500 B.C., groups of Scandinavian people began to migrate south into the Baltic states and Germany and east into Ukraine. As they fanned out across the land, their tribes took on a bewildering array of separate names: East Goths (Ostrogoths), West Goths (Visigoths), Burgundians, Franks, Saxons, and so forth. These were the tribes who traded with Rome and sometimes threatened its northern borders throughout the history of the empire.

Since the Germanic tribes had originally come from a small region in Scandinavia, they all shared many cultural similarities. Their settlements were based on clans—families joined in kinship groups. A whole tribe made up of many clans might number no more than 100,000 people, including only about 20,000 warriors. Historians studying their early history are hampered by the fact that they did not write and thus left no written records. Instead, we must piece together their history from archaeology, accounts of Romans who described them, and texts written centuries later, based on imperfect memories.

Well-preserved archaeological finds allow us to re-create the clothing these people adopted for their cold climates. Men and women alike depended on great capes to keep them warm. These folds of wool or skin were wrapped around the shoulders and fastened at the neck with a huge brooch, which was often elaborately decorated with gold and precious stones. (Poorer members of the tribe might have to settle for a large thorn to keep their cloaks fastened.) Beneath their cloaks, women wore ankle-length dresses of linen or woven wool, which they colored with vegetable dyes. They also dressed their hair with elaborate combs and hairpins and wore patterned jewelry as marks of wealth and prestige.

While archaeological finds offer much precise information, the written sources are more difficult to interpret, because the earliest descriptions by Romans are not objective. Some Roman accounts depict the Germans as "barbarians," that is, "outsiders," whose language sounded like babbling and whose personal hygiene was objectionable. The earliest and most famous text is that of Tacitus (A.D. 55?–120?). His *Germania,* written at the end of the first century, praises the Germans in order to criticize Roman society by contrast. Therefore, Tacitus portrays the Germans as strong and brave, people who care for their families and raise sturdy children. He writes: "with them good customs are of more avail than good laws elsewhere" (Tacitus 718). Readers must be cautious not to accept his descriptions uncritically—he was no objective reporter, and he was interested in urging Romans on to more virtuous customs. Nevertheless, by carefully using such imperfect sources in conjunction with archaeological finds, we can paint a picture of the lives of the early Germanic peoples. Within this re-creation, women emerge as central and valued figures.

Tacitus praised the Germans' devotion to marriage—"This they consider their strongest bond" (Tacitus 718)—and the children it produced. Although Tacitus somewhat romanticized the marriage bonds, without a doubt they forged the essential ties that bound society together. Within marriages, men and women had clearly defined and equally essential roles. Men cared for the cattle (a clan's greatest measure of wealth) and took primary responsibility for tending crops, working iron, and making war. Women owned property and received a share of their husbands' wealth upon marriage. Women also performed agricultural labor, but they were mainly responsible for pottery and textile production and household care. In addition, they brewed the all-important alcoholic beverages—honey-sweetened ale and mead, a fermented concoction of honey and water—that provided much of the caloric intake needed for survival.

Preserving knowledge of herb lore, women also cared for the sick and injured members of the clan. Perhaps in part because of their knowledge of brewing and healing, women were reputed to have a gift for prophecy, so men often consulted their wise female elders regarding important forthcoming enterprises. Tacitus re-

Figure 35. Girl's corpse from a bog at Windeby near Eckernforde, early centuries A.D. (Schleswig, Schleswig-Holsteinisches Landesmuseum fur Vor-und Fruhgeschichte, Schloss Gottorf)

marked in surprise at the respect accorded wise women, saying men "do not despise their counsels or make light of their answers" (Tacitus 713). As in so many instances, Tacitus's comments reflect both his observations of the Germanic peoples and by contrast his Roman opinions about women's advice.

In addition to being consulted for their wisdom, women were considered "peace-weavers," for through their marriages they were to bring peace between two families, although family feuds often transcended family ties. Unlike modern marriages, which are supposedly based on love and designed for the fulfillment of individuals, Germanic marriages emphasized the joining of families. For this reason, men were not limited to one wife. On the contrary, the more wives a man had, the larger his kin network became. Many Germans were polygynous; men had as many wives and concubines as they could support. Under these polygynous marriages husbands and wives did not necessarily live in the same household, so women had a good deal of independence and maintained close ties with their birth families. Although Tacitus claimed adultery was rare, anthropological studies indicate that polygyny may encourage infidelity among women, and there is no reason to doubt that adultery occurred among

these tribes. Adultery, however, deeply threatened the strong kinship ties that marriage forged and was severely punished.

Tacitus suggests quite plausibly that the children were raised in an active, outdoor life—"the children grow up naked and unkempt into . . . those sturdy limbs that we admire" (Tacitus 718). He praises the mothers for nursing their own infants (instead of using wet nurses as the Romans did), and the boys and girls played together until they reached puberty, when they were separated. Tacitus claimed that youths married later than the early Romans, who practiced prepubescent marriages, but their marriageable age was probably still low by modern Western measure—probably in their teens or early twenties.

Once boys learned to fight, they were initiated into the tribe by their fathers or male relatives, and we assume young girls were similarly taught necessary skills by the women of the tribe. Sometimes, however, the free-spirited girls who had grown up running naked in the fields forgot the requirement of purity in marriage.

Figure 35 shows the corpse of a fourteen-year-old girl who was executed in the first century A.D. by drowning, probably for committing adultery. Such bodies—well preserved by the northern European bogs—offer a wealth of information

Figure 36. Costumes of Germanic tribes, nineteenth-century reconstruction (Ann Ronan Picture Library)

about the lives of these early Germanic peoples. This young girl's head was shaved, and she was blindfolded before her death. Her right hand is frozen in an obscene gesture—perhaps her last act of defiance toward her executioners. This find offers eloquent, silent testimony to the importance of the marriage ties holding Germanic communities together and the gruesome penalty for violation.

Unlike the unfortunate girl in the illustration, most young women grew up to take an important place in the clan. Families and friends gathered in large halls made of branches and reeds woven on a timber frame and solidified their community bonds by eating and drinking together. The women "wove peace" as they strolled through the halls pouring beer for the noblemen

gathered there. These events served another crucial purpose as well. People used them to tell and retell the stories that preserved the great deeds of their heroic kin, and women took just as much pride in the family's accomplishments as their warrior husbands and fathers.

Consequently, warfare played a central role in this society. The Roman historian Tacitus remarked on the Germans' preference for war over work when he wrote: "They think it tame and stupid to acquire by their sweat what they can purchase by their blood" (Tacitus 716). Although Tacitus understated the agricultural productivity of the tribes, these warriors did prefer raiding and plundering. Through such adventures, they acquired both wealth and fame. In the evening gatherings after a day of war making, a poet might praise a particularly heroic deed, and the warrior's name would be permanently preserved in the "word-hoard" or poetry of his people.

Warfare permeated all aspects of this society. Sometimes when chiefs decided to conduct longer campaigns, they sent out a call to summon young, adventurous warriors who fought for their chief in return for arms, food, and with luck, treasure. Sometimes the whole tribe decided to move, bringing along all the related clans and escorting their women and children. According to Tacitus, women traveling with these fighting tribes stayed behind the battle lines, probably within a protective circle of oxcarts. If their men seemed to be losing, the women would goad the warriors to victory by baring their breasts behind the battle lines to remind them of their responsibility to protect their dependents. For centuries, until about A.D. 500 and beyond, Germanic clans and tribes moved from Scandinavia into other regions of Europe. As they interacted with other inhabitants of the continents, such as the Celts and the Romans, the women and men of the Germanic tribes left an important imprint on the future Europeans.

See also Boudicca; Clothing; Cosmetics; Mythology
Suggested Readings
Owen, Francis. *The Germanic People: Their Origin, Expansion & Culture.* New York: Dorset Press, 1960.

Piggott, Stuart. *Ancient Europe.* Chicago: Aldine Publishing, 1969.

Schutz, Herbert. *The Prehistory of Germanic Europe.* New Haven: Yale University Press, 1983.

Tacitus. "Germania." In *Complete Works of Tacitus.* Trans. A. J. Church and W. J. Brodribb. New York: Random House, 1942.

Glaphyra
Queen of Roman Client-State
(ca. 37 B.C.–A.D. 6)

During the time of Caesar Augustus (27 B.C.–A.D. 14), the emperor established a system of governance that was remarkably effective in bringing about the Pax Romana or Roman peace during which the Mediterranean world experienced an extraordinary degree of peace and prosperity for the ancient world. Augustus wisely used rulers in client-states to help him govern such a large empire with a relatively small bureaucracy, and he further encouraged intermarriage among the families of the client-rulers to try to cement peace. One ancient woman was reputed to have been so charming and desirable that she married three such kings. This was Glaphyra, daughter of the king of the powerful province of Cappadocia (see Map 7).

King Herod of Judea (r. 37–4 B.C.) clearly recognized the value of alliances, and though he usually married his sons and daughters to Jews, he made an exception for his son Alexander (the son of his first wife, Mariamne), and negotiated a marriage alliance with Cappadocia. Alexander married Glaphyra in 17 B.C., but the marriage was not well received in Herod's royal household.

Glaphyra had the title of "king's daughter," which was a higher rank than any of Herod's ten wives except the first, Mariamne, and Glaphyra boasted loudly and repeatedly of her high birth. The other women of the court grew to hate Glaphyra and her husband, Alexander, because of her imperious ways. The Jewish historian Josephus claimed that because of Glaphyra's unpopularity, rumors circulated about Mariamne's sons and ended with Herod's belief that the two boys were plotting against him.

As a good client-king, Herod then asked Caesar Augustus for permission to put his sons to death, which led the emperor privately to remark that he would rather be Herod's pig than his son. In 7 B.C., Herod tried and killed Mariamne's sons, and although he had questioned Glaphyra to test her loyalty, he freed her and sent her away with her dowry. Herod kept her two sons to be raised in Judea.

Shortly after Glaphyra left Judea, she must have met Juba, the king of the North African kingdom of Numidia (and husband of Cleopatra Selene Apene). Juba was traveling in Asia and was so captivated by the thirty-year-old Glaphyra that he married her, making her his second wife. Although Juba lived until A.D. 23, his marriage to Glaphyra must have ended in divorce sometime before about A.D. 7, because Glaphyra returned to Judea to marry once again.

According to Josephus, King Herod's son Archelaus, who succeeded his father in 4 B.C., had seen Glaphyra and instantly sent away his own wife in order to marry Glaphyra. This was against Jewish law, since Glaphyra had married and had borne sons with Archelaus's brother Alexander, but Archelaus was so smitten with her that he did not care and married her anyway. According to Josephus (who opposed the match), the marriage was ended quickly, almost by divine intervention.

Shortly after her marriage, Glaphyra had a dream in which her first husband, Alexander, stood at her side and reproached her for not being faithful to him. She had not only made a second marriage but had even come back and married her brother-in-law. The dream-husband said that he would now reclaim her as his own. She told the dream to her friends and died two days later.

Unfortunately, the sources do not allow us to see Glaphyra's motivations and inclinations in all these marriages. However, they do show us that in the system of client-kingdoms that shaped the early Roman Empire, a dynamic, attractive woman like Glaphyra was a force to be reckoned with.

See also Cleopatra Selene Apene; Mariamne
Suggested Readings
Josephus, Flavius. *Jewish Antiquities.* Trans R. Marcus. Cambridge: Harvard University Press, 1963.

———. *The Jewish War.* Trans. H. St. James Thackeray. Cambridge: Harvard University Press, 1927.

Kokkinos, Nikos. *The Herodian Dynasty: Origins, Role in Society and Eclipse.* Sheffield, UK: Sheffield Academic Press, 1998.

Macurdy, Grace Harriet. *Vassal-Queens and Some Contemporary Women in the Roman Empire.* Baltimore: Johns Hopkins University Press, 1937.

Sandmel, Samuel. *Herod: Profile of a Tyrant.* Philadelphia: J. B. Lippincott, 1967.

Richardson, Peter. *Herod: King of the Jews and Friend of the Romans.* Philadelphia: Fortress Press, 1999.

Greek Heroine Cults

Starting as early as the eighth century B.C., Greeks established cults of heroes—humans who had done extraordinary deeds that seemed to raise them to an almost godlike status. Tombs or small chapels were erected to these heroes, and these locations became the focal point for cult activities where local people periodically (usually annually) brought offerings to the tombs—often sacrificial animals or food or wine. At other times, Greeks brought small pottery items to the tomb shrine—perhaps pottery shields, figures, or vases dedicated to the hero. In return, people hoped the hero would bring protection to them and their community in the form of healing or general prosperity. Archaeological remains of many of these offerings tell us a good deal about early Greek worship, and among other things we have learned that these cults of heroes were not limited to men. Archaeologists and classicists analyzing the remaining tombs and cult sites have observed that about one in six included a woman, identified as a "heroine" in the worship. The cults of heroines offer another window into the world of Greek women.

Most heroines in a cult worship were associated with heroic family members, usually husbands or sons. Frequently the heroic couple were shown equal in size and offered joint worship; at other sites the women were portrayed smaller than the men and treated as satellite heroes. The oldest of such paired heroes was the cult of Helen and Menelaus near Sparta. In the earliest testimony of the cult, Helen was sup-

posed to have miraculously made an ugly child beautiful, and subsequent worshipers came asking for many kinds of benefits from each member of the couple. The offerings at the site included independent dedications to Menelaus and to Helen, suggesting that they had separate altars and that worshipers could appeal to either. Helen's worship derived from her status as Menelaus's wife, but Greeks noted that extraordinary women like Helen who fulfilled their family roles were worthy of cultic worship.

Another way scholars have analyzed whether the heroines were less important than the males at the same shrine has been to look at the local sacrifice records. Records from shrines in Athens of the fourth century B.C. may serve as good examples of ancient Greek attitudes. In most cases, the lists indicate that both the hero and heroine received sheep as sacrifice, but the hero's sheep was more expensive. In other examples, the hero received an ox and a sheep, while the heroine received only a sheep. These instances show two main principles of ancient Greek cultic activity: Greeks did value and venerate heroines but not as highly as heroes.

While people appealed to both heroes and heroines as they looked for supernatural help, there tended to be a gender difference between the kinds of requests worshipers made. For example, it was unusual to find a heroine presiding over a temple in which healing was practiced, presumably because real Greek women did not practice medicine. Women did serve as midwives, however, and consequently heroines more often than heroes presided over marriage, pregnancy, and childbirth. So, after their deaths, most Greek heroines continued many of the same roles they fulfilled during their lives.

While most heroines—such as Helen—were venerated because they admirably performed their family duties, others achieved notoriety precisely because they did not have the expected kinship ties. Some heroines were remembered for being sacrificial virgins, who committed suicide for the good of their city before they could become wives and mothers. One example of this type of heroine was Aglauros, a daughter of an Athenian. Apollo had given an oracle that Athens would win a war if someone killed himself for the city. The young virgin Aglauros threw herself off a cliff to save the city, and Athenians built a shrine for her as she became the focus of a heroine cult. In this typical example, people continued to venerate the dead heroine in hopes that she would continue to protect the city for which she had died.

Some cults arose over anonymous dead bodies washed ashore. These women seemed to represent the same kind of sacrifice—even if the context was not known. A lonely corpse washed up on shore must have been a disturbing sight to Greeks, who depended so much on the sea, and a significant number of heroic cults seemed to have grown up around the tombs of the unfortunate dead. These cults remember women (and men) who were separated from their families through premature death and who thus lacked a social tie that was so essential to the Greeks.

Some heroine cults arose around women who had been torn from their families by disaster and who through their death again offered protection for their cities. The heroine Polykrite was abandoned in a sanctuary by her family and was captured by an enemy when the island of Naxos was invaded. The victorious commander took her as a concubine, but while she was captive she showed remarkable bravery. She acted as a spy and sent secret information about the enemy back to her family. Although her city won its victory, defeating her rapist, Polykrite was killed during the struggle. Her tomb received cult status, and there were many such tombs from which wronged women offered their protection to those in the vicinity.

Many of the heroine cults dedicated to women who died before they had lived their lives fully became associated with the cult of the goddess Artemis. This is a goddess of transitional periods, and people invoked her when the normal transition—of girl to woman—went wrong. For example, Greeks said that women who died suddenly were "shot by the arrows of Artemis." Furthermore, people said that "Artemis made immortal" heroines who had died from sacrificial suicide or violence. One story may serve to show the frequent association between wronged heroine and Artemis: A dictator was planning to violate a young virgin and

placed his servant to guard her. The girl killed herself to escape being raped, but Artemis appeared to the guard to tell him to kill the dictator. The cult of the dead virgin became closely associated with her avenger goddess, Artemis.

In all these heroine cults, the Greeks reasserted their emphasis on family and on women's place within it. The social order—indeed, life itself—depended upon wives, mothers, and daughters fulfilling their expected roles. Sometimes when they did so, they were remembered as heroines within their families. Sometimes when women were torn from their families—through disaster, death, or sacrifice—they were also considered heroines and venerated precisely in the hope that they would help preserve the social order that had been lost for them. Greek society was a heroic one—one in which heroes of both genders protected the society that offered them worship.

See also Artemis; Clytemnestra; Helen of Troy in Greek Mythology

Suggested Readings

Burkert, W. *Homo Necans: The Anthropology of Ancient Greek Sacrificial Ritual and Myth.* Berkeley: University of California Press, 1983.

Cantarella, E. *Pandora's Daughters.* Baltimore: Johns Hopkins University Press, 1987.

Farnell, L. R. *Greek Hero Cults and Ideas of Immortality.* Oxford: Oxford University Press, 1921.

Larson, Jennifer. *Greek Heroine Cults.* Madison: University of Wisconsin Press, 1995.

Lyons, Deborah. *Gender and Immortality: Heroines in Ancient Greek Myth and Cult.* Princeton: Princeton University Press, 1997.

Greek (Athenian) Women

Athens was the largest and most prosperous of the ancient Greek city-states, and it was here that many of the ideas that we have come to know as Western civilization were formed. Athenians produced the greatest philosophers of the ancient world, defined ideals of beauty in the arts, and created a democratic political system. Because Athens was so influential in so many areas, historians have looked here to study women's position in Greek society and perhaps to seek some of the origins of Western attitudes toward women. As much as there is to praise about Athenian accomplishments, few today would advocate imitating their treatment of women.

Early in the sixth century B.C., as Athens struggled with economic and social problems, a reformer named Solon came to power, and he became the early architect of Athens's democracy. He reformed the political organization to strengthen the democratic assembly of male citizens, and he made economic and social reforms to help people become more prosperous. He also wrote laws regulating the lives of Athenian women. Solon's laws kept women out of sight and limited their influence. It may be that he saw women as a source of friction between men, and he wanted to limit this potential source of strife. His regulations on the lives of women continued to exert a tremendous influence over Athenian women throughout the classic period. Under the law, women were regarded as perpetual children, unable to speak for themselves. Consequently a woman remained under the care and control of a man—her father, husband, or other male relative.

Private Lives

Women lived in a separate women's quarter in the most remote and protected part of the house. The wife, any female relatives, and female slaves normally lived and worked in these accommodations. Some archaeological excavations of old homes show these women's quarters, and some that we have found indicate that the women's section of the house did not even have a door to the men's rooms. Wives would at times sleep with their husbands but more often probably slept with the other women and with infant children.

Respectable women did not leave the house even for shopping, not even for the food for the family. Men or slaves performed this function, believing they thus protected their women from the prying eyes of other men. It is difficult to know how strictly this ideal of seclusion was observed, for in poorer households wives or women slaves might have to leave to draw water for the household or engage in other activities. (Prostitutes were always exempt from the regulation of seclusion.) The ideal, however, was that

Figure 37. Girl with pigeons, grave relief ca. 450 B.C. (Metropolitan Museum of Art, Fletcher Fund, 1927)

men operated in the public arena while women remained in the private and ran the household.

Within their quarters, women associated with other women and did the household tasks. The sources say women cared for children, prepared the household food, spun and wove wool for clothing, and cared for the sick—including ill household slaves. Once boys were past their infancy, they joined their fathers and male tutors in preparing for their public lives, but girls grew up in seclusion, learning household work in preparation for marriage.

Young girls played with dolls and practiced their nurturing on pets. Images from gravestones show girls holding dolls and playing with pets such as geese or small birds. The girl in Figure 37 is shown affectionately nuzzling her pet pigeons, and this would have been a typical pet for young girls.

Further evidence from vase paintings suggests that at least some women learned to read while in the seclusion of their homes, for paintings show some women reading aloud to each other. In fact, from the hints of evidence we receive from artwork, it appears that women had close relationships with each other as they were hidden away from the world outside.

The central event of an Athenian girl's life was her wedding. When a girl reached puberty (at about the age of fourteen), her family arranged for her to marry a suitable man, who was usually in his late twenties or early thirties. The bride's parents provided her with a dowry that was to remain hers throughout her lifetime and used to ensure that she would never be left destitute. If a couple divorced, which was not uncommon, the husband had to return the woman's dowry to her male relatives so that she could continue to be supported. In addition to her dowry, she could bring a small trousseau—limited by Solon to three dresses and other small things of little value.

At the wedding, the bride rode in a simple chariot in a procession from her home to that of the groom. Here the young bride had to learn to accommodate to new circumstances of a new household. The playwright Euripides may have expressed the problems young women confronted when he wrote a speech for the character Medea, in which she complained about the difficulties of marriage:

First we have to buy a husband at a steep
    price [the dowry],
then take a master for our bodies. . . .
Confronting new customs and rules [in the
    new household],
she needs to be a prophet, unless she has
    learned
at home how best to manage her
    bedmate. . . .
A man, when he is tired of being with those
    inside
goes out and relieves his heart of boredom,

or turns to some friend or contemporary. But we have to look to one person only. (Fantham et al. 68–69)

The purpose of marriage was procreation, and when a woman produced a son, there was great joy in the family. Marriage did not mean there was much contact between men and women, however, since the household itself dictated separation. Custom said that men should have intercourse with their wives three times a month to fulfill their marital duties, and in a society that accepted homosexual relationships and male sexuality with slaves and prostitutes, women were no doubt often lonely. There were severe penalties against women's adultery, and literary sources suggest that men were fearful that women would somehow find a way to have affairs. Where would these secluded women meet their seducers? There were some situations in which even respectable women could venture outdoors, and it was at these times that their husbands feared contact.

Public Lives

One of the roles of women had always been to mourn for the dead. Before the time of Solon, women participated in large funerals for the wealthy: wailing, pulling their hair out, and scratching their faces as signs of grief. Solon regulated women's behavior at funerals, possibly to reduce the ostentation of the funerals for the wealthy. He said women could no longer mourn at funerals other than those of family members, which eliminated the practice of hiring paid mourners. Further, women were no longer to mutilate themselves or shout out loud lamentations. They continued to take part in the public mourning but in a more restrained way than before. The care of the dead did not end with the funeral and burial. The grave had to be continually visited and provided with offerings, and this responsibility fell to Athenian women. They brought wreaths and small jugs of perfumed oil or other goods. This was one more occasion when Athenian women left the seclusion of their homes.

Women also appeared in public when they engaged in religious ritual activities. From childhood on, girls participated in processions in which they carried offerings to the gods and goddesses of Athens. Young girls also could engage in races in honor of Artemis, and evidence from vase paintings suggests that women raced nude at these occasions. (Of course, there would be no training or opportunities for practice on the part of the secluded girls.) Some women must have celebrated the wild rituals of the god Dionysus, when they frolicked in uninhibited festivities in the woods. (*See* Maenads.)

One of the penalties for adultery was that a woman was no longer able to participate in the important (and enjoyable) public religious celebrations of Athens. That this regulation was considered serious shows how important these public celebrations were to Athenian women, who otherwise remained secluded.

There is controversy about whether or not Athenian women could have gone to the theater to see the magnificent plays that were produced in honor of Dionysus. Many of the plays—like those of Euripides mentioned above—featured women. It is hard to imagine that the playwright would not have expected women to witness these productions, so it may be that women could attend as part of their religious participation.

Because Athenian women had so few opportunities to appear in public, the accomplishments of few Greek women have come down to us. Ancient orators avoided naming living respectable women since that would bring them to the public eye and thus shame them. The memory of most of the ancient Athenian women was preserved on their tombstones, which repeatedly speak of their virtues and silent work within the home. Perhaps the fourth-century B.C. funeral inscription of one woman, Theophile, can serve as a memorial of the many good—but silent—Athenian women:

> The memory of your virtue, Theophile, will never die
> Self-controlled, good, and industrious, possessing every virtue. (Fantham et al. 83)

See also Artemis; Aspasia; Clothing; Maenads; Medea; Prostitution; Spartan Women

Suggested Readings

Fantham, E., et al. *Women in the Classical World.* New York: Oxford University Press, 1994.

Kraemer, Ross Shepard. *Her Share of the Blessings.* New York: Oxford University Press, 1992.

Lefkowitz, Mary R., and Maureen B. Fant. *Women in Greece and Rome.* Toronto: Samuel-Stevens, 1977.

Pomeroy, Sarah B. *Goddesses, Whores, Wives, and Slaves: Women in Classical Antiquity.* New York: Schocken, 1975.

Gynecology

The ancient Greeks took a dramatic new approach to medicine. Where previous ancient societies had assumed disease had a supernatural origin, the Greeks began to believe that the causes of disease could be attributed to things of this world—imbalances in critical bodily fluids (called *humors*), for example. Thus, they began a study of disease (and health) that shaped views in the West for over a thousand years. From the beginnings of this kind of medical study (in about the fifth century B.C.), physicians and theoreticians wrestled with the question of how women fit into their growing understanding of medicine. The first question was whether women had diseases peculiar to their sex or whether they were subject to the same conditions as men. A second question was whether, if the only difference of women was their different organs, a specialized branch of medicine was necessary to study the effects of their reproductive organs. From these questions, the study of gynecology and obstetrics was born. It was not a purely scientific study, however. Throughout the ancient world (and beyond) the "scientific" study of female physiology and disease was always shaped by men's perceptions of women and of their role in society.

Greek Medicine

In the fifth century B.C., a Greek physician named Hippocrates (460?–377? B.C.) is credited with inaugurating the modern practice of scientific observation in medicine and establishing standards of ethical medical practice. (Physicians today still take the Hippocratic Oath, promising to do no harm to their patients.) His ideas reputedly were collected in a body of about seventy treatises that were composed under his name. This *Corpus Hippocraticum,* or the Hippocratic Corpus, was written by several different physicians over a period of time, but it remained the central starting point of medical studies.

Eleven of the treatises are specifically gynecological, including discussions of women's sexual organs, menstruation, and "women's diseases." In this *Corpus,* women were seen as decidedly different from men, as one ancient doctor described: "I say that a woman's flesh is more porous and softer than a man's: since this is so, the woman's body draws moisture both with more speed and in greater quantity from the belly than does the body of a man" (Fantham et al. 184–185). In another entry the difference was described in terms of the categories by which physicians diagnosed imbalances: "The males of all species are warmer and drier, and the females moister and colder" (186). Thus, women were by nature different from men.

For the ancients, these differences accounted for all the observable differences between the genders. In a healthy woman, the excess moisture was excreted in the blood that was evacuated monthly, and in a pregnant woman, the excess blood (and moisture) went to the fetus. In a lactating woman, the excess blood was converted to milk.

All these processes seemed to offer a range of possibilities for things to go wrong. For example, since Greek men generally considered themselves more rational than women, they noted that women's bodies were more susceptible to diseases that would cause madness. For example, one physician wrote, "There is a thick vein in each breast. These contain the greatest portion of intelligence. . . . In one who is about to go mad the following is a warning indication: blood collects in the breasts" (Fantham et al. 187).

Other physicians believed that blood accumulation in the uterus might also lead to madness: virgins who had not yet menstruated might act erratically because of an excess of blood. According to the Hippocratic collection, however, menstruation was the salvation of most women, because this self-regulating purging mechanism frequently kept them from becoming too seriously ill.

The womb was seen to be a potential threat to female health and a cause of erratic behavior.

The Greek physicians believed that if a woman's womb became too dry and light (from lack of intercourse), it would move to the moister organs of her body—the liver, heart, brain, diaphragm, or bladder. If it settled on one of these, a woman might lose consciousness or suffer a symptom we designate by the word *hysteria* (which derives from the word *womb*). Physicians tried various means to draw the uterus back to its proper location. One of the most common was to use sweet- and foul-smelling substances to entice the uterus to move—burn sweet-smelling substances below the woman, allowing the smoke to fumigate her vagina, and burn foul-smelling substances under the nose. Then the womb would be drawn downward. The Greek physicians essentially believed that the womb had a consciousness of its own separate from the woman's body that was its host.

Finally, the Hippocratic collection believed that a woman ejaculated seed directly into her womb when she reached orgasm during sexual intercourse, paralleling men's ejaculation. In this analysis, women's pleasure was as important as men's to procreation. This theory was contrary to many Greek men's understanding of sexual pleasure, and a scientist even more influential than Hippocrates would offer a different explanation.

Aristotle differed from the Hippocratics in seeing a closer resemblance between the bodies of men and women. He believed that women were like men, but simply with the genital organs within the body instead of without. However, Aristotle believed that women were imperfect men. He wrote: "Just as it sometimes happens that deformed offspring are produced by deformed parents, and sometimes not, so the offspring produced by a female are sometimes female, sometimes not, but male. The reason is that the female is as it were a deformed male" (Fantham et al. 191).

For Aristotle, the problem with women was that they were cooler than men. Consequently they could not "concoct" (or cook) the food they ate sufficiently to change it into semen. Their "deformity" was a lack of heat that prevented them from being perfect males. Therefore, women had to menstruate to rid their bodies of the extra food that they had consumed, or they would become ill. Unlike the Hippocratics, Aristotle believed menstruation was a difficult—not a healthy—time for women. He said, "In all cases alike there is bodily distress until the attack be over" (Fantham et al. 191).

Their lack of vital heat also meant that women could not be as intelligent as men, and this made Aristotle believe that the Greek social structure that kept women strictly under men's control was justified by women's anatomy. These ideas would have a long-standing influence.

Since Aristotle believed women's bodies were not hot enough to produce semen, he departed from the Hippocratics' belief that women needed to have an orgasm to produce seed for conception. Therefore, Aristotle believed that a child was produced only from the male's seed—the woman was a passive vessel in which the seed was planted, and the woman's pleasure during sexual intercourse was irrelevant. This was another idea that had a deep impact on people's ideas of sexuality.

Hellenistic Medicine

The works of Aristotle and the Hippocratics formed the starting point of medical science after the Greek world became more cosmopolitan. Herophilus was a physician who lived and worked in Alexandria, Egypt, at the beginning of the third century B.C. Herophilus was particularly interested in gynecology, and he wrote a number of treatises on the subject. Unfortunately, we only have fragments that have survived.

Although Herophilus considered himself to follow the tradition of the Hippocratics, he accepted Aristotle's theory that the defining difference between men and women was that males possessed greater heat and that therefore women did not produce seed to contribute to conception. Herophilus was so wedded to Aristotle's views that even though he conducted dissections, scientific observation did not change his perceptions. Herophilus observed the fallopian tubes that led from the ovaries, but he said that since women did not contribute seed to conception, the woman's "seed" was excreted into her bladder and expelled with urine.

During the Hellenistic period, then, the ideas of Aristotle were passed on, including the no-

tion that women were inferior because of anatomy and governed by their weak bodies. However, Herophilus did make a practical improvement over his Greek predecessors—he wrote a handbook for midwives, recognizing that there was a place for women in the treatment of women's illnesses.

Roman Medicine

In the second century A.D., Soranus, a Greek doctor who lived in Rome, wrote a tract on gynecology that drew from the ancients and provided a model for the future. Like Herophilus, Soranus recognized the importance of midwives and wrote an extensive discussion on what constituted a good midwife. She had to be "well versed in theory" as well as a trained practitioner who understood diet, drugs, and surgery. Here, women seem to be included in the full range of medical practice.

Beyond this innovation, Soranus drew heavily from Aristotle. He, too, believed that women contributed no seed to conception, but he did acknowledge a place for women's pleasure during sexual intercourse: He said that pleasure relaxed the uterus, allowing an easier entrance for the sperm. Since he believed the essential contribution of women was their menstrual blood, he recommended that prospective bridegrooms inquire about a woman's menstrual flow before marrying her. Her flow was to be neither too heavy nor too light, and her uterus was to be straight to ensure that she would bear children. (Presumably, a midwife would be called to check the position of the prospective bride's uterus if a family were to take Soranus's advice.)

In Soranus, we can see the Roman preoccupation with childbearing, and many physicians worked to help couples bear more children. Rome always had a problem maintaining fertility, and thus for Rome's physicians gynecology in large part meant concern with conception.

The most authoritative medical authority in antiquity (and later) was Galen, who was active in Rome from the mid to the late second century A.D. He was a prolific writer who included discussions of female anatomy and gynecology within his larger medical works. Galen departed from Aristotle in asserting that women *did* produce seed. In fact, during their sexual pleasure and orgasm, their seed was ejaculated from the ovaries into the uterus, where it met the male's semen to bring about conception. Many modern women praise Galen for his restoration of the necessity of female pleasure to sexual intercourse and the contribution of mothers to their child's creation.

However, Galen did not depart too much from ancient medical theory. He, too, believed that women were naturally inferior because their sexual organs lay within them and because they lacked "noble" qualities like facial hair. Women would have to wait long after the ancient world before people believed that biology was not destiny and that anatomy did not dictate inferiority.

See also Abortion; Contraception; Hagnodice
Suggested Readings
Dean-Jones, Lesley. *Women's Bodies in Classical Greek Science.* Oxford: Oxford University Press, 1992.
Fantham, E., et al. *Women in the Classical World.* New York: Oxford University Press, 1994.
Lefkowitz, Mary R. *Heroines and Hysterics.* New York, 1981.
Lefkowitz, Mary R., and Maureen B. Fant. *Women in Greece and Rome.* Toronto: Samuel-Stevens, 1977.
———. *Women's Life in Greece and Rome.* Baltimore: Johns Hopkins University Press, 1982.
Rousselle, Aline. *Porneia: On Desire and the Body in Antiquity.* Trans. F. Pheasant. Oxford: Oxford University Press, 1988.
Temkin, Oswei. *Soranus: Gynecology.* Baltimore: Johns Hopkins University Press, 1956.

H

Hagnodice

Greek Physician (ca. fourth century B.C.)

In the Hellenistic period, many women received more education than they had previously, and many worked in trades and professions. It appears that perhaps a few women broke the traditional boundaries that kept them from becoming physicians. We have an account of one such woman named Hagnodice, and while many historians believe this tale was invented, it nevertheless points to some of the issues that faced women seeking medical treatment and offering it.

Hyginus, who recounted this story, said (inaccurately) that the ancients had no midwives, and therefore many women died in childbirth because they were too modest to consult a male physician. One girl, Hagnodice, wanted to learn the science of medicine. "Because of this desire, she cut her hair, put on male clothing, and entrusted herself to a certain Herophilus for her training" (Fantham et al. 168).

Herophilus was a physician who worked at Alexandria in Egypt at the beginning of the third century B.C. He was particularly interested in gynecological matters, and we have a number of surviving fragments of his works on female anatomy and gynecology. Herophilus also wrote a manual for midwives (now lost), which indicated that he expected some women to be working in this profession. Either Hagnodice really did study with this expert on gynecology, or the author of the fanciful tale of Hagnodice linked her name with a physician known to be interested in female matters.

Of course, as the story by Hyginus notes, Hagnodice had to disguise herself as a man to be trained as a physician, so the author recognized the limitations imposed on women at the time.

The story ends, however, by showing that Hagnodice's gender worked to her advantage: "After learning this science, when she heard that a woman was having labor-pains, she used to go to her. And when the woman refused to entrust herself [to Hagnodice], thinking that she was a man, Hagnodice lifted her undergarment and revealed that she was a woman. In this way she used to cure women" (Fantham et al. 168).

In this ancient story, we have a sensitive recognition that while there were some women who practiced medicine in the ancient world, the medical profession needed more.

See also Gynecology
Suggested Readings
Fantham, E., et al. *Women in the Classical World.* New York: Oxford University Press, 1994.
Lefkowitz, Mary R., and Maureen B. Fant. *Women's Life in Greece and Rome.* Baltimore: Johns Hopkins University Press, 1982.

Hannah

Hebrew Mother (ca. eleventh century B.C.)

The Bible tells of the life and accomplishments of the prophet Samuel, who was the last of the Hebrew judges—charismatic leaders who led the people by virtue of their strength of character. Samuel was the last of these leaders; in his old age, he succumbed to the people's pressure and agreed to name a king. He named Saul as the first king, and the Hebrew monarchy was established. Samuel is well remembered, but less famous was his mother, Hannah, who promised to dedicate her son to God's work.

According to the Bible, Samuel's father was Elkanah, who had two wives—Peninnah and Hannah. Peninnah had children, but Hannah had none, and she was greatly distressed. Every year Elkanah would go from his city to worship and give sacrifice to God at Shiloh, which was an important shrine in the times before the monarchy was established and before the Temple was built at Jerusalem. The worship at Shiloh was presided over by the priest Eli. On the day when Elkanah sacrificed an animal, he would give portions of the sacrificed meat to Peninnah and to all her sons and daughters, and "although he loved Hannah, he would give Hannah only one portion, because the Lord had closed her womb" (1 Sam. 1:5). Year by year this continued, and Hannah became more and more distressed. One year Hannah wept and would not eat, and Elkanah said to her, "And why is your heart sad? Am I not more to you than ten sons?" (1 Sam. 1:8). But she would not be consoled.

She left the table and went and prayed to the Lord. She made a vow that if God would grant her a son, she would "give him to the Lord all the days of his life, and no razor shall touch his head" (1 Sam. 1:11). As she continued to pray silently in her heart, her lips moved, though she made no sound. The priest Eli observed her and thought she was drunk. She responded, "Do not regard your maidservant as a base woman, for all along I have been speaking out of my great anxiety and vexation" (1 Sam. 1:16). Then Eli asked that God grant her petition and that she could go in peace.

When Elkanah and Hannah returned to their home, Hannah conceived and bore a son. She called him Samuel. When Elkanah and all his household went to Shiloh to make their annual sacrifice, Hannah did not go. She told her husband she would wait until the child was weaned, then take him there to live. He agreed to let her have her way. When the child was weaned, she took the child to make the sacrifice. She also took a three-year-old bull, a measure of flour, and a skin of wine, and she took all this to the house of the Lord at Shiloh. They sacrificed the bull and brought the child to Eli, and Hannah said, "For this child I prayed; and the Lord has granted me my petition which I made to him. Therefore I have lent him to the Lord; as long as he lives, he is lent to the Lord" (1 Sam. 1:27–28).

The Bible also includes a song of rejoicing that was attributed to Hannah, although the poem probably dates from much later than the context in which it is given. The beautiful poem is really a song of national thanksgiving, which praises God. It includes the stanza:

There is none holy like the Lord,
there is none besides thee;
there is no rock like our God. (1 Sam. 2:2)

Probably the greatest claim for this song of Hannah is that it became the model for Mary's song of thanksgiving (called the Magnificat) in the New Testament Book of Luke (Luke 1:46–55).

Elkanah and Hannah returned home, leaving the young Samuel to be raised by Eli the priest. Every year they returned to give the yearly sacrifice, and Hannah brought Samuel a little robe that she made for him. Every year, Eli blessed Elkanah and his wife, praying to God for them to have more children, and his prayers were answered. Hannah conceived and bore three sons and two daughters, and her first son, Samuel, grew up to shape the course of the Hebrew nation.

See also Jewish Women; Mary
Suggested Readings
Meyers, Carol, Toni Craven, and Ross S. Kraemer. *Women in Scripture.* New York: Houghton Mifflin, 2000.

Hatshepsut
"King" of Egypt (r. ca. 1479–ca. 1458 B.C.)
In about 1552 B.C., the strong pharaoh of Egypt, Ahmose I (1550–1525 B.C.), won military victories against foreign invaders and founded the eighteenth dynasty of rulers. Egyptologists consider Ahmose's reign the beginning of the New Kingdom, a period of Egyptian prosperity and expansion. Among the rulers of this dynasty was an extraordinary woman—Hatshepsut—who ruled Egypt for about twenty-two years. She was not content to be queen or regent as other Egyptian women had been; instead, she portrayed herself as "king" of Egypt, and her subjects accepted her and benefited from her wise rule.

The Egyptian pharaoh Thutmose I (1504–1492 B.C.) had two children by his favorite wife—one son who died in his youth, and a daughter, Hatshepsut. In the complex households of the pharaohs, the succession was never clear, for Thutmose I also had a son by a lesser wife. This son, Thutmose II, married his half-sister Hatshepsut and succeeded his father as pharaoh. Thutmose II apparently was sickly, and he died in 1479 B.C. after he and Hatshepsut had a daughter, Neferure.

The succession again went to a son by a concubine. This next son, Thutmose III, was younger than ten years old when his father died. The logical regent was his aunt-stepmother, Hatshepsut, and she began to rule in his name. For reasons we do not know, however, she decided to rule as king, and this politically astute woman seems to have cultivated the support of the powerful priests of the god Amon. Accompanied by young Thutmose III, she participated in one of the great feasts honoring the god, and during the ceremonies she had herself crowned king. Thutmose III served as a coregent—in effect, a minor king to Hatshepsut's lead.

Hatshepsut seems to have treated her young charge well. Contemporaries praised his extraordinary skills in reading and writing and his study of military arts. He was also healthy and a strong athlete. His remains show that he escaped even the severe dental decay that appears in many royal mummies. Thutmose III was probably married to his aunt's daughter, his half-sister Neferure, to guarantee the succession.

Hatshepsut grappled with two major challenges during her reign: how to forward her political vision for Egypt and how to ensure her credibility. She approached both tasks shrewdly, ever aware of the importance of appearances as well as policy. In her political vision, she focused attention on trade and peaceful pursuits, apparently trying to restore Egypt's former position of glorious isolation. She obviously kept the army strong, because Egypt's neighbors did not feel able to threaten the borders, but the accomplishments she seemed proudest of were in trade.

The king commissioned a great carving showing her successful trade mission to Punt, an African kingdom that we can no longer exactly identify, although some historians suggest it may be near modern-day Somalia. In any case, this wealthy sub-Saharan kingdom had been the destination of several trade missions during the Middle Kingdom, and all knew of the wealth that was available.

The carving Hatshepsut commissioned shows the pharaoh meeting with the queen of Punt—a heavy and powerful woman—and bringing back many luxury items of trade. Hatshepsut's ships were filled with incense, ebony, gold, ivory, animal skins, and even live baboons, sacred to the Egyptian gods. The pharaoh brought these great luxuries back to Egypt and used much of the wealth in her monumental building projects.

The king focused her attention on rebuilding and repairing many of Egypt's shrines—her inscriptions claim that she was the first pharaoh to repair the damages caused by the Hyksos, the Asian settlers who had taken over northern Egypt before the strong New Kingdom dynasty had expelled them. Hatshepsut's crowning architectural achievement was the beautiful funerary temple at Dais el-Bahri that was to be her burial location and her legacy for the future. All these buildings no doubt contributed to her popularity with her people—not just because she brought employment for many, but more than that, because Egyptians had traditionally viewed such evidence of prosperity as proof that the gods approved of their pharaoh.

In spite of Hatshepsut's clear success in domestic and foreign policy, she still confronted the problem of how to portray herself. To prove her right to rule, Hatshepsut used traditional Egyptian art as propaganda, but she brought her own unique view to gain acceptance for her role as king. In Figure 38, Hatshepsut is shown seated and dressed in the short skirt and headdress of a traditional male pharaoh. She is still shown as a woman, however, for her breasts are clearly visible. Her intention was not to pretend to be a man but instead to show herself as a king. In Figure 39, the king is shown in an even more traditional manner—she wears the false beard traditionally worn by pharaohs on ceremonial occasions.

Hatshepsut's reign lasted twenty-two years, a long time in the ancient world, but her death is a mystery. Some historians have speculated that

Figure 38. Pharaoh Hatshepsut shown with a female body wearing men's clothing (Bettman/Corbis)

Figure 39. Red granite sphinx of Hatshepsut showing her wearing a false beard (Metropolitan Museum of Art, New York, Rogers Fund, 1931)

her co-king Thutmose III, who had grown into a successful military leader, grew tired of his secondary role and displaced his aunt-stepmother. The early death of his wife, Neferure, weakened his ties to Hatshepsut, and the sources show that by about 1450 B.C. he began to take a major role at religious festivals. By 1482 B.C. his name appears alone as pharaoh. By that date, we assume that the woman pharaoh had died.

At some point during his reign it seems that Thutmose III tried to renounce Hatshepsut's rule, indeed, her very existence. Many of her monuments show that at some point after her death, a serious (but brief) attempt was made to physically remove her image and her name. Workmen gouged out many of her images, presumably to prepare to introduce another image in her stead. Many historians have suggested that Thutmose had resented Hatshepsut's rule and attempted to eradicate it after her death as he had been unable to do during her life. Other historians suggest, however, that the destruction was too haphazard and brief to have represented a policy instituted early in his reign. Thutmosis III ruled a long time—fifty-four years. If he had wanted to fully eliminate evidence of Hatshepsut's existence, he had plenty of time to do so. Perhaps he instituted a brief suppression at the end of his reign to make sure his wives and daughters did not follow her lead and try to rule on their own behalf.

We may never know the exact motivations behind the destruction of Hatshepsut's monuments; we can only be glad they were not all destroyed. Enough have survived to tell us the story of a remarkable woman who found a new role for herself. She had no models of sufficiently powerful queens of Egypt—when she took power, she redefined herself as a female king.

See also Cleopatra VII; Egyptian Women; Nefertiti
Suggested Readings
Gardiner, Sir Alan. *Egypt of the Pharaohs.* Oxford: Oxford University Press, 1961.
Tyldesley, Joyce. *Hatchepsut: The Female Pharaoh.* New York: Penguin, 1998.
Wenig, Steffen. *The Woman in Egyptian Art.* New York: McGraw-Hill, 1969.

Helen of Troy in Greek Mythology

One of the most popular myths in ancient Greece surrounded Helen, an extraordinarily beautiful woman whose beauty brought the destruction of men and societies. Helen stands for the most desired object in the heroic world, and Greek writers throughout the ancient world used the mythological Helen to explore questions of moral responsibility, desire, and beauty itself. In the mists of prehistory, Helen may have represented a fertility goddess, but by the historical period, her story was woven into the actual warfare of the Greeks in a way that combined myth with history. While there are varying versions of the story of Helen, the following account includes the general features.

Some stories say that Helen was the daughter of Zeus, who appeared to the mortal, Leda, in the form of a swan. Leda then gave birth to an egg from which Helen was hatched along with her brothers. (In a variant tale, the minor goddess Nemesis is Helen's mother, but she leaves Helen in an egg with Leda to be raised by her.) Helen grows up to be the most beautiful woman in the world and is given in marriage to the Greek king of Sparta, Menelaus.

Helen was swept into a controversy among the gods, when trouble began at the wedding of King Peleus and the nymph Thetis (who would become the parents of the famous hero, Achilles). All the gods and goddesses came to the wedding bringing gifts. Peleus and his bride had not invited Eris (or "discord"). The goddess came anyway and threw into the company a golden apple marked "for the most beautiful." Three goddesses—Hera, Athena, and Aphrodite

—each claimed the apple, so a contest was proposed to see to whom the apple should go. They selected the prince of Troy, Paris (who was living as a shepherd on the slopes of Mount Ida), to decide among the goddesses. As was usual in the ancient world, each of the goddesses offered the judge a bribe: Hera offered him an empire, and Athena promised him military prowess, but Aphrodite proffered the most beautiful woman in the world as his bride. Paris chose Aphrodite, and the goddess sent him to Sparta to seduce Helen and take her to Troy as his bride.

In response to the seduction, Menelaus gathered the Greek forces and set sail to reclaim his wife (and the goods she took with her). The Greeks reputedly besieged Troy (shown on Map 4) for ten years before that great walled city on the Hellespont fell. Archaeologists have excavated ancient Troy and ascertained that the city was destroyed by fire in about the thirteenth century B.C., so it seems possible that the Greek myths that talk of a great Trojan War have been recalling an ancient war between two growing powers that clashed in the eastern Mediterranean. Historians and archaeologists cannot ascertain whether the war was over economic and political power or about the theft of the beautiful Helen. Her role is preserved in the influential epics of Homer.

In about 700 B.C., a poet wrote the two great epics of ancient Greek society—*The Iliad* and *The Odyssey.* The Greeks attributed these works to one poet named Homer, and they were studied throughout the ancient Greek world as the great repositories of values, myth, and the heroic identity of the ancient Greeks. *The Iliad* tells of one incident during the ten-year war, and *The Odyssey* tells of the ten-year journey of Odysseus (in Latin, Ulysses)—a Greek hero who had fought in the war—as he tried to journey home to Greece. Homer places Helen at the center of *The Iliad* and portrays her as a very human woman—not a goddess in any sense.

In *The Iliad,* Homer claimed that the war was fought over the abduction of Helen and that she was in the besieged city watching the results of her flight with Paris. Homer did not blame Helen but instead saw her as one more pawn in the fate that binds everyone. Paris's father, who has to defend his city because of the whims of his son Paris, speaks kindly to Helen, saying: "You're not at all to blame in my eyes. It's the gods who to my mind are to blame. They stirred up against me the grievous wars of the Greeks." Helen, too, takes a fatalistic view of her plight: "I wish that evil death had been my pleasure when I followed your son here, leaving my bridal chamber, my husband, my kinsfolk and my darling daughter. . . . But that was not to be. So I waste with weeping" (Homer, *The Iliad* 68).

In *The Iliad,* a duel is proposed between the heroic Menelaus and Paris, after which the winner would have Helen back. Aphrodite, however, snatches up Paris, who would surely have lost the contest, and brings him to his bedroom. Aphrodite then seeks out Helen and tells her to go tend to Paris. Helen tries to demure, saying "It would be a blameable thing to make up that man's bed. All the women of Troy will reproach me from now on, and I've countless griefs in my own heart" (Homer, *The Iliad* 74). Helen's show of defiance stirs Aphrodite to anger; she warns Helen that the goddess can make both sides hate her, and Helen is frightened by the threat. She complies with the goddess's wishes and tends her husband. He lusts for her and draws her into his bed.

Throughout *The Iliad,* Helen is portrayed as innocent in causing the conflict, yet deeply suffering to be at the center of all the chaos. Through this portrayal, Homer creates a very human figure blessed (and cursed) with godlike beauty. *The Iliad* does not take the war to its conclusion, when the Greeks leave a hollow horse (filled with their soldiers) on the shore and pretend to abandon the siege. The Trojans, pleased with the apparent departure of the Greeks, bring the great horse within the walls of the city. At night the Greeks emerged from the horse and burned the great city. Menelaus reclaimed his bride and they returned home to Sparta, where Helen was replaced in her household.

Homer tells more of Helen in the narrative of *The Odyssey.* In *The Odyssey,* Odysseus's son Telemachus leaves to seek word about his missing father. He comes to Menelaus's home in Sparta, where he encounters a marriage feast for Hermione, Menelaus and Helen's daughter. She is to marry Achilles's son. When Helen enters the hall, she immediately notices Telemachus's resemblance to Odysseus, and all the company, including Helen, weep for the lost and missing from the war. Homer says that Helen prepares a drugged wine for Telemachus, which will make him forget his sorrows, and Homer claims that Helen learned the art of healing while she was in Egypt. Helen calls for the company to feast and to take pleasure in tales. Both Helen and Menelaus tell how Odysseus had distinguished himself in the Trojan War, which comforted Telemachus. Then Helen and Menelaus went to their marital bed together. The next day, Menelaus tells of his own adventures in returning—telling how he and Helen spent time both in Egypt and in Phoenicia. Later, Helen gives Telemachus a gift of a beautifully embroidered robe for him to give his bride in the future.

In *The Odyssey,* then, Homer once again portrays Helen as innocent in the catastrophe that swept over Greeks and Trojans. By showing her as a perfect and happy Greek wife presiding over a prosperous hall, Homer vindicates her once again. A sixth-century poet, Stesichorus, also vindicated Helen. According to legend, he had castigated Helen in his verses, then went blind as a punishment. A voice informed him that Helen's anger was the cause of his blindness, and to be cured he must publish a retraction. He complied and wrote an account that said that Helen was never in Troy, that instead a phantom of Helen was sent by the gods to Troy to provoke a war. This version fully absolved Helen from any guilt in the war. Future poets would not be so forgiving, however, and in the hands of other artists, Helen's role becomes more blameworthy.

After Homer, the most influential poet who wrote of Helen was the playwright Euripides. He wrote tragedies during the fifth century B.C. when Athens and Sparta were engaged in the devastating Peloponnesian War, a war that dragged on and destroyed the golden age of Athens. In two of his most famous plays—*The Women of Troy* and *Helen*—Euripides turned to the question of war and its devastating results. As war in fifth-century Athens seemed more destructive than heroic, Helen became more ambiguous.

In *The Women of Troy,* at the end of the war the women of Troy are enslaved, and Euripides shows the horror of warfare through their eyes. Helen as the symbol of desire is portrayed as obsessed with her vanity—her beauty is not a curse (as it was according to Homer), but a cultivated pleasure. Helen's claims that she was not at fault seem shallow, and even her husband, Menelaus, is not convinced: "She left my house willingly for a lover's bed. Her talk of Aphrodite is mere invention and pretense—Get out of my sight! Death by stoning is too short a penance for the long-drawn sufferings of the Greeks" (Euripides 124). Paris's mother Hecabe and the Greek chorus urge Menelaus to take revenge on his wayward wife, but he finally weakens in the face of her beauty and her pleas. In this play, Helen seems less a passive vehicle of unkind fate and more a willing participant in the catastrophe. In *Helen,* which is set in Egypt, Helen is once again vindicated, and the poet ends by wishing that many women would be able to share in Helen's beauty and virtue: "Women, I wish you joy in the virtuous heart of Helen—A joy which many women can have no hope to share" (Euripides 189).

Helen's death was treated differently in different legends and renditions of the story. Some said that she lived happily in Sparta with Menelaus until they died and went hand in hand into the Elysian Fields. In another version, the widow of one of the kings who died in the war avenged his death by sending some of her serving women to hang Helen. In yet another version, Helen was swept up to Olympus by the gods and became immortal.

So the figure of the beautiful Helen is seen once more to be a flexible one. The beautiful woman was a catalyst for great deeds in heroic societies, and sometimes was praised and sometimes blamed for that role. The mythological figure of Helen can symbolize the contradictory role of women in ancient societies—by turns praised and blamed.

See also Aphrodite; Athena; Greek Heroine Cults; Greek (Athenian) Women

Suggested Readings

Euripides. *The Bacchae and Other Plays.* Trans. P. Vellacott. New York: Penguin, 1982.

Grimal, Pierre. *The Dictionary of Classical Mythology.* Oxford: Blackwell Publishers, 1996.
Homer. *The Iliad.* Trans. E. V. Rieu. New York: Penguin, 1985.
———. *The Odyssey.* Trans. E. V. Rieu. New York: Penguin, 1976.
Lindsay, Jack. *Helen of Troy: Woman and Goddess.* Totowa, NJ: Rowman and Littlefield, 1974.

Helena

Christian Roman Empress
(ca. A.D. 250–ca. 330)

In the middle of the third century A.D., the Roman Empire was in turmoil; one emperor after another had been assassinated, and it seemed that the imperial power lay in the barracks of the troops in the provinces, who often raised their general up as emperor. The province of Illyricum (modern Balkans, shown on Map 7 as Illyria) was similar to many of the other regions—it had armies stationed there far from home, and lonely soldiers often struck up informal relationships with local women. This story was common, but in the third century a remarkable woman arose in this setting who would become the most powerful woman in the empire and who would later be venerated as a saint: Helena, the mother of Emperor Constantine.

There was nothing in her early life that suggested she was destined for greatness. We know nothing of her family, but apparently it was a humble one, and she allegedly worked in a tavern as a servant girl; in the Roman world, tavern girls were regarded as likely to be engaged in prostitution. The later biographer of Constantine (Eusebius) called Helena a woman of unusual character and of considerable energy and ability. These qualities seemed to have gained the attention of the soldiers who frequented the tavern, and one—Constantius Chlorus—fell in love with her and took her as his mistress. Like many frontier army families, Constantius and Helena settled down together, and before too long, Helena bore a son, named Constantine. Soon the dramatic events of the empire swept over this small family.

In A.D. 284, Diocletian became emperor, and he was the man who ended the turmoil that for fifty years had dominated imperial politics. He

Figure 40. Statue of a woman (probably Helena), early fourth century A.D. (Ann Ronan Picture Library)

established the Tetrarchy—an administrative system in which two emperors—called augusti—shared power. Each immediately adopted a successor—called caesar—who shared power and took the throne upon the retirement of the augustus. Diocletian chose Maximian as his co-augustus to rule in the west, and in 286 Maximian chose the successful provincial general—Constantius—as his caesar.

With Constantius as emperor, there was no place for a tavern girl at his side. He had to set aside Helena and solidify his position by marrying Maximian's stepdaughter, Theodora. The fourteen-year-old Constantine was sent away to be raised in the household of Galerius—Diocletian's caesar. Ostensibly, Constantine was to be educated there in a manner befitting the emperor's son, but in actuality, he was held hostage to ensure his father's loyalty. The system worked until A.D. 305, when Diocletian and Maximian retired, allowing their caesars to become augusti.

Constantius immediately invited his son to join him in Britain. Galerius did not want the young man to leave, but he grudgingly gave permission. Constantine left in the middle of the night before Galerius could change his mind and rode rapidly toward the coast to join his father, who was sailing to Britain. He made it just in time, and the two reunited after thirteen years. The reunion was brief, for Constantius became sick the following year and died in England.

Constantius's troops immediately declared Constantine the next augustus, but Galerius did not agree. He allowed Constantine only to become caesar, but Constantine had higher aspirations. He married Fausta, daughter of Maximian, then joined in the struggle for power that swept through the empire. Diocletian's tetrarchy fell apart, and instead of four peaceful leaders, there were four ambitious and warring augusti. Constantine won the battles, and by A.D. 324 was the sole ruler of the empire.

Through these years of struggle, Constantine did not forget his mother. Once he was caesar, she was returned to prominence. Her dutiful and affectionate son bestowed the title of empress on his mother and gave her the even more honorable title of "nobilissima femina," meaning "most honored and noble lady." The statue shown in Figure 40 dates from this period and is probably Helena. She is shown in the gracious reclining pose made famous by the statue of Cornelia, the mother of the Gracchi brothers. Here Helena is shown as an equally respected Roman mother, and she was even more influential.

Helena gave her son much advice, and it was probably she who persuaded Constantine to be sympathetic to Christians. Under her influence, Constantine ended the persecution Christians had suffered under the rule of Diocletian, and he even generously supported churches and gave privileges to Christians in his service. Constantine even called and presided over the influential Council of Nicaea in A.D. 325, which established the creed that became the basis of Christian faith for millennia.

Helena remained an active supporter of the church in her own right. She was extremely wealthy and used her resources to support the poor and to build Christian churches. Her piety did not prevent her from being involved in the brutal politics of Rome, however. In about A.D. 326, Constantine ordered the death of his son, Crispus, and—purportedly under his mother's influence—had his wife, Fausta, brutally killed by scalding her to death in the bath.

Helena's greatest impact on the future of Christianity came at the end of her life. In about A.D. 330, when she was eighty years old, she decided to go to Jerusalem to visit the holy spots of Jesus' life. Early Christians did not attach any particular significance to Jerusalem, because they believed that Christian holy spaces existed in the next life, not in this world. Helena and Constantine were Roman enough, however, to want to locate the spaces that were holy to her God, so Helena embarked on this journey.

Constantine had established churches in Bethlehem and on the Mount of Olives, and Helena traveled to Palestine and established more churches—one at the grotto that she believed had been the scene of Jesus' birth and another on the mount of his ascension. Sources dating from about fifty years after Helena's death claimed she discovered the True Cross during her travels, and while this story (and the precious relic) circulated widely, it is not likely to be true, since it was not mentioned by her contemporaries.

Shortly after her return to Constantinople, she knew her life was almost ended. She made her will, leaving her still-abundant property to her son and grandsons, and with Constantine by her side, died at the age of eighty. Constantine honored his mother in death as well as life; he escorted her body to a vast royal tomb and struck gold coins with her likeness. Helena later was proclaimed a saint and continues to be highly honored in the Eastern Orthodox Church. This tavern girl did much to shape the Christian empire of the fourth century and beyond.

See also Cornelia [Roman Matron]; Fausta; Melania the Elder; Valeria

Suggested Readings

Bowder, D. *The Age of Constantine and Julian.* London: Elek, 1978.

Eusebius. "Life of Constantine." In *Nicene and Post-Nicene Fathers,* vol. 1, ed. by Philip Schaff and Henry Wace. Peabody, MA: Hendrickson Publishing, 1995.

Holum, K. G. *Theodosian Empresses: Women and Imperial Dominion in Late Antiquity.* Berkeley: University of California Press, 1982.

Hera

Greek Goddess

Hera was the greatest of all the Olympian deities of ancient Greece; she was queen of the gods. She was the sister of Zeus, and both were born of Cronos and Rhea. Like all her siblings except Zeus, she had been swallowed by Cronus but restored to life by Metis's cunning and Zeus's strength. She had participated in the war against the Giants and was the protectress of the *Argo* as it sailed through its mythological adventures.

Hera married Zeus in a formal wedding ceremony. The poet Hesiod said that this was the third time Zeus had contracted a formal marriage. His first wife was Metis, and the next was Themis. The stories said, however, that the love between Zeus and Hera was long-standing, and the marriage assured the powerful goddess of her place as queen of heaven. Zeus and Hera had four children: Ares (the war god), Hephaestus (the smith-god), Eilithyia, and Hebe (a daughter, who personified children). The ancient traditions differ on the location of the divine wedding: Some place it in the Garden of the Hesperides in the heart of an eternal spring, which was the mystical symbol of fertility. Others say that they were married on the summit of Mount Ida in Phrygia. Sometimes the mythographers assert that Gaea—Mother Earth—gave Hera a tree of golden apples as a wedding gift.

As the lawfully wedded wife of Zeus, Hera was the protecting deity of wives, and festivals commemorating her marriage were celebrated almost everywhere in Greece. The statue of the goddess was dressed in the costume of a young bride and carried in procession through the city to a shrine where a marital bed was made ready. She was a powerful goddess who presided over the central ritual of a woman's life—marriage.

Hera was also a fierce, vengeful, and jealous wife, with good reason given Zeus's many infidelities with goddesses and humans alike. Since Zeus controlled the mighty thunderbolt, Hera could not rebel against him directly, but usually resorted to tricks to humiliate him or get her way. In a famous incident in *The Iliad*, she borrowed Aphrodite's magic girdle to entice Zeus sexually and thus get her way, but more often she punished her rivals and their children with implacable fury. For examples, she placed two snakes in the cradle of Heracles; she had Io guarded by a giant who had 100 eyes, and she drove the foster-parents of Dionysus mad.

Once, however, Hera and the other gods tried to rebel against Zeus's high-handed behavior directly. They surrounded Zeus while he was sleeping and bound him with rawhide thongs, knotted into a hundred knots, so he could not move. While they were celebrating their victory and jealously discussing who would be his successor, Thetis the sea-nymph hurried away to bring Briareus, a monster with a hundred hands, who swiftly untied Zeus. Since Hera led the conspiracy, Zeus hung her up from the sky with a golden bracelet around each wrist and an anvil fastened to each ankle. He finally released her when she promised never to rebel again.

The stories about the quarrels between these two powerful deities were often used to reveal truths about human nature. For example, in a famous story, Hera and Zeus were arguing as to whether the man or woman derived greater pleasure from the sexual act. Zeus said women enjoyed it more, but Hera said men did. They decided to consult Tiresias, who had experienced the sexual act both as a man and as a woman. Tiresias sided with Zeus, saying that women felt ten times the pleasure men did. Hera was so annoyed at being contradicted that she blinded Tiresias. From this story, people believed they learned about the nature of men and women and also learned to respect the wrath of the goddess.

See also Aphrodite; Athena; Gaea; Juno
Suggested Readings
Grimal, Pierre. *The Dictionary of Classical Mythology.* Oxford: Blackwell, 1996.

Herodias
Jewish Royal Woman (ca. 10 B.C.–A.D. 43)

The dynasty in Judea that was founded by Herod the Great (r. 39–4 B.C.) was plagued by violence and intermarriage. In this the royal family was solidly within the tradition of Hellenistic rulers whose members ruthlessly used everything from marriage to murder to seize and maintain power. One female member of this family—Herodias—was named in the New Testament of the Bible as one of the most notorious women of ancient Judea.

Herodias was the daughter of Aristobulus IV, son of Herod the Great (ca. 31–7 B.C.) and the old king's first wife, Mariamne I. Herodias's mother was Berenice, daughter of Salome I, the powerful sister of King Herod. Herodias seems to have inherited the love of ambition and fearful vengeance that had marked the first generation of the Herodian dynasty.

Herodias was married at an early age to her uncle Herod (although the Gospels of Matthew and Mark incorrectly said she was first married to a man named Philip). This Herod seems to have lived a quiet life with little ambition, which did not suit Herodias. Her life changed dramatically when Herod's half-brother Herod Antipas came to visit the couple. Antipas held the title of "tetrarch," which meant that he ruled one-fourth of Herod the Great's kingdom. The tetrarch and Herodias immediately fell in love, and Herodias promised to leave Herod and come to Antipas. Her lover was already married to the daughter of an Arab king, but Herodias made him divorce his first wife to marry her. This marriage took place sometime between A.D. 15 and 26.

While such rapid marriage alliances were common among the royalty of the Hellenistic world, they were not acceptable to Jews. There was a strict prohibition against a woman leaving a living husband to marry another, and it was particularly abhorrent for a woman to marry her husband's brother. What made it worse was that Herodias had already borne her first husband a daughter, named Salome. According to the Bible, a popular preacher in the tradition of the ancient prophets publicly criticized Herodias and Herod Antipas for their marriage, which was against Jewish law. This prophet was John the Baptist, and Herodias's revenge on him led to her long-lived infamy.

According to the Christian New Testament, Herod Antipas was unwilling to take revenge on John the Baptist because the preacher was so popular, but Herodias conceived of a plan to trick her husband. At a dinner party, Herodias sent in her very young daughter, Salome, to dance for Herod. The tetrarch was so delighted with the dance that he called Salome to him and offered her anything she wanted in reward for her lovely dance. Salome consulted with her mother and on her advice asked for the head of John the Baptist on a platter. Herod was appalled at the request, but he fulfilled it and John was executed.

At the end of her life, Herodias tried to fulfill her one ambition—to have the title "queen" instead of just tetrarch's wife. She persuaded Antipas to join her and go to Rome with gold and silver to plead with the emperor to award him the title of king. Although Herod was reluctant to be so forward, he yielded to her request. The two went together to Italy and were granted an interview by the emperor Caligula.

However, others had reached Caligula first. The emperor deprived Antipas of his tetrarchy and gave his money to Herodias's brother Agrippa, who like his sister was jockeying for political position. Caligula exiled Herod Antipas and sent him to Gaul, far away from Judea. When Caligula learned that Herodias was sister of his new favorite, Agrippa, he offered to let her keep her private fortune and return to Judea. Herodias (in an act that seems uncharacteristic for a reputedly ambitious woman) claimed that she had been her husband's partner in prosperity, however, and she would not forsake him in his change of fortune. Caligula was enraged at her response, gave her fortune to her brother as well, and sent her into exile with Herod Antipas.

The Jewish historian Josephus wrote that Herodias's fall from the wealth and power that she had so loved was God's punishment for her ambition and vanity. Others have suggested, however, that while Herodias had certainly been cruel and arrogant, she nevertheless stood faithfully by the husband that she had chosen in violation of all Jewish laws. Christians, however, would see no redeeming virtue in the woman who had arranged for the death of John the Baptist.

See also Mariamne; Salome I; Salome II

Suggested Readings
Josephus, Flavius. *Jewish Antiquities.* Trans R. Marcus. Cambridge: Harvard University Press, 1963.
———. *The Jewish War.* Trans. H. St. James Thackeray. Cambridge: Harvard University Press, 1927.
Kokkinos, Nikos. *The Herodian Dynasty: Origins, Role in Society and Eclipse.* Sheffield, UK: Sheffield Academic Press, 1998.
Kraemer, Ross Shepard. *Women and Christian Origins.* New York: Oxford University Press, 1999.
Macurdy, Grace Harriet. *Vassal-Queens and Some Contemporary Women in the Roman Empire.* Baltimore: Johns Hopkins University Press, 1937.
Meyers, Carol, Toni Craven, and Ross S. Kraemer. *Women in Scripture.* New York: Houghton Mifflin, 2000.
Richardson, Peter. *Herod: King of the Jews and Friend of the Romans.* Philadelphia: Fortress Press, 1999.

Hestia

Greek Goddess

Hestia was the Greek goddess of the hearth fire, and as such she presided over domestic life; every hearth on earth was her altar. According to the myths, she was the eldest sister of Zeus (and the oldest daughter of her parents Rhea and Cronus). She remained a virgin, for when her brother Zeus took control of the Olympians, Poseidon and Apollo came forward as rival suitors for her hand. She swore to refuse all offers and remain forever a virgin. At that, Zeus was very grateful because she had preserved the peace of Olympus by her refusal, and in exchange he awarded her the first victim of every public sacrifice. While other gods traveled throughout the world, Hestia remained quietly on Olympus, playing almost no role in myths. She remained an abstract idea of hearth and home.

Hestia was beloved for being the gentlest and kindest of all the Olympian deities. She was the only one who never took part in wars, and she protected people who fled to her for protection. She also symbolized the alliance of Greek mother cities with their colonies, because colonists took fire from the original hearth to keep it burning in the new city.

See also Vestal Virgins
Suggested Readings
Grimal, Pierre. *The Dictionary of Classical Mythology.* Oxford: Blackwell, 1996.

Hipparchia

Cynic Philosopher (ca. 370–285 B.C.)
The Hellenistic age (after the death of Alexander the Great in 323 B.C.) was one of great kingdoms, much violence, and increased poverty. The poignant figure of an old market woman shown in Figure 41 depicts the kind of scene that was increasingly familiar as people could no longer be certain of family ties or economic prosperity to ease their burden in their old age. During this time of uncertainty, many Hellenistic philosophers departed from their Greek counterparts and narrowed the focus of their inquiry. Most of them no longer tackled the lofty questions of truth and justice that had preoccupied Socrates and Plato. Instead, they considered how an individual could achieve happiness in an age in which vast, impersonal kingdoms produced the kind of pain and weariness embodied by the market woman.

The sensibilities of the Hellenistic age had

Figure 41. Old market woman, third century B.C. (Metropolitan Museum of Art, New York)

been first foreshadowed by Diogenes (400?–325? B.C.), an early proponent of the philosophic school called Cynicism. Diogenes was disgusted with the hypocrisy and materialism he saw around him in the transformed life of Athens as the traditional *polis* life deteriorated. Diogenes and his followers believed that the only way for people to live happily in a fundamentally evil world was to involve themselves as little as possible in that world. The Cynics therefore claimed that the more people rejected the goods and connections of this world—property, marriage, religion, luxury—the more they would achieve spiritual happiness. Although

Plato had dismissed Diogenes as "Socrates gone mad," Cynicism became popular during the Hellenistic world as people searched for meaning in their personal lives, rather than for justice for their *polis*. Some men and women chose to live an ascetic life of the mind instead of involving themselves in the day-to-day activities of the Hellenistic cities.

Philosophy, like other occupations in the ancient world, was often a family affair, with siblings following a beloved teacher together. Hipparchia from Athens, along with her brother Metrocles, established such a relationship with the Cynic philosopher Crates (368?–288? B.C.), whom Diogenes had persuaded to jettison all his worldly goods. The siblings met Crates when Metrocles, in despair after embarrassing himself in public while rehearsing a speech, confined himself to his home and determined to starve himself to death. Crates rescued Metrocles by teaching him the futility of despairing over worldly things.

Metrocles became a devoted follower of Crates and an accomplished philosopher in his own right. Yet Metrocles's sister Hipparchia, also captivated by Crates, earned a striking reputation of her own. As the ancient biographer Diogenes Laertes wrote, Hipparchia fell in love with Crates's "words and his way of life" (Hicks 6.7). Though Hipparchia's family was wealthy and her parents introduced many eligible suitors to the young woman, she rejected them all. Indeed, the passionate Hipparchia threatened suicide if her parents refused to permit her to marry Crates.

At the urgent request of Hipparchia's parents, Crates tried to dissuade the stubborn young woman by describing the rigors of life as a Cynic. When that failed, he rose from his seat and threw off his clothing. "Here," he announced, "is your husband-to-be, and this is all he owns; base your decision on this" (Hicks 6.7). Hipparchia accepted him, and they were married. The future Stoic, Zeno, reputedly covered his teacher Crates and Hipparchia modestly with his cloak when they consummated their marriage in the stoa of Athens. Hipparchia and Crates soon became parents to a son, Pasicles, who received a traditional Greek education

while also being strongly influenced by the philosophy of his parents.

Hipparchia lived the simple life of a Cynic, dressing in the same rough clothes as Crates and engaging in the public discourse of philosophers. An epigram attributed to Hipparchia states: "I, Hipparchia, have not followed the habits of the female sex, but with manly courage, the strong dogs [Cynics]. I have not wanted the jewel on the cloak nor bindings for my feet, nor headties scented with ointment; rather a stick, bare feet and whatever covering clings to my limbs, and hard ground instead of a bed" (Hicks 6.7).

Hipparchia joined Crates at public dinners, shocking Greek men who expected only prostitutes to appear at these gatherings. She also "confounded" one of her critics, Theodorus, by offering arguments in a philosophic style: "If it is not wrong for Theodorus to do a particular act, then it is not wrong for Hipparchia to do it. Further, if Theodorus slaps himself he does nothing wrong, therefore if Hipparchia slaps Theodorus she does nothing wrong either." The logic of the second statement, though questionable, had Theodorus stumped. At a loss as to what to do, he tried to embarrass Hipparchia by crudely pulling up her cloak. She refused to be bullied, and according to the text, "did not panic like a woman" (Hicks 6.7).

Theodorus attempted once more to criticize Hipparchia's "unwomanly" behavior, by reminding her of the traditional female role of working wool: "Is this the woman who left her carding combs beside her loom?" Hipparchia responded immediately, defending her choice of studying philosophy: "But do you think I have made a bad decision if instead of wasting my time at the loom I have used it for my education?" The biographer of this principled, spirited young woman closes his account of her life with this tantalizing hint at the many other memorable phrases she must have uttered: "These are among the numerous sayings of the woman philosopher" (Hicks 6.7).

While much of her intellectual heritage has been lost, her life remains an example of many of the trends characteristic of the Hellenistic world. In the larger, impersonal world of cosmopolitan cities, family ties broke down, and some young men and women began to choose their own partners for love instead of practical alliances. Many also rejected traditional religion and morality to find personal fulfillment as Hipparchia and Crates did, following philosophy and defying conventions. In making their own path, people like this couple opened the choices available to individuals in the West.

See also Philosophers, Greek
Suggested Readings
Hicks, R. D., trans. *Diogenes Laertius: Lives of the Eminent Philosophers.* Cambridge: Loeb Classical Library, 1922.

Honoria

Roman Empress (ca. A.D. 418–ca. 454)
Honoria (whose full name was Justa Grata Honoria) was the daughter of the strong-willed empress Galla Placidia. She proved to be as politically ambitious as her famous mother, but her actions endangered the empire and scandalized historians, both ancient and modern. Honoria, the elder child of Galla Placidia and Constantius III, was born about A.D. 418 and was given the names Justa and Grata after her mother's aunts, thus linking her solidly to the imperial household of Theodosius I.

During her youth, Honoria shared the exciting life of her mother, moving back and forth from Constantinople to Italy as political expediency dictated. The family even survived a shipwreck in about A.D. 424, and Galla Placidia erected a church dedicated to St. John the Evangelist in gratitude for the family's rescue. In the dedicatory inscription on this church, we learn a surprising detail about Honoria—she is described as augusta, or "empress." At the end of A.D. 425, when the inscription was dedicated, Honoria was eight years old at most, and it was unprecedented to crown a child princess as empress.

Galla Placidia arranged for Honoria's younger brother Valentinian to be crowned emperor at about the same time to ensure the succession within her family. It may be that she used the model of her famous relative Pulcheria, an empress who exerted a great deal of influence on her younger brother Theodosius II, to decide

that her young son could also use an empress-sister to help him rule. Whatever the motivation, the young empress grew up to imagine that she, too, could wield political power.

Honoria, like her royal relatives before her, lived in a special residence of her own—probably near the royal palace in Ravenna. A steward, named Eugenius, managed her estate, and Honoria had a sexual relationship with him. Some of the sources claim she became pregnant, but all agree that the liaison was discovered. Historians also dispute the date of the empress's "distress"—as one contemporary called it. Either it took place in A.D. 434, and she was an impetuous young girl of about sixteen, or in A.D. 449, when she was a mature, politically astute woman whose power was waning as her emperor-brother had grown stronger. The sources that argue for the earlier date attribute her motive to youthful passion. Modern historians who argue for the later date suggest, however, that this was a political action to produce an heir to compete with her brother's family.

Either way, her brother Valentinian would not tolerate the threat—he put Eugenius to death and drove Honoria from the palace in disgrace. To weaken her political power, Valentinian betrothed her to a respectable senator, who was both wealthy and loyal to the emperor. Honoria wanted nothing to do with the union, and she sought another champion. Like her mother before her, she turned to the "barbarians" outside Rome's borders.

In about A.D. 449, Honoria sent a trusted messenger—a eunuch named Hyacinthus—to Attila the Hun. Hyacinthus carried money, Honoria's ring, and a plea for the leader to support her cause against her brother. Attila, perhaps misinterpreting the ring as an offer of marriage, demanded that half Valentinian's territory be turned over to the empress, who would be his wife. The Hun also prepared to invade the western provinces to claim his territory and bride.

Valentinian was furious. He tortured the eunuch to find out the details of the intrigue, then beheaded him. Honoria's life was spared only because Galla Placidia interceded on her behalf. Attila sent an embassy to Ravenna to claim that Honoria be surrendered to him—along with half the empire. It was as her champion that Attila invaded Italy in A.D. 451. He was almost successful; in A.D. 452, he had Italy at his feet. Illness delayed him, however, and his death in A.D. 453 prevented him from coming to claim his bride.

After A.D. 452, we hear no more of Honoria; she may have lived a few years more. The ancient historians were not kind to her. The Romans called her a profligate girl who could not control her passions and who would betray Rome to the Huns for love. It is more likely, however, that her motive was ambition and her crime political. She was one more strong empress of the house of Theodosius who wanted to claim actual as well as titular power.

See also Flaccilla; Galla Placidia; Pulcheria
Suggested Readings
Bury, J. B. "Justa Grata Honoria." *The Journal of Roman Studies* 9 (1919): 1–13.
Holum, Kenneth G. *Theodosian Empresses: Women and Imperial Dominion in Late Antiquity.* Berkeley: University of California Press, 1982.

Hortensia

Roman Orator (42 B.C.)

One of the essential facts of Roman life was the importance of public oratory. Men made their political reputations and rose in power in part through their ability to speak in public and sway the people by their eloquence. Roman rhetoric also played an important role in the law courts of the age, where lawyers pleaded cases for clients who depended as much upon their speaking skills as on the justice of their cases. For the most part, women were excluded from this important public role, but during times of turmoil and civil war, when traditions broke down, some women became known—for better and worse—for their public speaking skills.

One woman—Afrania, wife of the senator Licinius Bucco—was much criticized because she preferred to defend herself in legal cases rather than hiring a lawyer. Her critic (Valerius Maximus) reports that she was "addicted to lawsuits" and "always pleaded her own case before the praetor, not for lack of friends to speak for her but because she was quite shameless. So from her constant harassment of the magistrate's tribunals with this unnatural yapping she became a notorious example of female abuse of court, so much so that the very name of Afrania is used as a charge against women's wicked ways" (Fantham et al. 273). Afrania died in 46 B.C., during the troubled times of the late republic. In spite of such negative comments, however, she seems to have continued her public life undeterred by her critics.

Another woman, on the other hand, was praised because she used her eloquence in the service of all women, not simply for her own gain. Hortensia came forward to plead the case for women who suffered financially under the civil wars that tore Rome during the late republic. During the civil wars that broke out after the murder of Julius Caesar in 42 B.C., men and women alike suffered if they supported the wrong party—not only did men sometimes suffer imprisonment or death, but they also had to pay large fines and taxes to the triumvirs, the strongmen who were ruling Rome. As Octavian, Mark Antony, and Lepidus struggled for power, a brave woman stepped forward to speak on behalf of the noble women of Rome who had not created this horrible civil war.

Hortensia was the daughter of a famous orator, Hortensius, and she delivered her memorable speech in 42 B.C. on behalf of the 1,400 wealthy women who were being taxed to pay the expenses of the triumvirs. The women had first approached Octavian's sister and mother and won them over, but Antony's wife, Fulvia, rudely turned them away. The women then forced their way into the forum, and Hortensia addressed the masses gathered there. A second-century historian, Appian, purports to preserve her speech in a Greek translation, and though it is probably not Hortensia's exact words, the sentiments are profound and are likely true to the orator's meaning:

> You have already deprived us of our fathers,
> our sons, our husbands, and our brothers
> on the pretext that they wronged you,
> but if, in addition, you take away our
> property you will reduce us to a condition
> unsuitable to our birth, our way of life, and
> our female nature.

If we have done you any wrong, as you claimed our husbands have, proscribe us as you do them. But if we women have not voted any of you public enemies, nor torn down your house, nor destroyed your army, nor led another against you, nor prevented you from obtaining offices and honors, why do we share in the punishments when we did not participate in the crimes?

Why should we pay taxes when we do not share in the offices, honors, military commands, nor in short, the government for which you fight between yourselves with such harmful results? You say "because it is wartime." When have there not been wars? When have taxes been imposed on women, whom nature sets apart from all men? Our mothers once went beyond what is natural and made a contribution during the war against the Carthaginians, when danger threatened your entire empire and Rome itself. But then they contributed willingly, not from their landed property, their fields, their dowries, or their houses, without which it is impossible for free women to live, but only from their jewelry. . . .

Let war with the Celts or Parthians come, we will not be inferior to our mothers when it is a question of common safety. But for civil wars, may we never contribute nor aid you against each other. (Appian 32–34)

In addressing the crowd in the forum, Hortensia wisely pointed out that she and the other women were patriots, ready to support Rome, but that they were not interested in supporting the civil wars that so tore their lives apart. Appian said that the triumvirs were angry that the women would dare to hold such a public meeting and criticize them. Nevertheless, the crowd supported the women, and the following day the triumvirs had to give way. They reduced the number of women subject to taxation to 400. Hortensia's eloquence had carried the day. Perhaps the most telling backhanded compliment to her oratorical skills came from Valerius Maximus, who regretted that there were no male descendants of Hortensius to carry on the inheritance of his eloquence.

See also Fulvia; Octavia; Turia

Suggested Readings

Appian. *Appian's Roman History*. Trans. H. White. Cambridge: Harvard University Press, 1964.

Fantham, E., et al. *Women in the Classical World*. New York: Oxford University Press, 1994.

Pomeroy, Sarah B. *Goddesses, Whores, Wives and Slaves: Women in Classical Antiquity*. New York: Schocken Books, 1975.

Hypatia

Alexandrian Philosopher (ca. A.D. 370–415)

Since its founding in the fourth century B.C., Alexandria in Egypt had grown to be a vibrant cosmopolitan center of the Mediterranean world. The great museum and library there that had been founded by Ptolemy Philadephus and his sister-wife Arsinoë II soon became the greatest intellectual center of the ancient world. Seven centuries later, the museum's reputation had only grown. The library contained thousands of volumes of scholarly readings, including the works of the great pagan philosophers, and the museum drew the greatest minds from all over the western world. Scholars studied physics, mathematics, philosophy, and science and came to listen to lectures by the greatest teachers in this cosmopolitan city. In the late fourth century A.D., the most charismatic and popular teacher was the philosopher and scholar, Hypatia.

Hypatia's father, Theon, was a mathematician and philosopher at the Museum of Alexandria, and it is fairly certain that Hypatia studied under her father's tutelage. According to the sources, she quickly surpassed her father, "since she had greater genius" than he had, and her growing fame rested upon her mastery of philosophy. According to one of her biographers, "the woman used to put on her philosopher's cloak and walk through the middle of town and publicly interpret Plato, Aristotle, or the works of any other philosopher to those who wished to hear her" ("Life of Hypatia").

Students flocked to her from everywhere, and letters reached her that were simply addressed to "The Muse" or "The Philosopher." We have some letters that survive from the famous Neoplatonic philosopher (and later Christian bishop) Synesius of Cyrene, and in them he praises her knowledge in many fields—Neoplatonism, astronomy, mechanics, and mathematics. He even asked her for practical advice on how to build an astrolabe (a navigational tool) and a hydroscope (a device used to determine the weights of different liquids). Synesius came to study with her in Alexandria because, as he wrote, she was "a person so renowned, her reputation seemed literally incredible. We have seen and heard for ourselves she who honorably presides over the mysteries of philosophy" ("Life of Hypatia"). At this time, Hypatia was only about twenty-three years old!

By about A.D. 400, she became the head of the Neoplatonic school in Alexandria. While it was not uncommon for the outstanding student in the school to inherit the position of teacher, one of the sources on her life suggests that Hypatia was paid by public funds, which meant that she would have received an official appointment. This would have been a remarkable honor for anyone and virtually unheard of for a woman.

Sometimes the fact of being a woman caused Hypatia some difficulty, for her position of teacher led her to live a public life (which was not common for a respectable woman). One of her biographers wrote that she was at ease in public: "On account of the self-possession and ease of manner, which she had acquired in consequence of the cultivation of her mind, she not unfrequently appeared in public in the presence of the magistrates. Neither did she feel abashed in going to an assembly of men. For all men on account of her extraordinary dignity and virtue admired her the more." However, another source describes how one of her students fell in love with her and was unable to control himself. To cure him, Hypatia reputedly gathered cloths that had been stained during her menstrual period (the equivalence of ancient sanitary napkins) and showed them to him, saying, "This is what you love, young man, and it isn't beautiful!" The source explains that "he was so affected by shame and amazement at the ugly sight that he experienced a change of heart and went away a better man" ("Life of Hypatia").

Hypatia wrote mathematical tracts—a commentary on Diophatus's *Arithmeticorum,* a commentary on Ptolemy's *Syntaxis Mathematica,*

and another commentary on the *Conic Sections* of Appolonius Pergaeus. One source reported that all of Hypatia's works had been lost, attributing this to the burning of the great library in Alexandria. Some scholars argue, however, that parts of these works have survived intact. Further, it appears that Copernicus—the famous sixteenth-century astronomer who demonstrated that the sun was the center of the universe—may have been influenced by Hypatia's writings.

None of Hypatia's philosophical writings have survived, but scholars assume that her position would have been similar to that expressed by her enthusiastic student, Synesius of Cyrene. He was a strong Neoplatonist, who believed that the soul could approach God through contemplation. Synesius had sent Hypatia one of his works—*Dion*—in which he reconciled Neoplatonism with the Christian views of the Trinity. However, Hypatia was not a Christian, and this caused her death.

As Alexandria was an intellectually vibrant city, not surprisingly, it also was a center of fourth-century Christianity. As we have seen, her student Synesius would become a bishop, and her Neoplatonic teachings deeply informed his Christian ideas. Other Christians, however, believed that the popular, charismatic teacher drew people to paganism and away from Christianity. One negative biographer of the philosopher wrote that "she was devoted at all times to magic, astrolabes and instruments of music, and she beguiled many people through her Satanic wiles." Furthermore, this biographer—John, Bishop of Nikiu—wrote that she had also "beguiled" the governor of the city, and this probably referred to her paid appointment as head of the school ("Life of Hypatia"). While to all appearances Hypatia was interested in philosophy, not politics, she was nevertheless drawn into the struggle between pagans and Christians in early fifth-century Alexandria.

Probably as a result of a political struggle between the Roman governor, Orestes (who was Hypatia's patron), and the Christian bishop of Alexandria, Cyril, Hypatia became the focal point of riots between Christian and pagans. A mob gathered near her—led by a man named

Peter—and dragged her from her carriage and took her to a church called Caesareum. There they stripped her and murdered her with tiles (the Greek word is *ostrakois,* which literally means "oyster shells," but the word also referred to the brick tiles used on the roofs of houses). The crowd then tore her body into pieces and burnt them.

However we might feel about the struggle between Christians and pagans, we must surely share the outrage of the author who described these events—Socrates Scholasticus—when he wrote: "Surely nothing can be farther from the spirit of Christianity than the allowance of massacres, fights, and transactions of that sort" ("Life of Hypatia"). The emperor was angry, but he was bribed not to take vengeance against her attackers. The ancient world lost one of its brightest women to bigotry and jealousy.

See also Arsinoë II; Philosophers, Greek

Suggested Readings

Kersey, Ethel M. *Women Philosophers: A Bio-Critical Source Book.* New York: Greenwood Press, 1989.

Lefkowitz, Mary R., and Maureen B. Fant. *Women's Life in Greece and Rome.* Baltimore: Johns Hopkins University Press, 1982.

"Life of Hypatia." Versions by John, Bishop of Nikiu, by Socrates Scholasticus, and by Damascius. http://cosmopolis.com/people/hypatia.html.

Waithe, Mary Ellen. *A History of Women Philosophers.* Vol. 1: *Ancient Women Philosophers.* Boston: Martinus Nijhoff Publishers, 1987.

I

Io
Mythological Greek Priestess

According to ancient Greek myths, Io was the daughter of the river-god Inachus and a priestess of the goddess Hera. Zeus fell in love with Io, and a dream told Io to go and submit to Zeus's embraces. She told her father about the dream, and her father consulted oracles to see what they should do. The oracles told him to obey, so Io was sent to Zeus. The god began an affair with the girl, and Hera became suspicious. To save Io from the goddess's jealousy, Zeus turned her into a cow. (Some analysts suggest that Io was an early moon goddess; horned cows are associated with the moon, since the horns resemble the crescent moon.) In the myth, Hera demanded that Zeus give her the cow, and she gave it to be guarded by Argus, who had 100 eyes.

Zeus felt sorry for Io and sent Hermes to fetch the beautiful cow for him. Hermes destroyed Argus and released Io, but the cow-woman's troubles were not over. Hera sent a gadfly to sting Io and chase her all over the world.

The legend describes the travels of Io as she went to Europe, Asia Minor, and Africa. She purportedly traveled down the Nile to a place where pygmies and cranes were in perpetual battle. Finally, she found rest in Egypt, where Zeus restored her to human form. She married there, but she gave birth to Epaphus, whose real father was Zeus. Io was credited with founding the worship of Isis—the Egyptian name she gave Demeter. Some people suggest that the myth of Io's travels was to explain the spread of the popular cult of Isis.

The legend seems to incorporate an old worship of a moon goddess into the Greek mythological pantheon. In this version, Io is swept into Zeus's infidelities and Hera's jealous rages.

Her grief was also incorporated into the worship of the mysteries of Demeter in various locations. It may also be that ancient women saw in this myth a woman who came to despair because of the lust of the powerful.

See also Demeter; Hera; Isis
Suggested Readings
Grimal, Pierre. *The Dictionary of Classical Mythology.* Oxford: Blackwell, 1996.

Ishtar
Mesopotamian Goddess

Ishtar was the goddess of love, sex, war, and fertility, and under various names she was the most important goddess throughout western Asia. For example, she was known as Inanna to the Sumerians, Astarte in Syria, Ashtoreth in the Bible, and Isis in Egypt. Her Sumerian name is probably derived from Nin-ana, which means "lady of heaven," and in all her aspects, she is described as a celestial body—perhaps the planet Venus. In art, Ishtar is often represented as a warrior-goddess, often winged and often naked. In this way she shows her combined functions of war and fertility.

At the heart of the worship of Ishtar was a myth that described how she entered the world of the dead. The Mesopotamian versions date from the seventh century B.C. (although the earlier composition probably dates from the end of the second millennium B.C.), and this myth is similar to the longer Sumerian version, called the "Descent of Inanna." The prevalence and popularity of this story testify to its centrality in the worship of the goddess.

According to the myth, Ishtar descends into the underworld of death. Although the myth is incomplete, scholars assume that she was seeking an elixir to restore people to life. She demanded to be admitted to the dark place where her sister Ereshkigal was queen:

> Here gatekeeper, open your gate for me,
> Open your gate for me to come in!
> If you do not open the gate for me to come in,
> I shall smash the door and shatter the bolt,
> I shall smash the doorpost and overturn the doors,
> I shall raise up the dead and they shall eat the living:
> The dead shall outnumber the living!
> (McCall 69)

As Ishtar gained entry, she had to go through various gates where she was stripped of her jewelry and attire. At the first gate her great crown was taken; at the second her earrings were removed. At the third gate she gave her necklace and at the fourth the ornaments from her breast that held her gown. At the fifth she gave up the girdle of birthstones from her waist, and at the sixth she gave the bracelets from her wrists and ankles. Finally at the seventh gate she was stripped of the cloak that covered her. At each gate, she complained to the gatekeeper, and at each she received the same answer, which suggests that this was ritual for initiation to the mysteries of the goddess:

> Gatekeeper, why have you taken away the great crown on my head?
> Go in, my lady. Such are the rites of the Mistress of Earth. (McCall 70)

Finally she was naked when she came before her sister, but still it was Ereshkigal who trembled at Ishtar's presence. The queen of the underworld summoned her vizier Namtar and instructed him to send out against Ishtar sixty diseases—to her eyes, her arms, her feet, her heart, her head, to every part of her. Meanwhile on earth, all sexual activity ended among people and animals, thus threatening all fertility and the very order of nature.

Therefore the great gods sent a messenger to the underworld to demand Ishtar's release.

Ereshkigal was forced to comply and sprinkled the waters of life on Ishtar; the fertility goddess then began her journey back through the seven gates of the underworld. At each one, she retrieved her possessions and emerged clothed in the trappings of her divinity. Ishtar paid for her release with her husband Dumuzi, the "lover of her youth," who would in future dwell in the underworld. On one day each year he returned to earth to enact fertility rituals and ensure the continuation of life on earth before he had to retreat back to the underworld.

The myth probably symbolically addressed ancient people's fear of famine and the time of year when nothing grew. The descent of Ishtar into the world of the dead expressed their hope in the resurrection of the crops and of life itself. This myth may have also been reenacted annually as people celebrated the mysteries of the return of the growing season. Perhaps more than anything else, the beautiful story of Ishtar expresses the importance that ancient men and women placed on the fertility goddess.

See also Clothing; Enheduanna; Isis; Mythology
Suggested Readings
McCall, Henrietta. *Mesopotamian Myths*. Austin: University of Texas Press, 1996.

Isis
Egyptian Goddess
The ancient Egyptians worshiped many gods and goddesses, recognizing a spiritual force in nature that inhabited many things. The Egyptians also treasured family life and recognized that family ties were at the heart of an ordered and peaceful world, so reflecting this importance, the ancient Egyptians gave special veneration for the family of deities who held a central place in their religious and political lives. Most beloved were the couple Isis and Osiris, who were sister and brother as well as wife and husband, and their child, Horus, of whom all pharaohs were said to be the living embodiment.

During the Hellenistic period (after 323 B.C.), the cult of Isis spread throughout the Mediterranean world and attracted converts from many lands. The goddess became universal, appealing to men and women seeking a particular form of spiritual satisfaction, and she became much more important than either her brother-husband or her son. Elements of the myth surrounding Isis have been found in the most ancient Egyptian texts, but in the first century A.D. the Greek writer Plutarch wrote the most complete version of the legend. It is this version that expresses the form of the beliefs during the Hellenistic world and the Roman Empire, and this is the myth as it is usually remembered today.

The earth god, Geb, and the sky goddess, Nut, had four children (two sets of twins). Isis and her sister, Nephthys, married their two brothers, Osiris and Seth. Osiris was the hero of the myth, for according to Plutarch, he "delivered the Egyptians from their destitute and brutish manner of living" (Plutarch 35) by showing them agriculture and by teaching them laws and how to honor the gods. He traveled all over the world spreading these fruits of civilization. While Osiris was away, Isis ruled in his stead, exerting supreme power over the land of Egypt, and some Egyptian queens looked to this goddess as offering precedent for their rule. Seth was jealous of his siblings, however, and contrived a plot to kill his brother.

When Osiris returned from his journeys, Seth promised to give a beautiful chest to whoever matched its measurements exactly. When Osiris took his turn lying in the chest, Seth's henchmen slammed down the lid and nailed it shut, capturing Osiris. They nailed it and sealed it with lead so he could not escape and put the chest in the river to let it float out to sea. Isis was frantic to find her beloved and searched the world for him. She discovered the chest had been washed ashore, and the foliage around the chest had grown into a great tree. A local king had so admired the tree that he had it cut down for use as a pillar in his palace.

Isis went to this household and became so intimate with the queen that she made Isis the nurse for her baby. Isis nursed the child by giving it her finger to suck instead of her breast, and in the night she would burn away the mortal portions of its body. The queen saw this one night and screamed and put the fire out, thus depriving the baby of its immortality. Isis revealed her

divinity and asked for the pillar—which also included the entombed body of Osiris. She brought it home to Egypt. While it was on the boat, she opened the coffin and laid her head on the dead head of Osiris and wept. She erected pillars in front of all Isis temples to represent the completion of her quest for her husband. Osiris was not to rest in peace, however.

Seth came upon the sarcophagus of Osiris and divided the body into fourteen parts and scattered them in different places. Once again the goddess had to search for her husband-brother. The myth says that in every place that Isis found a piece of Osiris, she erected a tomb and made effigies of him. In this way the cult of Osiris spread all over. Isis found all the parts of Osiris's body except his penis, which had been thrown in the river and eaten by a fish. But Isis made a replica of his penis to take its place, and according to Plutarch, Egyptians annually celebrate the creation of the new phallus. Isis was able to conceive a child with Osiris's reassembled body, and a son, Horus, was born.

To conceal Horus's existence from the murderous Seth, Isis hid him in the marshes, magically protecting him from the dangers of the riverside, including snakes and scorpions. She guarded him until he reached adulthood so he could take his rightful place as divine king—successor to Osiris. All Egyptian pharaohs considered themselves to be the incarnations of Horus, divinely destined to rule in Egypt. Because of Isis's fierce protection of her son, Egyptians considered her the paradigm of a perfect mother. As such, she was often invoked by mothers to protect their children, and the maternal goddess was frequently portrayed nursing her son, as she is in Figure 42.

Osiris appeared from the dead to visit his son Horus and train him for battle. After a time, Osiris asked Horus what he held to be the most noble of all things, and the son replied, "To avenge one's father and mother for evil done to them" (Plutarch 47). Osiris was pleased with his son and felt that he was prepared. Horus engaged a battle with Seth and defeated him, bringing him in chains to Isis. She did not have him killed, however, but released him. There were many more battles between Horus and

Figure 42. Isis nursing Horus (Field Museum of Natural History, Chicago)

Seth, for this brother represented chaos and formlessness—whether of the desert or the ocean—in opposition to the fecundity and cultivation personified by Isis and Osiris. The ongoing struggle between the siblings was the same struggle that always went on in Egypt, where an ordered world seemed to struggle to keep disaster at bay.

During the Hellenistic world, the worship of Isis became increasingly popular, and the goddess was less a fecund earth mother than a universal "mother of all things." There were elaborate festivals and processions in her honor, and every spring believers celebrated Isis's search for and resurrection of her brother-husband. In time, believers hoped that worship of Isis would bring immortal life to all followers of her cult.

See also Egyptian Women; Mythology

Suggested Readings
Martin, Luther. *Hellenistic Religions.* New York: Oxford University Press, 1987.
Plutarch. "Isis and Osiris." In *Moralia.* Trans. Frank Cole Babbitt. Cambridge: Harvard University Press, 1962.
Solmsen, Friedrich. *Isis among the Greeks and Romans.* Cambridge: Harvard University Press, 1979.

J

Jewelry

Humans have always adorned themselves with jewelry. Beginning in the Old Stone Age (Paleolithic) over 25,000 years ago, men and women took objects that they found, drilled holes in them, and wore them. Archaeologists have found necklaces of animal teeth, shells, pebbles, and bones, and in one communal grave from the Paleolithic, scientists found every body adorned with a necklace made of ivory beads. Why did early humans wear jewelry? We can only guess that the insights anthropologists draw from modern tribes applied in the long prehistory. If that is so, during our long history, humans have used jewelry for several reasons. One was that jewelry offered protection against adversity. Cowrie shells, for example, were widely favored from the Neolithic through early Egypt as a protection against sterility. Egyptian women wore fish amulets in their hair to protect against drowning, and earrings protected the wearer from the evil eye. A second reason to wear jewelry was to prove status: a chief's high position was marked by rare feathers or expensive jewelry of gold and jewels. Finally, jewelry was adornment to enhance sexual attractiveness.

While early jewelry was made of natural objects that were strung together, the real history of jewelry begins with a history of gold. Gold was one of the earliest metals sought, and by 3000 B.C. in Mesopotamia, goldsmiths skillfully worked gold in ways that are largely unchanged today. In the Bronze Age when people depended upon bronze for weapons and tools, they were drawn to gold even though it was too soft a metal to be used for anything other than adornment. It may be that people loved its color—the brilliant gold that did not tarnish made people believe that it held the powers of the sun. Furthermore, gold is very malleable—it can be hammered so thin that a mere ounce of the precious metal can be made into a sheet more than 100 feet square. The soft metal could be pressed into magnificent forms, engraved, spun into thin filagree wires, and cast. Early goldsmiths also learned to make beautiful jewelry by framing precious stones with gold. All these techniques were developed very early, and all the ancient societies valued jewelry made from gold. When gold was too expensive, they used the same techniques to adorn themselves with silver and other metals.

Sumerians

The peoples of the ancient Middle East—men and women alike—wore lots of jewelry. As archaeologists have excavated graves, they have found men and women buried with their magnificent adornments. Great headdresses made of gold and precious stones were buried with their owners. Women wore large earrings, occasional nose rings, and many necklaces of beads and gold. Their wrists and ankles sported bracelets that jangled as they walked. Figure 43 shows a dummy dressed in the headdress and jewels of the Sumerian queen Pu-Abi, which date from about 2500 B.C.

Egyptians

The Egyptians too were extremely skilled jewelers; they not only included finely wrought gold in their pieces, but they inlaid precious and semiprecious stones with a great deal of skill. Their favored stones were deep red carnelian, dark blue lapis lazuli, and blue-green turquoise. They also imported amethyst and amber. When these stones were too scarce or expensive, they used colored glass for the first costume jewelry.

Figure 43. Headdress, earrings, and necklace of Sumerian queen Pu-Abi, ca. 2500 B.C. (Werner Forman/Art Resource, NY)

gold and inlay. Finger rings were developed in the New Kingdom, and many included seals to identify the wearer's signature. These seal rings slowly replaced the more cumbersome seal cylinders or pendants that had been used for centuries.

Minoans

In the region of the Aegean, the great civilization of the Minoans (which flourished from about 2500 to 1100 B.C.) also prided itself on its jewelry. It is clear that these goldsmiths were influenced by the fine work of the Sumerians; nevertheless the Minoans left their own stamp on the goods they produced. They fashioned diadems from thin gold sheets and pounded simple designs in the gold out of dots. The nature of these designs—eyes, animals, and geometric patterns—suggests that their jewelry might have served as protective talismans. They also produced many hairpins with heads like daisies to support the elaborate hairstyles of Minoan women. They also had bracelets and pendants, but finger rings and earrings seem to have been unknown during the early periods of Minoan history.

Late in the Minoan period, the jewelry shows the influence of their far-flung trading empire. By 1600 B.C., Minoan craftsmen began to use fine gold filigree and imported a variety of stones for the jewelry. Egyptian influence in design and materials is strong. Hairpins became even more elaborate, and earrings make their appearance. Finger rings, too, became popular, and many had the Egyptian scarab on them, showing again the influence of the Mediterranean trade.

Greeks

Greek jewelers came into their own in the fifth century B.C., after the Persian Wars. Before this, there is little evidence for Greek jewelry because there were no local sources of gold, and Greek craftsmen must have worked for neighboring societies such as the Etruscans. As Greek city-states became heavily involved in trade, however, and wealth came to Greece, the craftsmen expressed their love of adornment.

Earrings were very popular by the fifth century B.C. and came in four basic designs: a boat

Tomb paintings and hieroglyphics help us to understand the specific uses for Egyptian jewelry. In addition to personal adornment, Egyptians used their jewelry as talismans—protection against various things. This explains the recurrence of various symbols: snakes, scorpions, and other vicious animals warded off evil spirits, while scarabs, falcons, and cowrie shells brought protection. Other jewels brought the wearer health, prosperity, and longevity—emeralds, for example, were thought to protect eyesight.

Crowns, collars, chokers, bracelets, and anklets were popular throughout Egypt's history. At the beginning of the New Kingdom (about 1560 B.C.), women began to wear earrings, a fashion that probably spread from Mesopotamia and the Middle East, where it had been popular for at least a thousand years. Egyptian women pierced their ears with huge holes so they could wear enormous pendant earrings made from shape with a fine wire that ran through the pierced ear, spirals, ear studs, and finally pendant earrings. Women also wore elaborate necklaces, mainly constructed from beads, and bracelets from simple plain loops to highly decorated pieces that had sculpted sphinxes or other animals created into the design. Finger rings also remained popular throughout the classical Greek age, and these rings were elegantly decorated. Figure 44 shows a beautiful gold ring engraved with the head of a woman, and the woman in the figure wears a boat-shaped earring made more elaborate by the addition of two dangling pendants.

Hellenistic Period

When Alexander the Great conquered much of Asia in the fourth century B.C., Greek culture spread east. At the same time, however, the Greeks were influenced by the skills and designs of peoples all the way to India. This blending introduced the richest period for jewelry and goldwork in the history of the Mediterranean world. Gold was more readily available owing to the increased trade, and a new class of rich merchants emerged who could afford beautiful jewelry.

Perhaps the most important innovation was the introduction of color—inlay and the use of precious stones were rare in ancient Greece, but in the Hellenistic period, jewelry exploded with color. Jewelers used garnets, emeralds, amethysts, pearls, and carnelians and supplemented these bright stones with enamels and glass. The designs were complex and filled with filigree. Earrings became huge—long pendants that dangled below the shoulders, or great hoops. Many people grew rich during this cosmopolitan era, and men and women alike proudly wore their wealth.

Romans

The early Romans inherited a fine tradition of jewelry-making from the Etruscans, who preceded them on the Italian peninsula. The Etruscans were magnificent craftsmen, and the Greeks and Romans accused them of being too fond of luxury. This combination of skill and love of beauty produced some magnificent treasures—goldwork that has fine filigree and that was pre-

Figure 44. Greek gold finger ring, ca. 400 B.C. (British Museum)

pared with a skill unequaled today. Etruscan men and women loved huge earrings, hair adornment made of spirals of gold, bracelets, and necklaces. Etruscans also developed elaborate pins to hold their great cloaks closed. These were called *fibulae* and were decorated with three-dimensional figures of lions and other animals. In about 250 B.C., the Etruscan civilization was absorbed into the expanding Roman Empire, and Romans adopted many of the Etruscan techniques. The early Romans were models of restraint, however, and many objected to the Etruscan ostentation.

In the fifth century B.C. and again in the third century B.C., Romans passed laws to limit the amount of gold the wealthy flaunted. The first law limited the amount of gold that could be buried with the dead, and the second law—the *lex oppia*—said that no woman should be allowed to wear more than half an ounce of gold. The republican Romans sought to regulate people's love of display, but that would not last.

This restraint ended with the huge expansion of the Roman Empire. By the imperial period, people had acquired the tastes of Hellenistic jewelry, and the wealthy sported huge amounts of gold and jewels to show that their status surpassed their neighbors'. One text claimed that a woman wore one bracelet of pure gold that weighed ten pounds! Romans wore all kinds of jewelry, from earrings to necklaces to bracelets to headdresses. However, more than in any previous society, they favored finger rings, and many people wore many rings on each hand. The Romans seem to have been the first to seal their betrothal with a ring.

Romans also seem to have been the first society to shift the emphasis in jewelry from gold to precious stones. In their love of color, they often used gold simply to outline precious gems in their bracelets and rings. They even carved exquisite cameos on stones, and the emperors gave these carved with their own image to their favorites. The Roman Empire vastly increased the range of jewelry that people found attractive.

Germans and Celts

The ancient tribes of northern Europe did not have the material wealth that characterized the southern Mediterranean world. Their lives were sparse, and much of their prosperity was counted in cattle and family. Nevertheless, personal adornment and jewelry played a large part in their culture. Kings—who were sometimes called "gold-givers"—distributed jewelry as a mark of their favor. Warriors who sported great gold necklaces and bracelets could let this wealth proclaim their own prowess.

Among the most remarkable finds of this northern world are the gold pieces made by the Bronze Age Celts in Ireland from the late third millennium B.C. on. These craftsmen made necklaces and fine goldwork. Sometimes they added stones and amber to the decorations. Figure 45, which shows a gold necklace made in Ireland in about the seventh century B.C., suggests how extraordinary it would have been to wear such a piece, which would seem to shine with the light of the sun itself as the wearer stood in the firelight.

The other Germanic tribes, too, perfected

Figure 45. Celtic gold necklace, ca. seventh century B.C. (Victoria & Albert Museum, London/Art Resource, NY)

their love of ornamentation by creating magnificent pieces in gold and silver, adorned with precious stones. By the time the German peoples invaded the Roman Empire, they were almost as elaborately decorated as the Romans. One of the motivations of the tribal raids, however, was to seek more of the gold that seemed so abundant in the empire.

Conclusion

The history of jewelry is as old as the history of humanity. As long as there have been humans, people have wanted to wear precious metals and stones. Gold has been valued as the defining ornamental metal from the moment people first discovered it, and stones and other metals quickly were added to the range of jewelry. Jewelry seemed to bring magical protection to the wearer, and it served to define a hierarchy of status. Finally, people were drawn to jewelry from the simple aesthetic appreciation of the beauty that comes with finely wrought jewelry.

See also Clothing; Cosmetics

Suggested Readings
Black, J. Anderson. *The Story of Jewelry.* New York: William Morrow and Company, 1974.
Gregorietti, Guido. *Jewelry through the Ages.* New York: American Heritage, 1969.

Jewish Women

In the early second millennium B.C., a Semitic people known as the Hebrews settled in the ancient Middle East. They had originally lived as nomads under patriarchs—such as Abraham—in the north of Mesopotamia, and about 1800 B.C. they moved to Palestine along the shore of the Mediterranean and settled among other Semitic peoples. Slowly the Hebrews adopted agriculture and settled in small villages. In about 1700 B.C. a group emigrated to Egypt, but their descendants returned to Palestine between 1300 and 1200 B.C. under their leader Moses. Their state enjoyed prosperity under kings and in about 900 B.C., Hebrews in the southern kingdom centered in Jerusalem began to be called Jews. The Hebrew and Jewish kingdoms were conquered in the sixth century B.C. by the Babylonians, and after that there were Jews dispersed throughout the ancient world.

Although the Hebrews shared many cultural characteristics with their neighbors, early in their history they departed from the religious beliefs of the ancient world by becoming monotheists. Instead of praying to many deities—including goddesses—as their neighbors did, the ancient Hebrews worshiped only a masculine God. We learn about the Hebrews from their sacred scriptures (which were later incorporated into the Christian Bible as the Old Testament), which were composed at various times ranging from about 1200 to 400 B.C. These texts include histories, stories, poetry, and laws, and they serve as our principal source of information about this early society—including the roles and perceptions of Hebrew women.

One of the central ideas of the ancient Hebrews was the idea of community—in the Hebrew scriptures, the word *community* appears some 160 times, and allied words, such as *assembly* and *people,* appear some 3,500 times. The definition of community in the sources excluded women, however; Hebrew men were the core of the community, at least as it appeared in the laws. For example, the contract between God and the Jews—or the "covenant"—that set Israelites as chosen people apart from others of the region was marked by the circumcision of sons. For a girl, there was no similar rite of passage

that marked her as a Jew, and women were excluded from many of the other religious requirements that continuously confirmed males as part of their religious community. For example, men were required to be educated in the Law and to observe many ritual activities—sounding the ram's horn, saying certain prayers, and so on—all of which were forbidden to women.

The center of the Hebrew cult in Jerusalem was at the Temple, where animals were sacrificed and prayers conducted by a male priesthood. Women were permitted to attend the Temple but were only allowed into an outer, less holy area, called the Court of Women (although men, too, were allowed to enter there). Foreigners, too, were permitted to enter this outer court, so Jewish women received no more privileged status with regard to the Temple than did nonbelievers. Furthermore, Jewish law required that "all Jews over twenty" be taxed to support the Temple, but in fact this law only applied to male Jews, so once again the official standing of Hebrews was restricted to men.

After the Temple was destroyed—first in the sixth century B.C. by the Babylonians, then again in A.D. 70 by the Romans—the heart of Hebrew worship moved to the synagogues, local places of gathering. The synagogues had both educational and liturgical purposes: to educate men in the Holy Law and to provide structured services of worship, prayer, readings, and sermons. Services could only take place if ten adult males were present (regardless of how many women were in attendance), and once the requisite number were there, men conducted the services. Women probably sat apart from the men and could listen but not read any of the prayers.

Probably one of the main reasons women were excluded from the priesthood and other ritual activities was that there were strong taboos against menstruation, and menstruating women were perceived as unclean. Men were forbidden to have sexual intercourse with a menstruating woman for fear of becoming polluted by the blood, and women were forbidden to enter even the outer courtyard of the Temple when they were menstruating. Furthermore, childbirth itself, with the attendant bleeding, also made a woman unclean, and the law describing this shows a further devaluing of the female: "If a woman conceives, and bears a male child, then she shall be unclean seven days. . . . But if she bears a female child, then she shall be unclean two weeks" (Lev. 12:2–5). These perceptions of feminine pollution continue throughout Jewish history and enter into Islam and Christianity as the heirs of much of Jewish thought.

Like other women in the ancient world, Hebrew women belonged to the private sphere of the home rather than the public spaces of town and Temple. When describing women's roles in this area, the scriptures offer a strikingly positive view of women, which contrasts with the negative image of pollution that emerges from the laws on public spaces. The *Song of Solomon* is a collection of about twenty-five lyric poems of love and courtship as might be appropriate to be sung at a wedding. While the poems have been interpreted metaphorically to speak of God's love of his people, nevertheless the beautiful erotic images of women's beauty have deeply shaped subsequent literature. The poet praises the woman's beauty, writing: "Your lips are like a scarlet thread, and your mouth is lovely. Your cheeks are like halves of a pomegranate behind your veil" (Song of Solomon 4:3), and he also praises sexual love between man and woman. These verses speak to a joyful pleasure behind the closed doors of the ancient homes.

Hebrew law strictly punished adultery, as the law aimed to preserve the ties of marriage. As scriptures say, "If a man is found lying with the wife of another man, both of them shall die" (Deut. 22:22). These laws are similar to the other Mesopotamian laws that also regulated adultery and rape. In the Hebrew law, however, a woman could be accused even if her husband was only jealous (without specific proof) (Num. 5:11–28), and the fear of accusation of such serious crimes appears in the literature of the times. (*See* Susanna.) Men could divorce their wives under Hebrew law, but women did not have the same rights of initiating divorce. In general, the strong emphasis on marriage demonstrates that women were at a disadvantage when they were not closely connected by family ties to men, and the literature bears this out.

Women also had a difficult time controlling property or wealth. They did not normally inherit property (although they could when there were no sons to inherit), but more often than not, they would bring any inherited property to their marriage and place it under the control of their husbands. Widows were often faced with poverty since they could not control property left them, and the scriptures contain repeated pleas for people to show charity to widows. (*See* Ruth.)

Scriptures also show how women's work within the household was essential. The fullest description of a woman's role may be found in Proverbs (31:10–31), in which the writer praises a good wife who "is far more precious than jewels." She rises every day while it is still dark and works until after dark. She provides food for the household and also spins, weaves, and makes clothing. She also works outside the home, sometimes in the fields: "She considers a field and buys it; with the fruit of her hands she plants a vineyard. She girds her loins with strength and makes her arms strong." The text also claims that she supports the family's income by selling some of the clothing that she makes. Through her hard work, she helps the family prosper and receives their praise in return: "Her children rise up and call her blessed; her husband also, and he praises her; 'Many women have done excellently, but you surpass them all'" (Prov. 31:28–29). This scriptural description of a perfect wife offers a clear model for Hebrew women to follow, and it is likely that most worked hard in the home as their husbands fulfilled the more public life outdoors.

While Proverbs may describe an ideal Hebrew woman, scriptures also show some examples of women who were extraordinary and give glimpses into women's lives that are not obvious from the standard idealized descriptions in the laws. Some texts—such as Judith or Maccabee 1 and 2—show women taking a politically active role to support Israel. Other texts—such as Ruth—show how women support each other and form communities to help themselves within the more formal structure of Judaism. While the formal dictates of the ancient Hebrew society were strongly patriarchal, with little room for women to participate in the religious or political life, the sources hint at strong, loyal Jewish women who played an important role in the continuity of Jewish life and beliefs.

See also Anna; Judith; Maccabean Martyrs; Naomi; Ruth; Susanna

Suggested Readings

Archer, L. J. *Her Price Is beyond Rubies. The Jewish Woman in Graeco-Roman Palestine.* Sheffield, UK: Sheffield University Press, 1990.

———. "Notions of Community and the Exclusion of the Female in Jewish History and Historiography." In *Women in Ancient Societies,* ed. by L. J. Archer et al. New York: Routledge, 1994.

Baron, S. *A Social and Religious History of the Jews.* New York: Columbia University Press, 1952.

Bird, P. "Images of Women in the Old Testament." In *Religion and Sexism: Images of Woman in the Jewish and Christian Traditions,* ed. by R. R. Ruether. New York: Simon and Schuster, 1974.

Meyers, Carol. *Discovering Eve: Ancient Israelite Women in Context.* New York: Oxford University Press, 1988.

Meyers, Carol, Toni Craven, and Ross S. Kraemer. *Women in Scripture.* New York: Houghton Mifflin, 2000.

Jezebel

Queen of Israel (ca. ninth century B.C.)

During the reign of King Solomon (ca. 961–922 B.C.), the Kingdom of Israel was consolidated, with its capital at Jerusalem. Solomon maintained close relations with Israel's neighbors, the Phoenicians, who had a prosperous trading civilization centered in the two city-states of Sidon and Tyre (see Map 5). The Phoenicians were talented builders, and Solomon had used many Phoenician artisans to build the great Temple at Jerusalem that would serve as the center of Hebrew worship. Not long after Solomon's death, however, the united kingdom broke apart into two: the Kingdom of Israel in the north and that of Judah in the south. The kings of both kingdoms maintained their ties with the Phoenicians, with some disastrous effects for King Ahab, who began to reign in Israel in the ninth century B.C.

According to the Book of Kings in the Bible, Ahab took as his wife Jezebel, daughter of the Phoenician king of Sidon, and this strong-willed woman brought some dramatic changes to the Hebrew kingdom. The new queen introduced the worship of her own gods to the land of the Hebrew God, Yahweh. She persuaded her husband to build altars to the Phoenician deities Baal and Ashtaroth (the goddess of fertility), and she brought 450 priests or "prophets" of Baal to the capital to preside over the worship. Shrines to her native gods began to spring up on hilltops throughout the kingdom, and a temple to Baal was even built in the palace itself. Even King Ahab began to offer worship to Baal in violation of the strict commandment against worshiping idols. Israelite priests who resisted were eliminated or driven into hiding.

Finally a strong voice was raised against these violations of religious law. Elijah the prophet suddenly appeared before the king dressed only in a leather loincloth and a cloak of hair. He predicted a drought in retribution for the king's lapses but disappeared before the king and queen could have him arrested. Elijah sought refuge across the Phoenician border and hid with a widow and miraculously provided food for himself and the widow through the drought.

After three years God told Elijah that the drought was ending and to once again confront King Ahab. Elijah proposed a contest between the two deities to see which was the true god. The prophet and the priests of Baal met on top of Mount Carmel, and each prepared a pile of wood with pieces of a bull laid on the pile. The test would see which divinity would send down fire to consume the sacrifice. All day the priests of Baal prayed for a flame, even slashing their bodies with knives and spears until the blood flowed, but there was "no voice; no one answered, no one heeded" (1 Kings 18:20). In the evening, Elijah stepped forward and prayed. At his cry, fire came down on the altar and consumed the sacrifice. Elijah had the priests of Baal seized and slain. The prophet told Ahab he could now descend from the mountain, for the rain was coming to end the drought.

When Jezebel heard what had happened, she sent word that the prophet should be killed. Once again he fled for his life and hid in the wilderness, but he would have a final confrontation with Ahab. While Elijah was away, the king had coveted a vineyard next to his winter palace in Jezreel, but the owner, Naboth, had refused to sell it. Jezebel arranged for Naboth to be falsely accused of blasphemy and stoned to death. Then his property was forfeited and claimed by the king. When Ahab went to his newly acquired vineyard, Elijah appeared before him and denounced him. The prophet predicted the fall of the house of Ahab and said that the dogs would eat Jezebel by the walls of Jezreel. Ahab tore his clothes, fasted, and repented, so according to the Bible, God delayed the fulfillment of Elijah's curse.

After a reign of twenty-two years, Ahab died and was succeeded by his son, Jehoram. Now Elijah's curse was to be fulfilled. An army commander named Jehu murdered Ahab's son and seized the throne. Now there was no one to protect Jezebel, but she met her fate proudly. As Jehu came through the gate of the palace in Jezreel, he saw the queen mother standing at the window with her eyes and face carefully made up and her hair beautifully dressed. She accused him of killing the king, and Jehu shouted out to her attendants to throw her out the window. They obeyed him, and the Bible relates her death in detail: "Some of her blood spattered on the wall and on the horses, and they trampled on her" (2 Kings 9:33). Jehu waited until he had eaten dinner before telling his servants to go and bury Jezebel's body. When they found her, however, all that was left of the corpse was the skull, hands, and feet. Jehu said that this was the fulfillment of Elijah's prediction that the dogs would eat her at her winter palace.

Jezebel remains the most notorious of the Israelite women—a Phoenician who married the king. During her lifetime, she was a strong queen, who expected to be able to administer various aspects of her kingdom. Her worship of Baal led to her downfall, however. The name of this woman who tried to bring the worship of her gods to the land of the Israelites became one of the most vilified in Judeo-Christian tradition, the symbol of female depravity.

See also Esther; Jewish Women

Suggested Readings

Ackerman, Susan. *Warrior, Dancer, Seductress, Queen: Women in Judges and Biblical Israel.* New York: Doubleday, 1998.

Meyers, Carol, Toni Craven, and Ross S. Kraemer. *Women in Scripture.* New York: Houghton Mifflin, 2000.

Judith

Hebrew Heroine (ca. fifth century B.C.)

The Latin Vulgate version of the Christian Bible contains fifteen Jewish books (or portions of books) written between 200 B.C. and A.D. 100 that were not included in the Hebrew canon of the Bible. These books are called the Apocrypha, and one of these—the Book of Judith—tells what is probably a fictional account of a brave Hebrew widow. Originally written in Hebrew at about the end of the second century B.C., it has remained a popular story that continues to stimulate numerous works of literature and visual arts to the present day. The author made no attempt at accuracy—it was set in an imaginary town called Bethulia, and it inaccurately claimed that King Nebuchadnezzar (the Babylonian king) ruled over an Assyrian kingdom. Nevertheless, the story captures the intensity of Hebrew pious national spirit, and it vividly tells the tale of a fictional woman whom many believed was real.

According to the Book of Judith, King Nebuchadnezzar was furious at some countries surrounding his land because they had refused to follow his orders. He called for his fiercest general—Holofernes—and told him to take vengeance against all who had disobeyed the king's command; included in that number were the Hebrew lands of Israel and Judea. When the people of Israel heard how Holofernes had devastated other nations and plundered and destroyed their temples, they were terrified at the approach of the general. Everyone feared for the Temple of Jerusalem that had been recently rebuilt after its destruction by the Babylonians, so Joakim, the high priest of Jerusalem, rallied the people. He told them to fortify the hilltops and the passes through the mountains that could be held against invaders, and particularly he sent word to the people of the (fictional) town of Bethulia, for it was located at a strategic position at a mountain pass. With prayers and fasting, the Israelites did as Joakim told them and readied themselves for battle.

When Holofernes heard that the people of Israel were preparing for war, he was furious. He called his advisers and asked about these rebellious people. He was told about the history of the Hebrews and about how they had the protection of God as long as they obeyed His commandments. Holofernes was warned that he could not defeat this religious tribe. These words only increased his anger and made him redouble his efforts. The general ordered his whole army and all their allies to move against Bethulia and to seize the passes up into the hill country to make war on the Israelites. The army laid siege to the town, surrounding it and cutting off the water supply. Then the invaders settled down to wait for the inhabitants to surrender from hunger and thirst. The water within the city ran out after thirty-four days of blockade, and the people despaired. The magistrates agreed to surrender if the Lord did not send help within five days. At this point a brave woman stepped forward.

Judith was a widow living in the region. Her husband, Manasseh, had died of the heat while in the fields harvesting barley, leaving his wife alone. Judith had lived as a widow for three years and four months, dressing in widow's clothing and fasting every day except for religious feast days. She was beautiful, and her husband had left her prosperous, but what characterized her the most was her piety. When she heard the words of the magistrates she stepped forward and reprimanded the people. She said, "Who are you, that have put God to the test this day?" (Jth. 8:12). She claimed it was not right to give God a five-day challenge for help, but instead they should accept this trial as a test from God and help themselves. The magistrate could not argue with her. He said, "All that you have said has been spoken out of a true heart, and there is no one who can deny your words. Today is not the first time your wisdom has been shown, but from the beginning of your life all the people have recognized your understanding, for your heart's disposition is right" (Jth. 8:28–29). Judith told them she had a plan, and within the five days she would deliver the city from its enemies.

After praying fervently, Judith removed her widow's clothing and dressed herself in her brightest clothes. She put on her precious jewelry—"anklets and bracelets and rings, and her earrings and all her ornaments" (Jth. 10:4)—and rubbed herself with precious oils and perfumes. She "made herself very beautiful, to entice the eyes of all men who might see her" (Jth. 10:4). She then left the house with her maid and persuaded the elders to open the gates of the city, and the two women crossed the valley toward the enemy camp. The Assyrian outposts seized the women and questioned them. Judith told them she had fled to escape the town's destruction and that she had information for Holofernes, claiming she could tell him of secret routes through which he could easily occupy the hill country. The women were taken to Holofernes's tent, where he was resting under a mosquito net richly decorated with jewels.

Judith told the king that the hungry people of Bethulia would soon lose God's protection by eating forbidden food, and then the Assyrians would be victorious. The beautiful woman said she would guide Holofernes all the way to Jerusalem herself and see him crowned king there. The general was captivated by her beauty, so he did not suspect any duplicity. Promising to treat her well, Holofernes gave instructions to the guards to let Judith and her maid pass freely through their lines to pray to the Lord. She promised to tell the general when the Hebrews had sinned so he would be free to attack. Holofernes invited her to dine with him, but she refused, claiming she could not offend God by eating the forbidden food, but she did accept his offer to sleep for a while.

For the next three days, Judith went out of the camp daily to bathe at a spring and pray, and then stayed in the tent and ate her food in the evening. On the fourth day, Holofernes held a banquet for his slaves, and he sent his eunuch to persuade Judith to join him. Judith agreed, dressed herself in her finest things, and went to the general's tent. She reclined before him on soft fleeces that her maid laid out for her and she ate and drank before him what her maid had prepared. "Holofernes's heart was ravished with her and he was moved with great desire to possess her" (Jth. 12:16). In his pleasure and passion, the general drank too much—"more than he had ever drunk in any one day since he was born" (Jth. 12:20). As the evening wore on, all the slaves left, and Judith was left alone with Holofernes. Judith dismissed her maid and told her to wait until she was ready to leave for her prayers as was her habit.

As Holofernes lay drunk on the couch, Judith prayed for strength and drew his sword from the scabbard by the bed. She grasped his hair, and with all her force struck twice at his neck, cutting off his head. She tumbled the body off the bed and went out and gave the head to her maid, who placed it in the food bag. Then the two went out together as they were accustomed to do for prayer, and none of the guards knew anything was amiss. They circled around to the gates of Bethulia and called out for the men to open. The guards rushed to let the women in and were astonished to hear Judith cry out, "Praise God, . . . who has destroyed our enemies by my hand this very night!" (Jth. 13:14). She showed them the head of Holofernes and swore to them that she had needed to commit no sin in order to be victorious. She told them to hang the head on the walls of the town and pretend to attack the Assyrians in the morning.

At dawn some Hebrews emerged armed from the town, and the Assyrians ran to the tent of Holofernes. Fear spread through the camp when they discovered their leader decapitated on the floor. The soldiers began to flee, and the Hebrews were able to slaughter many as they pursued the army. The people plundered the Assyrian camp and gratefully gave Judith Holofernes's tent and all his silver dishes, beds, and furniture. She piled these things high on carts and had her mule pull them away.

"Then all the women of Israel gathered to see her and blessed her, and some of them performed a dance for her" (Jth. 15:12). Judith danced with them and sang a long song celebrating her achievement, including the summary of her victory: "Her sandal ravished his eyes, her beauty captivated his mind, and the sword severed his neck" (Jth. 16:9). Judith went to Jerusalem and dedicated to God all the plunder that had belonged to Holofernes.

After the great celebration, everyone returned home, including Judith. She resumed her former life, and though many wanted to marry her, she remained a widow. She freed her maid who had helped her in her struggle against the Assyrians; then she lived to be 105 years old. She became more and more famous as the years passed, and she died in peace. She was buried with her husband, and the land mourned her for seven days. The story of Judith was told and retold to urge women and men alike to trust in God and to fight bravely against tyranny.

See also: Clothing; Cosmetics; Esther; Jewelry
Suggested Readings
Comay, Joan. *Who's Who in the Old Testament.* London: Routledge, 1971.
Enslin, Morton. *The Book of Judith.* Leiden: E. J. Brill, 1972.
Meyers, Carol, Toni Craven, and Ross S. Kraemer. *Women in Scripture.* New York: Houghton Mifflin, 2000.

Julia
Daughter of Roman Emperor
(39 B.C.–A.D. 14)
Julia was the daughter of Rome's first emperor, Octavian—known as Caesar Augustus—who ruled from 27 B.C. to A.D. 14. Octavian's first wife, Scribonia, bore Julia, but Octavian divorced her shortly afterward, claiming, "I could not bear the way she nagged at me" (Suetonius 88). He then married the great love of his life, Livia, who helped raise Julia. During Augustus's long reign (he died in A.D. 14), he created governmental structures that were effective and enduring, and he ushered in the two hundred years known as the Pax Romana—the Roman peace. Augustus did not limit his attentions to politics or foreign policy; he also promoted a number of laws that were designed to affect the personal lives of the Romans. He wanted to restore morality and family values and to promote policies designed to increase the birthrate among Romans; he wanted the new Rome to meet the standards of decency and seriousness that he believed had marked the great days of the early republic.

He set an example of such discipline in his personal life, living in a modest house, and he took measures to restrict ostentatious displays by private people. Furthermore, in 19 and 18 B.C., he introduced bills into the senate to regulate family life and restore morality. These "Julian laws" (named after him) strongly penalized adultery and tried to make sure that families provided the central order of Rome. All men between 25 and 60 were to be married, as were women between 20 and 50, and unmarried people were penalized by not being able to receive bequests from anyone other than close relatives. Beyond simply marriage, Augustus wanted to encourage these couples to have children, so a woman who bore three children was rewarded by being allowed to manage her own property. Fathers of three children were allowed to advance more quickly through the stages of their public career.

Augustus added legislation punishing adultery, which for the first time in Roman history moved the penalties for adultery from the family to the state. If adultery were proven, the wife and her lover were banished to different islands for life; the man lost half his property, and the woman lost a third of hers. Now the family as an institution came under the protective eye of the state, a situation that has extended in some form into the modern world. The new stern laws regulating morality took their toll in a surprising quarter—on Augustus's only daughter, Julia.

As the only child of the most important man in the empire, Julia's life belonged to Rome. Augustus made sure that she was raised strictly and modestly—she was taught to spin and weave as any republican woman would have done, and she was forbidden to do or say anything—either publicly or privately—that could not be proudly repeated in public. Augustus also took severe measures to prevent Julia from forming any friendships without his consent, and according to the imperial chronicler Suetonius, when a fine young man from a good family came to call on Julia, he received a terse letter from the emperor saying, "You were very ill-mannered to visit my daughter" (Suetonius 89). The young man did not repeat the error; no one was free to court the daughter of Augustus.

There were two main reasons for marriage to an only daughter of an emperor: to name a successor (her husband or son) and to prevent her from giving children of imperial blood to other families that were potentially rivals. Julia would be married three times, and her weddings were always arranged by Augustus with these motives in mind.

In 25 B.C., when she was fourteen years old, Julia was married to M. Claudius Marcellus, Augustus's nephew (son of his sister Octavia). Marcellus was a charming, popular figure and would probably have made a fine successor to Augustus (which is no doubt what the emperor imagined when he arranged the marriage). Fortune would not smile on this couple, however, for two years later Marcellus was dead, a victim of an epidemic that struck Rome. There had been no children produced by this marriage, so Julia would be married again soon.

The next candidate for the imperial title was an immensely capable man named Agrippa. As early as 23 B.C., Augustus entrusted him with many responsibilities, and two years later, Julia was given in marriage to Agrippa. The couple produced five children: three sons—Gaius Caesar, Lucius Caesar, and Agrippa Postumus—and two daughters—Julia and Agrippina. It seemed as if the succession was secure, but once again fate intervened. Agrippa died in 12 B.C. rather suddenly. He was only fifty years old and had been expected to outlive Augustus. The emperor had adopted his two grandsons, G. Caesar and L. Caesar, but they were still only children. Augustus had to secure the succession more clearly.

He then turned to Livia's surviving son—Tiberius—to prevent anyone else from challenging the succession of Augustus's two favored grandsons. The emperor forced Tiberius to divorce his wife Vipsania (daughter of Agrippa by an earlier marriage) so he could marry his stepsister Julia. It was clear that Tiberius was only a stopgap until Gaius and Lucius Caesar should reach maturity, and in any case the marriage was loveless. Tiberius withdrew from public life to Rhodes, leaving Julia alone in Rome. Julia seems to have believed that marriage to Tiberius was beneath her, and she resented being forced to conform to the role Augustus had decreed. In Tiberius's absence she began to take advantage of the exciting life that Rome had to offer.

When she was thirty-seven years old, Julia took lovers from among Romans ever eager to cultivate the family of the emperor. Later sources would accuse her of the most scandalous behavior—selling herself as a prostitute and becoming publicly drunk in the Roman forum. Augustus seems to have known that she was headstrong and amusing herself with company he did not like, for reputedly when the emperor saw Julia at a gladiatorial show with men who were not of the good character of those who accompanied her stepmother Livia, he reprimanded his daughter, but she simply responded defiantly. It may be that these sources underplayed any political motivation Julia had for her liaisons—did she hope to undermine her father's power? We will never know.

In 2 B.C. the storm broke. The strict laws that Augustus had passed gave informers the license to report Julia's scandalous behavior to her father. He was furious. In accordance with the very laws he had passed, he exiled his daughter to the island of Pandateria (today called Ventotene), which lies thirty-one miles west of the bay of Naples. The island is less than two miles long and according to the sources was full of field mice, which nibbled at the sprawling grapevines. The island had a small harbor and the imperial villa. Julia's mother, Scribonia, who was quite aged, accompanied her daughter into exile, and Augustus allowed no man to visit unless he was politically acceptable (and according to some sources physically unattractive). Finally, on the island that produced wine, Julia was forbidden to drink any. She was to be the sober, quiet daughter that Augustus wanted. Julia's lovers did not escape the emperor's wrath. Several were banished, and one committed suicide.

Many Romans protested Augustus's harsh treatment of his daughter, and after five years he relented a bit. He allowed her to continue her exile in Reggio in the south of Italy, which offered a few more amenities. Julia's son Agrippa Postumus and her daughter Julia also ended up being exiled for scandalous behavior. The elder Julia died in exile in A.D. 14, shortly after her ex-husband Tiberius became emperor at the death of her father. Her life showed that the lives of imperial princesses were governed by the politics of alliance and succession. Her experiences might also have shown Caesar Augustus that it was easier to legislate morality than it was to enforce it—a lesson that fell harshly on this first daughter of the Roman emperors.

See also Agrippina the Elder; Livia; Octavia
Suggested Readings
Balsdon, J. P. V. D. *Roman Women: Their History and Habits.* New York: John Day, 1963.
Hawley, R., and B. Levick, eds. *Women in Antiquity: New Assessments.* New York: Routledge, 1995.
Suetonius. *The Twelve Caesars.* Trans. Robert Graves. New York: Penguin, 1979.
Tacitus. "The Annals." In *Complete Works of Tacitus.* Trans. A. J. Church. New York: The Modern Library, 1942.

Julia Domna

Empress of Rome (early third century A.D.)

In about A.D. 180, a promising Roman general, Septimius Severus, was stationed with his army in Syria. He visited the temple of Baal and came to know the priest of the temple. The younger daughter of the priest, Julia Domna, was unmarried, and the ambitious general was most interested to find that the beautiful young woman had an auspicious horoscope: she was to become the wife of a king. Seven years later, after Septimius Severus's first wife died, he returned to Syria and married Julia Domna. He planned to share her fortunate horoscope, and he was not disappointed; by A.D. 197, Septimius had defeated all his rivals and became the emperor of Rome.

Julia gave him two sons. The elder was named Bassianus Antoninus, but history remembers him as Caracalla, the nickname that derived from the kind of hooded cloak he favored. The second son was named Geta, born just a year after Caracalla. The two boys grew up hating each other with a fierceness that neither parent could restrain.

By all accounts, the empress enjoyed the benefits of power. She was identified with the goddess Isis and shared the veneration that was accorded her husband. She seems to have ignored the persecution of Christians that took place during their reign and that claimed the lives of the famous martyrs, Perpetua and Felicity. Instead, Julia surrounded herself with philosophers and writers. The sources praise her literary circle, which included the authors of the most popular Hellenistic novels of the day, and Dio Cassius, the ancient Roman historian, wrote that "she was known for her love of learning and her wit" (Dio 233). Her pleasant life was disrupted with the death of her husband.

Septimius Severus died in A.D. 211 while campaigning in Britain. On his deathbed, he gave his sons final advice: "Be harmonious [with each other], enrich the soldiers, and scorn all other men" (Dio 271–273). Even their father's last wish did not still the animosity between the boys. They rushed back to Rome, each conspiring to kill the other. Finally, Caracalla tricked his mother into delivering her younger son to the assassin's blade. The elder persuaded Julia Domna to summon both sons to her apartment unattended so they could reconcile. As Geta saw centurions enter, who had been summoned by Caracalla, he ran to his mother and clung to her, pleading that she save him. The Roman historian described the subsequent events with horror: "And so she, tricked in this way, saw her son perishing in most impious fashion in her arms, and received him at his death into the very womb, as it were, whence he had been born; for she was all covered with his blood" (Dio 283).

The sources say that Julia Domna was not even permitted to mourn her younger son for fear of offending Caracalla, who was now sole emperor. Yet, it seems that Julia quickly became reconciled to the new situation and took an important role in the administration of her son. The sources say that Caracalla had "appointed her to receive petitions and have charge of his correspondence . . . and used to include her name, in terms of high praise . . . in his letters to the senate" (Balsdon 154). She continued to receive the most important politicians and thinkers of the empire, and the sources say that it was her love of power and authority that caused her to live harmoniously with Caracalla.

When she heard of Caracalla's death in A.D. 217, Julia was much affected, although the Roman historian was suspicious of her motives: "Thus she mourned now that he was dead, the very man whom she had hated while he lived; yet it was not because she wished that he were alive, but because she was vexed at having to re-

turn to private life" (Balsdon 155). Though she attempted some intrigue to take sole rule as emperor, she was unable to do so. Shortly thereafter she suffered from breast cancer, but instead of waiting for the cancer to claim her, she committed suicide by starving herself to death.

See also Felicity; Isis; Julia Maesa; Perpetua the Martyr

Suggested Readings

Balsdon, J. P. V. D. *Roman Women: Their History and Habits.* New York: John Day, 1963.

Benario, Herbert W. "Julia Domna—Mater Senatus et Patriae." *Phoenix* 12 (summer 1958): 67–70.

Birley, Anthony. *Septimius Severus: The African Emperor.* London: Eyre and Spottiswoode, 1971.

Dio Cassius. *Dio's Roman History.* Trans. E. Cary. Cambridge: Harvard University Press, 1961.

Salisbury, Joyce E. *Perpetua's Passion: The Death and Memory of a Young Roman Woman.* New York: Routledge, 1997.

Julia Maesa

Roman Empress (d. ca. A.D. 224)

The dynasty established by Septimius Severus in A.D. 197 was dominated by strong women who fought to keep their sons in power. They followed the example of Julia Domna, wife of Septimius Severus, and exceeded her in political savvy and ruthlessness. When Emperor Caracalla was murdered in A.D. 217, his powerful mother, Julia Domna, lost the influence she had held for so long—first with her husband, Septimius Severus, then with her cruel son, Caracalla. After being diagnosed with cancer, the empress committed suicide by starvation. Her death, however, would not end the influence of the women from this talented, strong-willed Syrian family. Her younger sister, Julia Maesa, stepped forward and shaped the rule of the empire for more than a decade.

Julia Maesa had been married to Julius Avitus, and they had two daughters—Julia Soaemias and Julia Mamaea. Avitus had died while Caracalla was emperor. Each of Julia Maesa's daughters was widowed, and each was left with one son. Julia Soaemias's son was fourteen years old when Caracalla was killed. His name was Varius Avitus, but he is remembered by the name of the sun-god Elagabalus, whom he worshiped. Elagabalus was a priest of this god, whose image was a black conical stone. His cousin (who would later be called Alexander Severus), son of Julia Mamaea, was a boy of ten. When Caracalla died, nothing seemed more improbable than that these boys would become emperors, yet the indomitable will of these women ensured it.

Upon Caracalla's death, a man named Macrinus was proclaimed emperor. One of his first acts was to send Julia Maesa a curt note insisting that she leave Rome and return to the east, taking her possessions with her. She obeyed his order, took her extraordinary wealth, and moved to Emesa. Life in the provinces did not suit her, however—she wanted to return to Rome and to the imperial palace. She saw her opportunity, for the big army that had been assembled in the east by Caracalla was not uniformly in favor of Macrinus. Julia Maesa had plenty of wealth to buy their loyalty, but she also hatched a scheme that would give the next heir the legitimacy of the imperial bloodline.

Julia Maesa and her daughter Julia Soaemias told the army that Elagabalus was really the illegitimate son of the emperor Caracalla himself, and thus the legitimate heir to both the throne and the loyalty of the troops. Astonishingly, the story was accepted, and the boy was smuggled into the camp. Elagabalus was an unusual candidate for the imperial purple—he was a beautiful young man whose interests seemed limited to worshiping his stone-god. He also insisted on dressing in the long robes of a priest with a tiara on his head, and it was in this guise that he appeared before the troops. The boy did have some courage, however, for when his troops met those of Macrinus, he fought bravely on horseback. At first, the rebels were pushed back, but the two Julias—Maesa and Soaemias—stopped the rout by jumping from their chariots and appealing to the troops to rally. The battle turned in their favor, and Macrinus fled to go to Rome to gather supporters for himself. He was murdered on the way.

Julia Maesa understood Roman politics and knew that installing this odd boy as emperor would be no easy task. Luckily the journey back to Rome took a long time—they had to spend the winter in the east, delaying their entrance into the city, which gave Julia Maesa time to prepare the city for her idiosyncratic grandson. Elagabalus regularly wore his priestly clothing—purple and gold silk, with necklaces and bangles, and on his head, a richly bejeweled miter. His grandmother and mother explained to him that it was a mark of decadence in Rome to wear silk, and he should dress more appropriately. They said that by Roman standards he looked more like a woman than a man. Instead of listening to the women, Elagabalus claimed that he would not wear traditional wool—it appeared cheap to him. Instead, he commissioned a portrait of himself in his full priestly regalia worshiping his stone. He sent it to be displayed in the senate house so the Romans could become accustomed to the appearance of their new emperor.

In July of A.D. 219, the party reached Rome. The Romans looked at his strange appearance and called him the Assyrian. The youth did not care but continued his single-minded devotion to Elagabalus. He built temples to his sun god, and in his extravagant devotion, Elagabalus further offended the Romans. He rid himself of his first wife and married one of the vestal virgins. He claimed: "I did it in order that godlike children might spring from me, the high priest, and her, the high priestess" (Balsdon 159). The Roman historian Dio Cassius probably spoke for most Romans when he wrote, "he ought to have been scourged in the Forum [for the violation of a vestal virgin]" (Balsdon 159). Elagabalus also dressed more and more like a woman, even having his beard hairs plucked out so his face would be smooth. He wore eye makeup and a hair net and took male lovers. He even shocked Rome by formally taking a "husband" in a wedding ceremony.

For all his extravagant behavior, Elagabalus seems not to have forgotten the debt he owed his mother and grandmother. They were both declared empresses and given the right to strike their own coins. Soaemias was given the titles "mother of augustus" and "mother of the army," and Maesa was called "mother of the army and the senate." No doubt under their influence, Elagabalus declared that since Rome had a senate of men, it should also have a senate of women. This body was established and met, but its only known achievement was to issue a complicated code of etiquette for women in Rome. It decreed what kind of clothing they might wear, who was to advance and kiss whom upon meeting, who might ride in a chariot or on a horse, and so on. Though the senate of women was dissolved at Elagabalus's death, it was revived occasionally later. It appears that the powerful Julias of the Severan dynasty were interested in bringing women's opportunities to the fore.

In spite of all the titles and privileges Julia Maesa received during the reign of her grandson, she was a realist. She knew that his incorrigible behavior would soon lead the army to raise another to the purple, and she did not wait for chance to choose the next emperor. She selected her other grandson, child of her daughter Julia Mamaea. In a repeat of the public relations ploy that had worked so well for Elagabalus, Julia Mamaea circulated the rumor that she, too, had been unfaithful to her husband and that her son had also been fathered by Caracalla. The twelve-year-old boy took the name Alexander Severus, and Julia Maesa persuaded Elagabalus to adopt his cousin to ensure his succession. Elagabalus commented at the strangeness of a sixteen-year-old boy adopting another of twelve: "I seem to have acquired a very large son" (Balsdon 162).

Alexander Severus was a serious and popular young man—the direct opposite of Elagabalus. The young emperor was jealous of his cousin and no doubt tried to murder him, but he was well protected by the three Julias. Finally, in A.D. 222, the Praetorian Guard lost patience with the eccentric emperor and raised Alexander Severus to the throne. The soldiers rampaged through the palace looking for Elagabalus, and they found him and Julia Soaemias in each other's arms hiding in the palace toilet. The soldiers quickly killed them both and dragged their corpses through the streets of Rome to the shouts and derision of the people.

Although Alexander showed none of the excesses of his cousin, his mother and grandmother were not going to take any risks. They controlled the administration of the empire and appointed a council of sixteen senators to advise

the young man. They set a new tone of seriousness and responsibility, much more to the liking of the conservative Romans. Even Elagabalus's god was prudently returned to Syria.

About four years later, Julia Maesa died a natural death. She had remained a popular and respected figure in Roman politics, and she was so well loved by the senate and people that she was declared a god after her death. Her daughter Julia Mamaea tried to continue the rule of empress after her mother's death.

See also Julia Domna; Julia Mamaea; Vestal Virgins
Suggested Readings
Balsdon, J. P. V. D. *Roman Women: Their History and Habits.* New York: John Day, 1963.
Dio Cassius. *Dio's Roman History.* Trans. E. Cary. Cambridge: Harvard University Press, 1961.

Julia Mamaea
Roman Empress (d. ca. A.D. 235)

The women of the Severan dynasty of Rome that had been established by Emperor Septimius Severus in A.D. 197 were extraordinary in the political power they wielded. First Septimius's wife, Julia Domna, withstood the murder of one son while she influenced the second. Then her sister, Julia Maesa, took over and was an effective leader behind the scenes of imperial power. When Julia Maesa died in about A.D. 224, she had accomplished all her goals (even if her life had not been easy). She had remained the most powerful person in Rome until her death and was loved and deified by the Roman people. Her grandson, Alexander Severus, was securely on the throne, and her daughter Julia Mamaea was his influential adviser. It only remained for her daughter to carry on in Julia Maesa's footsteps, but Julia Mamaea was not as skilled a politician as her mother.

As young Alexander began to grow up, he began to chafe at his mother's restrictions. Furthermore, he started to find something to criticize in his mother's otherwise impeccable behavior. She was hoarding money in a shameful fashion, and although she explained that she was doing so in order to have money to bribe soldiers if they should ever need to, her son was not satisfied. Julia and her mother had carefully raised the boy with staunch Roman virtues, and this did not include greed, so Alexander turned from his mother for a time.

He challenged her authority and married a woman who might take his mother's position in court. Julia Mamaea tried (in vain) to prevent her son from giving his wife the title of empress, and when that failed, she worked to have the marriage fail. Within two years, she had succeeded. The new empress was banished to Africa, and her father was executed. Alexander married again—perhaps even twice more—but he did not sire any children who survived. His mother remained the strongest influence during his reign.

It appears that Julia Mamaea was interested in Christianity. Even before her nephew Elagabalus had been proclaimed emperor, she had the church father, Origen, brought to her under military escort and had him preach her a sermon on Christian worship. She raised her son to be sympathetic to Christianity, for his private chapel included a range of statues from deified emperors to Abraham, Orpheus, and Christ. Later traditions suggest that Julia Mamaea had been a Christian, but the evidence cannot support so firm a commitment. Certainly she shared the interests in religion and philosophy that marked the women of this extraordinary family.

It may have been that Alexander and Julia's reign would have progressed peacefully, but the eastern borders of the empire were threatened by the Persians and Germans. When Alexander left Rome to campaign in the east in A.D. 231, Julia Mamaea joined him. Two years later, when he had to go north to deal with trouble on the Rhine, she went too. The troops had become disenchanted with their favorite, Alexander, during these years. He was not a good general, and although the Roman armies prevailed against the threats, they did not do so easily. The troops also disliked Julia Mamaea and her greed, and they hated the way she and Alexander showed favoritism to the soldiers who had come from the east. Finally the troops on the Rhine murdered both of them in A.D. 235. The dynasty of Severan women who had proven that Rome could be guided by empresses died out.

See also Julia Domna; Julia Maesa
Suggested Readings
Balsdon, J. P. V. D. *Roman Women: Their History and Habits.* New York: John Day, 1963.
Dio Cassius. *Dio's Roman History.* Trans. E. Cary. Cambridge: Harvard University Press, 1961.

Junia
Christian Woman (ca. A.D. 50)

The most important information we have about the spread of Christianity in the earliest years comes from the letters of St. Paul to the various Christian churches in the eastern Mediterranean. The first of Paul's letters in the Bible is his letter to the Romans, written about A.D. 55. Within this important letter, Paul explains his understanding of the gospel and discusses Christ's benefits. With these important lessons, this letter to the Romans was an influential early church document. At the end of this letter, Paul sends his greetings to important Christians in Rome. Within this list of names, he includes the name of a woman, Junia, who because of later translations of this letter became very controversial.

In his letter to the Romans (16:7), Paul greeted Andronicus and Junia, who he said were his relatives and fellow prisoners. He also said that they were distinguished apostles, and furthermore they were followers of Christ before Paul himself. This short passage is extraordinary because it implies several things about Junia. First, since Paul calls her an apostle, she must have claimed to have seen the risen Christ and have been engaged in missionary work. This means that she took a leadership role in the early church—just like other early Christian women such as Prisca.

The earliest copy of the letters of Paul comes from about A.D. 200, and there were many copies and translations after that. It appears that some early writers were uncomfortable with the concept of a female apostle (with the implied leadership role that entails) and began to write Junia as Junias—giving it a male ending and thus claiming the apostle was a man. Many biblical translations still use the masculinized form Junias, thus eliminating the existence of a female apostle. Modern textual criticism, however, is pretty convincing regarding the argument for the female form Junia. This was a popular name at the time; it occurs over 250 times among inscriptions from ancient Rome alone. At the same time, there is no ancient inscription of the hypothetical name Junias. Furthermore, the fourth-century church father John Chrysostom praised Junia as a female apostle, so in the text he had kept the name Junia.

It is highly likely that one of the apostles who saw the risen Christ was a female, since Jesus had included women in his following, and this new reading of Paul's letter to the Romans restores Junia to her rightful place among the influential early Christians.

See also Christian Women; Prisca
Suggested Readings:
Meyers, Carol, Toni Craven, and Ross S. Kraemer. *Women in Scripture.* New York: Houghton Mifflin, 2000.
Thorley, John. "Junia, a Woman Apostle." *NovT* 38 (1996): 18–29.

Juno

Roman Goddess

Juno was an early goddess on the Italian peninsula, who became one of the chief deities in Rome. She was one of three (along with Jupiter and Minerva) who shared a temple on the Capitoline Hill in Rome. These three deities were called the Capitoline Triad and were seen as the special protectors of Rome. By the late republic, Juno had acquired the title "queen," which she bore throughout the imperial period. In a land that valued family, she was praised as the wife of Jupiter and a special guardian of all women. At an early date, Juno became identified with the Greek goddess Hera, and all Hera's myths were attributed to Juno as well.

Many epithets were given to Juno to express her various aspects. For example, Juno Lucina was the goddess of childbirth, Juno Populonia blessed the people when they were at war, and Juno Sospita Mater Regina was a goddess mainly of fertility and protection. Juno Sororia was the goddess of protection of girls at puberty. While every man had his "genius," every woman had her "Juno"—a divine double that personified and protected her femininity. The temple of Juno Moneta at Rome was entrusted with keeping the

Figure 46. Juno, Roman goddess equivalent to Greek Hera. Marble statue (Ann Ronan Picture Library)

standard measure of a foot (about 11.65 inches), so that builders would come there for the standard. These few epithets show the many ways that the cult of Juno served the women of Rome.

There were many festivals dedicated to Juno, including those on 1 February, 1 June, 13 September, 1 October, and 10 October. One of the most popular celebrations, however, took place on 1 March to celebrate the foundation day of one of her temples in Rome. On this day husbands traditionally gave presents to their wives as a way of pleasing the goddess (and their wives). In a society that valued family and wives as much as the Romans did, it is not surprising that the queen mother of the gods would be so venerated.

See also Hera
Suggested Readings
Adkins, Lesley, and Roy A. Adkins. *Handbook to*

Life in Ancient Rome. New York: Oxford
University Press, 1994.

Grant, M. *Roman Myths*. London: Weidenfeld and
Nicolson, 1971.

Grimal, Pierre. *The Dictionary of Classical Mythology*.
Oxford: Blackwell, 1996.

Ogilvie, R. M. *The Romans and Their Gods*.
London: Chatto and Windus, 1969.

Justina

Mother of Roman Emperor
(d. ca. A.D. 389)

The late Roman Empire was dominated by instability and turmoil coming from many fronts. Emperors and dynasties quickly changed through powerful usurpers, Germanic tribes threatened the borders and even the stability of the empire itself, and religious disputes split the Christian congregations and the rulers who supported them. It took leaders with nerve and political shrewdness to negotiate these difficulties, and one such leader was Justina, who dominated the rule of her son, Valentinian II.

One of the strong generals who rose to imperial power in the mid-fourth century A.D. was Valentinian I. While he was still a general, he had married a woman named Severa, who died in A.D. 359 shortly after giving birth to a son they called Gratian. Valentinian then married Justina, who gave him several children: a son, Valentinian II, and three daughters, Galla, Justa, and Grata. (Some sources identify only the first two daughters.) In A.D. 364, Valentinian was proclaimed emperor, and the family entered into the struggle to establish a dynasty that would outlast Valentinian I.

To try to establish continuity, in about A.D. 368 Valentinian proclaimed his eight-year-old son Gratian as emperor—augustus—ruling with him. However, the violence of the times did not give the youth much time to consolidate his power. In A.D. 375, Valentinian I died, and the sixteen-year-old Gratian became sole emperor. But dynastic claims complicated the succession, for ministers also proclaimed Justina's son, Valentinian II (a child of four), as emperor. The sources are not clear about Gratian's response to this move, but he seems to have graciously accepted it—perhaps finding little threat

in the authority of his young half-brother. This status quo remained until violence again interrupted dynastic hopes.

In A.D. 383, Gratian was murdered by Magnus Maximus, a general who had been proclaimed emperor by his troops. Now the young thirteen-year-old Valentinian II began to rule in fact in the west. From A.D. 383 on, the sources indicate that Justina ruled in his name, using all her resources to make sure her son retained the title. Justina moved from the east to Italy and took up residence in the capital at Milan. There she brought the resources of the Catholic Church to bear in her efforts to preserve her son's crown by appealing to the popular bishop of Milan, Ambrose, to intervene with the usurper. Ambrose seems to have persuaded Magnus Maximus to leave Justina and Valentinian II ruling in Milan, so the bishop's political power grew.

At this point, Justina's religious views brought her into conflict with Ambrose. As she became involved in the religious controversies of the day, she established precedents that were to shape church-state relations in the west for centuries to come. Justina was an Arian—that is, she followed the belief that Jesus was created by God the Father, that there was a time before which Jesus did not exist. The orthodox Catholic Church (including Ambrose of Milan) strongly disapproved of this belief, but many of the Goths had supported it. Thus, Justina followed the faith of many of the strong Germanic armies that had become essential to imperial power, although it is impossible to know whether she followed her conscience or political expediency in her religious policies.

The controversy came to a head in A.D. 385, when Justina wanted to take over one of the churches outside Milan and devote it to Arian worship. Ambrose refused in no uncertain terms. The bishop wrote a letter to his sister telling of the conflict, showing his exasperation with Justina: "Each man is persecuted by some woman or other." Ambrose said he would not surrender the church: "The palaces belong to the Emperor, the churches to the Bishop" (Ambrose 371). It was a dramatic moment in church-state relations in the west, and the court gave way. Ambrose kept his church. Justina responded with an edict in A.D. 386 to reaffirm the right of assembly by Arians. Ambrose again opposed this, and with popular support, the bishop again prevailed over the royal court. Justina was in no position to confront the bishop, for the threat of the usurper Magnus Maximus always hung over her. She turned to a different means to ensure her son's rule.

Justina appealed to the emperor in the east, Theodosius I, to protect her son's interests against Magnus. To get his help, she used the traditional dynastic means of marriage. Theodosius's first wife, Flaccilla, had died, and Justina offered her beautiful, talented daughter Galla as wife for the older emperor. Theodosius agreed, and in A.D. 388 the marriage was sealed, and Theodosius marched west and defeated Magnus Maximus. Justina died the following year, so she did not live to benefit from the powerful mar-riage she had arranged. Nor did her son live very much longer; he died in A.D. 392, and the dynasty Justina had worked so hard to ensure moved to the east, where her daughter Galla bore the famous queen Galla Placidia. Justina also failed to ensure that Arianism could be practiced in the empire—orthodoxy and the power of bishops in the west were the ideas of the future.

See also Flaccilla, Galla Placidia

Suggested Readings
Ambrose. *Saint Ambrose: Letters.* Trans. Sister
    M. M. Beyenka. New York: Fathers of the
    Church, 1954.
Frend, W. H. C. *The Rise of Christianity.* Philadelphia:
    Fortress Press, 1984.
Jones, A. H. M. *The Later Roman Empire:
    284–602.* Baltimore: Johns Hopkins University
    Press, 1986.

L

Laodice I

Seleucid Queen (ca. 287–235 B.C.)

The Seleucid dynasty ruled in the eastern part of the region that was once Alexander the Great's empire (shown in Map 6). In 261 B.C. Antiochus II, son of Stratonice I, succeeded his father Antiochus I to the throne. By this date, it was not unusual for the Hellenistic monarchs to marry their relatives, and Antiochus married Laodice I, who was either his sister or his cousin (the sources are contradictory). She was a resourceful—and many said ruthless—woman, and though historians have had little good to say about this queen, she was so famous that her name became the dynastic name of princesses in the Seleucid family. Her reputation for violence came from her fierce protection of her children's right to rule in an age of violence and almost perpetual warfare.

While the date of her marriage is not recorded, it appears that Laodice married the king shortly after he was made coregent with his father in 267 B.C. She bore Antiochus four children—two sons and two daughters. Eventually, the daughters were married to kings, but the sons had a more stormy life. The first problem came in the family in 252 B.C., when Antiochus II decided to settle a long war against the Egyptian Ptolemy dynasty. To seal the peace, Antiochus agreed to take Berenice—the Egyptian king's daughter—as his wife. She would bring with her such a rich dowry that she was called "dowerbringer" by her contemporaries, who were astonished at such wealth. While it was usual for Hellenistic kings to take several wives, this high-born Egyptian princess was not to be a "second" wife. The arrangement seems to have called for Antiochus to set aside Laodice and displace her sons as heirs to the throne. Laodice was sent to live in her great estates near Babylon, where her wealth would assure her of a comfortable life. But she would await her chance to restore her sons to power.

The Egyptian king Ptolemy sent his daughter jars of Nile water to make her fruitful, so she could produce an heir that could join the two powerful dynasties. The charm seems to have worked, for Berenice produced a son—although he would not live long enough to take power.

After some years, Antiochus seems to have tired of Berenice and returned to live with Laodice on her estates. On his deathbed in 247 B.C., Antiochus named his elder son by Laodice —Seleucus—as his heir, renouncing Berenice's son. Some sources claim that Laodice poisoned Antiochus to prevent him from changing his mind again and returning to Berenice, but there is no other evidence of that. At the king's death, Laodice was again queen and coregent with her son. Like Alexander the Great and other rulers, she first had to ensure that her son would face no rival for the throne. Berenice was living in Antioch with her son, and her brother Ptolemy was marching from Egypt to save them. He was too late; Laodice sent assassins first to kill the boy, then Berenice herself, who had fled to the temple of Apollo.

The sources also report that Laodice was fierce in defending herself—and her son— against treason. In one instance, she called Sophron, one of her soldiers, to her presence because she believed he had been disloyal. Danaë, her lady-in-waiting, was the soldier's lover, and she warned him of the queen's intention to kill him. He escaped, but Danaë remained behind to feel the queen's wrath. Danaë refused to answer questions, and in her death speech accused the queen of murder. She said, despairing of justice in this world: "No wonder men despise the gods. I have saved my lover, who has been a husband to me, and this is my reward from heaven. Laodice has killed the man who was her husband and she receives all this glory" (Macurdy 86). Danaë was thrown from a cliff, and historians blame Laodice for a ruthless murder.

The queen was also reputed to have stirred up a war between her two sons—supporting the younger, Antiochus (who was only fourteen), against the elder, Seleucus. By 236 B.C., the two sons appear to have reconciled, and one of the sources (the Roman historian Appian) says that Laodice fell into Ptolemy's hands and he killed her. However she died, she lived as a typical Hellenistic queen, fiercely guarding power and her children against all threats.

See also Stratonice I
Suggested Readings
Appian. *Appian's Roman History.* Trans. H. White. Cambridge: Harvard University Press, 1964.
Macurdy, Grace Harriet. *Hellenistic Queens.* Baltimore: Johns Hopkins University Press, 1932.

Leah

Hebrew Matriarch
(ca. seventeenth century B.C.)
Leah and her sister Rachel are considered two matriarchs of the Hebrew people because they were married to Jacob—who later came to be called Israel—the father of the Jewish nation. The twelve Israelite tribes that occupied Canaan traced their descent and their names back to Jacob's sons, and the Hebrews were referred to collectively as the Children of Israel. Most of these children were born to Leah, the first but less-loved wife of the patriarch.

Jacob fell in love with Leah's younger sister, Rachel, who was more beautiful than Leah, who was only described as having "weak eyes" (Gen. 30:17). Jacob worked for Leah's father, Laban, for seven years to win Rachel as his wife. On the wedding night, however, Laban replaced Rachel with Leah, who was wearing heavy veils. The next morning, when Jacob discovered the substitution, he was angry, but Laban explained that in his culture the elder daughter had to marry first. Laban was also willing, however, to give Rachel to Jacob as a second wife if he

worked for another seven years. Jacob so loved Rachel that he was willing to do so.

Leah was in the position of being unwanted, but as the Bible says, "When the Lord saw that Leah was hated, he opened her womb; but Rachel was barren" (Gen. 30:31). Leah quickly bore four sons in succession, and after each, she hoped that Jacob would love her more—"Surely now my husband will love me"—she said poignantly (Gen. 30:32). When Leah ceased bearing children, she gave her maid, Zilpah, to her husband as a concubine. Zilpah bore two sons, who were also considered Leah's children.

One year, in the days when they were harvesting wheat, one of Leah's sons found mandrakes in the field, which were said to stimulate conception. The barren Rachel desperately wanted the mandrakes, but Leah said, "Is it a small matter that you have taken away my husband? Would you take away my son's mandrakes also?" (Gen. 30:15). Rachel then traded one night with Jacob for the mandrakes. Leah met Jacob as he came in from the fields and said, "You must come in to me; for I have hired you with my son's mandrakes" (Gen. 30:16). So Jacob lay with her and she conceived another son. Leah would bear two more children before Rachel finally conceived a child.

In all, Leah bore Jacob six sons—Reuben, Simeon, Levi, Judah, Issachar, and Zebulun—and one daughter—Dinah. In addition, her maid Zilpah gave Jacob two sons—Gad and Asher. As the Bible credits, these along with Rachel's sons would "build the house of Israel" (Ruth 4:11). Leah died and was buried in the family tomb in the Cave of Machpelah in Hebron before Jacob went to join his sons in Egypt.

See also Jewish Women; Rachel; Rebekah
Suggested Readings
Comay, Joan. *Who's Who in the Old Testament.* London: Routledge, 1993.

Leontium

Greek Epicurean Philosopher
(ca. early third century B.C.)
During the Hellenistic period after the death of Alexander the Great in 323 B.C., many people felt powerless and insignificant within the large

monarchies that had replaced the city-states that had spawned Greek culture. Some philosophers explored the question of how to live a happy life in such an uncertain setting, and one of the most influential was Epicurus (341–270 B.C.). Epicurus founded a "garden school" in Athens, in which he and his devoted disciples lived as they studied and practiced his philosophy, which has come to be called Epicureanism. Epicurus believed that the ultimate goal in life was to obtain happiness through tranquility, and in a practical sense, this meant withdrawing from a public life and living happily with friends in a community. His school was just such a community, where people grew their own food and studied and discussed philosophy—even developing a theory of atoms that in some ways sounds remarkably modern. Another unusual element of Epicurus's ideas was that he believed in an equality among people, and we know that the garden school included a number of women and slaves. One of the women who joined the philosopher was a courtesan, Leontium.

Leontium was a courtesan's name, and several women with such names were associated with the Epicurean school. The presence of such free women—in a cultural tradition when the only free women were courtesans (see Aspasia)—led to subsequent criticism and indeed ridicule of the philosopher. For example, Cicero (first century B.C.) used Epicurus's relationship with Leontium to attack weakness and hypocrisy in the Epicurean school. He describes Leontium contemptuously as a "little whore" who "dared" to write philosophy. Later, Plutarch (ca. A.D. 100) wrote a satirical work called "How a Pleasant Life Is Impossible according to Epicurus," in which he argued that Epicurus consorted with two courtesans, including Leontium. Contemporary and subsequent commentators clearly used Leontium's sexual freedom as a way of ignoring her interest in philosophy, and thus it is difficult to try to find the real woman among the critical gossips.

It appears that Leontium—who may certainly have been a Greek courtesan, for many were well educated, talented, and rich—entered into Epicurus's garden school. She studied under the master and seems to have become an accomplished philosopher. According to one letter, Epicurus had such respect for her intellectual talents that he made her president of his school for one day. She was also painted by Aristides of Thebes in a pose of meditation, which led later biographers to argue that she was devoted to philosophy. She wrote against an Aristotelian philosopher, and Pliny the Younger (first century A.D.) wrote in some awe, "I do not know how a woman has dared to write against Theophrastus, a man of such great eloquence that for this he has been called divine" (Kersey 147). So, while her writings have not survived in a way to let us know her philosophical position, it seems that Leontium—like Aspasia before her—was a courtesan who took advantage of the opportunities to study and discuss great ideas with great men.

In her personal life, she also seems to have forged her own path. She seems to have become Epicurus's mistress as well as his pupil, but the details of this relationship are unclear. Another source says she also was the mistress of one of Epicurus's principal followers, Metrodorus, and that the couple had two children. Diogenes Laertius, who wrote the *Lives of Eminent Philosophers,* also said she was Metrodorus's mistress. Unfortunately, beyond these shreds of evidence, we cannot find out more about the life of someone who clearly followed a sensual and intellectual life in the garden school of one of the most eminent philosophers of the day.

See also Aspasia; Hipparchia; Philosophers, Greek
Suggested Readings

Diogenes Laertius. *Lives of Eminent Philosophers.* Trans. R. D. Hicks. Cambridge: Harvard University Press, 1925.
Hawley, Richard. "The Problem of Women Philosophers in Ancient Greece." In *Women in Ancient Societies,* ed. by L. J. Archer et al. New York: Routledge, 1994.
Kersey, Ethel M. *Women Philosophers: A Bio-Critical Source Book.* New York: Greenwood Press, 1989.
Menage, Gilles. *The History of Women Philosophers.* Trans. Beatrice H. Zedlin. Lanham, MD: University Press of America, 1984.

Livia

Roman Empress (56 B.C.–A.D. 29)

After the turmoil of the civil wars at the end of the Roman Republic, a brilliant young man emerged as the clear victor. Octavian, who would later be known as Caesar Augustus, defeated his enemies and became the ruler of the Roman world. He introduced a new form of government—called the Principate—in which the old forms of the republic were preserved, but Rome would in fact be governed by one man: the "first citizen," who was later called the emperor. Augustus ruled for so long, from 27 B.C. to A.D. 14, that at his death there was hardly anyone left who remembered a different kind of rule. Thus, his role was centrally important to the stability of the state, and it was equally important that there be a clear succession to the next emperor. Every emperor from Augustus on knew the Principate depended on an heir, and for most emperors, the ideal remained that they would be followed by a son, grandson, or at worst, an adopted son.

Throughout his long reign, Augustus's partner was his much-beloved wife, Livia, who shared his triumphs and disappointments. In the end, she probably did not share Augustus's disappointment that her son by her first marriage, Tiberius, received the crown of emperor.

In the tradition of Roman parents, Livia's father had arranged for her to marry a prosperous, solid man—Tiberius Claudius Nero—and she bore him two sons, Tiberius (who became Augustus's heir) and Drusus. Her life took a sharp departure, however, from that of most modest Roman matrons. While she was still pregnant with Drusus, she and Octavian fell in love. At that time, Octavian was the heir of Julius Caesar and one of the three men (including Mark Antony) who were ruling Rome; he had not yet become sole ruler. Even though it was clear by then that marriage with Octavian would be a strong political match, the couple seemed most motivated by affection. In violation of modest Roman customs, they lived together for a few months until she bore Drusus. Then she rapidly obtained a divorce, and three days after the child's birth, Livia and Octavian married; her ex-husband gave her away in marriage.

There can be no doubt that the young couple were devoted to each other, but Livia's role as a wife took some unusual turns. According to the sources, she tolerated, and even encouraged, his acts of infidelity but was always the model of decorum and modesty herself. Augustus frequently consulted her, and it seems that she was able to mollify his anger and intervene to save some of his enemies. As we shall see, there were critics who claimed she exerted too great an influence on her husband, but the contemporary sources do not suggest that she was anything but a model Roman wife.

She was quite beautiful—as the cameo in Figure 47 shows—but she never showed anything but the greatest dignity in public. She presided over her complex household with grace and accepted tragedies with uncomplaining resignation. (She despised her sister-in-law Octavia's extremes of grief at the loss of her son.) It was to her (and Augustus's) great grief that she never bore him a child. Their household consisted of children born to their other spouses, and it was in this complex family that the future of the empire rested.

In addition to Livia's two sons by her previous marriage, the family included Julia, Augustus's daughter by his previous wife, Scribonia. It was to these children that Augustus looked for the succession. Julia had married Agrippa—an important political connection for her father, and the couple had achieved the important task of producing imperial grandchildren. Two sons were born (in 20 and 17 B.C.), and Augustus adopted them both, making them his official heirs and calling them C. Caesar and L. Caesar. Julia and Agrippa also produced two daughters, Agrippina and Julia, who were also raised in the palace under the emperor's supervision. It appeared as if the imperial succession was well established through Augustus's line, but life is never certain.

In 12 B.C., Agrippa died, and Augustus arranged for Julia to marry his stepson, Tiberius, perhaps to make sure that no other husband outside the family would think to produce an heir to threaten the grandsons. This was not a happy match (*see* Julia). The handsome and popular Drusus died while on campaign in Ger-

Figure 47. Livia, wife of Caesar Augustus, cameo (Burstein Collection/Corbis)

many in 9 B.C. He already had two sons—Germanicus (who would die young) and Claudius, who was considered something of a buffoon, but who would become emperor when he was nearly fifty. It may be that Livia was devastated over the death of her talented, popular son Drusus, but as a Roman matron of the old school, she hid her grief and carried on. Worse was yet to come. In A.D. 2, the promising grandson Lucius Caesar died and two years later his brother, Gaius Caesar, also died. Neither left widow or children, for although they were in their twenties, they had not yet married. The imperial grandsons were gone, and Augustus had run out of choices for an heir. In A.D. 4, he adopted Livia's less popular son, Tiberius, who would become the next emperor.

Augustus died in A.D. 14, when Livia was seventy years old. Reputedly, his last words were spoken to his wife, and he urged her not to forget the happiness of their married life. They had been married fifty-one years, which was a remarkable length of time for the ancient world. Livia lived for fifteen more years, preserving the gracious, dignified air that she had always held. She left the palace to her son Tiberius, the new emperor, but she had an abundance of property of her own. She had a house in Rome—the "house of Livia," which is open to tourists today. Her other house was nine miles north of Rome, where reputedly she was sitting when an eagle dropped a hen in her lap, and the hen held a laurel twig in its beak. She planted the laurel, and from this splendid bush came the laurel crowns that Augustus and his successors wore.

She was heavily involved in business matters, for she was immensely rich, owning property in Asia Minor, Gaul, and Palestine, and she had complete independence in administering this property. Her personal staff numbered over a thousand people. After Augustus's death, she continued to be venerated by the Roman people. She was appointed the first priestess of Augustus's cult and given other public honors. Her relationship with her son Tiberius was always correct. He never spoke ill of his mother, and in public he always deferred to her wishes. She died in peace.

In spite of the seeming upright quality of her life, subsequent Roman historians have treated her harshly. Tacitus (A.D. 56–120), for example, accused her of making sure that Tiberius received the coveted prize of emperor, even murdering the two grandsons of Augustus and others. Tacitus even suggested that she hated Augustus in the end. These charges probably came from the fact that Tiberius became very unpopular, and historians wanted someone to blame. There is no basis for believing in these accusations, however; it seems that Livia was what she appeared to be—an honorable Roman woman who made the best of life as it came and helped shape one of the greatest empires the world has known.

See also Cleopatra VII; Julia; Octavia; Turia
Suggested Readings
Balsdon, J. P. V. D. *Roman Women: Their History and Habits.* New York: John Day, 1963.
Hawley, R., and B. Levick, eds. *Women in Antiquity: New Assessments.* New York: Routledge, 1995.
Suetonius. *The Twelve Caesars.* Trans. Robert Graves. New York: Penguin, 1979.
Tacitus. "The Annals." In *Complete Works of Tacitus.* Trans. A. J. Church. New York: The Modern Library, 1942.

Lucretia

Republican Roman Heroine (ca. 510 B.C.)

Like other ancient civilizations, the early Romans were ruled by kings, but to work out the details of the monarchy, historians have to struggle with combinations of history and legend. Romulus (753?–715? B.C.) was the first king, and more unverifiable legends claim he was followed by four more monarchs. By the seventh century B.C., Rome seems to have been ruled by an Etruscan dynasty that governed for almost a century from about 616 to about 509 B.C. In the early sixth century B.C., Roman nobles seem to be chafing under the Etruscan rule and ready to throw off the dynasty. According to legend, the incident that sparked Rome's fight

for independence surrounded a brave woman named Lucretia. We cannot know whether she actually existed, but throughout their history Romans looked back to the story of Lucretia and held her up as a model of virtuous women.

During the reign of the Etruscan king Tarquin the Proud, the army was in the field besieging a city twenty-three miles south of Rome. As the men were drinking, there arose an argument between Tarquin's sons (one of them called Sextus Tarquinius) and their cousin Collatinus. They argued about whether their wives were behaving properly in their husbands' absence, so they decided to mount their horses and ride off to Rome to check. They arrived as darkness fell and discovered the princes' wives enjoying themselves at dinner parties, which was not considered a particularly virtuous pastime for women whose husbands were away at war. Then they rode another nine miles to Collatia, and it was late at night when they arrived. Collatinus's beautiful wife, Lucretia, was not in bed, however; she was hard at work, weaving with her slave women. Collatinus had won his bet, but he would have done well not to bet at all, for Sextus had seen his lovely wife and coveted her.

A few days later, Sextus called at Collatinus's house and asked for a bed for the night. Since he was a cousin, he was of course made welcome. When everyone was asleep, however, he went to Lucretia's bedroom and entered her bed. When she resisted his advances, he made a terrible threat: He said he would kill her, then kill a slave and leave his body naked in her bedroom. He would then tell the world that he had discovered them together making love and killed them immediately. Everyone would believe that she was a loose woman, and her reputation would be forever sullied. She allowed him to have his desire.

The next morning, when he had ridden back to camp, the unhappy Lucretia summoned her husband, her father (who had been placed in charge of Rome by the king in his absence), and her male relatives. These were the people who would have judged her had she been accused of adultery. She told them the horrible story of her rape and then challenged them, saying: "The mark of another man is in your bed. But only my body has been violated. My mind is guiltless, as my death shall testify. Swear that you will take vengeance on the adulterer" (Gardner 61). All the men swore and began to try to comfort her, assuring her that she was forced, and thus not at fault. Lucretia answered: "I absolve myself of wrongdoing, but I do not free myself from punishment; and hereafter no unchaste woman shall live through my example" (Gardner 61). She then pulled a sword and stabbed herself to death.

Her body was taken and exposed in the forum at Rome, and she became the example of the abuse of royal privilege, where a king's son believed he was above the law. The populace was inflamed to expel the king and inaugurate a republican form of government. Sextus Tarquinius was murdered by men who avenged Lucretia and other crimes he had committed. Lucretia was remembered as the perfect Roman matron who preferred honor above life itself.

The story of Lucretia has remained a riveting tale for writers and philosophers into the modern day. The overwhelming question that plagues commentators is: Why did she have to die? She was clearly innocent, so what purpose did her death serve? For the ancient Romans, her death was not about her own innocence or guilt, but instead the rape of Lucretia symbolized a serious disorder in a society that was ruled by family and decorum. Her death and her family's vengeance restored order to the Roman Republic, and the lesson of Lucretia continued to preach the values of family, responsibility, and order.

See also Etruscan Women; Verginia
Suggested Reading
Balsdon, J. P. V. D. *Roman Women: Their History and Habits.* New York: John Day, 1963.
Donaldson, I. *The Rapes of Lucretia: A Myth and Its Transformations.* Oxford: Oxford University Press, 1982.
Gardner, Jane F. *Roman Myths.* Austin: University of Texas Press, 1995.
Livy. *The Early History of Rome.* Trans. A. de Selincourt. Baltimore: Penguin Books, 1960.

Lydia
Christian Woman (ca. A.D. 50)
The Book of Acts in the Bible tells of Paul's travels through the eastern Mediterranean as he brought the message of Jesus to the cities in the region. In the course of his travels, Paul came to the Macedonian city of Philippi (see Map 8). Philippi was a prosperous town made up mostly of Gentiles (non-Jews), and Paul's conversions here were very important as Christianity began to spread to Gentiles. Philippi was also a religious center that seemed to have been important to women. The apocryphal Acts with their strong profemale message circulated here, pagan women honored the deified Livia (the wife of Augustus) with five huge statues, and many women followed the Diana/Artemis cult as well as the cult of Isis. It was to this city, where women had a tradition of prominence in religion, that Paul came with his message.

Acts says that Paul met a group of women who had gathered outside the gates of the city by a river at a "place of prayer." This passage is somewhat puzzling historically, because there were so many places of worship for women within the city that it is hard to imagine why these women gathered outside by the river; perhaps the place became one of prayer only after Paul began to speak. Nevertheless, the account says that Paul addressed a group of women here, and one was a wealthy woman named Lydia.

She was probably named for the region from which she had come, for the Bible says she was from Thyatira in Lydia (see Map 8). She was a merchant, dealing in the very lucrative trade in purple dye that was produced on the eastern shore of the Mediterranean and sold all over the ancient world. Purple dye was extremely valuable because anyone who was of royalty or was wealthy felt they had to wear garments dyed in purple to show their status. Thus, they paid premium prices to obtain purple cloth. Inscriptions in Philippi have been found that honor that city's guild of dyers, so it may be that Lydia was engaging in trade with them. There is no mention of a husband related to Lydia's household, so she may have been a widow. It was common for widows to continue to run family businesses after their husbands died, and it is most likely that this was the case with Lydia.

The Bible also tells us that Lydia believed in the Jewish God. Either she was Jewish or, perhaps more likely, she was one of those who actively supported Jewish communities—called

"God-fearers"—who went to services in the syn-
agogue and contributed money to the Jewish
community. According to the Bible, "the Lord
opened her heart to give heed to what was said by
Paul" (Acts 16:14). Lydia was converted to the
Christian message and was baptized along with
everyone in her household, which would have included slaves and perhaps family members. After
her baptism, Lydia prevailed upon Paul and his
company to come and stay at her house.

Some biblical scholars have argued that the
story of Lydia represents a conscious message
that the author of Acts (probably Luke) was
sending: The independent women of Philippi
should listen to the apostles and support them
with resources. The story also expressed how
wealthy, independent, ancient women like Lydia
followed their consciences, embraced the new
religion of Christ, and stepped forward to help
it grow.

See also Apocryphal Acts of the Apostles; Artemis;
Christian Women; Livia

Suggested Readings

Meyers, Carol, Toni Craven, and Ross S. Kraemer.
Women in Scripture. New York: Houghton
Mifflin, 2000.
Thomas, W. Derek. "The Place of Women in the
Church at Philippi." *Expository Times* 83
(1972): 117–120.

M

Maccabean Martyrs

By his conquests and policies of establishing Greek colonies in his wake, Alexander the Great (356–323 B.C.) had spread Greek civilization all the way to India. After his death, his great empire was divided up among some of his generals, who established monarchies to rule over the lands that they had been able to seize. These monarchs—the Ptolemies in Egypt and the Seleucids based in Syria—ruled what historians call the Hellenistic world, which means that their culture combined Greek (Hellenic) with Asian and African. (See Map 6.) In the Hellenistic kingdoms, enterprising native people quickly learned that the route to success was to learn to speak Greek, get a Greek education, and accept much of Greek culture. They then could join the Greek-speaking ruling classes. These policies brought a multicultural vitality to much of the ancient world, but in places it also brought cultural conflict that sometimes led to violence. The region that found it most difficult to reconcile Hellenization with traditional life was the ancient land of Judea, where the Jews had centered their worship in the holy city of Jerusalem.

Jews had proudly celebrated the rebuilding of their Temple in Jerusalem in 538 B.C., when the Persian great king Cyrus allowed Jews to return to their homeland from their captivity in Babylon. For the most part, Jews had continued to preserve their identity and religious freedom under the Hellenistic Seleucid rulers. Tensions began to grow from within and without the Jewish community, however. Many Jews compromised with Hellenism, learning Greek and taking advantage of the opportunities available to those who at least had the appearance of Hellenism. Some even forgot how to speak Hebrew, and in great cities, Jews gathered in traditional fashion but read scriptures in Greek. Others—particularly in Judea—scolded their fellows for turning away from the traditional Jewish Law of Moses.

These uncertainties within the Jewish community came to a head when the Seleucid king Antiochus IV (r. 175–163 B.C.) decided to quicken the pace of Hellenism. He decided his kingdom would be stronger if it were more homogeneous, so he decided to force the Jews to be more like his other subjects. As a Jewish chronicler wrote in 1 Maccabees (written in about 140 B.C.), "Then the king wrote to his whole kingdom that all should be one people, and that each should give up his customs." According to the text, even the high priest of Jerusalem supported the king and "exercised his influence in order to bring over his fellow-countrymen to the Greek ways of life" (1 Macc. 1:41). This pressure led to resistance, and among the earliest recorded martyrs in the Judeo-Christian tradition were a mother and her sons who refused to adhere to the decrees of Antiochus and in their stubbornness became models for subsequent Christian martyrs.

One of the main ways that Jews preserved their distinctive identity from their neighbors was in adhering to dietary and other purity restrictions that were in their sacred scriptures. The dietary laws in particular were the responsibility of women, who did the cooking and made sure their families did not eat food that was not ritually pure, or kosher. Antiochus's authorities sometimes used food as a measure of people's willingness to embrace the Greek way of life, and the first century B.C. text 4 Maccabees (which is included in some Old Testament Bibles as an "apocryphal" work, or not part of the approved scriptures) describes one such confrontation that led to violence and an extraordinary brave act by a pious mother.

4 Maccabees tells how an aged mother and her seven sons were brought before the authorities and told they had to eat pork, which is forbidden as unclean by Jewish law. The mother had to watch each son be tortured as he refused the forbidden food. Instead of wanting to save her sons, the mother urged each one to endure horrible pain rather than eat the pork that would cause them to lose their Jewish identity. The author wrote beautifully of the mother's love for her sons: "In seven pregnancies she had implanted in herself tender love toward them, and because of the many pains she suffered with each of them she had sympathy for them." Yet, in spite of this deep love, she did not try to save their lives, but instead "urged them on, each child singly and all together, to death for the sake of religion." Her sons "obeyed her even to death in keeping the ordinance." The mother, too, was killed after she watched each of her sons die. The author of the text was surprised at the mother's exceptional courage—"she fired her woman's reasoning with a man's courage" (4 Macc. 15:23)—but he recorded her deed as a model for preserving Jewish identity in the face of an oppression that threatened Jewish survival.

Judas Maccabee, a military leader, rallied Jews into an army that revolted successfully against the Seleucid rule, and an independent state emerged again centered around Jerusalem. Yet, the texts preserved the memory of the Maccabean martyrs—the mother and her seven sons—because their courage represented the center of Jewish identity, the family. The mother had made sure that her family kept the dietary laws that marked her family as Jewish, and this martyrdom was about preserving family piety in the face of oppression. The author of 4 Maccabees called the martyr "mother of the nation, vindicator of the law and champion of religion" (4 Macc. 15:21), and thus she also became a hero in the resistance. This mother/martyr also became a significant role model for Christian martyrs who found themselves having to choose between conscience and death.

See also Blandina; Felicity; Martyrs; Perpetua the Martyr

Suggested Readings

Frend, W. H. C. *Martyrdom and Persecution in the Early Church*. Grand Rapids, MI: Baker Book House, 1965.

Meyers, Carol, Toni Craven, and Ross S. Kraemer. *Women in Scripture*. New York: Houghton Mifflin, 2000.

Macha Mong Ruadh
Celtic Queen (ca. 377 B.C.)

The early chronicles of Ireland are difficult to use as historical sources; there is no independent confirmation of their information, for they recall times when there was no written language. The island was populated by Celtic tribes who had migrated there by 700 B.C. They lived in close-knit clans ruled by chieftains, who led the warrior classes in repeated raids on their fellows. The clans based their wealth on cattle—great long-horned beasts that served as draft animals to pull carts and plows and as sources of tough, boiled meat. Archaeological excavations in Ireland show that the Celts lived in settlements of round huts surrounded by walled fortifications to keep out would-be raiders. The early chronicles preserve accounts of chieftains who proved their strength in feats of arms, and these stories were told and retold in the evenings around the fires. Many historians accept some of the accounts as reasonably factual, including that of a queen who reputedly ruled all of Ireland for seven years.

Macha Mong Ruadh (Macha of the Red Hair) seized power after her father, Aedh Ruadh, drowned. Macha's father had ruled Ireland jointly with his two cousins (whom some texts identify as his brothers). At Aedh's death, the heads of the clans elected Macha to rule, but the two cousins disputed this vote since they wanted to rule without her. Macha raised an army and defeated one of the claimants—Dithorba—killing him and taking his five sons as hostages. She forced the sons to build a fortress to serve as her headquarters against the other cousin. Instead of fighting, however, Macha and the remaining cousin decided to marry and thus share the throne of Ireland. The Irish sources credit Macha with building the first hospital in Ireland, called Bron-Bherg (The House of Sorrow), which remained in use until A.D. 22.

See also Elen Luyddog; Germanic Tribal Women
Suggested Readings
Ellis, P. B. *Women in Celtic Society and Literature.*
Grand Rapids, MI: W. B. Eerdmans Publishing,
1995.

Macrina the Younger
Christian Woman (ca. A.D. 327–379)

By the fourth century A.D., many people in the Roman Empire were Christians. Since the time of Constantine (ca. A.D. 313), imperial patronage had strengthened and enriched the church, and new organizational structures—such as a strong hierarchy—were replacing the small congregations that gathered in house churches. By the fourth century, there was also a tradition of Christians who sought God by leading an ascetic life, sometimes retreating to the desert and wilderness areas, and sometimes living quietly within their homes. Communities of men and women began to gather together to live a simple Christian life, and these were the forerunners of monasteries. In the fourth century in Cappadocia, a brother and sister started such communities, and they are known as the founders of eastern monasticism. Basil of Caesarea and his sister, Macrina, shaped the direction of the fourth-century Christian church.

Macrina was the eldest child of a Christian family living in Cappadocia in modern Turkey (see Map 7). She is called "the younger" to distinguish her from her grandmother Macrina, who also was a Christian. Macrina the Younger's paternal grandparents had spent seven years hiding in the forests during the persecution of the emperor Decius (ca. A.D. 250), and one of their children became a bishop. Their other son, Basil, became a famous lawyer and the father of Macrina and her brothers, Basil, Naucratius, and Gregory (later called Gregory of Nyssa). Their mother was Emmelia, who was the daughter of a Christian martyr. Thus, the children grew up in a household that still had the vigorous spirit of the early Christians who had suffered for their faith.

When Macrina was twelve years old, her parents arranged for her to be betrothed to a young man who was planning to become a lawyer, and Macrina agreed to the match. The prospective groom died unexpectedly, however, and Macrina refused to accept any other suitor. Eventually, she vowed herself to a life of celibacy and contemplation.

Some two or three years before Macrina's engagement, her brother Basil had been born. His father gave him the best education he could in the hope that he would continue in his father's footsteps as a lawyer and orator. Young Basil studied first at Caesarea and later in Antioch, Constantinople, and Athens. This cosmopolitan experience caused Basil to feel proud of his wisdom and experience. His family connections immediately got him a job teaching rhetoric. His attitude caused Macrina to intervene, however. She bluntly told her brother that he had become conceited, acting as if he were better than anyone else. She further told him he would do well to study fewer pagan authors and spend more time on Christian ones. Basil ignored his sister's comments, thinking that she was simply uneducated. Soon events would cause Basil to turn to his pious sister, however.

Their father died, and a short time later, their brother Naucratius also died unexpectedly. Basil was greatly shaken since he and his brother had been very close, and in his bereavement, Basil turned to his sister. He resigned his teaching position and asked Macrina to teach him the secrets of religious life.

At Macrina's suggestion, the family withdrew to their land in nearby Annesi to live in renunciation of material things and contemplation of the divine. She said that happiness could only be found in the service of God and that to break all ties with the world, people should live as simply as possible and devote themselves entirely to prayer. Macrina thus proposed a life similar to that of the ascetics of the desert, yet within the household.

Macrina, her mother, and several other women withdrew to Annesi to live this life. Basil, following the desires of his sister, left for Egypt in order to learn more about the monastic life. Later Basil would write a rule for the monastic life, which was profoundly influential. Macrina spent the rest of her life in monastic retreat in Annesi. Years later, shortly after Basil's death, their brother Gregory of Nyssa (who had become a famous church father in his own right) came to visit Macrina. She had become so respected for her religious instruction that she was known simply as "the teacher."

Gregory was saddened to find that his sister was suffering from a severe asthma attack and on her deathbed. She let him shed his tears and then instructed him on the nature and destiny of the human soul, reminding him of the hope of resurrection. Gregory reputedly recorded her instruction in his dialogue *On the Soul and the Resurrection,* thus preserving her teachings. Gregory also wrote a biography of his saintly sister, which has maintained the memory of this influential woman. She died in great peace, and her brother closed her eyes, led the funeral service, and went out to continue her work.

Church leaders and theologians recognized the significant impact Basil, Gregory, and their friend Gregory of Nazianzus made on the future of the church. These three have been called the "great Cappadocians" to note their influence. Basil and Gregory, however, would no doubt not have made the same impact without the influence of their sister, Macrina the teacher. She, too, should be included in the list of the great Cappadocians of this generation.

See also Helena; Melania the Elder; Paula
Suggested Readings
González, Justo L. *The Story of Christianity.* New York: Harper and Row, 1984.
Gregory of Nyssa. "Life of Macrina." In *The Biographical Works of Gregory of Nyssa,* ed. by A. Spira. Cambridge: Philadelphia Patristic Foundation, 1984.
LaPorte, J. *The Role of Women in Early Christianity.* Lewiston, NY: Edwin Mellen Press, 1982.

Maenads

Greek Religious Celebrants

In the time of the ancient Greeks, Dionysus was a popular god whose attributes set him apart from the other Olympic deities. His birth was remarkable—according to the myth, he was snatched from the womb of his dying mother, Semele, by his father Zeus, and he was carried to term in his father's thigh. The Romans worshiped him as Bacchus. Throughout antiquity, he was first and foremost the god of wine, intoxication, and ecstasy, but his attributes also in-

Figure 48. Maenad, woman in ecstasy, detail of amphora Attic, ca. 500 B.C. (Museum Antiker Kleinkunst, Munich)

cluded the fictional world of the theater and the mysterious realm of death and afterlife. All these qualities show him to be a god whom people could worship when they wanted to transcend their everyday lives, when they wanted to glimpse something else. Women—particularly Greek women—were drawn to his worship, almost certainly as a release from their strictly circumscribed lives. These women who ecstatically worshipped Dionysus were called Maenads.

According to legend, Dionysus was first nurtured by nymphs. They were possessed by the god and inspired by him with a mystical frenzy, so they roamed about the countryside, drinking at springs and imagining that they drank milk or honey. They had power over wild animals; artists depicted them riding panthers and holding wolf cubs in their arms. Human followers of Dionysus sought to imitate their impassioned conduct.

Maenadic rituals took place in the rough mountains of Greece in the heart of winter every second year. Maenads (probably upper-class women) would leave the cities in great ceremony and walk into the mountains, shouting the cry "to the mountains." There they removed their shoes, let their hair hang loose, and clothed themselves in fawn skins. After a sacrifice of small cakes to the god, they danced every night, accompanied by drums and flutes and carrying a wand called a *thyrsus* as a mark of their religious devotion. The maenads would be stimulated by the high-pitched music, the flickering of the torches that lit their way, and the spinning and jumping of the dance until they collapsed to the ground in a euphoric ecstatic trance. The woman shown on the Greek vase in Figure 48 is in an ecstatic trance, holding her thyrsus and dressed in loose clothing.

One of the most famous descriptions of the maenads was in Euripides's play *The Bacchae*, written at the end of the fifth century B.C. The playwright offers a compelling but horrifying description of the mythical prototypes of worshipers of Dionysus. In the play, the women run wild in the mountains, tearing apart wild animals with their bare hands, and when they are thirsty, they strike rocks with a thyrsus wand, and a fountain magically spurts from the rock. When the daughter of Cadmus discovers her son, Pentheus, the king of Thebes, hiding in a tree disguised as a woman spying on the maenads, Dionysus makes her see Pentheus as a wild animal. In their trance, she and the others murder and dismember him, and it is only later that she discovers what she has done. The play ends with the worship of Dionysus firmly established in Thebes. This play offers the extreme example of the penalty for disobeying the gods; ordinary maenads did not kill people.

Historians have argued about whether Euripides's play described an existing cult or whether indeed it stimulated such ecstatic celebrations. While no consensus has emerged, the abundant portrayal of maenads in art and descriptions in other plays suggest that some form of the ecstatic celebration existed before Euripides and was popular with women of ancient Greece.

The writings of Plutarch from the second century A.D. contain several interesting references to women's ecstatic rites in honor of Dionysus. In one case he tells how a group of maenads was stranded during a severe winter storm and had to be rescued by a search party. In another case, he tells how a band of maenads in their ecstatic trance had strayed behind enemy lines and collapsed from exhaustion in the town square. The women of the town guarded the sleeping worshipers from the soldiers and arranged for them to have a safe escort home.

These stories and the popularity of the cult itself suggest that Greek women valued this opportunity to escape the constraints of their everyday lives and indulge in the wild abandon of ecstasy. By the Hellenistic period, when women began to have more freedom and other opportunities for creative expression, maenadism started to decline. By the second century A.D., it had virtually disappeared. But it remains a fascinating example of ancient women expressing their religious longings in wild abandonment.

See also Artemis; Greek (Athenian) Women
Suggested Readings

Dodds, E. R. *The Greeks and the Irrational.* Berkeley: University of California Press, 1951.
Evans, Arthur. *The God of Ecstasy.* New York: St. Martin's Press, 1988.
Grimal, Pierre. *The Dictionary of Classical Mythology.* Oxford: Blackwell, 1996.
Henrichs, Albert. "Greek Maenadism from Olympias to Messalina." *Harvard Studies in Classical Philology* 82 (1978): 121–160.
Kraemer, Ross Shepard. *Her Share of the Blessings.* New York: Oxford University Press, 1992.

Marcella

Christian Roman Matron (ca. A.D. 330–412)

In the fourth century A.D., Christian ideas had spread to Rome, and a number of people in the wealthy patrician families were drawn to these new ideas. Among the most famous and influential followers of the new religion were women, who used their wealth and influence to forward Christianity even as they renounced the trappings of wealth and power that were their birthright. One of these famous converts was Marcella, a wealthy widow who cultivated a close friendship with the influential church father Jerome (ca. A.D. 340–420).

Marcella was the daughter of a Roman family whose ancestors had served as leaders of the state, as consuls and other important officers. She had high rank and a great deal of wealth. When Marcella was only about ten years old, she came into contact with ideas of ascetic Christianity as practiced by holy men and women living in the deserts of Egypt and Syria. The eastern bishop, Athanasius, had taken refuge in Rome in about A.D. 340 and had been a guest in her home. Although she was a young girl at this time, she listened to his stories of the famous monk Anthony, whose life in the desert had served as a model for many others who followed him to seek God by living lives of strict renunciation and escape from society. Athanasius later wrote a biography of Anthony, which spread the ideas of monasticism throughout Christendom. His verbal account of the deeds of the great monk had already found fertile ground in the mind of the young, pampered Roman girl.

Although Marcella resolved to follow the ascetic life, she could not easily do so. As Jerome wrote, "In those days no highborn lady at Rome had made profession of the monastic life, or had ventured—so strange and ignominious and degrading did it then seem—publicly to call herself a nun" (Jerome 254). Marcella had to break new ground to introduce a monastic life to the patrician households of Rome. But first, the young girl had to obey her parents' wishes for her to marry. Her family arranged a good marriage for her, but her husband died less than seven months after the marriage. Her father died, too, leaving her and her mother alone.

As Marcella was a young, beautiful, and wealthy widow, she did not lack for suitors. A powerful Roman—named Cerealis—courted her, offering his great wealth and protection to the young widow. Her mother, Albina, supported his proposal, but the young woman adamantly refused. Her suitor was much older than she, but he pointed out to her that sometimes old men live long while young men die early—as her first marriage had shown. Marcella cleverly retorted: "A young man may indeed die early, but an old man cannot live long" (Jerome 253). She had decided to dedicate herself to perpetual chastity and to try to reproduce the monastic life as far as she was able in her magnificent mansion on the Aventine, the southernmost of Rome's seven hills and residential quarter of the rich.

Marcella persuaded her mother, too, to follow an ascetic life, and their household became a gathering place for widows and virgins who wanted to lead a monastic Christian life. Some—like her friend Lea—were extremely ascetic in their practices, living isolated in a small room and fasting constantly. Others, however, were more moderate in their practices, gathering for prayer and study and simply avoiding the luxuries of Roman society. The women wore modest widows' clothing and no makeup. Marcella wore no gold jewelry and never went anywhere without her mother and other modest women to keep her company. Marcella fasted in moderation, simply eating no meat, and drank wine sparingly. She donated much of her money to help the poor, but she was careful not to bankrupt the family for her mother's sake. The women renounced all the public entertainments that gave the Romans such pleasure—theaters and games—and instead confined their public visits to the basilicas where martyrs were buried. They probably visited the catacombs in Rome that held the remains of the faithful from the second century A.D.

Their lives were enriched in A.D. 382, when the educated church father Jerome came to Rome. He quickly became acquainted with the women gathering in Marcella's home. Marcella recognized that the scholar could help satisfy her curiosity on Christian matters. It is through her friendship with Jerome that we have learned so much about Marcella and her life, for he described her in his voluminous correspondence. According to Jerome, he was very shy in the presence of these patrician Roman women, yet Marcella approached him and pleaded with him to join them. Thus began a friendship that would last throughout her life. He met with the women in her household and helped them study the scriptures and other works.

Marcella was no passive student of the scriptures. She had an inquiring, probing mind and constantly questioned Jerome on fine points in the texts. Though their meetings were frequent, she often insisted that he set down his explanations on paper. Of this correspondence, sixteen letters from Jerome to Marcella survive. Many of her questions were linguistic—she wanted to understand passages of scripture that were obscurely translated from the Hebrew or to understand Hebrew words or phrases that the translators into Latin had left in Hebrew. It may be that Jerome's conversations and correspondence with Marcella confirmed his resolution to produce a new translation of the Old Testament from the Hebrew into Latin—which would later be his most influential life's work.

Sometimes in the correspondence, Jerome reveals some of the wonderful tensions that show their relationship to be a rich one. In one place he expresses impatience with his "task-mistress" for making him unravel baffling phrases in scripture, which imposed a "burden" on him. In another letter, he complains that he was kept up so late dictating his reply to her inquiries that he had to break off because of violent stomach pains. He also flatly refused to lend her texts that he believed were heretical. In other letters, however, he revealed the deep care he felt for the intelligent widow. When Marcella's friend Lea died in A.D. 384, Jerome wrote Marcella to console her by praising Lea's life and commitment to Christ: "So complete was her conversion to the Lord that, becoming the head of a monastery, she showed herself a true mother to the virgins in it, wore coarse sackcloth instead of soft raiment, passed sleepless nights in prayer, and instructed her companions even more by example than by precept" (Jerome 42). He insisted that Lea was happy in heaven now that she was gone from this earth.

Jerome left Rome in A.D. 386 to settle in Palestine. But he did not lose touch with Marcella, who had been such an important part of his life in Rome. In a letter written in A.D. 412 to Principia, one of Marcella's friends, Jerome tells of Marcella's death in the violent circumstances that swept through the empire in the early fifth century.

In A.D. 410, the Visigoths—a Germanic tribe—invaded the empire and sacked the city of Rome itself. This was a shocking event, as Jerome wrote: "The City which had taken the whole world was itself taken," and in the raiding that followed, Marcella's mansion on the hills was not spared. The raiders broke in, and she received them without alarm. They demanded gold, and she pointed to her coarse dress to show that she lived in poverty and had no wealth. Nevertheless, they "scourged her and beat her with cudgels." The old woman simply pleaded with tears for them to spare the other younger women in her household. Remarkably, the soldiers listened to her: "Christ softened their hard hearts and even among bloodstained swords natural affection asserted its rights." The soldiers sent Marcella and her young companion, Principia, to the church of the apostle Paul for safety and sanctuary. Marcella was said to be pleased that she had lived such a life of poverty that the devastation had taken nothing from her. The pain she suffered took its toll, however—she died a few days later, mourned by Jerome and the women upon whom she had made such an impact (Jerome 257).

It is impossible to overstate the importance of ancient women like Marcella. They were profoundly influential in bringing Christianity to Rome, and in their discussions with church leaders such as Jerome, they no doubt shaped the form of the writings that would become future doctrine. Marcella was a path breaker in establishing a new way of life for Roman women, and many others would follow her example.

See also Blaesilla; Cosmetics; Eustochium; Eve; Jewelry; Melania the Elder; Paula
Suggested Readings
Jerome. *Jerome: Letters and Select Works. Nicene and Post-Nicene Fathers,* vol. 6. Ed. Philip Schaff and Henry Wace. Peabody, MA: Hendrickson Publishers, 1995.
Kelly, J. N. D. *Jerome: His Life, Writings, and Controversies.* New York: Harper and Row, 1975.

Marcia
Concubine to Roman Emperor (ca. A.D. 190)
When the Roman emperor Marcus Aurelius died in A.D. 180, his nineteen-year-old son, Commodus, became emperor. Marcus Aurelius had been an excellent emperor and a fine Stoic philosopher who ruled with balance and care for the Roman people. His son was the complete opposite, so much so that Romans spread the rumor that he had been fathered by a gladiator instead of the upstanding emperor. Commodus enjoyed hunting and wrestling, and to the shock of the Roman people, he even appeared in the Colosseum and fought as a gladiator. During the empire, gladiators were condemned prisoners, so for the emperor to act as one was consid-

ered an appalling breach of custom. Commodus also arranged for the assassination of his critics, and all in all, he is remembered as one of the worst of Rome's emperors. His reign might have continued for even longer than the twelve years that he ruled but for the courage of his concubine, Marcia.

During the early years of Commodus's reign, his household was plagued by the rivalry of his sister, Lucilla, and his wife, Bruttia Crispina. In A.D. 182, Lucilla conspired with her cousin, Ummidius Quadratus, to assassinate Commodus and thus rid herself of both her brother and his wife. The plot failed, however, and most of the conspirators were killed. Lucilla was banished to the island of Capri and killed shortly thereafter. Bruttia Crispina did not survive much longer—in A.D. 187, she was found guilty of adultery and banished to Capri. She was executed shortly thereafter. Commodus did not marry again but instead took as his concubine Marcia, who had been the concubine of Quadratus who had conspired against Commodus in A.D. 182 and been executed.

According to the Roman sources, Marcia was courageous and intelligent, and she seems to have cared for the young emperor. She was also sympathetic to Christians, and while she held some power in the royal household, she did what she could to help them. Her affections for the emperor were misplaced, however. In A.D. 192, Commodus decided he would abandon the traditional and dignified formalities of the Roman New Year celebrations. Instead of dressing in the purple toga of an emperor, he decided to appear before the people as a gladiator. Furthermore, instead of leaving the palace, he decided to emerge from the gladiator barracks surrounded by an escort of gladiators. Marcia, who the sources tell us was concerned for the dignity of the imperial office, tried to dissuade him from his course of action, but he would not listen. Instead, he called the leader of the Praetorian Guard, Laetus, and the "groom of the bedchamber," Eclectus, to make the necessary preparations for him to spend the night in the gladiator barracks before his appearance on New Year's Day.

With these preparations made, Commodus was ready to retire for a rest, but before he did,

he made a list on a writing pad of the people he proposed to have executed that very night. He put it on his couch, not expecting that anyone would come into the room, and he left it there when he went out to the baths. While the emperor was gone, his favorite slave boy came into the room and picked up the writing pad; he was playing with it when he came out of the building and encountered Marcia. She noticed the pad and saw that it had writing in the emperor's hand on it, so she took it and read it to see if it was important.

She was horrified by what she saw. The list of people to be executed that night included her, Laetus, and Eclectus—the people closest to Commodus. The list also included the names of distinguished senators who had been friends of Commodus's father and who seemed to represent a constant criticism of his actions. They certainly would disapprove of his night in the barracks before the important New Year's celebration. Reputedly, Marcia cried out, "Well done, indeed, Commodus. This is a fine return for the kindness and affection I have lavished on you and for the drunken insults which I have endured from you all these years!" (Balsdon 149). She showed the document to Laetus and Eclectus, and the three decided what was to be done—Commodus would have to die if they were to live.

Marcia efficiently took matters into her own hands. As soon as Commodus returned from the baths, she gave him a cup of particularly fragrant wine that was heavily poisoned. He drank it down and fell deeply asleep. He woke quickly, however, and was very ill—he vomited so much that the conspirators were afraid that the poison would have been lost. Therefore the three secured a strong gladiator who was paid to strangle the emperor Commodus. Marcia, Laetus, and Eclectus quickly went to the house of Pertinax, a sixty-six-year-old veteran, and with the support of the senate and the army offered him the title of emperor.

Pertinax ruled for only three months before another man offered soldiers more money to kill this emperor. He was assassinated, and the three conspirators—Marcia, Laetus, and Eclectus—who had given Pertinax the throne were also killed. While the enterprising concubine efficiently killed the cruel young emperor to save her own life, the violence of the age consumed her shortly thereafter. Future emperors would know that their power rested on the strength of their armies.

See also Faustina the Younger; Julia Domna
Suggested Readings
Balsdon, J. P. V. D. *Roman Women: Their History and Habits.* New York: John Day, 1963.
Herodotus. *The History of Herodotus.* Trans. G. Rawlinson. Chicago: Encyclopaedia Britannica, 1952.

Maria

Niece of the Monk Abraham
(ca. fourth century A.D.)

During the fourth century A.D., many men and women moved away from society into the deserts of Egypt and Syria to try to seek a special relationship with God. They lived ascetic lives, eating and sleeping little, and praying often. Remarkably, the sources mention children living among the holy. Some men who became monks took their young sons with them to raise them in a holy life. Orphans, too, sometimes were put in the care of the holy people of the desert. At times, these children were sources of problems. For example, one monk was reputed to have warned: "Do not bring young boys here; four churches in the desert have been destroyed because of boys" (Ward 86–87). In one popular story, however, a young girl becomes a heroic model of piety, sin, and repentance. We cannot know whether this contemporary account of Maria, the monk Abraham's niece, was historically accurate, but we do know that it circulated widely and was treasured as true.

A literate churchman—Ephraim—lived closely with the desert hermits and wrote an account of the life of Abraham, a monk he admired deeply. In the last story of Abraham's life, Ephraim tells of the fortunes of Maria, Abraham's orphaned niece. The holy man's brother, who lived in the vicinity, died and left his seven-year-old daughter as an orphan. Friends of the girl's father took her to her uncle in the desert, and Abraham took on the responsibility for the young girl. He placed her in a room built onto the outside wall of his cell and placed a window between the two cells. Through the window, Abraham taught scripture and the methods of the ascetic life to his young charge, and his lessons were well learned. Ephraim writes: "Her uncle was glad to see how she at once made progress without any hesitation in all the virtues, that is to say, in tears, humility, modesty, and quietness . . ." (Ward 93). The two spent twenty years in each other's agreeable and pious company.

Then trouble came to the young woman. A monk "by name only" used to come to visit Abraham under the pretext of study, but really to try to see Maria. Although he could never catch a glimpse of her through the window of her cell, he "was filled with the urges of lust" and he spent a year "softening her thoughts by his words." Then one day when he came to her cell window, she climbed down to him: "At once he defiled and polluted her by intercourse out of wicked iniquity and lust" (Ward 93).

Poor Maria was overcome with dismay at the sin. "She beat her face with her hands, wishing, in such great grief, that she were dead" (Ward 93). She felt all her years of asceticism and prayer were useless in the face of such a fall. She could not bear to face her uncle, nor stay in the cell that reminded her of her holy life as a virgin. In despair, she fled away to a city and entered a brothel to work as a prostitute.

Abraham, meanwhile, knew nothing of the events, although he dreamed a serpent entered her cell and devoured a dove. The dream caused him to worry for her safety, and for two days he called eagerly to her through the window between their cells. Then he knew she was gone and "wept bitterly and said, 'Alas, a most cruel wolf has snatched my lamb away'" (Ward 95). For two years he missed her and prayed for her. Finally, his curiosity caused him to ask an acquaintance to make inquiries about Maria's whereabouts. The man found her in the brothel and with a heavy heart told Abraham what he had learned.

Without hesitating, the old monk decided to go after her. He disguised himself as a soldier, so he could enter the brothel without causing notice. Entering, he told the proprietor he had come a long way to "enjoy" the presence of a young woman whose fame had spread. The brothel keeper brought Maria, and Abraham had to kiss and stroke her to keep up pretenses in front of others. After they had eaten together and retired alone to her room, the monk was able to lift his disguise.

He spoke long to the devastated young woman, reminding her that no one is without sin. He reprimanded her not for her sin but for not accepting his help. Abraham promised her that he would take on her sin and answer to God for it if only she would leave the brothel and return with him to the desert. As written in Ephraim's beautiful prose, Abraham's plea was poignant and compelling. He said, "It is not new to fall, my daughter; what is wrong is to lie down when you have fallen" (Ward 98). She laid her head on his feet and wept the rest of the night away. In the morning they left together, and the old man put her on his horse and led her back to their cells.

This time he gave her the inner cell, and she spent years in prayer and weeping, asking God for forgiveness. After three years of such repentance, God showed his favor by giving her the gift of healing. Crowds of people came to her daily, and she would heal them all by her prayers. In this way everyone saw the power of God to forgive those who were repentant. Ten years later, when he was seventy years old, Abraham died; Maria lived five years after that, and both died in peace. Ephraim ended his account by lamenting his loneliness in the absence of his great friends and models, Abraham and Maria.

Ephraim had first written his account in Syriac, an ancient Middle Eastern language. It was soon translated into Latin and spread through western Europe as well as the east, circulating the fame of the pious family. In the tenth century, Hrosvit (also spelled Hroswitha or Roswitha) of Gandersheim, a German nun, wrote a play about these events, which further preserved their memory and popularity.

See also Mary Magdalene; Mary of Egypt; Pelagia; Prostitution; Thais

Suggested Readings

Brock, Sebastian P., et al. *Holy Women of the Syrian Orient.* Berkeley: University of California Press, 1987.

Hrosvit of Gandersheim. *The Plays of Hrosvit of Gandersheim.* Trans. Katherina Wilson. New York: Garland, 1989.

Ward, Benedicta. *Harlots of the Desert.* Kalamazoo, MI: Cistercian Publications, 1987.

Mariamne

Queen of Judea (ca. 50–29 B.C.)

In 37 B.C., the Roman senate made Herod king of Judea, which ended the previous Hasmonaean dynasty and introduced the Herodian one. Herod had come from a family of Idumaeans, Arabs whose land had been conquered by the Hasmonaean rulers and who had been forced to convert to Judaism. Therefore, many Jews taunted Herod as being only half Jewish and suggested that his commitment to Judaism was half-hearted at best. To eliminate such talk, Herod married Mariamne, granddaughter of the Hasmonaean ruler whom Herod had displaced. The new king no doubt hoped that such an alliance would silence critics and make their offspring fully royal children of the royal house. Mariamne's family seemed to pose a threat to the Herodians, however, and the king, supported by his sister Salome, would cruelly destroy the remnants of the Hasmonaeans.

Mariamne and her brother Aristobulus were strikingly beautiful children. Their mother, Alexandra, wanted to ensure that her children would rise to the height of power that was their Hasmonaean birthright. Mariamne married King Herod, which raised her to the highest state, but Herod did not want to make Alexandra's son, Aristobulus, high priest, for he believed that might threaten his own kingship. Alexandra turned to Cleopatra VII, queen of Egypt, and asked her to intercede with the Roman Mark Antony to make Herod give her sixteen-year-old son the priesthood. Antony had seen a picture of the beautiful young man and urged Alexandra to send him to Egypt. Herod was deeply suspicious of Alexandra's political machinations and ordered her not to meddle in political affairs. The king also eliminated Aristobulus's threat by having the young man drowned in a swimming pool. Cleopatra tried to make Antony punish Herod for this crime, but Antony was persuaded that Herod was more useful to him alive. The king remained deeply suspicious of his mother-in-law, however, which had disastrous consequences for Mariamne.

The young bride's archenemy at court was Salome, influential sister of King Herod. Salome was married to her uncle Joseph, who was left in charge of Mariamne while Herod was summoned by Antony to explain Aristobulus's death. Herod had left orders that if he did not return safely, Mariamne was to be killed. When Herod returned in good standing again, he went to his beautiful young bride, and while he was telling her of his passionate love for her, she told him that she knew of his order to kill her. Herod flew into a rage when he found out that she had been told of his plan, and he summoned his sister for an explanation. Salome lied and told him that her husband, Joseph, had seduced Mariamne in his absence. Herod went wild with jealousy and had Joseph put to death. He imprisoned Mariamne's mother, Alexandra, but his passion for Mariamne caused him to spare her life.

After a full year had passed—a year filled with bitterness and strife between Mariamne and Salome—Herod still deeply desired his wife. One day when the king lusted for her and called her to his side, Mariamne refused to yield to him and instead reproached him for the murders of her nearest relatives. Salome, who was nearby (as always, it seems), sent the royal cupbearer to the king with a false story that Mariamne had told him to give the king a love potion that the cupbearer feared was poison. To find out more, Herod tortured Mariamne's favorite slave; the king learned nothing more about the purported poison but did learn that Mariamne hated him. Once again burning with jealousy, Herod had the slave killed, believing that he had been Mariamne's lover, and placed the queen on trial for trying to poison her husband.

Salome wanted the king to execute Mariamne instead of imprisoning her, and in fear of Herod's wrath, Mariamne's own mother, Alexandra, betrayed her daughter and accused her of disloyalty to the king. Alexandra's conduct filled all with disgust and horror, but Mariamne stood calm and proud before her accusers, earning her a great deal of respect. The ancient Jewish historian Josephus described how Mariamne died bravely and showed fortitude and greatness of spirit to the last. She was killed in about 27 B.C. after a marriage of nine years. Josephus claimed that Mariamne was innocent of any wrongdoing and that Salome contrived to have her killed. Eventually, Salome had Mariamne's and Herod's two children, Aristobulus and Alexander, killed.

Mariamne was portrayed by the ancient historians as a beautiful and proud woman who was fully innocent and who was the victim of Salome's ruthless jealousy. Herod was described as being consumed by passionate love for her and being driven almost mad by her cold disdain for his passion. He was full of wild remorse and grief at having condemned her to death, and he could not believe she was dead. Some historians claimed that Herod was driven to even greater acts of cruelty after the death of his beloved Mariamne. It was this reputation for cruelty that led the author of the Gospel of Matthew in the Bible to write that Herod had ordered the slaughter of innocent children in the hopes of killing the newborn Jesus. Some historians question whether this event occurred, but the cruelty of the king that caused him to destroy his beloved Mariamne was certainly true.

See also Alexandra Salome; Cleopatra VII; Salome I

Suggested Readings

Josephus, Flavius. *Jewish Antiquities.* Trans R. Marcus. Cambridge: Harvard University Press, 1963.

———. *The Jewish War.* Trans. H. St. James Thackeray. Cambridge: Harvard University Press, 1927.

Kokkinos, Nikos. *The Herodian Dynasty: Origins, Role in Society and Eclipse.* Sheffield, UK: Sheffield Academic Press, 1998.

Kraemer, Ross Shepard, and Mary Rose D'Angelo. *Women and Christian Origins.* New York: Oxford University Press, 1999.

Macurdy, Grace Harriet. *Vassal-Queens and Some Contemporary Women in the Roman Empire.* Baltimore: Johns Hopkins University Press, 1937.

Richardson, Peter. *Herod: King of the Jews and Friend of the Romans.* Philadelphia: Fortress Press, 1999.

Sandmel, Samuel. *Herod: Profile of a Tyrant.* Philadelphia: J. B. Lippincott, 1967.

Martha

Christian Woman (ca. A.D. 30)

The Gospels that tell the story of Jesus' ministry also tell of many women who followed Jesus. Among the most famous were Martha and her sister, Mary. This same story of the two sisters has also led to much speculation about the expected roles of women in the early Christian communities. The basic story as told by the biblical author Luke is as follows:

> As Jesus traveled, he entered a village and a woman named Martha received him into her house. She had a sister called Mary, who sat at the Lord's feet and listened to his teaching. But Martha was distracted with much work. [The word translated as "work" is *diakonia,* which can mean "to serve"—as waiting a table—but it was also used to refer to Christian ministry. The modern term *deacon*—an official in the church—derives from the word *diakonia.*] Martha went to Jesus and said, "Lord, do you not care that my sister has left me to serve alone? Tell her then to help me." But the Lord answered saying, "Martha, Martha, you are anxious and troubled about many things; one thing is needful. Mary has chosen the good portion, which shall not be taken away from her." (Luke 10:38)

This story has been used to permit women to devote themselves to following Jesus instead of working with the many household tasks involved in maintaining life. Many future generations of nuns would look to Mary as the model of a contemplative life. Modern feminist authors suggest, however, that Martha had in fact stepped out of traditional women's roles of serving within the household; she was a deacon in the church working actively in a missionary and pastoral role. Since she was the one who invited Jesus to enter her home, it is likely that she was the leader of the household. In addition, since members of the early Christian communities referred to each other as brother and sister, we cannot even be sure that Mary and Martha were kin rather than Christians living together in a Christian household.

The story of Martha and her household is told in more detail and made more significant in the Gospel of John (John 11:1–45). John begins the account saying that in the village of Bethany (near Jerusalem), where Mary and Martha lived, their brother, Lazarus, was ill. (Again, we do not know if Lazarus was actually a blood relative or a fellow Christian.) Martha and Mary sent for Jesus to cure their brother. John then says, "Now Jesus loved Martha and her sister and Lazarus." Here again the text suggests that Martha was the head of this household. Jesus stayed with Lazarus for two days, then went to Judea to continue his ministry. While Jesus was away, Lazarus died, and Jesus told his disciples he would return to raise him.

When Jesus arrived, he found Lazarus had been in the tomb four days. Many people had come to Martha and Mary to console them on the death of their brother. When Martha heard that Jesus was coming, she ran to meet him, while Mary sat in the house. Martha told Jesus that she was sure if Jesus had been there, her brother would not have died. Jesus told her Lazarus would rise again. Martha said, "I know that he will rise again in the resurrection at the last day," but Jesus spoke to her and told her the significant Christian theology of the resurrection: Jesus said, "I am the resurrection and the life; he who believes in me, though he die, yet shall he live, and whoever lives and believes in me shall never die. Do you believe this?" Martha acknowledged this: "Yes, Lord; I believe that you are the Christ, the Son of God." When she had said this, she went and called her sister Mary and told her that Jesus was coming.

Mary went to Jesus, fell at his feet, and wept for her brother. When Jesus saw her weep, he was deeply moved and asked the Jews to show him where Lazarus was buried. Jesus came to the tomb, which was a cave with a stone in front of it. Jesus said for the stone to be removed. Martha objected, warning that after four days the odor of the dead flesh would be overpowering. Jesus reprimanded her, reminding her of his promise of the resurrection. They moved the stone and Jesus prayed. Then he cried with a loud voice, "Lazarus, come out." The dead man came out, his hands and feet bound with bandages, and his face wrapped in a burial cloth. Jesus bade them unbind him and let him go. The many Jews who had come with Mary were amazed and believed in Jesus' power. Jesus left and continued his ministry.

Six days before Passover, Jesus came again to Bethany and visited the house of Martha. The family gathered around—Martha served the meal, and Lazarus was at the table with Jesus. Mary took costly ointment and anointed Jesus' feet and wiped them with her hair. The house was filled with the scent of the costly ointment, and Judas Iscariot—one of the disciples (who would soon betray Jesus)—complained about the waste of the ointment. He said that money could have been used to help the poor. Jesus told him not to reprimand Mary and warned his followers that he would not be among them much longer.

Martha and her sister Mary were central to many significant points in Jesus' ministry. It was to Martha that Jesus explained the theology of the resurrection, and it was in response to Mary's ministrations that Jesus foretold his own imminent death. In addition, Martha and Mary remained two prototypes for women's activities in the newly emerging Christian world.

See also Christian Women; Junia; Lydia; Mary Magdalene

Suggested Readings
Meyers, Carol, Toni Craven, and Ross S. Kraemer. *Women in Scripture*. New York: Houghton Mifflin, 2000.

Martha
Persian Martyr (ca. A.D. 341)
As the Roman Empire grew strong in the west, its counterpart, the Persian Empire, prevailed in the east, centered in the regions dominated today by Iran and Iraq (see Map 3). The Persian Empire had developed its own powerful cultural and religious institutions, and the most significant of these was the religion of the prophet Zarathustra, known most commonly by the Greek form of his name, Zoroaster. The prophet was born in about 628 B.C., probably in northern Iran. Legend says he was a lover of wisdom who retreated to a mountain wilderness to seek the truth. There he received a revelation from

Ahura Mazda—whom he believed was the one true god and Lord of Light. Zoroaster recorded his revelation in the holy book of his new religion, the Avesta, and preached to his people. Zoroastrianism had much in common with the great monotheistic religions of the west—Christianity and Judaism—in that Zoroaster believed in one god and argued for people to live an ethical life in the expectation of an afterlife. Many in Persia converted to Zoroastrianism, and in fact, it became something of a national religion.

Centuries later—by the mid-third century A.D.—there were sizable numbers of Christians in the Persian Empire. These numbers swelled as third-century Persian victories over the Roman armies brought thousands of Christian captives as slaves into the Persian Empire. Just as in the Roman Empire, these Christians began to spread their message to other Persians, many of whom were Zoroastrians. Just as in the west, these conversions led to confrontation between Christians and Persian authorities. Since Persian officials identified Zoroastrians as loyal Persians, they identified Christians as loyal to their enemy, the Roman Empire. During the wars of the fourth century between the two great empires, Persians persecuted Christians within their borders, creating martyrs just as pagan Rome had done. Among these martyrs were Christian women whose stories of bravery were preserved in the Syriac-speaking east.

Among the early victims in the mid-fourth century was the king's master craftsman, Posi, a Christian who had been deported from Roman territory. Posi had married a Persian wife and converted her to Christianity. The couple had a daughter named Martha, who evidently had taken a vow of perpetual virginity—a practice particularly offensive to Zoroastrian culture. Posi was martyred, and shortly thereafter, Martha was arrested.

The king sent his chief Mobed (a Zoroastrian priest) to interrogate the girl, and the account tells how she spoke boldly to him. When asked about her religion, Martha said, "I am a Christian, as my clothing shows." Then Mobed continued: "Tell me the truth, are you the daughter of that crazy Posi who went out of his mind and opposed the king, with the result that he was put to an evil death?" (Brock et al. 68). Martha praised her father's faith and hoped that she was strong enough to share his fate. Then Mobed offered the king's clemency, saying that if she would show her loyalty to the Persian king of kings, she would be spared. The dialogue continued with Martha remaining firm in her faith.

The Zoroastrian then turned to her profession of virginity, what he called a "disgusting pretext" (Brock et al. 70), and urged her to marry. She claimed she was already betrothed, but to Jesus, and could not be forced to marry another. Then Mobed answered with anger: "I will spatter you from head to toe with blood, and then your fiancé can come along to find you turned into dust and rubbish; let him marry you then." Martha responded with joy: "He will indeed come in glory, riding on the chariot of the clouds, accompanied by the angels and powers of heaven, and all that is appropriate for his wedding feast . . ." (Brock et al. 70). In a rage, the chief priest informed the king of the stubborn girl's attitude, and the king ordered her sacrificed on the very spot where her father had been killed.

So they led the chaste virgin Martha to be put to death. When she reached the place appointed for the sacrifice, she threw herself down on the earth and prayed, thanking God for allowing her to be martyred as a virgin. When the officer came to tie her up, she laughed, saying "I am gladly sacrificed for my lord." According to the narrator of the events, the thousands of spectators who stood by were astounded at the chaste girl's courage, and everyone praised God for generating such a faithful following. Martha was "slaughtered like a lamb," and after some days, Christians were able to retrieve her body and bury it with ceremony beside her father (Brock et al. 72).

Martha joined the ranks of Christians who were persecuted by Zoroastrians in the Persian Empire. She shared much of the same experience as her counterparts in the west, who were also accused of treason for not worshiping the gods of the empire.

See also Martyrs; Tarbo; Thekla
Suggested Readings
Brock, Sebastian P., et al. *Holy Women of the Syrian Orient.* Berkeley: University of California Press, 1987.

Martyrs
(ca. A.D. 64–304)

Throughout history there have been people who were willing to suffer and die for their beliefs, just as there have been people equally willing to try to use force to change people's convictions. In the Judeo-Christian West, one of the most famous of the early martyrdoms was that of the Jewish Maccabean mother who encouraged her sons to die rather than give up their traditions and who then followed them in death. She became a prototype for subsequent Christian martyrs as they faced the largest suppression of belief that had been seen in the ancient world.

Conservative Romans looked askance at any innovations, particularly religious novelties. It was one thing for Christians to worship someone as a divinity who had died within living memory, but it was quite another for them to reject the traditional Roman assortment of gods. Furthermore, rumors circulated about misunderstood Christian rituals. One third-century Roman described the accusations against Christians: They gathered together with "the lowest dregs of society and credulous women" and engaged in incest, cannibalism, and orgies after indulging in shocking "love feasts." Such rumors came from misunderstandings of communion meals in which Christians commemorated Jesus' sacrifice and sealed their fellowship with "kisses of peace" (Salisbury, *Perpetua's Passion* 78). For Romans, early Christians seemed to violate the traditional social order by including the poor, slaves, and women as equals in their congregations, but the more shocking charges against them were never demonstrated. Even these earliest accusations indicate that women would feature prominently in the persecutions.

Emperor Nero implemented the first large-scale oppression of Christians in Rome in A.D. 64, when he needed scapegoats to blame for a large fire in the city. He executed hundreds of Roman Christians whom he "covered with the skins of beasts . . . to be torn by dogs, or nailed to crosses, or doomed to the flames" (Tacitus 381). This cruelty set a precedent that would be repeated periodically over the next two centuries. Even in this earliest persecution, women were present. Throughout subsequent persecutions

Figure 49. Procession of virgin martyrs, mosaic, ca. A.D. 560 (Scala/Art Resource, NY)

the same theme would emerge—weak women would prove themselves as strong as the mightiest athlete.

During the third century when the empire confronted many internal and external problems, its policy toward Christians grew harsher. Emperors decided that the imperial cult should constitute the single unifying rite of the empire, and everyone had to worship at the altar of the emperor. Jews were somewhat exempted from this requirement because of their long history of monotheistic worship. (The Romans did respect tradition.) Christians, however, lacked this lengthy history, and worse, struck the Romans as particularly traitorous in their obstinacy.

In A.D. 256, and then again under Emperor Diocletian in A.D. 304, all imperial residents were to sacrifice to the emperor and receive a document recording their compliance. But this widespread demand for conformity only provoked many more Christians to die for their beliefs. The persecution of Diocletian took the most Christians—some thousands throughout the empire.

These persecutions did not work. As Tertullian, the third-century church father, said, "The blood of martyrs is seed [from which new Christians would spring]" (Salisbury, *Perpetua's Passion* 166), and indeed watching brave Christians die seemed only to spur on others to convert. Emperor Constantine ended the persecution of Christians, and then Christianity itself became the religion of Rome. The age of the martyrs ended in A.D. 313.

Throughout all these sporadic persecutions, women had played important roles. Since women in the early Christian communities had been early converts, inevitably they were arrested with men. The texts that tell of the martyrdoms always mention the strong women who endured torture and death for their faith, and the presence of women in these trials no doubt persuaded other women that Christianity was a religion that offered something to them.

It is impossible to determine exactly how many people died. The earliest church historian, Eusebius, who wrote in the fourth century A.D., listed the names of 120 men and 15 women along with many more anonymous martyrs. Other later lists of martyrs yield the names of about 950 martyrs, of which 177 were women, and the heaviest proportion of the women martyrs was in North Africa.

The accounts of the martyrs—called "acts" or "passions"—often reveal a good deal of information about ancient women. For example, we learn that pregnant women were arrested and had to wait for childbirth before dying. We see married women and mothers who were arrested, to the chagrin of their families. We also see that the visions of the women martyrs included a great deal of concern for other people and images that are often described as containing feminine aspects: attention to clothing, descriptions of gardens and flowers, and a strong sense of modesty.

The way Christians transformed and remembered these female martyrs became even more important than the historical narratives of the actual women. One of the main transformations in the accounts of the female martyrs was that most became described as "virgins" whether they were actually virgins or not. The mosaic in Figure 49 shows a procession of virgin martyrs, each holding the palm of virginity and wearing the crown of martyrdom. The popular imagination began to see the procession of women who died for their faith as a parade of virgins, who died pure and untouched by the realities of the sexual world. Why did people make this transformation?

Part of the reason may simply be because ancient people associated the highest form of purity both with virgins and martyrs, so it made sense to combine them. There is a deeper symbolic meaning to the transformation, however, that grows out of the late Roman view of virginity. In the ancient world, virgins were (rather paradoxically) associated with fertility. Virgins who renounced their own fecundity were thought to bring fertility and prosperity to others. Since people believed martyrs brought benefits to the people in their vicinity, it seemed that martyrs were fulfilling the same role that the ancient virgins had.

Furthermore, there was a more symbolic reason to associate virgins with martyrs: in both blood flowed. Virgins continued to bleed monthly since they did not get pregnant, and martyrs bled through their torture and execution. Bleeding represented a mysterious sacrifice that in the minds of others brought fertility to the community. The fourth-century Spanish poet Prudentius expressed this relationship in his poem about the virgin-martyr Eulalia:

> Mighty and populous the city she blessed
> Drenching the soil with her blood there
>   outpoured,
> Hallowing it with her virginal tomb.
>   (Prudentius 129)

Prudentius's verse, at one level, is about martyrs' blood and a city hallowed by the martyr's burial. At a deeper level, it is about a city made prosperous by the blood from a virgin's tomb (and by association, a virgin's womb).

As people told the stories of women martyrs who spilled blood for their faith, they began to call these women virgins, who by their abstinence continued to spill blood monthly. The pure martyrs served not only as "seed" to bring new converts into the besieged church, but after the church became accepted, they continued to be venerated as women who brought prosperity to their communities. The old vestal virgins of Rome became the virgin martyrs of Christianity. And real women—who included mothers and wives—were converted to symbolic women—pure as the Virgin Mary.

See also Agnes; Blandina; Felicity; Maccabean Martyrs; Perpetua the Martyr; Vestal Virgins
Suggested Readings
Frend, W. H. C. *Martyrdom and Persecution in the Early Church*. Grand Rapids, MI: Baker Book House, 1965.
LaPorte, Jean. *The Role of Women in Early Christianity*. Lewiston, NY: Edwin Mellen Press, 1982.
Prudentius. *The Poems of Prudentius*. Trans. M. Clement Eagan. Washington, DC: Catholic University Press of America, 1962.
Salisbury, J. E. *Iberian Popular Religion, 600 B.C. to A.D. 700*. Lewiston, NY: Edwin Mellen Press, 1985.
———. *Perpetua's Passion*. New York: Routledge, 1997.
Tacitus. "The Annals." In *Complete Works of Tacitus*. Trans. A. J. Church. New York: The Modern Library, 1942.

Mary

Mother of Jesus (b. ca. 18 B.C.)

Mary the mother of Jesus was a central figure in Christianity, yet the references to her in the biblical texts are remarkably few; we can obtain only a shadowy picture of this most influential ancient woman. Stories of Mary's birth, life, death, and bodily ascension to heaven first appear in Christian narratives dating no earlier than the second century A.D. and usually much later. These were relegated to the Apocryphal Acts (outside the agreed-upon books of the Bible) and were composed only after the significance of the Virgin Birth was appreciated by Greco-Roman converts to Christianity. Within the Bible, the main references to Mary appear in the Gospel of Luke, which describes the miraculous birth of Jesus.

That Gospel says that the angel Gabriel appeared to Mary, a young woman engaged to Joseph the carpenter. Gabriel told her she would conceive a child, and she was to name him Jesus. Mary asked how she could conceive a child, since she had never "known a man." Gabriel reminded Mary of God's miraculous powers, telling her that her relative Elizabeth would bear a child even though she was too old. Mary's miracle would be even greater, however, for the Holy Spirit would father Mary's son. Mary submitted to God and agreed to the divine intervention, although she knew how shocking it would be for her—an unmarried virgin—to become pregnant. Such occurrences were the cause of much shame in the early Jewish communities in which Mary lived. Mary visited her relative Elizabeth and they took joy in her pregnancy.

The Gospel of Matthew, perhaps to underscore the difficulties inherent in Mary's social position, approaches the account from a different direction. Matthew says that when Mary was betrothed to Joseph, "before they came together" (Matt. 1:18), she was found to be with child of the Holy Spirit. Joseph, who was a "just man and unwilling to put her to shame" (Matt. 1:19), resolved simply to end the betrothal quietly. But then Gabriel appeared to Joseph in a dream and assured him that Mary's child had been fathered by the Holy Spirit and that he should take her as his wife. Therefore, they married, and Matthew says they had no intercourse until she had borne her son Jesus.

Mary appears in the Gospels several times later, and in each context she is shown as a good mother who took pride in her divine son. Joseph took her to Bethlehem for the imperial census, and there she gave birth to Jesus in a manger. When the shepherds came to worship him, "Mary kept all these things, pondering them in her heart" (Luke 2:19). As good Jews, Mary and Joseph had the infant circumcised and then took him to the Temple for ritual purification. There Simeon, the blind prophet, saw in Jesus the salvation of Israel. He took Mary aside and warned her about Jesus' future to prepare her for the troubles to come. Finally the young family returned to Nazareth, where Jesus grew up.

When the boy was twelve, the family was in Jerusalem for Passover. Jesus wandered off to the Temple without telling his parents. After a three-day search they found him, and as a dutiful mother, Mary scolded him. Jesus responded that he had simply been in his "father's house," and again Luke tells us that Mary "treasured all these things in her heart" (Luke 2:48–50).

The Gospel of Matthew tells us that when Jesus began to preach in his own land, his neighbors were astonished. They described his ordinary family life: "Is not this the carpenter's son? Is not his mother called Mary? And are not his brothers James and Joseph and Simon and Judas? And are not all his sisters with us?" (Matt. 14:55–56). This passage, which indicates how difficult it was for a prophet to be accepted in his own land, also implies some things about Mary's life and has generated a good deal of controversy. Did Mary and Joseph have a normal married life after Jesus' birth, so that Mary bore him four sons and many sisters? Some who argue for Mary's perpetual virginity suggest that these were her stepchildren. Alternative readings suggest that these were Jesus' cousins, born to a sister of Mary also named Mary. Matthew later refers to one of the followers of Jesus who was a companion of Mary Magdalene who was named "Mary the mother of James and Joseph" (Matt. 27:55), and Mark also refers to this Mary the mother of James (Mark 15:40, 16:1). Either these references were to Mary, mother of Jesus, or they referred to another follower of Jesus named Mary. Scholars disagree.

The Gospels give Mary virtually no role in Jesus' ministry (unless the Mary who was the mother of James and Joseph was in fact Jesus' mother). The Gospel of John even seems to suggest some tension between Jesus and his mother at the marriage at Cana (John 2:1–6). When the wine gave out, Mary came to Jesus to tell him of the problem. Jesus gave her a short reply, "O woman, what have you to do with me? My hour has not yet come" (John 2:4). This seemed to suggest that Jesus was not yet prepared to do miracles, but Mary was pushing him to do so. She told the servants to follow Jesus' instructions, and he then performed the miracle of turning water into wine for the wedding guests. This was the first of Jesus' miracles and began the significant part of his mission. The Gospel credits Mary with being the catalyst for this miracle.

Mary appears again in the Gospels on the day of Jesus' death. John tells us she appeared at the foot of the cross, and there Jesus entrusted her to the care of his beloved apostle John. Here at the end of his life, Jesus is the dutiful son, caring for his mother, just as she had been a dutiful and caring mother throughout his life. Based in part on this reference to John, subsequent tradition says that Mary lived out her life in Ephesus in Asia Minor (shown on Map 7), and today there is a church dedicated to Mary on the hill overlooking Ephesus, where she reputedly lived.

The Acts of the Apostles that told of the spread of Jesus' message after his death did not mention Mary. Nor did Paul refer to Mary in his letters. Perhaps she did not take an active role in the missionary activities. Nevertheless, countless generations of subsequent Christians have venerated her for her role in the birth of Christianity.

See also Apocryphal Acts of the Apostles; Elizabeth; Mary Magdalene

Suggested Readings
Brown, Raymond, et al., eds. *Mary in the New Testament.* Philadelphia: Fortress Press, 1978.
Gaventa, Beverly Roberts. *Mary: Glimpses of the Mother of Jesus.* Columbia: University of South Carolina Press, 1995.
Graef, Hilda. *Mary: A History of Doctrine and Devotion.* Westminster, MD: Christian Classics, 1985.
Meyers, Carol, Toni Craven, and Ross S. Kraemer. *Women in Scripture.* New York: Houghton Mifflin, 2000.

Mary Magdalene
Follower of Jesus (ca. A.D. 1)

The New Testament of the Bible contains references to more than three women named Mary (excluding Jesus' mother), and centuries later these women were often treated as the one named Mary Magdalene. The Gospels refer to one specific woman named Mary of Magdala in several places. Luke claims that Jesus was followed by several women "who had been healed of evil spirits and infirmities" (Luke 8:2), and among them he mentions Mary of Magdala (a town on the shores of the Sea of Galilee shown on Map 5), who had been "possessed by seven demons" (Mark 16:9). Jesus cured her of this possession, and she followed him in his ministry and joined the women who helped support Jesus and the Apostles. The Gospel of Mark also says that Jesus had cast out seven demons from Mary Magdalene (whose name may mean "Mary from Magdala").

This Mary stayed with Jesus until his crucifixion, when according to the Gospels of Mark and John, she watched the crucifixion and noticed where Jesus was buried. Then she and two other women (including another Mary, the "mother of James and Salome") brought spices so they could anoint the body and complete the burial rites. When they arrived, however, they discovered the tomb was opened and an angel was there, who told them Jesus had risen and gone ahead to Galilee, where he would meet them. The Gospel of John states that Jesus, too, appeared to Mary Magdalene at the tomb. Jesus said to Mary, "Woman, why are you weeping?" Thinking he was the gardener, Mary asked where he had moved the body so she could go there. When Jesus called her name, she recognized him and called him Rabboni, which means "teacher" in Hebrew. Jesus warned her not to touch him but told her to go to the disciples and say that Jesus was "ascending to my Father and your Father, to my God and your God" (John 20:13–18). Mary went and told the disciples, but they did not believe her. According to the Gospel of Mark, Jesus appeared to her the next day, and "she went and told those who had been with him, as they mourned and wept. But when they heard that he was alive and had been seen by her, they would not believe it" (Mark 16:9–12). But on the evening of that day, Jesus appeared to all the disciples, so they believed.

Very quickly, other women in the Bible came to be conflated with this Mary of Magdala. In part, this association came from Mary Magdalene's role as coming to anoint the dead body of Jesus; commentators began to associate her with other women who were mentioned in the Bible as anointing Jesus. For example, Luke describes an anonymous woman—"a woman of the city, who was a sinner"—who came to a Pharisee's house where Jesus was eating. She brought an "alabaster flask of ointment," and she "began to wet his feet with her tears and wiped them with the hair of her head, and kissed his feet, and anointed them with the ointment." Jesus forgave the woman's sins, "which are many," because she "loved much" (Luke 7:37–40).

Another anonymous woman appeared to Jesus when he was in Bethany eating at the house of Simon "the Leper." According to the Gospels of Mark and Matthew, she appeared "with an alabaster flask of very expensive ointment, and she poured it on his head as he sat at the table." When his disciples complained about the waste of the ointment, Jesus reprimanded them and said, "In pouring this ointment on my body she has done it to prepare me for burial" (Matt. 26:6–13; Mark 14:3–8). In this instance, the woman provides the opportunity for Jesus to predict his crucifixion, and it is perhaps not surprising that later commentators equated this woman with Mary Magdalene, who actually arrived at his burial to anoint his corpse. Both these instances linked Mary Magdalene with great love and great forgiveness of sins.

Finally, Mary Magdalene became linked with another Mary of the Bible, Mary the sister of Martha and Lazarus—those friends of Jesus with whom he stayed when he visited Bethany. This Mary, according to Luke, sat at Jesus' feet listening to him talk instead of helping her sister, Martha, serve them. Jesus defended her, saying "Mary has chosen the better part" (Luke 10:42). Thus, when Mary Magdalene became associated with this Mary, a contemplative life of prayer became associated with the new composite Mary Magdalene.

There is no scriptural authority that links all these women, and in fact, even a cursory reading of the Bible shows that these were separate women. Very soon after the composition of the texts, however, commentators and church fathers began to link the women. It is clear that the moral of the text was more important to them than its historical accuracy, and the figure of the composite Mary Magdalene offered a significant lesson that was greater than the sum of its parts.

The traditions about Mary Magdalene changed in the eastern and western traditions of the early church. In the east, particularly among groups who would later be known as Gnostic, she was given a great deal of respect and considered a prominent disciple of Jesus. The Gnostic Gospel, Gospel of Mary, gives Mary Magdalene an even more privileged position; she was recognized as the recipient of a special revelation from the risen Jesus, and when the disciples were discouraged, she rallied them. Peter within this Apocryphal Act called her the woman Jesus loved more than any other, but the apostle quarreled with her, claiming he should be the leader of the apostles, not a woman.

In the west, however, her reputation took a significantly different turn. The early church commentators added a significant feature to the slowly developing literary Mary: again without clear biblical authority, they claimed she was a reformed prostitute. The Bible only said she was a sinner, indeed that she had "many" sins and that she had been possessed by demons. By the sixth century A.D., she had been identified as a prostitute. Why?

Part of the answer may come from texts dating from about the second century A.D., which purport to be biblical stories but were excluded from the collection of the Bible. In several of these works—called Apocryphal Gospels or Acts—Mary Magdalene was described as Jesus' lover. In the Gospel of Philip, for example, the author wrote: "The companion of the Savior is Mary Magdalene. Christ loved her more than all his disciples, and used to kiss her often on her mouth" (Ward 15). It may be that such associations led people to associate Mary Magdalene with sexuality, and therefore sexual sins. It may be that the identification of Mary with prostitution served as an attempt to silence those traditions that attributed great authority to this woman who was so close to Jesus.

Perhaps the most likely reason for associating Mary with prostitution is that in the Bible she became a sinner who had been forgiven and redeemed. Therefore, in sermons and lessons, the story of Mary Magdalene became a story of salvation, and in the late Roman world the most striking example of redemption might have been a prostitute, who under Roman law could never change her status. Therefore, the image of a prostitute who was saved by Jesus offered a model of one of the most compelling transformations for a Roman audience. Mary Magdalene the sinner became Mary the prostitute. It is the memory of this Mary Magdalene that the West preserved in stories and churches and even in "Magdalene societies" designed to reform prostitutes. In this case the legendary woman was much more influential than the historical figure.

See also Apocryphal Acts of the Apostles; Martha [Christian Woman]; Mary of Egypt; Pelagia; Prostitution

Suggested Readings
Garth, H. M. *St. Mary Magdalene in Medieval Tradition.* Baltimore: Johns Hopkins University Press, 1950.
Meyers, Carol, Toni Craven, and Ross S. Kraemer. *Women in Scripture.* New York: Houghton Mifflin, 2000.
Ricci, Carla. *Mary Magdalene and Many Others: Women Who Followed Jesus.* Trans. Paul Burns. Minneapolis: Fortress Press, 1994.
Ward, Benedicta. *Harlots of the Desert.* Kalamazoo, MI: Cistercian Publications, 1987.

Mary of Egypt
(d. ca. A.D. 421)

In about A.D. 600, the patriarch of Jerusalem reputedly wrote down the account of a remarkable ascetic woman who had died in about A.D. 421.

He claimed to have faithfully recorded the account that had been preserved by oral tradition, and the written account proved a popular tale of a prostitute who had been redeemed by conversion to Christianity. Stories of reformed prostitutes were particularly popular during the Roman Empire, because although Romans accepted prostitution, they believed that once a woman was a prostitute, she could never be restored to respectability. Once a Roman woman was registered as a prostitute, she could never expect to have a legitimate marriage or lose the stigma of prostitution. It was in this context that Romans listened with wonder to stories of redeemed prostitutes.

The narrative of the life of Mary of Egypt begins with a monk, Zosimas, who had lived in a monastic community and had been a good and pious monk for fifty-three years. After all this time, he was still not content with his religious progress and hoped to learn more about God. His quest led him to the desert across the Jordan River. Zosimas wandered in the desert for twenty days, and one day when he was resting and praying at noon, he lifted his eyes to the east. There he saw what at first he thought was a ghost. It was a naked figure, skin blackened by the sun, clothed only in long hair like white wool. The figure began to flee deeper into the desert, but Zosimas pursued it. Finally he caught up with the apparition, which then addressed him by name, saying: "Father Zosimas, why do you chase me? Forgive me for not turning toward you, for I am a woman nude. Lend me your cloak so I may turn toward you and accept your prayers" (Salisbury 70). Zosimas was astounded that she knew his name, and he stripped off his garment and gave it to her.

Mary and Zosimas then argued over who should give the first blessing, each pleading unworthiness in the face of the other's sanctity. Mary argued that Zosimas deserved the honor because he was a priest. Zosimas, on the other hand, claimed that Mary was filled with the Holy Spirit because of her ascetic life, so she deserved precedence. Zosimas won the argument, persuading Mary to bless him first. The author of the account noted that by this, Mary the ascetic and woman was superior spiritually to the old, pious monk. After the exchange of benedictions, they entered into conversation.

Zosimas asked how Mary came to be in the desert, and she told her story: "Father, my country was Egypt. When I was twelve years old, I abandoned my parents and went to live in Alexandria. For seventeen years I sold my body, not to accumulate riches, but just to live a luxurious life. I abandoned myself to drinking, sleeplessness and lived a defiled life with laughter, ardor and friends" (Salisbury 71). When Mary was about twenty-eight years old, she saw a group of pilgrims from Libya preparing to cross the sea. She learned that they were going to Jerusalem to celebrate the redemption and ascension of Christ. Mary was interested in the procession and wanted to join the pilgrims. She was told she could join them if she paid the passage fee, as everyone else did. She did not have enough money for the passage, having spent all her earnings in luxurious living, but she offered to earn it, saying: "You may use my body for the passage fee" (Salisbury 71).

The voyage was hard, but the pilgrims arrived in Jerusalem and joined the procession of the cross that preceded the festival. At dawn on the morning of the feast day everyone hurried to the church. Mary tried to join the celebrants, but her past life caught up with her at the door of the church. A mysterious force repeatedly prevented her from entering. Her sins kept her from joining the community of the faithful. She retreated from the doorway and sat and wept, miserable at her sinfulness. Looking up, she saw an image of the Virgin Mary and prayed to her namesake for forgiveness. She renounced her previous life and was able to enter the church and worship the True Cross.

Upon leaving the church, she heard a voice saying: "If you cross the Jordan, you will find rest" (Salisbury 71). She felt herself divinely guided to her place of penance. A pious man gave her three coins with which she bought three loaves of bread to take with her to the desert. She crossed the Jordan with many tears of penitence and had lived in the desert ever since, seeing no one.

Zosimas asked how long she had been a hermit and about her labors in the desert. She responded that she had been in the desert for forty years and had subsisted for that time on the loaves of bread she had brought with her. She said it was the first seventeen years that had troubled her the most. During that time she was plagued with recollections of the carnal delights she had left behind. She overcame her sordid thoughts with many tears and, armed with prayer, she vanquished her burning passions. She said that the sweetness of overcoming these temptations more than compensated for her lack of food and clothing. She claimed to be clothed in the word of God.

Before the monk left, Mary asked him to return to the Jordan on Holy Thursday of the following year to bring her holy communion. Zosimas followed her instructions and met Mary at the Jordan to give her communion. He promised to return again the following year, but at that time, he found her dead. He saw written in the sand: "Father Zosimas, bury Mary in this place, and return her to the earth. I left this earth on the second day of April" (Salisbury 72). The old man then knew she had died after she had taken communion. He tried to dig a grave to satisfy her last request, but the ground was too hard. The story then tells about the appearance of a lion, who dug the grave for the holy woman.

Zosimas returned to his monastery and told the monks everything that had happened. They celebrated annually the death of the holy woman, and the narrator says that Zosimas lived in his monastery for a long time, surviving to an age of a hundred years. The patriarch of Jerusalem wrote down the account to preserve the story of Mary of Egypt, the prostitute who overcame her sinful life to become a venerated holy woman.

See also Mary of Magdalene; Prostitution
Suggested Readings
Salisbury, J. E. *Church Fathers, Independent Women.* London: Verso, 1991.
Ward, Benedicta. *Harlots of the Desert.* Kalamazoo, MI: Cistercian Publications, 1987.

Medb

Celtic Queen (before A.D. 400)
Before 600 B.C., Celtic tribes had settled in Ireland; there they lived in fortified settlements where they were ruled by a tribal king. The king

led his people in war and presided over a warrior class of young men who prided themselves on raiding, drinking, and telling stories of great escapades. There was also a priestly class of druids, wise men who preserved the wisdom of the tribe in a preliterate age, where memory was essential. Finally, there was a farmer class who worked the hard land and, even more important, tended the cattle that the Celts counted as their greatest wealth.

The early history of this society has been all but transformed into myth, preserved in stories that praise heroes and tell of battles, dreams, hopes, and losses. Scholars assume most of the tales were composed sometime between 200 B.C. and A.D. 400 and that most preserve traditions that were much older. While it is difficult to sort history from fantasy in these tales, many historians credit one series of stories—the Ulster Cycle—with preserving some genuine traditions of a conflict between two major tribes. Within this tradition appear accounts of the best-known Celtic heroine—Queen Medb (the English call her Maeve). It is particularly difficult to trace the story of Medb because there seem to have been at least two in the tales—one a queen (possibly historical) and the other a goddess, whom kings had to "marry" in order to achieve their sovereignty. Both these figures become confused in the various stories. While scholars have not agreed on whether Medb is a historical or a purely literary figure, all agree that the popular tales have made the Celtic queen a significant figure in the Celtic and Irish imagination.

Medb appears in the texts as the daughter of a king. She was described as independent and sexually active. She had many lovers before marrying Ailill Mac Mata, probably another tribal king, and Medb and her husband jointly ruled their combined kingdoms. The myths say that Medb preserved her independent ways even after marriage, saying "it would not suit me at all if [my husband] were jealous, for I have never denied myself the man I took a fancy to . . . and I never shall whatever husband I have now or may have hereafter" (Gantz 117).

The myths attribute to Medb all the skills of a good ruler—from warfare to wisdom. In the famous epic of "The Cattle Raid of Cuailgne,"

Medb appears as a forceful and sometimes violent queen. At the start, she finds her possessions are not as extensive as those of her husband, so she wants to acquire a fabulous brown bull from a neighboring kingdom. After unsuccessfully trying to buy it, she raises an army to seize the animal and stands in her chariot leading her warriors herself. In another story, Medb fights a single combat and wounds the opposing hero with an accurate cast of her spear.

In addition to skills in war, Medb is shown to be wise in counsel, giving her husband advice during times of difficult deliberation. For example, a neighboring king sends three warriors to Ailill for him to judge which should be made the champion. Ailill was placed in a difficult situation, for surely the two losers would bring violence to Ailill and Medb's kingdom in their rage. Medb develops a trick to avoid the problem. She tells her husband to tell each of the warriors that he is the champion, and swearing the men to secrecy, she gives each a symbol wrapped in cloth to take back to their king. When the warriors return home and present their king with their supposed symbol of championship, only one turns out to be made of gold. The king is thus readily able to see which is the winner, but by then the irate losers are safely out of Medb's kingdom. By such subterfuges, the queen gained a reputation for shrewd political dealings.

Medb and Ailill had seven sons and one daughter. The girl—Findbhair—takes a prominent place of her own in the myths. She is described as a prophet who had been trained by druids. The daughter is shown as a tender, loving woman who marries a fine warrior. The stories say that Medb continued to dominate her daughter, however, repeatedly interfering in her life. The young woman finally realizes that she had been controlled by her strong mother, and she cannot live with that knowledge. Findbhair drowns herself in a river, and her ring is found in the body of a salmon—the Celtic symbol for wisdom.

According to the myths, Medb dies violently. While bathing at the water's edge, the queen and her king are both killed by a spear cast by a young man from a different tribe. In another version, Medb is killed by her own nephew as an act of vengeance for a perceived insult against his mother. In both stories, the queen dies violently as a consequence of her own warlike life. She was reported to have been buried under a large mound, which still exists in Ireland, where for centuries it has been a custom to place a stone on the mound whenever one passes it.

What lessons did generations of Celtic women and men learn from the popular accounts of the legendary (or semihistorical) Queen Medb? Perhaps women learned that they could be shrewd warriors, inspiring such figures as Boudicca or Cartimandua. Perhaps they also learned of the difficulties of family ties as daughters and nephews clashed with the dominating Medb. It may have been enough if readers only learned about the richness of human experience from the skillfully drawn stories of the queen and her family. Whatever people took from these tales, they were and continue to be remarkably popular.

See also Boudicca; Cartimandua; Elen Luyddog; Macha Mong Ruadh

Suggested Readings
Dunn, Vincent A. *Cattle-Raids and Courtships*. New York: Garland, 1989.
Ellis, P. B. *Celtic Women*. Grand Rapids, MI: W. B. Eerdmans Publishing, 1996.
Gantz, Jeffrey. *Early Irish Myths and Sagas*. London: Penguin, 1981.

Medea

Sorceress in Greek Mythology

One of the oldest Greek legends tells of the hero Jason and his adventures on his ship, the *Argo*. Jason and his crew (called the Argonauts) sailed on the Black Sea and had many adventures that lived on in Greek myths. One of Jason's companions, who was central to his adventures, was the witch-princess Medea. This mythological woman became even more notorious than Jason in subsequent Greek literature.

The story of Jason and Medea began with royal struggles in Thessaly in northern Greece. A queen named Nephele was worried that her children would be placed in danger because their father had taken a new wife. She placed her children on a ram with a golden fleece. The ram delivered the boy, Phryxus, safely to the kingdom of Colchis on the eastern shore of the Black Sea. (The girl, named Helle, fell from the ram's back and drowned in the sea in the place named Hellespont after her. See Map 4.) In gratitude for his deliverance, the boy sacrificed the ram to Jupiter and gave the Golden Fleece to Aeetes, king of Colchis. Aeetes placed the fleece in a sacred grove under the care of a sleepless dragon. Medea was the daughter of King Aeetes.

Meanwhile trouble arose back in Thessaly. The king, Aeson, was tired of governing and entrusted the kingdom to his brother, Pelias, under the condition that Pelias would turn over the kingdom to Aeson's son Jason when the boy was grown. When Jason claimed his throne, Pelias suggested that he first go retrieve the Golden Fleece that was thought to be the property of the Thessalonians. Jason agreed and built the *Argo* for the adventure. The goddesses on Mount Olympus were interested in this enterprise, because they wanted their favorite, Jason, to win the fleece. Aphrodite persuaded her son, Eros, to send a magical arrow into Medea's heart, making her fall in love with Jason and thus help him with her knowledge of sorcery.

King Aeetes of Colchis consented to give Jason the Golden Fleece, but only if he could yoke two fire-breathing bulls, plow a field, and then sow it with serpent's teeth. (Aeetes knew that the serpent's teeth would sprout into armed men who would try to kill the farmer who sowed them.) Jason had no idea how he would accomplish these seemingly impossible tasks, but Eros's arrow had done its work. Medea approached Jason and promised to help him win the fleece if he would take her away in the *Argo* and marry her. Jason promised to be faithful to her forever.

Medea gave Jason a flask of lotion—the juice from the crocus flower—that would protect him from the bulls' fiery breath. Jason spread it all over his body, spear, and shield. Then he was able to subdue the bulls and harness them to the plow. When the armed men sprang from the ground, Jason followed Medea's advice and subdued them by throwing a stone into their midst, which caused them to fight among themselves instead of against him. Medea then led Jason and his men to the fleece and cast a spell on the dragon, putting it to sleep, allowing Jason to take the prize. The group fled to the *Argo* and escaped, and Medea cured most of their wounds by her magic potions.

Aeetes was furious and prepared his fleet to give chase, but Medea would stop at nothing to make her escape. She had taken her young half-brother Apsyrtus with her on the *Argo,* and when Aeetes approached, she killed Apsyrtus and cut him into pieces. She threw the body parts into the water, where they were caught by the strong current. Aeetes had to stop his pursuit to gather his son's remains to give them a decent burial, and the Argonauts escaped.

When the group returned to Thessaly with the fleece, the only thing that prevented Jason's joy was that his father was too old to enjoy the festivities. Jason pleaded with his wife to restore his father's youth. The night of the next full moon, Medea went forth and invoked the gods and goddesses of nature. A chariot pulled by flying serpents descended to her and took her where she could collect powerful plants. For nine nights she engaged in her search, then she was ready.

She erected two altars—to Hecate and to Hebe (goddesses of the underworld and youth). She laid Jason's father on a bed of herbs and began her mysterious ceremony (which no one was permitted to see). She mixed a huge cauldron with magic herbs and other items. When it was ready, Medea cut the throat of the old man and let out all his blood. She poured into his mouth the juice from the cauldron, and suddenly he was rejuvenated as if he were forty years younger. Jason was delighted. Medea also used her magic for revenge, however.

Jason's uncle Pelias was also old, and his daughters wanted Medea to make him young again too. This time, however, Medea prepared her cauldron in a different way. She told the daughters that they had to strike Pelias with swords first, and they entered his sleeping chamber to do so. (Medea had cast a spell on the guards to make them sleep.) The daughters struck him tentatively, but Medea dealt the death blow. They placed him in the cauldron, and Medea departed in her serpent-drawn chariot before they discovered her treachery. Pelias was not restored; his body was simply burned.

Medea and Jason lived for some time in Corinth, until King Creon wanted his daughter, Creusa (sometimes called Glauce), to marry Jason. Medea was furious and reminded Jason of the oath he had sworn to her, and she plotted her revenge. She sent a wedding gift to the wedding of Jason and Creusa—a beautiful golden crown and a long white robe. No sooner had Creusa put them on than unquenchable flames shot up from them and consumed her and all the wedding party except Jason, who escaped by leaping from the window. According to some accounts (most influential, the playwright Euripides), Medea completed her revenge on Jason by killing their two surviving children, so he would feel the deep pain of their loss.

Medea fled and had many adventures of her own. She visited the hero Heracles at Thebes and cured him of some madness. She married Aegeus, the old king of Athens, promising to use her magic to bear him a son. She bore a son named Medus, but when Aegeus's first son, Theseus, returned, Medea tried to poison him. She then had to flee again. She sailed to Italy and taught snake charming to the people there. She also sailed to Asia and married an Asian king. According to the myths, Medea never died but became immortal and reigned in the Elysian Fields. Some myths say that it was she (rather than the beautiful Helen) who married Achilles.

This Greek myth preserves the tale of a remarkably independent and destructive woman. She was remembered for her skill with magic and with herbs (traditionally female skills), and the stories told how she always gained what she wanted by her courage and ruthless determination. She is also remembered as the greatest example of feminine anger at being abandoned by her beloved. She cared more for revenge than she did for her children. She remained a frightening and compelling model of ancient womanhood.

See also Aphrodite; Helen of Troy in Greek
  Mythology
Suggested Readings
Corti, Lillian. *The Myth of Medea and the Murder of Children.* Westport, CT: Greenwood Press, 1998.

Euripides. *Medea, Hippolytus, Electra, Helen.* Trans. James Morwood. Oxford: Oxford University Press, 1998.

Grimal, Pierre. *The Dictionary of Classical Mythology.* Oxford: Blackwell, 1996.

Medusa
Greek Mythological Monster

Ancient Greek storytellers told of three fearsome monsters called Gorgons, who lived on an island far to the west. Their names were Stheno, Euryale, and Medusa, and all were daughters of two sea-gods, Phorcys and Ceto. They each had wings, huge tusks like those of a boar, hands of bronze, and hair of snakes, and any human who looked at them was turned instantly into stone. They were objects of fear and loathing to mortals and immortals alike. (Only Poseidon was unafraid of them, for he had fathered a child with Medusa.) Two of the Gorgons were immortal, but the third, Medusa, could die if anyone could figure out how to kill her. A young Greek hero—Perseus, son of Danaë—foolishly boasted that he would bring the head of Medusa back to King Polydectes. Fortunately for Perseus, two powerful gods watched over him and helped him in his adventure.

As Perseus wandered in search of the island of the Gorgons, the messenger god, Hermes, came to his aid. He told the young man that first he had to go to the Gray Women, who could tell him the way. The Gray Women were strange creatures because they had but one eye among the three of them. It was their custom to take turns with it, each removing it from her forehead when she had had it for a time and handing it to another. Hermes told Perseus he must rush forward and steal the eye as they passed it among them, then refuse to give it back until they told him how to reach the Gorgons. The plan worked perfectly, and Perseus forced the Gray Women to give him directions.

If Perseus were to prevail against the dreadful Medusa, however, he would need magical weapons, and the gods provided them. Hermes gave him a sword that could not be broken by the Gorgon's scales. But this sword would be useless if Perseus were turned to stone before he could approach the monster. Athena solved that problem: She took off the shield of polished bronze that covered her breast and gave it to him, telling him to use the shield as a mirror and with it to see the Gorgon without looking directly at her. As Hermes and Perseus continued, they stopped for a while in the land of a hospitable people called the Hyperboreans. They gave Perseus additional gifts: winged sandals to let him fly, a magic bag that would always become the right size for whatever was to be carried within it, and a cap that made the wearer invisible. Now Perseus was ready to confront Medusa.

He approached the Gorgons as they were sleeping, and Hermes and Athena told him which was Medusa. Perseus hovered over them with his magic sandals, and looking only in the bright shield, he located Medusa's head and cut it off with a single stroke of his sword. He quickly placed it in his magic bag, which closed tightly over it. He was now safe from Medusa's glance, which even in death would turn him to stone. From the stump of Medusa's neck two beings sprang forth: Pegasus, the winged horse, and Chrysaor, a man with a golden sword. The other two Gorgons had awakened and tried to pursue their sister's murderer, but Perseus's magic cap made him invisible so he could escape.

Perseus brought Medusa's head back and changed the evil king Polydectes into stone when he drew the monster's head from the bag. Then Perseus lived happily with his wife, Andromeda, and his mother, Danaë. He gave Medusa's head to Athena, who bore it always upon her aegis (her breastplate) or on her shield.

Medusa remained a popular subject in art, as the ancient Greeks remained drawn to this frightening and murderous ancient female monster.

See also Athena; Danaë

Suggested Readings

Grimal, Pierre. *The Dictionary of Classical Mythology.* Oxford: Blackwell, 1996.

Hamilton, Edith. *Mythology.* New York: Mentor, 1955.

Melania the Elder
Monastic Founder (ca. A.D. 341–410)

During the first centuries after the death of Jesus, Christians all over the Roman Empire had developed various ways to understand the

Christian message and to practice their faith. By the late fourth century A.D., church leaders eager to have a uniform worship found this diversity of thought and practice unacceptable, so religious controversies developed that split Christian communities. Many pious Christians found themselves on the wrong side of ideological differences—this happened to the wealthy, ascetic Roman woman, Melania. Melania was a well-known and influential woman during her lifetime, and her career as an ascetic monastic founder placed her in touch with the most famous church figures—men such as Augustine of Hippo, Palladius, and Paulinus of Nola wrote of her accomplishments, and the irascible church father Jerome condemned her for associating with religious dissidents.

Melania was born in about A.D. 341 into a wealthy Roman family in the province of Spain. Her family arranged a good marriage for her when she was about fourteen. Scholars believe her husband was Valerius Maximus, an important official in Rome and a man of considerable prestige. She became pregnant frequently in the early years of her marriage—bearing three living sons and enduring several stillbirths. The family seems to have moved outside Rome to live in one of their large estates in the provinces, but the country life did not improve their luck. In about A.D. 364, when Melania was only twenty-two years old, illness took two of her sons and her husband. The grief-stricken young widow moved with her remaining child back to Rome.

While in the city, Melania was drawn to Christian worship and joined a group of ascetics who gathered in the households of well-to-do Romans. For about eight years Melania developed her spiritual life, and finally at about the age of thirty, she decided to commit herself more dramatically to a religious calling. Her biographer said she kept her plans secret to avoid her relatives' interference, but she pursued her dream to escape the city of Rome. She appointed a guardian for her son (who was about ten years old), packed her goods, and as her biographer wrote, "put them on a ship, and then she sailed with all speed for Alexandria accompanied by various high-born women and children . . ." (Murphy 65). From there she planned to go on to Jerusalem—that holy city that had already drawn many pilgrims by the late fourth century.

Melania's first stop was Alexandria, where she sold her goods and met Rufinus—a scholar who became an influential force in her life. Melania's desire to learn from other ascetics was voracious, however, so she went into the desert to visit and learn from the holy men and women living there. She spent six months in the desert in about A.D. 377 and became involved in a great religious controversy. The monks in the Egyptian desert were engaged in a major disagreement over the relationship between God the Son and God the Father—the Arian controversy—that raged through the eastern portion of the empire. (The Arians believed that God the Father existed *before* the Son. This position was later condemned by the church.) The bishop of Alexandria banished several of the dissenting monks from Egypt, and they fled into Palestine. Melania went with them and used her own money to provide for them. Her biographer told how she dressed as a young male slave to minister to the holy men, but an official arrested her and threw her in prison "ignorant that she was a lady." She boldly announced who she was and insisted that she be treated with the respect because of her family connections. The judge "made an apology and honored her, and gave orders that she should succor the saints without hindrance" (Murphy 69).

After this, in about A.D. 378, she went to Jerusalem and founded a monastery, probably on the Mount of Olives. Rufinus, Melania's friend and spiritual director, joined her in the monastery, which was probably a "double monastery," one in which both men and women lived. Her monastery became a center for pilgrims as well. Visitors from the west often stayed with her and enjoyed her hospitality. In A.D. 385, the famous churchman Jerome and his companion, Paula, stayed with Melania. During these years, Melania's biographer credits her with healing religious breaches: "winning over every heretic that denied the Holy Sprit, [Melania and Rufinus] brought them into the Church" (Murphy 72). In the end, however, Melania and Rufinus could not escape being drawn into the controversies.

During her time at the monastery, Melania

spent much time in study: "She turned night into day perusing every writing of the ancient commentators, including three million lines of Origen. . . . Nor did she read them once only and casually, but she laboriously went through each book seven or eight times . . ." (Murphy 71). These studies ultimately led her into controversies that caused her reputation to be seriously damaged. Her friend and mentor, Rufinus, was an avid scholar of the works of Origen—a third-century Christian philosopher who had written prodigiously and speculatively about many topics. Rufinus had translated many of Origen's works from Greek into Latin to make them more accessible in the west. After A.D. 400, however, many of Origen's ideas were condemned—for example, he had cast doubts on the resurrection of the flesh and on eternal damnation. Rufinus refused to renounce his old master, so Jerome vituperatively condemned Rufinus and, by association, Melania.

Jerome's animosity did not seem to affect Melania during her life. In about A.D. 399, the holy woman returned to Rome for a visit to see her son and to guide her granddaughter and namesake, Melania the Younger. She strongly influenced the young Melania, who became a renowned holy woman in her own right. Then in about A.D. 404, Melania the Elder visited North Africa and the famous Bishop Augustine of Hippo on her way back to Jerusalem. She died in the Holy Land in about A.D. 410, at the venerable age of sixty-nine. Although her biographer detailed the events of her remarkable life, other church writers, who feared being tainted with the charge of heresy if they praised her, often omitted mentioning her in their accounts of the early years of the Christian church. We are fortunate not to have lost the story of her life and her accomplishments. She founded monasteries, helped spread Christian worship, and urged tolerance for differing ideas.

See also Egeria; Eustochium; Melania the Younger; Paula

Suggested Readings

Murphy, Francis X. "Melania the Elder: A Biographical Note." *Traditio* 5 (1947): 59–77.
Palladius. *Lausiac History.* Trans. R. T. Meyer. London: Longmans, Green, 1965.

Melania the Younger
Monastic Founder (A.D. 385–ca. 439)

In A.D. 385, a daughter was born into one of the oldest and wealthiest Roman families; she was named Melania and referred to as "Melania the Younger" in order to distinguish her from her grandmother, Melania the Elder, who had established a reputation for Christian piety. During Melania the Younger's life, she would exceed her grandmother in sanctity, and after her death, Gerontius, a priest who had lived with Melania the Younger in her old age, wrote a detailed biography of the extraordinary woman. Gerontius tells us that the young Melania was raised to fulfill the obligations of a dutiful Roman daughter and to marry and bear children to carry on the family name (and its wealth). From early childhood on, however, the young girl wanted to forgo marriage and live as a Christian holy woman like her grandmother, but her father would not allow it. Instead, as was customary in the Roman Empire, when Melania was fourteen years old, her parents arranged for her to marry Pinian, the son of another old Roman family. Pinian was not as wealthy as Melania, so the marriage was intended to better the prospects of his family.

With her longing for a Christian life, Melania pleaded with Pinian to allow her to practice chastity within marriage. She even tried to buy her way out of the marriage debt by offering Pinian control of all her wealth if he would leave her virginity intact. Pinian wanted first to ensure the succession of his family, however, so he told Melania that she must bear two children before he would consider her request to be freed from sexual intercourse. A daughter was duly born to the young couple, and at Melania's insistence, they dedicated her to a life of virginity. Again Melania pleaded with Pinian for a life of chastity, but he insisted on producing one more child. Melania considered fleeing the bonds of marriage (leaving her husband with her money), but she was persuaded by a holy man who suggested she stay and convert her husband to a holy life.

Melania began to practice austerities as a way of enhancing her religious life. For example, she began to wear a rough wool garment hidden under the soft silk clothing of the Roman upper classes so that her skin would be constantly scratched, reminding her of the frailty of flesh. Her ascetic practices continued even though she once again became pregnant. Late in her pregnancy, she spent many nights on her knees praying in the family chapel. Her self-sacrifices seemed to have taken their toll, for the child was born prematurely. The infant boy died shortly after being baptized, and Melania herself fell very ill after the birth. Melania told Pinian she would only survive if he vowed that they would henceforth live perpetually chaste. He agreed and the couple began a new stage of their lives, renouncing traditional Roman roles in favor of new Christian ascetic ones. Their daughter and Melania's father died shortly thereafter, and there seemed no longer anything to tie them to their past. Melania took the lead in deciding on the couple's new path.

The twenty-year-old woman moved the couple away from their wealthy estate, and they began to help the poor and the sick of Rome. Melania wanted to free herself and Pinian from the immense wealth they controlled, but since they had property all over the empire, it was very difficult. Melania asked the empress to help them liquidate the holdings, and Serena, the wife of Emperor Honorius, agreed to arrange for imperial agents to handle the sales. But even this did not quickly solve their problems. For example, Melania's town house was so valuable that no one in Rome, including the emperor, could afford to buy it. Melania's biographer explained that God provided a solution to the expensive house: "After the invasion of the barbarians they sold it for less than nothing since it was burned to the ground" (Salisbury 91).

Even as the property was being liquidated, Melania was faced with getting rid of the gold that was acquired with each sale. The young couple sent gold coins to holy men, founded monasteries, and even bought whole islands for holy men and women to live on. The barbarian invasions offered new opportunities for spending: the young couple ransomed captives with the seemingly unending flow of gold.

Like many others, Melania and Pinian fled Italy ahead of the invasions of the Visigoths. They first went to North Africa, where they lived for seven years, then they went on a pilgrimage to visit the holy places of Jerusalem and the eastern Mediterranean. Like many other pilgrims, they visited the holy men and women in the deserts of Egypt and Syria, and the biographer wrote that Melania was received by them "as if she were a man" (Salisbury 93). Finally the couple returned to Jerusalem, where Melania decided to build a monastery and surround herself with other women. During this period, Pinian died, and Melania arranged for a monastery for men to be built in his honor.

Through the rest of her life, Melania took advantage of many opportunities to travel to Constantinople and the court of the imperial household there. She was well received and enjoyed talking theology from dawn to dusk with wealthy pagans and Christians alike. She even became close friends with the new empress, Eudocia, who entertained Melania graciously whenever she visited. Finally, the fifty-four-year-old woman died in her monastery in Jerusalem, surrounded by her companions. The priest who would write her biography was at her side, and she was mourned by many. Melania's popular biography served as an inspiration for men and women who aspired to live ascetic Christian lives, and the monasteries she founded in Jerusalem offered shelter to thousands for centuries.

See also Christian Women; Egeria; Eudocia; Eustochium; Melania the Elder; Paula

Suggested Readings
Clark, Elizabeth. *The Life of Melania the Younger.* Lewiston, NY: Edwin Mellen Press, 1984.
Salisbury, Joyce E. *Church Fathers, Independent Virgins.* London: Verso, 1991.

Meryt-Neith
Egyptian Queen (ca. 2900 B.C.)

Before the dynasties of great pharaohs ruled Egypt, that land was divided up into many regions, each ruled by a chieftain. We have no historical records from this early period, and historians have had to illuminate this shadowy time with archaeological finds, surviving monuments, and later chroniclers' memories of this early Egyptian history. Sometime about 3000 B.C., Egypt was united by a king—named either

Menes or Narmer (historians disagree)—who joined the whole region along the Nile under his rule. Once upper (southern) and lower (northern) Egypt were united, subsequent kings continued to recognize this impressive accomplishment by doing many things by twos: they wore a double crown to symbolize the union of the two kingdoms; they maintained at least two official residences; and perhaps most important for Egyptians preoccupied with providing for their afterlife, they built two burial places.

With the union of Egypt, this ancient land began its historical period, for writing—in a mixture of pictograms and phonetic signs called hieroglyphs—was invented about this time. From then on, the early history of Egypt is preserved in tantalizing fragments of inscriptions that tell of the first two dynasties of rulers that date from about 3000 to 2650 B.C. We have not identified a clear chronology of these earliest rulers, but it appears that one of them—possibly the third ruler of the first dynasty—was a woman, one of a small number that seem to have ruled in dynastic Egypt from about 3100 to about 332 B.C.

In about A.D. 1900, when Egyptologists were excavating old tombs to try to understand the early history of Egypt, they discovered a large carved funeral monument bearing the name Meryt-Neith. Because of the impressive size of the memorial stone column, scientists accepted it as that of a king and assumed it was the third king of the first dynasty. As people began to improve their understanding of hieroglyphic writing, however, they realized that the name was actually one of a female—literally meaning "beloved of [the goddess] Neith." Then Egyptologists wondered if instead of a ruler, this was an unusually powerful queen consort. Or did a woman really rule Egypt in the formative years of the shadowy first dynasty?

Further excavations have lent support to the hypothesis that Meryt-Neith indeed ruled on her own, for archaeologists have excavated a number of tombs in Sakkara that belonged to high officials. These tombs contained goods bearing her name, as one might expect if she were the king, so these inscriptions further support the assumption that she ruled in her own right.

Her monuments were surrounded with all the ceremony accorded other ancient rulers. For example, she was given a solar boat that would let her spirit travel with the sun god in the afterlife, and this honor was normally reserved only for a king. Furthermore, each of her tombs was surrounded by the graves of at least forty attendants, while seventy-seven servants were buried in a neat U shape near her monument. Thus, all the evidence suggests that Meryt-Neith had been a powerful ruler in her own right. Unfortunately, there are not enough surviving sources to tell us anything more about her. Hardly more than her name survives to remind us of a time in the earliest dynasty of Egypt when a woman ruled and wielded enough power to be certain that her place in the afterlife was ensured.

See also Egyptian Women; Hatshepsut; Nefertiti; Nitocris; Sobeknofru; Twosret

Suggested Readings

Lesko, B. S., ed. *Women's Earliest Records from Ancient Egypt and Western Asia.* Brown Judaic Studies 166. Atlanta: Scholar's Press, 1987.

Tyldesley, Joyce. *Daughters of Isis: Women of Ancient Egypt.* New York: Penguin, 1994.

Messalina

Roman Empress (A.D. 25–48)

Caesar Augustus (Octavian) had established an empire that was virtually ruled by one man—the *princeps,* or "first citizen." One of the major problems with this new structure, however, was the question of succession. Augustus had ruled a long time—over forty years—and at his death, it seemed that he should be replaced by someone of his family. This introduced the "Julio-Claudian" dynasty of emperors, men who could trace their legitimacy to rule by having some blood relationship with the family of Augustus. The huge amount of power and wealth that came with the position and the importance of the succession led to corruption and violence among the Julio-Claudians, and many of their women were actively involved in the struggles for power that marked this dynasty. One young empress, Messalina (also known as Valeria Messalina)—who died when she was only twenty-three years old—created enough scandal that her name long outlived her short life span.

The Emperor Tiberius (r. A.D. 14–37) was succeeded by his grandnephew, known as Caligula (r. A.D. 37–41). Rome was thrilled because Tiberius had been very unpopular, but the celebrations were premature. Caligula would prove to be a disaster. He was cruel and autocratic, and assassins murdered him. A soldier of the elite Praetorian Guard searching the imperial palace discovered Claudius hiding behind a curtain, and the Praetorian Guard hailed Claudius emperor on 25 January 41. Claudius was proclaimed emperor because he was a member of the imperial family—he was the popular Germanicus's younger brother.

Claudius had never been considered imperial material because he had multiple handicaps and infirmities. He had weak knees, trembling hands, and a wobbly head; he dragged his right foot, walked with a limp, stuttered, and drooled uncontrollably. These very infirmities probably kept him alive, since his murderous relatives considered him as the subject of jokes, not as a threat to the imperial throne. Claudius had been well educated, and during his thirteen-year reign he consolidated many of the governmental structures established by Augustus and put the empire on a solid footing. Most historians—ancient and modern—conclude that Claudius's main failing was in his relationship with his wives. His first two marriages—to Plauta Urgulanilla and Aelia Paetina—ended in divorce. His third marriage, to Messalina, ended in scandal and death.

Messalina was born of the best Roman families, and indeed she was the great-granddaughter of Octavia (Augustus's sister). Claudius was her mother's first cousin; Claudius married Messalina in A.D. 39 or 40 (about one year before he was proclaimed emperor). She was only fourteen when she married, and Claudius was already forty-eight. Within seven years, they had two children—a daughter named Octavia and a son, Britannicus—and the young empress was at the height of her power, which she abused.

The sources accuse Messalina of taking lovers with abandon. Later her accusers would claim that she concealed her black hair under a blond wig and that under the assumed name of Lycisca she was regularly employed in a brothel. They further charged that she even set up a brothel in the palace, with women of the highest social standing as prostitutes and their distinguished husbands as pimps. Probably these charges were exaggerated if not completely false. Surely Claudius would not have been as blind as to overlook such goings-on under his own roof. Messalina's downfall, however, certainly came because of her great love for a handsome nobleman named Silius.

According to Tacitus, by A.D. 48 "adultery was such an everyday affair as to hold no further interest for Messalina" (Balsdon 97) and she fell hopelessly in love with Silius. She made him divorce his wife to accept Messalina as his mistress. She did not try to hide the affair: She came to his house attended by a huge crowd of followers, and she clung to his side when he went out. She gave him great presents and wealth, and at the end, the emperor's slaves, his freedmen, and even his heirlooms were to be found in the adulterer's house.

What brought the matter to a head was an outrageous event: As soon as Claudius left town to perform a necessary sacrifice, Messalina went through a formal marriage ceremony taking Silius as her husband. This was too much for the palace staff, because although the marriage could have no legal standing, it seemed to threaten Claudius's reign. Could Silius claim the right to the throne by being married to the empress who had Julio-Claudian blood in her veins? The freedmen (freed slaves who had influential positions in the court) decided to take action. If they were to tell Claudius, their own power would be enhanced if Messalina were removed. They decided to risk the emperor's wrath by bringing the bad news.

When he returned, a freedman fell to the ground at Claudius's feet and cried out: "Messalina is married to Silius" (Balsdon 99). He then called on others at the court to confirm the story. Claudius immediately called his most powerful counselors and verified the claims. The emperor set out for Silius's house and confronted the couple, who were having an extravagant party. Messalina was arrested. She sent word to her children, Britannicus and Octavia, to plead for her life and sent others to beg for mercy on her behalf. Claudius entered Silius's house and saw his own heirlooms displayed by the adulterer. Now the emperor was angry and worried at the implied threat to his rule. He ordered the troops to round up the offenders, and a number of accomplices who had facilitated the liaison were executed. Silius only asked to be killed quickly.

Messalina meanwhile was waiting in the gardens to find out her fate. With the optimism of youth, she still hoped to persuade Claudius to save her, but she would not have the opportunity. A freedman—who was perhaps also worried about her charms—told the soldiers that she was to be executed immediately. The soldiers found her lying on the ground in her mother's arms. Her mother told her: "Your only aim now should be to die honorably" (Balsdon 102). Messalina was crying when the executioners arrived. It was only now that Messalina realized there was no hope. She accepted the dagger and tried to commit suicide honorably, but her hand shook too much. So the officer killed her. Her mother was allowed to take the body. Claudius was at dinner when he was told she was dead, but he showed no emotion and simply asked for a drink and went on with the party.

What led to the tragedy of Messalina? Was it a young teenager faced with an old husband and more power than almost anyone could dream of? Was she seduced by a man greedy for power and longing for the throne himself? Perhaps. But even after her death, Claudius did not improve on his choice of wives. Agrippina the Younger would cause him even more grief, and Messalina would be portrayed in Roman sources as a woman dominated by sexual desire.

See also Agrippina the Younger; Octavia
Suggested Readings
Balsdon, J. P. V. D. *Roman Women: Their History and Habits.* New York: John Day, 1963.
Hawley, R., and B. Levick, eds. *Women in Antiquity: New Assessments.* New York: Routledge, 1995.
Suetonius. *The Twelve Caesars.* Trans. Robert Graves. New York: Penguin, 1979.
Tacitus. "The Annals." In *Complete Works of Tacitus* Trans. A. J. Church. New York: The Modern Library, 1942.

Minerva
Roman Goddess
Minerva was originally an Italian goddess of crafts and trade guilds, but as Romans became influenced by the Greeks, the goddess became identified with the Greek deity Athena. Minerva then acquired all the myths that the Greeks had associated with Athena. From then on, she was regarded as a goddess of handicrafts, wisdom, and war. Minerva was an important goddess in Rome: she was one of three (along with Jupiter and Juno) who shared a temple on the Capitoline Hill in Rome. These three deities were called the Capitoline Triad and were seen as the special protectors of Rome. The three marked the importance of family, work, and wisely fought wars.

Within Rome, the vestal virgins were charged with guarding a large statue of Athena within their temple. This statue was identified with Minerva, and the Romans believed it was a powerful talisman that brought good luck to the city.

The emperor Domitian (r. A.D. 81–96) particularly favored Minerva as his favorite goddess. In thanks for her protection, he founded a legion (one of his armies) in A.D. 83 and named it the I Minerva. In this, he emphasized the goddess's aspect of war, but this versatile goddess could equally give her support to guilds of craftspeople or women at their weaving.

See also Athena
Suggested Readings
Adkins, Lesley, and Roy A. Adkins. *Handbook to Life in Ancient Rome.* New York: Oxford University Press, 1994.
Grant, M. *Roman Myths.* London: Weidenfeld and Nicolson, 1971.
Grimal, Pierre. *The Dictionary of Classical Mythology.* Oxford: Blackwell, 1996.
Ogilvie, R. M. *The Romans and Their Gods.* London: Chatto and Windus, 1969.

Minoan Women
By 2000 B.C., the islanders living on Crete boasted the wealthiest, most advanced civilization in the Mediterranean. (See Map 4.) Early Greek historians identified an early (perhaps legendary) ruler of Crete as King Minos, and modern archaeologists named this society Mi-

noan after this legendary king. The Minoans were not Greek, nor even Indo-European, but were probably a Semitic people related to those living in the eastern and southern Mediterranean. With regard to women, however, this society seems to have been dramatically different from the related cultures in the eastern Mediterranean.

The Minoan ships were the best made in the Mediterranean. With their heavy construction and high front prows, these vessels cut effortlessly through rough seas and helped make the Minoans very wealthy from trade. Excavations show that the cities were not walled (unlike the equivalent sites in Mesopotamia or in early Greece), and historians suggest that this shows that this society was remarkably peaceful. Nor is there any evidence for a military presence on the island; soldiers were not part of the day-to-day culture. It may be that the Minoans depended upon their fleet to keep invaders at bay. It may also be that the lack of warrior society helped women take a prominent place in society.

Minoans made exquisite bronze weapons and tools and traded in valuable olive oil. One storeroom in a palace (at Knossos) contained clay jars for olive oil that totaled a remarkable capacity of 60,000 gallons. Minoans also learned writing from the Sumerians, and their script (called Linear A) was also a pictographic script written on clay tablets. As in Sumer, archaeologists have excavated clay tablets in Crete that seem to have been used for accounting and for tracking the movement of merchandise. So far, the symbols of Linear A have not been translated, so to learn about Minoan society, we must rely on archaeological remains, including their riveting artwork.

It is through the evidence in archaeological remains that historians suggest that women had an important position in Minoan society. Just as in the Stone Age finds at Çatal Hüyük, Minoan artifacts suggest that the people at Crete worshiped the goddesses over gods. One of the most popular images is the statue of the snake goddess shown in Figure 50. This goddess is shown wearing the standard fashion for Minoan women—a flounced dress with the breasts exposed. The goddess triumphantly holds a writhing snake in each hand. In many societies,

Figure 50. Minoan snake goddess, ca. 1600 B.C., Knossos, Crete (Nimatallah/Art Resource, NY)

snakes represented immortality (since they shed their skins and seem reborn from the old skin), and this goddess may offer a hope for immortality along with fertility.

The Minoans also decorated their great, rambling palaces (which the later Greeks called labyrinths) with beautiful frescoes painted on the walls. Within these images, we see men and women enjoying life at banquets with music and women participating in processions. The women are shown wearing fine clothing and using many cosmetics; their hair is elaborately coiffed. All these images suggest a prosperous, peaceful society with leisure and wealth.

The frescoes also show what might have been a religious ritual—a dangerous and athletic bull leaping—shown in Figure 51 (known as the *Toreador Fresco*). It was traditional in Minoan art to show men as dark skinned and women light, and thus in this image we see two women and a

Figure 51. Minoan Bull Ritual, fresco, ca. 1500 B.C., Knossos, Crete (Erich Lessing, Art Resource, NY)

man engaging in the bull ritual. The man is executing a somersault over the bull's back while the girl at the right holds out her arms to help him land. On the left, another girl prepares for her somersault by seizing the bull by the horns. Since bulls were sacred to the Minoans, we assume that this held some religious significance, but the details are lost. Certainly it was a dangerous ritual for both men and women.

In about 1450 B.C., Minoan society was destroyed. Excavations show that their great palaces were burned by invaders, and it seems clear that they were early warlike Greek invaders from the mainland who overwhelmed the peace-loving Minoans. Some historians suggest that a volcanic eruption on the nearby island of Thera created a tidal wave that may have destroyed the Minoans' protective fleet. We may never know exactly what happened to the Minoans of Crete, but the center of Aegean civilization then passed north to the Greek mainland.

See also Çatal Hüyük; Clothing; Jewelry
Suggested Readings
Cotterell, A. *The Minoan World.* New York: Scribner, 1980.

Miriam
Hebrew Woman (ca. thirteenth century B.C.)
Jacob (Rachel's husband) and his family settled in Egypt, in the northeast corner of the Nile delta. Their descendants lived and prospered

there for four centuries, but then the Hebrew scriptures (the Christian Old Testament) recounts that the Pharaoh turned against the growing community of Hebrews. Historians speculate that the Pharaoh in question might have been Rameses II, who needed many workers in his massive construction projects. According to the Bible, the Pharaoh first put the Hebrews to work—virtually enslaving the people—then when their numbers continued to seem too high, Pharaoh ordered the Hebrew midwives to kill every male infant at birth. The midwives evaded this decree on the pretext that "the Hebrew women are not like the Egyptian women; for they are vigorous and are delivered before the midwife comes to them" (Exod. 1:19). Pharaoh then ordered his people to throw the male babies into the river and drown them. This decree fell on one family of the priestly house of Levi. The parents, Amram and Jochebed, decided to defy the decree, and their children would play influential roles in the formation of the Hebrew nation.

The couple had two children—Aaron and Miriam—but Jochebed gave birth to a second son after Pharaoh's decree. To save the child, she kept him hidden for three months, then enclosed him in a basket woven of rushes and sealed with tar and concealed it among the reeds at the river's edge. She posted her daughter, Miriam, a little distance away to watch over him. Pharaoh's daughter came to bathe at this spot, and when she saw the basket, she sent a maid to fetch it. When she opened it, the baby started to cry. The princess felt pity for it, realizing it was one of the Hebrew children her father had ordered killed, and she decided to raise the child. Miriam came out and offered to find a Hebrew nurse to suckle the baby, and when the princess agreed, Miriam ran off to fetch the child's mother. When he was older, Pharaoh's daughter adopted him and gave him the name of Moses, which means "to draw out" because he had been drawn out of the water.

When Moses had grown, he and his brother Aaron confronted Pharaoh to free the Israelites from bondage. Moses brought many plagues upon the Egyptians before Pharaoh agreed to let them leave, but once permission was given, the great Exodus began in which Moses led his people from Egypt back to the promised land of Canaan. The Hebrews left in haste, fearing Pharaoh would pursue them, and their fears were warranted. Pharaoh regretted his decision and sent out a force that included 600 chariots. The Hebrews were trapped on the edge of the Sea of Reeds (that is incorrectly translated into English as the Red Sea), which may be in the area of the Bitter Lakes through which the Suez Canal now passes (see Map 2). According to the biblical account, Moses stretched out his hand and a strong east wind pushed the water aside so the Hebrews could cross to the other side. Pharaoh's pursuing chariots were engulfed as the waters swept back over them.

Miriam led the celebration of the Hebrews' liberation. The Bible calls her a prophet, probably because of her ecstatic rousing of worship through song and dance, and says she took a timbrel (tambourine) in her hand and led all the women in a dance. Miriam sang the following song:

Sing to the Lord, for he has triumphed gloriously;
The horse and his rider he has thrown into the sea. (Exod. 15:21)

This is reputedly one of the oldest poetic couplets in the scriptures. The Bible's account of Miriam's role suggests that she was perceived—along with her brother Aaron—as sharing some of the leadership during the Exodus. This perception would cause her to come into conflict with Moses—and the Lord.

At one point during the forty-year journey through the Sinai, Aaron and Miriam confronted their brother. They criticized him for marrying Zipporah, a "Cushite woman"—one of many Arabic peoples. In their confrontation, they said, "Has the Lord indeed spoken only through Moses? Has he not spoken through us also?" (Num. 12:2). In this speech, they reveal their jealousy of their brother's leadership, but God heard the speech and spoke to the three, saying: "Come out, you three, to the tent of meeting." The Lord appeared in a pillar of cloud and called Aaron and Miriam and confirmed that he had a special relationship with Moses: "With him I speak mouth to mouth" (Num. 12:4–8).

When the angry cloud disappeared, it was plain that God's anger had been directed toward Miriam, who had been struck by leprosy, and the illness made her skin "white as snow." Moses prayed for her, begging "Heal her, O God, I beseech thee" (Num. 12:9–14). The Lord told Moses that she had to be punished and to send her outside the camp for seven days, after which she would be restored. Moses halted the Exodus while they waited for his sister to be cured. After seven days, she was restored, and the people could set out again.

In the course of the travels, Moses revealed the laws that would bind the Hebrew nation, and in the forty years of wandering, the new nation was formed. Neither Moses nor Miriam would live to see the people successfully enter the Promised Land of Canaan. Miriam died and was buried in the wilderness, and Moses died reputedly at the age of 120 after glimpsing the new land. The experience of the Exodus and the laws that were generated in the wilderness have influenced Jews, Christians, and Muslims ever since. And Moses's sister, Miriam, played an influential role in this central event of Hebrew history.

Miriam was the first woman in the Bible to be called a prophet, so she begins a long tradition of female prophecy. Miriam's influence continued into the Christian era, for many women bore the Greek equivalent of her Hebrew name: Mary. The many Marys of the Gospels testify to the long-standing influence of this early prophet.

See also Jewish Women; Rachel; Zipporah
Suggested Readings
Burns, Rita J. *Has the Lord Indeed Spoken Only through Moses? A Study of the Biblical Portrait of Miriam.* SBL Dissertation Series 84. Atlanta: Scholars Press, 1987.
Comay, Joan. *Who's Who in the Old Testament.* London: Routledge, 1995.
Meyers, Carol, Toni Craven, and Ross S. Kraemer. *Women in Scripture.* New York: Houghton Mifflin, 2000.

Monica

Christian North African Mother
(A.D. 331–387)

One of the most famous mothers in the ancient Christian world was Monica, mother of the church father Augustine of Hippo (A.D. 354–430). She was immortalized in the writings of her devoted son in his autobiographical work, *The Confessions.* Since this work remained widely and popularly read for centuries (even today), his portrayal of his mother became the prototype for subsequent Christian mothers. Monica joined the Virgin Mary as an ideal mother.

Monica was born in North Africa in A.D. 331 into a Christian family. She was raised by an aged slave who had proven to be a long and faithful servant to the family. The nurse was very strict with young Monica, trying to bring her up as a model of virtue. For example, the servant would not allow the daughters of the household to drink anything—even water—between meals, for she did not want them to get into the habit of quenching their thirst, so that when they grew older they would not drink too much wine. Young Monica did acquire a taste for wine, however, because whenever her parents sent her to draw some wine from the cask, she rebelliously sipped a few drops. This habit was broken only when a servant girl quarreled with her young mistress and called her a drunkard, and Monica recognized her fault and renounced it. Even after she had grown, she always drank only in moderation.

Monica's parents arranged for her to marry Patricius, a pagan, who nevertheless had a mea-sure of prosperity and shared a desire for successful children. Augustine writes that his father had a bad temper, but Monica's patience and sweetness turned away his wrath. He offers insights into the plight of many Roman women when he writes that other women, "whose faces were disfigured by blows from husbands far sweeter-tempered than [Monica's]" (Augustine 195), complained about their treatment. Monica told her friends to remember that their husbands were their masters, and they should not anger them. Monica never quarreled with Patricius even though he was unfaithful to her.

Monica also had to withstand a difficulty faced by many other Roman women—conflict with her mother-in-law. At first during the marriage, servants sowed discord between Patricius's mother and his new bride. At first her mother-in-law disapproved of Monica, but in time the wife's patience and forbearance won her over. The mother-in-law told Patricius to beat any servant who told tales against Monica, and after a few whippings, the tales ceased and the two women lived harmoniously in the household.

Patricius and Monica had several children, but the favorite was the bright, talented Augustine. Once it was apparent that the boy had the intellectual skills to succeed in the best Roman career, the couple spared no expense to give him an excellent education. Patricius, who "had slender resources" (Augustine 45), saved his money so he could send Augustine to Carthage to study with the greatest teachers. Monica had an additional hope that her son's education would lead him to Christianity as well as to a successful career. This hope points to a conflict between Monica and Patricius that shaped much of Augustine's early life—her hope for his Christian salvation. One incident points up this tension: Augustine wrote that when he was sixteen years old and at the public baths with his father, his father was delighted to see signs of "active virility coming to life in me and this was enough to make him relish the thought of having grandchildren" (Augustine 45). He shared his excitement with Monica, but she only saw the possibility of sin in the young boy's growing maturity, and wept.

Monica began a career of praying and weeping for her son. Augustine in his conversation with God recalls, "my mother, your faithful servant, wept to you for me, shedding more tears for my spiritual death than other mothers shed for the bodily death of a son" (Augustine 68). By incessant weeping and prayer, Monica established a role for Christian mothers that persists today: They were to act as mediators for the salvation of their children. Monica was rewarded for her piety by visions that promised her that Augustine would eventually be saved. Monica converted Patricius when he was on his deathbed, so once again a Christian woman's role was shown to be one of bringing sinners to virtue. After Patricius's death, Monica focused all her prayers and attention on Augustine.

Augustine lived with a mistress and had a son, Adeodatus, so Monica felt he needed much prayer and guidance, and she was relentless in her determination that her son be saved. At one point, when Augustine was twenty-eight years old, he planned to sail from Carthage to go to Rome. His mother wanted to join him, and the young man slipped away on a ship while Monica was praying at a church. Eventually she followed him to Milan in Italy, where Augustine had obtained a post as a public teacher. In Milan both Monica and Augustine came under the influence of Bishop Ambrose, and Monica was certain that now Augustine would finally be converted to a Christian life. Her hopes were not misplaced. In A.D. 387 Augustine and his son, Adeodatus, were both baptized.

Monica became ill in that same year. While Augustine was at her deathbed, she assured him that now that her son was safely baptized, her work on this earth was over, and she could die in peace. She was fifty-six years old, and her beloved son was thirty-three. From Monica onward, Christian mothers were to pray and cry for their wayward children and be instrumental in bringing them to a virtuous way of life and to salvation in the next world. Few ancient Christian mothers pursued this ideal with the zeal of Monica.

See also Christian Women; Motherhood, Roman
Suggested Readings
Augustine. *The Confessions.* Trans. R. S. Pine-Coffin. New York: Penguin Books, 1980.
Brown, Peter. *Augustine of Hippo.* Berkeley: University of California Press, 1969.

Motherhood, Roman
Population Problems

As early as the end of the Roman Republic (ca. 20 B.C.), the Roman people recognized that they had a population problem. The first emperor—Caesar Augustus (27 B.C.–A.D. 14)—even attempted to correct this problem by legislation. He passed laws encouraging people to marry and to bear at least three children. The Roman sources suggest, however, that people found some attraction in remaining childless, perhaps in order to preserve family fortunes.

Such sources assumed that Roman women and men were *choosing* not to bear children. In part, that seems to have been so—they limited their children by various forms of birth control and by abortion. In part, however, Roman medical practices impeded fertility, and social practices caused high female mortality, which also limited childbearing. One Roman commented on the scarcity of women, noting "since among the nobility there were far more males than females, Augustus allowed all free men who wished to marry freedwomen" (Dixon 93). Noble women married very young—in their early teens, and sometimes even before they had menstruated, and youthful childbearing increased female mortality. The low birthrate had cultural as well as physical causes, however. For example, wealthy Roman men as well as women often wanted few children, so as to preserve their inheritance intact.

In spite of all these causes for a low birthrate, Augustus addressed his laws specifically to Roman mothers. He offered women special privileges before the law if they raised three children—that is, they would be given independence from their husbands' and fathers' control. This law is particularly interesting in its assumptions: it recognized women's desire for freedom before the law, and it assumed that women controlled their own fecundity. More than anything else, however, these laws and the Roman assumptions that lay beneath them recognized the importance of Roman mothers to the future of the state.

Childbirth and Infant Care

When a woman felt the beginnings of labor pains, she and her midwives secreted themselves

Figure 52. A woman nursing her child, watched by the father. She sits in a high-backed armchair, a sign of her upper-class status. Detail from a sarcophagus from the mid-second century A.D. (Louvre, Paris)

from the men of the household. Women bore children seated in a birthing chair, which helped the mother in the delivery by employing the force of gravity to help her. The chair had an opening through which the midwife could help deliver the child. If the woman died in childbirth, the midwives would cut the child from the mother's uterus in hopes of saving it. Even a successful delivery, however, would not guarantee that a healthy child would be raised.

Even after a safe birth, the newborn immediately faced further risks in the Roman household. When a child was born, the midwife inspected it even before the umbilical cord was cut to judge whether it was physically perfect. If it was not, she would likely cut the cord too closely, thus killing the child. A healthy newborn was placed at the father's feet. If he accepted the infant, picking up a boy or acknowledging a girl, then the child was raised. If he did not, the baby would be "exposed": placed outside to die or to be taken in and raised as a slave. Roman law required the father to raise only one daughter, but it is impossible to know how many children were exposed and how many died as a result. In one chilling letter, a soldier matter-of-factly instructs his pregnant wife to keep the child if it is a boy and to expose it if it is a girl. We can only conclude that the practice of exposure was not considered extraordinary.

Once the child was accepted, however, he or she received endless attention. Medical literature detailed explicit instructions on how to raise an infant, and all the child-rearing advice focused on molding the baby to be shapely, disciplined, and obedient. Newborns were tightly bound in strips of cloth for two months to ensure that their limbs would grow straight. Once a day they were unwrapped to be bathed in a tepid bath. Parents then stretched, massaged, and shaped the screaming babies before tightly wrapping them again. Noble children were usually breast-fed by a wet nurse (a slave woman who had recently had a child), although some Roman writers praised mothers who would nurse their own children. Figure 52 shows an idealized family in which a high-born mother nurses her infant while her husband looks on approvingly.

Many physicians recommended that children begin to drink sweet wine at six months of age, and infants sometimes needed to have supplementary feedings if their mothers had died or their wet nurses had insufficient milk. The pottery shown in Figure 53 is the equivalent of a baby bottle for feeding infants. Despite the recommendations of physicians and the attentions of loving parents, infant mortality was high—fewer than half of the newborns raised reached puberty.

Role of the Mother

Although Roman authors praised mothers who nursed their own infants, more often than not an infant was turned over to the care of a nurse,

Figure 53. A baby's feeding bottle (The University of Queensland Antiquities Museum)

who not only fed the child but served as a central influence. Roman authors recognized the importance of these surrogate mothers: "These nurses are the first people the child will listen to, it is their words the child will attempt to form by imitation and we are naturally most firmly influenced by the things we have learned when our minds were unformed" (Dixon 110). As Romans recognized the impact of the early nursemaids, many also criticized their importance. For example, they argued that other societies do not "hand their children over to slaves and nurses"; in contrast Roman babies are "handed over to some wretched Greek maidservant" (Dixon 125). The practice remained strong, however, and the child's nurse/slave remained an important part of the household. Furthermore, many adults seemed to retain a fondness for the nurses who raised them.

Mothers and fathers saw their role as different from the servant/nurturers who guided the small children. Both parents believed their roles were to educate and raise the children to be strong, moral citizens. Roman proverbs emphasized that mothers joined fathers as disciplinarians, and

Romans such as Tacitus, who longed for a "golden age" of Roman virtue, lamented the absence of "discipline and severity" that had characterized famous mothers such as Cornelia, mother of the Gracchi brothers. Indeed, the Romans believed severity was the way to build character, for only a child whose appetites were severely restricted could grow to be a model citizen.

Girls and boys could attend schools together from the ages of about seven to twelve. After that their lives diverged. Boys could continue into higher education to prepare for a public career, and girls returned home to prepare for marriage, which could come as early as twelve. If they did not marry right away, they worked in the household with their mothers, learning about the responsibilities of a Roman matron. When boys and girls came of age at eighteen, however, they still did not escape the influence of their parents.

Mothers of Adult Children

Roman sons and daughters remained under the authority of their fathers throughout his lifetime. For example, a grown man could take no legal action without his father's consent, nor could he even cultivate a career. Even many married daughters remained under their father's control if their marriage contract did not place them under their husband's. Mothers, too, retained an extraordinary influence over their grown children. This influence derived in large part from a mother's control over her own fortune that she brought with her to the marriage. Her position was further strengthened if she was a widow, for then she effectively controlled the portion of her husband's estate that he had left to her. Through their control of some family resources, Roman mothers retained a remarkable hold over their grown children, and the Roman sources repeatedly show this.

Seneca wrote of one young man left fatherless and a "ward in the care of guardians until his fourteenth year—but he remained perpetually in the guardianship of his mother" (Dixon 168). Sons were expected to visit their mothers regularly, even if they were divorced and remarried. Other sources criticized sons who neglected to visit their elderly mothers or even to listen to

their advice. Women who came from important families could use their family connections to help their adult sons and were expected to do so. All these factors combined to produce some formidable, influential women, many of whom used their relationship with their sons to make an impact on Roman society. Octavian's mother did not permit him to join a military expedition with his uncle Julius Caesar, and another young man—Metilius—claimed he could not serve in the military because he had to stay with his mother. Such loyalty might be scorned today, but Roman authors praised it.

Daughters, too, owed a great deal to their mothers. Women were expected to visit their mothers regularly, and the evidence suggests that grown daughters shared a good deal of affection with their mothers. Mothers were involved in selecting a good match for their daughters and in contributing to their dowries. Mothers throughout their lives offered their daughters financial assistance, advice, and protection and in return expected obedience, company, and perhaps the joys of grandchildren. (*See* Melania the Elder for an example of a Roman matron who made a point of traveling in order to exert influence on her granddaughter's life.)

The roles of Roman mothers were different from those of modern mothers. They served as minimal influences in the early nurturing of infants and in helping during those early formative and dangerous years of childhood. Romans remembered fondly the love and affection of their nurses, not their mothers. Roman mothers exerted considerable moral influence and guidance, however, and this influence grew even stronger as their children entered their adult lives as Roman citizens.

See also Abortion; Contraception; Cornelia [Roman Matron]; Gynecology; Melania the Elder

Suggested Readings
Dixon, Suzanne. *The Roman Mother.* Norman: University of Oklahoma Press, 1987.
Hallett, J. *Fathers and Daughters in Roman Society: Women and the Elite Family.* Princeton: Princeton University Press, 1973.
Phillips, J. E. "Roman Mothers and the Lives of Their Adult Daughters." *Helios,* n.s. 6: 69–80.

Figure 54. Muses of music and dance, left to right: Euterpe, Erato, and Terpsichore (Ann Ronan Picture Library)

Muses

Ancient Goddesses of Inspiration

Ancient Greeks treasured the creative impulses that allowed them to produce magnificent poetry, literature, and other arts, and they believed the origin of such creativity to be divine. The source of creative inspiration was the Muses—daughters of Zeus (the father of the gods) and the Titaness Mnemosyne. The Greeks believed that the Titans and Titanesses were a race of gods begotten by the union of Uranus (sky) and Gaea (earth), and the Greeks thought of them as gigantic beings who had ruled the world in a primitive age. Zeus had overthrown the Titans to take over rule of the ancient heavens. The goddess Mnemosyne the Titaness (whose name means "memory"), however, bore the Muses, who remained so influential in Greek thought. The name Muse denotes memory or "a reminder" and probably derives from a time when poets had no books to read from and relied on their memories. But in time, the Muses would come to bring inspiration to other arts along with poetry. All the Muses were goddesses, which linked the creative process with the female principle.

The Muses were generally depicted as winged and were said to live on mountains, particularly Helicon in Boetia and Pieria near Mount Olympus (see Map 4 of Greece). Originally there were believed to be only three muses—Melete ("practice"), Mneme ("memory"), and Aoede ("song")—and these three show their origin in poetry that was sung to an audience. At Delphi they were named after the three strings of the early lyre—bottom, middle, and top (*Nete, Mese, Hypate*)—which also shows their strong link to performed poetry. Hesiod, the influential Greek poet from the eighth century B.C., claimed, however, that there were nine Muses, and it is this number that became the standard understanding (although there always remained a difference of opinion on their exact functions).

The following are the names and disciplines of the nine Muses as they are usually identified:

Calliope ("fair voice")	Epic Poetry
Clio ("renown")	History
Erato ("lovely")	Lyric Poetry or Songs
Euterpe ("gladness")	Flute-Playing

Melpomene ("singing")	Tragedy
Polymnia ("many songs")	Mime
Terpsichore ("joy in the dance")	Lyric Poetry or Dance
Thalia ("abundance, good cheer")	Comedy
Urania ("heavenly")	Astronomy

The Muses were associated with Apollo, who as god of music and prophecy was their leader. Greeks believed they danced with him and the other deities—the Graces and the Hours—at festivals of the gods on Olympus, and they attended weddings. Philosophers—traditionally beginning with Pythagoras—took Muses as their special goddesses.

An open-air sanctuary and formal cult dedicated to the Muses was established below Mount Helicon (their sacred mountain) in the Vale of the Muses; it was the first Museum, and subsequent museums would be founded to invoke the Muses to generate creativity in study. This first Museum probably included a collection of poetic works, and later ones would become repositories of scientific and other texts. In the Hellenistic age, Ptolemy IV Philopater became a great patron of the musical contests sponsored in honor of the Muses. Occasionally, women who seemed particularly creative were called the "tenth Muse," suggesting that they were the embodiment of the divine creativity. The poet Sappho and the Hellenistic queen Arsinoë III both were praised by this designation.

While some women may have been praised in this way, Greek mythology suggested that the Muses jealously guarded their monopoly on creative talent. When the Thracian singer Thamyris boasted of being more talented than the Muses, they blinded him and deprived him of his memory. Similarly, when the nine daughters of Pierus—a Macedonian—challenged the Muses to a contest and lost, they were turned into crowlike birds called jackdaws. The Muses continued to be important through the Hellenistic world and under the Romans, and they were popular subjects in sculpture. Since ancient times, people have valued the creative products of the Greco-Roman world, and thus perhaps the Muses—who inspired this excel-

lence—are among the most influential of the ancient goddesses.

See also Arsinoë III; Gaea; Hypatia; Philosophers, Greek; Sappho of Lesbos

Suggested Readings

Grant, Michael, and J. Hazel. *Who's Who in Classical Mythology.* New York: Oxford University Press, 1973.

Grimal, Pierre. *The Dictionary of Classical Mythology.* Oxford: Blackwell, 1996.

Mythology

The ancient world expressed its understanding of the truths of the world and the gods by myths—stories of gods and heroes. These traditional stories were entertaining; poets told them by the fires in the evening, and women told them to children in the nurseries. These myths also contained symbolic concepts, however, that held deep meanings and dealt with fundamental issues of life in the ancient world. For example, myths explained the nature of human relationships—including the foundations of the social and political order—and the relations between humans and gods. Legends are related to myths and usually refer to some semilegendary historical event or person. (Although the terms *legends* and *myths* are often used interchangeably, *myths* usually refers more specifically to the activities of gods.)

Since myths are so central to ancient societies, they also reveal much about perceptions and status of ancient women. Since myths frequently use symbolic language, however, it is hard to draw direct meanings from these old stories, and historians therefore often disagree about what a myth reveals about ancient women's lives. In spite of these difficulties, it is possible to draw some understandings about how women were perceived. For example, Athenian myths told how males came to dominate women to keep chaos at bay, and Greek legends even explained why women wore the clothing they did. (*See* Clothing.)

Myths also explained the nature of the gods—who they were and what they did—and when women listened to stories of goddesses, they may have learned some things about themselves. For example, when women heard of the virgin huntress Artemis (or Diana), they might have come to some conclusions about virginity yielding independence. Myths also offered explanations for the origin of the world and for natural occurrences; as Greeks told the story of Pandora—the woman who brought evils into the world—or Hebrews recounted Eve's temptation, they also symbolically told of their fears about the influence of women. In these ways, the studies of mythology yield important (albeit general) insights into what ancient societies thought of women (and men and gods, for that matter).

Ancient cultures also used myths and legends to ascribe certain characteristics to natural regions. For example, when they situated murderous women on certain mountains, they were claiming that remote mountainous regions were dangerous. In contrast, myths that told of lovely maidens playing in meadows filled with flowers made lowland fields seem attractive and safe.

Finally, myths articulated a relationship between humans and gods and reminded people that there was an unbridgeable gap between the two. Mesopotamian myths made the deities fearful in their distance, but even Greek myths, which often made goddesses almost as real as humans, offered warnings against undue human pride. For example, when myths told of unhappy endings of love affairs between gods and humans, they stressed the unbridgeable gap between the two and reminded humans of their place in the religious order of the universe.

The ancient societies of the Middle East, Mediterranean basin, and northern Europe had myths (and deities) that resembled each other in many respects, and this was not purely by chance. In part the similarities came about because of a shared prehistory. Thus the Mesopotamian myth about a great flood resembles the account in the Hebrew Bible, and fertility goddesses are similar in many of the ancient societies. In other cases the myths are similar because ancient societies borrowed readily from each other. The early Romans, for example, had many deities, attributing a goddess or god for almost every space (natural and domestic), but they did not endow these deities with stories to explain them. When the Romans came in contact with the Greeks, who had elab-

orate myths for their gods, the Romans quickly superimposed the Greek myths onto their own deities. Thus, the Greek myths became part of the Roman heritage.

Individual entries within this volume give the myths and characters of the major goddesses of the ancient world. This general entry lists the major goddesses and gods of each ancient culture and gives an overview of the mythology of each. In the accompanying tables, the names of the goddesses are in italics. This outline gives a general background for the individual accounts and provides some comparisons among these ancient peoples.

Mesopotamia

Many of the myths from this region are from the earliest periods of human settlement. The many gods and goddesses overlap in their functions, and their names change as differing peoples conquered the region. Regardless of the names, however, the major deities remained a fertility goddess with her consort, the king of the gods, and a god of the underworld. In spite of this generalization, we can still identify many deities from the ancient Middle East, many of which are included here:

Deity	Function
Adad	Weather god, including the important rain
Annunaki	Sumerian gods of fertility and the underworld
Antum	Sky god's wife
Anu	Sky god
Damkina	Ea's wife
Dumuzi	Ishtar's lover. Fertility god.
Ea (Enki)	Lord of magic knowledge and arts and crafts
Ellil	Anu's son. Later became king of gods, displacing his father.
Ereshkigal	Queen of the underworld
Erra (Nergal)	God of plague and war
Igigi	Sumerian sky-gods headed by Ellil. (Paired with the Annunaki.)
Ishtar/Inanna	Goddess of love, sex, and war. The most important deity.
Marduk	Ea's son

Mulliltu	Ellil's son
Nabu	Marduk's son. God of wisdom and patron of scribes.
Namtar	Ereshkigal's vizier and much-feared god of plague
Nin-hursag (Aruru)	Mother goddess. Sometimes described as a spouse of Nergal.
Ninurta	War god and patron of hunting
Shamash (Utu)	Sun god
Sin	Moon god

The Mesopotamian myths were preserved on clay tablets inscribed with an ancient script called cuneiform. The most famous myth is the Epic of Gilgamesh, but other myths also have survived, including the story of the descent of Ishtar (*see* Ishtar). Archaeologists still hope that new excavations will yield tablets with new myths that will help us understand the religious ideas of these very ancient men and women.

Egypt

Like so many other ancient peoples, the Egyptians worshiped numerous gods and goddesses, believing that the divine spirit inhabited many parts of nature and the cosmos. In addition, the Egyptians believed that their king (in time known as pharaoh) was a living god. At different times in their history, the Egyptian rulers and priests favored worship of one god or another, but the principal ones remained Amen-Re, his consort-sister Isis, Osiris, and Horus, son of Isis. For a short period, the Egyptians worshiped one god—the sun disc named Aten (*see* Nefertiti)—but soon Egyptians returned to their long-standing list of deities.

Since there were many regional differences within Egypt where people worshiped various gods and goddesses, it is difficult to put together a definitive list of Egyptian deities. In fact, some texts of the early dynasties list some 200 deities and the later *Book of the Dead* supplies the names of nearly 500. When the names of other mythological Egyptian figures are added, the list might rise as high as 800. With this caution in mind, here follows a guide to the major Egyptian deities:

Deity	Function
Amen-Re	Creator and sun god
Anubis	God of the dead
Bastel	Cat goddess/daughter of Re
Bes	Dwarf god who guarded against evil spirits
Geb	God of the earth
Hathor	Cow goddess/symbolic mother of pharaoh
Horus	Son of Isis
Isis	Mother goddess; in Hellenistic times often worshiped as universal
Khonsu	Moon god
Maat	Goddess personifying cosmic harmony
Min	Fertility god
Mut	Wife of Amen
Nephthys	Goddess of the dead/daughter of Geb and Nut
Nut	Goddess of the sky and heavens
Osiris	God of the underworld and of vegetation
Ptah	Creator god/god of craftsmen
Qadesh	Goddess of love and beauty
Renenutet	Cobra-goddess/guardian of pharaoh
Sakhmet	Goddess of the rising sun/Daughter of Re
Serket	Scorpion goddess; helper of women in childbirth.
Seth	God of chaos
Taweret	Hippopotamus goddess and protector of childbirth
Thoth	Moon god/resides over scribes and knowledge
Wadjet	Cobra-goddess/northern Egypt
Wepwawet	God of war and funerals

Greece and Rome

The Greeks worshiped many gods and goddesses, from Zeus, the king of the gods, to heroes to nymphs who resided in rivers and woods. There were twelve main deities, however, who lived on Mount Olympus; these twelve were known as the "Olympians." Romans, too, worshiped many diverse gods and goddesses; indeed their list is even more numerous than that of the Greeks. Early in their history, however, the Romans adopted the names and mythology of many of the Greek deities, so for convenience they are listed here together. This list includes the main deities living on Mount Olympus:

Greek Deity	Roman Deity	Function
Aphrodite	Venus	Love and beauty
Apollo	Apollo	Sun god/healing
Ares	Mars	War
Artemis	Diana	Hunt/moon goddess
Athena	Minerva	War/wisdom/crafts
Demeter	Ceres	Harvest and fertility
Dionysus	Bacchus	Wine/revelry/rebirth
Hephaestus	Vulcan	Fire and forge
Hera	Juno	Sister-wife of Zeus. Queen.
Hermes	Mercury	Messenger
Poseidon	Neptune	Sea
Zeus	Jupiter or Jove	Ruler of the gods

Both the Greeks and Romans venerated other important deities, who are shown here:

Greek	Roman	Special Concern
Eros	Amor (Cupid)	Love
Hades	Pluto	Underworld/death
Helios	Sol	Sun
Hestia	Vesta	Hearth
Pan	Pan	Flocks
Persephone	Proserpina	Spring (reluctant bride of Hades)
Selene	Luna	Moon

Celtic

The Celts were an Indo-European people who from about 600 B.C. spread throughout much of Europe, including northern Spain and the British Isles. They dominated northern Europe until about the third century B.C., when Roman legions conquered and the more purely Celtic cultures were relegated to the fringes of Europe—mostly Ireland and Wales. Like other Indo-European peoples, the Celts worshiped many gods and goddesses. Since the early Celts

had no written texts, it is hard to gain direct information about their early worship. The Greeks and Romans who described the early Celts often associated the native gods with Roman ones—for example, calling the Celtic war god Mars.

Archaeological finds offer us some images of the deities that give clues about the functions and worship of these Celtic deities, and historians use these remains in conjunction with later records of Celtic myths to try to reconstruct early beliefs. The surviving Celtic myths themselves come from Irish and Welsh sources that were recorded no earlier than A.D. 600, and some even later. These sources presumably recorded old oral tales that told about Celtic gods and heroes, but it is impossible to tell what portion of the materials had been added by later societies that had been influenced by both Rome and Christianity. (The Roman territories were converted in the late fourth century, and the Irish shortly thereafter.) Many of the early Celtic legends purportedly recall ancient Celtic history, when tribes and heroes fought one another. These legends preserve the names of kings and queens more than gods and goddesses, which makes it even more difficult to sort out a list of Celtic divinities.

With all these cautions in mind, here is offered at least some of the names of the major deities as they appeared in the later Celtic myths. We can only assume that the ancient Celts worshiped a similar pantheon:

Deity	Function
Boann	River goddess; consort of Daghda
Daghda	Father god—provider and bringer of fertility
Dian Cecht	God of healing
Epona	Horse goddess
Lugh	God of light and crafts
Manannan	Sea god
Morrigan	Battle goddess; consort of Daghda
Nuadn	Temporary king and god of healing
Rigantona	Queen in some of the myths

The Celts, who were known for their skilled craftsmanship in iron and precious metals, also worshiped a triad of craft gods:

God	Craft
Creidhne	Metalworker
Goibhniu	Blacksmith
Luchta	Carpentry and construction

Persian

Like the Celtic material, our information about the early myths and deities of the ancient Persians (also known as the ancient Iranians) is drawn from texts of much later periods, and thus we can only get an approximate idea of the earliest gods. Much of our information can be found in the religious texts of the Zoroastrians, whose prophet Zoroaster may have lived somewhere in central Asia. Zoroaster lived sometime between 1000 and 600 B.C. (scholars disagree), and Zoroaster incorporated ancient myths in the holy book, the Avesta.

The original Avesta probably dates from between 1400 and 1200 B.C.; legends claim that this book was written in gold on prepared oxhides and that it was destroyed by Alexander the Great in about 323 B.C. Parts of the sacred text were assumed to have been saved and copied, but the present Avesta only dates from the thirteenth century A.D. It contains only a fraction of the original text, and as can be seen from the large span of dates, it is impossible to know how close these old stories are to the originals. The section of the Avesta that is assumed to contain the oldest material is known as the Yasht, and this contains the tales of the gods and goddesses. The following is drawn from the Yasht and gives a general idea of the major ancient Persian deities:

Deity	Function
Ahura Mazda	Creator and god of absolute goodness
Angra Mainyu or Ahriman	Evil god who wants to destroy the world
Ardvi Sura Anahita	Goddess of waters and fertility
Atar	God of fire/son of Ahura Mazda
Haoma	God of health and strength
Mithra	God of order and justice
Tishtrya	God of rains
Vayu	God of wind
Verethragna	Warrior god

Summary

The women and men of the ancient world venerated gods and goddesses who were responsible for the natural world. Divine families of deities married and produced divine children, and human worshipers could seek their protection when they were in need. Women and men prayed for peace, prosperity, health, and fertility, and in this they showed that their concerns were not so unlike our own. They had rich spiritual and ritual lives regardless of the many names of the gods and goddesses who populated their heavens and the deep underworld of their dead.

See also Aphrodite; Gaea; Hera; Ishtar; Isis

Suggested Readings
Curtis, Vesta Sarkhosh. *Persian Myths.* Austin: University of Texas Press, 1993.
Gardner, Jane F. *Roman Myths.* Austin: University of Texas Press, 1995.
Grimal, Pierre. *The Dictionary of Classical Mythology.* Oxford: Blackwell, 1998.
Hart, George. *A Dictionary of Egyptian Gods and Goddesses.* New York: Routledge, 2000.
Lefkowitz, Mary R. *Women in Greek Myth.* Baltimore: Johns Hopkins University Press, 1986.
McCall, Henrietta. *Mesopotamian Myths.* Austin: University of Texas Press, 1996.
Miranda, Jane Green. *Celtic Myths.* Austin: University of Texas Press, 1995.
Spence, Lewis. *Ancient Egyptian Myths and Legends.* 1915. Reprint, New York: Dover Publications, 1990.

N

Naomi
Biblical Mother-in-Law (ca. 1100 B.C.)

The Book of Ruth in the Bible shows readers one of the difficult aspects of life for ancient Hebrew women: Unless they were married, or otherwise in the care of a man who handled property, they could quickly descend into poverty. The story also shows, however, how women depended upon each other and through mutual loyalty transcended their circumstances. While the narrative features Ruth, a woman from Moab who married a Hebrew man, the Book of Ruth also describes another fine female character—her mother-in-law, Naomi. In the relationship between these two women, subsequent readers could find solid role models that would strengthen the family and community ties that helped preserve the Hebrew people.

The Book of Ruth tells how Naomi and her husband left a famine in Judah to go to the neighboring country of Moab (see Map 5). There they settled, and their sons married Moabite women. Naomi's husband and both sons died, however, leaving all the women as widows. The Moabite women could return to the protection and care of their own families, but Naomi had to try to return to Bethlehem, her original home, to try to find the charity that ancient peoples accorded widows. One of her daughters-in-law—Ruth—chose to remain with her mother-in-law and accompany her back to the land where Ruth, rather than Naomi, would be a stranger. The biblical author used Ruth's willingness to stay with Naomi as a way to emphasize the daughter's loyalty to her mother-in-law, for in an age when widows needed family protection, these two widows were indeed going off into an uncertain future together. Thus, Ruth's act was one of extreme love and self-sacrifice.

The two women set out alone along the arduous hundred-mile journey down the mountains, across the Jordan valley, and through the wilderness of Judea to Bethlehem. When they entered the town, the people were surprised to see the two and cried out: "Is this Naomi?" Making a play on her name, Naomi replied: "Do not call me Naomi [which means 'my pleasure'], call me Mara [which means 'bitter' in Hebrew], for the Almighty has dealt very bitterly with me" (Ruth 1:19–20). The text again reinforces the difficulty of life for widows, but the two women helped each other in their time of troubles.

Ruth went to gather spare grains of barley in a field of a wealthy relative of her dead father-in-law to feed the two women, and the owner—Boaz—treated her kindly. Naomi saw a prospect of gaining a more secure life for her beloved daughter-in-law, saying, "My daughter, should I not seek a home for you, that it may be well with you?" (Ruth 3:1). Naomi urged Ruth to look attractive while she was near Boaz in hopes that he would exercise the right of "redemption" that existed under Jewish law. This right said a relative could marry a widow in his family to protect her and preserve the family's property and lineage. The plan worked, and Boaz married Ruth. Naomi, too, prospered, for she stayed to care for the couple's new son, who proved to be a great comfort to her.

In this story, the Bible offered a model of female comportment within a world that was difficult for women who were disconnected from their families. It suggests that if women worked together and remained virtuous and loyal, they would soon be reconnected and cared for. No doubt all widows did not end up in such fortunate circumstances as Ruth and Naomi, but this much-beloved tale must have offered consolation and hope to many. It also offers a glimpse into the informal networks that must have sustained Hebrew women even though they were outside the public structures of official Judaism.

Scholars have differed widely on how to interpret the character of Naomi. Some assessments are highly positive: She is an independent woman who forges a deep friendship with Ruth and takes charge in a world in which she had little say. Others are negative: She is a domineering mother-in-law who denounces God for her troubles but fails to thank Him for her blessings. These varied judgments at least attest to Naomi's commanding, if ambiguous, presence in the Bible.

See also Jewish Women; Ruth
Suggested Readings
Meyers, Carol, Toni Craven, and Ross S. Kraemer. *Women in Scripture.* New York: Houghton Mifflin, 2000.

Figure 55. Nefertiti (Ann Ronan Picture Library)

Nefertiti

Egypt's "Sun Queen" (ca. 1366–ca. 1333 B.C.)
When the pharaoh Amenhotep III ruled (r. ca. 1391 to 1353 B.C.), the New Kingdom of Egypt was at the height of its power. (*See* Tiy.) When he died, the crown went to his younger son, Amenhotep IV (r. ca. 1353–1335 B.C.), whom everyone—especially his powerful mother—expected to perpetuate the prosperity. At first, he continued the building projects of his father, which in Egypt was a statement of continuity. Shortly, however, he embarked on a path of his own—one that would make him one of the most-remembered pharaohs of the ancient kingdom. What influenced his new direction? Some scholars suggest that he was molded by his beautiful and powerful consort-queen, Nefertiti.

In the tradition of the pharaohs, Amenhotep IV needed an official consort to create his royal house, and either shortly before or after his accession, he married an obscure woman whose history has been impossible to trace. Nefertiti—whose name means "a beautiful woman has come"—seems not to have been a royal sister, for she never took the title "king's daughter." Some scholars have speculated that she may have been

a foreign princess drawn from the king's harem, but we cannot know for sure. A famous bust of the queen shows that her name was accurate, for based on this statue (shown in Figure 55) Nefertiti has come to be regarded as one of the most beautiful women in history, and the epithets that her husband approved for her suggest that he, too, wanted her known for her beauty. She was called "fair of face," "mistress of joy," "endowed with charm," "great of love." This beautiful woman would soon become the most powerful woman in the kingdom, exceeding the influence of her powerful mother-in-law, Tiy.

Within a few years after Amenhotep's accession, the portrayals of Nefertiti begin to change in a strikingly unusual way. In the first departure from tradition, there are a disproportionate number of Nefertiti's images, many completely without the king at all. For example, the queen offers to the gods in the presence of one of her six daughters, again without the king. Furthermore, in some portrayals the queen is shown striking some enemies, and up to now, this warlike posture had been reserved exclusively for kings. Finally, the queen began to wear a dramatic blue headdress as an unusual symbol of power. This unique depiction of a queen-consort would have been enough to set Nefertiti and Amenhotep apart from other rulers, but they went further. They introduced a revolution in religion and art that continues to astonish historians.

Within five years of his succession, Amenhotep IV radically simplified Egypt's polytheistic religion by abolishing most of the established deities and replacing them with one sole god—the Aten, or "sun disc." To underscore this transformation, Amenhotep changed his name to Akhenaten, which means "he who is useful to the sun disc," and he began to build a new city—called Akhetaten, or "horizon of the disc" (see Map 2). (This location is now known as Amarna, so archaeologists call remains from Akhenaten's time the "Amarna period.") Nefertiti became known as the "Sun Queen" in honor of the new worship. The new god and the new city served to weaken the old established hierarchy of priests, opening the way for new, more naturalistic art forms and for a new role for the queen.

The new god was impersonal, distant, and without gender. As such, it made an unsatisfactory deity for Egyptians used to the divine family of Isis, Osiris, and Seth. The divine family was replaced by the royal one, however, and as the pharaoh represented Aten on earth, Nefertiti became his female complement, and believers were to offer prayers to the royal family instead of directly to the god. For example, burial petitions at Amarna show many addressed to Nefertiti, asking to be granted eternal life. Some were even addressed to Queen Tiy, who moved with the family to Amarna, but who seems to have faded in power in comparison with Nefertiti. Akhenaten and Nefertiti focused on their family life (see Figure 25, page 93), and the images of the couple with their six daughters served to promise the blessings of fertility on all Egyptians who followed the new religion.

The new worship of Aten has caused much dispute among historians. Some have seen the religion as an early turn to monotheism that reflected—or even borrowed from—the ancient Hebrews. Others have simply seen it as a shrewd political gamble on the part of a king who was insecure on his throne (evidence shows a large increase in personal bodyguards) and who wanted to weaken the traditional powers of Egyptian priests and nobles. Some have even credited Nefertiti with finding a new religion that would allow her power to increase. The truth remains elusive, but it probably lies somewhere in between these extreme positions.

In about the eleventh year of Akhenaten's rule, the royal family began dying—perhaps as a result of plague in the region. Within a few years, Queen Tiy and four of Akhenaten's six daughters were all dead. About this time, Nefertiti herself surprisingly disappears from view. The last clear portrayal we have of her is weeping over the lifeless body of one of her daughters. Perhaps she died at this time as well, although it is surprising that there is no reference in the sources to her demise, as devoted pharaohs often recorded and mourned the deaths of their consorts. Perhaps she simply retired in mourning and disappeared after her husband's death a few years later. A last hypothesis—not widely supported by experts—is that she changed her identity and became known as Akhenaten's coruler, the enigmatic Prince Smenkhkare.

It appears that toward the end of his life, Akhenaten took as coruler his heir, named Smenkhkare. The identity of this shadowy figure is unclear, and he has been variously identified as Akhenaten's daughter's husband, his son by his second wife, or even his own younger brother. Some suggest, however, that Smenkhkare was Nefertiti herself, renamed and regendered. The evidence supporting this hypothesis is slim: Smenkhkare appears in the archaeological record precisely at the moment that Nefertiti disappears, and one carving previously identified as Akhenaten and Nefertiti turned out to have an inscription identifying Smenkhkare.

Whoever Smenkhkare was, he (or she) was not to rule alone. After Akhenaten's death in about 1335 B.C., the throne went to Tutankamen, possibly Akhenaten's son by his second wife. Tutankamen was to undo all the religious and cultural reforms initiated by Akhenaten and Nefertiti. The capital returned to Thebes, and the worship of the old gods returned (as did the powerful priesthood) as this conservative pharaoh tried to bring Egypt back to ways of their ancestors. Future historians, archaeologists, religious scholars, and art historians, however, would instead focus intently on the brief moment in Amarna when a highly unorthodox king and queen created a religious and cultural revolution.

See also Egyptian Women; Hatshepsut; Isis; Tiy
Suggested Readings
Aldred, Cyril. *Akhenaten and Nefertiti*. New York: Viking Press, 1973.
Arnold, Dorothea. *The Royal Women of Amarna*. New York: The Metropolitan Museum of Art, 1996.
Tyldesley, Joyce. *Daughters of Isis*. New York: Penguin, 1994.
———. *Nefertiti: Egypt's Sun Queen*. New York: Viking Press, 1999.

Niobe

Mythological Greek Queen

The Greek myths tell of Niobe, who was the wife of the king of Thebes. She suffered from too much pride and was therefore destroyed by the gods. The queen and king of Thebes had many children, and the different versions of the myth give various numbers. Homer says six or twelve, Hesiod says twenty, Herodotus four, and Sappho eighteen. The playwright Euripides says fourteen—seven sons and seven daughters.

Niobe was inordinately proud, and she boasted that she was superior to Leto, the Titaness who was the mother of Apollo and Artemis. Niobe bragged that since Leto had borne only two children, she was inferior. Mante, the prophetic daughter of the prophet Tiresias, overheard this incautious remark and advised the women of Thebes to placate Leto and her children at once. She urged them to burn incense and wear laurel branches in their hair. Niobe, smelling the incense, appeared and interrupted the sacrifice, asking why Leto, a woman "with a mannish daughter and a womanish son," should be preferred to her. Abandoning the sacrifice, the terrified Theban women tried to placate Leto with murmured prayers, but it was too late.

Leto had sent her own divine twins to kill all Niobe's children. Apollo found the boys hunting and shot them down one by one, sparing only Amyclas, who had offered a propitiatory prayer to Leto. Artemis found the girls spinning in the palace, and with a quiverful of arrows, killed all of them except Meliboea, who also had prayed to Leto. Some myths say that the surviving children built a temple to Leto, but other myths say all the children were killed.

For nine days and nine nights Niobe mourned her dead children and found no one to bury them, because Zeus, supporting Leto, had turned all the Thebans into stone. On the tenth day, the Olympic deities themselves came to conduct the funeral for the children. Niobe fled, but Zeus turned her into a stone, which continued to weep every summer. The stone of Niobe is a crag of roughly human shape, which was probably a natural formation. It seems to weep when the sun strikes its winter cap of snow. It may be that the myth originated to explain the appearance of the rock.

A different version of the Niobe legend offers another explanation for the murder of her children. In this account, Niobe was the daughter of Assaon, who had married her to an Assyrian. Her husband was killed during a hunt, and Assaon fell in love with his own daughter. She refused to yield to him, and he then plotted his revenge. He invited all her children to a feast and set fire to the palace, burning his grandchildren alive. Stricken with remorse, Assaon then killed himself, and Niobe was either changed into stone or threw herself from the top of a rock.

The sadness of Niobe has captured the imagination of artists ever since. She is the symbol of grief—grief for lost children, but also the grief that comes to women so proud that they meet their destruction by challenging the gods. This was a lesson repeated over and over in the ancient world.

See also Artemis; Helen of Troy in Greek Mythology
Suggested Readings
Grimal, Pierre. *The Dictionary of Classical Mythology*. Oxford: Blackwell, 1996.

Nitocris

Egyptian Queen (ca. 2150 B.C.)

Throughout the long, over two-thousand-year history of ancient Egypt, people retained a remarkably consistent view of kingship. The monarch was the absolute head of all aspects of Egyptian life, and his word was law. He was supposed to administer and defend his country and in general bring prosperity to the land. Egyptians surrounded their kings—pharaohs—with a strong symbolic importance as well, for it was their role to ensure a cosmic order and justice, which Egyptians called *maat*. Egyptians believed *maat* had been established at the beginning of time, but it was fragile; chaos could overwhelm at any time. Egyptians believed their kings had established a kind of contract with the gods: The pharaoh was a god himself living on earth, and he ruled in the name of the gods. In return, the gods ensured that the Nile would flood annually, making the fields fertile, and the sun would shine, helping the crops grow. In short, with the god-king on the throne, *maat* reigned in the land.

Throughout the dynastic period of Egypt (from about 3100 to 332 B.C.) it was generally assumed that a man would serve as king. Kings had ritual duties to appease the gods, and it was important to ensure that kings would preserve *maat* by fulfilling these tasks and by providing a male heir to continue the divine dynasty. Kings frequently had several wives and concubines to be sure they would have an heir, and they often married their sisters or half-sisters to preserve their own divine bloodline. A few times during the long course of Egyptian history, this pattern was disrupted, and a woman came to the throne to rule on her own. All these women were first queen-consorts to their husbands, and all were probably of royal blood themselves (a close relative of their husbands). Perhaps most important, none produced a son to carry on the succession, so that when their husbands died, the women took the thrones during times when *maat* seemed absent.

It is difficult to find very much information about most of these enterprising ancient women, for there are few remaining sources. We know hardly more than the names of queens such as Meryt-Neith. Queen Nitocris presents the opposite problem for historians, however, for her life became surrounded with many legends. It seems probable that Queen Nitocris

took rule during a difficult time at the end of the sixth dynasty, just before Egypt plunged into a period of *maat*-less chaos.

The sixth dynasty king Pepi II is reputed to have ruled Egypt for over ninety years (ca. 2246–2152 B.C.), and his reign was marked by a gradual decline in the stability of the country. When he died with no clear successor, Egypt entered into a period of general unrest followed by what historians call the First Intermediate Period (ca. 2150–2040 B.C.)—a time of chaos and suffering when there was no clear ruler, and local leaders took control of a decentralized land. Just before the First Intermediate Period, there was a succession of little-known kings with very short reigns—a clear indication that all was not well within Egypt. One source records that Nitocris was the second or third of the rulers after Pepi II, and she ruled for about two years. For some reason, Nitocris captured the imagination of ancient historians who wrote centuries after her reign, and they have told such creative stories of her life that it is impossible to find the real ruler among the legends.

Manetho (ca. 280 B.C.) was an Egyptian priest and historian who wrote the history of the kings of his country, and his work became the basis for all subsequent chronologies. He described Queen Nitocris as "the noblest and loveliest woman of her time, rosy-cheeked and of fair complexion" (Tyldesley 217). He confused this queen with King Menkaure of the fourth dynasty and thus credited her with completing the third pyramid at Giza. Her reputed "rosy complexion" came from a confusion between Nitocris and a beautiful Egyptian prostitute who was said to have had such a beautiful rosy complexion that a king fell in love with her and made her his wife, eventually burying her in a great pyramid.

The earlier Greek historian Herodotus (ca. 484–424 B.C.) had heard these stories and scornfully rejected them as impossible. Yet he passed on another legend of the beautiful Nitocris that has become the prevailing memory of the queen:

Nitocris was the beautiful and virtuous wife and sister of an Old Kingdom monarch who had ascended the throne at the end of the Sixth Dynasty, but who had been murdered by his subjects soon afterwards. Nitocris then became the sole ruler of Egypt and was determined to avenge the death of her beloved husband/brother. She gave orders for a huge underground hall to be made that would connect to the Nile by a hidden channel. When the room was complete, she threw a great banquet, inviting all those whom she held responsible for the murder of her husband. When the guests were feasting, she commanded that a secret door be opened and, as the Nile waters flooded in, all the traitors were drowned. She then committed suicide by throwing herself "into a great chamber filled with hot ashes" and suffocating to death. (Tyldesley 218)

There is no way to test the accuracy of Herodotus's account, but it seems unlikely that he would have had access to any sources that would have detailed such a romantic tale from such a long-ago chaotic time. Yet, the story of Nitocris's loyal vengeance and brave sacrifice made more of an impact on subsequent listeners than any of the actual accomplishments of this Egyptian queen who ruled briefly during the twilight of the Old Kingdom before Egypt plunged into the dark chaos of the First Intermediate Period.

See also Egyptian Women; Hatshepsut; Meryt-Neith; Nefertiti; Sobeknofru; Twosret
Suggested Readings
Herodotus. *The Histories.* Trans. A. de Selincourt. London: Penguin Books, 1983.
Lesko, B. S., ed. *Women's Earliest Records from Ancient Egypt and Western Asia.* Brown Judaic Studies 166. Atlanta: Scholar's Press, 1987.
Tyldesley, Joyce. *Daughters of Isis: Women of Ancient Egypt.* New York: Penguin, 1994.

Nossis of Locri

Hellenistic Poet (ca. third century B.C.)
Some women during the Hellenistic period used their education and became much admired by their contemporaries as skilled poets. One such woman was Nossis of Locri in Italy. From hints about herself within her poetry, we know that Nossis was of the upper class, which is not sur-

prising since it would take money and leisure to acquire the poetic skills that Nossis reveals in her surviving poetry. She also frankly claimed that she had been influenced by the poet Sappho, who by then had been firmly identified with lesbian relationships.

Nossis wrote both lyrics and epigrams, but only the latter have survived. Even within the epigrams, readers can see how the poet gained her reputation as a poet of love, and perhaps of love between women. In one frankly erotic poem, Nossis claims that love is sweeter than anything, even honey:

Nothing is sweeter than desire. All other
    delights are second.
    From my mouth I spit even honey.
Nossis says this, whom Aphrodite does not
    love,
    knows not her flowers, what roses they
    are. (Fantham et al. 165)

Nossis also shows an appreciation of the visual arts and combines it with frank appreciation of women's appearance: "Let's go to the temple of Aphrodite to see how her statue is intricately worked from gold. Polyarchis set it there, with the great wealth she won from her own body's fame." Or in another instance: "This picture captures Thaumarete's form—how well he painted her looks and her beauty, her gentle eyes. If your little watch-dog saw you, he would wag his tail, and think that he saw the mistress of his house" (Lefkowitz and Fant 9).

These tantalizing bits of poetry can only serve to make us wish we had more of her lyrics and that we knew more of the ancient poet who composed them.

See also Anyte of Tegea; Corinna of Tanagra; Erinna of Telos; Sappho of Lesbos
Suggested Readings
Fantham, E., et al. *Women in the Classical World.* New York: Oxford University Press, 1994.
Lefkowitz, Mary R., and Maureen B. Fant. *Women in Greece and Rome.* Toronto: Samuel-Stevens, 1977.
Skinner, Marilyn B. "Nossis Thelyglossos." In *Women's History and Ancient History,* ed. by S. B. Pomeroy, 20–47. Chapel Hill: University of North Carolina Press, 1991.

Figure 56. Hermes with the Nymphs. Engraving of a detail from a vase. (Ann Ronan Picture Library)

Nymphs
Mythological Goddesses

In Greek mythology, nymphs were spirits of nature, and in the Homeric epics they were said to have been the daughters of Zeus. They are considered secondary deities, to whom prayers were addressed and who were sometimes to be feared. They were often worshiped in caves or woods (where they were called dryads or hamadryads) or by springs (where they were called naiads). They were always represented as beautiful young girls. Sometimes they were called daughters of Zeus and were said to inspire men with prophetic powers. At other times, they were portrayed as followers of Pan or participants in the cult of Dionysus. They are usually shown enjoying music and dance.

Within various myths, nymphs are portrayed as evil or benevolent. Sometimes they hurt humans, blinding or destroying those who offend them. Sometimes they are helpful, saving humans who come into their sphere. At other times, the nymphs themselves are the victims of the passions of gods or men—Daphne and Eurydice were both nymphs who suffered because of their beauty.

Their cult was widespread and continued into Roman times. The very flexibility of mythological stories of semidivine women probably contributed to their popularity. These beautiful women could be shown as villains and victims, and they could represent the natural world in its varied aspects. Even by the Christian era, nymphs remained popular symbols in art and literature.

See also Daphne; Eurydice; Maenads
Suggested Readings
Adkins, Lesley, and Roy A. Adkins. *Handbook to Life in Ancient Rome.* New York: Oxford University Press, 1994.
Grimal, Pierre. *The Dictionary of Classical Mythology.* Oxford: Blackwell, 1996.

O

Octavia

Sister of the First Roman Emperor
(69 B.C.–ca. 9 B.C.)

Through the tumultuous years of the late Roman Republic and the civil wars that ushered in the empire, marriage ties were central to forging political alliances. Men who sought power had to marry women of influential families, and divorces occurred when political winds shifted. Given this situation, it is not surprising that the sister of Octavian—who later became known as Caesar Augustus—became a vital figure in the strife that brought Augustus to power as the first emperor. Octavia was more than just a pawn in the power game, however, because her character and the way she comported herself became as much a political issue for the Romans as her husband's actions. In an age when violence and deceit often won political victories, Octavia was rightly known for being gentle, charming, kind, and good.

When Octavia was fifteen years old, her family arranged a marriage with C. Claudius Marcellus, a politically powerful man more than twenty years her senior. It was Marcellus who helped provoke Julius Caesar's invasion of Italy and the start of the civil war, so the teenaged bride must have recognized the coming storm of civil unrest, but in the tradition of good Roman matrons she concentrated on matters within her household. In the forties B.C., they had three children—a son named M. Claudius Marcellus and two daughters, each called Claudia Marcella. By 40 B.C. Octavia, however, was a widow and once more was brought into the politics of marital alliances.

By 40 B.C., Octavia's brother Octavian had emerged as one of the powerful leaders of Rome after the murder of Julius Caesar. To seal the al-

Figure 57. Coin with Antony and Octavia, 39 B.C. (British Museum)

liance between himself and the equally powerful Mark Antony, Octavian arranged for his sister to marry Antony, whose wife, Fulvia, had recently died. Antony's lover, the Egyptian queen Cleopatra VII, must have been horrified by this marriage, which threatened her political and personal alliance with Mark Antony as well as the status of her infants born to the Roman. She had to bide her time, however, while Antony established a household with the by-all-accounts beautiful and kindly Octavia. Antony even struck coins to celebrate his wedding to Octavia, and this was the first time a woman's portrait head appeared on a Roman coin (see Figure 57).

Late in 39 B.C., Antony and Octavia took up residence in Athens, where they were soon regarded as the model couple. She bore Antony two daughters—Antonia major (the elder) and Antonia minor (the younger). These daughters would in time be mothers and grandmothers to

Roman emperors. Octavia's household was complex; it included more than her children by Antony. She had her own son—Marcellus—by her first marriage, and she also took care of Antony's son by Fulvia—M. Antonius Antyllus. (In fact, when he was a teenager, Antyllus visited his father when he had returned to Cleopatra and reported on Octavia's unfailing kindness to him.) The couple's honeymoon period did not last too long, however.

As Octavian and Antony began to lose trust in each other, Octavia tried to keep an agreeable atmosphere between the men, but in 37 B.C., Antony sent her back to live with her brother (taking the children and stepchildren with her). He rejoined Cleopatra, thus insulting Octavian and all of Rome, who admired the virtues of Octavia. As the historian Plutarch wrote, "Octavia unintentionally did great harm to Antony's reputation, since he was naturally hated for wronging such a woman" (Plutarch 1135). The insults to Octavia mounted: In 36 B.C., Antony married Cleopatra. Although the marriage was not valid under Roman law, it did represent the final breach between Antony and Octavian—civil war began again. In 32 B.C., Antony sent Octavia formal notice of divorce.

By 31 B.C. Antony and Cleopatra were both dead, and by 27 B.C. Octavian—now called Caesar Augustus—was the undisputed master of the Roman Empire. Octavia, with a seeming unbounded generosity, took in Cleopatra Selene, the surviving daughter of Mark Antony and Cleopatra, and raised her with the kindness and care she had devoted to her own children. As the emperor's sister, Octavia continued to be an important political figure, but now her children became the focus for marriage alliances.

In his search for an heir, Augustus arranged for his daughter, Julia, to marry Octavia's promising son by her first marriage. Marcellus was charming and popular and would have made an excellent successor to Augustus. But it was not to come to pass, for two years later, Marcellus fell to an epidemic that swept the city. Octavia, who had been so courageous in facing the hardships of her earlier life, was inconsolable with the loss of her son. In the remaining twelve years of her life, she never discarded her mourning

clothes, and she built a library in memory of her son. The Stoic philosopher Seneca criticized the grief he thought was immoderate in a Roman matron: "She refused to have a portrait of her son whom she loved so dearly, and she never allowed his name to be mentioned in her presence. . . . Spending more and more of her time alone in the dark, with no regard even for her brother, she refused to listen to poems and other compositions in honor of Marcellus's memory, and to every attempt of consolation she simply closed her ears" (Balsdon 73).

Livia—Augustus's wife—had been admired for stoically withstanding the death of a beloved son, and Octavia was in the same measure condemned for giving in to a similar tragedy. It is perhaps ironic that the woman who won such honor as the perfect mother and stepmother was criticized at the end of her life for expressing such grief. But for highborn ancient women, children were to secure the future, and once they were dead, they could no longer fulfill the important political alliances that had so marked Octavia's life.

See also Cleopatra V Selene; Cleopatra VII; Fulvia; Livia

Suggested Readings

Balsdon, J. P. V. D. *Roman Women: Their History and Habits.* New York: John Day, 1963.

Macurdy, Grace Harriet. *Hellenistic Queens.* Baltimore: Johns Hopkins University Press, 1932.

Plutarch. *Lives of the Noble Grecians and Romans.* Trans. John Dryden. New York: Modern Library, n.d.

Pomeroy, Sarah B. *Women in Hellenistic Egypt from Alexander to Cleopatra.* New York: Schocken Books, 1984.

Suetonius. *The Twelve Caesars.* Trans. Robert Graves. New York: Penguin, 1979.

Olympias

Christian Deaconess (ca. A.D. 368–ca. 410)

By the fourth century A.D., the great city of Constantinople was the capital of the Roman Empire. There great debates raged that shaped the history of Christianity, and it was there that many church fathers preached, wrote, and guided the growing church. As during the earliest centuries of Christianity, some wealthy women used their money and influence in the service of the church, and in the late fourth century, one of the most influential was the deaconess Olympias.

Olympias was born into a pagan family of high rank in Constantinople. Her father, Seleucus, was a count of the empire, but he died when she was a young girl. She was then raised by her uncle, Procopius, who was a devout Christian and a friend of Gregory of Nazianzus (who was one of the "great Cappadocians" who along with Macrina were extremely influential in bringing ascetic Christian practices to the urban communities). Gregory took great interest in Olympias, and he spoke of her fondly in his letters. Her governess, Theodosia, was an extremely pious Christian woman, and Gregory urged Olympias to follow Theodosia's model.

The young Olympias was not only very beautiful, but she was an heiress of a large fortune. These qualities, combined with her important family connections, made her highly desirable as a bride, and she had many suitors. In A.D. 384, when she was about sixteen, she was married to Nebridius, a young man of high rank and irreproachable character. The marriage does not seem to have been happy, however; it may have been that Olympias had already chosen a life of religious chastity in her heart. When Nebridius died about two years later, Olympias was sure that God wanted her not to be married.

Emperor Theodosius I had different ideas. In the tradition of the Roman Empire, highborn heiresses were important to forging political ties, and the emperor wanted her to marry a young Spaniard, Elpidius, who was a relative of the emperor himself. Olympias refused, and the emperor was angered by her intransigence. He ordered her property to be confiscated until she turned thirty years old, unless she consented to the proposed marriage. Olympias remained firm, and in a letter to the emperor, she sarcastically thanked him for relieving her of the "burden of wealth." Theodosius, recognizing that she would not change her mind (and perhaps regretting his harsh measures), finally left her alone to enjoy her property as she wanted to.

From then on, her time and wealth were devoted to the service of the church. She cared for the sick and poor and gave so much money and land to the churches in Greece, Asia Minor, and Syria that even John Chrysostom, bishop of Constantinople, warned her against giving away so much of her wealth that there would be nothing left. Her generosity and activity for the church caused Chrysostom's predecessor, Bishop Nectarius, to ordain her deaconess even though she was not sixty years old, as required by church custom.

Olympias became the good friend of Bishop John Chrysostom, and seventeen of his surviving letters are addressed to her. In these letters, we can see their mutual care for each other; she urged him to care for himself and eat properly and not get ill. She herself practiced strict asceticism (as did many religious women of the time). She renounced bathing, wore only old coarse clothing, and ate and slept sparsely.

In A.D. 404, John Chrysostom came into conflict with the empress Eudoxia and other powerful people in the court, and he was exiled from Constantinople. Olympias, too, suffered from the persecution that plagued all Chrysostom's followers. She was accused of having caused a fire that broke out immediately after his departure and that destroyed the church and senate house. An official tried to frighten her into a confession of guilt, but her firm demeanor in the face of such pressure caused the people of Constantinople to admire her immensely. Chrysostom's letters to Olympias date from this period of exile and show the strong mutual support they gave each other during these difficult times.

Olympias was fined for her support of the bishop, and eventually she, too, left Constantinople, although we do not know whether she was exiled or simply left voluntarily. We have no information about the rest of her life and know only that she died sometime between A.D. 407 and 419. The example of this strong, Christian woman, however, shows how significant the wealth and influence of such women were to the growth of the church.

See also Christian Women; Eudoxia; Helena; Macrina the Younger

Suggested Readings

Clark, E. *Jerome, Chrysostom, and Friends.* Lewiston, NY: Edwin Mellen Press, 1979.

Schaff, Philip, ed. *Nicene and Post-Nicene Fathers.* Vol. 9: *Chrysostom.* Peabody, MA: Hendrickson Publishers, 1995.

Olympias

Macedonian Queen (ca. 375–316 B.C.)

Macedonia—the land to the north of Greece—played a formative role in the history of Western civilization in the fourth century B.C. The Macedonian king Philip I consolidated his rule over his kingdom and built a dynasty that soon strengthened Macedonia's political position. As was customary, such dynastic ties were bound by marriage, which linked the Macedonian royal house with the royal houses of its neighbors, and kings took many wives to forge as many ties as possible. By 357 B.C., Philip I had already arranged several marriages for his son and heir Philip II, but in that year he took Philip II to Samothrace, a sacred island where he would be initiated into religious mysteries. While there Philip II met and fell in love with a very young woman who would become his next wife. It was an excellent political match, and a marriage was soon arranged between Philip II and Olympias, the daughter of a king of Epirus (in modern Albania). Olympias would become a strong queen who shaped the destiny of Macedonia—particularly through her famous son, Alexander the Great.

Olympias and Philip had two children in quick succession: Alexander, born in 356 B.C., and Cleopatra, born two years later. According to the sources, both Philip and Olympias had wild and violent natures, and the marriage was marked by much passion. Olympias reputedly always hated the presence of Philip's other wives and children in the household, however, and the stormy relationship in time deteriorated into violence. One source claims she slowly poisoned one of Philip's sons to weaken his intellect so that he was left an imbecile.

The historian Plutarch wrote that Olympias introduced wild religious ritual into Macedonia, particularly among women who worshiped Dionysus, the god of wine. (*See* Maenads.) Reputedly, Olympias had the power of snake charming, and she taught the women to include live snakes in their religious procession. Their husbands did not like this practice, and Plutarch claims that even Philip grew to dislike his marriage bed because Olympias frequently slept with her pet snakes. It is impossible to know how ac-curate Plutarch's tales were, for he loved to repeat a good story, whether it was true or not.

The queen had a close relationship with her children, caring for their education and up-bringing. She made sure Cleopatra, too, was trained to rule, for she had hopes for both her children to take power. She was particularly close to Alexander, and throughout his life they exchanged letters. It was over her ambitions for her son that she and her husband had their final battle. After twenty years of marriage, Philip decided to marry yet another wife—a Macedonian noblewoman also named Cleopatra. Olympias found this offensive enough, but at the wedding, Cleopatra's father offered a toast hoping for a legitimate heir to be born of the union—suggesting that Olympias's children, since they were not Macedonian, should not rule. Alexander was furious, and so was his mother. Alexander took Olympias back to her native land, where she seems to have conspired against Philip.

Philip was murdered in 336 B.C. at the wedding of his daughter. Reputedly, Olympias had planned the murder, but that was never proven, for the assassin was killed. She does seem to have been responsible for killing Philip's last wife, Cleopatra, and their recently born infant. She refused to let Alexander face any competition for the throne of Macedonia, and she enjoyed a good deal of power as his mother. Olympias returned to Macedonia, and for the next five years she presided over the court while her son was away at the wars that would create a new Hellenistic world. Olympias's strength of will earned her many enemies, however. The regent, Antipater, wrote to Alexander complaining of the stubbornness, violence, and interference of the queen, but Alexander never renounced his mother. The sources claim that he told one of his followers that Antipater was unaware that one of his mother's tears would wash out the complaints of a thousand letters. The queen so alienated Antipater, however, that on his deathbed he warned the Macedonians never to let a woman rule over them.

In 331 B.C., Olympias had made so many enemies in Macedonia that she moved to Epirus, where her daughter, Cleopatra, was queen. She planned to wait there until her son returned from the wars, when she could return with him to Macedonia. Alexander's death in 323 B.C. changed that, but the indomitable woman did not give up her ambitions to rule. First, she tried to arrange a marriage between Cleopatra and a Macedonian who could rule as king. Powerful nobles led by Antipater foiled these plans, however. When Antipater died in 319 B.C., Olympias had one more opportunity to seize power. Some Macedonian nobles invited Olympias back to act as regent for Alexander's young son, Alexander. But another strong woman interfered—Eurydice, Philip II's granddaughter by his first wife.

The young Eurydice had been as determined as Olympias to place her husband on the throne of Macedonia, and the death of Antipater seemed to provide that opportunity. As the armies gathered, the two women appeared in front of their forces to fight for the throne. Olympias, who was almost sixty years old at this time, was dressed as a priestess of Dionysus, and Eurydice wore Macedonian armor. When the Macedonian soldiers saw the proud Olympias, looking so much like their beloved Alexander, they came to her side, and the battle was won without a blow. Eurydice and her husband were captured and turned over to Olympias, who showed them no mercy. She had Eurydice's husband, Philip, killed; then she sent Eurydice a dagger, a rope, and a bowl of hemlock poison, telling her to choose her own death. Eurydice cursed her, then took off her own girdle and hanged herself without a trace of fear. The brave Eurydice was only twenty years old.

As Olympias tried to kill more of her enemies, she lost the support of the Macedonians, who perhaps remembered Antipater's dying warning against following a queen. She was captured and imprisoned. Her captors sent some relatives of those she had killed, and these men stabbed her. She died bravely without begging for any mercy. Her daughter, Cleopatra, was also murdered by men who feared her potential for political power. Olympias's greatest contribution was her son, who changed the course of history by spreading Greek culture to the east with his conquests and who paved the way for the rise of the great Hellenistic kingdoms. Olympias also may have provided a model of a powerful queen who took it upon herself to be actively involved in the politics of the day. The women of the Hellenistic world would exert more freedom than any other women of the ancient world.

See also Egyptian Women; Eurydice I; Maenads; Phila

Suggested Readings

Macurdy, Grace Harriet. *Hellenistic Queens.* Baltimore: Johns Hopkins University Press, 1932.

Plutarch. "Alexander." In *The Lives of the Noble Grecians and Romans.* Trans. J. Dryden. New York: The Modern Library, n.d.

Olympic Games
(776 B.C.–ca. A.D. 390)

Greeks from all city-states gathered periodically at a religious festival dedicated to Zeus where they competed in athletic competitions—the Panhellenic, or Olympic Games, held in Olympia on the Peloponnesus in Greece. They so loved these sports that they even stopped their almost interminable warfare and came together to celebrate their love of the contest. The first Olympic Games were held in 776 B.C. In *The Odyssey,* Homer had written, "There is no greater glory for a man . . . than that which he gains through the speed of his feet or the strength of his hands" (Kebric 45), and Greeks everywhere trained for years and competed in preliminary trials in hopes of qualifying for these greatest of games. At first, the event consisted only of a foot race, but soon the games included boxing, wrestling, chariot racing, and the grueling pentathlon, which included long jumping, discus and javelin throwing, wrestling, and the 200-meter sprint. Olympic victors brought glory to their home cities and were richly rewarded there with honor and free meals.

Olympic organizers forbade women from competing in these contests, and except for some priestesses, women were not even allowed to watch the games. One woman, Callipateira, was remembered for bravely defying the convention, for she wanted desperately to watch her son compete. She dressed as a male trainer to enter the games, but after her son won, she was carried away by excitement and jumped over a

Figure 58. Female athletes, mosaic, ca. A.D. 350 (Erich Lessing/Art Resource, NY)

fence. In the process, her clothing flew up, revealing her gender. She could have been condemned to death by law for witnessing the games, but Olympic officials spared her out of respect for her father, brothers, and son, who had all been winners at Olympia. In order to avoid any similar future improprieties, officials passed a law requiring all trainers to attend the games in the nude to prevent further disguises.

Women were allowed to enter chariots and horses into the races as long as they were ridden by a man. A Spartan princess proudly erected a memorial recalling the victories of her chariot team in two different Olympics. Other women athletes, however, longed to participate more directly in games of their own. Some women's events were introduced into some of the games leading up to great ones at Olympia, but women were always forbidden from the grand games dedicated to Zeus.

Women did conduct games of their own separately from the men's. These games, dedicated to Zeus's wife, Hera, consisted only of foot races of virgins of varying ages, and the races were scheduled so the youngest ran first. They used a track similar to that at Olympia, but the distance

was shortened by one-sixth. The Greek sources describe the runners vividly: "Their hair hangs down on them, a chiton reaches to a little above the knee, and the right shoulder is bared as far as the breast" (Kebric 60). Women judged and sponsored the games and awarded the fastest competitors crowns of olive branches and a portion of the cow sacrificed to Hera. Furthermore, they had the right to dedicate statues with their names inscribed. Greek women, like men, enjoyed competing for the athletic honors that brought prestige to themselves and their cities.

The games continued even after Greece became part of the Roman Empire, but their emphasis changed. For the Romans, athletic competitions were for entertainment or business rather than for athletic pride. Many times athletic contests were held in the amphitheaters that dotted all the major cities of the Roman world, and sometimes in these settings women participated in the games. In one athletic contest in Rome in the early third century A.D., women wrestlers were so popular that they were banned from future games. The female athletes shown in the fourth-century mosaic in Figure 58 are dressed in the Roman, rather than Greek, style of athletic attire. We cannot know if this portrayal shows them actually competing in an athletic contest or practicing for one, but it does offer a view into the late history of the games.

The ancient Olympic Games were finally ended in the fourth century A.D. as Christian emperors banned the games as remnants of pagan worship. The events that had drawn the excited interest of men, women, and spectators alike came to a close, but the memory of an event that featured athletic excellence continued to capture people's imagination into modern times when the games were begun again—this time with women participating.

See also Greek (Athenian) Women; Hera; Spartan Women

Suggested Readings

Finley, M. I., and H. W. Pleket. *The Olympic Games: The First Thousand Years.* New York: Viking Press, 1976.

Kebric, Robert B. *Greek People.* Mountain View, CA: Mayfield Publishing, 1989.

Olivova, V. *Sport and Games in the Ancient World.* New York: St. Martin's Press, 1984.

Young, D. *The Olympic Myth of Greek Amateur Athletics.* Chicago: Ares Publishers, 1984.

P

Pamphila

Roman Encyclopedist
(ca. mid-first century A.D.)

In the cosmopolitan world of the Roman Empire, many men and women enjoyed educational opportunities. They had access to scrolls of ancient works that circulated through the empire, and perhaps even more important, they took advantage of erudite travelers as they moved through the cosmopolitan centers of the Roman world. One woman who made the most of this fertile learning environment was Pamphila, who wrote a number of books.

Pamphila, the daughter of an Egyptian scholar named Soteridas, married another scholar when she was young. Husband and wife lived in Greece, and Pamphila spent most of her time in study. In an introduction to one of her works, the narrator reported how she came to study and write:

After thirteen years of living with her husband since she was a child, she began to put together these historical materials and recorded what she had learned from her husband during those thirteen years, living with him constantly and leaving him neither night nor day, and whatever she happened to hear from anyone else visiting him (for there were many visitors with a reputation for learning). And she added to this what she had read in books. She separated all this material that seemed to her worthy of report and record into miscellaneous collections. (Fantham et al. 368)

Pamphila wrote some thirty-three books of historical materials (called the *Hypomnemata Historika*), which some ancient scholars ascribed either to her father or her husband, seemingly unable to believe that such works could have been written by a woman. She also composed several treatises: "On Disputation," "On Sexual Desire," and other titles.

Her works were collected into an encyclopedia, which was read a century and more after her death. Later (in the ninth century), the Byzantine anthologist Photius copied her works; he included the condescending remark that her style was "simple, being the work of a woman" (Fantham et al. 369). Yet, here was an ancient woman who found herself surrounded by scholars and who made the most of these surroundings by producing her own scholarly collection that she, herself, characterized as "enjoyable and attractive" (368).

See also Philosophers, Greek
Suggested Readings
Fantham, E., et al. *Women in the Classical World.* New York: Oxford University Press, 1994.

Pandora

Mythological Greek Woman

One of the creation myths of the ancient Greeks involved Zeus's creation of the first woman, Pandora. Zeus made Pandora to get revenge on Prometheus, a god who cared too much for humans. Prometheus had stolen fire from the gods to give to humans, and he had tricked Zeus into accepting bones and fat as a sacrifice, leaving the good meat for humans. For his revenge, Zeus made what the myths called "a great evil"—the first woman. Zeus made her beautiful to look at, in the form of a shy maiden. Then the other gods gave her gifts—beauty, grace, dexterity, and other virtues. Hephaestus, however, gave her lying and deceit. Because of all they gave

Figure 59. Pandora, center, being given gifts by Aphrodite, left, and Ares (British Museum)

her, her name was Pandora, which means the "gift of all." From her all women came, and the myths said that from her (and all later women) came all the evil for mankind. (The creation myth is similar to the ancient Judeo-Christian story of Eve, who purportedly brought all evil to humankind.)

In the Greek myths, Zeus sent Pandora to Epimetheus. Even though Epimetheus's brother Prometheus had told him to accept no presents from Zeus, Epimetheus was seduced by Pandora's beauty and made her his wife. Epimetheus had a great box. In it the gods had placed all the plagues and evils in the world. Pandora had hardly reached earth when, overcome with curiosity, she could not bear to leave the box closed. Finally, one day she decided to open it just a bit to peek in. As soon as she lifted the top all the plagues flew out. From then on humans were endangered by illness and storms and pain and sorrow. Pandora quickly slammed the lid back down, but it was too late. The troubles had already escaped. Then she heard a tiny voice

from within the box asking to be let out to save humanity. Pandora was afraid to open the box again, but the voice persuaded her. She opened it again and Hope flew out.

Other versions of the legend say that the box contained not all the world's evils, but every blessing, and that Pandora had brought it to Epimetheus as a wedding present from Zeus. By opening it carelessly, she let all the good things escape and return to the heavens instead of staying on earth. That is why humans are afflicted with every form of evil; only hope, a poor consolation, was left to them.

Some people believed that hope was a good thing—the salvation of humankind from all the ills she had released at first. But other people believed that hope was the worst thing she released from her box, because when people hoped for things, they were not satisfied with what they had. In either case, this story was how the ancient Greeks understood the creation of evil in the world—it came from the curiosity of the first woman, Pandora.

See also Eve
Suggested Readings
Grimal, Pierre. *The Dictionary of Classical Mythology.*
   Oxford: Blackwell, 1996.
Hamilton, Edith. *Mythology.* New York: Mentor,
   1955.
Lefkowitz, Mary R., and Maureen B. Fant. *Women's
   Life in Greece and Rome.* Baltimore: Johns
   Hopkins University Press, 1982.

Pasiphaë

Greek Mythological Queen

Pasiphaë was the daughter of Helios, the sun-god, and she married Minos, the king of Crete. They had several children, including daughters Ariadne and Phaedra and a son, Androgeus. But Minos had offended Poseidon, the god of the sea, and the deity decided to take revenge through Pasiphaë. Poseidon sent a magnificent white bull to the island for sacrifice, then he made Pasiphaë fall in love with the bull. She confided her passion to Daedalus, the famous craftsman who lived in Crete. Daedalus promised to help her, and he built a hollow wooden cow and covered it with cow's hide. Pasiphaë hid within the cow and in this form, mated with the bull. She became pregnant and gave birth to the Minotaur—a half-human–half-bull monster.

Minos consulted an oracle to know how he might best avoid scandal, and the prophet told him to build a great labyrinth at Knossos. The king did so and concealed the Minotaur and Pasiphaë within. Minos used the fierce Minotaur to get revenge upon Athenians because they had killed his son, Androgeus; he required an annual tribute of Athenian boys and girls to sacrifice to the Minotaur. The sacrificial youths were placed in the labyrinth from which it was impossible to escape and where the Minotaur could kill them at his pleasure.

One year, the Athenian hero Theseus came forward and offered to be one of the victims of the Minotaur. When the young victims arrived in Crete, they were paraded before the inhabitants on their way to the labyrinth. Minos's daughter Ariadne saw the captives and fell in love with Theseus. She sent for Theseus and told him she would bring about his escape if he would promise to take her back to Athens and marry her. He agreed, and she gave him a ball of thread to unwind as he went on through the labyrinth. That way he could retrace his steps and find the way out. Theseus did so and came upon the Minotaur while the monster slept. Having no weapons, Theseus killed the beast with his fists. He then followed Ariadne's thread back out of the labyrinth, taking the other captives with him.

They picked up Ariadne and fled to the ship and cast out to sea to head for Athens. On the way, they stopped at the island of Naxos. There, Theseus abandoned Ariadne, leaving her asleep on the island. (One story portrays Theseus in a better light and says that he was accidentally blown out to sea, leaving the young woman.) The god Dionysus found the desolate Ariadne, comforted her, and gave her several children. The ungrateful Theseus returned heroically to Athens. The stories of Pasiphaë and Ariadne continued to be very popular throughout the ancient world and into modern times.

See also Minoan Women
Suggested Readings
Grimal, Pierre. *The Dictionary of Classical Mythology.*
   Oxford: Blackwell, 1996.
Hamilton, Edith. *Mythology.* New York: Mentor,
   1955.

Paula

Roman Christian Widow (A.D. 347–404)

The fourth century A.D. was a critical time in the formation of Christian thought. The great persecutions were over, and writers that we have come to call church fathers produced many tracts that served to shape Christian ideas. One of these church fathers was Jerome (whose full name was Eusebius Hieronymus), later proclaimed a saint. Jerome was born sometime around A.D. 340 in Dalmatia, in the Balkans (shown on Map 7). He was highly educated in the Latin classics, he learned Greek, and in his youth he traveled to Rome to continue his studies. In Rome, he converted to Christianity and was baptized sometime before A.D. 366. In his search for a spiritual life, Jerome left Rome and traveled to Jerusalem and Antioch. There he became known as a scholar, was ordained a priest, and learned to admire the desert hermits who lived near Antioch.

Jerome, himself, lived as a desert hermit for two or three years while he continued his scriptural studies and learned Hebrew.

Jerome did not remain a hermit, however. In about A.D. 382, Pope Damasus in Rome commissioned Jerome to prepare a standard Latin translation of the Bible, and this became the great labor of Jerome's life. He went to Rome to work with his patron the pope, and at that time, he became acquainted with an extraordinary group of high-born Christian women and became their teacher, spiritual adviser, and friend. Modern feminists often criticize Jerome for his strong views against sexuality and his frequent antifeminist comments. The women he met in Rome befriended the irascible scholar, however, and supported him in his many controversies with other churchmen. One of the women who was most supportive and influential in Jerome's life was Paula, a Roman widow who became his lifelong companion.

Paula was a wealthy aristocratic Roman widow who was descended from the famous Roman family of the Scipios (the general who defeated Carthage; *see* Sophoniba). Her father was Rogatus and her mother Blaesilla, and as was appropriate to the exalted family, they arranged an excellent marriage for their daughter, Paula. She married Toxotius—descended from the family of Julius Caesar. She bore five children—four daughters and finally a son. After she bore her son—named Toxotius after his father—she renounced sexual intercourse and concentrated on her religious practices. When her husband died, she was not yet in her mid-thirties, and she mourned his demise. She found comfort in her religious beliefs, however.

She was lavish in her charity, offering money to the poor and comfort to the sick. Her family complained that she was so generous that she was robbing her children's patrimony, but she did not listen to such criticism and continued her care. Paula became acquainted with another intelligent, religious widow, Marcella, and the women gathered, studied, and discussed scripture. Their lives would change in about A.D. 382, when Jerome came to Rome to serve the pope. As soon as Jerome entered Rome, he was entertained at Paula's mansion in the company of other churchmen. He soon formed a friendship with Paula, for they both shared a love of the ascetic life—with fasting and other bodily mortifications—along with a passion for study.

Paula and one of her daughters, Eustochium, studied with Jerome. Paula knew most of the scriptures by heart and even learned Hebrew well enough to chant it with impeccable pronunciation. Paula lived an ascetic life—bathing only when ill and sleeping on the hard ground. Throughout the three years Jerome spent in Rome, the friendship grew, and even withstood the tragic death of Paula's daughter Blaesilla. With Pope Damasus's death in A.D. 384, Jerome lost his protector, and the enemies he made in Rome (who hated his argumentative style) began to make life unpleasant for him. He decided to leave for the Holy Land to take up a monastic existence there. Paula and Eustochium decided to accompany him, and this unorthodox traveling company generated even more scandal in Rome. Jerome wrote a letter to another high-born religious woman—Asella—reassuring her of the chaste motives and impeccable virtue of the three pilgrims.

Paula, too, ignored the scandals, for she longed to travel to the east to visit the sites where holy men and women retreated into the desert to live an ascetic life. Disregarding the demands of children and household, she planned to leave with Eustochium. As she boarded a ship, her children cried on the shore, and her small son, Toxotius, reached out to her. Jerome recounts how she was torn between her duties as a mother and her longings for a religious life: "She knew herself no more as a mother, that she might approve herself a handmaid of Christ. Yet her heart was rent within her, and she wrestled with her grief, as though she were being forcibly separated from parts of herself" (Jerome 197). One of the consistent themes of many of these early Christian women was the tension between the demands of family and their own desire to follow a different path. Paula sailed away in about A.D. 385 and traveled throughout the Holy Land.

Jerome recounts in detail her travels and the sites she saw, and he carefully mentioned the many shrines of ancient women that drew her attention. She stopped at the house of the early

Christian Cornelius (which by then was a church) to see the rooms where his daughters spoke prophetically. She stopped at the tomb of Rachel, where she had died giving birth to her son Benjamin, and she spent a good deal of time in Bethlehem, where Mary had given birth to Jesus. Paula entered the home of Sarah and saw the birthplace of Isaac. Finally, the group gathered in Palestine, outside Jerusalem, where they established two monasteries—one for men and one for women. During this time, Jerome worked on his Latin translation of the Old Testament based on the Hebrew texts, and the three friends continued their study and conversation.

Paula's son, Toxotius, had married a woman named Laeta, and Paula was delighted to hear that a granddaughter was born—named Paula in honor of her illustrious grandmother. The young child was dedicated to a life of virginity and her mother, Laeta, also converted to a life of chastity, perpetuating the circle of religious households that Paula and Marcella had established in the capital.

Paula became ill in Palestine, and Eustochium cared for her mother during her final sickness. She died in A.D. 404, at fifty-six years old, and was buried in Bethlehem. Jerome placed an inscription on her tomb, praising her background and her piety. In this final tribute to Paula, Jerome included the summary: "Seest thou here hollowed in the rock a grave, 'Tis Paula's tomb; high heaven has her soul. Who Rome and friends, riches and home forsook Here in this lonely spot to find her rest" (Jerome 212). Like many other Christian women, Paula gave up all her social connections to seek God in the remote Holy Land. Her heritage included her influence on the works of Jerome, and her daughter Eustochium, who stayed with the church father until her death.

See also Blaesilla; Eustochium; Marcella; Rachel; Sarah (also Sarai); Sophoniba

Suggested Readings

Jerome. *Jerome: Letters and Select Works. Nicene and Post-Nicene Fathers,* vol. 6. Ed. Philip Schaff and Henry Wace. Peabody, MA: Hendrickson Publishers, 1995.

Kelly, J. N. D. *Jerome: His Life, Writings, and Controversies.* New York: Harper and Row, 1975.

Paulina

Roman Woman (ca. A.D. 30)

When Tiberius (r. A.D. 14–37) became emperor of Rome after the death of Augustus, he was already in his mid-fifties. He was a morose and sullen man, who was suspicious of almost everyone and who worried constantly about conspiracies. By A.D. 26, he left Rome to live a secluded life on the island of Capri, from where he guided the empire while surrounded by a limited number of trusted advisers (including his favorite astrologer). Among the many things that aroused Tiberius's suspicions were various religious cults. One that particularly suffered under his watchful eye was the cult of the Egyptian goddess, Isis, and the Roman historian Josephus (who was not a fan of the cult of Isis) records what he claims is the incident that sparked the emperor's hostility. It is impossible to know how accurate this rather remarkable tale is, but we cannot discount it completely because of the level of detail. We may approach his story of the noble woman, Paulina, with some skepticism, however.

According to Josephus, there was a woman named Paulina who was descended from the noblest families of Rome and who was held in high regard because of her own virtuous conduct. She was beautiful and wealthy and was married to a man named Saturninus, who was her equal in reputation. Another man, Decius Mundus, was in love with her, however. He sent her abundant gifts to persuade her to have relations with him, but she scorned them all because of her virtue. His passion was so inflamed, he even offered her 200,000 Greek drachmas (a king's ransom) if he could share her bed a single time. When even this failed to shake her resolve, Mundus decided to starve himself to death rather than suffer any longer from unrequited love.

As Mundus began his fast, a freedwoman named Ida who lived in his household intervened. She had no patience with his self-sacrifice and went to him with a plan that held out hope that he might succeed in enjoying intimate relations with Paulina. She informed him that she would need no more than 50,000 Greek drachmas to gain his desire. Mundus gave her the money, and Ida instituted her plan. She knew better than to approach the virtuous Paulina directly, but since she knew that Paulina was much devoted to the worship of Isis, Ida went to the goddess's priests. She offered them 25,000 drachmas payable at once and as much more after the success of the plot. She told them of Mundus's passionate desire for Paulina and urged them to think of a way to satisfy his lust. Swayed by greed, the priests agreed.

The eldest priest went to Paulina's house and requested a private talk with her. He said that he had been sent by the god Anubis to say that the god had fallen in love with her and wanted her to come to him. Paulina was much flattered; she told her friends of the invitation and even told her husband of her summons to dine with and share the bed of Anubis. Since her husband had no doubt of his wife's virtue, he gave his permission.

She went to the temple, and after supper when it came time to sleep, the priest shut the doors within the shrine and took away the lamps. Mundus, who had been concealed within the temple, appeared and was not rejected when he sought intercourse with Paulina, since she believed he was the god Anubis. The next morning, Paulina went to her husband and described in detail the divine manifestation of Anubis, and in front of the ladies who were her friends, she bragged about the god. Those who heard could hardly believe it, but knowing her reputation and her position in society, they could not argue.

Two days later, however, Mundus appeared before her, saying: "Well, Paulina, you have indeed saved me 200,000 drachmas which you could have had, yet you rendered to perfection the service I urged you to perform. Since you rejected Mundus, I took the name Anubis as my own" (Kebric 115). With this speech, he departed. When Paulina heard these words, she understood the horrible deed that had been done to her. She went to her husband and begged him to get vengeance. He brought the matter to the notice of Tiberius.

Tiberius examined the priests and discovered the full story. He crucified both of the priests and the woman, Ida, for their role in compromising the lady's honor. Furthermore, he destroyed the temple and ordered the statue of Isis to be cast into the Tiber River. Mundus escaped with his life; he was sentenced to exile, since

Tiberius believed his crime had been committed under the influence of passion. And the historian, Josephus, concluded, "Such were the insolent acts of the priests in the temple of Isis" (Kebric 115).

See also Isis; Livia; Julia
Suggested Readings

Josephus. *Jewish Antiquities.* Vol. 9. Loeb Classical Library. Cambridge: Harvard University Press, 1965.
Kebric, Robert B. *Roman People.* Toronto: Mayfield Publishing, 1993.

Pelagia
Prostitute and Holy Woman (ca. A.D. 457)

Pelagia was a beautiful prostitute who lived in Antioch (shown on Map 8) in the fifth century A.D. Shortly after she died, the story of her transformation from prostitute to holy woman spread rapidly, and a churchman named Jacob the Deacon recorded the story of her life. From then on, her story was read and reread, and in many churches she was venerated as a saint. Jacob wrote that this is a story of "splendid repentance" (Salisbury 99), and its popularity probably grew from its message of forgiveness.

The story began when the bishop of Antioch convened a council of eight bishops. Among those summoned was Bishop Nonnus, who can probably be identified as the bishop of Edessa who lived ca. A.D. 451. Nonnus came to the council accompanied by his deacon, Jacob (who became Pelagia's biographer). The bishops gathered in the forecourt of a church, and as they listened to Bishop Nonnus speak, they were distracted by the approach of a beautiful woman. She appeared riding on an ass, and she was so elaborately ornamented that observers could only see gold and pearls and precious stones adorning her. A train of young men and women clad in rich robes with gold jewelry at their necks accompanied her, and the very air was scented with rich perfumes as she passed by. Upon seeing this impudent woman who rode with not even a veil to cover her head modestly, most of the bishops turned their faces away. But Bishop Nonnus did not turn his head; he gazed at her long and carefully.

After the woman had passed, Nonnus fell to

his knees and shed many tears. Sighing heavily, he asked the other bishops: "Did not the beauty of the woman delight you?" The bishops did not answer him, but Nonnus was not deterred. He said again: "In truth, it greatly delighted me, and well pleased was I with her beauty" (Salisbury 99). Nonnus spoke of the time the woman spent adorning herself so that there would be no stain or flaw in her body's beauty. Thus, the bishop said, she was careful to please all men's eyes and not disappoint her earthly lovers. In contrast, Nonnus felt that they were trying to please God, an immortal lover, and they could not clean their souls or make them nearly as beautiful as the prostitute's body.

This account of the impact of the vision of the prostitute's beauty on Nonnus is quite remarkable. In all the patristic writings, the fathers warned that the mere vision of any woman could lead a man to sin. In this case, the vision of a beautiful fallen woman had led a bishop to the recognition of a higher level of holiness. This is a reversal of the standard Roman warnings against prostitutes, and the standard Christian admonitions against women's beauty. Nonnus claimed that his perspective was validated by a dream in which he saw a filthy black dove that dove into the water and emerged clean and white. The bishop believed he was called to cleanse the beautiful prostitute.

The narrator went on to describe that Bishop Nonnus was preaching in the church, but by chance the prostitute heard him and "she, who had never before thought of sin, was moved to tears by his words." She sent a note to the bishop asking for an audience. Nonnus received her, and she promptly asked to be baptized. The bishop asked her name, and she answered: "At birth the name I received was Pelagia. However the townspeople of Antioch call me Margarite because of the pearls with which I was adorned" (Salisbury 101). Nonnus then agreed to baptize her as Pelagia after she completed the necessary preparation. The names were related—Pelagia means "belonging to the sea," and Margarite means "pearl." In a Christian context, the name Pearl was an unusual one for a prostitute, because it means purity. Perhaps the narrator wanted to show that even as a prostitute, Pelagia had an inner purity that the bishop discovered.

During Pelagia's preparation for baptism, she was tormented by the devil, who tempted her with recollections of her wealth. He said: "Were you not decorated in precious stones and pearls? Were you not covered in gold and silver?" (Salisbury 102). The young woman was not swayed, however; she sent her servant to her house to give up all her wealth for the church to distribute to widows and orphans.

Finally, after eight days of preparation, she was supposed to put off her white robes of baptism and dress as a modest Christian woman. Instead, Pelagia once again set out on an unusual path. She rose in the night and laid aside her white robes and dressed in the clothing of Bishop Nonnus. She disappeared in the darkness and was not seen again in the city of Antioch.

About three years later, Nonnus's deacon Jacob longed to go on a pilgrimage to Jerusalem. Nonnus suggested that Jacob visit a certain holy eunuch in Jerusalem named Pelagius, who had acquired a reputation for holiness. Jacob found Pelagius in a cell on the Mount of Olives, and they prayed together for a while. Jacob left much impressed with the holy eunuch's piety. After some travels, Jacob returned again to the Mount of Olives to confer with Pelagius. There was no response to his knock on the cell. Peering in, Jacob discovered that Pelagius was dead. When the other monks gathered to prepare the body for burial, they discovered that Pelagius was a woman. Jacob then knew who the holy eunuch really was—the ex-prostitute, Pelagia. Her reputation spread after her death, and many came to venerate the prostitute who transcended not only her sinful past but her gender as well.

See also Euphrosyne (Castissima); Jewelry; Melania the Younger; Prostitution

Suggested Readings

Brock, Sebastian P., et al. *Holy Women of the Syrian Orient.* Berkeley: University of California Press, 1987.

Bullough, Vern L., and Bonnie Bullough. *Cross Dressing, Sex, and Gender.* Philadelphia: University of Pennsylvania Press, 1993.

Salisbury, J. E. *Church Fathers, Independent Virgins.* London: Verso, 1991.

Ward, Benedicta. *Harlots of the Desert.* Kalamazoo, MI: Cistercian Publications, 1987.

Penelope

Legendary Greek Wife

During the Trojan War between the Greeks and the Trojans (immortalized by the poet Homer), the Greek soldiers were gone from home for ten years besieging the city of Troy. Even after the war was over, some men took a long time returning to their homes. The most famous of the delayed Greek heroes was Odysseus, who took ten more years returning to his home, and his legendary adventures are preserved in Homer's popular work, *The Odyssey.*

Homer portrays Penelope as a faithful wife (unlike Clytemnestra, who took a lover in her husband's absence). Penelope suffered, however, from the Greek tradition that required that a woman take a husband or live with her family. Many suitors gathered in the household, eating and drinking and urging Penelope to select one of them as her husband to replace the long-absent Odysseus. She staved them off by a ruse: She said she first must finish weaving a shroud for her father-in-law, Laertes. She then wove all day, but every night she unraveled what she had created. After three years of this delay, the suitors discovered her trickery and told her she must finish it and choose.

Finally, twenty years after Odysseus's departure, the wanderer washed ashore on his native land. Athena disguised him as an old beggar and clothed him in rags. Odysseus waited at a beggar's hut while he planned how to rid his household of the 112 insolent suitors. Athena brought Odysseus's son, Telemachus, to meet his father, and the two had a tearful reunion. They agreed not to tell Penelope of his return yet. The two went to the household, where Odysseus was given the hospitality accorded beggars. Penelope invited him to talk to her to see if he had word of her husband. Maintaining his disguise, Odysseus spun a long tale but promised Penelope that her husband would return soon.

On the following day at a banquet, one of the suitors finally exerted more pressure on Penelope to choose her next husband. Penelope announced that she was ready to accept any suitor who could match Odysseus's skill and shoot an arrow through the rings of twelve axes that were set in a straight row. She further told them they

had to use Odysseus's bow, which was very hard to pull. Some suitors tried but did not have enough strength even to string the great bow. No one could accomplish the feat. Then Odysseus in his disguise as an old beggar came forward amid jeers and insults. Taking careful aim, he shot an arrow through every one of the twelve axe rings. Then with his bow, Odysseus began to kill all the suitors. After a difficult battle, all were killed, and Odysseus was reunited with Penelope.

They were not to have a peaceful life together, however. The relatives of the dead suitors came to exact vengeance, and Athena brokered a truce among the fighters. Under the terms of the truce, Odysseus was to go into exile for another ten years while the suitors' families paid reparations to Telemachus, who was the new king. A prophecy had said that Odysseus would be killed by his son, but it was not to be Telemachus who would kill his father. Instead, Telegonus, Odysseus's son by the goddess Circe, whom he had fathered during his long trip home from Troy, raided the seacoast. Odysseus set out to repel the invaders without knowing who was there. Telegonus killed him on the seashore with a spear tipped with the spine of a sting ray.

Telegonus had to spend a year in exile to compensate for killing his father. But then he returned and married Penelope. Telemachus then married Telegonus's mother, Circe, and both branches of the family became closely united. Penelope was not remembered for the incestuous second marriage, however. Instead, she was remembered as the model of the faithful, patient wife.

See also Clytemnestra; Helen of Troy in Greek
   Mythology
Suggested Readings
Grimal, Pierre. *The Dictionary of Classical Mythology.* Oxford: Blackwell, 1996.
Homer. *The Odyssey.* Trans. E. V. Rieu. New York: Penguin, 1976.

Perpetua the Martyr

(ca. A.D. 181–203)

In the late second century A.D., the Roman Empire seemed at its height of territorial and military might. Yet many people felt a spiritual long-ing that led them to join new cults even as they worshiped the traditional pagan gods and god-desses of Rome. This spiritual quest was partic-ularly evident in Carthage, a city in North Africa (shown on Map 7). Carthage was a cos-mopolitan city of about 100,00 people, second only to Rome itself in power and wealth, and here people (and ideas) from all parts of the em-pire mingled. In the northern suburbs of the city, there was a large Jewish community (prob-ably at least 5,000 strong), and this neighbor-hood also included small groups of people who gathered together several times a week to wor-ship Jesus Christ. Most Romans had never heard of the "Jewish prophet" who had been crucified as a criminal almost two hundred years earlier. But members of the small Christian communi-ties believed he was God who had come to earth to satisfy people's spiritual longings. In Carthage when Perpetua was born, there were probably about 2,000 Christians who met regularly to-gether in joyful celebration.

Perpetua herself was raised in a prosperous Roman family who worshiped the pagan gods in the traditional fashion. Well educated by her family, Perpetua could read and write in three languages—Greek, Latin, and the local dialect called Punic. When she was about twenty years old, the young woman married and by the fol-lowing year was nursing an infant son. In spite of a pampered upbringing, Perpetua was drawn to Christianity sometime in her late teens. She must have attended some Christian services and decided she wanted to learn more about the new religion. Therefore, she became a catechumen—that is, she was studying about Christianity to prepare herself to be baptized as a full member of the church. The power of Rome intervened, however, to challenge the strength of the young woman's faith.

In A.D. 202, the emperor Septimius Severus decided to stop the spread of Judaism and Christianity, so he passed a law forbidding any-one to convert to either of these religions. In the next year, the local Carthaginian governor sent soldiers to Perpetua's home, where they ar-rested two Christian slaves and Perpetua her-self. Perpetua's father was distraught by his daughter's insistence upon proclaiming her Christian faith and begged her to renounce her beliefs and avoid jail. The young woman was adamant, however, and while under house ar-rest, she was baptized, thus defying the em-peror's law. She and five other Christians were tried and sentenced to be killed by wild beasts in the arena on the occasion of the birthday of the emperor's son.

Through this sentence Perpetua was to share the fate of many similar Christian martyrs. This young woman set herself apart, however, be-cause while in prison she kept a diary of the last few days of her life. This diary offers us a rare glimpse into the mind and feelings of a young Roman woman and remains a moving docu-ment. Perpetua tells of her arrest and of her fear and concern for her infant son: "I was terrified, as I had never before been in such a dark hole. What a difficult time it was! . . . I was tortured with worry for my baby there" (Salisbury 85). She describes her final trial where she pro-claimed her Christianity in spite of her father's pleas and how her parents took her son away from her. She returned to prison to await the day of her death.

Most of her diary describes four dreams she had in prison. Within these dreams we can see her belief that she would go to heaven after her ordeal. She also dreamed that she could help ease the suffering of her little brother who had died years before of cancer. Perpetua ended her diary after these reassuring dreams by giving the text to another member of the Christian com-munity. This narrator completed the story by recording what happened to the other prisoners and by describing their death in the arena. The narrator told how Perpetua and her female com-panion, Felicity, were brutally buffeted by a wild long-horned cow while the crowd cheered. He also wrote how her male companions were at-tacked by leopards and bears. Finally, he de-scribed the deaths of the badly wounded Chris-tians: They were brought to a scaffold where a gladiator slit their throats. Perpetua was the last to die, and the gladiator missed her throat, painfully cutting her shoulder. She bravely guided his hand and gave herself the death blow across her own throat.

Many pagans converted to Christianity after watching the brave young people face death, and the bodies of the martyrs were buried with care and awe. After Christianity became accepted in the Roman Empire (ca. A.D. 313), their bodies were moved to a great church, and every year Christians conducted a celebration on the date of their martyrdom. Perpetua's influence continued because for centuries priests read her diary annually to the congregation to remind them of the young woman's strength and vision. Today, many look to the text of Perpetua's diary to argue for women to serve as priests and leaders in the church. Other Christians see proof in her dreams of the existence of heaven and of the benefits of praying for the dead. For all readers, however, Perpetua's writing offers precious insight into the mind and life of a brave, talented woman of the ancient world.

See also Felicity; Isis; Julia Domna

Suggested Readings

Fiorenza, Elizabeth Schussler. *In Memory of Her: A Feminist Theological Reconstruction of Christian Origins.* New York: Crossroad, 1983.

Ide, Arthur Frederick. *Martyrdom of Women: A Study of Death Psychology in the Early Christian Church to 301 C.E.* Garland, TX: Tangelwüld Press, 1985.

Laporte, Jean. *The Role of Women in Early Christianity.* Lewiston, NY: Edwin Mellen Press, 1982.

Musurillo, H., comp. and trans. *The Acts of the Christian Martyrs.* Oxford: Oxford University Press, 1972.

Salisbury, Joyce E. *Perpetua's Passion: Death and Memory of a Young Roman Woman.* New York: Routledge, 1997.

Persian Women

(539–330 B.C.)

In the sixth century B.C., the political history of the ancient Middle East took a dramatic turn: Cyrus the Great (ca. 601–ca. 530 B.C.) seized the crown of the Persians—a people who lived on the plateau in modern Iran. (See Map 3.) In the 540s B.C., Cyrus conducted an astonishing series of military campaigns that won him a wide empire stretching from India through Mesopotamia into Lydia. Shortly after Cyrus's death, the Persians conquered Egypt, thus creating a single empire out of the ancient peoples in this region. The Persians were tolerant rulers—the Jews were able to return to their homeland and rebuild their temple, and all peoples were allowed a generous degree of religious and cultural autonomy.

The imperial structure reached its fullest development under Darius the Great (521–486 B.C.). The court was centered at a great fortress-palace at Persepolis (see Map 3) ruled by an absolute hereditary monarchy assisted by a central council of nobles. The provinces were administered by local governors called *satraps.* Although the provinces, or *satrapies,* retained much local control, the king kept close watch over them through a network of imperial inspectors, who tried to make sure the satraps remained both honest and loyal. Commerce was stimulated by an extensive network of roads and the introduction of imperial coinage. This powerful empire confronted the growing strength of the Greek city-states and fought wars against the Greeks, which were immortalized by the Greek historian Herodotus (ca. 484–424 B.C.) and which stimulated the rise of Athens. The Persian Empire remained a vigorous force until it was conquered by Alexander the Great in 331 B.C.

For the 200 years of its history, the Persian Empire stimulated much writing on the part of the Greeks, who found their powerful enemy interesting and very foreign. This empire has also captured the imagination of subsequent historians, who have tried to rise above the ancient Greek negative propaganda to understand the life of the enterprising Persians. Perhaps one of the most difficult areas to reconstruct from the Persian Empire is the role and position of the Persian women—the women of the royal household in Persepolis, the noble women of the satrapies, and the everyday women of the empire. Part of the problem is that the most detailed sources are from the Greeks—particularly the historian Herodotus—and they neither understood nor liked Persian customs. The description offered here of some of the information from the Greek sources is contrasted with what information we can glean from other sources to try to glimpse a fuller picture of Persian women.

Unlike the Greeks, the Persian kings—and perhaps the nobility—took many wives. Marriages were used as political alliances, so many wives meant more alliances. The earliest Persian kings entered politically motivated marriages with daughters of Persian nobles and with daughters of non-Persian royalty, and these marriage practices reflect the need of the Persian kings to expand their political dominance. In addition, the kings seemed to have a number of concubines who often also reflected political alliances: the daughters of lower officials than kings did not have the right of becoming wives but could still bind an alliance by becoming concubines. With all these women at the court, the Greek historians credited Persian women with exerting a great deal of influence over the king, but the reality was more complicated.

In one highly implausible example, Herodotus describes how Cambyses (530–521 B.C.), the son of Cyrus, was killed and his place taken by an impostor named Smerdis (or Gaumata), who pretended to be Cambyses. One of the Persian nobles, Otanes, suspected that there was an impostor on the throne, and he sent a message to his daughter, Phaedyme, who was one of Cambyses's wives. He asked her if the man with whom she slept was Cambyses or someone else. According to Herodotus, Phaedyme did not know with whom she slept. Otanes told her how to tell: the suspected pretender had had his ears cut off as punishment, so when Phaedyme slept with him she was to secretly feel for his ears—if they were missing, then he was not the son of Cyrus the Great. She bravely felt for his ears and discovered they were missing. Then the Persian nobles came in and removed the impostor, and Darius the Great took the throne.

The details of the Greek version of this story seem a little far-fetched—surely the wife would have other ways to recognize her husband beyond the presence of ears! All the Persian sources, however, confirm that this was a turbulent time during which a palace revolt brought Darius to power. We also know that Darius consolidated his rule by marrying royal daughters. He married Cyrus's daughter Atossa and Otanes's daughter Phaedyme, who had previously been married to Cambyses. In this way, the Greek belief that the palace women were important to Darius's rule seems accurate. The new king also married several other noble daughters. His position thus ensured, Darius continued on to consolidate his rule and earn the appellation "the Great."

Darius responded to a Greek revolt in Asia Minor by invading the Greek mainland in the first of the Persian Wars. The great Persian army was defeated at the Battle of Marathon in 490 B.C. While the motivation for Darius's invasion was surely the revolt of the Greeks within the empire, Herodotus attributes his desire to invade to Atossa—Darius's favorite wife. She came to know of Greece through a talented Greek physician who had cured a sore that had erupted on her breast. She urged Darius to expand his empire by invading Greece, and according to Herodotus, he did so. While this is another story that is not likely to be accurate (for example, the invasion of Greece was twenty years after the event of her cure, so that seems too long to be linked causally), it once again reflects the Greek tendency to call the Persians weak by being dominated by their too-independent women.

What was the reality of the influence of the royal women? It is clear that at least two women in the royal court had a good deal of influence—the king's mother and the mother of the royal heir. Once Darius had declared Xerxes to be his heir, Xerxes's mother, Atossa, gained considerable status at court. Herodotus's animosity toward Atossa probably increased because her son Xerxes continued the Persian Wars by invading Greece again (only to be repulsed again at the Battle of Salamis in which Artemisia, a woman admiral, led a portion of the Persian fleet). Persian women's political influence, however, must have been fairly limited.

With so many women at the court, they did not have unlimited access to the king. They had to wait for an audience or talk to him when he chose to visit their beds. Furthermore, it appears that the women were frequently separated from one another, so this was not a setting like later harems of women. For example, Phaedyme claimed she could not consult with Atossa on the question of whether or not her husband had ears, for the women did not see each other. Their political influence was limited and probably did not extend much beyond household and family matters. In one area royal women did seem able to exert influence with the king—this was to ask for clemency for family members who had fallen out of favor. In this circumstance, it seems that the Persians believed that women's roles were to look out for their relatives. After all, it was for this that their fathers had arranged their marriages to the king—such political influence was certainly expected.

If the Greek sources overstated the political influence of some of the Persian royal wives, they completely underestimated the amount of freedom Persian women did have. Persian women appeared in public and in many cases seemed to enhance the status of their royal husbands. The statue of the Persian woman in her elegant robes shown in Figure 60 gives an example of their official appearance. The Persian sources refer to noblewomen as appearing at banquets and eating and drinking with the men (a practice that shocked the Greeks). Even Alexander the Great met his wife, Roxane, who was the daughter of a local king, when she joined a feast with thirty other young women. So, Persian women mingled with men in a number of informal settings.

Perhaps even more surprising to the Greek observers, Persian women accompanied their noble husbands and lovers on hunting trips or even military campaigns. One Persian nobleman foolishly took his Greek concubine to war with him against the Greeks, and when she got close to her homeland, she escaped. Xerxes entrusted his family to his admiral, Artemisia, after the Battle of Salamis so she could return them safely to Persia. Perhaps the most famous example of a family going to war with the great king was when Darius III (336–330 B.C.) confronted Alexander the Great. The account of the battle told how Persian women accompanied their men to battle riding in golden chariots and bringing their furnishings and jewelry. At the Battle of Issus in 330 B.C., Alexander captured Darius's family and used the occasion to show his generosity to captive women.

Noble Persian women also traveled on their own without being accompanied by their husbands, which is further indication of the independence they experienced. Persian records

Figure 60. Woman in Persian dress (Brooklyn Museum)

show one woman who traveled to Syria to persuade her husband to abandon a revolt, and Parysatis, mother of Cyrus the Younger, traveled to Babylon to supervise the return of her son's body. Persian economic records show the amounts of rations allocated to female members of noble families for their travel expenses, and these indicate both the frequency of travel and the extent of the entourage that accompanied the noblewomen. For example, when the daughter of Darius I took a trip in 498 B.C., she

Figure 61. Persian miniature from a manuscript depicting lovers (Ann Ronan Picture Library)

was issued 176 quarts of wine for the four-day excursion. So women had a good deal of freedom of movement, but the really striking indication of the freedom of some Persian women was their economic status.

The Persian records also indicate that noblewomen owned and managed huge amounts of property on their own. Even some of the Greek sources recognize the wealth of noblewomen. For example, the Greek philosopher Plato referred to the vast amount of property owned by Amestris, the mother of the Persian king Artaxerxes I (465–424 B.C.). Similarly, the Greek Xenophon describes the wealth of Parysatis, mother of Cyrus the Younger, who had such vast estates in Syria that she could draw from them and supply troops for her son to use in his revolt against Artaxerxes II (404–358 B.C.). Such extensive landholding by Greek women was uncommon, so the Greek authors mentioned it as remarkable, but it was expected of many of the Persian noblewomen.

Texts that list supplies and production in the Persian Empire matter-of-factly list noblewomen as the owners and indeed the managers of many estates. Darius's wife, Artystone, wrote letters ordering supplies for her estates and sealed the letters with her personal seal. From the surviving records, it appears that Artystone had at least three large estates throughout the empire, each of which was administered by a steward to whom she addressed her orders. And she was not unique. It was typical for many noblewomen to own and run large estates and to gain great personal wealth from these sources.

These economic sources also shed some light on nonnoble Persian women, for they list large numbers of skilled and unskilled workers who labored on the estates. These lists included women and children as well as men, and the women were frequently paid the same rate as the men who worked alongside them. Unfortunately the vocabulary of the lists is unclear, and the records are incomplete, so we do not know exactly what kind of work these large workforces did. Nevertheless such lists are a clear testimony to women's involvement in the economy, from the richest royal women to the poorest workers on the estates. The system was so different from that of the Greek city-states that it is perhaps no wonder that the Greek sources felt so compelled to comment negatively on the influence of women in the Persian Empire.

Persia fell to the Macedonian armies of Alexander the Great, who spread Greek culture throughout the whole region. In the process, Greek culture itself was transformed, becoming what we call the "Hellenistic culture." One of the characteristics of the Hellenistic world was that women gained more freedom to own land, work, and participate in many aspects of life than they ever had in the classical Athenian society of the city-states. Furthermore, Hellenistic

queens from Alexander's mother, Olympias, to the famous Cleopatra VII exerted a remarkable amount of authority. Many scholars have attributed the position of women in the Hellenistic world to the Macedonians, who seemed to have expected their women to be strong and outspoken. It may also be that the many women in the Persian Empire who had become used to exerting a good deal of economic power also influenced the Greeks as they moved east. The Greek armies may have conquered the Persian Empire, but perhaps some of the sovereignty of the little-understood Persian women influenced the ways of the Greeks.

> *See also* Artemisia; Cleopatra VII; Egyptian
>   Women; Esther; Greek (Athenian) Women
> **Suggested Readings**
> Brosius, Maria. *Women in Ancient Persia (559–331*
>   *B.C.).* Oxford: Clarendon Press, 1996.
> Cook, J. M. *The Persian Empire.* New York:
>   Schocken Books, 1983.
> Curtis, J. *Ancient Persia.* Cambridge: Harvard
>   University Press, 1990.
> Dicks, B. *The Ancient Persians.* North Pomfret, VT:
>   David and Charles, 1979.
> Herodotus. *The History.* Trans. D. Grene. Chicago:
>   University of Chicago Press, 1987.

Phila

Macedonian Queen (r. 294–289 B.C.)

When Alexander the Great was campaigning in the east, conquering the vast territories that ultimately created the Hellenistic kingdoms, he left his trusted friend, Antipater, in Macedonia as regent to rule on his behalf. Antipater's greatest rival had been Alexander's mother, Olympias, and with his dying breath the regent warned Macedonians not to ever accept rule by a queen. In spite of this attitude, Antipater shared with other ancient men the desire to ensure power for their grandchildren through good marriages for their daughters. Antipater had many sons and daughters, and three of his daughters married successors of Alexander the Great who became kings. One of his daughters—Phila—married two successors and remarkably in a violent age earned a reputation for virtue and kindness.

In 322 B.C., less than one year after Alexander's death, Antipater gave his daughter Phila to

Craterus, his close friend who seemed certain to rise in fame and power. Phila had been Antipater's favorite, and even when she was a girl her father had consulted her about affairs of state and valued her judgment. In addition to wisdom, the sources say she had the virtues of kindness and pity, and her father had found a splendid husband for her. Craterus was hugely popular—charming, handsome, and brave on the battlefield. The couple had one son named Craterus after his proud father. The marriage was brief, however, for Craterus died in battle.

Antipater very quickly found another politically expedient marriage for Phila—to Demetrius, the son of Antigonus, the governor of Asia. The marriage was arranged so rapidly that when Phila received the body of Craterus for burial, she had already been remarried. Demetrius was only eighteen when he married Phila, a woman of thirty, and Phila once again found herself married to a man of heroic beauty. Demetrius was so handsome that strangers followed him in the streets for the pleasure it gave them to see him. Demetrius valued Phila's wisdom and political acumen as much as her father had and consulted her regularly on matters of state.

The sources all say that Phila deeply loved her husband, even though he was famous for his many lovers; his longest-standing mistress was Lamia, a woman as old as Phila. Demetrius and Phila had a son named Antigonus, and even though the Macedonian kings were polygamous, Demetrius did not take another wife until 307 B.C. Then he married an Athenian woman named Eurydice, who bore him a son. This marriage did not seem to affect Phila very much, for Demetrius only visited Eurydice occasionally, and the Athenian was not highly placed politically. More threatening was Demetrius's marriage in 303 B.C. to Deidameia, sister of the king of Epirus. This high-born princess could well displace Phila as Demetrius's most important wife. Deidameia bore Demetrius a son, named Alexander, but she died shortly thereafter.

By now, Phila lived as queen in Macedonia, much beloved by the people there. Her position was secure, and her son, Antigonus, was his father's second-in-command. The sources claim that Macedonia had never before had a queen of such wisdom. For example, the Greek historian Diodorus wrote: "She strove to see that justice was done and she was generous with her wealth" (Macurdy 66).

Demetrius perhaps should have rested on his laurels at this point, but he did not. Ever seeking more glory and new adventures, the bold man began with a new wedding. In 292 B.C., he agreed to marry a princess—Lanassa—who brought the island of Corcyra as her wedding gift to him. At the wedding, Demetrius acted with such pride—claiming to be king of kings—that he alienated his Macedonian troops. Then disaster struck—he lost an important battle and lost with it the throne of Macedonia exactly at a time when he was preparing to invade Asia. The Hellenistic kings were all against him, and the Macedonians told Demetrius that they were sick of a spendthrift king and that he had better leave to save his life. He went into his tent and changed his royal purple cloak for a plain black one and went to where Phila was staying. Phila could not endure the loss of her country and the sight of her beloved king in flight. She took poison. She did not live to see her husband marry again and recover much of his wealth and power. Nor did she live to see the splendid funeral procession that brought the ashes of Demetrius home for burial. The unselfish woman would probably have been pleased for her husband. In spite of her tragic death, she was remarkable in living through the violent times after the death of Alexander the Great, preserving her reputation for wisdom and kindness. She died beloved by her people and her children and remembered as a fine queen.

See also Eurydice I; Olympias [Macedonian Queen]
Suggested Readings
Macurdy, Grace Harriet. *Hellenistic Queens.*
    Baltimore: Johns Hopkins University Press, 1932.

Philomela
Legendary Greek Woman
Early Greek myths told of the origins of the royal house of Athens. Among the stories of the legendary founders of the royal family, the most

tragic (and one of the most popular) was that of the misfortunes of the two sisters of an Athenian king. Their names were Procne and Philomela.

Procne, the elder sister, was married to Tereus of Thrace, a son of the war-god Ares. The two had a son named Itys, and when he was five years old, Procne begged Tereus to let her invite her sister, Philomela, to visit her, for she was lonely for her family. He agreed and said he would go to Athens himself to escort Philomela to his home. As soon as he set eyes on the young woman, however, he fell in love with her, for she was as beautiful as a nymph. The lovely Philomela readily agreed to travel with Tereus, for she suspected nothing of his motives. All went well on the voyage, but when they landed and traveled overland for the palace, Tereus told Philomela that he had received news of Procne's death and that her father had consented to his marrying her. He forced her to bed with him.

The sources agree on the horrible consequences of Tereus's betrayal, but they differ on the details. In one version he hides Procne and cuts out her tongue so she cannot tell of his betrayal. In another, it is Philomela who was imprisoned and mutilated by removing her tongue. Whichever sister was imprisoned, she managed to tell the other of her plight by means of a message woven into a piece of tapestry.

The sisters determined to rescue each other and take revenge on Tereus. When they had again found each other, they wept in each other's arms. Then the instrument of their revenge appeared: Procne's little son, Itys, came into the room. At that instant the mother realized how much like his father was the beloved son, and a plan came into her mind. She grabbed the boy and killed him with one stroke of a dagger. She dismembered his body, and the sisters cooked him in a large kettle. Procne then served the horrifying dinner to Tereus that night. She watched him as he ate; then she told him what he had eaten.

In his first horror, he could not move, and the sisters fled. He overtook them, however, and was about to kill them when suddenly the gods turned them into birds. Philomela became a nightingale and Procne a swallow. The legends say that the nightingale sings a mournful song, ever mourning the death of Itys. The swallow cannot sing, since Procne had no tongue, so it just screams. (Some versions reverse the transformations, making Procne the nightingale.) Tereus too was changed into a bird—an ugly beaked bird or a hawk. It is perhaps because of the particularly horrible nature of the revenge taken by the sisters that this legend was repeated throughout the Roman period.

See also Nymphs

Suggested Readings

Grimal, Pierre. *The Dictionary of Classical Mythology.* Oxford: Blackwell, 1996.

Hamilton, Edith. *Mythology.* New York: Mentor, 1955.

Philosophers, Greek

Philosophy is a Greek word that originally meant "love of wisdom," and early Greek philosophers established a new way to look at the world. Abandoning the emphasis on the supernatural that shaped other ancient western societies, the Greeks used rational thought—logic—to explore the world and the place of humans and gods within it. In doing so, famous philosophers such as Socrates, Plato, Aristotle, and others established an approach that continues to form the basis of modern philosophical speculations. From the dawn of philosophy, women were excited about the new ideas and became "lovers of wisdom." The constraints experienced by women in ancient Greek society, however, restricted their participation, so the numbers of women philosophers from ancient Greece are few, and many are connected to family members who engaged in philosophy. This is not surprising, because since women did not have free access to move about and choose their interests, women with direct contact with philosophers would most easily become engaged in the study. In spite of the constraints, a number of women made an impact in the history of philosophy of ancient Greece.

Probably the first school to have encouraged the study of philosophy by women was that of the Pythagoreans in the mid-sixth century B.C. The Pythagoreans believed that reason, which was the most important human characteristic, was unaffected by gender, so women could engage in philosophic study. Tradition holds that Pythagoras himself studied under the Delphic priestess Themistoclea, which not only links him to a woman but also gave his philosophic musings divine authority. Pythagoras established a community—and school—for studying philosophy, and in a striking departure from traditional Greek practice, women were welcome to attend. The *Life of Pythagoras,* written in about the fourth century A.D., records seventeen women followers of Pythagoras, whom the author describes as "the most illustrious." That perhaps implies that there were also others. This lifestyle also generated criticism; at least two ancient comedies written in the fourth century B.C. by Cratinus the Younger and Alexis bore the title *The Woman Who Pythagorises,* which no doubt made fun of the participation of women in the Pythagorean community.

Pythagoras married one of his female pupils, Theano, who followed him as the leader of the school. His daughters—Myia, Arignote, and Damo—also became Pythagoreans. Late Pythagorean women—from the fourth century B.C. to about the first century A.D.—included Phintys, Aesara of Lucania, Perictione, and possibly another Theano. We know little about most of these women because we only have some fragments of their writings (or of writings attributed to them), but from these fragments we can identify something of their interests.

While these women shared the interests of male philosophers in the basic principles of science, mathematics, and human behavior, the women also frequently added commentaries on topics of specific interest to women. For example, Aesara of Lucania said that human nature provided the standard for law and justice in the home as well as in the city; thus the principles of philosophy had relevance to women. A surviving fragment attributed to Theano (probably the later one) shows how she applied the Pythagorean principle of "harmony" to a woman who was coping with an unfaithful husband and showed how this principle could help such a woman decide what she ought to do and how she ought to act. Phintys and Perictione applied the concept of harmony to the question of how

women ought to act in public and private life. These Pythagoreans show how fruitful the interaction of men and women in the schools and communities could be, but subsequent philosophic schools were not as inclusive.

The pursuit of philosophy in Athens took a giant leap forward with the life and career of Socrates (469–399 B.C.), a stonemason by profession but a philosopher by calling. He spent his life talking to people in the marketplace of Athens and asking questions designed to lead students to insights into such large questions as truth, beauty, and justice. Socrates left no writings himself, but his pupils recorded many of his conversations, which allow us to study some of the ideas of this influential thinker.

Socrates thought that women were equally capable as men of attaining wisdom, but the surviving texts show that Socrates's followers (and likely the master himself) shared the Greek notion of differential treatment for women. For example, Xenophon in his *Oeconomicus* limits women's learning to domestic duties, and a later writer, Theophrastus, said that women should just have enough knowledge of letters to manage the household, which was their own sphere. Socrates offended many Athenians in the course of his long career of questioning, and they placed him on trial in 399 B.C. for impiety and corrupting youth. The Athenians sentenced him to death, and he drank a cup of poison hemlock to fulfill the sentence rather than stop his life of philosophy. His work was taken up by his brilliant student, Plato, whose writings have marked him as one of the greatest philosophers in western culture.

Plato established a school called the Academy in an olive grove outside Athens, where he drew many of the brightest minds of the day. At the core of Plato's philosophy was the idea that everyone had a soul that was immaterial, eternal, and nonsexual; only our bodies are different. Thus the souls of men and women alike could study philosophy, and the goal for everyone was to try to focus on our souls and detach from the material world, including gender. Perhaps not surprisingly, given the equality at the heart of his philosophy, the sources record women connected with Plato's academy.

There was a tradition that Plato's mother, Perictione, was a philosopher, but it is difficult to substantiate this claim, and it may just be a later literary convention. Other women certainly studied with Plato. Diogenes Laertius in his *Lives of the Philosophers* records two women—Axiothea and Lasthenia—who were pupils of Plato and of his successors.

According to one source, Axiothea lived in Arcadia, a region in the southwest of Greece, and she read Plato's *Republic,* in which he outlined how an ideal society should be governed. She was so impressed by the work that she traveled to Athens to become a follower of Plato. Although *The Republic* maintains the equality of women with men as potential members of the guardian class, Axiothea had to dress as a man to gain admittance to Plato's lectures; Plato's ideal world had certainly not been implemented. Axiothea also studied under Plato's successor as head of the Academy, Speusippus. Diogenes Laertius also mentions Lasthenia in connection with Axiothea as a student of Speusippus. He tantalizingly tells us only "one may learn philosophy too from your female disciple from Arcadia" (Waithe 209), but he offers no more information about what Lasthenia taught. We would like to know more about these women who studied under Plato, but the sources unfortunately offer nothing more than the evidence of their presence.

One of Socrates's followers was a man named Aristippus, who went to North Africa to the city of Cyrene to found his own school of philosophy. Aristippus made Socrates's definition of virtue concrete by equating "good" with pleasure, and thus the Cyrenaics held that true happiness depended upon an absence of wants. While this school is considered one of the first proponents of hedonism—or the search for pleasure as a way of life—its followers nevertheless claimed that education and intelligence were necessary as guides to proper enjoyment. Aristippus's daughter, Arete, succeeded her father as head of the Cyrenaic school. The sources report that she taught philosophy for thirty-five years to well over a hundred students and that she wrote forty books. Unfortunately, none has survived. She was the mother of Aristippus the Younger, who went by a nickname that means "taught by his mother." An epigraph on her tomb records the accomplishments of this remarkable woman: "She was the splendor of Greece and possessed the beauty of Helen, the virtue of Thirma, the pen of Aristippus, the soul of Socrates, and the tongue of Homer" (Waithe 198). One could not wish for a better epigraph.

Plato's greatest student was Aristotle (384–322 B.C.), who departed from Plato in a number of areas. Aristotle did not share Plato's belief in the basic similarity of men and women. His scientific and biological studies led him to think of women only as connected to their physical nature, and he maintained that women were biologically inferior to men (*see* Gynecology). In effect, he claimed that men were perfect and that when nature made a mistake, a woman was formed. He believed that since women were weaker than men, their mental capacities were also weaker, so women could not be real philosophers. It is perhaps not surprising that we have no evidence for any female pupils of Aristotle.

Aristotle was a teacher of the Macedonian Alexander the Great, whose conquests transformed the classical culture of the ancient Greek city-states and in turn changed the position of women. When Alexander conquered his great empire, Greek culture spread eastward and mingled with the older culture of the east. When Alexander died, his empire broke into large monarchies—the Hellenistic kingdoms—and within these large states, the small city-states no longer held such sway. As city life changed, so did the tight family life that restricted Greek women to the household. In the Hellenistic world, there is much evidence for women who emerged from the shadows and became poets, rulers, and philosophers.

The participation of women in philosophy was also increased by new schools of philosophy that grew up in response to new situations. No longer were philosophers primarily interested in the large questions of truth and justice that consumed Plato, but instead they wondered how individuals could live a good life in a chaotic world. Neopythagorean communities flourished in Alexandria and southern Italy, and these included women philosophers just as the earlier communities had. Scholars still debate whether or not a number of fragments of writings from Neopythagoreans were written by women. Certainly they discuss topics that had been traditionally linked with women—the education of children, choice of a nurse, control of slaves, manner of dress, and so on—and they were attributed to women. There is no real reason to doubt their authorship, and at the very least, they demonstrate that writings purportedly written by women could circulate and be taken seriously in the world of Hellenistic philosophers.

The Epicureans of the early fourth century B.C. developed a philosophy that claimed that the good life could be had by studying in a community of companions. The woman Leontium (*see* Leontium) was a member of this community and shows the appeal to women of this kind of life. Cynics believed the good life could be attained by despising things of this world, and some women, too, followed this philosophy. (*See* Hipparchia.)

Another significant philosophic school of the Hellenistic world was the Stoic, founded by the Greek Zeno (third century B.C.). The Stoics claimed there was no difference between men and women, and all should study philosophy. Although we do not have any record of women Stoics, a number of the later Stoic writings encouraged women to study philosophy so that they, too, could enjoy an easier life. The Roman Stoic Musonius Rufus (first century A.D.) wrote essays called "That Women Too Should Study Philosophy" and "Should Daughters Receive the Same Education as Sons," which explicitly support the study of philosophy by women. We do not know in what specific incidents women were affected by such writings.

The ambiguity of women's participation in Stoic philosophy might serve as an appropriate conclusion to this brief summary of ancient women's participation in philosophy. Our sources can tell us what philosophers believed about women—Aristotle dismissing their potential while Pythagoras, Epicurus, and Plato supported it—but we do not have any substantial information about how those ideas affected the lives of many real women. Where philosophers founded communities and gathered pupils together, there was more opportunity for women to enter along with their relatives or lovers, but most participants remained anonymous and thus forgotten by history. We can identify a few women, however, who made their mark in a field that had been dominated by men, and perhaps the very difficulty of the task makes these "lovers of wisdom" all the more admirable.

See also Aspasia; Diotima of Mantinea; Greek (Athenian) Women; Hipparchia; Hypatia; Leontium; Theano

Suggested Readings

Diogenes Laertius. *Lives of Eminent Philosophers.* Trans. R. D. Hicks. Cambridge: Harvard University Press, 1925.

Hawley, Richard. "The Problem of Women Philosophers in Ancient Greece." In *Women in Ancient Societies,* ed. by L. J. Archer et al. New York: Routledge, 1994.

Kersey, Ethel M. *Women Philosophers: A Bio-Critical Source Book.* New York: Greenwood Press, 1989.

Menage, Gilles. *The History of Women Philosophers.* Trans. Beatrice H. Zedlin. Lanham, MD: University Press of America, 1984.

Waithe, Mary Ellen, ed. *A History of Women Philosophers.* Vol. 1: *600 B.C.–500 A.D.* Boston: Martinus Nijhoff Publishers, 1987.

Plancia Magna

Roman Benefactress (b. ca. A.D. 100)

By the first century A.D., the cities of the provinces of the Roman Empire offered great opportunities for people to prosper, and these territories drew enterprising Romans from Italy. In the first century B.C. at the end of the republic, one such family—the Plancii—came to Perge in Asia Minor (in modern southwest Turkey) from Italy (see Map 7 of the Roman Empire). They came to make their fortune as traders and succeeded in becoming very wealthy. By the late first century A.D. the head of the family, M. Plancius Varus, rose to the governorship of a province in Asia. Plancius was in a position to arrange a fine marriage for his daughter, Plancia Magna.

Plancia Magna married C. Julius Cornutus Tertullus, a man who was at least as old as her father—probably in his sixties when they married. Tertullus was a wealthy provincial, who also had achieved high office in the empire. Both Tertullus and Plancius Varus owned many estates far away from Perge, which brought even more wealth into their coffers. In the tradition of Rome, one would expect Plancia Magna to have lived modestly in the shadows of her illustrious father and husband, but remarkably she emerges from the past as a woman who rose to prominence in her own name. How was she able to do so? She used money combined with what must have been her own ambition for public position.

It was unusual for a woman (especially one in her twenties as Plancia must have been when she married) to control her own wealth. Public inscriptions indicate that Plancia spent her own money—and spent it lavishly—without control of her husband. Therefore, her father must have split a substantial inheritance between Plancia Magna and her brother. While her brother used his funds in a traditionally Roman way to advance his own career, Plancia Magna used hers to acquire public status. It may be that the men of her family were pursuing their public careers in Rome while Plancia upheld the family's status at Perge.

During the Roman Republic and on into the empire, Romans—usually men—frequently used their wealth to contribute to public causes. They built great buildings or other public monuments, endowed and supported priesthoods, or paid for public spectacles such as games. In return for such largesse, the patron's political and social eminence was celebrated by the grateful populace. Wealth for a Roman was used primarily to buy the respect—indeed adulation—of the community. This system—called evergetism—lay at the heart of the public life of the Hellenistic Greek and Roman civilizations and helped contribute to many of the accomplishments that have endured. Both sides of Plancia Magna's family engaged in this kind of public display. Her father had dedicated a city gate of Nicaea to the imperial house, and in return he was called the patron of that city. A husband and wife of the Cornuti family had dedicated a gymnasium at Perge and were commemorated publicly by at least four inscriptions. Plancia's largesse and her accolades far exceeded those of these relatives, and it is through the grateful inscriptions that we can glimpse this ancient woman.

At the beginning of the second century A.D., a complete renovation was undertaken on Perge's gate and its two round towers. The new gate included a courtyard; a new marble, two-storied, columnar facade; and a new monumental triple arch. There were also statues included in the niches and arch. The statues' bases establish Plancia Magna as the donor of the renovation, which must have cost a fortune. The statues included images of five of the Olympian deities, and in the upper niches stood statues of Plancia's father and brother. The inscriptions of those statues identified them in that way, as related to Plancia, instead of as notable in their own right. This identification shows that Plancia Magna had been the instrumental donor in the courtyard. The great arch that was the highlight of the construction further shows that Plancia Magna was the patron, for the inscription proclaims that Plancia Magna dedicated the arch to her city.

The existence of this monument to Plancia Magna's wealth and generosity alone would have been enough to set her off as an extraordinary ancient woman, but her grateful city awarded her an impressive list of public titles that further show that she played an active role in her city's life. She was designated "daughter of the city" as well as being given the title *demiourgos,* which made her a public official whose name was used for dating purposes. She also held three of the most significant priesthoods: She was priestess of Artemis, the most important deity in Perge; also priestess of the "mother of the gods"; and finally she was the priestess of the imperial cult of the emperor—perhaps the most political of the religious appointments. In addition, she received one more highly public appointment: she was the director of the gymnasium, which was the physical and intellectual school for young men, and the heart of the Hellenistic cities. Clearly, Plancia Magna took an active and influential role in the life of her city, and this was probably made possible as a result of the wealth that she controlled. But it also must have been owing to her own energetic determination to gain a public reputation.

Was she unique in this? She had other models of public women, and it seems that the presence of role models is one of the factors that help women step out of their expected roles. There were imperial women who often traveled with the emperors, and during Plancia Magna's lifetime, Plotina, Trajan's wife, had intervened on behalf of the Jews in Alexandria. This kind of activity was not limited to the imperial household, for the wives, daughters, and other relatives of Roman governors traveled in the provinces and gave donations and were publicly honored. After Plancia Magna's generous endowment, another woman in a neighboring city also built a city gate with her own money (though it was not as grand as Plancia's), and other wealthy women in the provinces also received important public offices.

In the eastern provinces of the Roman Empire, in the world heavily influenced by the Hellenistic kingdoms and influential Hellenistic women, some Roman women rose to local prominence. If they had wealth and inclination, they could contribute materially to their cities, and in return, the grateful populace awarded them respect, honors, and public position. If today many of these women have faded into the ancient shadows, during their day they stood out brightly in the center of their world.

Figure 62. Plotina (Araldo de Luca/Corbis)

See also Plotina; Roman Women

Suggested Readings

Boatwright, Mary Taliaferro. "Plancia Magna of Perge: Women's Roles and Status in Roman Asia Minor." In *Women's History & Ancient History,* ed. by Sarah B. Pomeroy. Chapel Hill: University of North Carolina Press, 1991.

Van Bremen, R. "Women and Wealth." In *Images of Women in Antiquity,* ed. by A. Cameron and A. Kuhrt. Detroit: Wayne State University Press, 1983.

Plotina

Roman Empress (ca. A.D. 76–ca. 122)

Beginning in A.D. 96, the Roman Empire experienced a period of fine government marked by responsible leadership. This era, known as the "good emperors," extended from A.D. 96 through 180 and included the rules of Nerva, Trajan, Hadrian, Antoninus Pius, and Marcus Aurelius. Many people saw in emperors such as Trajan (r. A.D. 98–117) a restoration of the old virtues of the Roman Republic and the virtuous rule of Augustus. Trajan was considerate, diplomatic, and respectful of the Roman senate. He married a strong, intelligent woman—Plotina—who also left her mark on his reign.

Plotina had been born at Nîmes in modern France (shown on Map 7) to a reasonably distinguished family. Reputedly, she knew the dangers of power and wanted to preserve her integrity even while wielding immense influence. By all accounts, Plotina achieved her goal, and her reputation is preserved (and perhaps enhanced) by the praise offered her in the surviving works of Pliny the Younger. His extravagant prose praised Trajan's wife (and by association, the emperor himself): "Your wife has brought you nothing but renown and distinction. No woman alive has greater integrity or represents more perfectly the best tradition of Roman womanhood. If the High Priest had to choose a wife, she—or some woman like her—would be his certain choice" (Balsdon 134). Plotina was awarded the title of augusta—meaning "empress"—in A.D. 105, after first modestly turning it down. What did she do to earn such praise?

First, she presided over a harmonious household. This included Trajan's sister, Marciana, and Marciana's daughter, Matidia. Marciana was much beloved by her brother, and she, too, received the title of augusta, the first time a woman other than a wife of an emperor had received such a title. The honors increased, for in A.D. 112 both women were given the right to issue coins in their own names (and bearing their own images). One of the things the ancient commentators found remarkable about Plotina was that she and her sister-in-law Marciana lived together peacefully in the household, with no trace of jealousy or animosity. Pliny wrote to Trajan in respectful wonder: "They respect each other, they defer to each other; both are so deeply devoted to you that neither thinks it of the slightest consequence to her which of the two you love better" (Balsdon 136). This wonder was probably heightened by the long history of women's animosity that marked the Julio-Claudian dynasty.

The public honors bestowed by Trajan tell us little about the ways Plotina influenced life within the household or the empire itself. We do have some tantalizing bits of evidence to suggest that she was able to exert some of her opinions. For example, when Trajan betrothed his grandniece Vibia Sabina to Hadrian, the historical records indicate that he was not happy with the match but agreed to it because of Plotina's support. Plotina was also involved in the management of the provinces: when Trajan let his officials extort excessive money from the provinces, Plotina reproached him because she said that such injustice affected his own good name, so Trajan began to reform.

Second, Plotina was an educated woman who was interested in philosophy, in particular Epicureanism (*see* Philosophers, Greek). Inscriptions survive in which she wrote to Hadrian after Trajan's death asking the new emperor to confirm the right of the head of the Epicurean school of philosophy to name his own successor even if that person were not a Roman citizen. Plotina prefaced her request by writing, "How much I am interested in the sect of Epicurus you know very well" (Fantham et al. 353), and this reveals her long-standing interest in philosophy.

Third, Plotina's influence was most felt in the controversial naming of Trajan's successor. For some reason, Trajan had not yet named a successor, even though he was sixty years old. He was healthy and perhaps had not yet decided to name the obvious successor, his second cousin Hadrian, or perhaps Trajan was not yet sure that Hadrian was the best choice. It was rumored that Plotina cared too much for Hadrian (who was about her own age), and she must have supported his succession, since it was she who had insisted that Trajan's grandniece marry Hadrian, thus strengthening his claim to the throne. Thus, the all-important succession was still up in the air when Trajan went to the east to fight a major war in Mesopotamia. Plotina and Hadrian accompanied Trajan on campaign when he left in A.D. 113. Plotina's presence on a military expedition is also suggestive of her influence on him.

Along the way, the people erected statues to the illustrious couple—some to Trajan and some to Plotina. Once in Syria, Trajan left Plotina and moved to the front. In A.D. 114 and 115 his troops claimed a large portion of Mesopotamia as a province, and the following year he took Arabia. Trouble then followed, however. There was an uprising of Jews in Egypt, and in the winter of A.D. 116 Trajan fell ill. He had a stroke, and though he recovered sufficiently to talk of resuming military operations, he was forced to realize (perhaps persuaded by Plotina, who was with him) that he had better take things more easily. He left Hadrian as governor of Syria and began to return home to Rome. His health continued to deteriorate, however, and he had not yet adopted Hadrian as his heir. Finally, on his deathbed it was said he adopted Hadrian, and a declaration to this effect was sent to the Roman senate—but it was signed by Plotina, not Trajan.

Some of Hadrian's critics in Rome claimed that this was all a plot by Plotina to make sure her favorite, Hadrian, would be emperor. It may have been; the sources will not allow us to know for sure. There really was no other candidate for the succession, however, and Plotina may have simply wanted to ensure that the transition would be smooth. In any case, Hadrian proved to be a good emperor, so the succession was a reasonable one.

Plotina lived a few years longer under Hadrian's rule, and when the emperor spoke at her funeral oration, he said, "She often made requests of me, and I never once refused her anything" (Balsdon 138). Hadrian also proclaimed her a goddess at her death, and a temple was erected in her honor. He could well afford to be grateful to the intelligent woman who ensured that his succession to the imperial throne would be smooth. All of Rome, too, might well have thanked her for her intervention.

See also (Julia) Berenice; Philosophers, Greek
Suggested Readings
Balsdon, J. P. V. D. *Roman Women: Their History and Habits.* New York: John Day, 1963.
Fantham, E., et al. *Women in the Classical World.* New York: Oxford University Press, 1994.

Pompeia

Roman Wife of Julius Caesar (ca. 50 B.C.)
Julius Caesar was the brilliant politician who became "dictator for life" at the end of the Roman Republic before it formally became the Roman Empire. In addition to being known as a superior general and a fine writer and being popular with the Roman people, Caesar was known for his marriages and love affairs. Although he scandalized Rome with his affairs with the Egyptian queen Cleopatra VII and with his long-standing mistress, Servilia, Caesar insisted that the women in his life adhere to the strictest standards of behavior expected from Roman matrons. The ancient biographer Plutarch describes how this high standard affected one of Caesar's wives, Pompeia.

After Caesar's first wife, Cornelia, died, he married a woman named Pompeia, about whom little is known except that she was a beautiful woman. This beauty led to an appearance of scandal. A wealthy patrician, Publius Clodius, who was known in Rome for the licentiousness

of his life, fell in love with Pompeia. According to Plutarch, she "had no aversion to him" (Plutarch 859), but they had no opportunity to be alone together. Caesar's mother, Aurelia, lived with the couple and kept a close watch on her daughter-in-law, making any conversation with Clodius dangerous and difficult. An opportunity seemed to arise, however, during a religious ceremony dedicated to the goddess, known as Bona Dea.

Women who celebrated her festival did so within their homes, and it was not permitted for any man to be there. Therefore, at festival time, the husband left the house with every male in the household, and the wife took over the ceremonies. She arranged the celebration, and the ceremonies were performed during the night while the women visited together and listened to music of various kinds.

It was Pompeia's turn to celebrate this feast, and Clodius, who as of yet had grown no beard, thought to enter the house in disguise. He dressed as a singing woman and took on the walk and demeanor of a young girl. He entered the house and bribed a maid to be part of the conspiracy. The maid ran to tell Pompeia, but she was gone a long time. Clodius grew uneasy waiting for her and went through the house from one room to another, taking care to avoid the lighted areas. Finally Aurelia's servant met him, and as Plutarch wrote, "invited him to play with her, as the women did among themselves" (Plutarch 860). He refused to comply, and she pulled him forward and asked him who he was. Clodius told her he was waiting for Pompeia's maid, but his voice betrayed his gender.

The woman began shrieking and ran into the room where there were lights and cried out that she had discovered a man. The women were all frightened. Aurelia covered up the sacred things and stopped the ceremonies. She ordered the doors barred and went through the house until she found Clodius. The women recognized him and drove him out of doors. That very night, they went home and told their husbands the story. By morning, it was all about the town that Clodius had offended not only Caesar but the very gods whose ceremonies he had invaded. The principal senators came together and gave evidence against him, charging him not only of profaning the holy rites, but of other vile crimes, including incest with his own sister.

Caesar was in a difficult situation, because his political support came from the lower classes, and he wanted to retain Clodius's political support. Caesar immediately divorced Pompeia, but when he was summoned as a witness against Clodius, he said he had no charge against him. The accusers asked him about this paradox: Why did he divorce Pompeia if he had no knowledge of any wrongdoing? Caesar replied with a famous retort: "Members of my household should not be even so much as suspected" (Plutarch 860). According to Plutarch, some people thought this was Caesar's real thought, while others believed he simply wanted to let Clodius go. Whatever the real motive, Clodius was freed, and Pompeia was divorced. Caesar was free to marry again and chose the faithful Calpurnia.

See also Calpurnia; Cleopatra VII; Servilia
Suggested Readings
Grant, Michael. *Caesar*. Chicago: Follett Publishing, 1975.
Plutarch. *The Lives of the Noble Grecians and Romans*. Trans. J. Dryden. New York: The Modern Library, n.d.

Poppaea Sabina
Roman Empress (ca. A.D. 31–65)
During the reigns of the Julio-Claudian emperors, one of the most important problems was the succession—the emperors drew their legitimacy from their descent from the family of Augustus. (See Chart 4 of the Julio-Claudian house.) Power followed bloodlines, which made marital alliances crucial. This principle also provided a way for some women to use their attractiveness to enter the imperial household and exert a good deal of power on their own. Perhaps one of the most notorious of such women was Poppaea Sabina, who won the heart of the ruthless emperor Nero.

Poppaea was born in about A.D. 31 of a fairly undistinguished Roman family of the equestrian order, and she thus did not mingle in the imperial circles. In spite of the fact that she was beautiful and intelligent, her family could thus only arrange a fairly ordinary marriage for her. In about A.D. 44 (when she was thirteen years old) she married Rufrius Crispinus, who was a leader of the Praetorian Guard who served the palace. Poppaea's mother (Poppaea Sabina the Elder) had run afoul of the women of the imperial household. Messalina (*see* Messalina) seems to have been furious at Poppaea the Elder because she supplanted the empress in the affection of a handsome pantomime actor. The elder Poppaea was driven to suicide, and the younger Poppaea must have taken some lessons from this event. She set her sights at the highest levels of power.

In A.D. 51, the younger Poppaea's husband was displaced by Agrippina (Nero's mother). It seemed as if Poppaea would never be close enough to the court to exert any influence, but that situation changed in A.D. 58. When Poppaea was twenty-seven years old, a handsome young senator, M. Salvius Otho, fell in love with her. She divorced her husband and married him. Otho was madly in love with his bride, and he made the mistake of speaking lyrically of her charm in such high praise that Emperor Nero asked to meet her. She soon became Nero's mistress.

The emperor easily got rid of her husband—he was sent to govern a distant province of the empire, yet it seems he never lost his love for his wife. As the mistress of the emperor, Poppaea must have begun to calculate her chances of becoming empress. There were a few obstacles in her way: Nero was already married to Octavia, the daughter of Emperor Claudius and Messalina. Nero hated this wife, but she not only had the Julio-Claudian blood in her veins, she had the support of Nero's formidable mother, Agrippina. Nero also already had a mistress—the freedwoman Claudia Acte, who had been brought as a slave from Asia and who had captured Nero's attentions when the emperor turned from his wife, Octavia.

According to the Roman historian Tacitus, Poppaea worked to have Nero renounce his mother's influence and marry her. She taunted him about his mother, and purportedly Agrippina responded by acting seductively toward her son to keep his affections from Poppaea, whom she hated. Finally, Nero and Poppaea arranged the death of Agrippina in A.D. 59, yet Nero still did not immediately marry Poppaea; perhaps he did not want to formally divorce Octavia, who was popular with Romans. In A.D. 62 the moment came, however; Poppaea was pregnant, so it was time to marry to legitimize the child.

Nero divorced Octavia and married his pregnant mistress twelve days later. The Roman people were outraged; they rioted in Rome and destroyed Poppaea's statues while they decorated those of Octavia. Nero sent Octavia to an island exile and eventually had her killed. Octavia's head was chopped off and sent to Poppaea. In A.D. 63, the child was born, a girl named Claudia. Both Poppaea and the child were given the title of augusta, but the public celebrations had hardly died down when the child died at the age of four months.

Two years later, in A.D. 65, Poppaea was expecting a second child. It was the year when Nero was celebrating games in which he participated in the music, gymnastics, and horse racing. Nero returned to the palace late from these activities, and Poppaea reprimanded him. In the ensuing fight, Nero kicked her, causing a miscarriage. Poppaea died from loss of blood. For all her efforts, she was not able to leave a child to inherit the imperial throne.

Historians—ancient and modern—have been ambiguous in their assessment of Poppaea's life and influence. Some have condemned her for her ambition and her presumed role in eliminating Agrippina and Nero's first wife, Octavia. Others have emphasized her beauty and how she used it to the best effect: She was supposed to have kept a herd of 500 wild asses to provide milk for a regular beauty bath to soften her skin. She also introduced a new hairstyle that remained popular after she died. People claimed that she said that she wanted to die before she ceased to be attractive.

These accounts of her vanity and cruelty were strangely united with spiritual interests that seemed unexpected in Nero's household. She was interested in Judaism and seems to have used her influence to secure the release of Jews who had been sent under arrest to Judea. Some historians have suggested, however, that she used her pro-Jewish sympathies to persuade Nero to institute the first persecution against Christians in A.D. 64.

All these bits of evidence and analysis perhaps allow us to glimpse some of the many facets of one influential ancient woman—extraordinarily beautiful, charming, and intelligent—who used her attributes to gain power and who lost everything by cultivating the ruthless emperor Nero. Nero did not long outlast Poppaea. Rebellions broke out in response to his cruel and extravagant rule, and he fled and was forced to commit suicide in A.D. 68. Nero ended the Julio-Claudian line of emperors. In the year that followed his death, four men briefly seized the imperial power, and one of them was Otho—Poppaea's first husband. He accomplished little in his three-month reign, but he did restore Poppaea's statues that had been destroyed during the riots in Nero's lifetime. Otho never forgot his beloved wife, and his actions helped preserve her memory.

See also Agrippina the Younger; Boudicca; Messalina; Octavia

Suggested Readings

Balsdon, J. P. V. D. *Roman Women: Their History and Habits.* New York: John Day, 1963.

Suetonius. *The Twelve Caesars.* Trans. Robert Graves. New York: Penguin, 1979.

Tacitus. "The Annals." In *Complete Works of Tacitus.* Trans. A. J. Church. New York: The Modern Library, 1942.

Porcia

Roman Wife and Conspirator (d. 42 B.C.)

The last decades of the Roman Republic were times of turmoil when powerful men struggled to control the wealthy state of Rome, which by now encompassed much of the Mediterranean. The towering figure from this time was Julius Caesar, who managed to wrest power for a time and who is remembered as one of the best politicians and generals of all time. Almost as famous as Caesar, however, was Brutus, one of the architects of the plot to assassinate the dictator. There was only one woman who was privy to the secrets of the conspirators as they planned to kill Caesar—Brutus's wife, Porcia.

Brutus was first married in 54 B.C. to the daughter of Appius Claudius, which connected him to an old and prominent patrician family but also shaped his alliance in the power politics of the day. During this time, Rome was ruled by an informal arrangement among three strong men—Julius Caesar, Pompey, and Crassus. This organization, later called the First Triumvirate, was intended to prevent the kind of battles that had gone before when strong men engaged in civil war with each other. Brutus's marriage linked him to the party of Pompey, whom he hated because Pompey had arranged for the death of Brutus's father. The politics of the late republic led to strange bedfellows, however, and for a time Brutus joined Pompey.

The First Triumvirate fell apart into war between Caesar and Pompey, and Caesar crushed Pompey's army in 48 B.C. It would seem that Brutus would have been killed for his support of Pompey, but Caesar was in love with Brutus's mother, Servilia, and thus forgave Brutus and took him into his own government. Brutus's beloved uncle, Cato the Younger, continued to fight against Caesar, however, and Caesar defeated him as well. Cato committed suicide, and Brutus reacted strongly to his uncle's death. Within a year of Cato's suicide, Brutus divorced his wife and married Cato's daughter—his own cousin—Porcia.

Porcia was a widow who had been married to Bibulus, who was an old adversary of Caesar, and she had one surviving son. There was no particular political advantage to Brutus's marriage—perhaps he loved her, or perhaps he wanted to identify more closely with his dead uncle Cato. This marriage may have offered him some solace, but it caused other family problems for Brutus. His mother, Servilia, had openly opposed the marriage, and she and Porcia quarreled constantly. Servilia must have also viewed Brutus's marriage as a purposeful affront to Caesar, for Porcia openly hated Caesar. Porcia held Caesar responsible for Cato's death, and she had resented him for having humiliated her first husband years before. By 44 B.C., as Brutus began to organize the conspiracy to kill Caesar, he could expect Porcia to lend a sympathetic ear. Brutus did not readily share the secret, however. The historian Plutarch relates how the devoted wife persuaded her husband.

Porcia loved Brutus deeply and was full of "spirit and good sense," and when she sensed a change in his behavior, she wanted to find out what was troubling him. Porcia sent her attendants away, pulled out a small knife, and gave herself a deep gash in the thigh. She lost a great quantity of blood, after which the wound became intensely painful and brought on a high fever. When she saw that Brutus was deeply distressed for her, she said to him: "Brutus, I am Cato's daughter, and I was given to you in marriage not just to share your bed and board like a concubine, but to be a true partner in your joys and sorrows. . . . I know that men think women's natures too weak to be entrusted with secrets, but . . . now I have put myself to the test and find that I can conquer pain" (Plutarch 1193). She showed him her wound. Brutus was amazed and prayed to be worthy of such a wife, and he shared the secret.

On the day appointed for the assassination, Porcia discovered that she was not as calm as she imagined. She was highly disturbed in anticipation of the event and could hardly stand the anxiety. She started at every noise, and finally her mind was so overcome with doubts and fears that she fainted dead away. At this sight, her servants made a loud cry, and many of the neighbors went running to Brutus to say that Porcia was dead. With her women's help, Porcia was restored, and when Brutus received this news, he was extremely troubled. Yet, he was not so carried away by his grief that he gave up his purpose. He continued the plan, and on the Ides of March (15 March) in 44 B.C., Brutus and fifty-nine other senators stabbed Julius Caesar to death as he came to the senate.

Brutus and the other conspirators had to flee, as Caesar's followers began to seek vengeance for his murder. He sent Porcia back to Rome without him, although she was fearful to be separated from him. By 42 B.C., Porcia was dead; she might have died from illness, although there is some evidence that she committed suicide. In 42 B.C., Brutus's forces were defeated in Greece by Caesar's heir, Octavian, at the Battle of Philippi, and Brutus killed himself by falling on his sword. He and his wife—coconspirators—were dead. The future lay with Octavian, who became known as Caesar Augustus.

See also Calpurnia; Servilia
Suggested Readings
Kebric, Robert B. *Roman People.* Toronto: Mayfield
  Publishing, 1993.
Plutarch. *The Lives of the Noble Grecians and
  Romans.* Trans. J. Dryden. New York: The
  Modern Library, n.d.

Prisca

Christian Woman (ca. A.D. 50)

During the early years after Jesus' death and resurrection, his message was spread by missionaries traveling primarily through the eastern portion of the Roman Empire. These missionaries stopped at various cities, established meetings in households, and gathered a group of believers around them. Then they moved on, leaving the house church in the hands of newly converted local Christians. The Bible tells of an influential couple who worked with the apostle Paul to establish house churches: Prisca and her husband, Aquila.

Prisca (called Priscilla—meaning "Little Prisca"—in Acts) is mentioned six times in the New Testament—in Acts and in Paul's letters. Prisca is always mentioned with Aquila, but usually her name is placed first in the pair (which was an unusual order since a husband was usually mentioned first). This order suggests that the authors of scripture placed Prisca in a more important role. Both were tent makers (like Paul), and they obviously had enough wealth to move at will and to establish houses that were large enough to allow local congregations to assemble.

Prisca and Aquila were Jews who had converted to Christianity in the early years. They were living in Rome (although Aquila was originally from Pontus on the southern coast of the Black Sea). In A.D. 49, the emperor, Claudius, expelled all Jews from the city of Rome because they were engaging in disturbances, as the Roman historian Suetonius wrote, "at the instigation of Chrestus" (Suetonius 202). This is widely interpreted to refer to quarrels between Jews who believed in Christ and those who did not. Rome responded by sending all Jews out of the city.

Paul met Prisca and Aquila in Corinth soon after their arrival from Rome. When Paul left Corinth to go to Ephesus, Prisca and Aquila were with him. When he wrote his letter to the church in Corinth (1 Cor. 16:8), Paul sent the warm greetings of the couple to their old congregation in Corinth.

After the edict banning Jews was lifted in A.D. 54, Prisca and Aquila must have returned to Rome, for when Paul wrote to the community of that city in A.D. 56, he sent his greetings first of all to them. Again they used their home to establish a house church, which Paul greeted as well. In his letter to the Romans, Paul gives praise for Prisca's and Aquila's contributions to his missionary work: He asserts that they risked their lives for him and thanks them for their work. The Book of Acts credits Prisca and Aquila for teaching, specifically for instructing Apollos, an early missionary remembered for his eloquent speech.

According to one legend, the fourth-century church Saint Priscae in Rome was built on the site of Prisca's house church. It has also been suggested that Prisca was the author of the anonymous letter to the Hebrews, but this cannot be confirmed. What is certain, however, is that Prisca was an influential missionary of the early church and that her work was long remembered.

See also Christian Women; Junia; Lydia
Suggested Readings
Meyers, Carol, Toni Craven, and Ross S. Kraemer.
  Women in Scripture. New York: Houghton
  Mifflin, 2000.
Suetonius. *The Twelve Caesars.* Trans. Robert
  Graves. New York: Penguin, 1986.

Priscilla

See Prisca

Proba

Roman Poet (ca A.D. 351)

Throughout the Roman Empire, the favorite poet was Virgil (70–19 B.C.), who praised the greatness of Rome in his much-beloved epic poem, *Aeneid,* which told of the founding of Rome by the Trojan, Aeneas. This monumental work became the centerpiece of a Roman education, and for centuries Romans learned about values, history, and language by reading the works of Virgil. In addition to the famous *Aeneid,* Romans prized Virgil's less majestic works: the *Eclogues*—pastoral poems about the countryside—and the *Georgics*—poetic descriptions of country life and work.

Since Romans praised Virgil's accomplishments as a high point of poetic endeavor, many Romans used his poetry as a basis of new creative works that echoed the master. The literary form that copied the lines of one poem to make a new one is called a *cento;* in fact the word itself is thought to have meant a "patchwork cloak," indicating that it was composed of pieces of the old. In this form lines were copied and rearranged to tell a different story from the original one. In the fourth century A.D., a well-educated Roman matron named Proba composed such a work using Virgil's lines to explore a new subject, Christianity.

We know nothing of Proba except the tantalizing bits of information that may be gleaned from her *cento,* but from that we can at the very least know she was a pious Christian. Furthermore, she was a married woman of the privileged Roman upper class, of the famous family of the Anicii. She had two sons, and she may have written her work for her sons. Proba must have been well educated, for her knowledge of Virgil was impeccable, and she was well read in many other Roman and Christian writings. She had written an earlier poem on war, which treated a rebellion against Emperor Constantius II in A.D. 353. Some years later, however, Christians fell on hard times, and Proba brought her poetic skills to a Christian purpose.

In A.D. 361, Julian—known as "the Apostate"—became emperor, and desiring to restore pagan worship, he issued an edict forbidding Christians from teaching classic texts. The basis for Julian's edict is interesting to modern educators, for he said that in order for someone to teach, they had to be in good "mental health." He further argued that Christians who taught one thing—the pagan classics—while they believed another—the Christian texts—were automatically mentally unfit to teach. It may be that in reaction to this, Proba composed her long verse that combined classical texts of Virgil with the story of Christianity. In this text, she showed that there was no contradiction between pagan and Christian classics. In her *cento,* she wrote "that Virgil put to verse Christ's sacred duties" (Wilson-Kastner 45). Proba affirms that Virgil, when correctly understood, testifies to Jesus.

Proba's *cento* consists of 694 verses that retell biblical tales from Genesis through the life of Christ; however, it does not attempt to cover the whole Bible. Instead it concentrates on the stories of the creation and fall and on selected episodes of Jesus' life, with heavy emphasis on the birth, infancy, and death of the savior. Throughout her selections, Proba reveals her interests in traditional Roman families and their values as well as her privileged upper-class status. For example, she does not emphasize charity, but stresses the need to pass wealth on to one's family. Nor does she praise Mary's virginity, but instead emphasizes her maternity. Jesus throughout is portrayed as an epic hero rather than a New Testament suffering servant. At the end of the work, she addressed her husband, saying "O sweetest spouse, embrace them [Christian ideas] also, and if our devotion merits it, grant that our children remain pure and holy in Thy religion" (Wilson-Kastner 685). It may be that Proba's portrayal of Christ as a Virgilian hero might have made him more acceptable to her husband and son.

By using the beloved words of Virgil, Proba ensured that Romans would take her work seriously. Modern literary critics have not been kind to Proba's efforts, for her insistence on using Virgil's lines makes much of her narration of sacred history forced and awkward. Yet, her work was very successful in subsequent centuries, because it was used as a textbook to teach about both Christianity and Virgil. We do not know if she was successful in her hope of educating her husband and children, but she certainly made an impact on many subsequent generations of schoolchildren.

See also Christian Women; Paula
Suggested Readings
Clark, E. A. *Ascetic Piety and Women's Faith: Essays on Late Ancient Christianity.* Lewiston, NY: Edwin Mellen Press, 1986.
Clark, E. A., and D. F. Hatch. *The Golden Bough,*

The Oaken Cross: The Vergilian Cento of Faltonia Betitia Proba. Chico, CA: Scholars Press, 1981.

Wilson-Kastner, Patricia. *A Lost Tradition: Women Writers of the Early Church.* New York: University Press of America, 1981.

Procne

See Philomela

Prostitution

The Ancient Middle East

Prostitution is among the oldest professions. The Sumerian word for female prostitute (*kar.kid*) occurs in lists of jobs dating back to about 2400 B.C. Prostitutes are listed on clay tablets as waiting at taverns, presumably to find clients, and a prostitute ("harlot") even appears as an important figure in the ancient *Epic of Gilgamesh.* In this work, the wild man is brought to civilization and given wisdom by having sex with a harlot who was sent to educate him. All these references suggest that from the earliest history of cities, some women sold sexual favors.

Commercial prostitution probably came from the practice of taking female slaves in military conquests. The violence that repeatedly swept the ancient Middle East led to captives who sometimes became the concubines or slaves of conquerors and at other times were simply enslaved and put to work as prostitutes for their masters. Another source of prostitutes came from free women who were forced by poverty to sell sexual favors. By the middle of the second millennium B.C., prostitution was well established as an occupation for the daughters of the poor.

By that time, the region of the Fertile Crescent was conquered by the Assyrian Empire, and its leaders introduced a harsh, militaristic rule over the conquered peoples. Among their laws was one that regulated prostitution, and this law shows that this society had become increasingly concerned to separate "respectable" women from prostitutes. The Assyrian law stated that respectable women—women under the care of a man—must veil themselves when they appeared in public. This included wives and daughters,

and even a concubine who "goes out on the street with her mistress" had to veil herself. The law even stated that a sacred prostitute "whom a man married" must veil herself. In all these cases, the veil would mark the woman as dependent and unavailable to other men. The law concluded: "A harlot must not veil herself; her head must be uncovered" (Lerner 248).

The law also provided penalties for violators. "He who has seen a harlot veiled must arrest her" (Lerner 248). This raises the question of how a man would know if a veiled woman walking past him were a harlot. Presumably this penalty was to prevent men from treating their prostitutes as respectable women by veiling them. Women who attempted to hide their profession would receive harsh penalties. A free prostitute who wore a veil in public would be publicly stripped and whipped and have pitch poured over her head. She would probably be disfigured for a long time because she would have to shave her head to remove the tar. Slave prostitutes received even stiffer penalties: they would have their ears cut off.

From the time of the ancient world on, prostitution was established as an occupation for women and men, and as sex was recognized as a marketable commodity, its sale also began to separate respectable from unrespectable women. From this early period, then, prostitution may have been the oldest profession, but it was also one that brought public shame. Two classes of working women were established—respectable and improper. This structure persisted to varying degrees throughout the ancient world.

Ancient warfare led to women being captured and turned into prostitutes outside Mesopotamia. In fact, ancient writers claimed that Egypt was filled with prostitutes/slaves who served either in harems of the rich or in the markets of the cities. Marriage was considered an important institution in Egypt, and moralists frequently warned young men against the foreign women serving as prostitutes who tempted them.

The Greek historian Herodotus (484–424 B.C.) recorded what he called famous Egyptian prostitutes, and in his stories he seems to show that prostitution was perhaps even more central in the Egyptian economy than in that of ancient

Mesopotamia. In one example, Herodotus tells of the pharaoh Cheops who ran short of money to build his pyramid. To raise funds, he sent his daughter into a brothel but kept her fees to pay for his pyramid. According to Herodotus, his daughter did not seem to object to the work, but she wanted her own immortality ensured as well, so she required all her customers to bring a stone for her in addition to the regular fee that she passed on to the pharaoh. From these stones, she built herself a pyramid that measured over 150 feet. Herodotus delighted in such tales of successful Egyptian prostitutes, but we cannot tell how accurate they are. At the very least, however, they serve to confirm other sources that indicate that prostitution was not rare in the ancient land of the pharaohs.

The Hebrew scriptures also testify to the commonplace existence of prostitution among the ancient Jews. While the Bible periodically opposes prostitution—as when Moses forbade fathers from prostituting their daughters (Lev. 19:29)—for the most part the Bible treats prostitution as a fact of life. Israelite priests were prohibited from marrying harlots, but others could do so without penalty. Biblical accounts tell how some women dressed in the veils of a prostitute and sold themselves by crossroads to men who came by. Further, it seems that children of prostitutes did not bear any particular stigma because of their mothers' profession.

One of the famous passages of the Bible concerns an argument between two "harlots" who appeal to King Solomon. The two prostitutes claimed to live in the same house, and each had borne an infant. One child died, and the king had to decide to whom the other belonged. In his famous ruling to cut the child in half, the wise king ruled that the prostitute who was willing to give up the child rather than to see him killed was the real mother. This story reveals that prostitutes seem to have lived together and raised their children in a common house. It also shows a remarkable lack of criticism about prostitution—the biblical king did not bother reprimanding the women for their chosen profession, which by this time was well established everywhere in the ancient Middle East.

Greece

Commercial prostitution that extends as far back as historical records was also prevalent in the city-states of classical Greece. Large cities on the seacoasts supplied huge numbers of prostitutes who served the sailors as they beached their ships every night. Athens, which took the lead in so many Greek developments, was not to be outdone in the market for prostitutes. It established state-owned brothels, staffed by slave women, to attract the trade of sailors and others who passed through the city. There was a wide-ranging hierarchy among the prostitutes in ancient Greece, which encompassed women from the lowest slaves to highly influential courtesans.

The lowest-status prostitutes lived in the state-owned brothels, where they collected very small fees from their clients. A special official was appointed to oversee the brothels and to make sure the "prostitute tax" was collected. Slightly above these slaves were the streetwalkers, who sought out their customers in streets or taverns. Many of these women were possibly aging courtesans, whose popularity had waned, so they were reduced to advertising on the streets. Many were blatant in their solicitation. For example, archaeologists have found one shoe that has the words "follow me" on the bottom, so her footprints included the invitation to anyone who passed along the dirt road behind her. One Greek satirist wrote that these aging streetwalkers entertained customers in rooms so poorly lit that "any could look like Aphrodite" (Bullough and Bullough 34).

Entertainers were prostitutes who had more status than streetwalkers, and their talents helped them command higher prices for sexual favors. Musicians, acrobats, and dancers tempted members of the audience by erotic dances, sexually explicit songs, and skimpy clothing. Sources describe how dancers might "bare their thighs" seductively, and the entertainers boasted of the riots they had provoked. The most famous entertainer was Lamia, who was reputed to have entertained both the kings of Egypt and Macedonia. The Greek writer Plutarch said that she was called Lamia—"vampire"—because of her "depravities" (Bullough and Bullough 36), but no one doubted her influence with the kings with whom she consorted.

The Greek prostitutes who had the highest status (and were most highly paid) were the *hetairai,* or "companions to men." These courtesans were well educated and highly trained in the arts of cosmetics, conversation, and entertainment. Greek sources discuss many highly influential *hetairai,* and certainly the most renowned was Aspasia, mistress to Pericles, the leader of Athens. All the sources accuse the women of commanding exorbitant fees for their services and consequently of amassing large personal fortunes. These were the rare women in ancient Greek society who controlled their own fortunes, but they were never accepted in "respectable" society, and their fortunes depended on their own talents and attractiveness.

The prevalence of prostitution in ancient Greece derives in part from the way the Greeks structured the basic relations between men and women. Especially in Athens, where respectable women were strictly separated from mixed company, men shared their recreational times with other men or with less respectable women. Figure 63 shows a drinking bowl with an image of a courtesan relaxing at a drinking party, and this image demonstrates how prostitutes were intimately tied to parties and social activities, which were forbidden to wives and daughters of Athens's citizens. As the Greek orator Demosthenes wrote, the Greeks had "*hetairai* for delight, concubines for the daily needs of the body, and wives in order to beget legitimate children and have faithful housekeepers" (Bullough and Bullough 44). In this setting, women's roles were carefully separated, and the institution of prostitution was central to the social structure.

Rome

After the conquests of Alexander the Great, the small city-states of classical Greece were overshadowed by the great cosmopolitan cities of the Hellenistic world, and prostitution flourished in the great urban centers. For centuries, prostitutes in cities such as Alexandria and Antioch were reputed to make huge fortunes, and in this new Hellenistic world, fortunes brought independence and a measure of power. When Rome

Figure 63. Courtesan at a drinking party, fifth century B.C. (Fogg Art Museum, Harvard University)

conquered the Hellenistic cities, it took over the ancient commerce in sexual favors, but these cautious, conservative people gave the vocation its own particular stamp.

Roman women were not as secluded as their classical Greek counterparts, so respectable, educated women served as companions for their husbands. Perhaps for this reason, the Greek courtesans, who were highly influential, were not prevalent in Rome. While there were some influential mistresses and concubines, Roman prostitution—while accepted—was even less respectable than it had been before. Where Greeks had called their best prostitutes "companions of men," Romans simply and practically called them all "earners"—*meretrices.* The practical Romans saw that this was an economic relationship between men and women.

Roman prostitutes (even if they lived outside Rome itself) were required to register with the state. While some prostitutes solicited customers on the street (or during shows at the theaters or Colosseum), most prostitutes were slaves who worked in brothels. In Rome, these brothels were located close to the city walls, on the outskirts of the city. Each brothel contained a room for each of the prostitutes—her name was sometimes inscribed above the door, occasionally along with a list of her prices. Within the room was a small bed or a blanket on the floor and a lamp. The brothels were forbidden to open until late in the afternoon, to prevent young men from being drawn away from their work or exercise. Most of the women who worked in the brothels were slaves.

Romans considered prostitutes to be like gladiators and performers—lowest-status workers—and legislated accordingly. Just as in the strict Assyrian law code, Romans insisted that registered prostitutes wear particular clothing—a togalike garment instead of the modest dress of a matron. Furthermore, prostitutes often bleached their hair blond to attract the eye of admirers. Once a woman registered as a prostitute, Roman law never allowed her to return to respectable status, even if she stopped selling sexual favors. Becoming a prostitute defined a woman once and for all, and an upper-class Roman was not even permitted to marry a prostitute. Furthermore, the stigma extended even to the next generation, for an upper-class Roman could not even claim as legitimate any daughters he had fathered with a prostitute. Similarly, upper-class Roman women were not permitted to register as prostitutes.

During the Roman Empire there no doubt were as many prostitutes working in all the great cities as there had ever been in the ancient world. People—men and women alike—accepted prostitution as a fact of life and as an economic and social necessity. Just like the Assyrians, however, the Romans wanted to make sure that there remained a clear difference between "respectable" and "unrespectable" women, and they did so by passing laws to make sure that women did not cross from one category to another. It was in this setting that Christianity made a striking claim—even prostitutes can be redeemed. After Christianity became the prevailing religion of the empire, prostitution became a sin, a job, but most important, a temporary state that could be put aside.

See also Aspasia; Mary Magdalene; Mary of Egypt; Pelagia; Prostitution, Sacred

Suggested Readings

Bullough, Vern L., and Bonnie Bullough. *The History of Prostitution.* New York: University Books, 1964.

Edwards, Catherine. "Unspeakable Professions: Public Performance and Prostitution in Ancient Rome." In *Roman Sexualities,* ed. by J. P. Hallett et al. Princeton: Princeton University Press, 1997.

Lerner, G. "Prostitution in Mesopotamia." *Signs* 11 (Winter 1986): 236–254.

Pomeroy, Sarah B. *Goddesses, Whores, Wives, and Slaves: Women in Classical Antiquity.* New York: Schocken Books, 1975.

Prostitution, Sacred

From as long ago as the fifth century B.C., historians have been fascinated by the possibility of women who served various goddesses by selling sexual favors, and this interest has not waned. The Greek historian Herodotus (484–424 B.C.) gave the first detailed account of this purported activity, and it has drawn the attention of scholars ever since. Herodotus claims to tell of an ancient Babylonian custom:

> The most shameful custom the Babylonians have is this: every native woman must go sit in the temple of Aphrodite, once in her life, and have sex with an adult male stranger. . . . They sit in the sanctuary of Aphrodite, these many women, their heads crowned with a band of bow-string. Roped-off thoroughfares give all manner of routes through the women and the strangers pass along them as they make their choice. Once a woman sits down there, she doesn't return home until a stranger drops money in her lap and has sex with her outside the temple. When he drops it he has to say, "I call on the goddess Mylitta." Assyrians call Aphrodite Mylitta. The money can be any value at all—it is not to be refused, for that is forbidden, for this money becomes sacred. She follows the first one who drops money and rejects none. When she has had sex, she has performed her religious dues to the goddess and goes home. (Beard and Henderson 482–483)

The Greek geographer Strabo gives a similar account of "temple prostitution" in the city of Corinth, saying that there were more than a thousand men and women who sold sexual favors in the service of Aphrodite.

These few citations have generated much controversy about whether the practice ever existed or whether these Greeks used such titillating tales to attract their audiences and to prove that the "exotic east" had values and practices utterly foreign to the Greek ones. Perhaps the most compelling modern argument against the existence of this practice is the absence of references to such large-scale trafficking in any of the Babylonian cuneiform records. Many clay tablets have survived that record all kinds of commerce for the temples, and any activity that embraced the whole female population would presumably have yielded records. It therefore seems highly unlikely that the large-scale practice that Herodotus and Strabo described ever existed.

While the ancient goddesses seem not to have required a ritual sex act from every woman, there is evidence for some kinds of cultic sexual activity. The ancient Babylonians (and other Mesopotamian peoples) believed that the gods and goddesses actually dwelled in the temples and that they had physical desires. The priests and priestesses were to care for the needs of the deities, providing food, music, and even cosmetics. Within this context and in a society that regarded fertility as essential to survival, it is not surprising that care for the gods meant offering them sexual favors.

The heart of religious sexual acts lay in the idea of a sacred marriage in which a priestess representing a goddess would have intercourse with a priest or king representing a god. It may be that this rite originated in the Sumerian city of Uruk as early as 3000 B.C. Uruk was dedicated to the goddess Inanna, and poems have survived that seem to celebrate the successful union in the sacred marriage, after which the goddess promised to bless the house of her husband, the king.

Other priestesses also participated in some kinds of sexual rituals, although these are not so clearly documented as the important sacred marriage. Some women were listed as "temple servants" who were required to "remain fallow," thus forgoing childbearing. These women lived cloistered lives and were at times listed as scribes. Since they were described specifically as chaste, it suggests that others were not. In con-

trast, other temple servants were listed as serving as wet nurses for wealthy patrons, who then contributed the money to the temple. In this case, these temple women must have recently given birth themselves, so we might assume they also served the goddesses as prostitutes. Finally, ancient law codes mention low-level temple workers, probably slaves, who served as prostitutes whose earnings went to the goddess.

In sum, ritual prostitution of a certain kind existed in the ancient temples of Mesopotamia. Just as almost every other commercial activity was conducted at the bustling temples, people made money from sexual activities. The scandalous large-scale ritual prostitution that some Greek historians attributed to the "barbaric" east probably did not exist, however. Of course, in addition to such ritual prostitution, there were always prostitutes engaging in the oldest profession outside of the temple complexes.

See also Aphrodite; Ishtar; Prostitution; Venus

Suggested Readings
Beard, Mary, and John Henderson. "With This Body I Thee Worship: Sacred Prostitution in Antiquity." *Gender and History* 9 (1997): 480–503.
Lerner, G. "Prostitution in Mesopotamia." *Signs* 11 (Winter 1986): 236–254.

Pudentilla

North African Roman Widow (ca. A.D. 180)
In the second century A.D., North Africa was a prosperous province of the Roman Empire. Fields in the great North African estates produced great yields of high-quality grain—so much so that the region around Carthage was seen as the breadbasket for Rome. (See Map 7.) The sunny land also produced magnificent olive orchards, which yielded valuable oil, and vineyards to grow grapes for wine. To exploit these productive agricultural resources, the land was organized in large estates cultivated by slaves or peasants who reaped little benefit from the production—but the patrician owners lived very well from the wealth of the land. Most of the texts from this period tell of wealthy men and the comfortable lives they led as they pursued a public career, but it is difficult to reconstruct the lives of the women who shared this good life.

One text, however, allows us to tell of one late second-century wealthy widow, and the details of her life can shed light on the experience of many other forgotten ancient women. She is the wealthy widow—Aemilia Pudentilla—whose story is preserved because of her marriage to the brilliant, if controversial, North African philosopher Apuleius of Madaura.

In addition to being a wealthy province, North Africa—and especially its cosmopolitan center, Carthage—was an intellectual center for the whole Roman Empire. Apuleius had come from the provincial town of Madaura to Carthage to complete his education, and he became a masterful orator and philosopher. He spoke to the cosmopolitan audiences in the public forum of Carthage and praised its learning. People there spoke in many languages—from Latin to Greek to the native North African Punic—and discussed ideas from all over the empire. Eventually, the Carthaginians recognized the greatness of their native son Apuleius and erected a statue in his honor. Many North Africans felt honored by the friendship and visits of the philosopher. One such was Pontianus—the elder son of the widow Pudentilla.

As he was traveling to Alexandria, Apuleius became ill, and he took refuge at the estate of his friend Pontianus. He stayed there through the winter, and came to know the widow Pudentilla. She had been a widow for fourteen years by then and had two sons—Pontianus and a younger son, Pudens. Her father-in-law was interested in keeping the family's resources intact, so he urged Pudentilla to marry her deceased husband's brother to keep the inheritance in the family. She refused and thus remained a widow. Once her father-in-law died, Pontianus became the legal head of the family. We have the account of what happened next from Apuleius.

Pudentilla became ill, and in accordance with current medical understanding, the doctors claimed that her illness was due to her long years of chastity. Apuleius explained:

[She was] made ill by the long inactivity of her organs—the insides of her uterus were damaged—and began to suffer internal pains so severe that they brought her to the

brink of the grave. Doctors and wise women agreed that the disease had its origin in the absence of a marriage, that the evil was increasing daily and her sickness steadily assuming a more serious character; the remedy was that she should marry before her youth finally departed from her. (Apuleius 114)

Pontianus began to urge his friend Apuleius to marry his mother in spite of the age difference between them. According to the text, Pudentilla loved the young orator, and they married.

In the meantime, Pontianus had married, and his new father-in-law, Rufinus, opposed the marriage that Pontianus had worked to arrange. Rufinus also engaged the support of Pontianus's uncle Aemillianus (the second brother of Pudentilla's deceased husband). Together they began to spread rumors that Apuleius had illegally taken possession of Pudentilla's extensive property. Apuleius formally challenged them to sue him if they dared, but since they did not have a good case, they trumped up a charge of magic against the philosopher and charged him with "bewitching" the chaste matron to get her property. Pontianus died before the case came to trial, but he had repented bringing the lawsuit, and was fully reconciled to Pudentilla and Apuleius. The wheels had been set in motion, however, and the younger son, Pudens, formally brought the charge.

The information we have about this case comes from Apuleius's defense at his trial—published in English as the *Apologia,* or sometimes the *Apology.* Needless to say, this is not an objective account since it was written in his own defense; nevertheless, historians believe they can obtain a good—if somewhat ambiguous—picture of Pudentilla. The first thing the record makes clear is the amount of money involved. Apuleius described the huge amount of capital she had in addition to various country houses with lots of servants and slaves. Apuleius also indicates that Pudentilla took an active interest in the estates, for he disproves her alleged madness by reminding her sons that "she showed the utmost shrewdness in her examination of the accounts of the bailiffs, grooms, and shepherd" (Apuleius 136–137). Furthermore, Apuleius reminds the judges that he persuaded his wife to offer her sons large portions of her estates—"exceedingly fertile lands, a large house richly decorated, a great quantity of wheat, barley, wine and oil, and other fruits of the earth, together with not less than four hundred slaves and a large number of valuable cattle" (Apuleius 145). If this offering was intended as a friendly gesture, we can realize what a large financial interest was at stake in this trial.

While we can learn much about Pudentilla's wealth and her active involvement with its management, we can know much less about the woman herself. Even her age is uncertain, although most scholars assume she was in her mid-forties when they married, and Apuleius's accusers argue that she was in her sixties. Apuleius also rather ungenerously claims she was not attractive—"a woman of plain appearance"—suggesting that he could have held out for a more attractive match. Yet, he proved that he did not marry for money—since her will gave him little advantage, and he was absolved of the charge of magic. In fact, he claimed that any of those actions would have been "unworthy of a friend and a philosopher" (Apuleius 119).

This is all the information we have about this enigmatic woman. She seems not to have attended the trial, and we have no record of her own opinions on this whole matter. The tantalizing bits of information perhaps allow us to speculate about the character of this wealthy woman. She refused to marry when she did not want to and did marry the young philosopher who was the pride of Carthage. She ran her estates, controlled her finances, and prepared her will in which she left the bulk of the property to her sons, not her second husband. Perhaps the main reason historians find her story so fascinating is that it offers a glimpse of an impressive, yet not unusual woman of the Roman upper classes. No doubt she is also fascinating because her story is within a trial record of accusations of magic.

See also Gynecology; Sexuality
Suggested Readings
Apuleius. *The Apologia and Florida of Apuleius of Madaura.* Trans. H. E. Butler. Westport, CN: Greenwood Press, 1970.

Fantham, Elaine. "Aemilia Pudentilla, or the Wealthy Widow's Choice." In *Women in Antiquity: New Assessments,* ed. by R. Hawley and B. Levick. London: Routledge, 1995.

Hunink, Vincent. "The Enigmatic Lady Pudentilla." *American Journal of Philology* 119.2 (1998): 275–291.

Pulcheria
Roman Empress (A.D. 399–453)

When Arcadius, emperor of the eastern portion of the Roman Empire, died in A.D. 408, he left only minor children to inherit the throne. His heir, Theodosius II, was only seven years old, and Arcadius's daughter, Pulcheria, was only nine. There were also two younger sisters. The children grew up in the palace, sheltered from the politics of empire by an able administrator and regent, Anthemius. They were well educated in secular studies, and Pulcheria was drawn to Christian studies and earned a strong reputation for piety. She also quickly acquired a shrewd political sense, and throughout her life she exerted a great deal of influence on the events of the Roman Empire in the east.

Pulcheria's mother, Eudoxia, and her grandmother, Flaccilla, had both earned the title of empress by producing heirs for the Theodosian dynasty. (See Chart 1 of the Theodosian dynasty.) Pulcheria would forge a different path to imperial power. When the young girl was fourteen years old—old enough for marriage—she showed a precocious astuteness and began to take control of her fortunes. She announced that she would take a vow of virginity and insisted that her sisters do the same. With this act, Pulcheria dashed the hopes of the regent, Anthemius, who had planned on a royal marriage for one of his grandsons, but she also helped ensure the safety of her brother. As one of the contemporary commentators noted, she wisely saw that this vow would "avoid bringing another male into the palace and . . . remove any opportunity for the plots of ambitious men" (Holum, *Theodosian . . . ,* 93).

Anthemius disappeared from the scene, and Pulcheria became her brother's most important adviser. As a source wrote, "she took control of the government, reaching excellent decisions and swiftly carrying them out with written in-

Figure 64. Coin showing Pulcheria, minted in Constantinople, ca. A.D. 450 (Dumbarton Oaks)

structions" (Holum, *Theodosian . . .* , 97). Theodosius recognized her importance by awarding her the title of augusta—"empress"—in A.D. 414. Her mother and grandmother had earned the rank through childbearing, but Pulcheria broke new ground by accepting the title as a single woman. Coins were minted that proclaimed to everyone that the emperor's sister was now empress, and the coin in Figure 64 shows Pulcheria in the same way that her mother was depicted—she wears the royal robes and crown jewels and is blessed by the hand of God above her head.

The people of the empire credited Pulcheria with setting a pious tone to the administration and helping the Christian church as it grew in power and wealth. Further, many credited her piety with bringing prosperity and even military victories to the empire. In A.D. 421, when her brother's armies won a decisive victory over the Persian armies, the grateful populace erected a victory column to commemorate the accomplishment. The inscription also praised Pulcheria's contribution, for it lauded Theodosius as victor "through the vows of his sisters" (Holum, *Theodosian . . .* , 110). It appeared that the Empress Pulcheria had reached a perfect partnership with her brother. Dynastic necessity intervened to create a change in fortunes, however. Theodosius needed a wife.

In A.D. 421, Theodosius married Eudocia, an intelligent, beautiful, and strong-minded woman in her own right. When Eudocia was also named empress, dissent entered into the household of the emperor. After A.D. 431, Pulcheria had withdrawn from the court to live in the suburbs, and it seemed that her years of influence were at an end. Her greatest contribution to political and religious history was yet to come, however.

By the 440s, Theodosius's marriage to Eudocia had become strained. The empress was living alone in Jerusalem, and there was no longer any hope of a male heir. Theodosius turned again to his sister for advice and guidance. In July 450, however, the emperor had a hunting accident and died two days later. There was no heir named, so the empress Pulcheria ruled alone for a month. The Roman Empire had no precedent for a woman ruling alone, however, so Pulcheria with her political acumen recognized that she needed to marry in order to continue to govern.

In A.D. 450, in spite of her vow of virginity, she married Marcian, a Roman official who owed his power only to her. Breaking all tradition, she conveyed the title of emperor on him, and in return, he pledged to respect her vow of virginity. Their marriage was to be a political one of convenience only. Pulcheria kept her authority without concern for producing heirs for the next generation. Without a doubt, many Christians were concerned about a dedicated virgin marrying for political reasons, but in Roman fashion, the court issued a coin as a propaganda piece to praise the wedding. Figure 65 shows the commemorative coin, on which

Figure 65. Marriage coin showing Pulcheria and Marcian, minted in Constantinople, ca. A.D. 450 (Glasgow, Hunterian Collection)

the couple are depicted as joined together by Christ, who is depicted thus giving his blessing to the marriage in name only of his virgin bride.

Pulcheria's final accomplishment was in the area of religious controversy. In the fifth century A.D. the eastern empire was torn by religious factions who argued over the nature of the union of divinity and humanity in Christ. Pulcheria strongly supported a formula that preserved Christ's full humanity and full divinity (against those who emphasized one over the other). Under her influence, Marcian called a council of bishops to meet to resolve the issue, and the empress appeared in person before this body (which was highly unusual). The Council of Chalcedon that met in A.D. 451 adopted a formula that agreed with Pulcheria's view, and churchmen

praised her role, saying "Many years to the Augusta! You are the light of orthodoxy! Because of this there will be peace everywhere! . . . You have persecuted all heretics!" (Holum, *Theodosian . . .*, 215). This was the crowning achievement of the empress who for the first time ruled as a virgin, not a wife. In spite of the blessings of the bishops, Pulcheria did not have many years left. She died in A.D. 453.

See also Eudocia; Eudoxia; Helena
Suggested Readings
Holum, K. G. "Pulcheria's Crusade and the Ideology of Imperial Victory." *Greek, Roman and Byzantine Studies* 18 (1977): 153–172.
Holum, Kenneth G. *Theodosian Empresses: Women and Imperial Dominion in Late Antiquity.* Berkeley: University of California Press, 1982.

R

Rachel

Hebrew Matriarch
(ca. seventeenth century B.C.)

According to the Hebrew scriptures (the Christian Old Testament), four women were considered the matriarchs of the Jewish people, from whom all were descended. Along with Sarah and Rebekah there were two sisters, Rachel and Leah, both of whom married the same man and competed for his affections.

The Book of Genesis in the Bible tells how Jacob, son of Rebekah and Isaac, went to find a wife among his mother's relatives. Jacob met Laban, his maternal uncle, and stayed with him while working for a month. Laban had two daughters, Leah—the elder—and Rachel. The Bible says, "Leah's eyes were weak, but Rachel was beautiful and lovely" (Gen. 29:17). Jacob fell in love with Rachel and offered to work for Laban for seven years in order to win his bride. The many years "seemed to him but a few days because of the love he had for her" (Gen. 29:20).

At the end of the time, Laban prepared a great wedding feast and brought in the bride, who wore heavy veils covering her face as was customary. Instead of Rachel, however, Laban had brought the elder daughter, Leah, to be Jacob's bride. In the morning, when Jacob discovered the deception, he confronted Laban. His father-in-law responded that it was customary among his people for the elder daughter to marry first. He said that Jacob could also marry Rachel as a second wife if Jacob would work for Laban for another seven years. Jacob agreed, and after years of labor took Rachel as another wife.

Leah bore him many sons, but for a long time Rachel had no children. She was jealous of her sister's fecundity and said to Jacob, "Give me children, or I shall die!" (Gen. 30:1). Jacob grew angry with her, claiming it was God's decision to withhold children. In desperation, Rachel gave Jacob her maid, Bilhah, so he could produce a child for Rachel by her maid. Bilhah conceived two sons whom Rachel named Dan and Naphtali. After Leah had borne six sons, God finally "remembered Rachel, and God hearkened to her and opened her womb" (Gen. 30:22). She gave birth to a son named Joseph.

Jacob became very wealthy after he had lived with Laban for twenty years and decided to take his large family and go to his own country. He left for Canaan with his two wives, his two concubines (the servants of his wives), and his twelve children—including Rachel's son, Joseph. Laban pursued them and accused Jacob of taking his family away in secret, but Jacob responded that he was afraid Laban would take his daughters away from their husband by force. Then Laban accused Jacob of stealing his household gods (which according to ancient custom were small idols that ensured a man's leadership of the family and his claim on the property). Jacob urged Laban to search for his gods and said that anyone who had stolen them would be killed, but he did not know that his wife Rachel had stolen them.

Rachel had put the gods in the camel's saddle within the tent and was sitting on it when her father came in to search. She apologized to her father for not standing in his presence, but she claimed she was menstruating—"the way of women is upon me" (Gen. 31:35)—so could not rise. Laban did not find his images, so he gave up. He and Jacob did make peace, and the family departed with all in harmony.

Rachel became pregnant one more time, and when she came to term, she had a difficult labor. During the delivery, she knew she was dying and named her newborn son Benoni—which means "son of my sorrow." Jacob changed the boy's name to Benjamin—"son of my right hand." Rachel was buried where she died, and Jacob set up a pillar on her grave. The traditional site of Rachel's tomb is today marked by a small white structure standing at the side of the main road near Bethlehem. It is venerated by Jews and Muslims alike as a holy place. Women have traditionally come to this spot to wind threads of cotton around the tomb, thinking this would secure healthy sons for their daughters.

See also Jewish Women; Leah; Rebekah
Suggested Readings
Comay, Joan. *Who's Who in the Old Testament.* London: Routledge, 1993.
Meyers, Carol, Toni Craven, and Ross S. Kraemer. *Women in Scripture.* New York: Houghton Mifflin, 2000.
Niditch, Susan. *Underdogs and Tricksters: A Prelude to Biblical Folklore.* San Francisco: Harper and Row, 1987.

Rahab
Canaanite Prostitute
(ca. thirteenth century B.C.)

According to the Bible, Moses led the Hebrews out of Egypt through the wilderness to the Promised Land along the eastern coast of the Mediterranean. Moses died as they were within sight of the land, and leadership went to Joshua. God promised Joshua victory over all who lived in that land, and the story of Joshua's life is one of warfare and conquests. His first victory was over the ancient walled city of Jericho, and he was helped by the prostitute Rahab.

Jericho was the largest settlement in the lower Jordan valley, and as such it was the gateway to western Palestine. Joshua knew he had to take this city first, and he sent two spies into the city. They came first to the house of a prostitute named Rahab, whose house was situated along the walls of the city. In the meantime, the king of Jericho had heard that Joshua was sending spies, and he sent word to Rahab, saying "Bring forth the men that have come to you, who entered your house; for they have come to search out all the land" (Josh. 2:3). But Rahab protected the two. She first hid the men under stalks of flax that she had laid on the roof and then sent word to the king that the men had gone.

Then Rahab spoke to the two spies. She told them she knew that the Lord had promised them that land, and she said her people knew of the power of their God because they had heard of the miracles that had occurred when Moses led them out of Egypt. Therefore, she offered a bargain: "Now then, swear to me by the Lord that as I have dealt kindly with you, you also will deal kindly with my father's house, and give me a sure sign, and save alive my father and mother, my brothers and sisters, and all who belong to them, and deliver our lives from death" (Josh. 2:12–13). The men agreed to exchange her silence for her safety.

Then she let them down by a rope through her window, which placed them outside the city wall. And she told them to go into the hills and hide for three days until the men who were searching for them gave up. Then they could go their own way. The spies told her to bind a scarlet cord in the window and gather all her family into her house. The invaders would spare all in this house, as long as no one went outside into the streets. She sent them away and tied the scarlet cord in her window.

When Joshua came with his army, they did not have the weapons to break through the thick walls of the city, but according to the Bible, God told Joshua how to bring down the walls. Every morning for six days, the Israelite force circled silently once around Jericho, with seven priests in their midst carrying the ark of the covenant (that reputedly contained the Ten Commandments Moses had received from God) and blowing on rams' horns. On the seventh day, they went around seven times. The priests blew a long final note, and at a signal from Joshua all the Israelites gave a loud shout. The city walls miraculously tumbled down, and the soldiers rushed in from all sides. They slaughtered all the inhabitants of the city—"both men and women, young and old, oxen, sheep, and asses, with the edge of the sword" (Josh. 6:21).

But the Hebrews did not forget the promise made by their spies, and Joshua told them to go and get Rahab and all her family. They brought them all safely out of the city and took them to the Israelite camp. Then they burned the city to the ground. "But Rahab the prostitute, and her father's household, and all who belonged to her, Joshua saved alive; and she dwelt in Israel to this day, because she hid the messengers whom Joshua sent to spy out Jericho" (Josh. 6:25).

Archaeologists have argued for generations about the account of the fall of Jericho as it is given in the Bible. The city is regarded as one of the oldest fortified cities in the world—walls and a tower have been excavated that date back 9,000 years, and that is 6,000 years before Joshua, and 3,000 years before any other fortified cities. Jericho was destroyed by an earthquake and fire in about the fourteenth century B.C.—about 100 years or more before Joshua's invasion. According to excavations, the city was restored and re-settled only several centuries later, during the time of the Hebrew monarchy. Some analysts suggest that the archaeological evidence is in-complete and that indeed the city had been re-built by the time of Joshua. Others suggest that a later Hebrew attack felled the city, and chroniclers attributed its fall to Joshua. Whatever the actual events, the account of the fall of Jericho was considered a turning point in the Hebrew expansion, and people credited the prostitute Rahab with helping the conquest and becoming the oracle of Israel's occupation of the land.

See also Jewish Women; Prostitution; Zipporah
Suggested Readings
Comay, Joan. *Who's Who in the Old Testament.* London: Routledge, 1993.
Meyers, Carol, Toni Craven, and Ross S. Kraemer. *Women in Scripture.* New York: Houghton Mifflin, 2000.

Rebekah

Hebrew Matriarch
(ca. seventeenth century B.C.)

According to the Hebrew scriptures (the Christian Old Testament), Rebekah was the second of the biblical matriarchs (after Sarah) who lived at the dawn of Hebrew history. Rebekah was the granddaughter of Nahor, Abraham's brother, and this branch of the family had stayed behind in northern Syria when Abraham moved to the land of Canaan with his wife, Sarah. One

evening, Rebekah went to fill her water jar at the well as usual. But as she returned, a stranger who was leading a caravan of pack camels stopped to ask her for a drink. She gave him one and offered to draw water for his camels as well. In thanks, he gave her a gold ring for her nose and two gold bracelets.

The man was Abraham's trusted servant, sent to find a wife for the patriarch's beloved son Isaac. Abraham wanted his son to have a wife from his kinfolk and made the servant swear that he would go there on this errand. An angel had told the servant that the chosen girl would be one who was drawing water from the well, so he inquired who her parents were and whether he could lodge there overnight. She courteously invited him to do so.

The servant told the family of his mission and gave them the gifts Abraham had sent—jewelry and beautiful clothing for Rebekah and "costly ornaments" for her family, including her brother Laban. Rebekah consented to the marriage and received the blessing of her family: "Our sister, be the mother of thousands of ten thousands" (Gen. 24:60). Then she started the long journey that would lead her to Canaan to be the wife of Isaac. As they neared their destination, Rebekah saw a man walking through the fields, and the servant told her this was Isaac. She descended from the camel, veiled her face, and walked to meet him. Isaac found out from the servant who she was, took her into his tent, and she became his wife. He loved her and "was comforted after his mother's death" (Gen. 24:67).

In spite of the blessings of her family, Rebekah remained barren for many years. Then Isaac prayed to God for children, and his prayer was granted. Rebekah became pregnant with twins, and she asked God why these children struggled within her. He answered: "Two nations are in your womb, and two peoples, born of you, shall be divided; the one shall be stronger than the other, the elder shall serve the younger" (Gen. 25:23). When she came to term, she delivered twin boys: the first was named Esau; the second, Jacob. Isaac was sixty years old when she bore the twins. When the boys grew up, Esau was a skillful hunter, while Jacob was a quiet man, dwelling in tents. Isaac loved Esau, because of the game he brought, but Rebekah loved Jacob.

Once when Jacob was boiling lentils, Esau came in and asked for food, for he was hungry. Jacob said, "First sell me your birthright" (Gen. 25:31–34), which meant the leadership of the family and the double share of the inheritance that was due the elder son. Esau was so hungry, he quickly agreed to trade his rights for food.

During a famine, Rebekah moved with Isaac into the territory of Abimelech, who was the king of the Philistine city of Gerar (between Beersheba and Gaza). The couple told everyone that she was Isaac's sister, because she was so beautiful that they feared Isaac would be killed for her. After they had lived there for a long time, Abimelech looked out his window and saw "Isaac fondling Rebekah his wife" (Gen. 26:9). The king was angry at the deception, for he said, "One of the people might easily have lain with your wife, and you would have brought guilt upon us" (Gen. 26:10). But Abimelech did not harm the couple and indeed warned everyone to keep them safe under penalty of death. The family prospered in this land, and Isaac became rich. He had flocks and herds and a great household.

When Isaac was old and his eyes so dim he could not see, he called his older son, Esau, to him. He told Esau to go out in the field and catch some game and prepare it for his father. Then Isaac would give his son his blessing before he died. Rebekah had heard this conversation and thought of a plan by which her favored son Jacob would receive his father's blessing instead of his elder brother. She told Jacob to bring two good kids from the flock, and she would prepare the food for Jacob to take to his father and receive the blessing. Jacob was afraid he would be caught in the ruse, saying: "Behold, my brother Esau is a hairy man, and I am a smooth man. Perhaps my father will feel me . . ." (Gen. 27:11–12). His mother reassured him. She dressed Jacob in Esau's best clothing and put the skins of kids on his hands and his neck, and she sent her son to his father with the savory food.

Jacob went to Isaac, and when his father asked who he was, Jacob said, "I am Esau your first-born." Isaac felt his son's hands and because they were hairy like Esau's, he gave Jacob a blessing. Then Isaac ate the savory food and called his son to him. Jacob came near his father, and Isaac smelled the smell of his garments and blessed him, thinking again that he was Esau. Shortly after Jacob had gone, Esau returned. He cooked the savory food for his father and asked for his blessing. Isaac realized that Jacob had stolen his brother's blessing as well as his birthright. Esau vowed revenge against his brother.

Hearing of Esau's rage, Rebekah persuaded Isaac to send Jacob away to her brother Laban, where he could find a wife among Laban's daughters. Jacob left and married both Leah and Rachel. When Rebekah died, she was buried in the family tomb in the Cave of Machpelah in Hebron. Jacob fathered many children through which the faithful trace the history of the chosen people of God. That is why Rebekah is considered one of the founding matriarchs of the Jewish people.

See also Jewish Women; Leah; Rachel; Sarah (also Sarai)

Suggested Readings

Meyers, Carol, Toni Craven, and Ross S. Kraemer. *Women in Scripture.* New York: Houghton Mifflin, 2000.

Rhea Silvia

Legendary Vestal Virgin (ca. 750 B.C.)

According to legend, the founders of Rome were born in an Italian kingdom called Alba Longa. The king, Numitor, was deposed by his younger brother, Amulius. To prevent the rise of avengers, Amulius made Numitor's daughter, Rhea Silvia (also called Ilia), a vestal virgin to be sure she would never bear children. Although she lived the secluded life of a virgin, she was nevertheless impregnated by Mars, the god of war himself. She bore twins, named Romulus and Remus.

Amulius was furious. He ordered the twins to be thrown into the Tiber River, and a slave placed them in a wooden trough to carry them down to the river. The river was in flood, however, and the slave was afraid to approach too closely to the rushing river, so he placed the trough at the edge of the Tiber, from where it was swept gently into the water and floated ashore. There a she-wolf tended and suckled the twins. Plutarch, the later biographer, adds that a woodpecker also fed them—both wolves and woodpeckers were sacred to Mars, the twins' father.

They were found by Faustulus, the royal herdsman, who raised the twins as his own. The boys grew up strong and bold, and in time they met Numitor and came to know about their background. Together they rose against Amulius, killed him, and made Numitor king again. Romulus went on to found the city of Rome, but what happened to his mother, Rhea Silvia? The legends offer various versions of her fate. Some said she was put into prison and died; others claimed that her sons released her from prison. Yet other tales claimed she was thrown into the river, and the river-god married her. The legend offers little that historians might consider factual in understanding the origins of the founders of the great city, but it did give subsequent Romans a pride in their origins. What greater genealogy might there be for a mighty people than a priestess of Vesta and the god of war?

See also Sabine Women; Vestal Virgins
Suggested Readings
Grimal, Pierre. *The Dictionary of Classical Mythology.* Oxford: Blackwell, 1996.
Livy. *History.* Trans. B. O. Foster. Cambridge: Harvard University Press, 1963.
Plutarch. "Romulus." In *The Lives of the Noble Grecians and Romans.* Trans. J. Dryden. New York: The Modern Library, n.d.

Rizpah
Hebrew Concubine and Mother
(ca. eleventh century B.C.)
According to the Hebrew scriptures (the Christian Old Testament), Saul was the first Hebrew king. The prophet Samuel had bestowed upon him the title of king at a time when the Israelites were threatened by their neighbors and felt in need of a single leader who could unite the people. The king successfully attacked the neighboring Philistines and other tribes and brought security to the land for a while. Saul had many children, including two sons by his concubine, Rizpah. After Saul had ruled for

about twenty years, the Philistines again attacked, and this time they were victorious. They killed three of Saul's sons, and the king killed himself so he would not be taken prisoner. After his death, the united kingdom split into two—Judah in the south and Israel in the north—and a civil war began between them. The south was ruled by Saul's eldest surviving son, Ishbosheth, and the north by David, who had been Saul's friend, rival, and military officer. David's ultimate victory was precipitated by the concubine Rizpah.

Ishbosheth was a weak king, and his claim to the throne depended on the military support of his able commander, Abner. The king foolishly offended the general, however, by accusing him of having relations with Rizpah. The general was so angry that he sent a message to David saying, "Make your covenant with me, and behold, my hand shall be with you to bring over all Israel to you" (2 Sam. 3:12). David agreed and the country was reunited under the new king. Rizpah would still face tragedy, however.

Late in David's reign, there was a three-year famine in the country. David was told that the famine was due to a delayed punishment given the Hebrews because of Saul's slaying of a number of inhabitants of Gibeon, a hill town five miles northwest of Jerusalem. David asked the Gibeonites what they would need for atonement, and they said David had to hand over to them seven of Saul's descendants. David gave them five grandsons by Saul's eldest daughter as well as Rizpah's two sons. The Gibeonites hanged all seven and left their bodies unburied.

Rizpah so mourned her sons that she "took sackcloth and spread it for herself on the rock" (2 Sam. 21:10) and kept watch over the bodies. She "did not allow the birds of the air to come upon them by day, or the beasts of the field by night" (2 Sam. 21:10). This watch continued throughout the harvest season, until the rains came. When King David was told what Rizpah had done, he gathered the bones of the hanged men and buried them together with the bones of Saul and his son Jonathan. And Rizpah, about whom so little is known, is remembered for being a dedicated and tenacious mother.

See also Jewish Women
Suggested Readings
Comay, Joan. *Who's Who in the Old Testament.*
London: Routledge, 1995.
Meyers, Carol, Toni Craven, and Ross S. Kraemer.
Women in Scripture. New York: Houghton
Mifflin, 2000.

Roman Women

Ancient Roman women lived from the founding of the ancient city in about the eighth century B.C. to the fall of the empire in the west in about the fifth century A.D., and during this long history, their circumstances changed enormously. The Roman people preserved the ideal of semimythological women, such as Verginia or the Sabine women, who were said to have shaped the formation and ideals of the city itself by embodying strong values of modesty and family honor. Then as time passed, many women used dramatically changing political situations, which turned Rome from a small city-state to a huge empire, to gain personal autonomy and exert some public influence. Thus, the history of Rome is peppered with the lives of famous women who left a mark on the enduring empire. Reading beyond the myths and even beyond the lives of strikingly individual Roman women, historians have come to some general conclusions about the lives and status of Roman women, and most agree that Roman women claimed a surprising degree of independence for the ancient world.

Republican Women

In the founding ideals of the city, there was no hint of the autonomy that later Roman women would claim. In the earliest laws (purportedly established by the founder of the city, Romulus), citizens were admonished to raise every boy-child, but they had to raise only one daughter. This law suggests that women were not valued. Records do not indicate how many infant girls were exposed to die (or to be adopted as slaves), but certainly some were. When an infant girl was born, she was placed at her father's feet, and if he told the midwife to feed her, then she was accepted into the family and raised. She was to be strictly under the control of her father, however, who continued to hold the power of life and death over her. If he determined that his daughter somehow had shamed the family, he could execute her with impunity.

The early Romans were highly influenced by the Etruscans, a neighboring tribe that actually ruled Rome for a time. Although Romans learned much about engineering and divination from the Etruscans, they seem to have been unaffected by the freedom enjoyed by their Etruscan women. Instead, Roman women were to be strictly controlled by their fathers.

In about 509 B.C., the Romans overthrew the Etruscan kings and established a new government—the republic—in which male citizens participated actively in government. In the struggles that took place during the early republic, the people forced the nobility—the *patricians*—to record the laws so that they would exist beyond human whim. In these earliest codes, called the Twelve Tables, which date from about 450 B.C., women's position before the law mirrored earlier traditions that placed them under the control of their fathers. One law read: "Women, even though they are of full age, because of their levity of mind shall be under guardianship" (Lefkowitz and Fant 174). In other words, women were not supposed to control their own property or bring cases before the law but were to be represented by the *pater familias,* the father of the family. Upon the death of the father, custody passed to the nearest male relative.

By the late republic, however, it seems that many women were not burdened by these laws of guardianship. We have many examples of women, such as Terentia and Cornelia, who clearly conducted their own business affairs and controlled their own wealth, so the written laws do not give the full story of life for women during the republic. Although most women were probably satisfied with their status and role within the family, some women seem to have used Rome's marriage laws to gain some autonomy.

As these laws suggest, a girl's father could be more important than her husband. Marriages were centrally important to the ancient Romans (as to all other ancient societies), for they served to bind families together in ties of kin and loyalty. In Rome there were two different kinds of marriage, however. In the most common form, called *sine manu* ("without authority"), the bride remained under the authority of her father. If she married *cum manu* ("with authority"), she was completely transferred to the authority of her husband. This system had strong religious origins because family members worshiped their ancestors, so if a daughter completely moved into the family of her husband, she then celebrated the rites for the husband's family instead of those of her birth family.

Remaining under the control of her father while married actually probably offered some freedom for some women. Living apart from her father, she could have a good deal of control over her own affairs. Furthermore, the males of her birth family continued to make sure she did not suffer abuse at the hands of her husband. We see examples of women (such as Cicero's daughter Tullia) who returned to their father's house to escape from abusive situations, and marriage *sine manu* made such escapes easier.

Fathers also preferred to keep control over their daughters to simplify divorces, which were very common in Roman society. Since most marriages were conducted for political reasons among the upper classes, when political circumstances changed, so did the marriage partners. For example, Julius Caesar forced his daughter, Julia, to divorce her first husband and marry another to solidify a political alliance. Such divorces were further simplified if the wife's family continued to control her resources and dowry, so they could enforce the return from the husband.

In the case of a divorce, the children remained with their father, since they were part of his family, not his wife's. The sources show that mothers remained in close touch with their children, however. For example, Scribonia, the mother of Octavian's (also known as Caesar Augustus) daughter Julia, accompanied Julia into exile even though she had been divorced from Octavian for thirty-seven years, and Julia had been raised in Octavian's household.

While these marriage and family patterns suggest that women were kept under close supervision by the men in their families, in reality many women claimed a great deal of autonomy.

Upper-class Roman women were well educated, for both daughters and sons were provided with tutors. Cornelia, the famous mother of the Gracchi, had acquired a taste for literature from her father, and other women (such as Hortensia) learned the art of public speaking from their fathers. Many women translated this education into artistic pursuits and into exerting some influence over the men of their families who participated actively in public affairs.

The most important factor in a woman's ability to guide her own destiny was money. By the late republic many women (as well as men) had become wealthy as Roman armies conquered far-flung lands, and this trend only continued later in the Empire. Wealthy women such as Terentia (Cicero's wife) and Clodia earned notoriety throughout Rome by their ability to do as they pleased because of the freedom their money brought them. Many other women throughout the empire used their money in philanthropic ways to benefit their community, however, and in turn received their community's thanks in the form of inscriptions that have survived. One wealthy woman in Egypt was given the title "father of the city" in thanks for her generosity, and there were many other similar recognitions left in stone monuments. Through these inscriptions, we can see that Roman women—particularly wealthy ones—played an instrumental role in the growing empire.

The wealth that was controlled by women was periodically raised as a political issue in Rome. Sometimes this wealth saved the city, as in 390 B.C. when the Gauls had captured and sacked most of Rome, and the women gathered up 1,000 pounds of gold to pay the invaders to leave. Such largesse from women seems to have been ignored when Rome was threatened again during the devastating Second Punic War. At that time the Carthaginian, Hannibal, brought his army into Italy and handed Roman armies devastating defeats. As Roman men died in 216 B.C., their wives inherited much more money. Were the women flaunting this new wealth even as Rome was threatened? We do not know, but the Roman men believed they did, and in the following year passed a law known as the Oppian Law that tried to restrict both women's

Figure 66. Roman marriage ceremony, copperplate engraving after antique painting in the Aldobrandin, Paris (Alinari/Art Resource, NY)

wealth and its display. The Oppian Law limited the amount of gold women could have to half an ounce. Furthermore, they were forbidden to wear dyed clothes, and they lost the privilege to drive in carriages within Rome. (Many believed the women had originally won that right in thanks for their saving the city with their gold in 390 B.C.) The war lasted for thirteen more years, and in spite of the Oppian Law, many women continued to be enriched by the deaths of their male relatives.

After the defeat of Hannibal in 201 B.C., Rome swiftly recovered. Men were allowed to display their prosperity, but the Oppian Law remained in effect, curtailing displays by women. In 195 B.C. women demonstrated in the streets to obtain the repeal of this law. The historian Livy preserves a speech that the conservative orator, Cato, was supposed to have delivered, warning Romans to restrict the freedom their women had obtained during wartime. He reputedly said, "Women have become so powerful that our independence has been lost in our own homes and is now being trampled and stamped underfoot in public. We have failed to restrain them as individuals, and now they have combined to reduce us to our present panic" (Lefkowitz and Fant 177). Against this argument, the tribune Valerius spoke in favor of repealing the law. He argued that men's horses could be dressed better than their wives and that the women of Rome's allies could wear more ornamentation than Roman women. Finally, he claimed that men "should

not make slaves of your women and be called their masters; you should hold them in your care and protection and be spoken of as their fathers or as their husbands" (Balsdon 36). He prevailed, and the Oppian Law was repealed. Two hundred years later, Valerius Maximus looked back on this decision and saw it as a moment when women were able to exert their power, and it opened the way for scandalous new freedoms on the part of women.

Was it this decision that led to Roman women's taking more freedom for themselves? Or was it simply that during the many years of war and in the absence of men who were serving as soldiers, women stepped in and took more control over their lives, and more important, over their finances? Whatever the reason, it soon became clear that women of the empire not only lived more extravagantly than their republican predecessors, but they received even more public honors.

Imperial Women

Once Caesar Augustus (r. 27 B.C.–A.D. 14) ended the devastating period of civil wars and established what has come to be called the empire, Roman women gained even more honors and liberty. After the emperor's death, Augustus's widow was awarded the title "augusta," showing that she shared the honor and rule of her husband. Other imperial family members gained the titles "empress" and "mother of the army and senate" or were even proclaimed goddesses. Female members of influential families were honored by the erection of statues and buildings, giving them more public recognition.

The statue in Figure 67 shows that wealthy women—even if they were unrelated to the imperial family—became involved in public affairs and were rewarded by public recognition of their contributions. This statue is of a woman named Eumachia, who sometime before A.D. 64 erected a number of public buildings in Pompeii and served as a patron to the cloth workers. Her example is just one of many that indicate that imperial women, while they had no formal role in government, were highly influential nevertheless.

The growing involvement and visibility of imperial women were not lost on Roman men, and some objected to this growing presence. Tacitus recorded a debate conducted in the senate in A.D. 21 in which one Roman tried to pass a law forbidding women to accompany their husbands during their administrative services in the provinces. The man arguing in favor of this law claimed there had been incidents when women actually commanded military parades and maneuvers for their commander-husbands or directly participated in provincial corruption. He argued that the Oppian and similar laws had kept women in their places, but women now "in these emancipated times control households, law courts—even armies" (Tacitus 120).

Only a few members of the senate applauded his speech. Most shared the ideas of the opposing speaker, who said that times had changed and the circumstances that had led to the Oppian Law no longer existed. He argued that it was worse for marriages and households for husbands and wives to be separated for extended periods and that men would serve more willingly if their wives were with them. He pointed to the example of the great Augustus, who took his wife, Livia, with him on his imperial tours. That argument prevailed, and the freedom of wealthy imperial women was secured. The subsequent history of the empire is full of accounts of empresses and noblewomen traveling in the provinces and exerting their influence as they went.

Perhaps the most remarkable example of Roman women's public involvement was reputed to have occurred during the reign of the emperor Elagabalus (r. A.D. 222–235), when the

Figure 67. Statue of Eumachia erected in gratitude for her public donations, Naples (Alinari/Art Resource)

emperor (probably under the influence of his grandmother, Julia Maesa) established a senate of women. The body met and issued a complicated code of etiquette for women, determining what kind of clothing they should wear and other matters of behavior. The body was disbanded at the death of Elagabalus, but it may have been revived again briefly by Emperor Aurelian (r. A.D. 270–275). All these examples and trends refer to noblewomen, whose family ties and wealth ensured they had a large measure of freedom and autonomy. They were not the only women who inhabited ancient Rome.

Slaves and Workers

In the course of Rome's conquests, it captured tens of thousands of slaves, a situation that transformed Roman society. Wealthy Romans owned hundreds or thousands of slaves, and even poorer households owned several. While male slaves outnumbered female ones by a ratio of about three to one, that still left many female slaves in the Roman Empire. Female slaves took care of their owners' needs as clerks, secretaries, ladies' maids, hairdressers, masseuses, entertainers, and midwives. As this list indicates, many women slaves were well educated.

Women slaves were also used for sexual purposes, either in brothels or in their own households. The master had access to all his slave women, and he could also give permission to male slaves in his household to have sexual relations with female slaves. Records indicate that some masters charged their male slaves a fixed fee for intercourse with their female slaves.

The children born to a slave were automatically slaves and belonged to the household of the father of the family. There were many opportunities for slaves to gain their freedom, however, either through purchase or through the generosity of their owners. These freedwomen might also continue to belong to the household and be paid a wage for their labors.

Freedwomen and poorer Roman women born of citizens worked in many occupations. Many worked in textiles, spinning, and weaving wool for sale. Others ground grain in mills, and still other women worked in construction as bricklayers and stonecutters. Throughout the imperial period, trade was a significant component of Roman life, as goods moved through the extensive lands, and women worked as shopkeepers. They sold everything from exotic merchandise, such as purple dye or perfumes, to everyday items, such as nails, fish, and beans.

Conclusion

Roman culture spanned centuries, and it is not surprising that during that time the position of women changed. Under the republic, the ideal woman was much like her Greek counterpart—modest, silent, and invisible. From the beginning, however, this ideal was never achieved in Rome, because women who felt the same fierce loyalty to their city as their husbands and fathers periodically came to the fore to defend it. Republican women expected to share the dangers of expansion but also expected to share the benefits. As Romans became wealthier, so did many women, and they used their wealth to be more influential in their society. By the time of the empire, many upper-class women exerted a great deal of influence.

It is not surprising that such active involvement generated some criticism. Some of the women who involved themselves in politics (such as Plotina) came under scathing attacks. Women who involved themselves in local politics and philanthropy, however, were praised and rewarded by the appreciation of citizens. The historian Plutarch (writing about A.D. 100) dedicated his tract "On the Bravery of Women" to his great friend Clea, a Greek woman. In the introduction, Plutarch said he disagreed with the traditional Greek view that held that the best woman is one no one had ever heard of because she stayed inside her house. He said, on the contrary, "Best for all seems the Roman custom, which publicly renders to women, as to men, a fitting commemoration after the end of life" (Fantham et al. 390). While Plutarch advocated praising women only after their death, he missed the implications of such praise: Living Roman women saw what their predecessors had done and used their example to participate actively in their society. Perhaps the greatness of Rome was due in part to the activity of resourceful Roman women.

See also Cornelia [Roman Matron]; Etruscan Women; Hortensia; Livia; Plancia Magna; Rhea Silvia; Terentia

Suggested Readings

Balsdon, J. P. V. D. *Roman Women: Their History and Habits.* New York: John Day, 1963.

Fantham, E., et al. *Women in the Classical World.* New York: Oxford University Press, 1994.

Lefkowitz, M. R., and M. B. Fant, eds. *Women's Life in Greece and Rome: A Source Book in Translation.* Baltimore: Johns Hopkins University Press, 1982.

Pomeroy, Sarah B. *Goddesses, Whores, Wives, and Slaves: Women in Classical Antiquity.* New York: Schocken Books, 1975.

Tacitus. "The Annals." In *Complete Works of Tacitus.* Trans. A. J. Church. New York: The Modern Library, 1942.

Ruth

Biblical Woman (ca. 1100 B.C.)

One of the books of the Hebrew scriptures (the Christian Old Testament) tells a story of a great friendship between Ruth and her mother-in-law, Naomi. According to the Bible, this tale was set in the "days when the Judges ruled," or about 1100 B.C. Some scholars speculate, however, that the book was actually composed sometime after 539 B.C. when the Jews had returned to Jerusalem after their exile in Babylon, because the tale offers a positive view of marriage between Jews and foreigners. This lesson might have been more readily received after some Jews had experienced intermarriage during their exile. Regardless of its date of composition, the story of Ruth offered a sympathetic view of foreigners who put themselves under the care of Israel's god, but it also portrayed a strikingly positive view of a woman and her mother-in-law. It has been held up as a model of such family feeling ever since.

According to the Book of Ruth, there was famine in Judea that led a Hebrew family to flee their hometown of Bethlehem. Naomi, her husband, Elimelech, and their two sons moved eastward beyond the Dead Sea to the mountain plateau of Moab. (See Map 5.) There Elimelech died, but the two sons married Moabite women—Orpah and Ruth. Ten years later, both sons had died, and the three widows were left to their own devices. Naomi decided to return to Bethlehem, but she urged her two daughters-in-law to return to their own families in Moab. Orpah went back to her original home, but Ruth refused to be parted from Naomi, saying the much-quoted phrase, "where you go I will go, and where you lodge I will lodge; your people shall be my people, and your God my God; where you die I will die, and there will I be buried" (Ruth 1:16). Naomi offered no more protests, and the two women left for Bethlehem.

They arrived at the beginning of the wheat and barley harvest. Hebrew law allowed the poor to enter the fields behind the harvesters and pick up, or "glean," what was left in the fields after the reapers had passed (Lev. 19:9–10). Ruth joined the gleaners to gather food for the two destitute widows. By chance, her gleaning brought her into a barley patch owned by Boaz, a wealthy relative of Naomi's late husband. Boaz noticed the young woman and asked who she was. When she was identified to him, he told her she should glean only in his fields where she would be safe and protected. She was so grateful, she fell on the ground before him, saying "Why have I found favor in your eyes, that you should take notice of me, when I am a foreigner?" Boaz answered her, "All that you have done for your mother-in-law since the death of your husband has been fully told me, and how you left your father and mother and your native land and came to a people that you did not know before" (Ruth 2:10).

Ruth brought plenty of barley back to Naomi, and the women did not go hungry. Naomi told Ruth of another Hebrew law that might help the widows. According to the law, a dead man's next of kin had the right to marry a widow—or "redeem" her—and if the nearest relative did not want her, the right to redeem her would pass on to the next nearest male relative. Naomi urged Ruth to continue working in Boaz's field in hopes that he might eventually be willing to marry her.

One night, Naomi heard that Boaz was going to spend the night on the threshing floor after the harvest was finished. She urged Ruth to go and wait for him. When Boaz had laid himself down to sleep, Ruth quietly lay down at his feet. In the middle of the night, Boaz awoke and was surprised to find Ruth, but the hardworking widow simply asked him to redeem her, "for you are next of kin" (Ruth 3:9). Boaz explained that there was another closer relative who held the right first, but if he did not want to exercise his right, Boaz would do so and marry her. Before daybreak, he sent her back to Naomi with plenty of barley and told her to wait.

That morning, Boaz waited at the city gate for the other relative to pass. They sat down together in the presence of ten elders whom Boaz had invited, and Boaz asked if the man was prepared to redeem the dead man's land along with his widow. The kinsman was unwilling to marry the widow, so renounced his right of redemption, opening the way for Boaz's suit. The agreement was sealed in the customary way—the kinsman took off his sandal and handed it to Boaz in the presence of witnesses. Boaz then declared that he was acquiring the property and also Ruth to be his wife.

Ruth bore Boaz a son, who gave Naomi much joy. The midwives handed Naomi the child, saying "He shall be to you a restorer of life and a nourisher of your old age; for your daughter-in-law who loves you, who is more to you than seven sons, has borne him" (Ruth 4:15). Naomi took the child and served as his nurse. This boy—Obed—in turn became the father of Jesse, who was the father of the great king David, all born from the Moabite woman who became a Hebrew to follow her beloved mother-in-law home to Bethlehem.

See also Naomi; Susanna
Suggested Readings
Meyers, Carol, Toni Craven, and Ross S. Kraemer. *Women in Scripture.* New York: Houghton Mifflin, 2000.

S

Sabina

Roman Empress (ca. A.D. 88–136)

The household of the emperor Trajan (r. A.D. 98–117) included a number of women who played an important part in his rule—a reign that was remembered as one that brought expansion and honor to the Roman Empire. These women included Trajan's wife, Plotina; his sister, Marciana; and Marciana's daughter, Matidia. Plotina and Matidia even traveled with the emperor on his last campaign and brought his ashes home to Rome when he died in the east. The household also included Matidia's daughter, Vibia Sabina (who is usually known as Sabina). All these women lived harmoniously together (a fact that contemporaries noted with some wonder), but when the young Sabina became empress, she did not have as happy a household as Trajan and Plotina.

Matidia had been widowed while her two daughters (Matidia and Sabina) were young, and she was determined never to marry again but simply to devote herself to her husband's memory. This was why she and her daughters joined the household of the emperor Trajan. The young girls were raised in a circle of pleasant company that was presided over by Plotina, the intelligent and virtuous (and childless) wife of Trajan.

Since Trajan had no children of his own, it fell to his nieces to ensure the succession by marriage. Plotina and Matidia favored a second cousin of Trajan—Hadrian—and urged Trajan to arrange a marriage between him and Sabina. This would link Hadrian to the family and prepare the way for Sabina to become empress. Trajan was said to have objected to the match, but he acceded to the wishes of the women of his household, and the marriage was arranged.

Sabina married the twenty-six-year-old Hadrian when she was about twelve, but the marriage was never happy. Hadrian described her as a tiresome and irritable woman whom in any other walk of life he would have divorced. On her part, she reputedly remarked that she had taken care to ensure that she would not bear him a child so that she would not perpetuate a character as inhuman as his. The evidence for the unhappiness in the marriage appeared as early as A.D. 112, even before Trajan died, because when Trajan, Hadrian, Plotina, and Matidia accompanied Trajan on his ill-fated last journey to the east, Sabina did not join them. Perhaps the estrangement between her and Hadrian was already there. In the East, Trajan died, and Plotina sent a document to the senate saying that he had adopted Hadrian on his deathbed. Although some were skeptical, he became the next emperor, and his marriage to Sabina conferred a measure of legitimacy on the succession.

There were some good times in the imperial household. When Hadrian took the title "father of the country" in A.D. 128, Sabina was given the title of augusta—"empress." Like her great aunt and her mother, she also traveled with Hadrian on many of his imperial tours, and Hadrian was an emperor who spent little time in Rome, so there were many trips. She was certainly with him in A.D. 130 when he toured Egypt, and this voyage seems to have been marked by good comradeship and interesting company. During this trip, Hadrian was accompanied by the handsome young man named Antinous, who was Hadrian's favorite. Indeed, the emperor was in love with the young man in a way he was never drawn to Sabina. Sabina seems to have been on perfectly good terms with Antinous, and they all traveled together.

They were also joined by a remarkable poet named Julia Balbilla, who historians assumed was invited to join the party by Sabina herself. Balbilla composed Greek epigrams on the thigh of the statue of the Colossus of Memnon. Balbilla was a Greek noblewoman, and her epigrams were written in the archaic language of the ancient woman poet Sappho, who had lived almost a thousand years before. In her poem, she honored Sabina, urging the statue to "be keen to welcome by your cry the August wife of the Lord Hadrian." Balbilla also made herself immortal in the inscription, writing, "For pious were my parents and grandparents. Balbillus the wise and Antiochus the king, father of my father. From their line do I draw my noble blood and these are the writings of Balbilla the pious" (Fantham et al. 354).

The pleasant trip on which the royal couple was joined by their favorites ended in tragedy. It was probably only a few days later that Antinous drowned. Hadrian was plunged into despair and had his favorite proclaimed a god, and statues of the beautiful young man were erected in his memory.

In spite of some travels, there were obviously times of high tension in the royal household. For example, Hadrian believed that Sabina was too close to other men in the imperial palace, and the emperor dismissed the leader of the Praetorian Guard and the emperor's private secretary for being too intimate with Sabina. In fact, when Sabina died in A.D. 136, some rumors declared that Hadrian had poisoned her. There is no way to know for sure whether this unhappy imperial marriage ended in murder, but Hadrian himself died two years later.

See also Faustina the Younger; Plotina; Sappho of Lesbos

Suggested Readings
Balsdon, J. P. V. D. *Roman Women: Their History and Habits.* New York: John Day, 1963.
Fantham, E., et al. *Women in the Classical World.* New York: Oxford University Press, 1994.

Sabine Women
(ca. 750 B.C.)

According to the Romans' traditions and legends, their community began without women.

Romulus, son of the vestal virgin Rhea, left Alba with other young men to establish a new city. He chose the Palatine Hill by the Tiber River, and they began to build what became the greatest city of the ancient world. Romulus offered asylum to fugitives from nearby communities to increase the population, but even in their legends, Romans could not imagine that they would welcome fugitive women; they wanted only women of the highest virtue. The strong young men of the new community were faced with a dilemma, for of course the city needed women and children to flourish.

The men first sent representatives across its borders to negotiate alliances and the right of intermarriage for the newly established state. The neighbors were unwilling, however, to allow their virtuous daughters to go to what appeared to be a ragged bunch of rough youths. So Romulus devised a scheme to acquire the needed brides.

Romulus announced that they would celebrate the Consualia, a solemn festival in honor of Neptune, patron god of the horse. On the appointed day crowds flocked to Rome, and men brought their wives and daughters to see the new town and to admire the festivities. The crowd included the Sabines, a neighboring tribe. At the height of the celebration, when everyone was riveted watching the show, Romulus gave a signal, and all the able-bodied Romans broke through the crowd and each seized the most attractive young woman he could find and carried her off. The Roman poet Ovid (43 B.C.–A.D. 17) wrote a romantic view of this rape (or capture) of the Sabine women:

> The king gave the sign for which
> They'd so eagerly watched. Project rape was
>   on. Up they sprang then
>   With a lusty roar, laid hot hands on the
>   girls,
> . . .
> So this wild charge of men left the girls all
>   panic-stricken
>   Not one had the same color in her cheek
>   as before—
> The same nightmare for all, though terror's
>   features varied;

Some tore their hair, some just froze
Where they sat; some, dismayed kept
   silence, others vainly
Yelled for Mamma; some wailed; some
   gaped;
Some fled, some just stood there. So they
   were carried off as
Marriage bed plunder: even so, many
   contrived
To make panic look fetching.
(Fantham et al. 218)

The women's families escaped, but not without bitter comments on the treachery of their hosts to act so at a holy festival. Romulus made sure all his men treated the women kindly and harmed none.

The next morning Romulus told the women of the superiority of the new marriage institution that he had founded as part of his new city. The heart of Rome was to be the family, with an indissoluble form of marriage. Women would be virtuous and under the control of their husbands, but at the same time they could share their property and inherit their wealth. The Sabine virgins were promised that they would share in the fortunes of Rome. Romulus urged the women to forget their wrath and give their hearts to their captors. The men, too, appealed to the women's hearts by kind words and high praise. The women finally agreed and were married to the Roman youths. The new city now had all it needed to flourish.

Even though the women had consented to their own abduction, their families still believed they had to avenge the rape of their daughters. The Sabines took some months and gathered their forces to attack Rome. They surrounded the Roman citadel on the Capitoline Hill and gained access to the citadel by means of the perfidy of a Roman vestal virgin named Tarpeia. The virgin showed the Sabines a secret way up to the citadel, but Roman legend claimed that she was punished for her treachery. The tale relates that as her reward, Tarpeia asked for "what you wear on your left arms," coveting the gold bracelets worn by the soldiers. Instead, the Sabine soldiers crushed her with the shields that they carried on their left

Figure 68. Coin, reverse of a denarius of L. Titurius Sabinus (89–88 B.C.), showing the death of Tarpeia (British Museum)

arms—the coin dated 89 B.C. shown in Figure 68 shows the Sabines crushing Tarpeia. Through this story, Roman men and women alike learned of the dangers of putting the love of finery before love of country.

While Tarpeia betrayed the Romans holding the Capitoline Hill, the other Romans who held the stronghold on the Palatine Hill attacked the Sabines. All parties fought bravely enough for honor to be reestablished, but the war was ended by the Sabine women themselves who had been stolen from their families. The women, who by this time were pregnant, intervened to separate the combatants. Peace was made, and the Romans and Sabines joined to form a single community.

See also Rhea Silvia; Vestal Virgins

Suggested Readings

Fantham, E., et al. *Women in the Classical World.* New York: Oxford University Press, 1994.

Livy. *History.* Trans. B. O. Foster. Cambridge: Harvard University Press, 1963.

Ovid. *Erotic Poems.* New York: Penguin Classics, 1983.

Plutarch. "Romulus." In *The Lives of the Noble Grecians and Romans.* Trans. J. Dryden. New York: The Modern Library, n.d.

Salome I

Sister of King Herod of Judea
(ca. 70 B.C.–A.D. 10)

Salome and her brother, Herod, were born into a prominent family of Idumaeans, an Arab people whose capital was Hebron, a city south of Jerusalem (shown on Map 5). During the time of their grandfather, Idumaea had been conquered by Jewish armies led by the Hasmonaean dynasty of Judea, and the Idumaeans had been forced to convert to Judaism. Herod's grandfather and father served members of the Hasmonaean dynasty with distinction, so the family was well placed to rise to power.

In the early 40s B.C., Julius Caesar became a force in the Near East, and Salome's father, Antipater, provided Caesar with military support. For this, Caesar rewarded Antipater and allowed him to name his son, Herod, as governor over the area of Galilee. Shortly after Caesar's murder, Antipater, too, was assassinated, a murder that Herod himself avenged. In the Roman civil wars that followed, Herod showed himself a skilled politician, and for his support of Mark Antony and Caesar Augustus, the Roman senate made Herod the king of Judaea. By 37 B.C., he had consolidated his control and began his long rule (from 37 to 4 B.C.) that earned him the somewhat dubious appellation "the Great." Throughout his reign, one of the most influential figures at court was his fierce and ambitious sister, Salome.

Like her brother, Salome showed a shrewd political awareness that their fortunes were linked to that of the Roman Empire. She seems to have had an intimate correspondence with Livia, the influential empress, for Herod's son planted forged correspondence between Livia and Salome, thinking this relationship would forward his own ambitions. Salome was constantly at her brother's side, and he consulted her on many matters. Josephus, the ancient historian who preserved her history, condemns her for brutality and selfish ruthlessness. It is hard to dispute his evidence. The king continued to value his sister, however, and in his will he left her a vast fortune for her unswerving loyalty to him.

Salome was first married to her uncle, Joseph, who like herself was an Idumaean. Later, he was killed by Herod's order after Salome accused Joseph of adultery with the king's wife, Mariamne (*see* Mariamne). Salome married a second time to another Idumaean named Kostobar, who was the governor of that province. Salome quarreled with him as well and denounced him, claiming that he was conspiring against her brother. Contrary to Jewish law, she sent him a bill of divorce (instead of waiting for him to divorce her). Kostobar was killed by Herod in 25 B.C.

Salome then had an affair with an Arab, Syllaeus, who was the prime minister of the king of Arabia, and she fell violently in love with him. She wanted Syllaeus to be circumcised, but he refused, claiming that if he did so he would be stoned by the Arabs in his own country. Salome was so deeply in love with him, she wanted to marry him anyway, even though it would have been in violation of Jewish custom. Only the influence of the empress, Livia, persuaded Salome to obey her brother, Herod, and marry the king's friend Alexas, who was a more appropriate husband for the Jewish royal woman. For the remainder of her brother's reign, she remained a central influence in the Herodian household, causing troubles, spreading rumors, and having her rivals killed.

After Herod's death, Salome and her husband, Alexas, took temporary charge of the affairs of the kingdom. The only gracious act recorded of Salome came at this time: Reputedly Herod had imprisoned many Jews in the Hippodrome who were to be killed as soon as the king died. Salome and Alexus released them all instead of following the old king's command. Perhaps this was an effort to gain popularity after her long career of betrayals. She then thanked the army for its loyalty and turned over the reins of power to Herod's son, Archelaus.

The aging Salome was not through with her political machinations, however. She traveled to Rome with other members of her family to appear before Augustus and challenge Archelaus's inheritance. Salome's own son, Antipater, delivered a powerful indictment of Archelaus before Augustus and brought Salome's testimony to the fore as evidence that Archelaus should not rule. Salome was not fully successful in this final intrigue, for Augustus embraced Archelaus, showing he did not believe the charges. Nevertheless, the emperor tried to find a compromise that would quiet the quarreling Herodian family. He divided the lands among the claimants and rewarded Salome by confirming her huge inheritance from Herod and giving her another royal residence. Salome lived another fourteen years after the death of her brother, and although she fades from the pages of history, she surely enjoyed the great wealth that her loyalty to her brother earned her. It seems she did not have to pay for the many murders and conspiracies she instigated at the Herodian court.

See also Alexandra Salome; Calpurnia; Livia; Mariamne; Salome II

Suggested Readings

Kokkinos, Nikos. *The Herodian Dynasty: Origins, Role in Society and Eclipse*. Sheffield, UK: Sheffield Academic Press, 1998.

Macurdy, Grace Harriet. *Vassal-Queens and Some Contemporary Women in the Roman Empire*. Baltimore: Johns Hopkins University Press, 1937.

Richardson, Peter. *Herod: King of the Jews and Friend of the Romans*. Philadelphia: Fortress Press, 1999.

Salome II

Queen of Judea (ca. A.D. 20–ca. 58)

King Herod the Great (r. 39–4 B.C.) of Judea, who was a client-king of the Roman emperors, established a dynasty that held power in Judea for about a century. These Herodian rulers balanced precariously between the power of Rome and the strength of a resident Jewish population who did not particularly trust this dynasty. To protect their authority, most of the family intermarried with their relatives, and many of the Herodians ruled ruthlessly, which caused them to confront the new Christian movement and to be vilified by the writers of the Christian Bible. One of these rulers was Queen Salome, namesake of the murderous sister of the original King Herod.

Salome II's parents were Herodias and her first husband, Herod. When Salome was just an infant, her mother caused a scandal by leaving her husband and marrying his half-brother, Herod Antipas. Salome was raised in her mother's household, and when she was still a girl, she performed a dance for which she is still remembered: According to the Bible, Herodias hated the prophet John the Baptist for criticizing her marriage. Her husband, Herod Antipas, did not want to offend the people by killing the prophet. At a dinner, Herodias sent her daughter Salome to dance for Herod, and the dance so pleased her stepfather that he offered her any reward she would like, even up to half his kingdom. Under her mother's guidance, Salome asked only for the head of John the Baptist on a platter. Herod reluctantly agreed, and the two women were forever implicated in the ruthless killing (Mark 6:17–28; Matt. 14:1–11; Luke 3: 19–20).

When Salome was a young teenager, her parents arranged for her to marry her uncle, Philip, who was also the half-brother of her own father, Herod. The Jewish historian Josephus claims he was a good and honorable prince, but he was considerably older than Salome. The couple had no children, and after Philip's death Salome married again (sometime after A.D. 34), this time to her cousin Aristobulus the younger. Under this second marriage, Salome received the title of queen (which her mother had so coveted), and her husband struck coins with Salome's image on them. She is the only one of the Jewish queens to have her image and title on a coin in the manner of the Hellenistic rulers. Salome and her second husband had three sons— Herod, Agrippa, and Aristobulus.

Little is known about Salome's life, so she is remembered for two things only: her youthful dance for her stepfather and the coin bearing her image. She died sometime before A.D. 60.

See also Herodias; Salome I

Suggested Readings

Josephus, Flavius. *Jewish Antiquities*. Trans R. Marcus. Cambridge: Harvard University Press, 1963.

———. *The Jewish War*. Trans. H. St. James Thackeray. Cambridge: Harvard University Press, 1927.

Kokkinos, Nikos. *The Herodian Dynasty: Origins, Role in Society and Eclipse*. Sheffield, UK: Sheffield Academic Press, 1998.

Kraemer, Ross Shepard. *Women and Christian Origins*. New York: Oxford University Press, 1999.

Macurdy, Grace Harriet. *Vassal-Queens and Some Contemporary Women in the Roman Empire.* Baltimore: Johns Hopkins University Press, 1937.

Richardson, Peter. *Herod: King of the Jews and Friend of the Romans.* Philadelphia: Fortress Press, 1999.

Sappho of Lesbos

Greek Poet (b. ca. 612 B.C.)

In Greece in the seventh century B.C. there emerged a tradition of brilliant poetry—called lyric poetry because it was recited accompanied by a lyre or other musical instrument. The poetry was probably much older, but by the seventh century B.C., some poets appear whose work is wonderfully direct and beautiful. The island of Lesbos in eastern Greece (see Map 4) produced some well-known poets; probably the most famous was a woman—Sappho—who has been a controversial figure since ancient times.

We know little about Sappho's life for certain. She was born about 612 B.C. on the island of Lesbos. Her father was probably a rich wine merchant named Scamandronymus, and her mother was probably called Cleis. The poet had three brothers: Charaxus and Larichus, who served in the government in Lesbos, and Eurygyius, about whom nothing more is known. The oldest brother—Charaxus—reputedly fell in love with a courtesan, which displeased Sappho, but she often praised her brother Larichus. She was probably married, and she had a daughter named Cleis, whom she praises in her poetry. There was political turmoil in Lesbos (as in so many other city-states of the time), and in about 600 B.C., Sappho went into exile in Sicily for a short time. By then, she was already well known for her poetry.

Sappho's poetry must also have been formed by the particular circumstances of the culture of Lesbos. Not only did the island spawn lyric poets, offering Sappho models for her art, but it also seems to have offered a particular freedom for women unusual in the Greek world. In a Greek culture that admired male beauty, the residents of Lesbos seem to have greatly admired and praised their women's beauty—apparently even holding beauty contests. Other Greeks gave women of that island a reputation—real or imagined—for excessive sexual behavior, and by the sixth century B.C. the word *lesbian* began to take on the modern connotations of female homosexuality, as the poet Anacreon indicates in his poem:

> Not that girl—she's the other kind,
> one from Lesbos. Disdainfully,
> nose turned up at my silver hair
> she makes eyes at the ladies. (Kebric 73)

Within this context at Lesbos, scholars interpret the remnants of Sappho's poetry. It appears that Sappho surrounded herself with young girls on the island. She did not exactly run a school, but her poetic and musical talents made her so well known that apparently parents sent their daughters to associate with her informally. Thus they could acquire the talents that would perhaps make them more attractive marriage partners. Apparently there were other groups like Sappho's, and they had rivalries in singing and dancing. Sappho's poetry shows how emotionally involved she was with her young charges.

Sappho's work consisted of nine books, but only one complete poem survives. The rest ranged in completeness from several full lines to one word. Many of the lines lack beginning, middle, or end because they have survived on mummy wrapping in Egyptian tombs, the papyrus having been ripped off the roll of a poetry book. Other lines have survived because ancient literary critics quoted them to praise Sappho's style. The surviving poetry consists primarily of passionate love poems addressed to the young women in her circle. The one complete poem— "Ode to Aphrodite"—pleads with the goddess to help her win the love of a girl, and the goddess promises "soon she will love you, even if she doesn't want to" (Lefkowitz and Fant 4).

When Sappho's girls came to marriageable age, they left the poet's circle, and sometimes Sappho wrote of the loss she felt as the young girl went to her husband: "Cold sweat pours down me, and shuddering grasps me all over, and I am greener than grass, and I seem to myself to be little short of death" (Lefkowitz and Fant 4).

Sappho's poetry has been praised for its expressions of direct, stark emotions that reveal

Figure 69. Sappho of Lesbos surrounded by three young women in her circle, Athenian vase painting ca. 440 B.C. (National Archaeological Museum, Athens)

is thanks to their diligence that the few surviving fragments have been saved to give us an intense yet tantalizing glimpse into the emotions of at least one woman of the ancient Greek world.

See also Muses

Suggested Readings
Barnard, Mary. *Sappho: A New Translation.* Berkeley: University of California Press, 1958.
Brooten, Bernadette J. *Love between Women: Early Christian Responses to Female Homoeroticism.* Chicago: University of Chicago Press, 1996.
Burnett, Ann Pippin. *Three Archaic Poets: Archilochus, Alcaeus, Sappho.* Cambridge: Harvard University Press, 1983.
Kebric, Robert B. *Greek People.* Mountain View, CA: Mayfield Publishing, 1989.
Lefkowitz, Mary R., and Maureen B. Fant. *Women in Greece and Rome.* Toronto: Samuel-Stevens, 1977.
Robinson, David M. *Sappho and Her Influence.* New York: Cooper Square Publishers, 1963.
Snyder, Jane M. *Lesbian Desire in the Lyrics of Sappho.* New York: Columbia University Press, 1998.

the passions of the human heart. During the golden age of Athens (in the fifth century B.C.), her poetry was much admired, and even the philosopher Plato referred to her as the "tenth muse" as a form of highest praise for her creative talents. Her reputation was not sustained, however. Although there is nothing in her surviving poems that describes actual sexual contact between Sappho and the girls she loved, many assumed (probably correctly for the ancient Greek world) that her poetry praised homosexual love. By the third century B.C., comic playwrights made fun of her and accused her of being "masculine" for taking up a man's profession of poet. Perhaps more than anything else, the poetry of Sappho has contributed to the use of the word *lesbian* to mean female homosexuality.

Later Christian authorities condemned the poet's works, calling them licentious and corrupting, and as late as A.D. 1073, Pope Gregory VII ordered a public burning of her writings in Rome and Constantinople. It was only in the Renaissance and again in the nineteenth century that scholars once again began to appreciate the skillful and directly moving poetry of Sappho. It

Sarah (also Sarai)

Hebrew Matriarch (ca. eighteenth century B.C.)

The first Hebrew patriarch was Abraham—the founder of the Hebrew nation. He came originally from Ur, a Sumerian city in the Euphrates valley, near the head of the Persian Gulf (shown on Map 1). Abraham married his half-sister, a beautiful woman named Sarai, who is considered the first of the four biblical matriarchs (along with Rebekah, Leah, and Rachel). With his father, wife, and nephew Lot, Abraham moved up the river until they settled in a trading city in modern Syria, and eventually God told them to go to Canaan, where the Lord promised Abraham he would found a great nation. When famine came in the land, however, the family had to go to Egypt to find food.

In Egypt, Sarai's great beauty caused Abraham to worry: He said, "I know that you are a woman beautiful to behold; and when the Egyptians see you they will say, 'This is his wife'; then they will kill me" (Gen. 12:11–12). So Abraham told Sarai to pretend she was his sister. Indeed, Pharaoh heard of her great beauty and paid Abraham a handsome sum for his "sister" and took Sarai into his household as a concubine. The Lord intervened and brought a plague on the pharaoh and his household. When Pharaoh learned the truth of Sarai's relationship, he reprimanded Abraham for his ruse, saying "Why did you say 'She is my sister,' so that I took her for my wife? Now then, here is your wife, take her and be gone" (Gen. 12:19). Thus Sarai was restored to her husband, and the couple went on their way in peace. A similar incident occurred on a later journey, when the ruler of Gerar near Gaza also was captivated by Sarai's beauty and acquired her after he was told she was Abraham's sister. God disclosed the truth in a dream, and the ruler returned her to her husband.

For all her physical attractiveness, Sarai was unable to conceive a child. This seemed particularly troubling because God had promised Abraham that the whole land of Canaan would belong to his descendants. Sarai suggested a solution: she offered Abraham her Egyptian slave, Hagar, who became pregnant by the patriarch. There was a good deal of tension between Hagar and Sarai, perhaps because of God's promise that his heir would inherit the land of Canaan, which raised the prospects of any child born of Hagar. One passage in Genesis (Gen. 16) tells that Sarai believed the pregnant maid looked at the childless woman with scorn, thus implicitly renouncing the servant relationship (Gen. 16:4–7). Sarai beat Hagar and drove her away from the household, but an angel appeared to Hagar and told her to return and behave appropriately to Sarai. In return, the angel promised that her son would also father many generations. Hagar obeyed the angel's command, returned, and bore a son named Ishmael.

When Abraham was ninety-nine years old—and Sarai ninety—God appeared before him and said that he would become a father of nations. At that time, Sarai's name was changed to Sarah, which means "princess." As a physical token of Abraham's covenant with God, the Lord told him to circumcise himself and all members of his household. From then on circumcision became central to Jewish religion and culture. God made Abraham another promise: that Sarah would finally bear a child. When he heard this, Abraham laughed, saying: "Shall Sarah who is ninety years old, bear a child?" But the Lord said yes, and they should name him Isaac, and it was this son who would inherit the lands that the Lord had promised him. Although Sarah, too, did not believe she would finally bear a child, the Lord's promise came true.

Sarah bore Isaac, and Abraham circumcised his son when he was eight days old, as God had commanded. When Isaac grew older and was weaned, Abraham gave a great feast to celebrate that day. At this time, the old animosity between Hagar and Sarah resurfaced. Sarah saw Ishmael playing with his young half-brother, and she did not want Isaac's birthright to be threatened by Abraham's older son. She told Abraham to send Hagar and Ishmael away. Although Abraham was reluctant to do so, the Lord told him to listen to Sarah but promised that Ishmael, too, would found a great kingdom. Hagar and Ishmael were sent away, and Isaac was left as the sole heir.

God tested Abraham's faith through his beloved son, Isaac. The Lord told the aging patriarch to take his son and sacrifice him on an altar. As much as Abraham loved the boy, he was willing to follow God's command. He built the altar and raised a knife to slay Isaac. An angel stayed his hand and told him he had passed the test. He did not need to sacrifice his son but could sacrifice a ram instead. And the Lord promised Abraham that he would bless his son and multiply his descendants.

Sarah died at the age of 127 at Hebron (shown on Map 5), where Abraham had purchased the Cave of Machpelah from the Hittites, and here Sarah was laid to rest. Abraham took another wife and had many children by her before he died at the age of 175. He was buried with Sarah in the Cave of Machpelah.

Historians have no independent evidence for the details of this biblical account of Sarah, but Jews, Muslims, and Christians alike have venerated the ancient matriarch of the Hebrews.

See also Rachel; Rebekah
Suggested Readings

Bledstein, Adrien Janis. "The Trials of Sarah." *Judaism* 30 (Fall 1981): 411–417.
Meyers, Carol, Toni Craven, and Ross S. Kraemer. *Women in Scripture.* New York: Houghton Mifflin, 2000.

Sarai

See Sarah (also Sarai)

Servilia

Roman Republican Mother and Mistress
(ca. 100–after 42 B.C.)

The Roman Republic ended by 27 B.C. when Caesar Augustus took rule and established an imperial form of government. This transition was not smooth; instead it came after years of civil war during which brilliant politicians and ruthless generals vied for power over this giant, wealthy state governed by a republican constitution that no longer functioned. The most famous man who took power during these years was Julius Caesar, but perhaps equally famous was Brutus, one of his assassins, who killed Caesar to try to restore the republican constitution. An important role was also played by an influential noblewoman, Servilia, who was mistress of Caesar and mother of his killer.

Servilia was born into one of the patrician families of Rome, but her parents died while she was young; she learned early to be resourceful and was successful throughout her life. Before she was fourteen, she was married to a man named Marcus Junius Brutus. In 85 B.C., when she was fifteen, she bore a son named Brutus after his father. Her first husband was murdered by Pompey—one of the powerful figures of this age, who fought Julius Caesar for power. Servilia was the half-sister of Cato the Younger, another influential orator and philosopher who became Caesar's bitterest political enemy. Young Brutus was very fond of his uncle Cato and found himself at times at odds with the powerful Caesar.

Throughout these years, Rome was split between two factions: The *optimates* represented conservative nobles and their followers longing for the old, traditional forms of government and life. The second faction was the *populares,* who recognized the need for changes and who looked to the support of the common people to achieve such change. Cato was on the side of the optimates, and Caesar supported the populares. As Brutus grew up he confronted the tensions surrounding these political divisions.

In 77 B.C., Servilia married for a second time;

she had three daughters with her second husband, an elderly statesman, Decimus Junius Silanus. Sometime during her marriage to Silanus, she began a love affair with Julius Caesar, who at that time was beginning to rise in prominence in Rome. They were about the same age—in their thirties—when they began their affair. Caesar was captivated by her cleverness, and the two remained lovers for twenty years.

In 63 B.C., the republic was challenged by a conspiracy conducted by a bankrupt patrician named Catiline. The Catiline conspiracy was uncovered by the famous orator Cicero, who eloquently presented his case against the conspirators in the senate. (Cicero considered this his finest hour and credited himself with saving the republic.) During the debate in the senate, Cato and Caesar were both standing up, arguing about the best approach to quell the conspiracy. At that time, a little note was delivered to Caesar, which he read silently to himself. Seeing this, Cato cried out aloud, accusing Caesar of corresponding with enemies of the state, and when many other senators joined the call against Caesar, he delivered the note to Cato. Upon reading it, Cato discovered that it was a love letter from his own half-sister, Servilia. Furious, Cato threw the note back to Caesar, saying "Keep it, you drunkard" (Plutarch 1189), and returned to the debate. Plutarch told this incident as an example of how open and notorious was Caesar and Servilia's relationship. After the death of Servilia's husband in about 60 B.C., she did not remarry. She apparently preferred to be Caesar's mistress, and in this role she was able to exert influence upon him and help her son, Brutus.

It appears that Brutus was the person originally destined to marry Caesar's only child, Julia. When Caesar needed some way to bind an alliance with Pompey to seal the First Triumvirate that he had formed to control the Roman government, however, Julia was given to Pompey. Were Brutus (and Servilia) disappointed to lose such a match to the man who killed Brutus's father? The sources do not say, but we do know that in the following year (59 B.C.) Caesar gave Servilia a magnificent pearl, worth a million and a half denari. Some scholars suggest that the gift was to soothe Servilia's disappointment at the failed marriage, but others suggest that this was simply the first time the debt-ridden Caesar had enough money to give his mistress a gift worthy of his love for her. Where did Caesar get the money? He had just received a fortune from Cleopatra VII's father to keep him on the throne in Egypt, and a few years later, Caesar would go to Egypt and fall in love with the Egyptian queen herself.

Caesar showed his affection for Servilia in other ways as well. When the civil war finally came in 49 B.C. with the breakdown of the First Triumvirate, Brutus had to choose between supporting Pompey or Caesar. Brutus hated Pompey, and as late as 52 B.C. had attacked him as an enemy of freedom; but Pompey had the support of the optimates (and his uncle Cato). Brutus did not want to support Caesar either; he may have resented Caesar's long-standing affair with his mother, or perhaps he sincerely believed that the party of change was not good for Rome. In any case, Brutus threw his support to Pompey. When Caesar crushed Pompey's army in 48 B.C., Caesar made sure that Brutus was not harmed—according to the ancient sources, out of affection for Servilia. Brutus was reconciled to Caesar, who gave him a high office in Gaul. Brutus did not even openly object when his uncle, Cato, was defeated by Caesar and committed suicide.

By 44 B.C., Caesar had taken control of Rome. He was the dictator and began his program of reform that he thought would rejuvenate the state. He rewarded Servilia's loyalty and affection by giving her great estates that he had confiscated. But opposition began to grow. Brutus probably knew that in Caesar's will he left everything to his grandnephew, Octavian, which eliminated any hope that Brutus would benefit from their long relationship. Brutus may also have strongly returned to his philosophic position as an optimate opposing change. Brutus was also influenced by Cassius, an older, more experienced man who was married to Junia—Servilia's daughter and Brutus's half-sister. Junia may well have resented her mother's affair throughout the years her father was alive. It is perhaps ironic that the two chief conspirators in the assassination of Caesar were Servilia's son and son-in-law.

On the Ides of March in 44 B.C., about sixty senators surrounded Caesar in front of the senate meeting and stabbed him to death. Suetonius's account includes the final words Caesar supposedly uttered to Brutus before the end—"you, too, child?" (Suetonius 51)—and this phrase was repeated by Shakespeare and others who look back to Brutus's disloyalty as an ultimate betrayal of a man who had been as a father to him. Perhaps Caesar's repeated last words were recorded as a more direct allusion to the affair with Servilia. (Another Roman author—Plutarch—claimed Caesar died too quickly to say a word, and this is probably more accurate.) Caesar's death did not bring peace to Rome.

Although the senate met and proclaimed an amnesty for the conspirators, Caesar had been too popular for such a forgiveness to hold. The Roman people had loved Caesar and longed for revenge, which came at the hands of Caesar's heir, Octavian (later to be known as Caesar Augustus). In 42 B.C., the conspirators were defeated at the Battle of Philippi in Greece. First Cassius, then Brutus, committed suicide.

Servilia lived to see her beloved men die. When Caesar was killed, she kept his gifts and continued to refer to him as the love of her life. We do not know how she reacted to her son's and daughter's involvement in the murder. After Brutus's suicide in 42 B.C., the victors sent her his ashes for burial. The sources do not permit us to know exactly what influence Servilia had on the great events that surrounded and engulfed her, but as the woman who had the longest relationship with Caesar, she could not help but have been consequential. At the very least, without her, Caesar would not have spared his eventual murderer, and the future of Rome might have been different.

See also Calpurnia; Cleopatra VII; Cornelia [Roman Matron]; Julia; Pompeia

Suggested Readings

Kebric, Robert B. *Roman People*. Toronto: Mayfield Publishing, 1993.

Plutarch. *The Lives of the Noble Grecians and Romans*. Trans. J. Dryden. New York: The Modern Library, n.d.

Suetonius. *The Twelve Caesars*. Trans. Robert Graves. New York: Penguin, 1979.

Sexuality

From the earliest humans, women have been associated with sexuality; people believed women were profoundly sexual beings whose associations with fertility shaped their cultural identities. The Stone Age Venus figurines emphasize women's sexual features and suggest how important women's sexuality was to our ancient ancestors. We cannot know more about people's attitudes toward female sexuality, however, until the historical period when written texts supplement visual portrayals.

In Mesopotamia, where writing first appeared, some early texts show that women and their sexuality were centrally important to religion and society. The most famous Sumerian work—the *Epic of Gilgamesh*—purportedly collects stories of a king of the city-state of Uruk (shown on Map 1) who ruled in about 2700 B.C. In one of these tales, the author tells how the mother goddess created a counterhero named Enkidu to check Gilgamesh's tyrannical power. First Enkidu had to be civilized and brought to the city, however, and the only one who could do this was a harlot sent to seduce the wild man:

> The lass freed her breasts, bared her bosom,
> And he possessed her ripeness.
> She was not bashful as she welcomed his
> ardor.
> She laid aside her cloth and he rested upon
> her.
> She treated him, the savage, to a woman's
> task,
> As his love was drawn unto her.
> For six days and seven nights Enkidu comes
> forth
> Mating with the lass. ("Epic of Gilgamesh" 75)

After this, Enkidu was dramatically transformed. The woman tells him he has become wise, and it is time to go to the city and challenge Gilgamesh. This story shows poetically the perceived transformative power of women's sexuality and perhaps helps explain the existence and importance of temple prostitutes, who served the goddess by offering their sexuality.

The ancient Hebrews, too, recognized the significance of female sexuality. In many interpretations of the story of the Garden of Eden in which the first woman, Eve, tempts Adam with the apple, the apple represents intercourse. The couple—like Enkidu—are transformed by the experience of sexual intercourse and acquire a certain wisdom from the experience. (Of course, in the process, they lose the innocence of the presexual state.) In this analysis, the fact that the *woman* is the one who introduces sexuality and tempts the man places the responsibility for sexual intercourse on her. This again recognizes the ancient world's belief that sexuality resides most strongly in women.

Ancient Jewish law acknowledged the importance of sexual relations within marriage and specifically noted that wives had the right to sexual pleasure (and to the children it would produce). For example, men were exempt from military service and business obligations that might take them away from their brides during the first year of their marriage, for a husband was to be home specifically "to cause his wife to rejoice" (Deut. 24:5). Furthermore, even after the first year, husbands were required to have sexual intercourse with their wives periodically to satisfy their needs and to give them children.

One of the most beautiful praises to sexuality exists in the Bible in the Song of Songs. This poem is full of magnificent images that celebrate the young bodies of the two lovers. The man rejoices in the woman's breasts, hair, lips, neck, and so on, and she loves his dark hair, fragrant cheeks, lips, and strong limbs. Many scholars from the ancient world and beyond interpreted this work as allegory, but at a literal level there has seldom been a more beautiful celebration of sexuality.

These biblical references recognized the importance of sexuality to women (and men), but its expression was supposed to be limited to marriage. The Bible forbids "cult prostitution" of both men and women (Deut. 23:17), thus separating Jews from the practices of their neighbors. Recognizing the centrality of female sexuality, the Bible warns men to avoid the seduction of women, perhaps assuming that men would not stray from the marital bonds without temptation. For example, Proverbs describes a seduction scene as a man walks in the street:

> She seizes him and kisses him, and with impudent face she says to him: "I had to offer sacrifices, and today I have paid my vows; so now I have come out to meet you, to seek you eagerly, and I have found you. I have decked my couch with coverings, colored spreads of Egyptian linen; I have perfumed my bed with myrrh, aloes, and cinnamon. Come, let us take our fill of love till morning; let us delight ourselves with love. For my husband is not at home. (Prov. 7:14–19)

The man is warned to ignore her temptations and to return to his wife and enjoy married sexuality. The incident also shows, however, the degree to which ancient men believed that women's sexual urges drove them to illicit liaisons.

These early literary works offer tantalizing glimpses into ancient people's attitudes toward female sexuality, but we can begin to get a fuller account of perceptions with the Greeks, who articulated their views in texts from literature to medicine. Greek attitudes shaped subsequent ancient societies and contributed a great deal to our own perceptions of women's sexuality. The Romans adopted and transmitted Greek ideals of sexuality.

The Greeks'—and later the Romans'—view of sexuality was overwhelmingly shaped by their understandings of what it meant to be male and female. They believed men were supposed to be active—in the world and in the bed—and women were to be passive. Therefore, women's sexuality, while demanding, was expressed in an open passivity. Medical views also shaped their understanding. They believed men were hot and dry and women cold and moist, and it was men's heat and energy that allowed them both to make semen and to make an impact in the world. Ancient men did not separate these two activities. Indeed, Roman texts warned men against too much sexual intercourse, for if they expended too much semen, they would be cooled and thus be made more like a woman. Sexuality was threatening to men, and thus women's sexuality was also threatening.

Most physicians did not believe that women were weakened by sexual intercourse. Instead, they believed that women desired the beneficial effects of the hot semen and would be strengthened by intercourse just as men were weakened. (This analysis, of course, ignored the significant dangers of childbearing, which took many women's lives.) Perhaps the most vivid story that explains classical views on female sexuality is the mythological account of an argument between the deities Zeus and Hera over whether men or women experienced more pleasure in intercourse. Zeus claimed women did, while Hera insisted that men did. They approached the prophet Tiresias, who had lived part of his life as a man and part as a woman. He said that women enjoyed intercourse nine times more than men did. This oft-repeated story was taken as divine proof of women's sexual nature and indeed of their insatiable desire.

Some gynecology texts concerned themselves with women's pleasure in intercourse (see Gynecology), hoping that women's orgasm would help conception. The influential Greek philosopher Aristotle, on the other hand, believed that women produced no seed, so under his influence, the issue of women's pleasure receded from medical consideration. Since women were believed to be particularly sexual, it seems that their pleasure was taken for granted. The texts continued to warn men against the enervating effects of intercourse, however. Thus, one of the legacies of ancient beliefs about female sexuality was that it was threatening to men.

Roman beliefs about the power of women's bodies extended into fears about menstruation and menstrual blood. The Roman encyclopedist, Pliny the Elder (A.D. 24–79), recounted many warnings about menstrual blood: it can put bees to flight, stain linens black, dull razors, tarnish bronze, ruin dyes, and cause abortions. He warns that intercourse with menstruating women can be deadly. The power he attributes to women's bodies—and their sexuality—is impressive, and this power can also be beneficial. In an example that raises a humorous image, Pliny says that headaches can be cured by wearing a woman's brassiere on the head, thus perpetuating the view of the force of women's sexuality.

When Christianity began to spread through the Roman Empire, Christians began to think about their views of sexuality. In many respects, they preserved the Roman fear and caution about sexuality and its association with women. Isidore of Seville, who was a seventh-century A.D. compiler of Roman knowledge, expressed the classical view of women's sexuality: He said, "the word *femina* [woman] comes from the Greek derived from the force of fire because her concupiscence is very passionate: women are more libidinous than men" (Salisbury 23). Much of the misogynist expressions in the writings of the early church fathers comes from the association between women and sexuality. The fear was directed against sexuality, and unfortunately the result was misogyny: The third-century church father Tertullian called women the "devil's gateway" through which all humankind fell. The early church fathers rejected all the senses because they led men to a "feminine" sexuality that was both unmanly and sinful. By relegating women to the sensual realm, Christians devalued them dramatically.

There are some texts that offer a different view of female sexuality. In collections of saints' lives about women, we can see that obviously many women did not share the negative view of women and their sexuality that many church leaders were advocating. In the anonymous Saint's Life, "Life of Melania the Younger," for example, the saint reputedly said that vaginas could not be "filthy" because through them were born the saints of the church. This points to a more positive view of sexuality than that of Tertullian's "devil's gateway." In another example, Constantina reputedly wrote that everyone needed to please God through their bodily members. Here we can see Christian women using sensuality in the service of spirituality—they did not see any contradiction between inhabiting a woman's body and seeking religion. The church fathers built on the medical and philosophical "wisdom" of the Greco-Roman world and incorporated a deep suspicion of women's sexuality into Christian Europe. Throughout the first few centuries after the birth of Christ, however, there were women who clearly knew there was nothing to fear in their own sensuality, and even some writings by women who had renounced sexual intercourse praised women, their bodies, and their sexuality.

Homoeroticism: Love between Women

Before the Roman times, writers hardly mention erotic attraction between women. (The Hebrew Bible prohibits male homosexual behavior in Leviticus 18 and 20 but does not mention women.) Ancient texts probably in part ignored the practice because writers saw sexual intercourse as centered on the phallus and penetration. Women's sexual expression with other women either was too general or simply not necessarily recognized as sexual by male writers.

The famous sixth-century B.C. poet Sappho from the Greek island of Lesbos wrote magnificent poetry that expressed love for the girls who were in her charge. This poetry remained hugely respected throughout the ancient world. Modern scholars argue about whether her poetry expresses sexual love between women or whether it was simply the poetic expression of a passionate, affectionate woman. As time passed in the ancient world, similar arguments arose: Was this the first female homoerotic poetry?

One of the earliest unambiguous references to female homoeroticism in Greek literature seems to have been by Plato, in "The Symposium," in which one of the speakers refers to women who are attracted to other women. In spite of Greek acceptance of male homoerotic attraction, Plato claimed that comparable female behavior was unnatural. This condemnation may have grown out of the violation of cultural norms of female sexuality: If two women made love, they could not both be passive, so at least one had to violate the norm for passivity. (Greeks also condemned men who were passive partners in a homoerotic relationship for precisely the same reason—it violated their maleness. Active male homosexual acts were perfectly in accord with masculine norms, and thus acceptable.)

The Romans condemned female lovers even more strongly. When Roman literature—from the plays of Plautus to a rhetorical exercise by Seneca—mentioned the practice, it was to note that female lovers were against nature, against the gods, and against custom. Jews during the

Roman times also began to become aware of women's sexual relations and prohibit them: A rabbinical commentary from about A.D. 220 on the Levitical prohibition against male homosexual behavior expanded it to ban women marrying women. New Testament Christian writers lived during this time of increasing suspicion and continued the prohibitions that pagan writers expressed. Paul, for example, in his letter to the Romans, wrote to condemn "women [who] exchanged natural relations for unnatural . . ." (Rom. 1:26), and this prohibition was further developed by church fathers who continued the condemnation of female homoeroticism.

In spite of all this rhetoric, how do we know there were actually women who loved other women? Perhaps the strongest evidence is the existence of surviving magical binding spells in which one woman tried to make another fall in love with her. These date from about the second to the fourth centuries A.D. and match the same formulas used by heterosexual lovers. Long spells urge the goddesses to cause the women to love: "Burn, set on fire, inflame her soul, heart, liver, spirit with love for Sophia" (Brooten 86). The spells further ask that the lovers be bound together. These spells indicate that when Roman or early Christian authors condemned sexual relations between women, they were responding to a social reality.

The church father Clement even claimed that some women married other women, but we do not know any details about such alliances. A medieval scribe who was commenting on Clement's mention of marriages wrote "Lesbian" in the margin. This indicates that at least by then, the word *lesbian*—which initially simply meant "from the island of Lesbos"—had come to refer to female homoerotic activity. It may be that over time Sappho's poetry had become sufficiently associated with love of women to have the name of her home island mean the activity.

Some texts from the late Roman and early Byzantine period indicate that some believed that female homoerotic behavior was a medical problem. They claimed that some women had an enlarged clitoris that led them to behave like men. Medical texts offered information on how

to shorten the clitoris surgically to try to make the woman act in a more "normal" fashion. We do not know how often this surgery was practiced, but the existence of texts that advocate such painful mutilation gives silent testimony to how ancient people perceived women's sexuality. Women were thought to be highly sexual temptresses yet supposed to be passive recipients of men's affections. Variations of this formula were considered highly threatening to the established cultural norms.

See also Gynecology; Melania the Younger; Prostitution; Prostitution, Sacred; Sappho of Lesbos; Stone Age Art; Sulpicia; Theano

Suggested Readings
Brooten, Bernadette J. *Love between Women: Early Christian Responses to Female Homoeroticism.* Chicago: University of Chicago Press, 1996.
Cosby, Michael R. *Sex in the Bible.* Englewood Cliffs, NJ: Prentice Hall, 1984.
"Epic of Gilgamesh." In *Ancient Near Eastern Texts Relating to the Old Testament,* ed. by J. B. Pritchard. Princeton: Princeton University Press, 1969.
Hallett, Judith P., and M. B. Skinner, eds. *Roman Sexualities.* Princeton: Princeton University Press, 1997.
Rouselle, Aline. *Porneia: On Desire and the Body in Antiquity.* Oxford: Basil Blackwell, 1988.
Salisbury, Joyce E. *Church Fathers, Independent Virgins.* London: Verso, 1991.

Sibyls
Prophetesses

The name Sibyl was first used in Hellenistic Greek to refer to an inspired prophetess, who was said to have entered into ecstatic trances and delivered oracles from Apollo. There were Sibyls in several places—Varro, the great scholar of the Roman Republic, listed ten, and the origins of the Sibyls go far back to the Greek times. According to some traditions, the first Sibyl was the daughter of a Trojan; according to other traditions the earliest was a daughter of Zeus who uttered prophecies. Some said the first Sibyl was born before the Trojan War and predicted that the land would be laid waste through the fault of a woman from Sparta (Helen).

The most famous of the Greek Sibyls was from Erythrae, in Lydia. She was said to have been born in a cave on Mount Corycus, and immediately after her birth she began to prophesy in verse, so her parents dedicated her to Apollo in his temple. She was said to have lived for 110 years. One tradition maintained that she was the same as the famous Roman Sibyl of Cumae.

The most famous Roman prophetess was the Sibyl of Cumae in Italy. (See Map 7.) It was related that she had asked Apollo for a long life, but at the same time she forgot to ask him for youth. So as she aged she became smaller and shriveled, and she ended up looking like a cicada (a kind of beetle). She was hung up in a cage in the temple of Apollo at Cumae. Children would ask her, "Sibyl, what do you want?" and she would reply, "I want to die."

In Virgil's magnificent epic, which became the poetic history of Rome's greatness, when Aeneas landed in Italy, he was first directed to the Sibyl of Cumae. She then led him into the underworld to visit his father.

The original Sibyl of Cumae was said to have produced a series of oracular sayings that were collected in volumes called the *Sibylline Books*. According to legend, an old woman offered nine oracular books to the Etruscan king Tarquin the Proud, who ruled Rome. When Tarquin refused to buy them at the price asked, she went away and burned three of them. Then she came back and asked the same price for the remaining six. Everyone laughed at her and thought her crazy to think she could get for six books what the king was unwilling to pay for nine. She went away again and burned three more, then came back and asked for the same price for the remaining three. Surprised at her determination, Tarquin sent for augurs to read the signs. They told him he had rejected a blessing sent by the gods and warned him to buy the remaining books at whatever price she asked. Tarquin did so and saved the books and appointed special keepers to guard them.

The books were kept in a chest in a stone vault under the temple to Jupiter in Rome, and during the republic, people consulted the *Sibylline Books* in time of crisis. The oracles were supposed to contain the key to guidance for the state. The temple was destroyed by fire in 83 B.C. and the books with it. A new collection of oracles was made from different copies of the original oracles that existed in many places. These new Sibylline books were placed by Augustus in the temple of Apollo in Rome.

Over time, there were additions made to the books that included Judeo-Christian interpolations in the oracles. Because of these, the Sibyls were later considered equal to the Old Testament prophets, and they appear in Christian art and literature. These books continued to be consulted until the fourth century A.D., when they were burned again by the order of General Stilicho. Fourteen books of so-called Sibylline prophecy still exist, however, which purport to bring the words of the ancient Sibyl into the modern world.

See also Delphic Oracle; Helen of Troy in Greek Mythology

Suggested Readings

Adkins, Lesley, and Roy A. Adkins. *Handbook to Life in Ancient Rome.* New York: Oxford University Press, 1998.

Gardner, Jane F. *Roman Myths.* London: British Museum Press, 1993.

Grimal, Pierre. *The Dictionary of Classical Mythology.* Oxford: Blackwell, 1996.

Radice, Betty. *Who's Who in the Ancient World.* New York: Penguin, 1980.

Sirens

Greek Mythological Creatures

In ancient Greek mythology, Sirens were birdlike women who lived on an island in the sea. In Homer's writings they were presented as two sisters, but later authors increased their numbers to three or four. The Sirens were threatening creatures, for they had enchanting voices that lured sailors to crash into the island's rocks and drown. In some early myths, the Sirens were presented as daughters of Earth, who escorted (or fed on) the dead. The most popular myths of the Sirens tell how the Greek heroes Jason and Odysseus escaped their seductive song.

Jason was the famous captain of the ship *Argo,* and he and his Argonauts had many legendary adventures. According to some versions, they were accompanied by Orpheus, a great musician whose songs could quiet wild beasts and

Figure 70. Sirens lure Odysseus, detail from a Greek red-figured Stamnos from Vulci, early fifth century B.C. (Ann Ronan Picture Library)

move inanimate objects. As the Argonauts sailed near the island of the Sirens, they heard the enchantingly sweet song that drove out all thoughts except to go closer and hear more. As the sailors turned their ship toward the island, Orpheus snatched up his lyre and played a tune so clear and ringing that it drowned out the sound of the fatal voices. The sailors came to their senses and steered their ship out of the Sirens' danger.

Odysseus, too, had to sail past the Sirens' island in his journey home from the Trojan War. The nymph Circe had warned him about the Sirens, and Odysseus told his men to stop up their ears with wax so they would not hear the fatal song. Odysseus himself, however, was determined to hear the song, so he told his crew to tie him to the mast so strongly that he could not get away however much he tried. As they drew near the island, Odysseus heard the song. The words were even more enticing than the melody, for they promised wisdom and a growth of the spirit. Odysseus's heart ached with longing, but the ropes held, and the deafened crew safely rowed the boat out of range of the deadly Sirens. Figure 70 shows the birdlike Sirens luring Odysseus as he is tied to the mast.

In some classical texts, the Sirens lose their evil nature and are remembered by their beautiful music. For example, the philosopher Plato claimed that the Sirens provided the perfect notes that made up the music of the heavenly spheres. In later folklore tradition, the Sirens were shown with fish tails like those of mermaids. Although their images changed, these mysterious female creatures of the sea maintained their hold on the imaginations of storytellers for centuries.

See also Eurydice; Medea; Penelope

Suggested Readings

Grimal, Pierre. *The Dictionary of Classical Mythology.* Oxford: Blackwell, 1996.

Hamilton, Edith. *Mythology.* New York: Mentor, 1955.

Plato. "The Republic." In *Great Dialogues of Plato.* Trans. W. H. D. Rouse. New York: Mentor, 1956.

Sobeknofru

Egyptian Queen (ca. 1785 B.C.)

From about 21,500 B.C. to about 2000 B.C., Egypt experienced a period of decentralization and chaos that is called the First Intermediate Period—a time between strong dynasties. During this Intermediate Period, people saw that the land lacked order (what the Egyptians called *maat*), and many longed for a strong king. (*See* Nitocris.) In about 2000 B.C. a powerful king (named Montuhotep) in the southern city of Thebes was able to break the power of the local nobles and reestablish a strong central government centered in the new capital of Thebes. A pharaoh—Amenemhat I—ruled again over a united kingdom, and he introduced the twelfth dynasty and a prosperous era called the Middle Kingdom. During this dynasty, building, art, literature, and international commerce flourished.

The kings of the twelfth dynasty seem to have recalled the importance of securing the succession of pharaoh to preserve Egypt's prosperity, so many of them practiced the policy of coregency—as he grew old, a reigning king appointed his successor, and both kings ruled jointly for a time. Thus, when the elder king died, there was no break in the rule and no opportunity for civil disruption. This policy was successful for centuries, but in about 1789 B.C. there seemed to have been no male successor, and the twelfth dynasty ended with the reign of a woman—Queen Sobeknofru.

King Amenemhat III (ca. 1832–1797 B.C.) probably fathered several children, including his son and heir Amenemhat IV (ca. 1797–1790 B.C.), whom he dutifully appointed as coregent. The elder king also had at least one daughter, Princess Sobeknofru. In the tradition of Egyptian royal families, the younger Amenemhat married his sister, although we are not certain whether the stone monument mentioning the queen refers to Sobeknofru or another sister. Amenemhat IV ruled briefly and left no remarkable accomplishments. He also left no male

heirs. His sister, Sobeknofru, became the last ruler of the twelfth dynasty.

We do not know the reasons behind Sobeknofru's ascent to the throne. Some historians have suggested that there was a feud within the royal family, with the princess successfully conspiring to wrest power from her brother. There was probably a less dramatic cause, however, for the unusual ascent of a woman: There were no male heirs from the highly successful family of Amenemhat. There is no evidence that her reign raised any controversy, and it was duly recorded in the official lists of rulers. Archaeologists have recovered a number of statues of the queen, and she is portrayed as a regal woman.

Sobeknofru ruled for only about three years, and her accomplishments were as unremarkable as those of her brother. Nor was she able to produce an heir to continue the rule of the twelfth dynasty—it ended with her. We do not know exactly what ended her brief reign—historians simply assumed she died. With her death, however, Egypt's prosperous Middle Kingdom came to an end, and the chaotic Second Intermediate Period once again brought decentralization, violence, and foreign invaders into the Nile valley. The last queen of the twelfth dynasty had been unable to prevent new desolation.

See also Egyptian Women; Hatshepsut; Meryt-Neith; Nefertiti; Nitocris; Twosret

Suggested Readings

Lesko, B. S., ed. *Women's Earliest Records from Ancient Egypt and Western Asia.* Brown Judaic Studies 166. Atlanta: Scholar's Press, 1987.

Tyldesley, Joyce. *Daughters of Isis: Women of Ancient Egypt.* New York: Penguin, 1994.

Sophoniba

Carthaginian Heroine (ca. 205 B.C.)

By the fourth century B.C., two great powers had emerged in the western Mediterranean. Carthage—the magnificent North African city founded in about 800 B.C. by Queen Dido (shown on Map 7)—controlled lands as far away as Spain; it had grown wealthy and powerful on a vast trade that moved goods all around the Mediterranean basin. Rome had begun as a small settlement in about 750 B.C. and had successfully conquered its neighbors on the Italian peninsula. It, too, had begun to grow wealthy and powerful, and it seemed inevitable that these two powers would clash. In 264 B.C., the two city-states came into direct conflict over a disputed region in Sicily. This began the first of three Punic Wars between Rome and Carthage. (*Punic* came from the Roman word for "Phoenician," which recalled Carthage's early history as a Phoenician colony.) The Punic Wars were extraordinarily destructive, and at the end they destroyed Carthage and established Rome as a major imperial power.

During the Second Punic War (218–201 B.C.) it seemed as if Rome itself would be conquered as the Carthaginian general Hannibal marched across the Alps with his armies and elephants and defeated Roman forces all across Italy. Rome was saved by its dogged determination and by a bold general—Scipio—who took the war to Carthage's North African homeland. While all students remember the Carthaginian general Hannibal, few remember his niece Sophoniba (often spelled Sophonisba), who secured Carthage's North African allies in a way that almost led to Rome's defeat.

Throughout the Punic Wars, the native North African princes carefully played one side against the other to gain power and to try to ally with the ultimate winner. To the west of Carthage was the large kingdom of Numidia, led by the talented, but aging, King Syphax. Syphax had been inclined to support Rome to free himself from the strong presence of the Carthaginian armies, and in the summer of 206 B.C., the Roman general Scipio met with the Numidian king and was certain that he had secured the king's alliance. The general believed Carthage would be pressed from the west as well as from Rome's armies. Scipio did not reckon, however, with the beautiful and talented Sophoniba, daughter of the Carthaginian general Hasdrubal.

The Carthaginians knew that their security depended upon making an alliance with Syphax, so they sealed the king's friendship by his marriage with Sophoniba. The Roman sources say that she was young, beautiful, educated, and a fine musician. She was also "gifted with wit as well as charm" and completely "en-

slaved" Syphax (Lancel 399). But the elderly Syphax could not hold his own territory, and in 203 B.C. his palace and country were captured by a rival claimant to the throne—Massinissa.

Carthage was placed in a difficult position by this palace coup, because Massinissa had supported Rome in the past and was now in a position to deliver the powerful Numidian forces into Rome's camp. Once again, however, Sophoniba came to her country's aid. Massinissa was immediately captivated by the talented woman and fell in love with her, but this great love was not enough to stop the conquering armies of Scipio. At the end of the Second Punic War, as Rome won a decisive victory, Sophoniba asked her new lover, Massinissa, to put her to death rather than let her be captured by the hated Romans. He agreed and prepared poison for her. Once again in the land founded by Queen Dido, a remarkable Carthaginian woman preferred to die rather than succumb to an enemy.

Carthage's final defeat took place at the end of the Third Punic War in 149 B.C. The Romans were determined to destroy their old rival completely; the Roman general Scipio Aemilianus blockaded the city and presided over street fighting for six days and nights, and his troops struggled up the Byrsa hill to take the fortification at the top. Finally, the stronghold itself could not hold, and the Carthaginian general, Hasdrubal, surrendered, pleading at Scipio's feet for mercy.

Here at the final moments of the independent Carthaginian civilization, its history was once again dramatically punctuated by the suicide of a brave woman. As the general surrendered, his unnamed wife reproached him for cowardice. In a final gesture, she cursed her husband: "Upon this Hasdrubal, betrayer of his country and her temples, of me and his children, may the gods of Carthage take vengeance." With these words, she killed their children, flung them into the fires that were consuming the city, and plunged in after them. The Roman historian Appian, who recounted these events, concluded his account of the incident with his own reproach of the husband: "With these words . . . did the wife of Hasdrubal die, as Hasdrubal should have died himself" (Salisbury 54).

According to legend, ancient Carthage was founded by a woman who committed suicide rather than succumb to another's will, and the ancient city's independent existence also ended with the same act. For better or worse, the tradition of sacrifice was strong in North Africa, and the stories of these women helped to perpetuate it.

See also Dido
Suggested Readings
Appian. *Appian's Roman History.* Trans. H. White. Cambridge: Harvard University Press, 1964.
Lancel, Serge. *Carthage: A History.* Oxford: Basil Blackwell, 1992.
Livy. *History.* Trans. B. O. Foster. Cambridge: Harvard University Press, 1963.
Salisbury, Joyce E. *Perpetua's Passion.* New York: Routledge, 1997.

Sosipatra

Philosopher (ca. A.D. 300s)
Ephesus (shown on Map 8) was a prosperous merchant city in Asia Minor where ideas circulated along with goods, so it was a vibrant intellectual town as well as a rich one. The apostle Paul had preached in Ephesus, and there was a well-established Christian community there by A.D. 300. Like other areas in the Roman Empire, however, Ephesus boasted competing sects as people sought to understand the mysteries of the universe through many differing paths. Sometime in the fourth century A.D., a girl named Sosipatra was born in Ephesus, and she would grow up to take a prominent place in the intellectual life of her city.

When Sosipatra was a young girl, she was placed in the care of two elderly male guardians, who were reputed to have extraordinary powers. Many people in the fourth century claimed to have prophetic or magical powers, and Sosipatra's guardians called themselves "Chaldeans," which probably meant that they thought of themselves as soothsayers, astrologers, or seers practicing some other form of magical divination. They taught Sosipatra all they knew, and by the time she grew up, she had gained a great reputation for clairvoyance.

Her reputation for philosophy eclipsed her skill in magic, however.

When she reached marriageable age, a match was arranged with the Sophist philosopher Eustathius. Sosipatra quickly eclipsed her philosopher husband. Her biographer wrote that "her surpassing wisdom made her own husband seem inferior and insignificant" (Kersey 191). In the course of their marriage, she bore three sons. One, named Antonius, became known in his own right as a philosopher-seer, so it seems he learned a great deal from his mother. After her husband died, she continued her career, surpassing her previous reputation.

She moved from Ephesus to Pergamon, a larger and more cosmopolitan city deeper in Asia. There she took another philosopher—Aedesius—as her consort, and together they founded a school. She held a chair in philosophy that was as prestigious as Aedesius's, and Eunapius, her biographer, wrote that after students had attended Aedesius's lectures, they would go immediately to hear Sosipatra's. Unfortunately, we know no more about this philosopher-seer, but we may assume that she continued her teaching.

There are no surviving writings by Sosipatra, so scholars cannot identify what kind of philosophy she favored or what her impact was on the students she taught. The ease with which she could maintain her reputation as a seer, soothsayer, and philosopher does reveal the way these enterprises were mixed in the fourth century A.D. During that time, many people were longing to be more closely in touch with the gods—whether by magic or by reason, and Sosipatra's career illustrates this yearning. She was another ancient woman who used all her talents to make her way in the dynamic, cosmopolitan cities of the late Roman Empire.

See also Hypatia; Philosophers, Greek
Suggested Readings
Eunapius. *The Lives of the Philosophers and Sophists.* Trans. W. C. Wright. New York: Putnam, 1922.
Kersey, Ethel M. *Women Philosophers: A Bio-Critical Source Book.* New York: Greewood Press, 1989.
Menage, Gilles. *The History of Women Philosophers.* Trans. Beatrice H. Zedler. Lanham, MD: University Press of America, 1984.

Spartan Women

The Greek city-state of Sparta (shown on Map 4) had a way of life strikingly different from that of the other classical Greek cities. When the early Greek invaders marched into the Peloponnese (the southern peninsula of the Greek mainland), they conquered a resident population, whom they enslaved and called *helots*. These Spartan overlords constantly feared the revolt of the *helots*, who greatly outnumbered the ruling invaders, so they structured their city as a military encampment. Boys lived in barracks from their youth through most of their mature lives and trained rigorously all the time. The Spartans created strong soldiers who were the envy (and fear) of the other Greek city-states. At the same time, the strictly regulated lives of the men created a way of life for Spartan women that was dramatically different from that of the secluded lives of women in other Greek city-states. The Spartan women have been both admired and vilified from the ancient times to the present.

While the job of a Spartan man was to become a good soldier, that of a woman was to produce good soldiers. To this end, the semi-legendary founder of Sparta's constitution, Lycurgus, reputedly broke with traditional Greek practice. He said that for women to bear strong children, they should avoid the secluded life of most Greek women, who were to stay inside and weave wool. He believed slave women could weave enough to supply all the needed clothing. Free women were to be educated and engage in vigorous athletic training just as men, and these strong women would then bear strong children.

Sparta was the only Greek city-state that provided a public education for its girls. These girls studied Greek myths, poetry, and philosophy. At the end of the seventh century B.C., a poet named Alcman composed choral lyrics that were performed by Spartan girls, and many of these are beautiful and, indeed, erotic. Women who participated in these artistic activities reputedly knew how to sing and dance beautifully. Unlike Athens, Sparta produced at least two female poets; though their names are known, their works are lost. As late as the fourth century B.C., the philosopher Plato remarked that Spartan women were well educated in philosophy. While Spartan

Figure 71. Statuette of a female athlete, sixth century B.C. (Foto Marburg/Art Resource, NY)

men who spent all their time in military training were notoriously uneducated, it seems that Spartan women received a fine classical education.

Greek commentators remarked in even more wonder about Spartan women's exercise habits, as Lycurgus's recommendation for physical exertion was embraced vigorously. Women raced, wrestled, and threw the discus and javelin. While they probably did not exercise completely nude as men did, they did appear in scanty dresses that offered freedom of movement. Figure 71 shows a statuette of a young woman athlete dressed as a Spartan woman would be for racing. The healthy young women were reputedly beautiful—with golden hair and shining complexions uncovered by cosmetics.

According to the ancient sources, the Spartans developed unusual marriage practices that they believed would also enhance the strength of children. After marriage, husbands and wives were kept separate, and the men had to sneak out of the barracks and stealthily enter their wife's room without being seen. Reputedly this restriction on intercourse was supposed to keep their mutual desire strong, with the result that strong children would be conceived during these passionate, stolen interludes. Other Greeks commented negatively on this unusual marital situation, which also permitted the possibility for adulterous relationships to develop. It seemed, however, that the important thing was that strong children were conceived, regardless of the father.

The Greek biographer Plutarch (ca. A.D. 46–ca. 120) recorded a series of quotations that were supposed to be the words of Spartan women. It is impossible to tell how many of these quotations were accurate, or when they were composed, but they serve to give a sense of the reputed wit of Spartan women (unlike their supposedly silent men) and of the values that they held dear. If the quotations are accurate, Spartan women during the early centuries of Sparta's history shared the militaristic values and loyalty to the state of their husbands. One saying describes the strength of a mother's resolve:

After hearing that her son was a coward and unworthy of her, Damatria killed him when he made his appearance. This is the epigram about her: Damatrius who broke the laws was killed by his mother, She a Spartan lady, he a Spartan youth. (Plutarch 459)

Another woman was burying her son when an old woman came up to her and said, "Ah, what bad luck you have had you poor woman." "No, by heaven," the Spartan mother responded, "but good luck; for I bore him that he might die for Sparta, and this is the very thing that has come to pass for me" (Plutarch 463).

These brave Spartan women also earned a reputation for unprecedented freedom among Greek women. In one of the sayings Plutarch preserved, a Spartan woman who had been captured in war was being sold as a slave. When the slave master inquired of her what she knew how to do, she simply answered: "To be free" (Plutarch 469). By late in Sparta's history, after its victory in the Peloponnesian War, some commentators claimed that feminine freedom caused Sparta's decline. The philosopher Aristotle (384–322 B.C.) said that Spartan women, who had the right to own and manage their own property, had accumulated so much money that they had become corrupted by it. Aristotle claimed that nearly two-fifths of the land was owned directly by women. Furthermore, he said Spartan women were using their wealth frivolously, rather than for the good of the state.

It is impossible to know how much truth there is in Aristotle's accusations. Certainly women controlled property more in Sparta than elsewhere in the Greek world, but there is no evidence that this control contributed to the decline of the military state. Women did spend money on nonessential items, but so did many men from other Greek states. For example, Spartan women were the first to join men in owning racehorses to run in the Olympic Games. Like wealthy male owners, they did not themselves race, but hired charioteers. One inscription of Olympic victories in 396 B.C. proudly proclaimed the novelty of one woman's achievement:

My father and brothers were kings of Sparta. I, Cynisca, victorious with my chariot of fleet horses, erected this statue. I declare that I am the only woman in all of Greece, who has won this crown. (Fantham et al. 64)

The city-state of Sparta produced a harsh military society in which men gave up individual freedoms for the glory of the state. Yet, at the same time, this city offered opportunities for women that were unheard of in the rest of the ancient Greek world. Women were educated, physically fit, and self-reliant. They controlled property and expressed themselves creatively. Their experiences offer rare examples of voices of independent women of the ancient Greek world.

See also Greek (Athenian) Women
Suggested Readings
Fantham, E., et al. *Women in the Classical World.* New York: Oxford University Press, 1994.
Plutarch. *Moralia, III.* Trans F. C. Babbitt. Cambridge: Harvard University Press, 1961.
Pomeroy, Sarah B. *Goddesses, Whores, Wives, and Slaves: Women in Classical Antiquity.* New York: Schocken Books, 1988.

Stone Age Art

ca. 40,000–ca. 4000 B.C.

For most of human history people lived in small tribal groups, moved slowly but consistently as they sought food and shelter, and survived by gathering plants that grew wild and by hunting wild animals. During this early period, people depended upon tools and weapons made of stone, and what we know of their life is mostly extrapolated from the remains of the stone tools they carefully made. Therefore, scholars have called this period the Stone Age. In time, scholars began to subdivide this long period based on the quality of the tools that people made: The first appearance of men and women who used tools was about 40,000 B.C., and this Old Stone Age (Paleolithic) extends to about 8000 B.C. (Of course the scarcity of the evidence makes all these dates approximate, and the dates vary all over the world.) During this time, the great ice ages that covered many continents with glaciers took place. The Middle Stone Age (Mesolithic), which extended from about 8000 to 5000 B.C., marked a warming climate and the retreat of glaciers. (Once again these dates vary depending on the location; the Mesolithic ended in the Near East in about 7000 B.C. and in Britain in about 4000 B.C.) Now, peoples could settle around lakes and other places where food was abundant. Finally, the New Stone Age (Neolithic) began about 7000 B.C. in the Near East and extended as late as the second millennium B.C. in northern Europe. In the Neolithic, some people slowly made the revolutionary change from hunting and gathering to agriculture. Society from then on in many places of the world would take on a dramatic new form.

The evidence for the lives of ancient women in the Stone Age is scarce. The remnants of stone tools tell us nothing about who made them or who used them. Archaeologists have discovered that Stone Age people carefully buried their dead, many placing them in a fetal position and covering them with a red pigment called red ochre; some scholars suggest the red represents blood—perhaps of the childbirth that had ushered the person into the world in the first place. The most tantalizing information about beliefs about women comes from the

Figure 72. Venus of Willendorf, ca. 25,000 B.C. (Ann Ronan Picture Library)

Stone Age art that has remarkably survived for so long.

Paleolithic artists focused on two principal kinds of artwork—sculpture and painting. The most famous sculpture is a small (about 4 1/2 inches high) carving of a woman found in Willendorf, Austria, which was made in about 25,000 B.C. Figure 72 shows this statue, which was carved from limestone and was originally dyed with red ochre. Scholars have come to call these figures Venuses, named after the Roman goddess of love, and the Venus of Willendorf is just one of many that have been found all over Europe. The small female figure has no facial features, which implies that she is more a symbol than an individual, and many scholars believe that she represented a supernatural appeal to fertility.

The large breasts on which she rests her arms hint at an abundance of food, and her heavy belly and thighs celebrate an excess of calories rarely available to hunting-gathering societies. The figure's prominently displayed genitals may express either sexuality or childbirth, or both. We do not know whether the figure represents a fertility

Figure 73. Goddess statue from Malta, ca. 2500 B.C. (J. Allan Cash Ltd., London)

"goddess," a celebration of—or hope for—general abundance, or a magical invocation of fecundity. The red ochre dye may have represented the blood of menstruation or childbirth, which suggests that Stone Age people may have had awe and respect for that aspect of womanhood.

The portrayal of female figures continued into the Neolithic (*see* Çatal Hüyük), and perhaps the most dramatic surviving fragments of female statues come from the island of Malta, where archaeologists have excavated a large Neolithic temple complex. Within the temples, there is evidence of sacrifices of animals and of stone statues that must have represented goddesses. Figure 73 shows the stone fragment of one such goddess. All that has survived of this figure is her body and legs. Her large legs, like those of other statues found here, leave no doubt that in their original state these were imposing—indeed gigantic—figures. One colossal statue was surrounded by many smaller obese female figures, and they suggest the presence of a fertility cult. A number of them were ritually covered around the legs with red ochre, again suggesting the blood of childbirth or menstruation.

Even more impressive than the fine stone carvings were great cave paintings that have survived deep in caves of limestone in Spain and France and in other areas of the world, including Africa and Australia. The paintings were mostly of great animals—bisons, horses, stags—that must have represented impressive hunts. People returned seasonally to the same caves and painted new figures near earlier ones, and sometimes over them. Some caves show evidence of repeated painting over an astonishing span of 10,000 years, revealing the endurance of these early cultures as they preserved their traditions over lengths of time that are almost unimaginable today. Scholars believe that the paintings were done for some ritual purpose—perhaps to ensure the continued abundance of the great game animals they painted. The interpretation is made more complicated because many of the animals they feature were not the principal ones they hunted. It may also be that the repeated visits to the deep caves coincided with the periodic gathering of groups for trade and other interactions, and perhaps the paintings preserved tribal memories.

The cave paintings offer tantalizing bits of information for scholars studying the history of ancient women, but there is little consensus on what the images signify, because the paintings, while realistic, seem to portray a ritual life that may or may not have coincided with real life. Nevertheless, some suggestions emerge. In the European paintings, the animals are portrayed most realistically, but there are small figures of hunters, and these are all male. This has led some scholars to speculate that—as in many modern hunting-gathering societies—men did most of the hunting while women gathered the important vegetable products that actually made up most of the caloric intake. (The Australian cave paintings do show women and men together hunting kangaroos, so it is impossible to generalize based on such scanty evidence.)

Some of the most interesting speculation on the paintings comes not from the figures themselves, but from abstract symbols that often surround the magnificent images. Figure 74 shows a wonderful horse from the caves of Lascaux, France. The horse's body suggests pregnancy

Figure 74. Horse from Lascaux, France, ca. 15,000 B.C. (Ann Ronan Picture Library)

and the imminent delivery of a foal, so scholars see the presence of the female and the important fertility in the figure of the animal. There are two diagonal forms in this image—one near the horse's neck and the other overlapping its lower outline—and these have been identified either as plants or as arrows. They are similar to hunting harpoons that have been found in the Stone Age sites, so they may be hunting figures. Some archaeologists identify the harpoons as phallic symbols, and therefore male signs. Above the horse is a rectangle, which some scholars interpret as a female symbol. These interpretations are similar to many that emerge from the study of the strange symbols surrounding the cave paintings, and if they are accurate, they suggest a society that was deeply concerned about fertility and survival, and one that also profoundly understood the importance of both men and women to contribute to the totality of their world. We are so removed from those Stone Age times, however, that we can hardly do more than admire in wonder their magnificent, mysterious creations.

See also Çatal Hüyük; Clothing; Jewelry; Work
Suggested Readings

Bandi, Hans-Georg, and Henri Breuil. *The Art of the Stone Age: Forty Thousand Years of Rock Art.* London: Methuen, 1970.
Ehrenberg, M. *Women in Prehistory.* Norman: University of Oklahoma Press, 1989.
Gimbutas, M. *The Civilization of the Goddess: The World of Old Europe.* San Francisco: HarperCollins, 1991.
Graziosi, Paolo. *Paleolithic Art.* New York: McGraw-Hill, 1960.

Stratonice I

Queen in Seleucid Dynasty
(r. ca. 295 B.C.– 254 B.C.)

After Alexander the Great's death in 323 B.C., the empire he had briefly forged broke apart, and the most powerful of his followers—the "successors"—became kings in what have come to be called the Hellenistic kingdoms. (See Map 6.) In 305 B.C., one of his followers—Seleucus I—was able to secure the eastern part of the empire, including Mesopotamia and regions to the east. He introduced the Seleucid dynasty that ruled for centuries. As was traditional with the Macedonian kings, Seleucus consolidated his power with strong polygamous marriages. His first wife, Apame, was Persian and had been given to Seleucus by Alexander himself at a great wedding in 324 B.C. in which Macedonians married Persian women. Apame was Seleucus's only wife until 298 B.C., when he sealed a treaty with the Macedonian king, Demetrius, by accepting Demetrius's young daughter, Stratonice, as his next wife. Stratonice proved to be as popular as her wise and kind mother, Phila.

Stratonice bore one daughter by Seleucus, named Phila after her mother, but then her marriage took a strange turn. The Roman historian Appian tells the story in great detail. According to him, Antiochus, Seleucus's son by his first wife (Apame), grew very ill. Seleucus called his best physician and was told that the young man was sick with love for his stepmother, Stratonice. Seleucus preferred his son's happiness and health to his young wife, so he arranged for Stratonice to marry her stepson. Furthermore, Seleucus sent the couple to the eastern provinces as king and queen of the east, and he told the couple not to worry about their unorthodox union, for as he said, "what the King holds as right *is* right" (Macurdy 79).

Antiochus and Stratonice had four children, most of whom were caught up in the stormy politics of the age. Their son Seleucus shared his father's throne for a time, but Antiochus put the youth to death, charging him with treason. Antiochus II inherited his father's throne and ruled from 261 to 246 B.C., but then he was perhaps poisoned by a wife he had repudiated. Stratonice and Antiochus's daughters made good marriages: Apame became the mother of Berenice II of Egypt, and Stratonice II married her cousin, Demetrius II of Macedonia.

Stratonice I was a religious woman, and she used much of her great wealth in offerings to the gods. She bore the title of empress and was worshiped in local cults as Aphrodite Stratonikis, which suggests that she had won the love and respect of many of her subjects. Her husband was said to have loved her greatly, and he took no

other wives—remarkable for the Hellenistic kings. For all this, Stratonice seems to have been little interested in wielding political power, but she lived relatively calmly as her mother had done before her. She died in 254 B.C., outliving her husband by seven years.

See also Laodice I; Phila

Suggested Readings

Appian. *Appian's Roman History.* Trans. H. White. Cambridge: Harvard University Press, 1964.
Macurdy, Grace Harriet. *Hellenistic Queens.* Baltimore: Johns Hopkins University Press, 1932.

Sulpicia

Roman Poet (b. ca. 40 B.C.)

The reign of Caesar Augustus (r. 27 B.C.–A.D. 14) introduced the imperial period of Rome and began what has become known as the Pax Romana (Roman peace), a time of relative peace and prosperity for the Roman world. During Augustus's reign, there was also a flourishing of literature—the Augustan era has been called the golden age of Latin literature—fostered by brilliant poets under imperial patronage. The great poets of the age included Horace (65–8 B.C.) and Ovid (43 B.C.–A.D. 17), but the greatest of them all was Virgil (70–19 B.C.). Virgil's fame rests chiefly on the *Aeneid,* the great Roman epic that tells a gripping story of the origins of Roman civilization. In this poem, Virgil tells of Dido, the Carthaginian queen who sacrificed honor and power for love of Aeneas, who abandoned her and founded the city of Rome. The *Aeneid* also includes a praise of Augustus and his policies that brought a golden age to Rome. From this age that fostered poetry, the works of only one female poet survive—those of Sulpicia. Thus, her works are important for shedding light on at least one woman's feelings about love, sex, and poetry.

Sulpicia was the daughter of Servius Sulpicius Rufus, and her mother was Valeria, the sister of one of Augustus's generals. Like most well-born girls, Sulpicia was educated, and she clearly seems to have read the works of the poets that were circulating during her lifetime. Fragments of her poems were preserved among the works of Ovid's contemporary, Tibullus, and most scholars agree that they were written by a

Figure 75. Roman woman with stylus and writing pad, Pompeii, first century A.D. (Scala/Art Resource, NY)

woman (not by a man using a woman's identity). Figure 75 shows an anonymous Roman girl of the first century A.D. holding a stylus and a writing pad. She is shown in concentration, perhaps much as Sulpicia would have looked as she was composing her poetry.

The poet speaks in the voice of a young unmarried woman from an upper-class family. Her guardian still has control over her, but she nevertheless conducts a passionate love affair with a man whom she calls Cerinthus. In the first excerpt, the poet complains about having to spend her birthday in the country:

My hateful birthday is at hand, which I
    must celebrate
without Cerinthus in the irksome country-
    side. (Fantham et al. 324)

Later, however, she writes a poem that says that the plans were changed, and she is able to celebrate in Rome after all:

Do you know of the dreary journey just
    lifted off your girl's mind:
Now she gets to be in Rome on her
    birthday!

Let's all celebrate that day of birth,
which has come to you by chance when
you least expected it.
(Fantham et al. 324)

At first glance, such poems celebrate young life and high spirits. Her works express anger at being taken for granted and joy in delighted passion. Some scholars, however, have seen a more complex message in the poems of Sulpicia, seeing in them an alternative presentation of women's passion and sexuality from that articulated by Virgil and by Augustus, who so rigorously legislated morality. (*See* Julia.)

Virgil had portrayed Dido as sacrificing her public reputation by her open passion for Aeneas, and readers of the *Aeneid* find Augustus's strict moral codes reinforced. Sulpicia, on the other hand, subtly renounces the public opinion that is supposed to preserve private morality. She writes:

But I delight in my wayward ways and
loathe to dissemble
for fear of Rumor. Let me be told of:
I am a worthy woman who has been
together
with a worthy man. (Fantham et al. 324)

Throughout Sulpicia's six short elegies, the poet repeatedly evokes the relationship of Dido and Aeneas by using Virgilian diction, themes, and images. Her work offers a different glimpse of women's sexuality and an alternative moral compass, however, from that articulated by the poets writing to please and mirror Augustus's moral sense. Unfortunately, we know no more about Sulpicia's life than these incidents left in her poetry. Did she live to violate convention as fully as she claimed? Were her desires suppressed? We will likely never know, but we can be grateful for the poetry of this ancient Roman woman who expressed her feelings with such passion and freshness.

See also Dido; Julia

Suggested Readings

Fantham, E., et al. *Women in the Classical World.* New York: Oxford University Press, 1994.

Keith, Alison. "*Tandem venit amor:* A Roman Woman Speaks of Love." In *Roman Sexualities*, ed. by J. P. Hallett and M. B. Skinner. Princeton: Princeton University Press, 1997.

Susanna

After the conquests of Alexander the Great (ca. 330 B.C.), the Jewish homeland of Judea came under the rule of Hellenistic rulers who prided themselves on their Greeklike ways. For centuries, there was little trouble between the two cultures as they coexisted, but in time trouble arose as more Jews adopted Greek customs and other Jews objected to such accommodation. The fundamental problem was how much cultural compromise there could be before Jews lost their distinct religious and cultural identity. The problems came to a head under the rule of the Hellenistic king Antiochus IV (r. 175–163 B.C.). For reasons that are still unclear, the king decided to institute policies to force Jews to give up their traditional practices and take on the Greek ways of the Hellenistic world. Some Jews responded with rebellion, and some (such as the Maccabean martyrs) died for their faith. Others, however, reacted by creating magnificent literature to argue for preserving one's faith in the face of persecution. One such author was the writer of the Book of Daniel of the Bible.

The author of Daniel—who probably wrote during the persecutions of Antiochus—set his stories in an earlier time of troubles for the Jewish people: the Babylonian captivity. In 586 B.C., the Babylonian king Nebuchadnezzar had conquered Judea and destroyed the great temple in Jerusalem. Many Jews were taken into exile to Babylon, where they lived until 539 B.C., when the Persian king Cyrus conquered the Babylonians and allowed the Jews to return to Jerusalem and rebuild their temple. During their exile, Jews confronted the same question as Jews did under Antiochus—that of how to preserve their traditional ways while living among people with other religions. By setting his stories in the time of the Babylonian captivity, the author of Daniel could remind his readers how faithful Jews had practiced their religion under difficult circumstances before and tell how virtue could triumph over evil.

The Book of Daniel was originally written in Aramaic (the official language of the Persian Empire) and Hebrew, and sometime in the late second or first century B.C. it was translated into Greek. When it was, someone added the story of

Susanna, which is considered one of the finest short stories in western literature. In some Bibles the story is included at the beginning or the end of the Book of Daniel; in others it is in the Apocrypha as the Book of Susanna. Like the other Daniel stories, it was a tale of virtue triumphing over evil, and it was set in Babylon during the exile. While Susanna was probably a fictional character, subsequent Christians valued her engaging story and believed her to be a real woman whose honesty and bravery were supposed to serve as a model for men and women alike. Here is her story.

In Babylon during the exile, there was a very rich man named Joachim who married a beautiful woman named Susanna. The young woman had been raised by pious and righteous parents who had "taught their daughter according to the law of Moses" (Sus. 1:3). The Jews of Babylon came regularly to Joachim's house, where they met and talked and often enjoyed the spacious gardens adjoining Joachim's residence. One year, two elders from the Jewish community were appointed as judges, and they, too, came often to Joachim's house as they advised people who had pending lawsuits.

At noon, when all the visitors left, Susanna went into the garden to walk. The two elders saw her pass every day, and they "were overwhelmed with passion for her" (Sus. 8). They finally confessed to each other their lustful desire for Susanna and conspired to find her alone. Their opportunity came one hot day when Susanna told her maids she wanted to bathe. "Bring me oil and ointments, and shut the garden doors" (Sus. 17), she told her servants as she prepared for her bath. The servants obeyed her wishes and left Susanna alone.

The lustful elders, who had been hiding in the garden, saw their chance. They ran to her and offered her a horrible choice: "Give your consent and lie with us. If you refuse, we will testify against you that a young man was with you, and this was why you sent your maids away." Susanna recognized the extent of her peril, for if she did not submit to their lust, she could receive the death penalty for adultery after being accused by two such respected judges. On the other hand, if she agreed to their demands

she would "not escape their hands." She chose to face death rather than to "sin in the sight of the Lord" and commit adultery. The elders shouted for the servants and took Susanna into custody (Sus. 28–40).

The next day when the people gathered at Joachim's house as usual, they were astounded at what confronted them. The "two elders came, full of their wicked plot to have Susanna put to death." They sent for the woman, who appeared veiled as was appropriate for a modest matron. But the judges still longed for her and ordered her veils removed "that they might feast upon her beauty." The elders testified that while they were in the garden, they saw Susanna dismiss her maids. Then a young man appeared and "lay with her." The elders claimed they were shocked by witnessing such wickedness and rushed out to catch the couple, but the young man was too strong and escaped, so they took Susanna into custody (Sus. 48–49).

Because the men were elders and judges, the assembled people believed them and condemned Susanna to death. The woman protested her innocence and prayed to God for help. The Lord heard her plea, and as she was being led away to death, God roused a champion on her behalf—a young man named Daniel. He shouted, "Are you such fools you sons of Israel? Have you condemned a daughter of Israel without examination and without learning the facts? Return to the place of judgment. For these men have borne false witness against her" (Sus. 48–49). And Daniel thought of a clever way to trap the elders in their lie.

The people returned, and Daniel told them to separate the two elders so he could question them apart. Then he tricked them into telling conflicting versions of the story: He asked each under what kind of tree the couple had been intimate. Each man said a different tree, showing that they lied. "Then all the assembly shouted loudly and blessed God who saves those who hope in Him." They rose against the two elders, "for out of their own mouths Daniel had convicted them of bearing false witness," and they pronounced the sentence on them that had been planned for Susanna. The wicked elders were put to death. Susanna's parents, husband, and all her family praised God for the beautiful and virtuous woman "because nothing shameful was found in her" (Sus. 54–63).

The story of Susanna long outlived the crisis in Hellenistic Judea that had generated its creation. Instead of a story about being true to tradition in the face of persecution, it became one of honesty and bravery in the face of individual oppression. Subsequent writers wrote of the brave woman, and later artists portrayed her in the bath. Susanna has become an important part of the tradition of Western culture.

See also Maccabean Martyrs

Suggested Readings

Meyers, Carol, Toni Craven, and Ross S. Kraemer. *Women in Scripture.* New York: Houghton Mifflin, 2000.

T

Tabitha
Christian Woman (ca. A.D. 40)

As the apostles traveled throughout the Mediterranean world after the death of Jesus, they spread the word and deeds of Christ and brought many to the new religion. According to the Bible, the apostles converted people most readily through the performance of miracles, and one of the miracles that caused a sensation in the ancient Holy Land was Peter's raising Tabitha from the dead.

The story is told in the Acts of the Apostles in the Bible and takes place as the apostle Peter visits Joppa, a port city on the coastal plain of Judea (shown on Map 8). Joppa had been a predominantly Jewish city since its conquest in 143 B.C. by Simon Maccabeus, and it was a center of the Jewish revolt in A.D. 66, when it was de-

Figure 76. Tabitha raised from the dead, Sarcophagus of St. Sidonius (U. D. F.—La Phototeque)

stroyed by the Romans. Although Acts was written after the destruction of Joppa, the story of Tabitha was set between A.D. 30 and 40, while the city still had a strong Jewish community.

The Bible calls Tabitha a "disciple," which is the only New Testament occurrence of the feminine form of the word *disciple* in Greek. That usage strongly suggests she was known as a close follower of Jesus. The author of Acts gives us the Greek translation of Tabitha's name—Dorcas—which means "gazelle." This was probably a nickname, and it seems to have originated in the first century A.D. among the slave population. Therefore, Tabitha was probably a slave or a freedwoman of slave origins.

The Bible says that Tabitha had done many good works and acts of charity, but she had recently died. Her sad friends laid her out in the upper room of her house, and the disciples, hearing that Peter was nearby, sent two men to him entreating him to come quickly. When Peter arrived, they took him to the upper room where widows were weeping around the body. The women showed Peter the lovely tunics and other garments that Tabitha had made, indicating how industrious she was. Peter sent all the women outside the room and knelt down and prayed. Then he turned to the body and said "Tabitha, Rise" (Acts 9:40). She opened her eyes and when she saw Peter, she sat up. "And it became known throughout all Joppa, and many believed in the Lord" (Acts 9:42). Figure 76 is a detail from a burial sarcophagus, and it shows Peter giving his hand to raise Tabitha, while the widows look on.

Some scholars consider that Tabitha may have lived with a community of women who earned their living (and kept their independence) by making cloth. This sort of group of widows was important somewhat later in the Christian communities, and this story might indicate how early in the spread of Christianity these women's communities developed. The account of Tabitha as an early female disciple within the important city of Joppa is also indicative of how central women were in the early conversions.

See also Christian Women; Lydia; Maccabean Martyrs

Suggested Readings

Meyers, Carol, Toni Craven, and Ross S. Kraemer. *Women in Scripture.* New York: Houghton Mifflin, 2000.

Witherington, Ben, III. *Women and the Genesis of Christianity.* Cambridge: Cambridge University Press, 1990.

Tarbo

Persian Martyr (ca. A.D. 341)

In the fourth century A.D., the Persian Empire was ruled by an able and warlike king—Shapur II (r. A.D. 309–379). Throughout his reign, the powerful Persian Empire engaged in three major wars against the Roman Empire, during which Persians were particularly alert for people within their lands who seemed to support Roman interests. Among those who came to the attention of the authorities were Christians, who followed a religion of the Roman Empire rather than the Persian Zoroastrianism. Thus, in the fourth century, Christian texts written in Persia tell of martyrs who died at the hands of Persian authorities. One such martyr was Simeon, bishop of a city south of Baghdad (see Map 3). Simeon had refused to raise extra taxes from his congregation to support the war effort and was martyred for his intransigence. Simeon's sister, Tarbo, a virgin dedicated to God, also came to the attention of the authorities, and the account of her martyrdom preserves some interesting information about beliefs in the ancient Persian Empire.

According to the text, it happened that the Persian queen fell ill, and to find the source of her illness she consulted Jews with whom she was friendly. The Jews accused local Christians: "The sisters of Simeon have put spells on you because their brother has been put to death." Once this reached the queen's ears, she arrested Tarbo, a "daughter of the covenant" (a virgin dedicated to God); her servant, also a "daughter of the covenant"; and Tarbo's married sister. The queen's soldiers brought the women to the queen's residence for interrogation. The head *mobed* (Zoroastrian priest) and two officers were summoned to serve as judges. When the women were introduced to the judges, they were surprised at Tarbo's "beautiful looks and her fine appearance, excelling that of all other women."

All three judges secretly entertained "disgusting intentions concerning her" (Brock et al. 73).

They accused the women of casting a spell on the queen, the "mistress of the entire orient." Tarbo replied boldly, denying all charges of sorcery, claiming that the scriptures forbid Christians to practice evil arts. She concluded, "How then could we perform sorcery? Sorcery is in the same category as the denial of God; in both cases the sentence is death." All three judges listened in silent awe at her beauty and her wisdom, and each thought: "I'll rescue her from death so that she can be my wife" (Brock et al. 74).

The women were sent off to prison after the initial interrogation, and the *mobed* sent a message to Tarbo saying he would save all three from death if she would agree to be his wife. She responded with horror: "Shut your mouth, you wicked man and enemy of god; don't ever again utter anything so disgusting." She claimed to be a bride of Christ and would die before submitting to his wishes. The other two judges sent similar messages and received the same indignant reply. The three angry judges then decided to bring false testimony and a "wicked verdict," saying that the three women were indeed witches (Brock et al. 74–75).

The Persian king gave them one opportunity to save themselves: If they would worship the sun, they need not be put to death on the grounds that they might really not know how to cast spells. The women refused this offer, saying they would never worship the created sun instead of the uncreated God. The king then granted the judges the right to impose any means of execution they liked. They proposed some magic of their own: The women's bodies would be "cut in two and the queen should pass between the two halves, after which she would be healed" (Brock et al. 75).

The three holy women were taken outside the city, where they were tied to the ground by four stakes. They were stretched out, attached by hands and feet, "like lambs about to be shorn." The judges then sawed their bodies in halves, leaving six portions. Then they placed the body parts in "six baskets, which they suspended on six forked pieces of wood. These they

thrust into the ground, three on each side of the road. These were shaped like half crosses, carrying half a body each" (Brock et al. 76).

The narrator wrote that all who watched wept for the pure and chaste women who did not deserve to die in such a horrible way. "Who got any joy out of this lugubrious spectacle? Who took any pleasure in this awesome sight? Who could look with dry eyes?" (Brock et al. 76). Through this heartbreak, the judges completed their sorcery to try to cure the queen: The king's entourage came along the road flanked by the dismembered bodies, and the queen got out and stood between the bodies. The narrator does not say whether she was cured of her illness.

This account serves as an interesting source of information not only about the brave Christian martyrs who withstood the pressures of Zoroastrian priests and the Persian king but also about folk beliefs of medicine and sorcery. People readily believed that the queen had been bewitched and that it would take extreme measures—and violence—to lift the spell. The people of the ancient world would also believe in the power that came with the blood of many martyrs such as Tarbo.

See also Martha [Persian Martyr]; Martyrs; Thekla
Suggested Readings
Brock, Sebastian P., et al. *Holy Women of the Syrian Orient.* Berkeley: University of California Press, 1987.

Tarpeia
See Sabine Women

Terentia
Roman Wife and Mother
(ca. 98 B.C.–ca. A.D. 4)
Marcus Tullius Cicero was a great statesman who served Rome through the crises in the last years of the republic. He came from a well-to-do family outside Rome that had never been patrician, or served in the senate, but Cicero quickly showed the intelligence and promise to rise to the ranks of the Roman patriciate. Cicero's fame rests less on his political accomplishments than on his writings—through his speeches, treatises, and letters, he transmitted Rome's cultural and

political values. Furthermore, his style of rhetoric and prose became models for posterity and is still much studied today. Cicero could not have risen to the highest ranks of Roman politics solely on his own, however. His wife, Terentia, was instrumental in helping him, but the statesman was shown to be less than honorable to his intelligent and loyal wife.

Terentia married Cicero in about 79 B.C. when she was about seventeen and he twenty-seven. We know nothing about her family except that her half-sister, Fabia, was a vestal virgin. Terentia brought with her a large dowry that included at least two blocks of tenement apartments in Rome that brought her an excellent annual income. She also owned some woods in the suburbs of Rome and a large farm that brought in more income. Terentia was an extremely wealthy woman, and there can be no doubt that her money helped Cicero rise in Rome's political ranks.

The wealthy bride did not turn over her fortune to Cicero when she married. Instead she continued to manage her own properties with the assistance of her steward, named Philotimus. In fact, the biographer Plutarch wrote that she was "neither weak nor timid, but on the contrary ambitious, and as her husband tells us, taking a larger share in Cicero's political activities than she allowed him to take in her affairs" (Plutarch 1052). She had a great talent for managing her own affairs, and she regularly increased her own wealth and landholdings. Through her expert management, Cicero benefited financially and could concentrate on his political life. They had two children: a girl, Tullia, and a boy, Marcus Cicero.

Cicero became involved in some of the central controversies of the day. In his most famous enterprise, Cicero fought against an aristocratic conspiracy led by Catiline to seize the government. Cicero uncovered the plot and ordered the conspirators arrested and called for their summary execution. It was against Roman law, however, to execute citizens without the right of final appeal to the people of Rome. In Cicero's famous Catilinarian orations, he persuaded the senate to follow his lead. Cicero prevailed and saw himself as a savior of Rome, but the incident brought with it repercussions.

In 58 B.C. Cicero's enemy, Publius Clodius Pulcher, introduced a bill to exile anyone who had put Roman citizens to death. While he did not mention Cicero by name, the bill was clearly aimed at him. Terentia actively urged Cicero to take on the powerful Clodius because she hated Clodius's sister, Clodia, who lived in their wealthy neighborhood. According to Plutarch, Terentia was jealous of the attentions Cicero paid to the attractive Clodia and wanted revenge. Plutarch wrote that Terentia was "a woman of a violent temper and having the ascendant over Cicero, she urged him on to taking a part against Clodius . . ." (Plutarch 1057). In this instance, Terentia's advice did not turn out well. Cicero was forced to leave Rome in about 58 B.C., and Clodius and his followers tore down Cicero's house and persecuted Terentia.

In Cicero's letters written to Terentia during these dark times, we can see how much he depended upon his wife. He wrote: "To think that a woman of your virtue, fidelity, uprightness and kindness should have fallen into such troubles on my account!" He urged her to guard their resources for their two children but also cautioned her to care for herself: "Do not, as you love me, overtax your delicate constitution. . . . I see that everything depends on you" (Carcopino 143–144). Terentia took care of their fortunes brilliantly in Cicero's absence, and her concern to make sure that their fortunes remained intact led to some criticism. In fact, by about 47 B.C., we have a letter in which Cicero complains to a friend of his about her stinginess. While early in their relationship, Terentia was more than willing to sell property when Cicero needed funds, now, after thirty years of marriage, she was more reluctant to support Cicero's luxurious tastes. Struggles over money and its control began to sour their marriage.

Cicero began to warn his friends not to let Terentia know about his financial affairs, and she was equally guarded. The marriage as a partnership had already failed, but Cicero could not get a divorce until he had accumulated enough money to return Terentia's substantial dowry. Some months later the opportunity appeared. The aging orator—now over sixty—began to be seen in the company of Publilia, a young woman still in her teens. Publilia's father had died leaving a huge fortune, and the girl's father had made Cicero the trustee of the funds with the understanding that the money would go to Publilia at her marriage. While Rome teased the old man for falling for the fresh beauty of the girl, Cicero in 45 B.C. divorced his wife of over thirty years and married his young ward Publilia, thus gaining her fortune. This new marriage lasted only a few months before Cicero arranged with Publilia's brother to gain another divorce and return her fortune. This divorce followed suspiciously closely upon Cicero's large inheritance from a recently deceased friend; perhaps he no longer needed Publilia's money.

Cicero's political fortunes fell soon afterward. After Julius Caesar's assassination in 44 B.C., Cicero hoped to restore the republic, but in doing so he offended the new men who were coming to power. Mark Antony's supporters hunted Cicero down and assassinated him. Antony's wife, Fulvia, reputedly gloried in the orator's death, and Antony placed Cicero's head and hands on the speaker's platform (rostra) in the forum to disgrace the orator who had so often spoken against the powerful.

Terentia did not share Cicero's disgrace. In fact, her intelligence and force of character (and her great wealth) attracted other suitors. She married the historian Sallust after he divorced his wife, and the couple lived together until his death. Even then the aging Terentia married again, to the orator Messalla Corvinus who was about the same age as her son. Terentia lived until she was over one hundred years old, and this remarkable Roman matron is fine proof of the ability of strong, wealthy women to make their own way in the Roman world.

See also Caerellia; Clodia; Fulvia; Tullia; Vestal Virgins

Suggested Readings

Bailey, D. R. Schackleton. *Cicero.* New York: Charles Scribner's Sons, 1971.

Carcopino, Jerome. *Cicero: The Secrets of His Correspondence.* New York: Greenwood Press, 1969.

Plutarch. *Lives of the Noble Grecians and Romans.* Trans. John Dryden. New York: The Modern Library, n.d.

Teuta

Queen in Illyria (r. ca. 231 B.C.)

In 231 B.C., the area of the Illyrian coast (shown on Map 7) was one of the many regions plagued by seemingly endless warfare among the Hellenistic kingdoms. The Romans were beginning to negotiate with local rulers as they slowly sought to exert their authority over the region. In that year, a widow succeeded to the throne of her husband in one of the kingdoms. Ancient Roman historians recorded that she ruled in the traditional Germanic and Celtic fashion, with an advisory council of her chieftains, but the Roman sources also record the many difficulties they had dealing with this strong queen. Teuta wanted to expand her territory, and she successfully invaded a neighboring kingdom. The Greek historian Polybius wrote with scorn about this political expansion that caused trouble for the Romans who wanted to keep peace in the region. In his critique, however, Polybius blamed Teuta's gender rather than her ambition, writing: "She suffered from a typically feminine weakness, that of taking the short view of everything" (Ellis 81).

Teuta's initial military successes were followed by problems within her kingdom. She had to suppress an uprising among some of the Illyrians she ruled; they may have resented her extensive use of Celtic forces in her armies, but we cannot be certain of the cause of their distress. In the course of putting down the rebellion, Teuta's forces seem to have hurt Roman citizens living in the area. Rome sent an embassy to Teuta to warn her against causing trouble in the future. The ambassador seems to have been arrogant and offensive to the queen, and Polybius criticized the queen's response as "a fit of womanish petulance" (Ellis 81), rather than seeing her actions as those of a proud sovereign. The queen simply reacted in the manner of many ancient monarchs and ordered the Roman ambassadors assassinated while they were preparing to return to Rome.

Rome lost patience with the high-handed queen and sent a fleet of 200 ships to attack Teuta's territories. Rome's virtually invincible land army slowly conquered her cities, and Teuta was forced to retreat to one of her strongly fortified cities. Remarkably, she was able to negotiate a peace with Rome that allowed her to retain her rule. She agreed to pay reparations to the conquering army and assured Rome she would no longer threaten her neighbors. The Romans celebrated their victory in 228 B.C., and the enterprising queen disappeared from the pages of Roman history.

See also Dynamis; Zenobia

Suggested Readings

Ellis, P. B. *Women in Celtic Society and Literature.* Grand Rapids, MI: W. B. Eerdmans Publishing, 1995.

Magie, D. *Roman Rule in Asia Minor.* Princeton: Princeton University Press, 1950.

Polybius. *The Histories.* Trans. W. R. Paton. Cambridge: Harvard University Press, 1954.

Thais

Prostitute and Holy Woman

(ca. fourth century A.D.)

Among the communities of Christian holy men and women living in the deserts of Egypt and Syria during the fourth century, many stories circulated about some men and women who had done extraordinary deeds or whose lives offered particular examples for other Christians. It is impossible to know how many of these stories describe real individuals or how narrators embellished the accounts of real lives to make the moral better. These tales were profoundly influential, however, in shaping how Christians viewed themselves and their lives, and in that way, the stories themselves expressed moral truths that transcended strict historical accuracy. Some of the most popular tales were those about the redemption of prostitutes, for people believed if even those great sinners could be saved, there was much hope for all of them. One such "holy prostitute" whose life was told all through the deserts of Egypt was Thais the harlot. Her story is as follows.

Once there was a harlot called Thais, who was so beautiful that many men sold their goods and reduced themselves to utter poverty for her sake. Her beauty also caused much jealousy, and quarrels arose among her lovers so that often the doorstep of her house was soaked in the blood of young men. When Father Paphnutius (a renowned ascetic living in the desert) heard of this state of affairs, he decided to go to her city (probably Alexandria) to talk to Thais. He dressed in secular clothes and appeared at her home. He paid her a silver piece "as the price for committing sin" (Ward 83), and she invited him inside.

When he went in, they sat on a bed draped with precious covers, and the monk said, "If there is a more private room, let us go in there." Thais answered, "There is one, but if it is people you are afraid of, no one ever enters this room; except, of course, for God, for there is no place that is hidden from the eyes of divinity." When Paphnutius heard this, he said, "So you know there is a God?" When the harlot acknowledged she did, Paphnutius continued his reprimand: "But if you know this, why are you causing the loss of so many souls that you will be condemned to render an account not only of your own sins but of theirs as well?" (Ward 83). When Thais heard this, she threw herself at the monk's feet, crying and begging him to give her a penance through which she might earn forgiveness. She begged him to wait three hours for her, after which she would do whatever he bid her. Paphnutius agreed and arranged a meeting place.

After the monk left, Thais went and collected all the goods she had earned from prostitution and piled them all in the middle of the city. As the people surrounded her, watching in wonder, she burned all the goods, which were valued at forty pounds of gold—an extraordinary amount of wealth. Thus released from her worldly goods, the young woman went to meet Paphnutius at the appointed place.

The holy man took her to a monastery of virgins and placed her in a small cell. He then sealed the door with lead so she could neither leave nor receive visitors. He left only a small opening through which food could be passed to her, and he ordered the sisters to give her daily a little bread and a little water. When Thais realized that the door was sealed, she said to him, "Father, where do you want me to urinate?" and he replied, "In the cell, as you deserve." Then she asked him how she should pray to God and he said to her, "You are not worthy to name God, or to take his divine name upon your lips, or to lift up your hands to heaven . . . only stand facing to-wards the east and repeat often only this: 'You who made me, have mercy upon me'" (Ward 84).

After three years, Paphnutius began to be anxious about the reformed harlot, so he went to consult with another holy monk, Father Antony, to ask him if her sins had been forgiven. Father Antony called together all his disciples, and they all agreed to pray that God might reveal to one of them the answer to Paphnutius's question. Each retired to his cell and began to pray continuously. Then one of them named Paul suddenly saw in the sky a bed adorned with precious cloth and guarded by three virgins whose faces shone with brightness. A voice spoke to him saying the bed was "for the harlot Thais" (Ward 84).

Paul went quickly and reported what he had heard and seen, and Paphnutius recognized the will of God in the vision. He went quickly to Thais's cell and opened the door. He said to her, "Come out, for God has forgiven you your sins." She replied, "I call God to witness that since I came in here my sins have always been before my eyes as a burden; they have never been out of my sight." Father Paphnutius said to her, "God has forgiven your sins not because of your penances but because you have always had the remembrance of your sins in your soul" (Ward 84). When he had taken Thais out, she lived for fifteen days and then passed away in peace.

This story of the harshness of Father Paphnutius and the forgiveness of God captured the imagination of Christians for centuries. In the tenth century, a nun wrote a beautiful play preserving the story, and a nineteenth-century novelist retold the tale, so the account of the harlot of Alexandria has lived on in people's imagination.

See also Maria; Mary Magdalene; Mary of Egypt; Pelagia; Prostitution

Suggested Readings

France, Anatole. *Thais.* Trans. B. Galati. Chicago: University of Chicago Press, 1996.

Hrotswitha of Gandesheim. "Paphnutius." In *The Plays of Hrotswitha.* Trans. C. St. John. New York: B. Blom, 1966.

Ward, Benedicta. *Harlots of the Desert.* Kalamazoo, MI: Cistercian Publications, 1987.

Theano

Greek Philosopher (ca. 500s B.C.)

In the early sixth century B.C., some Greek intellectuals made a striking break with the past. Instead of looking to the gods and goddesses for understanding about the nature of the universe, they searched for more worldly explanations. In doing so they became the first philosophers and contributed a rational approach to the world to subsequent generations in the west. One of the earliest philosophers was Thales of Miletus (ca. 585 B.C.), and he suggested that the whole world was unified by the composition of one substance—water. Others posited other unifying substances or principles to explain the nature of the world, and one highly influential philosopher was Pythagoras (ca. 580–500 B.C.).

Pythagoras was born on the island of Samos (shown on Map 4), but as a mature man he emigrated to the Greek colony of Croton in southern Italy, and there he made his intellectual mark that continues to influence us today. Pythagoras emphasized numbers and their relations—or mathematics—as the key to understanding the unifying principle of the world. In working out his theories, Pythagoras discovered principles of geometry (the best known is the Pythagorean theorem, which is used to calculate the sides of a right triangle) and analyzed music to see the mathematical ratios of harmonies. Pythagoras and his followers—the Pythagoreans—lived almost monastic lives in communities that sought to live in harmony with each other. Unlike many other Greek associations, the Pythagoreans were open to both men and women, and consequently there were a number of women Pythagoreans. One was the great mathematician's wife, Theano.

Theano was the daughter of Brontinus, an aristocrat of Crotona. She became the pupil of Pythagoras and later his wife. They had three daughters—Arignote, Myia, and Damo—who also became philosophers. Purportedly Pythagoras died in a violent fire that destroyed his daughter Myia's home, and after his death, Theano took over the direction of the Pythagorean school. Theano and her daughters continued their practice of philosophy, and the fragments of their writings that survive shed light on this early school of philosophy and some of the women who studied it.

Theano shared Pythagoras's belief that numbers can illuminate the nature of things and can show the harmony in the universe. Furthermore, Theano shared the Pythagorean belief in immortality and transmigration (or reincarnation) of souls. In one of her works, Theano argued that the transmigration of souls was essential to restore justice in the universe. As she wrote: "If the soul is not immortal, then life is truly a feast for evil-doers who die after having lived their lives so iniquitously" (Waithe 14). For her, such injustice could not be; people who do wrong must return to this world as less than human in order to restore the balance they had disrupted.

While Theano shared many of the ideas of male Pythagoreans, she and her daughters also applied these principles to the particular circumstances of women. Theano believed that a wife's sexual activity was to be restricted to pleasing her husband, but that marital intercourse did not lead to any kind of impurity. Her daughter Myia wrote a letter to another woman, named Phyllis, who had just given birth. Myia offered advice about how to choose a nurse and raise the child in a way that was moderate and balanced. Her advice was simple and full of common sense. For example, she wrote, "It is best to put the newborn to sleep when it has been suitably filled with milk, for then rest is sweet to the young. . . . Hold off altogether from wine, because of its strong effect, or add it sparingly in a mixture to the evening milk" (Waithe 16).

Myia's and Theano's writings about women share characteristics of other women Pythagoreans. They wanted to urge everyone—including women—to be moderate in their lives and to bring harmony and balance into their homes and into their world. Theano wrote, "Better to be on a runaway horse than to be a woman who does not reflect" (Waithe 15). In this saying, she shows the principle that had governed her own life—she was a woman who thought and reflected. She was truly an ancient philosopher— a lover of wisdom.

While the information about Theano (and the other women philosophers) is very interesting, we do have to note that much of our information about Theano is legendary, written after their death. Nor can we be sure that the works attributed to them were actually written by them, since the editions were written long after their deaths. In spite of these cautions, however, it is clear that many people in the ancient world believed that women could and did do philosophy.

See also Diotima of Mantinea; Philosophers, Greek
Suggested Readings
Kersey, Ethel M. *Women Philosophers: A Bio-Critical Source Book.* New York: Greenwood Press, 1989.
Philip, J. A. *Pythagoras and Early Pythagoreanism.* Ann Arbor: University of Michigan Press, 1966.
Waithe, Mary Ellen. *A History of Women Philosophers.* Vol. 1: *Ancient Women Philosophers.* Boston: Martinus Nijhoff Publishers, 1987.

Thecla
Christian Follower of Paul (ca. A.D. 50)

In the first few centuries after the birth of Jesus, Christians began to write down events of the lives of Jesus and the apostles to preserve their deeds. In the process, there grew up a varied collection of such stories. Centuries later, when churchmen assembled the official, or canonical, version of the Bible, many of these early Christian tales were relegated to the realm of literature (or folklore) and left out of the Bible. These old writings are called "apocryphal" to distinguish them from the scriptural works that were included in the Bible. They remain fascinating stories, however, that reveal the attitudes and beliefs of at least some early Christians. One ancient and popular apocryphal act tells of a woman named Thecla, who purportedly followed the apostle Paul. While the story is generally believed to be a fictional account, there may have been a first-century follower of Paul named Thecla, for her cult appeared early and spread widely in the east, and many pilgrims visited what was reputed to be her tomb. (*See* Egeria.) Her story in the Acts of Paul and Thecla was widely circulated, and many ancient women and men enjoyed reading her exciting tale.

According to the Acts, Thecla was a virgin who lived in Iconium (in modern-day Turkey, shown on Map 8); she was engaged to marry a man named Thamyris. The apostle Paul came to the city and began to preach, however, and Thecla, who was sitting at a window, heard him. She was riveted by his words of prayer and his praise of virginity, and she could not move. She spent three days and nights at the window staring longingly at the direction of the voice. Both her mother and her fiancé tried to persuade her to come away, but she ignored them. Thamyris became angry and urged the Roman governor—the proconsul—to arrest Paul, calling him a magician who was corrupting the wives and women of the city.

Paul was arrested, bound, and jailed until the proconsul could have more time to interrogate him. Thecla heard of his imprisonment and took her bracelets to bribe the guard to let her into the prison cell. She sat at Paul's feet, kissed the bonds that tied him, and listened to him tell of "the great things of God." Thamyris came looking for his betrothed and was furious to find her at the apostle's feet. The governor called Paul and Thecla before him. He asked Thecla why she did not obey Thamyris "according to the law of the Iconians." But she gave no answer and just looked longingly and lovingly at Paul. Her mother was equally furious, and shouted, "Burn the wicked wretch; burn in the midst of the theater her that will not marry, in order that all the women that have been taught by this man may be afraid" ("Acts of Paul and Thecla" 488–489).

The proconsul agreed with this recommendation—he had Paul whipped and sent out of town, and Thecla was condemned to be burnt in the theater. The servants brought a huge pile of sticks for the fire, and Thecla climbed on top. When a great fire was blazing, it miraculously did not touch her. Then, according to the text, God brought a huge rain that put the fire out, and Thecla was saved and released. She left the town to find Paul, and when she did, she rejoiced. She said, "I shall cut my hair, and follow thee wherever thou mayst go" ("Acts . . ." 489). Paul agreed to have her follow him, and he urged her to wait patiently for her baptism.

They went next to Antioch, where a man named Alexander fell in love with Thecla as soon as he saw her. He approached Paul to win the beautiful virgin, but the apostle claimed he had no control over her. Alexander tried to embrace Thecla and take her by force. She fought back, tearing his cloak and pulling off his crown, and she "made him a laughing-stock." Alexander denounced her to the governor, who condemned her to the wild beasts. The women in the crowd leaped to her defense, shouting "Evil judgment! Impious judgment" ("Acts . . ." 489), and one woman agreed to take Thecla into her home to keep her safe until the day she was to face the beasts in the arena. On the appointed day, Thecla faced a wild lioness, who simply licked the virgin's feet. Again the women in the crowd shouted their support for her.

On another day Thecla was brought again to the arena. She was stripped naked and thrown in to lions, bears, and a fierce lioness. The lioness ran to her and lay at her feet. The lioness first killed the bear that tried to attack Thecla, then died killing a lion who also threatened the young woman. With the lioness dead, Thecla had no more protection against other wild beasts that were being released. She thought surely she would die, but she saw a ditch filled with water and wild seals. She prayed, and said, "Now it is time to wash myself. And she threw herself in [the water], saying: In the name of Jesus Christ I am baptized on my last day." Even the governor shed tears because he thought "the seals were going to devour such beauty." But once again God intervened. Lightning struck and all the seals "floated about dead" ("Acts . . ." 489). The women in the audience cried out for her and threw sweet-smelling herbs, and none of the wild animals would touch Thecla.

Alexander persuaded the governor to try one more torture, and he had Thecla bound to two wild bulls so they would tear her apart. As the bulls ran, however, a sacred fire that surrounded Thecla burned the ropes so she was once again spared. The governor summoned Thecla out of the wild beasts and asked her why nothing could harm her. She explained that she was a follower of God, who kept her safe. The governor ordered that her clothing be brought, and he freed her. The women in the audience shouted their praise so loudly at her release that "the foundations of the theater were shaken by their voice" ("Acts . . ." 490).

Thecla sewed her garments so they made a man's cloak, and she once again went to find Paul, who was preaching the word of God. Paul was astonished to see her, and when she saw him, she said, "I have received the baptism, Paul." And Paul told her to go and teach the word of God. She returned to her home in Iconium and discovered that Thamyris had died. Her mother was still alive, and she visited her and testified to her faith. Then Thecla left Iconium and "lived in a cave for seventy-two years, living on herbs and water" ("Acts . . ." 491). Many people came to see her, and she miraculously cured many who were ill. Finally she died when she was ninety years old. Other traditions say that Thecla did not die naturally; instead, she was magically sealed into a rock cave to avoid being raped.

This story had several elements that made it popular with ancient (and some modern) women and distinctly unpopular with some church leaders. For example, the second-century church father Tertullian specifically disputed this book because it supported what he called the "heretical" opinion that women should teach and baptize (because Thecla had baptized herself in the seal pool). It also showed the women spectators supporting Thecla in a solidarity that defied civil authority. In fact, some modern analysts have suggested that this work (and other apocryphal stories) were written by and for women. We may never know the author or the circumstances of the composition, but the Acts of Paul and Thecla remained extremely popular, even though they were declared untrue.

See also Apocryphal Acts of the Apostles; Egeria

Suggested Readings
"Acts of Paul and Thecla." In *Ante-Nicene Fathers.* Vol. 8, *Fathers of the Third and Fourth Centuries.* Ed. A. Roberts. Peabody, MA: Hendrickson Publishers, 1995.

Burrus, Virginia. *Chastity as Autonomy: Women in the Stories of Apocryphal Acts.* Lewiston, NY: Edwin Mellen Press, 1987.

Davies, Stevan L. *The Revolt of the Widows: The Social World of the Apocryphal Acts.* Carbondale: Southern Illinois University Press, 1980.

MacDonald, Dennis R. *The Legend and the Apostle: The Battle for Paul in Story and Canon.* Philadelphia: Westminster, 1983.

Thekla

Persian Martyr (fourth century A.D.)

Most of the Christians martyred in the lands of the old Persian Empire were killed because of perceived political loyalty to the Roman Empire or religious disloyalty to Zoroastrianism, the religion of Persia. One group of martyrs, however, seems to have been persecuted less for political or religious reasons than for the human inclination toward greed. The narrator of the story of Thekla, who was martyred with some companions, wrote both to remember the brave deaths of the women and to remind readers about the dangers of clinging to material possessions.

The tragedy began with a Christian priest named Pawle, who presided over a congregation in a village near the Tigris River. He came to the attention of the authorities because he was very rich and owned much property. The greedy Persian authorities looked for a reason to arrest him so they could confiscate his property, but their desires caused tragedy for innocent victims along with the wealthy priest. When they arrested Pawle, they also took four virgins dedicated to God (called "daughters of the covenant" in the Persian sources), including their spokeswoman, Thekla.

The judge first addressed Pawle, saying "If you do the king's will, by worshiping the sun and eating blood [in violation of biblical law], I will return to you everything that has been confiscated from you." While the judges no doubt expected Pawle to refuse as was the custom among Christians, this priest turned out to care more for his property than the state of his soul: "Hungering after his riches, and yearning for his money, [Pawle] did everything he was told to do" (Brock 78). The judge was thus frustrated in his desire to confiscate Pawle's wealth, so he tried another strategy. He decided to try the women, and if they persisted in their faith, he would make Pawle kill them. The judge believed the priest would recoil from that deed, and then he would have a pretense for taking his money.

The judge ordered the women to "do the

king's will, worship the sun, and get married." The holy women refused, crying out in loud voices: "You proud and insolent man, don't try to frighten or beguile us with these deceiving words." The judge ordered them beaten with a hundred strokes of the rod, but they still persisted in their faith. The judge then issued a sentence of death upon them and turned to the impious priest, saying "If you kill these daughters of the covenant you can have back all that has been taken from you." Even the prospect of committing this deed did not cause Pawle to stop longing for his goods. "Lured by his possessions . . . the grasping Pawle hardened his heart and put on a brazen face, took the sword and had the audacity to lift it against the holy women" (Brock 79–80).

The women reprimanded him, reminding him that he was supposed to guard his congregation as a good shepherd, not kill the "lambs" in his care. Furthermore, they issued a prophetic warning, saying he would not live long enough to enjoy his ill-gotten possessions. He did not listen, however, and decapitated each of the women with his sword. The narrator wondered how a novice executioner had been able to sever their heads so effectively, and in his speculations, he warned his readers against the greed that could turn a shepherd into a wolf: "Maybe it was the love of his money that gave him strength; perhaps he was fortified by his lust for gold?" (Brock 80–81).

The holy women died bravely, but their prophecy about Pawle was to come true. After scheming so long to claim Pawle's money, the judge was not going to lose it now, in spite of all that the priest had done to try to preserve it. Furthermore, the judge was afraid that Pawle would complain to the king about the treatment he had received. Therefore, that very night before Pawle's release, the judge sent men to the prison and hanged him. Thekla had been right—he would not live long enough to enjoy the goods he had worked so hard to preserve. This story preserved two central Christian messages: hold fast to faith in spite of persecution and do not value material goods over spiritual ones.

See also Martha [Persian Martyr]; Martyrs; Tarbo

Suggested Readings
Brock, Sebastian P. *Holy Women of the Syrian Orient.* Berkeley: University of California Press, 1987.

Tiy

Egyptian "King's Great Wife" (ca. 1370 B.C.)
Amenhotep III (r. ca. 1391–1353 B.C.) became pharaoh during the height of Egypt's prosperous New Kingdom, when the ancient land was safe from foreign invaders (for a time) and benefited from a strong economy fueled by the bustling trade with its empire. The new pharaoh was the great-grandson of Thutmose III, who had succeeded the woman pharaoh, Hatshepsut, to the throne, and perhaps enough time had gone by that this king did not fear sharing power with his consort. Egypt's noble families enjoyed a leisurely life of hunting, fishing, and banqueting, and men and women alike indulged new tastes in elaborate garments, precious and semiprecious jewelry, heavy makeup, and long, heavy wigs. When Amenhotep became king as a teenager, he surrounded himself with able administrators who kept Egypt's business flourishing, while the king enjoyed the good life.

Egypt's kings were polygamous, and Amenhotep was no exception. He kept many wives in his harem, and they enjoyed a good deal of independence as they produced children who never rose to political prominence. Foreign kings also sent prized daughters to add to Amenhotep's harem, thus hoping to cement an alliance with the most powerful ruler of his time. For example, we have the record of the arrival of Gilukhepa, daughter of the king of a Middle Eastern state—the Mitanni—who arrived in Egypt with "the chief women of her entourage, totaling three hundred and seventeen women" (Tyldesley 28). Amenhotep's residence for women must surely have been strained by the arrival of so large a company of women. All these wives and other women could not, however, satisfy the pharaoh's need for an official consort. Unlike most pharaohs, Amenhotep did not choose his principal wife from among his own family; instead he chose a nonroyal woman who became one of the most influential of

Egypt's queen-consorts—Tiy, honored with the title of "king's great wife."

Tiy was the daughter of a nonroyal couple named Yuya and Thuyu who came from a prosperous town on the east bank of the Nile. Her father, Yuya, had held important posts at court, and her mother had been a talented musician in the service of the state god Amen. Although Thuyu had held many posts at court as well, on her tomb she repeatedly had her artists engrave her favorite title, "royal mother of the chief wife of the king." Tiy was not strikingly beautiful from the standards of the time—the wood carving of her shown in Figure 77, however, shows an intelligent and determined woman who wore the latest fashions in wigs and jewelry. Amenhotep clearly valued his chief wife, and she soon assumed unprecedented privileges.

Tiy became the first queen whose name was consistently linked with that of the king on both official inscriptions and more private objects. One statue designed for Amenhotep's mortuary temple even shows Tiy the same size as her husband, which was a new convention in a land where artistic size was directly equated with status. Tiy also began to take a prominent role in religious rituals, becoming the first queen we know of to serve as both consort and priestess, and this religious role led to her assuming more respect and importance in the life of the empire. Tiy had her own living quarters as well as maintaining a position at the court, and she owned a good deal of property in her own name. She therefore controlled much personal income derived from her estates, which were administered by her servants. For all her independence, Tiy's life remained centered in her royal family, and from all evidence, she and Amenhotep were devoted to each other.

Tiy bore her husband at least six children: two sons, Tuthmosis and Amenhotep, and four daughters, of whom the eldest—Sitamen—was her father's favorite. As was the case with a number of royal Egyptian families, Amenhotep in time took his daughter Sitamen as one of his wives and eventually even gave her the coveted title "great king's wife," although we can see from contemporary illustrations that she never took precedence over her mother.

Figure 77. Head of Queen Tiy, carved wood (Foto Marburg, Art Resource, NY)

Amenhotep ruled over thirty years—an extraordinary feat in an age when people died young from disease. The old king seems to have suffered badly from toothaches, and contemporary illustrations show him as fat with a somewhat lazy demeanor. Some historians have argued that this king who enjoyed his luxuries was more than willing to let his able queen-consort exert a great deal of power from behind the throne. When Amenhotep III died, the throne went to his younger son, Amenhotep IV (the elder seems to have predeceased his father). Tiy continued to be an influential figure in the reign of her son and his even more famous wife, Nefertiti.

We have evidence of Tiy's continuing influence upon the accession of her son because archaeologists have discovered a number of letters dating from this period, some of which were addressed directly to Tiy. In one, a foreign king wanted the new pharaoh to send him gold that had been promised by Tiy's husband, and in his letter he implied that she had been involved in the political affairs of Egypt. He wrote: "You are the one who knows that I always showed love to your husband. . . . You are the one that knows much better than all others the things that we said to one another. No other person knows them as well as you" (Tyldesley 44–45). Kings outside Egypt hoped that Tiy would provide some continuity in rule, and she certainly continued her influence at least for the first few years of her son's reign.

On one tomb, the artists created a family scene that shows Tiy eating with her son, his wife, and her royal grandchildren. Such depictions further suggest Tiy's continuing presence in the court. The portrayals of Tiy caused Egyptologists for many years to assume that Tiy was the most powerful influence in her son's highly unorthodox rule. Most now believe that role belongs to Nefertiti, another powerful Egyptian consort who forged an important role for herself in the history of ancient Egypt.

See also Clothing; Egyptian Women; Hatshepsut; Jewelry; Nefertiti

Suggested Readings

Arnold, Dorothea. *The Royal Women of Amarna.* New York: The Metropolitan Museum of Art, 1996.

Tyldesley, Joyce. *Nefertiti: Egypt's Sun Queen.* New York: Viking, 1999.

Tullia

Roman Daughter (76–45 B.C.)

One of the closest relationships during the Roman Republic was that between father and daughter. Obedient daughters forged political and social ties for the head of the family (the *pater familias*), and the daughter's obedience was often rewarded with paternal love. Many Roman texts describe the great affection that existed between fathers and daughters, and such bonds of affection allow us to know a great deal about one beloved Roman daughter, Tullia, the daughter of the famous orator Cicero.

Tullia was born in 76 B.C., the eldest child of her parents, Cicero and Terentia. Her father was very fond of his daughter; he commented on her affection, her modesty, and her quick intelligence. Indeed, he was delighted to see that she resembled him in her voice, her features, and her mind. The first task of fond Roman parents was to negotiate a good marriage for their daughter, and when Tullia was in her teens, they arranged for her to marry Caius Piso Frugi, who was in his late thirties. This marriage was a coup for a daughter of a man whose family was only recently entering into the upper classes of Rome, for Piso's family was one of the noblest of the senatorial aristocracy. The marriage seems to have been a happy one, but it was brief. Within five years Piso died of natural causes, and the young widow was inconsolable. But the daughters in ancient Rome did not stay unmarried for long.

Within a year (by 56 B.C.), Tullia married another very wealthy patrician husband named Furius Crassipes. Crassipes owned a beautiful house by the river in Rome, and Cicero wrote how much he enjoyed spending time there with his new son-in-law and his daughter. The marriage was not a happy one, however. Sometime between 53 and 51 B.C., the couple began negotiations for a divorce, which was completed by 51 B.C. Once again the parents had to find a suitable husband for their beloved daughter. In 50 B.C., while Cicero was absent from Rome as governor of Cilicia, Terentia and Tullia decided on a third husband, Cornelius Dolabella.

Dolabella was an unfortunate choice for Tullia. He was already notorious in Rome for disorders and violence and was considerably younger than Tullia. Cicero had twice saved him from persecution for crimes he probably committed. There was little possibility that this would be a happy marriage, but Dolabella, who supported Julius Caesar, may have helped the family survive the civil wars. But as a husband, the man was all but useless. Tullia became pregnant in 49 B.C., but she lost the child when it was born prematurely at seven months. Tullia's troubles were only beginning.

For the next two years, Dolabella engaged in drunken revels and broke into the houses of neighbors with his drunken friends. He took mistresses without any concern about the scandal this caused or the pain it brought Tullia and her family. By 47 B.C., Tullia had returned to her father's house, where she stayed—secluded, ill, and in mental distress. By now, Cicero should have arranged for a divorce, but his own financial problems got in the way; the marriage was patched up again for a while. In May 46 B.C., Dolabella returned to Rome from his army duties in Africa and resumed life with his wife. Tullia became pregnant again, but this did not mean the couple was happy—within a few months of the pregnancy, they had decided to finally divorce. Tullia had moved back to her parents' house and there bore a son, named Lentulus, who probably died within a few weeks. Tullia did not recover from the childbirth and the sadness that her marriage had brought. She died in their country house a short time later.

Tullia's last year had also been troubled because her father was divorcing her mother, ending a marriage of over thirty years. Cicero had married a woman younger than Tullia herself, but after Tullia's death, Cicero divorced his new bride. The sad father missed his daughter and wanted to build a shrine in her honor, but ended up writing a book of his grief. It is through her eloquent father's grief that the young Roman woman who died in her early thirties was so remembered. Thanks to Cicero's works, her life that included several marriages and tragedies was retold many times in ancient Rome, and perhaps her life can illuminate the lives of many anonymous ancient Roman women who probably experienced similar heartbreaks.

See also Terentia

Suggested Readings

Bailey, D. R. Schackleton. *Cicero*. New York: Charles Scribner's Sons, 1971.

Carcopino, Jerome. *Cicero: The Secrets of His Correspondence*. New York: Greenwood Press, 1969.

Hallett, Judith. *Fathers and Daughters in Roman Society*. Princeton: Princeton University Press, 1984.

Turia

Roman Wife (ca. 30–8 B.C.)

In the last half of the first century B.C., the Roman Republic was in turmoil. The city of Rome and much of the Mediterranean world were plagued by civil wars, and people had to take sides in conflicts with no certain outcome. Many lost their lives as powerful men struggled to take control of the mighty Roman state. Most of the sources record the fortunes of the powerful men and women who engaged in this struggle—such as the famous Egyptian queen Cleopatra VII. Yet, as always, great events strike humble people as well, even though the sources often leave out their fortunes. We have one fascinating source, however, in the form of an inscription of a funeral eulogy from the period. It tells how one couple survived the turbulent times, thanks to the devoted wife, Turia, whose husband praised her at her death.

Turia and Quintus Lucretius Vespillo, a Roman senator, were married in 49 B.C. This was the very year that Julius Caesar crossed the Rubicon River with his armies into Italy, beginning the civil war among the three great men—Julius Caesar, Crassus, and Pompey. Vespillo tells how their wedding day was saddened because both of Turia's parents were killed in the war. Vespillo then immediately left for Greece to fight with Pompey against Caesar, leaving Turia and her sister to cope with the problems of the murder. The women did not want to leave the murder of their parents unavenged, so they made inquiries and demanded punishment. We do not know the outcome of these inquiries, but Vespillo indicates that they were successful; he said he could not have done better.

Their problems increased as the civil war continued, for Pompey was defeated at the Battle of Pharsalus in 48 B.C. Luckily Vespillo escaped, but he was not out of danger. He described his wife's efforts to keep him safe: "When my political enemies were hunting me down, you aided my escape by selling your jewelry; you gave me all the gold and pearls which you were wearing and added a small income from household funds. We deceived the guards of my enemies, and you made my time in hiding an enriching experience." She warned him of dangers in time for him to escape and carefully advised him throughout. As he said, "You did not permit me to be swept away by my foolhardy boldness; how, by calm consideration, you arranged a safe place of refuge for me and enlisted as allies in your plans to save me your sister and her husband, Gaius Cluvius, even though the plans were dangerous to all of you. . . . Let it suffice to say that you hid me safely" (Kebric 101).

The assassination of Julius Caesar in 44 B.C. brought new power struggles. Vespillo was granted a pardon by Octavian (who later became known as Caesar Augustus). It looked as if the family's political troubles were over, but Turia had to intervene yet again on behalf of her husband, for Octavian's colleague, Lepidus, opposed the pardon. Turia threw herself on the ground before Lepidus to plead for her husband. Vespillo wrote painfully of her treatment: "He grabbed you and dragged you along as if you were a slave. You were covered with bruises, but with unflinching determination you reminded him of Augustus Caesar's edict of pardon. . . . Although you suffered insults and cruel injuries, you revealed them publicly in order to expose him as the author of my calamities" (Kebric 102). By 27 B.C., Augustus's final victory ended the civil wars, and the couple's political troubles were over. For the rest of their lives they were to enjoy the Pax Romana (Roman peace) that Augustus introduced. They had to confront the personal disappointments that plagued many Roman couples, however.

The couple settled down and "enjoyed quiet and happy days," but they were disappointed that they were not able to have children. Turia was depressed by her infertility and even offered to divorce Vespillo to allow him to marry another woman who might give him children. She said she would arrange for a suitable new wife and live in the household to help out. Vespillo writes strongly of his response: "I must confess that I was so angered by your suggestion that I lost my mind. I was so horrified that I could scarcely regain control of myself. . . . How could the desire or need for having children be so great that I would break faith with you!" (Kebric 102). Many Roman couples suffered from infertility, and Turia and Vespillo lived into their old age without children.

Vespillo wrote how Turia did help other relatives—bringing young women into their home and providing dowries for them so they could make good marriages. Furthermore, he praised their ability frugally to maintain their inheritances intact in an age when many lost their money through profligate behavior.

Finally, Vespillo praised Turia's personal virtues, which reveal the values of Roman society. He praises "your modesty, obedience, affability, and good nature, your tireless attention to wool making, your perfomances of religious duties without superstitious fear, your artless elegance and simplicity of dress" (Kebric 101). He closes by wishing that he had died first, so he would not have to live the rest of his life without Turia. Vespillo lauded their marriage of forty-one years during which there was no unhappiness—a remarkable claim for families who lived through the horrible times of the civil wars that claimed so many lives. This insight into this long-standing, loving marriage offers a reminder that all Romans were not engaged in the political bonds that changed rapidly and that even in the ancient world, sometimes people found happiness in marital comfort.

See also Cleopatra VII; Fulvia; Roman Women
Suggested Readings
Kebric, Robert B. *Roman People.* Mountain View, CA: Mayfield Publishing, 1993.

Twosret
Queen of Egypt (ca. 1197 B.C.)

In about 1550 B.C., Egypt recovered from the Second Intermediate Period, a time of decentralization and hardship, and rulers of the new, strong seventeenth dynasty crushed the hated Hyksos invaders and began a period of expansion all their own. They created an Egyptian empire, controlling lands far to the north into modern Syria. During this New Kingdom, which was dominated by military and economic might, Egypt became the most powerful state in the ancient Middle East. The New Kingdom had produced two remarkably powerful women—Hatshepsut and Nefertiti—and toward its end, one more rose to power—Queen Twosret, of the nineteenth dynasty.

The nineteenth dynasty began auspiciously bringing order after the religious disruptions at the end of the eighteenth dynasty (*see* Nefertiti). This dynasty reached its apex with the rule of Ramses II (ca. 1290–1224 B.C.), who won great military battles and who commissioned huge building projects as testimony to the prosperity of his reign. Following the death of Ramses and his successor Merenptah, however, law and order disintegrated, and there was a confusing succession of pharaohs who ruled briefly. Contemporary documents used standard phrases to record a time of turbulence and unrest. In addition, Egypt's borders were not even secure against foreign invaders, and many peoples attacked, stretching Egypt's resources. In the midst of these growing troubles, a resourceful woman rose to power to become the last truly Egyptian queen who actually ruled in her own right.

Twosret never had the title "king's daughter," so she may not have been of royal blood. Her tomb does give her the title "mistress of all the land," however, which implies she was the principal wife of Pharaoh Seti II. Twosret seems to have borne no children, so when her husband died, the throne went to Merenptah Siptah, the son of a minor wife of Twosret's polygamous husband. Therefore, Twosret was the stepmother of the new child-king.

As one might expect of a young boy, Siptah was a weak and ineffectual king who left few monuments and who died while still young. His mummy shows that he had suffered from a debilitating illness, possibly cerebral palsy. Throughout his short reign, Siptah was controlled by his forceful stepmother, who gradually took over the role of joint ruler. It is not clear whether Twosret actually married her young stepson so that she could be actual queen-regent. Some paintings show her standing behind Siptah in a pose usually reserved for a wife, but in most of her memorials Twosret preferred to be shown in association with her first husband, Seti II.

After Siptah died, a wave of civil unrest swept through the country. There was no clear successor to the throne, and Twosret took full advantage of the confusion to extend her rule, reinforcing her claim by adopting the full titles of a male king of Upper and Lower Egypt (perhaps recalling the successful rule of Hatshepsut). In addition to ruling as coregent with Siptah for about six years, Twosret ruled alone for less than two years. Mirroring the concerns of all the Egyptian kings, Twosret wanted to ensure her immortality with a monumental tomb, but she did not live long enough to see the work completed. Her place in the afterlife was further undermined because her male successor, Sethnakht, usurped the tomb and tried to efface her name and her image from its walls.

The sources do not tell how Twosret's reign ended. Was she deposed, or did she die a natural death? We know only that she was the last ruler of the nineteenth dynasty, for Sethnakht emerged to found the twentieth dynasty. The height of Egyptian power was ended, however. By 1090 B.C. Upper and Lower Egypt had separated again, and pharaohs could not keep out foreign invaders. The twenty-seventh dynasty began a series of Persian rulers, which ended with the Macedonian conquests of Alexander the Great (332 B.C.). Twosret was the last of the Egyptian women to rule the ancient land, but in time the Macedonian Ptolemies would produce female rulers who exerted impressive power over the land of Egypt.

See also Cleopatra VII; Egyptian Women; Hatshepsut; Meryt-Neith; Nefertiti; Nitocris; Sobeknofru

Suggested Readings

Lesko, B. S., ed. *Women's Earliest Records from Ancient Egypt and Western Asia.* Brown Judaic Studies 166. Atlanta: Scholar's Press, 1987.

Tyldesley, Joyce. *Daughters of Isis: Women of Ancient Egypt.* New York: Penguin, 1994.

V

Valeria

Roman Empress (ca. A.D. 305)

In A.D. 285, the half century of civil war that had plagued the Roman Empire came to an end with the ascension of an emperor who restructured the empire and autocratically established an organization that preserved it for over a century. Diocletian (r. A.D. 285–305) recognized that for the empire to continue, he had to solve two significant problems: the administration of so large a unit and the succession to the imperial throne. To address the first problem, Diocletian divided the empire into four sections for administrative purposes. In this system—called the Tetrarchy—four men shared power but worked together. To ensure a peaceful succession, Diocletian established a coemperor who shared power. These two main emperors—called augusti—each chose their successors—called caesars—who inherited their predecessors' positions as augusti and then chose their own caesars. The first two augusti were Diocletian (with his capital in the east at Nicomedia) and his old friend Maximian (with his capital at Milan, Italy; see Map 7.) Their caesars were Constantius in Gaul and Britain and Galerius on the Danube.

What could tie these powerful men together in alliance? It soon became clear that dynastic marriages played the same important part in government as they had at the beginning of the empire with the Julio-Claudian marriages. Galerius was tied to Diocletian by marriage to the emperor's daughter, Valeria, and Constantius was to discard his concubine, Helena, and marry Theodora, Maximian's stepdaughter.

Valeria and her mother, Prisca, were sympathetic to Christians, and though they were not baptized, they probably attended Christian worship services. Valeria must have had a difficult time in her household because Galerius's mother believed strongly in the traditional gods of Rome, and she seems to have induced Galerius to persuade Diocletian to issue edicts in A.D. 303 that authorized the persecution of Christians. This launched the worst of the Christian persecutions, which created many martyrs.

Diocletian resigned his power two years later to retire to his villa and enjoy the pleasures of gardening. He persuaded Maximian to follow his example, and the succession briefly went smoothly to the two caesars—Galerius and Constantius. Now Valeria received the titles of empress and "mother of the army," and she and Galerius began to rule. The couple had no children, but Valeria served as a good mother to Galerius's bastard son, Candidianus. During the next few years, Valeria may have softened Galerius's animosity toward Christians, for in A.D. 311, when he was a dying man, the emperor revoked the edicts authorizing their persecution. Also on his deathbed, he entrusted the care of his wife and son to Licinius, who had been his fellow augustus since A.D. 308. The boy Candidianus fell into Licinius's hands and was eventually killed. Valeria seemingly did not trust Licinius and fled to Maximin Daia, who was caesar in Asia.

Diocletian's orderly succession was rapidly falling apart. The sons of Constantius and Maximian (Constantine and Maxentius) all asserted their rights to be emperors along with Licinius and Maximin Daia. Once again marriage alliances seemed to be the key to succession. Therefore, when Valeria arrived at the court of Maximin Daia, his first thought was to divorce his wife and marry this daughter of Diocletian. Christian writers at the time claimed that he was motivated by lust for the young widow, but politics probably had as much to do with his proposal as love. Valeria, however, refused him. She claimed she was still in mourning, and she would not think about marriage while the ashes of her husband were not yet cold. Maximin Daia probably saw a political motive in her refusal and banished Valeria and Prisca to a remote part of Syria. Diocletian sent protests from his retirement, but he was too old to do much more.

In A.D. 313, Licinius defeated Maximin's army, and Licinius died shortly thereafter. Prisca and Valeria were no longer safe in their exile, as great men once again battled for supremacy of the Roman world. They set out in disguise, perhaps hoping to reach the safety of Diocletian's villa. That hope was dashed by news of Diocletian's death, and so they wandered for fifteen months. Then in Thessalonica they were recognized; they were publicly beheaded, and their bodies were thrown into the sea. Historians write in praise—and perhaps wonder—that Diocletian had been able to give up the power he held as emperor and to live out his life in peaceful retirement. Few mention, however, that he was not able to ensure such a tranquil existence for his daughter, the kindly Valeria.

See also Helena; Julia Maesa; Zenobia
Suggested Readings
Balsdon, J. P. V. D. *Roman Women: Their History and Habits.* New York: John Day, 1963.

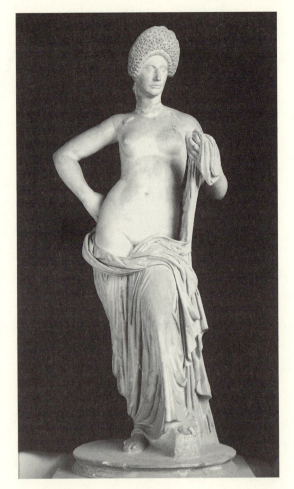

Figure 78. Tomb statue of a Roman woman depicted as Venus, late first century A.D. (Araldo de Luca/Corbis)

Venus
Roman Goddess

Venus was originally an Italian goddess, probably presiding over the fertility of vegetable gardens, fruit, and flowers. The oldest known temple of Venus dates back to 293 B.C., and within a century many other temples were dedicated to Venus. By the second century B.C., under Greek influence, Venus became identified with the Greek goddess of love, Aphrodite, and the Greek goddess's myths and attributes became associated with Venus.

Various cults arose that recognized the goddess's many aspects. For example, Venus Genetix was the universal mother, while Venus Verticordia was the "changer of hearts." (This latter represents Venus in her role most similar to that of Aphrodite, whose myths relate her many adulterous relationships.) There was also a festival of Venus Victrix (victorious Venus).

By the second century A.D., sometimes deceased women were portrayed as the goddess Venus as a way to enhance the virtues of the deceased. A tomb statue (Figure 78) shows one such woman posed as Venus, yet sporting the highly curled contemporary hairstyle.

The cult of Venus became particularly important to the Romans because Aphrodite was said to have been the mother of Aeneas, the founder of Rome. Later influential Romans took Venus as their patron, thus also enhancing her importance. For example, the dictator Sulla claimed her as his protectress, as did Pompey. The most important family to claim descent directly from the goddess, however, was that of

Julius Caesar and his nephew Caesar Augustus (Octavian). By linking themselves to the family of Venus through Aeneas, these men helped consolidate their power to rule what had become a huge empire. The goddess that brought love had become one that bestowed power.

See also Aphrodite; Calpurnia; Dido; Livia
Suggested Readings
Adkins, Lesley, and Roy Adkins. *Handbook to Life in Ancient Rome.* New York: Oxford University Press, 1994.
Fantham, E., et al. *Women in the Classical World.* New York: Oxford University Press, 1994.
Gardner, Jane F. *Roman Myths.* Austin: University of Texas Press, 1993.
Kraemer, Ross Shepard. *Her Share of the Blessings.* New York: Oxford University Press, 1992.

Verginia

Roman Maiden (ca. 464–449 B.C.)

After Rome had thrown off the Etruscan monarchy and established a republic, the Romans experienced power struggles within the growing state. During the earliest republic, power rested in the hands of an aristocracy, known as the patricians, who were members of old families that had probably gained special status under the monarchy. These patricians had the exclusive right to hold important religious offices, and they had the authority to approve decisions made in citizen assemblies. During the early fifth century B.C., Rome experienced military difficulties and economic recession. Not surprisingly, it was the poorer citizens—called the plebeians (or plebs)—who suffered most. To improve their lot, they took matters into their own hands, and in 494 B.C., the plebs withdrew from the city and formed their own assembly and elected their own officers (called tribunes). Slowly plebeians were able to exert power, and over the next two centuries (a time called the struggle of the orders) a balance was struck that established a constitution that provided for power to both patricians and plebeians.

The struggle was not peaceful; at times it was punctuated by violence even to innocent bystanders. One such victim was a young girl named Verginia. Historians cannot be sure whether her story as told by the Roman historian Livy is true, or whether it was a legend that Romans told and retold to remember a significant turning point in their history. Ancient men and women believed the story, however, and Verginia joined Lucretia as a model of a virtuous Roman woman.

In 451 B.C., the constitution of Rome had been suspended, and a Commission of Ten (the Decemviri) had been set up to publish laws. These ten men were reelected in 450 B.C., but then when they were supposed to renounce their temporary power, they were unwilling to give it up, so in 449 B.C. they remained in office illegally. In that year, while most Romans were in the field defending the city from its enemies, the commission's chairman, Appius Claudius, remained behind. There he suffered a scandal that was to bring down this threat to the growing constitution.

Appius Claudius saw a beautiful plebeian virgin—Verginia—and he set his mind on debauching her. Appius Claudius had arranged a scheme to capture the girl with his client (supporter), named M. Claudius. Verginia was fifteen years old, and while that was old enough to marry in ancient Rome, she was still a schoolgirl. One day while she was on her way to school (which was near the forum), she was modestly accompanied by her governess. M. Claudius was waiting for her and arrested her, claiming that she was the daughter of one of his own female slaves. He said that she had been stolen as a baby by Verginius's wife and falsely represented as her own daughter. He dragged the girl to Appius Claudius, who was prepared to judge this fantastic claim.

Verginia's fiancé, L. Icelius, who had served as a tribune of the plebs, quickly intervened, however, and had the hearing delayed for a day. This allowed time for her father, L. Verginius, to rush home from the army to be with her. The next day, Appius Claudius heard the case, and disregarding all the evidence, he adjudged Verginia to be a slave girl of his client. The historian Livy wrote: "He was not by nature sound of mind, and now was spoiled by the greatness of his power, his soul turgid and his bowels inflamed because of his love for the girl" (Livy 145).

There seemed no legal way to save Verginia from the clutches of the power-mad Appius Claudius.

The girl's father was not going to allow her to become a slave, but he knew of only one way to save her honor. He grabbed a large butcher knife and stabbed her dead. Like Lucretia's, her corpse was exposed in the forum, and the people were horrified at the sight of the poor innocent girl. "Matrons and maidens ran out of their houses lamenting her fate, some throwing flowers and garlands upon the bier, . . . others their childhood toys, and others perhaps even locks of their hair that they had cut off" (Livy 147–157).

The people rioted, the army mutinied, and the plebs once again left the city to establish their own government. The Decemvirs were deposed, and the republican constitution was restored. Appius Claudius was arrested, and although he appealed to the tribunes not to imprison him with lowly burglars and thieves, the tribunes—remembering Verginia—did not listen to his protestations. Before the case was heard, he killed himself, and his client M. Claudius was banished from Rome. According to the Roman historian, the spirit of Verginia was satisfied: "The ghost of Verginia, happier in death than in life, had wandered through many a home to ensure that the crime should not go unpunished; but now that not a single one of the criminals was left, it was at rest" (Livy 199). Later Romans remembered the sacrifice of Verginia whenever they believed tyranny threatened their constitution.

See also Lucretia
Suggested Readings
Balsdon, J. P. V. D. *Roman Women: Their History and Habits.* New York: John Day, 1963.
Gardner, Jane F. *Roman Myths.* Austin: University of Texas Press, 1993.
Livy. *The Early History of Rome.* Trans. A. de Selincourt. Baltimore: Penguin Books, 1960.

Vestal Virgins

From the time of its legendary founding, Rome held the family sacred. Within the small round huts of the earliest Romans, the open hearth at the center of the house marked the heart of the family. The goddess of the hearth was Vesta (the Greek goddess Hestia), and her presence was marked by the undying flame in the hearth. Tending the family hearth was the responsibility of the daughters of the households, and the family believed that their care of the fire guaranteed the survival and continuity of the family.

At some point in the remote past of Rome, a state cult to Vesta was inaugurated (some claimed it was instituted by Romulus, the original founder of the city), and a temple was set up in the forum of the city to worship the goddess. This public shrine was a circular building, intended to represent the earliest houses of the Romans, and instead of a statue of Vesta, it contained her sacred fire. This was viewed as the fire that kept the state safe in the same way as the household hearth offered safety to the family within. The state fire was tended by a group of priestesses called vestal virgins.

At first there seem to have been one or two vestals dedicated to the goddess, but by the historical period there was a college of six vestals who varied in age. Their primary duty was to tend the fire in the temple, and any vestal who let the fire go out was severely whipped. They also had charge of sacred objects within the inner sanctum of the temple, such as the palladium—an image of the Greek goddess Athena, who was identified with the Roman goddess Minerva. The Romans believed the palladium was a powerful talisman that protected Rome. Finally, the vestal virgins made a sacred cake—called *mola salsa*—which was a mixture of grain and salt used in public sacrifices.

Vestal virgins were recruited from patrician families and chosen between the ages of six and ten. They served for thirty years, during which time they had to preserve their virginity intact; after this time they were permitted to marry. Few chose to marry after their term, however, and some historians suggest that they may have found the ties of marriage onerous after the relative independence they had had as the most respected priestesses in Rome.

Even though the vestals had to adhere to the strict rules of virginity throughout their tenure of office, they still had many freedoms. As early as the issuing of the Twelve Tables (ca. 450 B.C.), laws stated that a vestal was to be freed from her father's control. She had the right to make a will

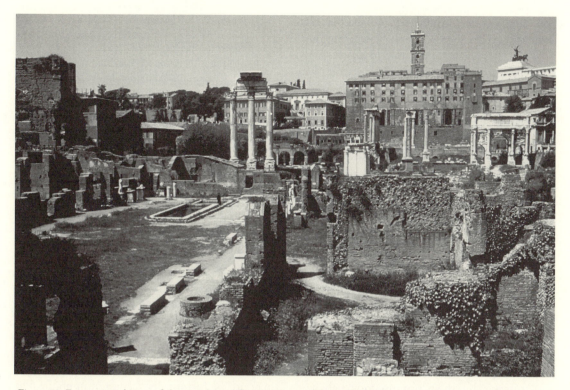

Figure 79. Forum row, house of the vestals on left (Ann Ronan Picture Library)

and control her own resources. Vestals answered only to the chief priest of the state—the *pontifex maximus.* Vestals also had a public presence— they were the only women permitted to drive through the city of Rome in a *carpentum,* a two-wheeled wagon that conferred high status on its occupant. Furthermore, like the highest magistrates, they were preceded in the streets by an attendant—a *lictor*—who cleared the way before them. Their privileges were such that some emperors granted the women in their family the rights of vestals, and they were at times shown on coins as vestal virgins even though they were not actually priestesses.

Another benefit the vestals held was good seats in the arena. When Caesar Augustus required that all women had to sit at the top tiers of seats at theatrical performances and in the arena for gladiator shows, the vestal virgins retained their places in front with the emperor's party. The vestals' intimate presence at gladiator games called forth criticism on the part of people who believed their pleasure in the carnage verged on the sexual. The fourth-century A.D.

Christian critic of the games, the poet Prudentius, included a scathing critic of the vestals' enjoyment of the games. He begins with sarcasm: "What a sweet and gentle spirit she has! She leaps up at each stroke, and every time that the victorious gladiator plunges his sword into his opponent's neck, she calls him her sweetheart . . ." (Prudentius 175).

Prudentius suggests that the vestals were neither sweet nor gentle, and their passions generated by the violence raised questions about their very purity. Prudentius was interested in banning gladiator contests completely, but his concern about the purity of the vestals was widely shared.

The Romans believed that the prosperity of Rome depended upon the dedication of the vestal virgins. Not only did they have to keep the sacred fire burning, but they had to keep their virginity intact throughout their tenure. Perhaps not surprisingly, there were incidents when virgins did not keep to their vows. Even Romulus's mother, Rhea Silvia, had been a vestal virgin who became pregnant, and though the founding legends of Rome claimed that her husband was no less than Mars, the god of war himself, later vestals were not able to claim divine intervention if they were caught violating their vows. The penalties were severe: Vestals judged guilty of violating their chastity were condemned to be entombed alive with a bed, a lamp, and a little food. The theory was if she were innocent, Vesta herself would rescue her entombed priestess, but none was ever saved.

Fewer than ten vestals are known to have undergone this execution in the long history of the cult. In part this was because at times in its history, Romans overlooked the deportment of the vestals. Sometimes the government found itself in difficult times, however, and looked to the virtue of the vestals as a reason for Rome's declining fortunes. For example, when the Romans lost the Battle of Cannae (216 B.C.) to the Carthaginian general Hannibal during the Second Punic War, they executed two of the six vestals, accusing them of causing the military disaster by their promiscuous behavior. The emperor Domitian (r. A.D. 81–96) wanted to restore public virtue, and as part of his campaign, he held trials of vestals and their lovers. In the first trial, the guilty vestals were allowed to commit suicide and their lovers to go into exile. In the second trial, however, the guilty vestal was buried alive and her lover beaten to death.

Such scandal and severity were rare. For most of their long history, the vestal virgins were highly respected and bore their responsibilities with dedication and virtue. Many Romans continued to attribute the success and endurance of the empire to their care of the home fires of the state. The last known chief vestal virgin was Coelia Concordia, who presided in A.D. 380. The cult was finally abandoned in A.D. 394, when the empire was officially Christian, and the fire of Vesta was extinguished.

See also Athena; Rhea Silvia; Sabine Women
Suggested Readings
Hallett, Judith. *Fathers and Daughters in Roman Society.* Princeton: Princeton University Press, 1984.
Kraemer, Ross Shepard. *Her Share of the Blessings.* New York: Oxford University Press, 1992.
Pomeroy, Sarah B. *Goddesses, Whores, Wives, and Slaves: Women in Classical Antiquity.* New York: Schocken Books, 1975.
Prudentius. *The Poems of Prudentius.* Vol. 2. Trans. M. C. Eagan. Washington, DC: Catholic University Press, 1962.

Veturia
Roman Mother (ca. 490 B.C.)

In the fifth century B.C., Rome was struggling with the formation of its constitution to accommodate the patrician and plebeian classes. At the same time, however, Rome was repeatedly threatened by its neighbors. Roman legend and history record wars with nearby peoples—the Sabines, the Volsci, and the Gauls, among others. It is very likely that every year—in the summer, after planting season—Romans participated in some military campaign. Slowly Rome conquered the peninsula and much more, but in the early years such victories were not automatic. According to one legend (which may or may not be historically accurate), in about 490 B.C., Rome was threatened by an invasion and was saved only by a heroic Roman mother, who could demand her son's obedience. Veturia, the mother of Coriolanus, was remembered by a grateful Rome.

In 493 B.C., a Roman patrician led the armies to a glorious victory over the Volsci, a neighboring tribe. He had captured the town of Corioli, and to mark his achievement he was forever known as Coriolanus (Gnaeus Marcius Coriolanus). He was a conservative patrician, who despised the plebeians (or plebs) and scorned their representatives, the tribunes. He opposed the distribution of grain to the starving plebs, and the people of the city grew so tired of his arrogance that in spite of his military glory he was banished.

Angry at his city, he placed his military genius at the service of the Volscians, who welcomed him and were pleased to place him at the head of their armies. In two devastating campaigns he captured a number of Latin towns and led his forces to the gates of Rome itself. He refused to see deputations from the Roman government, but at last a group of women arrived at his camp. They were led by his mother, Veturia, and joined by his wife, Volumnia. (Later traditions followed by Plutarch and Shakespeare call his mother Volumnia and his wife Vergilia.) His mother reprimanded him and reminded him of a son's duty to his parent. Duly chastened, Coriolanus turned away from Rome and marched the Volscian army home.

There are two accounts of Coriolanus's end. One tradition says (quite reasonably) that the Volscians killed him for betraying them. Plutarch and Shakespeare believed this version of the story. Another Roman tradition claims he lived into old age in exile. It is possible that the whole story is a fabrication, designed to remember a time when Rome was threatened by outsiders. The senate at Rome did remember and marked the women's triumph over treason by erecting a temple to Fortuna Muliebris (the "fortune of women") on the spot where Veturia commanded her son and saved Rome. A respect for Roman mothers joined legend in the growing history of the Roman people.

See also Lucretia; Motherhood, Roman; Verginia

Suggested Readings

Balsdon, J. P. V. D. *Roman Women: Their History and Habits.* New York: John Day, 1963.

Gardner, Jane F. *Roman Myths.* Austin: University of Texas Press, 1995.

Livy. *The Early History of Rome.* Trans. A. de Selincourt. Baltimore: Penguin Books, 1960.

W

Work

Prehistory

Women have always worked as hard as men to support their families and build the cultures that dominated the ancient world. During the early Stone Age, when humans first appeared and lived by hunting and gathering, archaeologists assume that women did most of the gathering while men did most of the hunting. They base this assumption on anthropological studies of modern hunting and gathering societies in which this is the case, but we cannot necessarily generalize to humans' earliest history. Even if it is so, this in no way devalues women's contribution. Indeed, in most hunting-gathering societies, almost 75 percent of the caloric intake consists of gathered food, not hunted meat. Thus, women may have provided most of the foodstuffs that sustained the family, and we may perhaps get tantalizing evidence for people's respect for women in the small carvings of females that were produced in this dawn of the human era. (*See* Stone Age Art.)

Women's skill at gathering may have led to further contributions by women. The earliest records indicate that women were skilled in knowledge of herbs and their medicinal value. Therefore, women were probably the earliest healers. Women's skill in preparing food also probably led to their discovery of some of the early important cooking techniques: brewing ale, making wine, and baking yeast breads. These skills seemed so remarkable that women were also reputed to have skills in magic, and this reputation continued throughout the ancient world.

It is also probable that women during the prehistoric times took the lead in curing hides and sewing them together for clothing. These skills led to important technological developments because the earliest boats were sewn together (not pegged with wooden nails).

Finally, at the dawn of the historical period, some Stone Age societies in Mesopotamia began to develop agriculture and to domesticate animals. Some archaeologists suggest that if indeed women were the principal gatherers of vegetable crops, they might have been the likely ones to have first planted the all-important grains that created the agricultural revolution that dramatically changed human society. With the development of agriculture, societies grew larger and more complex. The increased population also permitted more specialization of labor, and women's labor remained essential and varied.

Ancient Middle East

In Mesopotamia and the eastern coast of the Mediterranean, agriculture and herding allowed relatively large populations to grow. This was always a hard land, however, and agriculture required more work than the old hunting-gathering existence. Furthermore, the availability of water meant the difference between survival and famine in this hot, dry land. Scholars who have studied changing patterns of men's and women's work note that in regions that require irrigated land, both men and women must put in hard work in the fields to ensure a sufficiency.

In the fertile river valleys and coastal plains men and women probably worked in the irrigation of crops. With organization and prosperity, cities grew, and with them more of a division of labor. Some men and women could specialize in crafts—pottery and later textile production—for sale. Women also sold some of the surplus ale and wine they had produced for the family. Thus, at the beginnings of urban work, women participated in all aspects. In the earliest Mesopotamian records, we even have evidence of women who were scribes, the highest educated of the workforce. (Later in their history, women began to be excluded from the scribal schools.) Mesopotamian women also engaged in the "oldest profession" of prostitution within the ancient cities.

In the Iron Age, people—including the ancient Israelites—began to settle in the difficult highlands surrounding the fertile Jordan valley. The men and women in this frontier land faced even more hardships. There was little reliable water, and the earliest settlers had to dig cisterns in the rock to store rainwater. They also had to practice terraced agriculture in which fields were cleared, leveled, and surrounded with rock to prevent runoff of the precious water. In this difficult land, labor was essential. Men and women not only cleared the land and cultivated the precious grain, but they had to dry the fruits as they ripened to be sure the scarce but late rains would not spoil the crop. The animals had to be tended—goats milked and sheep sheared. Women not only worked hard alongside men, but their job also included producing as many children as possible to help work the difficult land. This was the context in which men had multiple wives, who between them shared the work and the childbearing.

In ancient Egyptian society, the Nile River was more predictable than the Tigris and Euphrates Rivers of Mesopotamia, and very early irrigation allowed for a highly developed society. Within this culture, poorer women always continued to work alongside their husbands in family enterprises. For example, we have records of a woman who supervised the delivery of grain for her husband's business. Some women who had been fortunate to be educated enough to learn to read and write worked as administrators or supervisors—for example, in the large linen-making enterprises. Other women worked in the female-dominated music, weaving, and mourning industries. Finally, women who had no specific training entered domestic service.

While the Egyptian records indicate that many women were employed—and earned their own money—there emerged a gender-based work ideal: Men worked outside the home, and women worked indoors. Even when they were serving as administrators in weaving or brewing, women were not supposed to work out in the hot sun. (Even the highly stylized artworks often show this ideal, portraying light-skinned women next to their sun-darkened husbands.)

During these centuries of early agricultural development, neither men's nor women's work was devalued. Everyone's labor was essential to the group's survival. With prosperity, warfare, and conquests, slaves were acquired to help with the hard labor of society. As slaves began to perform more and more work, however, labor itself became devalued. The ideal was to be wealthy enough to have someone else do your labor, and this ideal had a strong impact on women, particularly in Greece.

Greece

In Greek society—particularly Athenian culture—neither upper-class men nor women intended to work. Men wanted to live off the income generated by hardworking slaves (of both genders), and women stayed within the household to supervise the household slaves in the production of the necessities for life. Even upper-class women continued to work on things that were by now considered women's work: caring for children, nursing the sick, spinning and weaving cloth for clothing, and preparing food. Wealthy women did not even go out to shop, for that involved leaving the house. Purchases were done by their husbands or slaves.

Poorer women, even citizens, went out to work, most of them engaging in occupations that were an extension of women's work at home. They worked as laundry women and in the clothing industries. They also engaged in trade, selling food, clothing, or flowers. Other women worked as nurses of children and midwives. Finally, some women continued to work as prostitutes.

The devaluation of working outside the home had a long-standing effect on women in Western culture because it established the idea that women of quality did not work at all, which restricted women's opportunities. This ideal hardly outlasted classical Athenian society, however, because with the conquest of Alexander the Great, Greek culture was transformed, and more women worked.

Persia and the Hellenistic Kingdoms

In the Persian Empire, women had taken more of a visible role than they had in the Greek world. At all levels, the records show women controlling and managing their own property and engaging in trade and other work. (*See* Persian Women.) It is important to remember, however, that women remained primarily responsible for child care, clothing, and food production, so that other activities were added to these responsibilities. Wealthy women owned slaves to handle many of these chores, but they always had supervisory responsibilities over the slaves in their charge. Persian women seem not to have been affected by the Athenian notion of seclusion, and they took the opportunity to work in more arenas.

In Macedonia, to the north of Greece, there was a tradition of strong, independent women in the ruling families. Olympias—mother of Alexander the Great—even appeared in front of the armies as she jockeyed for political power. When Alexander conquered Greece and the Persian Empire (in 323 B.C.), he introduced an era that we have come to call Hellenistic, meaning "Greeklike." As Alexander spread Greek culture east all the way to India, he transformed the local Persian culture somewhat. Greek culture too, was transformed in the process, and in the large kingdoms that were established with Alexander's death (shown on Map 6), women had more opportunities than they had ever had before. These included opportunities for work.

In the fluid Hellenistic world with its cosmopolitan cities, women appear working in many fields, from sales to manufacturing to the arts. The documents repeatedly reveal how these new work opportunities were transforming traditional life. For example, in 220 B.C., an Egyptian father writing in Greek appealed to the king to help him resolve a domestic dispute. He claimed that his daughter, Nike, had abandoned him in his old age. According to the father, Nike had promised to get a job and pay him a pension every month out of her wages. To his dismay, she instead became involved with a comic actor and neglected her filial duties. The father implored King Ptolemy IV to force Nike to care for him in his old age instead of running off with the comedian named Dionysus. Here we can see a woman engaged in working and following her own interests with the money she generated. She was only one of many such women.

Some women engaged in the public life of their cities by using their money to help their cities. For example, inscriptions remember female magistrates, such as Phile of Priene, who was the first woman to construct a reservoir and aqueduct to provide water for her city. Another woman—Aristodama—was given citizenship because of her magnificent poetry. Within the Hellenistic kingdoms, then, many women worked in many occupations. These kingdoms were subsequently conquered by Rome, and these conquests would in turn increase the opportunities for Roman women to work outside the home.

Rome

The ideal work for early Roman women was "working in wool." Like Greek women, women of the Roman Republic were supposed to stay secluded and spend their time—and labor—on domestic pursuits, specifically making cloth and clothing. But this ideal was strictly limited to the noble upper classes. Upper-class women slowly gained more freedom to participate in the public life of the empire (*see* Roman Women). Throughout its history, however, many women continued to work in all occupations. After all, the poor of both genders could not afford to be out of the workforce.

Women of the lower classes—and ex-slaves—worked in many professions. Not surprisingly, freedwomen who worked dominated the textile industry, although men also worked as weavers. Unlike the situation in Greece, men worked alongside women doing laundry work as well, and these instances show that in the Roman world there was less division of labor by gender. Working men and women did what they could to turn a profit.

The occupations of women listed in the city of Pompeii (which was destroyed by a volcano) can serve as an example for the diversity of women's work in the Roman world. Women worked at mills grinding grain, and the Pompeian records mention a landlady and a female moneylender. Women were involved in selling in all kinds of shops, from nails to wine to clothing to fish. Freedwomen, who often had originally come from the east, sold luxury items or exotic merchandise such as purple dye or perfumes. Women's names stamped on pipes and bricks record their involvement in building activities from ownership to working as a mason. Women also worked as waitresses in taverns and continued to work in brothels as prostitutes.

Conclusion

Women in the ancient world worked hard. They were always overwhelmingly responsible for care of children and the ill and for providing food and clothing for the household. In addition, most women took on the duties of bringing in some income for the family or working in the family businesses. These facts remained constant. What did change over time was the degree to which women's contribution was valued: As life became more urban, women's contribution within the home was valued less than it was when life was more rural. It was with city life that labor outside the home—which brought in money as a profit—was valued more than labor within the home. This shift caused women's work to be devalued. This devaluation began in the ancient world and continues into the present—to the detriment of women without whose labors families and societies would not have survived.

See also Clothing; Persian Women; Prostitution; Stone Age Art

Suggested Readings

Boserup, E. *Women's Role in Economic Development.* London: G. Allen and Unwin, 1970.

Friedl, E. *Women and Men: An Anthropologist's View.* New York: Holt, Rinehart and Winston, 1975.

Pomeroy, Sarah B. *Goddesses, Whores, Wives, and Slaves: Women in Classical Antiquity.* New York: Schocken Books, 1975.

Xanthippe

Wife of Greek Philosopher (ca. 380 B.C.)

Historians, philosophers, and many others hold the Greek Socrates (469–399 B.C.) to be one of the greatest philosophers and moralists of all time. Socrates left no writings but spent his life talking to and teaching the young men of Athens as he walked about the marketplace. Although he was the son of a sculptor and probably worked in that trade himself, he claimed that he was like his mother, who was a midwife, because he gave birth to ideas. Throughout his life, he questioned his neighbors, trying to spur them on to greater virtue, but in the course of this enterprise, he offended many. Finally, in 399 B.C. he was placed on trial on charges of corrupting the young and of impiety (not believing in the gods). In spite of a lack of evidence, he was found guilty and sentenced to death. He drank a bowl of hemlock (poison) and died, and his life and death have served as a model of a man living a virtuous life of the mind.

We know most about Socrates's life from the writings of his student, Plato, who was most interested in describing the sage's ideas. Yet, he (and other subsequent writers) included a few bits of tantalizing information about Socrates's wife, Xanthippe. Due to Socrates's fame, Xanthippe's name, too, lived on through the ages.

Socrates must have married Xanthippe when he was elderly and she was much younger than he, because when he died at the age of seventy, his son by Xanthippe (named Lamprocles) was described as being a "small boy." Even if the child were as old as ten (which hardly qualifies as a small boy), Socrates would have been sixty when Xanthippe conceived the child. Plato did not comment on this age discrepancy, so it must not have been remarkable.

What was remarkable for the ancient Greek world was Xanthippe's temperament. In a society that insisted that respectable women be silent and unobtrusive, Xanthippe had a reputation for being a "shrew"—shouting at Socrates in public and berating him. She was known throughout Athens for her sharp tongue and her quick temper. Socrates once jokingly said, "As I intended to associate with all kinds of people, I thought nothing they could do would disturb me, once I had accustomed myself to bear the disposition of Xanthippe" (Plato 109). It is this reputation that has survived through the ages, for centuries later, artists portrayed Socrates being ridden by his domineering wife.

Plato does reveal one moment of humanity in Xanthippe that perhaps offers us a glimpse into the real woman (instead of the caricature of the nagging wife). In the dialogue "Phaedo," Plato describes Socrates's death. On the day the philosopher was to die, his friends came to him, and in Plato's words: "We went in, and found Socrates . . . and Xanthippe, you know her, with his little boy, sitting beside him. Then when Xanthippe saw us, she cried out in lamentation and said as women do, 'O Socrates! Here is the last time your friends will speak to you and you to them!' Socrates glanced at Criton and said quietly, 'Please let someone take her home, Criton.' Then some of Criton's people led her away crying and beating her breast" (Plato 462–463). In banishing his wife, Socrates was banishing emotions—embodied in a woman—from his death.

Here we see the wife and mother mourning her husband. At the same time, we can see that in this traditional Greek city, she was not included in Socrates's final words to his friends. The philosopher died as a Greek man, surrounded by the male friends who formed the core of his life. Xanthippe was closed out of the room and lived in history as an angry shrew.

See also Aspasia; Greek (Athenian) Women

Suggested Readings

Diogenes Laertius. *Lives of Eminent Philosophers.* Trans. R. D. Hicks. Cambridge: Harvard University Press, 1942.

Plato. "Phaedo." In *Great Dialogues of Plato.* Trans. W. H. D. Rouse. New York: Mentor, 1965.

Z

Zenobia

Queen of Palmyra (ca. A.D. 260)

In the half century after the death of emperor Alexander Severus, the Roman Empire entered into a period of administrative chaos. There were scores of claimants to the imperial throne, and some ruled (and survived) for only a few months. At the same time, invaders began to penetrate the borders of the empire—Goths threatened the north and Persians the east. In the course of this chaos, Palmyra, a small client kingdom on the eastern edge of the Roman Empire between Rome and Persia, rose to prominence (shown on Map 7).

Palmyra was a wealthy city that lay on the caravan routes between Phoenicia, Syria, and Egypt. Lists of commercial taxes show that goods came all the way from China and India through the hands of merchant aristocrats. In this cosmopolitan city, people spoke Latin, Greek, Aramaic, and Egyptian, and since the second century A.D., some of its illustrious citizens had risen in the ranks of Rome. One such successful man was Odenathus, whose grandfather had been a Roman senator in about A.D. 230 and who had become a Roman consul himself in A.D. 258. Events and the breakdown of central authority brought Odenathus even more prominence.

In A.D. 260, the Roman emperor Valerian was defeated and held captive by the king of Persia. Odenathus took to the field with archers and spearmen of Palmyra and the cavalry of the desert Arabs, and he defeated the Persian forces. According to one chronicler, they even captured the magnificent treasure of the Persian emperor. A year later, Odenathus scored another victory against a Roman general in Syria who had set himself up as emperor. The new legitimate em-

peror, Gallienus, gave Odenathus the title of king in Palymra and created an alliance with him to help secure the eastern borders. Odenathus enjoyed his title for only a few years, however, for in about A.D. 266, he was assassinated. In the same attack, Odenathus's heir was also killed. Then his second wife, Zenobia, took power, ostensibly serving as regent on behalf of her own young son. Zenobia's accomplishments eclipsed those of her husband, and she captured the imagination of ancient and modern historians.

A collection of Roman biographies written in the fourth century A.D. (called the *Scriptores Historiae Augustae*) included an account of Zenobia's life. The authors praised her beauty, calling her "the noblest of all the women of the East" and "the most beautiful" (Fraser 114), with black eyes and dark skin and teeth so white that many believed she wore pearls in her mouth. These historians also attributed to her a measure of chastity, claiming that she only allowed her husband in her bed in order to conceive her sons and did not permit him near her at other times. There is no evidence to corroborate that story, and she did bear three sons. Zenobia claimed that she was descended from the famous Egyptian queen Cleopatra VII, and she seems to have planned to claim the same power as that famous queen. She certainly had the same ambition.

Once Odenathus was dead, Zenobia quickly took control and was not content to hold Palmyra; she began to expand at the expense of the beleaguered Romans. By A.D. 269, her general Zabdas had secured most of Egypt, and at the same time Zenobia had annexed most of Syria. A year later, Zenobia conquered as far north as the Black Sea. Palmyra was now a respectable empire in its own right, and more importantly, it controlled much of the commerce that was so vital to Rome. To add a final insult, Zenobia took a step her husband had not—she declared herself formally independent of Rome. Confirming this independence, Zenobia called herself empress, and in A.D. 271, she had coins struck on behalf of herself and her son. Rome did not let this insult go unanswered.

In the midst of its chaos, Rome acquired an emperor—Aurelian (r. A.D. 270–275)—whose military skill restored most of the lands that were falling away from the empire. He first reconquered Egypt, and then marched north, slowly retaking the lands that Zenobia had claimed as her own. Zenobia led her army against Aurelian, riding her horse in the thick of battle while transmitting orders through her generals. The Palmyran cavalry lacked the discipline of the Roman legions and were lured into a horrible slaughter. Zenobia escaped across the desert to her home city of Palmyra, but Aurelian pursued her and besieged the city.

During this time, Aurelian and Zenobia were said to have exchanged correspondence. Aurelian asked her to surrender, writing "How, O Zenobia, have you dared to insult Roman emperors?" (Fraser 123). Zenobia reputedly responded with defiance worthy of Queen Cleopatra. Zenobia then was going to seek help from the Persians and planned to escape the siege of Palmyra by fleeing on a female camel, which was supposed to be faster than the fleetest horse. She escaped the city and made it as far as the Euphrates River, where she was captured as she was boarding a boat—she was either recognized or betrayed. She was brought before Emperor Aurelian as a captive and was unable to do anything to save her city, which was captured and sacked.

At this point, Zenobia's instinct for survival overrode her pride. She claimed that she was a "simple woman" who had been led astray by her advisers. She even renounced the bold letter that she had sent to Aurelian, claiming it had been written by someone else (although another scholar swore that Zenobia herself had dictated it to him). These claims earned her some clemency, for Zenobia was taken to Rome as a captive. She was forced to march in Aurelian's triumph, during which she walked shackled by golden chains and weighed down by the heavy jewels that she had once worn so proudly.

Perhaps remarkably, Zenobia's career did not end in chains. At some point, the Roman state allowed her to retire in affluence to a villa near Tivoli. She married a Roman senator and had more children. At the same time, she entertained lavishly in Rome, and the only scandal that remained attached to her was that she spoke Latin with an outlandish accent. Her command of Greek, Aramaic, and Egyptian, however, made her an exotic hostess.

Aurelian had to return to Palymra again to put down another rebellion, and this time he sacked the city so thoroughly that the distinctive Palmyran civilization disappeared. Zenobia, however, continued to thrive in Rome, a testament not only to a bold warrior-queen but to a survivor who could find some victory even in military defeat.

See also Cleopatra VII; Julia Maesa; Julia Mamaea
Suggested Readings
Balsdon, J. P. V. D. *Roman Women: Their History and Habits.* New York: John Day, 1963.
Fraser, Antonia. *The Warrior Queens.* New York: Alfred A. Knopf, 1989.
"Historia Augusta." In *Scriptores Historiae Augustae.* Trans. D. Magie. Cambridge: Harvard University Press, 1967.

Zipporah

Hebrew Wife and Mother
(ca. thirteenth century B.C.)

The Hebrew scriptures (the Christian Old Testament) tell of a crucial turning point of the Hebrew people—when they were led out of Egypt by Moses. In this Exodus, they were forged into a nation. The great Hebrew leader and lawgiver, Moses, was joined by his wife, Zipporah.

According to the Book of Exodus, Moses grew up in the Egyptian pharaoh's household, but he remained aware of his Hebrew origin (since his mother had served as his nurse). One day, once he was grown, he decided to go off alone to find out what was happening with his people. He saw an Egyptian overseer whipping an Israelite slave, and Moses intervened. Thinking that no one was watching, Moses killed the

Egyptian and buried the body in the sand. The next day, he intervened in a fight between two Israelites and was alarmed when one of them said: "Who made you a prince and a judge over us? Do you mean to kill me as you killed the Egyptian?" (Exod. 2:14). Moses realized that he had been observed and grew afraid. Indeed, Pharaoh heard of the killing and sought to kill Moses, but he fled to the land of the Midianites—a Semitic people who were distantly related to the Hebrews.

Moses sat by a well to rest, and while he was there the seven daughters of Jethro, the priest of Midian, came to draw water and fill long troughs for their father's flock of sheep to drink. Some shepherds came and tried to drive the women away, but Moses intervened. Then he helped the women water the flocks. When they came to their father, he was surprised to see them return so soon. So they told him about the Egyptian who had helped them, and their father told them to call him and invite him to eat with them. Moses then came to live with the priest and married his daughter Zipporah. She bore him a son; Moses named him Gershom, because *ger* means "stranger," and Moses was a stranger living in a strange land.

One day while Moses was watching the flock of his father-in-law, he led the sheep to Horeb, which people believed was the mountain of God. According to the Bible, an angel appeared to him in a flame of fire out of a bush, and Moses saw that the bush was burning, yet it was not consumed. Then Moses heard God address him and tell him that the Lord would lead the Israelites out of bondage in Egypt to a Promised Land "flowing with milk and honey" (Exod. 4:17). God gave Moses powerful signs of leadership to persuade the people—a rod that would turn into a snake and water that would turn to blood. God also promised Moses that the people would not leave Egypt empty-handed: "Each woman shall ask of her neighbor, and of her who sojourns in her house, jewelry of silver and of gold, and clothing, and you shall put them on your sons and on your daughters; thus you shall despoil the Egyptians" (Exod. 4:22). So the Hebrew men and women were to be led out of bondage by

Moses, but first Zipporah had to help him return to Egypt.

Moses told his father-in-law that he had to return to Egypt, and with Jethro's blessing, Moses took his wife and placed her on an ass to travel. Along with Zipporah went Gershom, the elder son, and a newly born son named Eliezer. As they traveled, Moses came into difficulty. "The Lord met him and sought to kill him" (Exod. 5:24). This may have meant that Moses became ill or suffered some other attack, and Zipporah believed that Moses had omitted some ritual act. To appease the Lord, Zipporah took a sharp stone of flint and "cut off her son's foreskin, and touched Moses's feet with it, and said, 'Surely you are a bridegroom of blood to me!'" (Exod. 5:25). Then Moses was restored, or as the Bible put it, "[God] let him alone" (Exod. 5:26).

Biblical scholars have offered some suggestions about the meaning of this passage. It is clear that Zipporah—and the author of the passage—believed that the blood spilled during the circumcision would ward off the adverse effects of the attack. In addition, since God had required all Hebrew infant boys to be circumcised, Zipporah may have worried that since the infant was not yet circumcised, this was the offense. But the passage offers yet more complexities due to her words. In the Bible, the word *feet* is sometimes a euphemism for sexual organs, so this passage implies that Moses was not circumcised, and by her acts Zipporah cleansed him of that impurity. In some ancient cultures, circumcision was a puberty or marriage ritual, so Zipporah's words "bridegroom of blood" may have been an old expression for a young man who was circumcised before marriage. This whole passage may suggest that Zipporah prepared Moses for leading the Hebrews by symbolically accomplishing his circumcision with the blood of their newly circumcised son. Whatever the full meaning of the passage, Moses was cured and continued on to confront Pharaoh and free his people.

At some point during the confrontation, Moses must have sent Zipporah and his sons back to her father, and the Hebrews escaped

Pharaoh and began their long travels in the desert of Sinai. Later, Jethro brought Zipporah and her sons to meet Moses again in the wilderness. They were welcomed and continued to travel with Moses. Zipporah disappears from the biblical narrative at this point, but her inclusion offers her a small but central role in the majestic story of the Exodus.

See also Clothing; Jewelry; Jewish Women; Miriam

Suggested Readings
Comay, Joan. *Who's Who in the Old Testament.* London: Routledge, 1995.
Meyers, Carol, Toni Craven, and Ross S. Kraemer. *Women in Scripture.* New York: Houghton Mifflin, 2000.

INDEX

ABOUT THE AUTHOR

Joyce E. Salisbury is Frankenthal Professor of History and Humanistic Studies at the University of Wisconsin–Green Bay, where she has taught undergraduates for almost twenty years. She received her Ph.D. in medieval history from Rutgers University in New Jersey and is a respected historian who has published many scholarly articles and has written or edited more than ten books, including the critically acclaimed *Perpetua's Passion: Death and Memory of a Young Roman Woman,* and *The Beast Within: Animals in the Middle Ages.* Salisbury is also an award-winning teacher who was named "Professor of the Year for Wisconsin in 1991" by CASE (Council for Advancement and Support of Education), a prestigious national organization, and has coauthored a college-level Western civilization textbook, *The West in the World.*